Wissenschaftliche Untersuchungen
zum Neuen Testament

Herausgegeben von
Martin Hengel und Otfried Hofius

106

Richard H. Bell

No one seeks for God

An Exegetical and Theological
Study of Romans 1.18–3.20

Mohr Siebeck

RICHARD BELL, Born 1954; 1979 Ph. D. in Theoretical Atomic Physics at University College London; 1991 Dr. theol. at the University of Tübingen; 1990–97 Lecturer in Theology at the University of Nottingham; since 1997 Senior Lecturer at the University of Nottingham.

Die Deutsche Bibliothek – CIP-Einheitsaufnahme:

Bell, Richard H.:
No one seeks for God : an exegetical and theological study of Romans 1.18–3.20 /
Richard H. Bell. – Tübingen : Mohr Siebeck, 1998
   (Wissenschaftliche Untersuchungen zum Neuen Testament; 106)
   ISBN 3-16-146864-3

© 1998 J.C.B. Mohr (Paul Siebeck), P.O. Box 20 40, D-72010 Tübingen.

This book was printed by Gulde-Druck in Tübingen on non-aging paper from Papierfabrik Niefern and bound by Heinr. Koch in Tübingen.

ISSN 0512-1604

To my mother

Preface

Why write a book on Romans 1.18-3.20? And why write a book with such a negative title as "No one seeks for God"? The first reason for doing so is that the section Rom. 1.18-3.20 is a preparation for what Paul says about justification by faith. If the bad news of Rom. 1.18-3.20 is not understood, there is little chance that the good news of Rom. 1.16-17; 3.21-26 will be understood. A second and related reason for this investigation is that many Christians, including protestants, have questioned the idea of salvation *sola fide, sola gratia*. They support a salvation by faith *and works* or even a view of salvation by works, independent of faith in Jesus Christ. I have often found ministers and theologians appealing to Romans 2 to justify such views. So, for example, it is argued that Rom. 2.6, 12-13 and 14-16 point to a possible way of salvation by works. This is a serious issue and needs addressing. My third reason for this investigation is that Roman 2 is often seen as a stumbling block for a "Lutheran" understanding of Romans. I have no desire to argue for an infallible Martin Luther, but if Romans 2 is indeed a problem for such an interpretation, there is again a serious issue to address. The fourth reason for this study is that Rom. 1.18-32 has had a particular fascination for me in regard to the issues of natural theology and natural revelation. This has partly come about because of my previous research in theoretical atomic physics. There is no shortage of books written by theologians and scientists regarding the knowledge of God possible through observing the created universe. In the present work I pay particular attention to what Paul in Romans has to say about this issue.

My present work is not simply a commentary. This can be seen in two respects. First, the verses in Rom. 1.18-3.20 are not treated equally. Rather I have tried to follow the argument through focusing on certain questions issues related to the theme "No one seeks for God". For example natural revelation and natural theology are treated in some detail as is the fall and the question of a possible justification according to works. Secondly, part of my task has been to try to relate Rom. 1.18-3.20 to some of the great themes of dogmatics such as natural revelation, natural theology, the fall and judgement according to works. One problem in today's theological scholarship (and a particularly acute problem among anglo-saxon scholars) is the scarcity of work done on the relationship of the New Testament to systematic theology. Systematicians often have a limited grasp of the New Testament and New Testament scholars seem to be increasingly uninterested in systematics. I therefore present something which I hope may be of use to both groups.

Although I have developed a number of new insights, what I offer may to some seem rather old fashioned. There are no great paradigm shifts, there is nothing about social scientific approaches to Paul and much of the work stands firmly in the protestant tradition. Further I have made extensive use of older works. In response to such possible criticisms I should say that Pauline studies, like many other areas, seem to be under the tyranny of novelty. New Testament scholars are under enormous pressure to show that they have made some great new discovery and that, for example, "Romans will never be the same again". My experience is that in many cases of recent alleged "breakthrough" in biblical studies, the element of novelty has been grossly exaggerated (and it is of course in the interests of scholars to do so). Also precisely those who claim to have made the greatest breakthroughs often do the greatest violence to the texts. Conversely, those who are perhaps not so radical in their approach often turn out to be the best exegetes. Whether my exegesis is good, the reader will have to judge. But I believe that we ignore the past richness of the Christian tradition at our peril. This, unfortunately, is what many modern works on Paul do. Looking through bibliographies one can sometimes get the impression that Pauline scholarship began in 1900 (or even later). I have therefore attempted to attain a balance in the secondary liturature, not necessarily giving the greatest attention to the latest literature and trying to give attention to the older works.

In my book *Provoked to Jealousy*, Tübingen 1994 I spent some time putting Paul and his letter to the Romans in historical perspective. In the present investigation I will not repeat what I wrote there and the reader should refer back to my earlier work in regard to the historical context of

Romans. In this work I have tried to address what I consider the fundamentally important issues and the ultimate aim of my work is unashamedly to know God. I make no apology for this. Historical approaches to the New Testament are vital; but if, at the end of it all, one is unable to say anything about God himself, I believe one has failed as a theologian. My work is therefore both scientific and confessional.

Much of the research for this book was carried out at the Faculty of Theology, University of Uppsala. I wish to thank especially Dr Tord Fornberg and Mr Kay Svensson for organising my visit to that fine University. My thanks go also to the University of Uppsala, the British Academy and the University of Nottingham for financing my travel and my accommodation.

Various colleagues have been very kind in reading my work in whole or in part. I am grateful to Edward van 't Slot of Utrecht whose comments helped make my argument more coherent. The advice of Dr Friedrich Avemarie of Tübingen has been invaluable, especially regarding Paul's relationship to Judaism. Dr Olle Christofferson formerly of Uppsala but now at the teologiska högskolan Stockholm made a number of penetrating criticisms of my work and the Very Revd Dr N.T. Wright, Dean of Lichfield was extremely helpful in alerting me to a number of weaknesses in the argument. Dr Clive Garrett of St. John's College Nottingham and Prof. Brendan Byrne S.J. of the Jesuit Theological College, Parkville, Victoria made a number of helpful comments especially regarding natural theology and have helped to sharpen my arguments. Prof. John Heywood Thomas, Emeritus Professor in Christian Theology at Nottingham, Canon Vernon White, Chancellor of Lincoln Cathedral and my student Mr Matthew Howey made various helpful suggestions regarding some of the sections regarding systematic theology and Prof. J.H.W.G. Liebeschütz, Emeritus Profesor of Classics at Nottingham advised on images in Graeco-Roman religion. Dr Stephen Travis of St John's College, Nottingham read the whole work and made a number of helpful suggestions. In addition I would like to thank colleagues at the University of Nottingham who have given me advice on various issues which have arisen in the work: Dr Carl Trueman, Dr Seth Kunin, Mr Ed Ball, Frau Wiebke Sievers and especially my New Testament colleague, Dr Maurice Casey. I also wish to thank Prof. Anthony Thiselton, head of the Department of Theology at the University of Nottingham, for providing a congenial atmosphere in which to work. Looking further back I want to acknowledge my debt to Professors Peter Stuhlmacher, Martin Hengel and Otfried Hofius who have taught me more than anyone else how to study the New Testament.

I wish to express my gratitude to those who have given practical help and prayer support during some difficult months when the project was nearing completion. I particularly wish to mention Dr Paul Stafford, Dr David and Mrs Anne Curnock, Mrs Carol Scothern, Mr Ed and Mrs Daphne Ball, Dr Günther and Frau Susanne Richter and my sister Mrs Susan Lofts. A special mention must be made of my two sons, Jack and Cameron, with whom I have shared great joy and laughter. They have been a welcome distraction in my study. Finally I thank my mother for the help and support she has so generously given over the years. I dedicate this study to her.

I thank Vandenhoeck & Ruprecht for permission to use material from my article "Extra ecclesiam nulla salus? Is there a salvation other than through faith in Christ according to Romans 2.14-16?", in J. Ådna, S. Hafeman and O. Hofius (ed.), *Evangelium - Schriftauslegung - Kirche: Festschrift für Peter Stuhlmacher zum 65. Geburtstag*, Göttingen: Vandenhoeck & Ruprecht 1997, 31-43, and Sheffield Academic Press for permission to use material from my articles "Sin Offerings and Sinning with a High Hand", *JPJ* 4 (1995) 25-59, and "Teshubah: The Idea of Repentance in Ancient Judaism", *JPJ* 5 (1995) 22-52.

Unless indicated otherwise, bible quotations are from the RSV and Babylonian Talmud quotations are from the Soncino version. For some works which exist both in German and in English translation, I have used sometimes the English translation and sometimes the German original. There are a number of reasons for this, one of them being that sometimes the German original has an elegance which the translation lacks and another being that in some cases the translation is somewhat misleading.

March, 1998   Richard H. Bell
Nottingham

Table of Contents

Abbreviations

1. Biblical books

The abbreviations used for books of the OT, NT and Apocrypha will be readily understood.

2. Pseudepigrapha and Early Christian Writings

2 Bar.	Syriac Apocalypse of Baruch
3 Bar.	Greek Apocalypse of Baruch
1 En.	1 Enoch
2 En.	2 Enoch
3 En.	3 Enoch
Jub.	Jubilees
Apoc. Abraham	Apocalypse of Abraham
Apoc. Moses	Apocalypse of Moses
Ps. Sol.	Psalms of Solomon
Test. Ash.	Testament of Asher
Test. Is.	Testament of Issachar
Test. Jud.	Testament of Judah
Test. Lev.	Testament of Levi
Test. Naph.	Testament of Naphtali
Test. Reub.	Testament of Reuben
Test. Zeb.	Testament of Zebulun
Test. Ben.	Testament of Benjamin
Test. Job	Testament of Job
Test. Moses	Testament of Moses
1 Clem.	1 Clement
Sib.	Sibylline Oracles

3. Dead Sea Scrolls

1QH	Hymns of Thanksgiving
1QpHab	Pesher Habakkuk
1QS	Community Rule
4QFlor	Florilegium
4QMMT	Miqṣat Ma'aśe Ha-Torah

4. Targumim

Targ. Is.	Targum of Isaiah
Targ. Onk.	Targum Onkelos
Targ. Neof.	Targum Neofiti I
Targ. Yer. I	Targum Yerushalmi I (otherwise known as the Targum of Palestine or Pseudo-Jonathan)
Targ. Yer. II	Targum Yerushalmi II (otherwise known as the Jerusalem Targum or Fragment Targum)

5. Tractates of the Mishnah, Tosephta, Babylonian and Palestinian Talmudim

For the Tosephta, Babylonian and Palestinian Talmudim the letters t., b. and y. are placed before the tractate respectively.

Aboth	Aboth
Abod. Zar.	Abodah Zarah
Bab. Bat.	Baba Bathra
Bab. Kam.	Baba Kamma
Bab. Met.	Baba Metzia
Bek.	Bekhoroth
Ber.	Berakoth
Erub.	Erubin
Hag.	Hagigah
Hul.	Hullin
Kel.	Kelim
Ker.	Kerithoth
Ket.	Ketuboth
Kid.	Kiddushin
Mak.	Makkoth
M. Kat.	Moed Katan
Nid.	Niddah
Ohol.	Oholoth
Sanh.	Sanhedrin
Shab.	Shabbath
Sot.	Sotah
Suk.	Sukkah
Yeb.	Yebamoth
Yoma	Yoma

6. Midrashim

Gen. R.	Midrash Genesis Rabbah
Ex. R.	Midrash Exodus Rabbah

Lev. R.	Midrash Leviticus Rabbah
Num. R.	Midrash Numbers Rabbah
Dt. R.	Midrash Deuteronomy Rabbah
Ruth R.	Midrash Ruth Rabbah
Eccl. R.	Midrash Ecclesiastes Rabbah
Sg of Sgs R.	Midrash Songs of Songs Rabbah
Lam. R.	Midrash Lamentations Rabbah
Mek. Ex.	Mekhilta Exodus
Midr. Tann.	Midrash Tannaim
Midr. Ps.	Midrash on the Psalms
Pes. R.	Pesikta Rabbati
Sifre Dt.	Sifre Deuteronomy
Sifre Num.	Sifre Numbers

7. Reference works

ABD	D.N. Freedman (ed.), *The Anchor Bible Dictionary*, 6 vols, New York: Doubleday 1992
ANEP	J.B. Pritchard (ed.), *The Ancient Near East in Pictures*, Princeton: Princeton University Press ²1969, (¹1954)
BA	W. Bauer, *Wörterbuch zum Neuen Testament*, Berlin/New York: Walter de Gruyter ⁶1988 (bearbeitet von K. und B. Aland)
BAG	W. Bauer, W.F. Arndt, and F.W. Gingrich, *Greek-English Lexicon of the New Testament*, Chicago and London: University of Chicago Press 1961
BDB	F. Brown, S.R. Driver, and C.A. Briggs, *A Hebrew and English Lexicon of the Old Testament based on the Lexicon of W. Gesenius*, Oxford: Clarendon Press 1978 (repr.)
BDF	F. Blass and A. Debrunner, *A Greek Grammar of the New Testament*, translated and revised by R.W. Funk, Chicago/London: University of Chicago Press 1961
BGU	Ägyptische Urkunden aus den staatlichen Museen zu Berlin. Griechische Urkunde I-IX 1895-1937
Denzinger	H. Denzinger, *Enchiridion symbolorum definitionum et declarationum de rebus fidei et morum* (ed. P. Hünermann), Freiburg: Herder 1991
EB(C)	T.K. Cheyne - J. Sutherland Black (ed.), *Encyclopaedia Biblica*, 4 vols, London: A. & C. Black 1899-1903
EDNT	H. Balz - G. Schneider (ed), *Exegetical Dictionary of the New Testament*, 3 vols, Grand Rapids: Wm. B. Eerdmans 1990-93
EJud	*Encyclopaedia Judaica*, 16 vols, Jerusalem: Keter Publishing House 1978 (repr.), (¹1971-72)

HDB   J. Hastings (ed.), *A Dictionary of the Bible*, 5 vols, Edinburgh: T.
              & T. Clark 1898-1904

HGR   J. Hastings (ed.), *Dictionary of the Bible* revised by F.C. Grant and
              H.H. Rowley, Edinburgh: T. & T. Clark ²1963

HWP   J. Ritter and K. Gründer (ed.), *Historisches Wörterbuch der
              Philosophie*, Basel: Schwabe & Co. 1971ff

IB   G.A. Buttrick (ed.), *The Interpreter's Bible*, 12 vols, New
              York/Nashville: Abingdon-Cokesbury Press 1952-57

IDB   G.A. Buttrick (ed.), *The Interpreter's Dictionary of the Bible*, 4
              vols, New York/Nashville: Abingdon-Cokesbury Press 1962

IDBSup   Supplementary volume to IDB, 1976

Jastrow   Marcus Jastrow, *A Dictionary of the Targumim, the Talmud Babli
              and Yerushalmi, and the Midrashic Literature*, 2 vols, New York:
              Pardes Publishing House 1950

JE   I. Singer (ed.), *Jewish Encyclopedia*, 12 vols, London/New York:
              Funk and Wagnalls 1901-6.

KP   K. Ziegler and W. Sontheimer (ed.), *Der Kleine Pauly: Lexikon der
              Antike*, 5 vols, München: Deutscher Taschenbuch Verlag 1979

LPGL   G.W.H. Lampe (ed.), *Patristic Greek Lexicon*, Oxford: Clarendon
              Press 1961-68

LSJ   H.G. Liddell and R. Scott, *Greek-English Lexicon*, Oxford:
              Clarendon Press 1985 (revised by H.S. Jones and R. McKenzie with
              a Supplement 1968)

LEHC   J. Lust, E. Eynikel, K. Hauspie and G. Chamberlain, *A Greek-
              English Lexicon of the Septuagint: Part I, A-I*, Stuttgart: Deutsche
              Bibelgesellschaft 1992

LThK¹   M. Buchberger (ed.), *Lexikon für Theologie und Kirche*, 10 vols,
              Freiburg: Herder 1930-38

LThK²   J. Höfer and K. Rahner (ed.), *Lexikon für Theologie und Kirche*, 11
              vols, Freiburg: Herder 1957-67

MTH   J.H. Moulton, N. Turner and W.F. Howard, *A Grammar of New
              Testament Greek*, 4 vols, Edinburgh: T. & T. Clark 1978-80
              (repr.), (¹1908-76)

NIDNTT   Colin Brown (ed.), *The New International Dictionary of New Testa-
              ment Theology*, 3 vols, Exeter: Paternoster Press 1975-78

PW   *Paulys Realencyclopädie der classischen Altertumswissenschaft*,
              Neue Bearbeitung von Georg Wissowa, Wilhelm Kroll, Karl Mittel-
              haus et al., Stuttgart: Alfred Druckenmüller Verlag 1894ff., 2.
              Reihe 1914ff.

PWSup   Supplement to PW, 1903ff.

RE[3]	A. Hauck (ed.), *Realencyklopädie für protestantische Theologie und Kirche*, 22 vols, Leipzig: J.C. Hinrichs'sche Buchhandlung [3]1896-1909.
RGG[3]	Kurt Galling (ed.), *Die Religion in Geschichte und Gegenwart: Handwörterbuch für Theologie und Religionswissenschaft* (UTB), 7 vols, Tübingen: J.C.B. Mohr (Paul Siebeck) 1986 (repr.), ([3]1959)
SVF	Ioannes ab Arnim (ed.), *Stoicorum veterum fragmenta*, 4 vols, Stuttgart: In aedibus B.G. Teubner [2]1964 ([1]1903-24).
TDNT	G. Kittel and G. Friedrich (ed.), *Theological Dictionary of the New Testament* ET, 10 vols, Grand Rapids, Michigan: Wm. B. Eerdmans 1964-76
ThWAT	G.J. Botterweck and H. Ringgren (ed.), *Theologisches Wörterbuch zum Alten Testament*, 6 vols, Stuttgart/Berlin/Köln/Mainz: W. Kohlhammer 1973-89
ThWNT	G. Kittel and G. Friedrich (ed.), *Theologisches Wörterbuch zum Neuen Testament*, 10 vols, Stuttgart: W. Kohlhammer 1933-78
TRE	G. Krause and G. Müller (ed.), *Theologische Realenzyklopädie*, 17 vols, Berlin/New York: Walter de Gruyter 1977-88

8. Sources

ANF	A. Roberts, J. Donaldson and A.C. Coxe (ed.). *Ante-Nicene Fathers*, 10 vols, Peabody: Hendrickson 1994 (repr.), ([1]1885-1896)
AV	Authorised Version
BHS	Biblia Hebraica Stuttgartensia
BSELK	*Die Bekenntnisschriften der evangelisch-lutherischen Kirche*, Göttingen: Vandenhoeck & Ruprecht [10]1986
CC	Calvin's Commentaries
CCSL	Corpus Christianorum, Series Latina
CSEL	Corpus Scriptorum Ecclesiasticorum Latinorum
GCS	Die griechischen christlichen Schriftsteller der ersten drei Jahrhunderte
GNT[3]	K. Aland, et al. (ed.), *The Greek New Testament*, New York: United Bible Societies [3]1975
GNT[4]	K. Aland et al. (ed.), *The Greek New Testament*, Stuttgart: Deutsche Bibelgesellschaft [4]1993.
JB	Jerusalem Bible
LCC	Library of Christian Classics
LCL	Loeb Classical Library
MPG	J.-P. Migne, *Patrologia Graeca*
MPL	J.-P. Migne, *Patrologia Latina*
NA[26]	K. Aland et al., (ed.), *Novum Testamentum Graece*, Stuttgart: Deutsche Bibelstiftung [26]1979
NEB	New English Bible

NPNF1	P. Schaff (ed.), *Nicene and Post-Nicene Fathers: First Series*, 14 vols, Peabody: Hendrickson 1994 (repr.), ([1]1886-1889).
NPNF2	P. Schaff and H. Wace (ed.), *Nicene and Post-Nicene Fathers: Second Series*, 14 vols, Peabody: Hendrickson 1994 (repr.), ([1]1890-1900).
NRSV	New Revised Standard Version
OCT	Oxford Classical Texts
OECT	Oxford Early Christian Texts
PS	Patrologia Syriaca
PTS	Patristische Texte und Studien
RSV	Revised Standard Version
RT	Rabbinische Texte
RV	Revised Version
SC	Sources chrétiennes
VTS	Vetus Testamentum Syriace
WA	*D. Martin Luthers Werke, kritische Gesamtausgabe*, Weimar: Hermann Böhlaus Nachfolger

9. Periodicals

AJT	American Journal of Theology
BA	Biblical Archaeologist
Bib	Biblica
BJRL	Bulletin of the John Rylands Library, University of Manchester
BZ	Biblische Zeitschrift
CBQ	Catholic Biblical Quarterly
EvTh	Evangelische Theologie
ExpT	Expository Times
ETL	Ephemerides theologicae Lovanienses
GPM	Göttinger Predigtmeditationen
GTJ	Grace Theological Journal
HeyJ	Heythrop Journal
HTR	Harvard Theological Review
HUCA	Hebrew Union College Annual
IMJ	The Israel Museum Journal
JAAR	Journal of the American Academy of Religion
JAC	Jahrbuch für Antike und Christentum
JBL	Journal of Biblical Literature
JJS	Journal of Jewish Studies
JPJ	Journal of Progressive Judaism
JR	Journal of Religion
JRE	Journal of Religious Ethics
JSNT	Journal for the Study of the New Testament
JSS	Journal of Semitic Studies
JTS	Journal of Theological Studies

Jud	Judaica
KuD	Kerygma und Dogma
NovT	Novum Testamentum
NTS	New Testament Studies
OCP	Orientalia Christiana Periodica
OTS	Oudtestamentische Studien
RB	Revue biblique
RBén	Revue bénédictine
RechSR	Recherches de science religieuse
RQ	Revue de Qumran
RSO	Rivista degli studi orientali
RTR	Reformed Theological Review
SBET	Scottish Bulletin of Evangelical Theology
SEÅ	Svensk Exegetisk Årsbok
SHAW.PH	Sitzungsberichte der Heidelberger Akademie der Wissenschaften, Philosophisch- historische Klasse
SJT	Scottish Journal of Theology
SR	Studies in Religion
StTh	Studia Theologica
ThBl	Theologische Blätter
ThLZ	Theologische Literaturzeitung
ThPh	Theologie und Philosophie
ThR	Theologische Rundschau
ThStKr	Theologische Studien und Kritiken
ThZ	Theologische Zeitschrift
USQR	Union Seminary Quarterly Review
VF	Verkündigung und Forschung
VT	Vetus Testamentum
WTJ	Westminster Theological Journal
ZAW	Zeitschrift für die alttestamentliche Wissenschaft
ZNW	Zeitschrift für die neutestamentliche Wissenschaft
ZThK	Zeitschrift für Theologie und Kirche
ZWTh	Zeitschrift für wissenschaftliche Theologie

10. Series

AB	Anchor Bible
AGAJU	Arbeiten zur Geschichte des antiken Judentums und des Urchristentums
AMT	Abhandlungen zur Moraltheologie
AnBib	Analecta Biblica
ANTJ	Arbeiten zum Neuen Testament und Judentum
ASNU	Acta seminarii neotestamentici Upsaliensis
ATD	Das Alte Testament Deutsch
AThANT	Abhandlungen zur Theologie des Alten und Neuen Testaments
AUS.TR	American University Studies, Series 7: Theology and Religion

AUU	Acta universitatis Upsaliensis
AUU.HR	Acta universitatis Upsaliensis: historia religionum
BEThL	Bibliotheca ephemeridum theologicarum Lovaniensium
BEvTh	Beiträge zur evangelischen Theologie
BFCTh	Beiträge zur Förderung christlicher Theologie
BHTh	Beiträge zur historischen Theologie
BJS	Brown Judaic Studies
BKAT	Biblischer Kommentar: Altes Testament
BLG	Biblical Languages: Greek
BNTC	Black's New Testament Commentaries
BVSAW.PH	Berichte über die Verhandlungen des Sächsischen Akademie der Wissenschaften zu Leipzig, Philologisch-historische Klasse
BZAW	Beihefte zur Zeitschrift für die alttestamentliche Wissenschaft
BzBETh	Beiträge zur biblischen Exegese und Theologie
CB	Century Bible
CCWJCW	Cambridge Commentaries on Writings of the Jewish and Christian World 200BC to AD200
CGTC	Cambridge Greek Testament Commentary
CRINT	Compendia rerum Iudaicarum ad Novum Testamentum
CThM	Calwer Theologische Monographien
EKGB	Einzelarbeiten aus der Kirchengeschichte Bayerns
EKK	Evangelisch-katholischer Kommentar zum Neuen Testament
Étbib	Études bibliques
FRLANT	Forschungen zur Religion und Literatur des Alten und Neuen Testaments
FzB	Forschung zur Bibel
GThA	Göttinger theologische Arbeiten
GThW	Grundriß der theologischen Wissenschaft
HzAT	Handbuch zum Alten Testament
HzNT	Handbuch zum Neuen Testament
HThKNT	Herders theologischer Kommentar zum Neuen Testament
HThKNTSup	Herders theologischer Kommentar zum Neuen Testament, Supplementbände
HUTh	Hermeneutische Untersuchungen zur Theologie
ICC	International Critical Commentary
JC	Judaica et Christiana
JSNTSup	Journal for the Study of the New Testament Supplement Series
JSPSup	Journal for the Study of the Pseudepigrapha Supplement Series
KzAT	Kommentar zum Alten Testament
KEK	Meyers kritisch-exegetischer Kommentar über das Neue Testament
KzNT	Kommentar zum Neuen Testament
LD	Lectio Divina
LDSS	Literature of the Dead Sea Scrolls
LJC	Library of Jewish Classics
LL	Lutterworth Library
MF	Missionswissenschaftliche Forschungen

MNTC	Moffatt New Testament Commentary
MRvB.BÖA	Monographische Reihe von 'Benedictina': Biblisch-ökumenische Abteilung
MThS	Marburger theologische Studien
MTL	Marshall's Theological Library
NCB	New Century Bible
NClB	New Clarendon Bible
NICNT	New International Commentary on the New Testament
NICOT	New International Commentary on the Old Testament
NIGTC	New International Greek Testament Commentary
NovTSup	Novum Testamentum Supplements
NTA	Neutestamentliche Abhandlungen
NTD	Das Neue Testament Deutsch
NTF	Neutestamentliche Forschungen
NTL	New Testament Library
OTL	Old Testament Library
PLO	Porta Linguarum Orientalium
PVTG	Pseudepigrapha Veteris Testamenti Graece
RVV	Religionsgeschichtliche Versuche und Vorarbeiten
SBLDS	Society of Biblical Literature Dissertation Series
SBT	Studies in Biblical Theology
SJLA	Studies in Judaism and Late Antiquity
SLJC	The Schiff Library of Jewish Classics
SNTSMS	Society for New Testament Studies Monograph Series
SNTU	Studien zum Neuen Testament und seiner Umwelt
SPIB	Scripta Pontificii Instituti Biblici
SPS	Sacra Pagina Series
SSEJC	Studies in Scripture in Early Judaism and Christianity
SSS	Semitic Study Series
STDJ	Studies on the Texts of the Desert of Judah
StNT	Studien zum Neuen Testament
SVTP	Studia in Veteris Testamenti Pseudepigrapha
ThBü	Theologische Bücherei
ThHK	Theologischer Handkommentar zum Neuen Testament
ThSt	Theologische Studien
TNTC	Tyndale New Testament Commentaries
TPINTC	Trinity Press International New Testament Commentaries
TaS	Texts and Studies. Contributions to Biblical and Patristic Literature
TSAJ	Texte und Studien zum Antiken Judentum
TU	Texte und Untersuchungen zur Geschichte der altchristlichen Literatur
UNT	Untersuchungen zum Neuen Testament
UTB	Uni-Taschenbücher
WBC	Word Biblical Commentary
WC	Westminster Commentaries
WdF	Wege der Forschung

Chapter 1

Introduction

1. The Context of Romans 1.18-3.20

The passage under consideration, Rom. 1.18-3.20, is sandwiched between two crucial sections of Romans: 1.16-17 and 3.21-26. Both these sections deal with the revelation of the righteousness of God.

Rom. 1.16-17 may be said to set forward the theme of the letter:

Οὐ γὰρ ἐπαισχύνομαι τὸ εὐαγγέλιον, δύναμις γὰρ θεοῦ ἐστιν εἰς σωτηρίαν παντὶ τῷ πιστεύοντι, Ἰουδαίῳ τε πρῶτον καὶ Ἕλληνι· 17 δικαιοσύνη γὰρ θεοῦ ἐν αὐτῷ ἀποκαλύπτεται ἐκ πίστεως εἰς πίστιν, καθὼς γέγραπται, Ὁ δὲ δίκαιος ἐκ πίστεως ζήσεται.

Rom. 1.16a gives a clue to the purpose of the whole letter. Paul is not ashamed of the gospel, implying that some thought he ought to be ashamed of it (or at least he ought to be ashamed of *his* gospel, i.e. the gospel entrusted to Paul). In the letter Paul therefore defends his gospel of justification against charges brought against him by Jewish Christians.[1]

In Rom. 1.17 Paul writes that in the gospel, the righteousness of God is revealed. The righteousness of God I take to be a subjective genitive which can be translated as "salvation of God".[2] The word δικαιοσύνη is

---

[1] On these charges brought against Paul and the whole issue of the occasion of Romans, see R.H. Bell, *Provoked to Jealousy: The Origin and Purpose of the Jealousy Motif in Romans 9-11*, Tübingen 1994, pp. 63-79. See also the discussion below on Rom. 1.16b.

[2] I defend this translation on the basis of the LXX. In a number of texts the Greek δικαιοσύνη (Hebrew צְדָקָה) means God's righteous acts in the sense of his saving acts. God's δικαιοσύνη then takes on the meaning "the saving activity of God" or "God's salvation". This is to be found in the oldest text where צְדָקָה occurs, Judg. 5.11. See also 1 Sam. 12.7; Mic. 6.5; Ps. 103.6; Dan. 9.16; 1QS 10.23. Of special importance are a number of texts in Isaiah and the Psalms where δικαιοσύνη takes on the meaning "salvation" (Is. 45.8, 22-24; 51.6, 8; Ps. 71.19 (70.18); 89.17 (88.17); 96.13 (95.13); 98.9 (97.9); 111.3 (110.3). See, for example, Is. 51.6c: וִישׁוּעָתִי לְעוֹלָם תִּהְיֶה

used rather than σωτηρία (or σωτήριον) to emphasise the forensic aspect of salvation (just as δικαιόω is used rather than σώζω to speak of salvation in terms of acquittal). I have argued elsewhere that this righteousness of God is the major theme of the whole letter.³ This righteousness then is revealed in the gospel, which v. 16 says is the power of God for salvation. The gospel has this power precisely because it is God's word.⁴ So faith does not place a condition on the power of God for salvation. The words παντὶ τῷ πιστεύοντι of Rom. 1.16b do not place any limit on the power of the gospel. Faith is not the condition of salvation; rather it is the mode of salvation.⁵ So the person who hears the gospel is made a believer through the gospel and as this believer is saved.⁶

וְצִדְקָתִי לֹא תֵחָת (τὸ δὲ σωτήριόν μου εἰς τὸν αἰῶνα ἔσται, ἡ δὲ δικαιοσύνη μου οὐ μὴ ἐκλίπῃ): "but my salvation will be for ever, and my righteousness will never be ended". Although δικαιοσύνη can parallel words other than σωτήριον or σωτηρία, I believe the idea Paul has picked up in Rom. 1.17 and 3.21 is δικαιοσύνη in the sense of "salvation". For the parallelism of righteousness and salvation in Paul see Rom. 10.10: καρδίᾳ γὰρ πιστεύεται εἰς δικαιοσύνην, στόματι δὲ ὁμολογεῖται εἰς σωτηρίαν.

³ See my *Provoked to Jealousy*, pp. 44-55. My analysis of the whole letter is as follows:
1.1-17:   Introduction and theme (16b-17)
1.18-5.21:   Righteousness of God for Jews and Gentiles through Jesus Christ
6.1-8.39:   The Righteousness of God as a reality of eschatological freedom
9.1-11.36:   The Righteousness of God "to the Jew first and also to the Greek"
12.1-15.13:   The Righteousness of God in the life of the Church
15.14-16.25:   Conclusion

⁴ I follow O. Hofius in rejecting Bultmann's view that the gospel is to be equated with the apostolic preaching (see O. Hofius, "Wort Gottes und Glaube bei Paulus", in *Paulusstudien*, Tübingen 1989, 150-51 (148-74)). For Bultmann's view see *Theologie des Neuen Testaments*, Tübingen ⁹1984 (durchgesehen und ergänzt von O. Merk), (¹1948), p. 89: "Als technische Bezeichnung für die christliche Verkündigung erscheint im hellenistischen Christentum alsbald das Subst. τὸ εὐαγγέλιον . . ."

⁵ I would therefore agree with Hofius, "Wort Gottes", 158, in rejecting the view of B. Weiß, *Der Brief an die Römer*, Göttingen ⁹1899, (⁶1881), p. 70, which would seem to paralyse the power of the gospel for salvation: "Der Glaube ist auf Seiten des Menschen die Bedingung, ohne welche ihm das Evangelium jene Kraft nicht sein kann".

⁶ See A. Schlatter, *Gottes Gerechtigkeit: Ein Kommentar zum Römerbrief*, Stuttgart ⁵1975, (¹1935), p. 33: "Es ist aber nicht möglich, Paulus eine synergistische Theologie zuzuschreiben, nach der der Mensch Gott wirksam macht. Bei Paulus wirkt

This power for salvation is for the Jew first and also for the Greek (i.e. the Gentile). Two important points are to be noted here. First, by writing Ἰουδαίῳ τε πρῶτον καὶ Ἕλληνι Paul hints that Israel's special role in salvation history has not been abolished.[7] It is essential to keep this to the fore in the discussion of Rom. 1.18-3.20; too often commentators of Rom. 1.18-3.20 have been insufficiently aware that Paul does *not* relativise Israel's election. Secondly, Paul points to the universal nature of the gospel. The gospel is not only for Jews but also for Gentiles.

Clearly, the place of the Gentiles was a fundamental problem for the early Church and Paul was one of the key Christians to fight for the full acceptance of Gentiles. However, I believe the text of Rom. 1-3 is distorted if the key theme is seen as "God's impartiality". This is an important point and I want to spend some time dealing with it.

Bassler has argued that divine impartiality is the fundamental theological principle in Rom. 1-3,[8] justification by faith being a "continuation of the basic theological principle of no distinction".[9] No doubt divine impartiality is *a* theme in Rom. 1-3 (and in Rom. 4 and certain parts of Rom. 9-11, 14-15) and occurs explicitly in Rom. 2.11; 3.22; 3.29-30 (see also 10.12). But I do not believe it is the major theme. Even if the discussion is restricted to Rom. 1.16-2.29, divine impartiality fails to be the dominant theme.[10] Much more fundamental in Rom. 1-3 is the theme that both Jews and Gentiles need the righteousness of God which they can only gain through faith.[11] After all, divine impartiality would only estab-

---

Gott und der Mensch wird gewirkt. Er wird durch die Botschaft zu einem Glaubenden gemacht und deshalb, weil er dies geworden ist, gerettet".

[7] I believe one of the objections of Jewish Christians to Paul's gospel was that Paul smoothed over the distinction between Jews and Gentiles in salvation history. He answers this charge in passages such as Rom. 1.16-17; 3.1-2; 9.1-5. See Bell, *Provoked to Jealousy*, p. 75.

[8] J.M. Bassler, "Divine Impartiality in Paul's Letter to the Romans", *NovT* 26 (1984) 55 (43-58). See also J.M. Bassler, *Divine Impartiality*, Chico 1982. Bassler also argues for the dominating principle of "divine impartiality" in Rom. 9-11 (*Divine Impartiality*, pp. 160-62) and in 14-15 (*Divine Impartiality*, pp. 162-64).

[9] Bassler, "Divine Impartiality", 58.

[10] See my discussion of Rom. 2.11 in chapter 4, section 5. Bassler, "Divine Impartiality", 45, argues that 2.11 is the pivotal point in the section 1.16-2.29.

[11] Cf. D. Moo, *The Epistle to the Romans*, Grand Rapids 1996, p. 93 n. 6.

lish that Jews and Gentiles are treated on the same basis.[12] Paul is arguing
for much more profound truths in Rom. 1.16-3.31.[13] First, there is the
devastating argument in Rom. 1.18-3.20 that no one does good, therefore
no one will be justified by works.[14] Secondly, Paul therefore establishes
the necessity of the revelation of the righteousness of God to be received
through faith in Jesus Christ. This is dealt with in Rom. 1.16-17 and
3.21-31.

I add four further points which put in question the centrality of divine
impartiality. First, the principle of divine impartiality will not necessarily
issue in a theology of justification by faith. Divine impartiality works just
as well for justification by works as Rom. 2.11 makes abundantly clear.
In Rom. 2.1-16 Paul considers justification by works, which, at this point
in the argument,[15] could give a way of salvation for Jew and Gentile
alike. Justification by faith is not a "continuation of the basic theological
principle of no distinction"; rather, it is something which arises out of the
view that no one will be justified by works.[16]

Secondly, justification by faith gives further reason for divine
impartiality. Therefore to some extent divine impartiality is logically
dependent on Paul's gospel of the justification of the ungodly through
faith. This is suggested by my view that the righteousness of God is the
dominating theme in Romans itself.[17] It may be objected that Rom. 3.28-
30 actually proves precisely the opposite. Bassler argues that to establish
what Paul says in Rom. 3.28, in Rom. 3.29-30a he "appeals to the common affirmation of monotheism" and then in 3.30b "draws . . . his own

---

[12] This is a point with which Bassler, "Divine Impartiality", 54, seems to agree.

[13] I take this unit for it is this which Bassler considers in her article (see, for example, "Divine Impartiality", 55).

[14] See the discussion on the theme of Rom. 1.18-3.20 below (section 2).

[15] See the exegesis of this passage in chapter 4 below.

[16] See the discussion below on the relationship of Rom. 1.16-17 to Rom. 1.18-
3.20. Note also that the basis for what Paul writes in Rom. 3.22a (δικαιοσύνη δὲ θεοῦ
διὰ πίστεως Ἰησοῦ Χριστοῦ εἰς πάντας τοὺς πιστεύοντας) is not simply Rom. 3.22b
(οὐ γὰρ ἐστιν διαστολή) but 3.23 also (πάντες γὰρ ἥμαρτον καὶ ὑστεροῦνται τῆς
δόξης τοῦ θεοῦ).

[17] See my analysis in n. 3 above and the discussion in Bell, *Provoked to Jealousy*,
pp. 54-55.

innovative conclusion".[18] "Both Jew and Gentile must fare alike, for God is one and thus the God of both. Therefore faith, not works, is the basis of salvation".[19] However, I do not think this does justice to Paul's argument in Rom. 1-3. He did not simply argue that God justifies by faith apart from works of law because God is one, so treating Jew and Gentile on the same basis. Indeed, earlier he argued for the possibility of a justification by works for Jew *and Gentile* (Rom. 2.12-16; 2.25-29).[20] Justification by works is not impossible because of any idea of divine impartiality; justification by works is impossible because no one does good (Rom. 3.9-20). Paul's line of thinking in Rom. 3.27-30 is that justification by works, if that were possible, would give rise to boasting in one's achievement (Rom. 3.27-4.2).[21] But such boasting is excluded by the law of faith. For justification is by faith apart from works of law (Rom. 3.28). From this point he establishes the universality of justification by alluding to Dt. 6.4 LXX.[22] But Dt. 6.4 acts more as a *confirmation* of justification by faith and not as the fundamental basis of justification by faith. If it were the essential basis, why did Paul not make use of it earlier in his argument? Likewise Rom. 4 shows that justification by faith is in harmony with scripture, developing the idea of Rom. 3.31b νόμον ἱστάνομεν.[23]

---

[18] "Divine Impartiality", 55.

[19] "Divine Impartiality", 55.

[20] See the exegesis in chapters 4 and 5 below.

[21] See my discussion of this passage in chapter 7, section 5.

[22] There has been some discussion as to whether Paul alludes to the shema here (see E. Peterson, *Eis theos*, Göttingen 1926; A.J. Guerra, *Romans and the Apologetic Tradition*, Cambridge 1995, pp. 84-101). I believe Paul is probably alluding to Dt. 6.4, despite the fact that Dt. 6.4 LXX has κύριος εἷς and not εἷς θεός as in Rom. 3.30. I suggest Paul here uses εἷς ὁ θεός rather than εἷς ὁ κύριος because he wanted to refer to God and not Christ (cf. 1 Cor. 8.6).

[23] Paul does this by taking the examples of Abraham (and David). On the relationship of Rom. 3.31 to Rom. 4 see J. Jeremias, "Zur Gedankenführung in den paulinischen Briefen", in *Abba: Studien zur neutestamentlichen Theologie und Zeitgeschichte*, Göttingen 1966, 272 (269-76); "Die Gedankenführung in Röm 4: Zum paulinischen Glaubensverständnis", in M. Barth and C.K. Barrett (ed.), *Foi et Salut selon S. Paul (Épitre aux Romains 1,16)*, Rome 1970, 51-58; O. Hofius, "'Rechtfertigung des Gottlosen' als Thema biblischer Theologie", in *Paulusstudien*, Tübingen 1989, 128 (121-47).

The logical dependence of divine impartiality (in the sense that the gospel is open to both Jews and Gentiles) on justification by faith can also be detected in Paul's theological development. I believe the justification of the ungodly by faith alone was developed at an early period in Paul's Christian life, and from this he inferred divine impartiality in the sense that the gospel was for Gentiles as well as Jews.[24] The idea of the justification of the ungodly developed out of Paul's Damascus Road experience.[25] It is easy to underestimate the trauma of this life-changing experience before Damascus.[26] Paul was overwhelmed by Jesus Christ in his glory. But this was the same Jesus who had suffered the ignoble death of crucifixion. Right from the start Christ's person and work were therefore of fundamental importance[27] and they became inextricably intertwined with his theology of justification.[28] Paul had to rethink all his assumptions about Jesus and about the law. When he realised that salvation was to be

---

[24] Contrast K. Stendahl, *Paul among Jews and Gentiles and Other Essays*, London 1976, p. 40: "Paul's thoughts about justification were triggered by the issues of divisions and identities in a plualistic and torn world . . ." For Stendahl justification is simply a means of bringing Jew and Gentile together. However, Paul's view of justification cannot be reduced to a doctrine of the Church. See E. Käsemann, "Rechtfertigung und Heilsgeschichte im Römerbrief", in *Paulinische Perspektiven*, Tübingen ²1972, (¹1969), 108-139. K. Stendahl's view of justification as simply a means for bringing Jews and Gentiles together has been addressed in my earlier work (see *Provoked to Jealousy*, pp. 48, 203-3, 286).

[25] See S. Kim, *The Origin of Paul's Gospel*, Tübingen 1981, pp. 269-311.

[26] Cf. Chr. Dietzfelbinger, *Die Berufung des Paulus als Ursprung seiner Theologie*, Neukirchen-Vluyn 1985, 115, who is critical of Wrede, Schweitzer and Strecker, for not taking full account of the Damascus Road experience in their consideration of Paul's theology.

[27] Cf. M. Hengel and A.M. Schwemer, *Paul between Damascus and Antioch*, London 1997, p. 98: "The starting point could only be the person of the exalted Christ who had encountered Paul before Damascus and his saving work. At the beginning stands a personal encounter, a being overwhelmed by the crucified and exalted Christ".

[28] See G. Bornkamm, *Paulus*, Stuttgart ⁶1987, (¹1969), pp. 128-29: "Die Zusammengehörigkeit der christologischen und soteriologischen Aussagen, genauer gesagt: die Entfaltung der Christusbotschaft *als* Rechtfertigungsbotschaft und umgekehrt, ist vielmehr ein entscheidendes Anliegen seiner ganzen Theologie" (Bornkamm's emphasis). See also G. Bornkamm, *Paulus*, pp. 249-51; "Paulus", *RGG*³ 5:177 (166-90).

found through Jesus and not through the law,[29] he first applied this to himself. This would be natural in view of the extreme personal and intellectual upheaval he experienced. So following the ideas in Phil. 3.2-11, he realised that all his privileges and efforts (Phil. 3.5-6) were worthless in view of the incomparable value of coming to know Jesus Christ (Phil. 3.7-8). Paul was taken out of himself and was found in Jesus Christ, not having a righteousness which comes from the law but a righteousness from Christ. Having experienced this existential displacement, Paul *then* came to conclusions about salvation (and justification) being for both Jew and Gentile. So first came a realisation of justification by faith;[30] then came the idea that salvation and justification were open to both Jews and Gentiles.[31] The precise nature of the universality of the

---

[29] These were central issues for Paul (cf. P. Stuhlmacher, "Das paulinische Evangelium", in *Das Evangelium und die Evangelien*, Tübingen 1983, 160-75 (157-82)). I therefore reject the following view of G. Strecker, "Befreiung und Rechtfertigung: Zur Stellung der Rechtfertigungslehre in der Theologie des Paulus", in J. Friedrich, W. Pöhlmann, and P. Stuhlmacher (ed.), *Rechtfertigung: Festschrift für Ernst Käsemann zum 70. Geburtstag*, Tübingen/Göttingen 1976, 480 (479-508): "In der Frühphase scheint — wie in der Anfangszeit der Urgemeinde überhaupt — die jüdische Tora mehr im Sinn eines 'Adiaphorons' von Paul gehandhabt worden zu sein".

[30] Cf. P. Stuhlmacher, "'Das Ende des Gesetzes': Über Ursprung und Ansatz der paulinischen Theologie", in *Versöhnung, Gesetz und Gerechtigkeit*, Göttingen 1981, 182 (166-91): "Mit der Damaskusepiphanie gewann Paulus also die Erkenntnis Jesu Christi als des Endes des Gesetzes und vollzog sich, zugleich und ineins mit dieser Christuserkenntnis, die Rechtfertigung des Gottlosen ohne Werke des Gesetzes allein aus Gnaden am Apostel selbst". See also R. Riesner, *Die Frühzeit des Apostels Paulus: Studien zur Chronologie, Missionsstrategie und Theologie*, Tübingen 1994, who argues that although Paul may have made his view on the law more precise through the Galatian conflict, his thinking was a development of the revelation of Christ on the Damascus Road. I reject Wrede's view that justification for Paul was a "Kampfeslehre" (see "Paulus", in K.H. Rengstorf (ed.), *Das Paulusbild in der neueren deutschen Forschung*, Darmstadt 1982, 67 (1-97)).

[31] See also J. Dupont, "The Conversion of Paul, and its Influence on his Understanding of Salvation by Faith", in W.W. Gasque and R.P. Martin (ed.), *Apostolic History and the Gospel: Biblical and Historical Essays presented to F.F. Bruce on his 60th Birthday*, Exeter 1970, 192-93 (176-94), who suggests that it was salvation through the Christ and not through the law which was the primary idea for the converted Paul; the mission to the Gentiles was derived from this. (Note, however, my criticism of another part of Dupont's article in *Provoked to Jealousy*, p. 304 n. 61.) On Gal. 1.16a (ἀποκαλύψαι τὸν υἱὸν αὐτοῦ ἐν ἐμοί ἵνα εὐαγγελίζωμαι

gospel clearly developed over a period of time.[32] So justification by faith, far from being a development of the principle of divine impartiality, is actually the source of an important aspect of that principle.[33]

The third reason for questioning the centrality of divine impartiality is that even in Rom. 1-4 and Rom. 9-11, there are sections which actually *contradict* the idea. Israel's priority is, as we have seen, expressed already in Rom. 1.16 (Ἰουδαίῳ τε πρῶτον καὶ Ἕλληνι) and then again in Rom. 3.1-2[34] and 9.1-5.[35] This partiality to Israel is further seen in Paul's claim that "all Israel" (πᾶς Ἰσραήλ) will be saved (Rom. 11.26) but only "the fulness of the Gentiles" (τὸ πλήρωμα τῶν ἐθνῶν) will be saved

---

αὐτὸν ἐν τοῖς ἔθνεσιν), Dupont, "Conversion", 193, writes: "He did not claim that Christ had given him the command to evangelize the Gentiles and there is nothing to allow us to imagine that this injunction was given him explicitly at this time". For an alternative view, see J.D.G. Dunn, "'A Light to the Gentiles': the Significance of the Damascus Road Christophany for Paul", in L.D. Hurst and N.T. Wright (ed.), *The Glory of Christ in the New Testament: Studies in Christology*, Oxford 1987, 251-66.

[32] One of the important texts in this regard was Is. 49.1-6, alluded to in Gal. 1.15-16 (see Bell, *Provoked to Jealousy*, p. 317). Note that Paul clearly did not have the idea of a world-wide mission from the beginning. M. Hengel, "The Origins of the Christian Mission", in *Between Jesus and Paul: Studies in the Earliest History of Christianity*, London 1983, 50 (48-64), points out that for 14 years Paul's activity "was limited to the Roman province of Syria and Cilicia, to which according to Acts 13 and 14 we must add nearby Cyprus and the immediately adjacent areas of Asia Minor". Note also that Paul's earliest missionary activity was in the territory of the Nabataeans (I take Gal. 1.17 to refer to missionary activity among the Nabataean Arabs) and the theological reason for going there was because Arabs were considered by Jews to be descendants of Ishmael and were therefore at that time the closest kins-folk of the Jews who were still Gentile (Hengel and Schwemer, *Paul between Damascus and Antioch*, pp. 110-111). Although the Idumaeans, descendants of Esau, were more closely related, they had already been converted to Judaism by John Hyrcanus I.

[33] It is true that the Damascus Road experience also influenced Paul's view of the mission to the Gentiles. He may well have seen a parallel between his call and that of Jeremiah (appointed a "prophet to the nations", Jer. 1.5) and that of the servant of Is. 49.1-6 (see n. 32 above). But I suspect that the overwhelming thought coming to his mind was not so much the parallel between his call and that of the servant of Is. 49.1-6, but rather the personal encounter with Jesus, who was crucified but now was reigning in glory.

[34] See the discussion of these verses in chapter 5 below.

[35] See Bell, *Provoked to Jealousy*, pp. 172-79.

(Rom. 11.25).[36] Further, Paul's theology of predestination suggests that God does in fact show partiality and always has done.[37]

The fourth argument to consider is that going outside Rom. 1-4 and Rom. 9-11, the idea of divine impartiality receives no particular prominence in Rom. 5-8[38] or Rom. 12-13, although it does emerge again in Rom. 14-15.[39] On the other hand, the theme of the righteousness of God is one running through the whole letter.[40] God declares those who believe in Christ to be not guilty, and in giving this verdict makes them not guilty.[41]

So in Rom. 1.16-17, Paul sets forward the theme of his letter, the revelation of the righteousness of God. This theme is taken up again in Rom. 3.21-26. In fact it is striking that in 3.21 Paul points again to this righteousness being witnessed to by the law (i.e. the Pentateuch) and the Prophets. But whereas in 1.16-17, where Paul speaks of ἀποκάλυψις, in Rom. 3.21-26 the emphasis is on φανέρωσις.[42] Another way of putting it is that whereas in Rom. 1.16-17 Paul emphasises the reconciling *word* (i.e. the gospel), in 3.21-26 he emphasises the reconciling *act* (i.e. the atoning death of Christ). Christ is publicly set forward as a ἱλαστήριον

---

[36] On Rom. 11.25-32, see Bell, *Provoked to Jealousy*, pp. 126-53.

[37] So he chose Isaac rather than Ishmael (Rom. 9.7-9) and Jacob rather than Esau (Rom. 9.10-13). See Bell, *Provoked to Jealousy*, pp. 179-80.

[38] This is acknowledged by Bassler, *Divine Impartiality*, p. 160. However, R.D. Kaylor, *Paul's Covenant Community: Jew & Gentile in Romans*, Atlanta 1988, extends Bassler's approach, applying divine impartiality to Rom. 5-8 as well (see, for example, *Covenant Community*, pp. 103-5).

[39] I identify the weak largely with Jews and the strong largely with Gentiles. See Bell, *Provoked to Jealousy*, pp. 72-73, 77-78.

[40] Again, see my analysis in n. 3 above and the discussion in Bell, *Provoked to Jealousy*, pp. 54-55.

[41] God's verdict is therefore a creative verdict, not an analytical verdict. See Hofius, "Rechtfertigung des Gottlosen", 130, who makes use of a formulation of H. Stoevesandt, "Meditation zu Joh 1,35-42", *GPM* 35 (1981) 344 (336-45): "Dieses Urteil 'stellt nicht fest, was ist, sondern stellt her, was zuvor nicht war' und was ohne es 'nimmermehr wäre'". If this creative verdict is taken seriously, there is no problem of a "legal fiction" when it comes to the matter of justification.

[42] Cf. M.N.A. Bockmuehl, "Das Verb φανερόω im Neuen Testament", *BZ* 32 (1988) 95-96 (87-99). Note, however, my critical comments on Bockmuehl's article in my exegesis of Rom. 1.19 (see chapter 2 below).

(Rom. 3.25).[43] The emphasis in 3.21-26 is on salvation-historical events.[44]

Therefore Rom. 1.18-3.20 is bracketed by Rom. 1.16-17 and Rom. 3.21-26, both of which concern the revelation of the righteousness of God. Between these two passages, Rom. 1.18-3.20 forms a unit and it is to the theme of this unit that I now turn.

2. The Theme of Romans 1.18-3.20

In recent years there has been much disagreement on the precise theme of Rom. 1.18-3.20. In an article questioning much of the protestant exegesis of Romans 2, Snodgrass suggests that the theme of 1.18-3.20 is the vindication of God.[45] He says that the usual explanation given, that Paul is attempting to prove the sinfulness of both Jews and Gentiles, is a "distortion of 1.18-3.8".[46] He argues that if Paul were trying to prove that all humans are sinners "it is strange that ἁμαρτία and its cognates hardly appear before 3.9". This is a strange argument. Although these words may not be frequent in 1.18-3.8 (ἁμαρτωλός, 3.7; ἁμαρτάνω, 2.12 (twice)) it is clear from other words and phrases that Paul is concerned with sin. The word ἁμαρτία and its cognates do not occur in the catalogue of vices in Rom. 1.28-31, but these vices of course refer to the

---

[43] In a future work I wish to focus on the issue of the sacrificial death of Christ. For the time being I refer to P. Stuhlmacher, "Zur neueren Exegese von Röm 3,24-26", in *Versöhnung, Gesetz und Gerechtigkeit*, Göttingen 1981, 117-35; "Sühne oder Versöhnung?", in U. Luz und H. Weder (ed.), *Die Mitte des Neuen Testaments. E. Schweizer FS*, Göttingen 1983, 291-316; O. Hofius, "Erwägungen zur Gestalt und Herkunft des paulinischen Versöhnungsgedankens", *ZThK* 77 (1980) 186-99; "Sühne und Versöhnung. Zum paulinischen Verständnis des Kreuzestodes Jesu", in W. Maas (ed.), *Versuche, das Leiden und Sterben Jesu zu verstehen*, München/Zürich 1983, 25-46. See also R.H. Bell, "Sin Offerings and Sinning with a High Hand", *JPJ* 4 (1995) 56-58 (25-59).

[44] Note that νυνὶ δέ in v. 21 has a temporal aspect.

[45] K.R. Snodgrass, "Justification by Grace — to the Doers: The Place of Romans 2 in the Theology of Paul", *NTS* 32 (1986) 76 (72-93).

[46] "Romans 2", 76.

sin of humanity. Likewise Rom. 1.21b refers to the sin of humanity without using ἁμαρτία; Rom. 2.21-23 refers to sin of the Jews without using ἁμαρτία. Such examples could be multiplied. Such an argument based on a word study therefore proves nothing. I believe the whole argument of 1.18-3.20 concerns the universal sinfulness of humankind. Paul wishes to prove that all, Jews and Gentiles, will be condemned on the day of judgement. He thereby demonstrates the necessity of the revelation of the righteousness of God (see again Rom. 1.16-17; 3.21-26). I believe this is the only way of making sense of Paul's argument, and the particularly difficult chapter, Romans 2, only makes sense if Rom. 1.18-3.20 is so understood.

Some have objected to making a break between 3.20 and 3.21. R. Hays, for example, believes Rom. 3 has to be seen as a unit. So "vv 21-26 close the circle by answering the objections raised in vv 1-7".[47] So for Hays 3.1-8 asks whether "God has abandoned his promises to Israel"; 3.9-20 show "All such objections are invalid: humanity, not God, is guilty of injustice"; 3.21-26 argues "God has not abandoned his people", for he has revealed his justice/righteousness in a new way.

I find Hays' analysis unconvincing. If 3.1-8 concern Israel, is it not better to take these verses with 2.17-29 which do concern Israel and not with 3.9-20, where Paul enters a discussion about all humanity being guilty before God. Also Rom. 3.21-26 is not about God not abandoning his people.[48] The issue is about a righteousness revealed apart from law for Jews and Gentiles. In fact Hays' analysis flounders on his understanding of δικαιοσύνη θεοῦ. In 3.21 it is a righteousness χωρὶς νόμου. So δικαιοσύνη θεοῦ is a saving righteousness. But Hays equates this righteousness of God (which he describes as "God's own salvation-creating power"[49]) with the δικαιοσύνη of 3.5. I agree that in both cases we have a subjective genitive. But in 3.5 it is a *iustitia distributiva* and in 3.21 it is a *iustitia salutifera*.[50] Rom. 3.5 is concerned with the situation

---

[47] R.B. Hays, "Psalm 143 and the Logic of Romans 3", *JBL* 99 (1980) 113 (107-15).

[48] Hays compares Rom. 11.1.

[49] Hays, "Psalm 143", 108.

[50] Contrast the approach of J. Piper, "The Righteousness of God in Romans 3,1-8", *ThZ* 36 (1980) 3-16, who objects to such a dichotomy.

before the revelation of the righteousness of God; Rom. 3.21 is concerned with the situation after. That a change has occurred is clear from the temporal νυνὶ δέ in 3.21.

However, despite these disagreements with Hays, I do not wish to say there is no link between 3.20 and 3.21. Paul quotes Ps. 143.2 (142.2) in Rom. 3.20 (οὐ δικαιωθήσεται πᾶσα σὰρξ ἐνώπιον αὐτοῦ) and it may be, as Hays suggests, that vv. 3.21ff takes up some ideas from this Psalm.[51] However, such a link does not necessarily mean that Paul is not starting a new section in 3.21.[52]

So I affirm with many commentators that Rom. 3.20 marks the end of the major section which began in Rom. 1.18.[53]

Having argued for seeing Rom. 1.18-3.20 as a unit (but not an independent unit), it is necessary to examine the relationship of Rom. 1.18 back to 1.16 and forward to 1.19-3.20. Rom. 1.18, as I will show, has a pivotal role in the structure of the argument.

3. Relation of Romans 1.18 to 1.16-17

One of the most difficult questions we are faced with in 1.18-32 is how exactly to relate 1.18 back to 1.16-17 and forward to 1.19-32 and to 1.19-3.20.

Rom. 1.18: Ἀποκαλύπτεται γὰρ ὀργὴ θεοῦ ἀπ᾽ οὐρανοῦ ἐπὶ πᾶσαν ἀσέβειαν καὶ ἀδικίαν ἀνθρώπων τῶν τὴν ἀλήθειαν ἐν ἀδικίᾳ

---

[51] Hays, "Psalm 143", 113, writes that Ps. 143 "provides the point of departure for what *follows*" (Hays' emphasis). Hays quotes Ps. 142.1 (where I would argue that salvific view of righteousness predominates (cf. Hays, 115, who says this righteousness is a "power of deliverance")): Κύριε, εἰσάκουσον τῆς προσευχῆς μου, ἐνώτισαι τὴν δέησίν μου ἐν τῇ ἀληθείᾳ σου, ἐπάκουσόν μου ἐν τῇ δικαιοσύνῃ σου. One may add also Rom. 3.23 (πάντες γὰρ ἥμαρτον καὶ ὑστεροῦνται τῆς δόξης τοῦ θεοῦ), which clearly refers back to Rom. 1.18-3.20.

[52] Compare later parts of the letter. So Rom. 9.1 clearly begins a new section. Yet Rom. 9 is linked to Rom. 8 (cf. Rom. 9.3 and Rom. 8.39). Also Rom. 12.1 begins a new section. Yet Rom. 12.1 relates back to Rom. 11.32. See Bell, *Provoked to Jealousy.* p. 53.

[53] See A. Nygren, *Commentary on Romans* ET, Philadelphia ⁶1983, (¹1949), p. 140, and W. Sanday and A.C. Headlam, *A Critical and Exegetical Commentary on*

κατεχόντων, . . . The γάρ of 1.18 has been understood in a variety of ways. Some are unhappy about giving γάρ its normal sense "for". Lagrange does translate it by "car" but speaks of it indicating "une légère opposition".[54] Moffatt renders it "but" and Dodd in his commentary (based on the Moffatt translation) writes: "The adversative conjunction *but* in 1.18 shows that the revelation of God's *anger* is contrasted, and not identified, with the revelation of His righteousness".[55] Although γάρ can in special circumstances have an adversative force[56] there is no lingustic reason why γάρ should not mean "for" in 1.18. There may, however, be theological objections for one would expect the δικαιοσύνη θεοῦ, which I understand to refer to the salvation of God,[57] and the ὀργὴ θεοῦ to be contrasted.

Those who accept the translation "for" understand it in a variety of ways. Barth relates it to v.16a, v.18 so giving another reason why Paul has no need to be ashamed of the gospel.[58] Sanday and Headlam seem to understand the "for" as giving the reason for the revelation of the δικαιοσύνη θεοῦ.[59] Käsemann's view is somewhat similar.[60] Michel translates γάρ as "denn" and writes:

Im Kreuz Jesu und in der Botschaft vom Kreuz liegt das Gericht Gottes über die Welt, die Enthüllung der Sünde des Menschen, die Strafgewalt Gottes, die dem zukünftigen Gericht voranläuft. Gerechtigkeit und Strafgewalt schließen sich nicht aus, sondern ein. Röm 1,17 und 1,18 entsprechen einander.[61]

Cranfield understands these two revelations as "two aspects of the same process".[62] "In the gospel the divine mercy and divine judgement are

---

the Epistle to the Romans, Edinburgh ²1896, p. 76, whom Hays, "Psalm 143", 113 n. 27, quotes critically.

[54] M.-J. Lagrange, *Saint Paul: Épitre aux Romains*, Paris ²1922, (¹1915), p. 21.

[55] C.H. Dodd, *The Epistle of Paul to the Romans*, London ¹²1949, (¹1932), p. 45.

[56] See C.E.B. Cranfield, *A Critical and Exegetical Commentary on the Epistle to the Romans*, 2 vols, Edinburgh 1 ²1977, (¹1975); 2 1979, 1:106; *LSJ*.

[57] See the discussion above on Rom. 1.16-17.

[58] K. Barth, *A Shorter Commentary on Romans* ET, London 1959, pp. 25-26.

[59] Sanday and Headlam, *Romans*, p. 40.

[60] E. Käsemann, *An die Römer*, Tübingen ⁴1980, (¹1973), p. 31.

[61] O. Michel, *Der Brief an die Römer*, Göttingen ¹⁴1978, (¹⁰1955), p. 111 (Michel's emphasis).

[62] Cranfield, *Romans*, 1:110.

inseparable from each other."[63] Like Barth, Cranfield relates the wrath of God in 1.18 to the cross.[64]

Michel and Cranfield make interesting theological comments about wrath and mercy in the cross which to some extent may well be true. However, I do not believe Paul is making *precisely such* comments about Calvary in 1.18ff.[65] Neither is he speaking of the wrath of God manifest in history.[66] Rather Paul is referring to the eschatological judgement. Eckstein points to the apocalyptic nature of the words ὀργή, ἀποκαλύπτεσθαι and ἀπ' οὐρανοῦ of 1.18[67] and rightly argues that the present tense ἀποκαλύπτεται refers to a future eschatological judgement.[68] In the Patristic period this future understanding is to be found in

---

[63] Cranfield, *Romans*, 1:110.

[64] Barth sees the revelation of the wrath of God in the cross of Christ and with the preaching of the gospel sees this as being "zugeschrieben, zugerechnet, imputiert" to the Gentiles (*KD* 2.1:181).

[65] See also the criticism M. Lackmann makes of Barth's exegesis (*Geheimnis der Schöpfung*, Stuttgart 1952, p. 181). "Paulus sprach mit dem 'ἀποκαλύπτεται' weder von der Kreuzigung Christi noch von seiner Rede als Apostel". Later he comments (p. 182): "Diese Auslegung Barths ist eine für sein Denken theologisch folgerichtige Konstruktion, aber sie ist keine Wiedergabe dessen, was bei Paulus steht".

[66] Contrast G. Stählin, in H. Kleinknecht, O. Grether, O. Procksch, J. Fichtner, E. Sjöberg and G. Stählin, ὀργή κτλ, *TDNT* 5:431 (382-447): "There can not be the slightest doubt that a present revelation of God's wrath is proclaimed here". The only texts in Paul where this is clearly found is 1 Thes. 2.16c: ἔφθασεν δὲ ἐπ' αὐτοὺς ἡ ὀργὴ εἰς τέλος. Rom. 13.4-5 is not so clear: θεοῦ γὰρ διάκονός ἐστιν ἔκδικος εἰς ὀργὴν τῷ τὸ κακὸν πράσσοντι. 5 διὸ ἀνάγκη ὑποτάσσεσθαι, οὐ μόνον διὰ τὴν ὀργὴν ἀλλὰ καὶ διὰ τὴν συνείδησιν. The ὀργή may well refer to the punishment of the state, not the wrath of God. For this use of ὀργή see H. Kleinknecht, ὀργή, 5:384.

[67] On ἀποκαλύπτεσθαι, A. Oepke, καλύπτω κτλ, *ThWNT* 3:586 (558-97), writes that "in den Briefen hat der Begriff der Offenbarung seinen eigentlichen Sitz in der Eschatologie". Note that although ἀποκαλύπτεται also occurs in 1.17 for a present event, it is not qualified by ἀπ' οὐρανοῦ (ἀπ' οὐρανοῦ refers to ἀποκαλύπτεται and not to ὀργὴ θεοῦ (contra H.-M. Schenke, "Aporien im Römerbrief", *TLZ* 92 (1967) 888 (881-888), Cranfield, *Romans*, 1:110-11, U. Wilckens, *Der Brief an die Römer*, 3 vols, Zürich/Einsiedeln/Köln/Neukirchen-Vluyn 1 1978; 2 1980; 3 1982, 1:102)). Note the contrast: the δικαιοσύνη θεοῦ is revealed in the gospel (1.17); the ὀργὴ θεοῦ is revealed from heaven. On the eschatological nature of the day of wrath see Zeph. 1.18, Dan. 8.19. See also the discussion in A. Ritschl, *Die christliche Lehre von der Rechtfertigung und Versöhnung Bd II: Der biblische Stoff der Lehre*, Bonn 1874, pp. 140-41.

[68] H.-J. Eckstein, "'Denn Gottes Zorn wird vom Himmel her offenbar werden'.

Irenaeus,[69] Chrysostom,[70] Theodore of Mopsuestia,[71] Gennadius of Constantinople,[72] Theodoret,[73] Oecumenius,[74] and Theophylact of Achrida.[75] In the 19th century the same idea is found again.[76] Some commentators have objected to the future sense precisely for the reason that ἀποκαλύπτεται is a present tense.[77] However, in New Testament Greek, as in classical Greek, the present tense can be used for a future event

---

Exegetische Erwägungen zu Röm 1₁₈", *ZNW* 78 (1987) 74-89, points to the tradition of understanding a future reference in 1.18.

[69] Note Irenaeus' earlier quotation of Eph. 5.6-7 and the translation of ἀποκαλύπτεται by the Latin future *revelabitur enim ira Dei de caelo* (*Adversus haereses* 4.27.4, A. Rousseau (ed.), *Irénée de Lyon: Contre les hérésies IV* (SC 100.1-2), Paris 1965, pp. 752-53; English translation in *ANF* 1:500).

[70] Although Chrysostom does speak of God's wrath being expressed through famines, pestilence and wars, such present revelation of wrath is for chastisement. But the future revelation is for vengeance. So he writes: τότε δὲ φανερὰ ἔσται ἡ παρὰ τοῦ θεοῦ κόλασις, ὅταν καθήμενος ἐπὶ τοῦ φοβεροῦ βήματος ὁ κριτής, τοὺς μὲν ἐπὶ τὰς καμίνους ἕλκεσθαι κελεύῃ, τοὺς δὲ ἐπὶ τὸ σκότος τὸ ἐξώτερον, τοὺς δὲ ἐπ᾽ ἄλλας ἀπαραιτήτους καὶ ἀφορήτους κολάσεις (*Commentarius in epistulam ad Romanos* homilia 3, *MPG* 60:411 (391-682)). For an English translation, see *NPNF1* 11:351 (335-564).

[71] See K. Staab, *Pauluskommentare aus der griechischen Kirche*, Münster 1933, p. 115: ἐν γὰρ τῷ νῦν αἰῶνι καλύπτεται ἀνεξικακοῦντος θεοῦ καὶ μὴ παραχρῆμα τιμωρουμένου, ἵνα μὴ ἀποκλείσῃ τῆς μετανοίας καιρόν, ἵνα ἢ μεταγνόντες σωθῶσιν ἢ καταφρονήσαντες ἀπολογίας μὴ σχῶσι πρόφασιν.

[72] Staab, *Pauluskommentare*, p. 356.

[73] Eckstein, "Zorn", 74-75, points out that Theodoret refers to the coming Son of Man of Mk 13.26 (τότε ὄψεσθε τὸν υἱὸν τοῦ ἀνθρώπου ἐρχόμενον ἐπὶ τῶν νεφελῶν τοῦ οὐρανοῦ — note the future ὄψεσθε and οὐρανός) and understands ἀπ᾽ οὐρανοῦ ἀποκαλύπτεται of Rom. 1.18 as future: ὡς τοῦ θεοῦ καὶ σωτῆρος ἡμῶν ἐκεῖθεν ἐπιφανησομένου (see *Interpretatio epistulae ad Romanos*, *MPG* 82:61).

[74] Eckstein, "Zorn", 75, points out the present ἀποκαλύπτεται is explained by ἐν τῆς κρίσεως ἡμέρᾳ (*MPG* 118:340).

[75] *In epistulam ad Romanos* caput I (*MPG* 124:352).

[76] See F.A. Philippi, *Commentar über den Brief Pauli an die Römer*, Frankfurt am M./Erlangen ²1856, p. 34, and Ritschl, *Rechtfertigung und Versöhnung Bd II*, p. 146, who writes that Paul "im Einklang mit allen seinen übrigen Aeußerungen auch 1;18 den Zorn Gottes eschatologisch versteht".

[77] B. Weiß, *Römer*, p. 77; Th. Zahn, *Der Brief des Paulus an die Römer*, Leipzig ³1925, p. 86.

especially when one is sure that the event will take place.[78] In the New
Testament there are a number of instances where this future present is
used, interestingly in eschatological texts. In 1 Cor. 3.13 and Lk. 17.30
the future present of precisely this verb, ἀποκαλύπτεται, occurs. More
frequent is the future present of ἔρχομαι.[79] Note also the present
participle ἐπιφέρων in Rom. 3.5, which, from the context, must have a
future meaning. Eckstein's conclusion seems right especially as the wrath
of God is eschatological in other texts (e.g. Rom. 2.5). Further, when this
future eschatological understanding of ἀποκαλύπτεται is adopted, 1.18
relates well back to 1.16-17 and forward to 1.19-32 and 1.19-3.20.

How is γάρ in 1.18 to be understood? I believe Sanday and Headlam
and Käsemann are on the right tracks. In 1.16-17 Paul has spoken of the
revelation of the righteousness of God. In 1.18-3.20 he explains the

---

[78] For New Testament Greek see *BDF* §323 and L. Radermacher, *Neutestamentliche Grammatik*, Tübingen ²1925, p. 152, and for classical Greek see E.
Schwyzer/A. Debrunner, *Griechische Grammatik*, vol. 2, ⁴1975, 273.4. *BDF* do not
mention ἀποκαλύπτεται in Rom. 1.18 as such a case but their list is far from exhaus-
tive (neither do they give ἀποκαλύπτεται in 1 Cor. 3.13 — but this is certainly a case
of a future present).

[79] See Jn 14.3 and Mt. 17.11 and especially Col. 3.6 and Eph. 5.6. Many commentators seem to agree that Col. 3.6 refers to a future wrath (δι' ἃ ἔρχεται ἡ ὀργὴ
τοῦ θεοῦ). See E. Lohse, *Colossians and Philemon* ET, Philadelphia 1971, p. 139 and
J. Gnilka, *Der Kolosserbrief*, Freiburg/Basel/Wien ²1991, (¹1980), p. 183, who
writes: "Gewiß ist mit dem Zorn Gottes auf das Endgericht verwiesen, das so sicher
kommen wird, daß im Präsens von ihm geredet werden kann". However, there is
more uncertainty concerning Eph. 5.6 (διὰ ταῦτα γὰρ ἔρχεται ἡ ὀργὴ τοῦ θεοῦ ἐπὶ
τοὺς υἱοὺς τῆς ἀπειθείας). J. Gnilka, *Der Epheserbrief*, Freiburg/Basel/Wien ⁴1990,
(¹1971), writes: "Der Zorn Gottes betrifft dabei auch etwas gegenwärtig Wirksames,
nicht bloß etwas in der Zukunft Hereinbrechendes", although, as we have seen, he
opts for a future eschatological understanding in the Colossian parallel (cf. M. Barth
and H. Blanke, *Colossians*, New York 1994, p. 405 and M. Barth, *Ephesians*, 2 vols,
Garden City, New York 1974, 2:566). Those favouring a future understanding of
ἔρχομαι are H.A.W. Meyer, *Critical and Exegetical Handbook to the Epistle to the
Ephesians and the Epistle to Philemon* ET, Edinburgh 1880, p. 270 and A.T. Lincoln, *Ephesians*, Dallas, Texas 1990, p. 326.

necessity of this revelation. The γάρ of 1.18 is therefore to be understood as giving the grounds for the revelation of the righteousness of God.

4. Relation of Romans 1.18 to 1.19-32 and 1.19-3.20

But what is the relation of Rom. 1.18 to 1.19-32? Many commentators believe that the revelation of the wrath of God in 1.18 is manifest in the "giving up" in 1.24, 26 and 28.[80] Such an interpretation must then go with a non-eschatological understanding of ἀποκαλύπτεται in 1.18. I have already given reasons for understanding ἀποκαλύπτεται as future and eschatological and a number of additional points can be made. The first point is related to the nature of the verb ἀποκαλύπτειν. F.A. Philippi writes:

Ἀποκαλύπτειν, *etwas Verborgenes enthüllen*, bezieht sich wie das Subst. ἀποκάλυψις im N. T., wenn Gott das offenbarende Subject ist, immer auf eine *ausserordentliche* Offenbarung durch wunderbare That, durch Wort der Propheten und Apostel oder innerlich durch den Geist Gottes.[81]

In the light of this, it seems unlikely that the ὀργὴ θεοῦ is simply manifested in normal historical events. The second point is related to the ὀργή. Wilckens writes: "Aber von der ὀργή Gottes spricht Paulus nie als einem innergeschichtlichen Handeln Gottes, sondern durchweg als von einem endzeitlichen".[82] The third point against understanding the wrath of God as an inner historical event is that the situation described in 1.18-3.20 (in particular 1.18-2.16) is only made possible through God's χρηστότης, ἀνοχή and μακροθυμία (2.4). That the people who according to the δικαίωμα θεοῦ are guilty of death (ἄξιοι θανάτου) are still alive is dependent entirely on the gracious delay of God's wrath (2.4; cf. 9.22).

---

[80] Διὸ παρέδωκεν αὐτοὺς ὁ θεός (v. 24), διὰ τοῦτο παρέδωκεν αὐτοὺς ὁ θεός (v. 26) and παρέδωκεν αὐτοὺς ὁ θεός (v.28). See, for example, F.L. Godet, *Commentary on Romans* ET, Grand Rapids 1977 (repr.), (¹1883), p. 102; E. Weber, *Die Beziehung von Röm 1-3. zur Missionspraxis des Paulus*, Gütersloh 1905, p. 39.

[81] Philippi, *Commentar über den Brief Pauli an die Römer*, p. 33 (Philippi's emphasis).

[82] Wilckens, *Römer*, 1:101 n. 155. However, Eckstein, "Zorn", 78 n. 33, points to the inconsistency of Wilckens when he proceeds to entitle 1.18-32 "Die Offenbarung des Zornes Gottes".

So I take 1.18 to refer to the eschatological judgement. If this is done, it is found that the whole argument of 1.18-2.16 corresponds to the single elements of 1.18.[83] So 1.19-20 concerns the availability of the truth (ἀλήθεια), 1.21-32 concerns the ἀσέβεια and ἀδικία of men and their suppression of the truth in unrighteousness (cf. τὴν ἀλήθειαν ἐν ἀδικίᾳ κατεχόντων), 2.1-4 speaks of the universality of the ungodliness and unrighteousness (cf. ἐπὶ πᾶσαν ἀσέβειαν καὶ ἀδικίαν ἀνθρώπων) and 2.5-11 and 2.12-16 concern the revelation of God's wrath (cf. Ἀποκαλύπτεται γὰρ ὀργὴ θεοῦ ἀπ' οὐρανοῦ). Further, if 1.18-2.16 is taken as a unit we have an inclusio[84]: both 1.18 and 2.16 refer to the final judgement and both verbs ἀποκαλύπτεται (1.18) and κρίνει (2.16) although present in form are to be understood as future.[85]

But 1.18 is not only related to the section 1.18-2.16; it is also related to the whole section 1.18-3.20. Although the first subsection finishes at 2.16 the final conclusion does not occur until 3.20.

5. Analysis of Romans 1.18-3.20

Having discussed the question of 1.18 and its relation to 1.19-3.20 I put forward my analysis of the passage which will be defended in the exegesis in the following chapters.[86]

---

[83] Eckstein, "Zorn", 88.

[84] The inclusio is characteristic of Paul's style. See D. Garland, "The Composition and Unity of Philippians: Some Neglected Literary Factors", *NovT* 27 (1985) 141-73, and F. Siegert, *Argumentation bei Paulus gezeigt an Röm 9-11*, Tübingen 1985, p. 197 n. 78.

[85] See the discussion of Rom. 2.16 in chapter 4 below.

[86] I am grateful to some helpful ideas of Prof. L. Hartman (Uppsala) concerning the analysis.

1.18-3.20 All, Jews and Gentiles, will be condemned on the day of judgement thereby demonstrating the necessity of the revelation of the righteousness of God[87] from faith to faith.

1.18-2.16 God will judge the ungodliness of men.

    1.18 Thesis

    1.19-2.16 Development

        1.19-32 Men suppress the truth in unrighteousness

            1.19-20 Truth available to all men.

            1.21-32 The ἀσέβεια and ἀδικία of men.

            1.21 Thesis (cf. v. 18: τὴν ἀλήθειαν ἐν ἀδικίᾳ κατεχόντων).

            Development in three steps:

            1.22-24; 25-27; 28-31.[88]

            1.32 Conclusion.

        2.1-16 All, Jews and Gentiles, will be judged according to their works

            2.1-4 The self-righteous judge

            2.5-16 The revelation of God's wrath from heaven.

                2.5-6 The coming wrath.

                2.7-11 Two possible outcomes.

                2.12-16 Judgement based on keeping the law for Jew and Gentile. Judgement is actually according to the gospel.

    2.17-3.8 The self-righteous Jew.

        2.17-24 Jew is just as guilty as the Gentile.

        2.25-29 Circumcision by itself will not save.

        3.1-8 Objections.

    3.9-18 Jew and Gentile under the power of sin.

    3.19-20 Conclusion: there will be no justification by works of law.

This analysis will be defended in the following chapters. I now proceed as follows. Chapter 2 is largely an exegesis of Rom. 1.18-32. This is followed in chapter 3 by a discussion of some of the issues raised in these verses, paying particular attention to the Jewish and Greek background

---

[87] See Käsemann's analysis of 1.18-3.20: "die Notwendigkeit für die Offenbarung der Gerechtigkeit Gottes" (*Römer*, p. 30).

[88] This division will be discussed in the exegesis below.

and the issues of natural revelation, natural theology and the fall, including some dogmatic discussion. Chapter 4 will deal with Rom. 2.1-16, the excursuses focusing especially on issues related to natural law. Chapters 5 and 6 examine Rom. 2.17-3.8 and 3.9-20 respectively. Finally chapter 7 discusses some of the main theological issues raised in Rom. 1.18-3.20 which have not already been dealt with in chapter 3 or in the excursuses in chapter 4.

Chapter 2

Romans 1.18-32: Introduction and Exegesis

1. Introduction

Before engaging in the exegesis of Rom. 1.18-32 I deal with some background issues.

Many have seen Paul's missionary preaching reflected in Rom. 1.18-32[1] and the relationship of Romans 1-3 to this preaching has been investigated in some detail by E. Weber earlier this century.[2] He points out that when considering Paul's missionary preaching, the Areopagus speech (Acts 17.22-31) is an unsatisfactory source for it is secondary.[3] In view of the stress Paul places in his letters on preaching Christ crucified,[4] he argues that it is unlikely that Acts 17 represents the sort of thing Paul would preach.[5] I believe Weber has overstated his case. Although there

---

[1] See, for example, Michel, *Römer*, p. 96: "Wir haben in Röm 1,18-32 ein Beispiel der *Missionspredigt* des Paulus vor uns, wie er sie häufig genug vor Heiden gehalten hat" (Michel's emphasis). Cf. E. Klostermann, "Die adäquate Vergeltung in Rm 1_{22-31}", *ZNW* 32 (1933) 6 (1-6): "Das Pathos aber, mit dem hier der Gedanke von dem Gott durchgeführt wird, der sich nicht spotten läßt (Gal 6_7), ist das Pathos des Predigers . . .".

[2] Weber, *Missionspraxis*.

[3] Weber, *Missionspraxis*, 9. Although his comments were written nearly a century ago, a number of scholars do just the same today.

[4] See especially 1 Cor. 2.2: οὐ γὰρ ἔκρινά τι εἰδέναι ἐν ὑμῖν εἰ μὴ Ἰησοῦν Χριστὸν καὶ τοῦτον ἐσταυρωμένον.

[5] Weber, *Missionspraxis*, p. 9, writes: "Ist es nach dem Bilde, das uns die Briefe von dem Apostel der Kreuzespredigt zeichnen, denkbar, daß Paulus mit der 'natürlichen Theologie' von Act. 17 aufgetreten sein sollte, um sich erst ganz allmählich mit dem Skandalon der eigentlichen christlichen Botschaft hervorzuwagen (Act. 17,30f.)?" Weber concludes (*Missionspraxis*, p. 10): "Die Apostelgeschichte bietet uns kein sicheres Material für die Frage nach der Missionspredigt des Paulus". Cf. P. Vielhauer, "On the 'Paulinism' of Acts", in L.E. Keck and J.L. Martyn (ed.), *Studies in Luke-Acts: Essays presented in honor of Paul Schubert*, London 1968, 34-

are clear differences between what we find in Acts 17.22-31 and in the letters of Paul,[6] many scholars like Weber have exaggerated the differences.[7]

If Rom. 1.18-3.20 sets the scene for the revelation of the righteousness of God (3.21) it would seem reasonable to assume that it does in fact tell us something about Paul's missionary preaching. A number of scholars have pointed to the rhetorical nature of Rom. 1.18-3.20.[8] Could not this rhetorical flavour be accounted for by relating the material to the sort of thing Paul would use in his mission? Paul addresses his hearers directly.[9] This in itself may not seem unusual for Paul. But the people he addresses appear to be strangers and seem loath to recognise his authority.[10] In short, they seem to be non-Christians. The idea that Rom. 1.18-3.20 is related to Paul's missionary preaching receives confirmation in that the theme of the judgement of God is prominent in this section[11] and, as I will

---

37 (33-50) and Käsemann, *Römer*, p. 47. For a bringing together of Rom. 1.18-32 and Acts 17 see Wilckens, *Römer*, 1:115.

[6] For example, one may point to the fact that in 1.18-3.20, human beings sin "with a high hand" (i.e. deliberately) whereas in Acts 17.30a Paul is reported to have said τοὺς μὲν οὖν χρόνους τῆς ἀγνοίας ὑπεριδὼν ὁ θεός (see Bell, "Sin Offerings", 56-59.

[7] One of the commonly believed differences is the status of natural theology in Acts 17.22-31 and Rom. 1.18-32 (see Vielhauer, "Paulinism", 34-37). However, I argue in the section on "Natural Revelation and Natural Theology" in the next chapter that the two passages are not so different as regards natural theology.

[8] See Guerra, *Romans*, pp. 43-72.

[9] Weber, *Missionspraxis*, p. 18, points to the personal address in Rom. 2.1, 3, 4, 5, 17-24.

[10] See Weber, *Missionspraxis*, p. 18: "Es ist ein Fremder, den der Apostel vor sich hat, gar nicht geneigt, seine Autorität von vornherein anzuerkennen. Der Apostel redet auf ihn ein, hält ihm Tatsachen vor, sucht ihm Folgerungen abzunötigen".

[11] Weber, *Missionspraxis*, pp. 44-45 writes: "Es ist eine der sichersten Tatsachen aus der Geschichte der Paulinischen Mission, daß das Gericht in der ersten Verkündigung eine große Rolle gespielt hat. Die ganze propädeutische Einwirkung des Apostels läuft auf die Anerkennung des drohenden Gerichts hinaus; erst muß diese Tatsache gegen allen Einwand festgestellt sein, ehe von der Gerechtigkeits-offenbarung geredet werden kann". See, for example, 1 Thes. 1.9-10 (cf. 2 Thes. 1.8; Acts 17.30-31). The theme of the coming judgement was also important for other preachers of the early Church. On the wrath of God see the discussion below on Rom. 1.18.

argue, the nature of judgement according to works in this section is unique to Paul.[12] Although Weber overstates his conclusion, there is an element of truth in it: "der Abschnitt ist eben selbst ganz aus der Missionstätigkeit des Apostels herausgeboren".[13]

If Rom. 1.18-32 can be related to Paul's missionary preaching, what is then exactly the background for this preaching? Some have suggested a link with the "apologetic tradition". This "apologetic tradition" could be either related to the Jewish wisdom apologetic and/or the later second century Christian apologetic. So Guerra argues that Paul "stands at the decisive crossroad of Jewish apologetic tradition and what was to become the Greek Christian apologetic tradition".[14] So in Jewish apologetic use was made of natural theology[15] and scholars have pointed to Paul's concern with this in Rom. 1.19-21a. However, in the following discussion I hope to demonstrate the difference between Paul and this tradition. Similarly there is a considerable gap between Paul and the later Greek Christian apologetic tradition.[16] Paul's preaching may have contained certain elements of Jewish wisdom tradition. But the crucial point about Rom. 1.18-32 is that it acts as an accusation[17] and a more likely background for Paul's argument is the tradition of Jewish apocalyptic.[18]

---

[12] See the discussion in chapter 7 below.

[13] Weber, *Missionspraxis*, p. 31.

[14] Guerra, *Romans*, p. 48.

[15] E.g. Wis. 13.1-9.

[16] As I point out in my review of Guerra's *Romans and the Apologetic Tradition* (*JTS* 47 (1996) 228 (226-30)), Paul inhabits a different world from that of the second-century apologists.

[17] See A. Klöpper, "Die durch natürliche Offenbarung vermittelte Gotteserkenntnis der Heiden bei Paulus. Röm. 1,18ff.", *ZWTh* 47 (1904) 179-80 (169-80), and Weber, *Missionspraxis*, pp. 32ff.

[18] Here and in a number of places below I refer to "apocalyptic". I use this term to refers to the kind of material found in apocalypses (cf. J.J. Collins, "Genre, Ideology and Social Movements in Jewish Apocalypticism", in J.J. Collins and J.H. Charlesworth (ed.), *Mysteries and Revelations: Apocalyptic Studies since the Uppsala Colloquium*, Sheffield 1991, 13 (11-32)). For a helpful summary of the genre of apocalypses, see K. Koch, "Einleitung", in K. Koch and J.M. Schmidt (ed.), *Apokalyptik*, Darmstadt 1982, 12-13 (1-29). But in using "apocalyptic" in this narrow sense, I do not intend to suggest that groups such as the Qumran sectaries did not have "apocalyptic" ideas even though the number of apocalypses found there are few (cf. J.J. Collins, *Apocalypticism in the Dead Sea Scrolls*, London 1997, p. 9). It has

Schulz rightly points out that "der Abschnitt 1,18-32 primär und wur-
zelmäßig von der Anklage im Stil der Apokalyptik und nicht von der
spätjüdisch-apologetischen Weisheitsrede des Hellenismus geprägt ist".[19]
The background to Rom. 1.18-32 will be discussed further in chapter 3
below.

The next issue is who is actually addressed in 1.18-32? In the discussion of Rom. 1.18ff there are two main views: first, that Paul is addressing the Gentiles[20] and second that he is addressing both Jews and
Gentiles.[21] I believe that Rom. 1.18ff runs on two different levels. In one
sense Paul is speaking of humankind generally. There are allusions to
Adam,[22] to the fall of Israel[23] and, of course, to the sins of the Gentiles.[24]

---

become customary to use the term "apocalypticism" for the world view which may be
extrapolated from apocalypses (P.D. Hanson, "Apocalypticism", *IDBSup* 30-31 (28-
34); J.J. Collins, "Early Jewish Apocalypticism", *ABD* 1:283 (282-88)).

[19] S. Schulz, "Die Anklage in Röm. 1,18-32", *ThZ* 14 (1958) 165 (161-73).

[20] See O. Pfleiderer, *Urchristentum*, 2 vols, Berlin ²1902, (¹1887), 1:211-13;
Dodd, *Romans*, p. 19 (1.18-32 entitled "Sin and Retribution in the Pagan World");
E. Kühl, *Der Brief des Paulus an die Römer*, Leipzig 1913, pp. 61-63; Michel,
Römer, p. 95; P. Feine, *Theologie des Neuen Testaments*, Berlin ⁸1953, p. 274; P.
Boylan, *St. Paul's Epistle to the Romans*, Dublin 1947, p. 17; H. Schlier, *Der
Römerbrief*, Freiburg/Basel/Wien 1977, p. 47; J. Fitzmyer, *Romans*, New York
1993, p. 269; Nygren, *Romans*, p. 98.

[21] See J. Jervell, *Imago Dei: Gen 1,26f. im Spätjudentum, in der Gnosis und in
den paulinischen Briefen*, Göttingen 1960, pp. 317-18. W.L. Knox, *St Paul and the
Church of the Gentiles*, Cambridge 1939, p. 183, writes that "the conventional Jewish
argument against idolatry is turned into an attack on Judaism" (see also *Church of the
Gentiles*, p. 196).

[22] Although some have warned of seeing too much of Adam in Rom. 1 (see the
response to M.D. Hooker by A.J.M. Wedderburn "Adam in Paul's Letter to the
Romans", in E.A. Livingstone (ed.), *Studia Biblica 1978 III*, Sheffield 1980, 413-30)
there are undoubted allusions to Adam. I mention just two. First, note the allusion in
Rom. 1.23 to Gen. 1.26a LXX: "Then God said, 'Let us make man in our image,
after our likeness (καὶ εἶπεν ὁ θεός Ποιήσωμεν ἄνθρωπον κατ᾽ εἰκόνα ἡμετέραν καὶ
καθ᾽ ὁμοίωσιν)". Secondly, compare Paul's discussion of sexual immorality in Rom.
1.24-27 to traditions of the serpent tempting Eve to unchastity (e.g. 4 Mac. 18.7-8; 2
En. 31.6; b. Shab. 146a; b. Yeb. 103b). As regards this second point, there are differences between Rom. 1 and Jewish traditions about Eve's fall. As Wedderburn,
"Adam", 416, points out, in Jewish texts Eve is seduced whereas in Rom. 1 "sexual
perversions are a further development of man's decline and not its cause". He adds
that if Genesis were to influence Rom. 1 at this point, Gen. 6.1-4 is a more likely
influence, with its story of the unnatural union of the sons of God with the daughters

These allusions suggest Paul is referring to Jews and Gentiles.[25] But on another level the reader (especially the Jewish reader) is expected to see

---

of men. Note also that Paul's argument concerning natural revelation may be understood against a text like 1 En. 36 (see chapter 3, section 2 below), 1 En. 12-36 being related to the story of fallen angels. To some extent Wedderburn has a point. But note that there is a link between Gen. 3 and Gen. 6 in 1 En. 69.4-6. Here one of the fallen angels, Gader'el, is said to have "misled Eve". Also, I hope the discussion of the texts in the following exegesis and the material in chapter 3 below on natural revelation and natural theology will make it clear that the tradition of the fall of Adam does solve some aspects of the text which at first may appear baffling (cf. M.D. Hooker, "Adam in Romans I", *NTS* 6 (1959-60) 298 (297-306), commenting on H.P. Owen's puzzlement in "The Scope of Natural Revelation in Rom. I and Acts XVII", *NTS* 5 (1958-59) 141-42 (133-43)). Note also my discussion in chapter 3 below on "Jewish Views of the Fall" and "Paul's View of the Fall" where I deal with Paul's theological motives for changing the emphasis found in Gen. 3.

[23] Compare Rom. 1.23 with Ps. 105.20 LXX: καὶ ἠλλάξαντο τὴν δόξαν αὐτῶν ἐν ὁμοιώματι μόσχου ἔσθοντος χόρτον (δόξαν αὐτῶν, כְּבוֹדָם meaning "glory of God" (A.A. Anderson, *The Book of Psalms*, 2 vols, London 1972, 2:742). Ps. 106.19-23 concerns the golden calf incident. See also Jer. 2.11: εἰ ἀλλάξονται ἔθνη θεοὺς αὐτῶν; καὶ οὗτοι οὐκ εἰσιν θεοί. ὁ δὲ λαός μου ἠλλάξατο τὴν δόξαν αὐτοῦ, ἐξ ἧς οὐκ ὠφεληθήσονται. Also compare Rom. 1.21 and Jer. 2.5: τάδε λέγει κύριος Τί εὕροσαν οἱ πατέρες ὑμῶν ἐν ἐμοὶ πλημμέλημα, ὅτι ἀπέστησαν μακρὰν ἀπ᾽ ἐμοῦ καὶ ἐπορεύθησαν ὀπίσω τῶν ματαίων καὶ ἐματαιώθησαν (see also 4 Reg. 17.15: καὶ τὰ μαρτύρια αὐτοῦ, ὅσα διεμαρτύρατο αὐτοῖς, οὐκ ἐφύλαξαν καὶ ἐπορεύθησαν ὀπίσω τῶν ματαίων καὶ ἐματαιώθησαν καὶ ὀπίσω τῶν ἐθνῶν τῶν περικύκλῳ αὐτῶν, ὧν ἐνετείλατο αὐτοῖς τοῦ μὴ ποιῆσαι κατὰ ταῦτα). Those who see a reference to the sin of Israel are M. Barth, "Speaking of Sin", *SJT* 8 (1955) 291 (288-96); J.B. Lightfoot, *Notes on the Epistles of St. Paul*, Peabody 1993 (repr.), ([1]1895), p. 253; Michel, *Römer*, p. 102; Schlatter, *Gottes Gerechtigkeit*, p. 64. Note also that 1.18-32 can be compared to Test. Naph. 3-4 (K. Berger, *Exegese des Neuen Testaments*, Heidelberg [2]1984, ([1]1977), p. 26). Here Jews, who are in a position to know God from the created order (3.4), actually engage in the sins characteristic of the Gentiles (4.1).

[24] See, for example, the references to homosexual practices (Rom. 1.26-27).

[25] Despite the allusions to the fall of Israel there is disagreement whether Paul is actually attacking Israel. Michel, *Römer*, p. 102, seems to believe Paul is still referring to the Gentiles: "*Die Heiden tun, was Israel ausdrücklich verboten wurde, und die Schuld der Heiden ist eine Schuld, die auch Israel in der eigenen Geschichte nachzuweisen ist*" (Michel's emphasis). Another possibility is that Paul is using Israel as an example for Gentiles (cf. 1 Cor. 10.18-20, discussed in Bell, *Provoked to Jealousy*, pp. 251-55). But the most likely explanation is that Paul is indeed referring to both Jews and Gentiles in Rom. 1.18-32.

just Gentile sins in this passage. Paul, however, turns on the self-righteous judge in Rom. 2.1ff[26] and on the self-righteous Jew in 2.17.

A final general issue to be discussed is the time dimension of 1.18-32. As far as the verba finita are concerned, the *tenses* may be set out as follows: 1.18-19a is present; 1.19b is aorist; 1.20 is present; 1.21-28 are aorist; 1.32 is present. Note also the use of the aorist participles in vv. 21, 32. The two most controversial points regarding the tenses are how the present in 1.18 and in 1.19-20 is to be understood. As regards v. 18, I argued in chapter 1 that ἀποκαλύπτεται is to be understood as a future present. As far as vv. 19-20 are concerned, the use of the present has been seen as highly significant for those who have advocated a "natural theology" in Paul.[27] This point will be discussed in some detail in chapter 3 below but I need to anticipate some of the points made there in order to make a start on the exegesis.

A key to the time dimension of the passage is to be found in Paul's idea of the "fall". When Paul speaks of this "fall", to what is he referring? Is he referring to the "fall of Adam", the "fall of Israel" or the "fall of every generation"? I believe he is referring to all three. First, there are several allusions to the fall of Adam (and Eve) in this passage.[28] Secondly, there are clear allusions to the fall of Israel, in particular the episode of the golden calf.[29] Thirdly, Paul clearly believes this "fall" relates to his present generation and presumably to every previous generation.[30] So this fall from "knowing God" to "suppressing the truth" to

---

[26] Jervell, *Imago Dei*, p. 319, argues that διό in Rom. 2.1 is not to be understood simply as rhetorical. Rather it has full consecutive meaning (as it always does in Paul). "In 1,20 heißt es, daß die Menschen ohne Entschuldigung sind, ἀναπολογήτους, und 2,1 fährt fort: *Deshalb, διὸ ἀναπολόγητος εἶ.* Sinn gibt es erst, wenn der in 2,1 Angeredete schon 1,18-32 erwähnt ist".

[27] Pointing to the present in Rom. 1.19-20, P. Althaus argues: "Die Kundgebung Gottes ist also nicht eine einmalige, der Vergangenheit, dem Urstande angehörige, sondern eine andauernde, gegenwärtige, auch an den sündigen Menschen, an alle Geschlechter ergehende" (*Die christliche Wahrheit*, Gütersloh ³1952, (¹1947), p. 38).

[28] See the discussion above on the addressees in Rom. 1.18-32, especially n. 22.

[29] Again, see the discussion on the addressees.

[30] A number of scholars have taken this view but there are a number of variations on this theme. See Weber, *Missionspraxis*, p. 27, and the discussion on Paul's view of the fall in chapter 3 below.

becoming "futile in their thinking" seems to relate not only to Adam and to Israel, but also to every generation of Jews and Gentiles and means they are without excuse (ἀναπολόγητος, v. 20). In view of these three sorts of "fall", there must be some sort of historical perspective in Rom. 1.18-32. I am therefore skeptical of Porter's view that 1.18 has an "emphatic timeless present" and continues with the "timeless aorist" in vv. 19-25.[31] As I argued in chapter 1 above, ἀποκαλύπτεται is to be understood as a future present. The emphasis in Rom. 1.19-32, however, is on the past. I therefore understand the aorists as referring to past events.[32] Likewise I understand the present tenses as historic presents, or, using the "Verbal Aspect" theory, "the present form draws added attention to the action to which it refers".[33] So in 1.19a, special attention is paid to God in his knowability being manifest to them (διότι τὸ γνωστὸν τοῦ θεοῦ φανερόν ἐστιν ἐν αὐτοῖς). Such a manifestation, though, was in the past. The same is true of Rom. 1.20, where Paul argues that God's invisible nature has been clearly perceived in the things that have been made so that they are without excuse (τὰ γὰρ ἀόρατα αὐτοῦ ἀπὸ κτίσεως κόσμου τοῖς ποιήμασιν νοούμενα καθορᾶται, ἥ τε ἀΐδιος αὐτοῦ δύναμις καὶ θειότης, εἰς τὸ εἶναι αὐτοὺς ἀναπολογήτους).[34]

2. Exegesis of Romans 1.18-32

2.1 Romans 1.18

1.18: Ἀποκαλύπτεται γὰρ ὀργὴ θεοῦ ἀπ' οὐρανοῦ ἐπὶ πᾶσαν ἀσέβειαν καὶ ἀδικίαν ἀνθρώπων τῶν τὴν ἀλήθειαν ἐν ἀδικίᾳ κατεχόντων. It has

---

[31] S.E. Porter, *Idioms of the Greek New Testament*, Sheffield ²1994, (¹1992), p. 39.

[32] These verbs are ἐφανέρωσεν (19), ἐδόξασαν, ηὐχαρίστησαν, ἐματαιώθησαν, ἐσκοτίσθη (21), ἐμωράνθησαν (22), ἤλλαξαν (23), παρέδωκεν (24), μετήλλαξαν, ἐσεβάσθησαν, ἐλάτρευσαν (25), παρέδωκεν, μετήλλαξαν (26), ἐξεκαύθησαν (27), ἐδοκίμασαν, παρέδωκεν (28).

[33] Porter, *Idioms*, p. 31.

[34] See the exegesis below of Rom. 1.19-20 for a precise translation of these verses.

already been argued that the verb ἀποκαλύπτεται is to be understood as a
future present. But what is the nature of the ὀργὴ θεοῦ? This wrath is not
an emotion of God,[35] not even an emotion which is constant (as opposed
to capricious).[36] Rather it is an objective entity, related to God's role as
just judge and the consequence of this wrath is that sinners will be condemned on the day of judgement. Two objections could be made against
this view. First, if God shows love and mercy which have an emotional
perspective, can not his anger have this perspective too? Secondly, is not
the view that God's wrath is an objective entity rather than an emotion of
God totally removed from the God of the Old Testament? In answer to the
first point, it can be a dangerous argument to say that just because the
love of God in an "emotion" so must the wrath of God. Each aspect of
God must be judged on its own terms. Also one must avoid the argument
of analogy (i.e. because human wrath is an emotion so must God's

---

[35] This fits in with Paul's view of reconciliation whereby human beings need to be
reconciled to God (Rom. 5.6-11; 2 Cor. 5.14-21) but God does not need to be reconciled to humankind. The enmity between God and man is therefore *not mutual*. We
are God's enemy; but God is not our enemy. This seems to put in question the whole
view of propitiation (and "penal substitution") of scholars such as L. Morris (see his
view on propitiation in *The Apostolic Preaching of the Cross*, Leicester [3]1965,
([1]1955), pp. 144-213). See also the view of Godet, *Romans*, p. 102, who points to the
addition of the word θυμός in 2.8 "which denotes the *feeling* at its deepest" (Godet's
emphasis). However, see the discussion in chapter 4 on Rom. 2.8.

[36] Note that although Morris does not see God's wrath as capricious, it is nevertheless an emotion: "Those who object to the conception of the wrath of God should
realise that what is meant is not some irrational passion bursting forth uncontrollably,
but a burning zeal for the right coupled with a perfect hatred for everything that is
evil" (*Apostolic Preaching*, p. 209). Because Morris believes that God has enmity
against human kind, Christ's death has to be understood as propitiatory. The same
logic is found in R.V.G. Tasker, *The Biblical Doctrine of the Wrath of God*, London
1951. He speaks of propitiation in Rom. 3.25 (p. 9) and goes on to defend the view
that God's wrath is an emotion, although it is not "fitful, wayward, and spasmodic"
like human anger but is "stable, unswerving and of set purpose" (p. 11). Tasker
points to Lactantius, *De ira Dei* 22 (21), who makes the same distinction: "I might
say that the anger of man ought to be curbed, because he is often angry unjustly; and
he has immediate emotion, because he is only for a time (*temporalis*). . . . But God is
not angry for a short time (*ad praesens*), because he is eternal and of perfect virtue,
and He is never angry unless deservedly" (*De ira Dei* 21, *ANF* 7:277 (259-80)).

wrath).[37] As regards the second point it is the case that God's wrath in the Old Testament is portrayed in graphic terms suggesting God's wrath is in fact an emotion of God.[38] But in the Old Testament itself there is a development. In the earliest texts God's wrath is certainly an emotion and is manifested directly towards those who have offended him.[39] In Deuteronomy the wrath of God is fully moralised and is inflicted indirectly. Then in the prophets wrath, whilst being an emotion of God, generally seems more controlled[40] and is related to questions of righteousness and punishment.[41] Indeed it is here that the idea of the eschatological wrath of God begins.[42] After the exile two tendencies can be detected.[43] First, there is the tendency to depersonalise God's wrath which can be seen as a development from Deuteronomy.[44] Secondly, there continues among the Prophets (and taken up in apocalyptic) the personal view of wrath but it is directed against Gentiles as well as against Israel and although in some of these texts wrath has an emotional element, it is not

---

[37] See the problems with *analogia entis* in the discussion on natural theology in chapter 3 below.

[38] The most common term for wrath is אַף and derives from אָנַף, "to be angry", originally "to snort" (Grether-Fichtner, ὀργή *TDNT* 5:392). So when God's anger waxes hot (חָרָה אַף) smoke comes from his nostrils (Ps. 18.8).

[39] See especially 2 Sam. 6.7-8; 24.1. Note also the vivid expressions of God's wrath in Ps. 18 (see the previous note). Ps. 18 has a close parallel in 2 Sam. 22 and contains a number of archaic features. Anderson, *Psalms*, 1:153, has suggested that this Psalm was composed by a court poet for the use of Davidic kings and says a date in the reign of Josiah (640-609) may well be too late.

[40] Hos. 11.8b-9a: "My heart recoils within me, my compassion grows warm and tender. 9 I will not execute my fierce anger, I will not again destroy Ephraim; for I am God and not man".

[41] See Hos. 5.9-10.

[42] See Is. 13.9, 13 (cf. 66.15); Zeph. 1.14-16, 18; 2.2.

[43] Cf. A.T. Hanson, *The Wrath of the Lamb*, London 1957, p. 37.

[44] Fichtner, ὀργή, 396, points out that in later Old Testament literature there is "an attempt to loosen and even dissolve too close an association of God with wrath". Wrath tends to be used absolutely in the post-exilic writings (so, for example, in P קֶצֶף יהוה does not occur at all). Also, Hanson, *Wrath of the Lamb*, p. 22, points out that in P God's wrath is only referred to five times, and in two cases it is expressed "in strangely impersonal terms". See Num. 16.46b: "for wrath (קֶצֶף) has gone forth from the LORD". The same tendency is seen in the Chronicler.

so prominent as in the earlier Old Testament texts. Punishment is the central idea.[45] These two strands are found also in post-biblical Judaism, the first in "Hellenistic Judaism"[46] and the second in apocalyptic.

There are cases in later texts where God's wrath is vividly portrayed[47] but the general tendency to lessen the anthropopathism is undoubtedly there.[48] This general development is also found in Rabbinic texts.[49] Then

---

[45] Cf. G.P. Wetter, *Der Vergeltungsgedanke bei Paulus*, Göttingen 1912, p. 17. Note also that if in later texts the wrath of God becomes associated with the day of the Lord, the implication is that God's wrath is not so impulsive but waits for that day. The first texts dealing with the day of the Lord are from the eighth century prophets. Note also Ex. 34.6: "The LORD, the LORD, a God merciful and gracious, slow to anger (אֶרֶךְ אַפַּיִם), and abounding in steadfast love and faithfulness . . . " (cf. Num. 14.18; Neh. 9.18; Ps. 86.15; 103.8; 145.8; Jon. 4.2).

[46] See Aristeas, 254; Philo, *Quod Deus immutabilis sit* 52 (commenting on Gen. 6.7) writes: "some on hearing these words suppose that the Existent feels wrath and anger, whereas He is not susceptible to any passion at all" (Philo (LCL) 3:37)). I put the term Hellenistic Judaism in quotation marks because all Judaism in Paul's time was hellenised and "Hellenistic Judaism" only has a relative meaning (i.e. Judaism which has been strongly hellenised). See M. Hengel, *The 'Hellenisation' of Judaea in the First Century after Christ* ET, London 1989, p. 53: "Since after a more than three-hundred-year history under the influence of Greek culture Palestinian Judaism can also be described as 'Hellenistic Judaism', *the term 'Hellenistic' as currently used no longer serves to make any meaningful differentiation in terms of the history of religions within the history of earliest Christianity*" (Hengel's emphasis).

[47] See Sib. 4.159-61: "Even then know that God is no longer benign but gnashing his teeth in wrath and destroying the entire race of men at once by a great conflagration" (translation by J.J. Collins, in J. Charlesworth, *The Old Testament Pseudepigrapha*, 2 vols, London 1 1983; 2 1985, 1:388).

[48] Interestingly, some confirmation of the view of this development is seen in the fact that any ideas of propitiation are to be found in the earlier texts of the Old Testament. So in 1 Sam. 26.19b David says to Saul: "If it is the LORD who has stirred you up against me, may he accept an offering". See also 2 Sam. 24.25. But in the later writings (e.g. P) there seems to be no idea of propitiation. Cf. J. Barr, who concludes that "propitiation or appeasement of an angry but fickle deity appears at an early stage in Israelite religion" ("Propitiation", *HGR*, 810). On the view of atonement in the Priestly writing, see the important article by H. Gese, "Die Sühne", in *Zur biblischen Theologie*, Tübingen ³1989, (¹1977), 85-106.

[49] See, however, E. Sjöberg, ὀργή, *TDNT* 5:416, who stresses the role of God's wrath in the Rabbinic writings as an emotion of God. He points out that God's wrath can be compared to human anger (for example it is likened to that of a father being angry with his son (Mek. Ex. 14.15, J.Z. Lauterbach, *Mekilta de-Rabbi Ishmael*, 3 vols, Philadelphia 1 ²1949, (¹1933); 2 ²1949, (¹1933); 3 ²1949, (¹1935), 1:218)). But,

in the New Testament, the wrath of God has become virtually devoid of any emotion of God[50] and this is especially so for Paul. How has this come about? Perhaps one reason is the hellenisation of Judaism.[51] Another reason is that in the New Testament the wrath of God is predominantly eschatological.[52]

In the context of this development how is Paul's view of the wrath of God to be understood? First of all, Paul cannot simply be slotted into

---

as Sjöberg argues, God's wrath is always righteous. Sjöberg contends that although in fairly late Rabbinic texts the anger of God is often hypostatised, this is not due to fear of anthropopathism. "It rests on the one hand on the love of a concrete and plastic mode of depiction which is distinctive of Rabbinism, and on the other on the general growth of angelological speculations" (ὀργή, 416). However, I wonder whether this is a satisfactory analysis. P. Billerbeck, *Kommentar zum Neuen Testament aus Talmud und Midrasch*, 4 vols, München 1-3 ³1961; 4 ²1956, 3:30, writes: "Das Streben nach Beseitigung von Anthropomorphismen in Verbindung mit dem Grundsatz, daß bei Gott nichts Böses (Schlimmes) wohne, hat die jüdische Schriftgelehrsamkeit hier u. da veranlaßt, den 'Zorn' oder den 'Grimm' oder den 'Groll' Gottes in einen Engel des Verderbens מַלְאַךְ חַבָּלָה umzudeuten". In view of Ex. 34.6 the angel of wrath is far from God (see Tanh. תזריע (155ᵇ), quoted in Billerbeck, *Kommentar*, 3:30). Note also that the very development of angels was probably linked to a fear of anthropopathism.

[50] M. Pohlenz, *Vom Zorne Gottes. Eine Studie über den Einfluß der griechischen Philosophie auf das alte Christentum*, Göttingen 1909, p. 10, writes: "Die im Alten Testament so häufige sinnliche Ausmalung des Zornes als eines psychischen Vorganges fehlt im Neuem Testament vollkommen".

[51] Pohlenz, *Vom Zorne Gottes*, p. 5 points out: "Daß für die Gottheit selber die ἀπάθεια ein notwendiges Attribut sei, darüber sind natürlich alle Philosophen einig". So, for example, Xenophon and Plato criticised the poets for attributing emotions to the gods. This tendency to take away the emotion of God is found to some extent in the LXX. For example נחם in Gen. 6.6-7 is translated with ἐνθυμεῖσθαι. Note, however, that in a text like 1 Sam. 15.35 κύριος μετεμελήθη is allowed (see Pohlenz, *Vom Zorne Gottes*, p. 7). Then in "Hellenistic Judaism", one can find that anger is something quite unworthy of God. Aristeas 254: γινώσκειν δὲ δεῖ, διότι θεὸς τὸν πάντα κόσμον διοικεῖ μετ᾽ εὐμενείας καὶ χωρὶς ὀργῆς ἁπάσης. See, however, the texts from the very hellenised book of 4 Maccabees (4.21; 9.32).

[52] Pohlenz, *Vom Zorne Gottes*, p. 10: "Denn die eschatologischen Schilderungen des Zorngerichts haben mit den seelischen Erregungen nichts zu tun". Pohlenz also points out that even though Ritschl may have gone too far in believing the wrath of God to have only an eschatological significance, "so ist es doch wirklich der zukünftige Zorn Gottes, der im Vordergrunde steht" (p. 13). Note that already in the Old Testament the wrath of God was tending to become eschatological in the prophetic "day of the Lord".

some category of Jewish thought, for he was a creative theologian. But I
can make the following points. Paul did not have an impersonal view of
God's wrath such as one finds in the Chronicler.[53] This impersonal view
of wrath was put forward by Dodd. He wrote that Paul "retains the concept of 'the Wrath of God' . . . not to describe the attitude of God to man,
but to describe an inevitable process of cause and effect in a moral
universe".[54] Dodd is followed by Hanson.[55] But is this a fair understanding of the Pauline concept of wrath? On the one hand Hanson is
quite right to point out that "God is never described as angry, and no verb
describing anger is ever used of him by St Paul, or any writer of the New
Testament".[56] So there is no evidence for wrath being an emotion of God
according to Paul. Further there are arguments against wrath being an
emotion of God when one considers Paul's view of the atonement.[57] But,
that is not to say wrath is impersonal and that it is simply "a process
which sinners bring upon themselves".[58] Wrath originates in God (as is
clear in Rom. 3.5; 9.22; 12.19).[59] Further, the wrath of God is related to
God's role as a righteous judge. Just as God is completely involved in
judgement, so he is completely involved in wrath. I suggest therefore that
the impersonal view of wrath found in the Chronicler does not correspond
to Paul's understanding. Is then apocalyptic a more appropriate back-

---

[53] Contrast Hanson, *Wrath of the Lamb*, p. 23: "The significance of this treatment
of the divine wrath in the Chronicler's work must not be underrated. We need to look
no further for the origin of Paul's doctrine of the wrath of God".

[54] Dodd, *Romans*, p. 23. Cf. Wetter, *Vergeltungsgedanke*, p. 22-23. On Rom.
1.18-32 he writes: "Diese Vergeltung tritt in Aktion ohne Gottes persönliches
Eingreifen, es ist, als ob immanente Gesetze in der Menschheit wirksam wären".

[55] Hanson, *Wrath of the Lamb*, p. 69.

[56] Hanson, *Wrath of the Lamb*, p. 69.

[57] See above n. 35.

[58] Hanson, *Wrath of the Lamb*, p. 69.

[59] Further, although the expression ὀργὴ τοῦ θεοῦ only occurs in Rom. 1.18 among
the seven letters generally considered genuine (elsewhere the apparently impersonal
expression ὁ ὀργή is used), it is illegitimate to conclude that wrath must be
impersonal. Paul also often refers simply to χάρις but that is no argument for taking
grace to be impersonal (see S.H. Travis, "Wrath of God (NT)", *ABD* 6:997 (996-
98)).

ground? Paul in Rom. 1.18 certainly does share apocalyptic views.[60] His views of wrath are concerned with judgement and eschatology. But he does not share the view, found in many apocalypses, that God's wrath has an emotional element. I believe Paul's view is that God's wrath is personal, but not emotional.

Now this wrath of God will be revealed ἐπὶ πᾶσαν ἀσέβειαν καὶ ἀδικίαν ἀνθρώπων. Pohlenz makes the point that although for Paul ἀσέβεια and ἀδικία are linked, this was by no means obvious for someone like the Stoic Marcus Aurelius.[61] Note that in Rom. 1.18 the wrath of God is directed not against people themselves but against their godlessness and unrighteousness.

In apposition to ἀνθρώπων there is τῶν τὴν ἀλήθειαν ἐν ἀδικίᾳ κατεχόντων. What is the nature of this ἀλήθεια? Michel's idea that ἀλήθεια here means behaviour seems unlikely.[62] Neither does the term simply mean the true knowledge of God;[63] nor does it refer to the reality of the created order.[64] Much more likely is the idea of Bultmann, who sees ἀλήθεια here as meaning the "revealed reality" of God.[65] This view is shared by Lackmann,[66] Käsemann,[67] and Hübner,[68] and coheres with

---

[60] 1 En. 91.7-9. See chapter 3 section 2 below ("The Relation of Romans 1.18-32 to Apocalyptic", pp. 82-84).

[61] See *Meditations* 9.1. It is striking that the link between unrighteousness and godlessness is very much taken for granted in many Christian cultures.

[62] Michel, *Römer*, p. 99. Cf. Schlatter, *Gottes Gerechtigkeit*, p. 50: "ἀλήθεια ist aber bei Paulus ein Tätigkeitsnomen, der Name jenes Verhaltens, durch das der Mensch das, was ihm gezeigt wird, anerkennt und nicht entstellt und ebenso sich selbst zeigt, wie er ist, und sich nicht durch Lüge und Schein der Gemeinschaft entzieht".

[63] H. Menge, *Die heilige Schrift*, Stuttgart 1926, translates the term of Rom. 1.18 as "die wahre Erkenntnis Gottes".

[64] Schlier, *Römerbrief*, pp. 50-51, writes that in view of 1.25, ἀλήθεια is "die offenbare und gültige Wirklichkeit der Schöpfung Gottes". Cf. his earlier work, "Von den Heiden", 30: "Die 'Wahrheit' ist hier nicht die rechte Gotteserkenntnis oder auch die rechte Religion, sondern die wahre, unverdeckte Wirklichkeit der Dinge, in der sich Gottes Anspruch verbirgt und offenbart". May we compare Barth's view of Theology being not just about God but about everything?

[65] R. Bultmann, ἀλήθεια κτλ, *TDNT* 1:243 (238-251).

[66] Lackmann, *Geheimnis der Schöpfung*, p. 183, writes concerning ἀλήθεια: "Im Munde des Israeliten und Apostels wird er aber nur in Anlehnung an die Schöpfervorstellung des Alten Bundes verwandt worden sein, so daß 'Wahrheit' hier

the non-partitive understanding of τὸ γνωστὸν τοῦ θεοῦ of 1.19 adopted below.

The next important issue is what is meant by the verb κατέχειν (ἐπὶ πᾶσαν ἀσέβειαν καὶ ἀδικίαν ἀνθρώπων τῶν τὴν ἀλήθειαν ἐν ἀδικίᾳ κατεχόντων). J.H. Bavinck suggests the translation "repress". He believes this translation is especially fitting, for in modern Psychology "repression" is something done unconsciously.[69] "We may justifiably interpret Paul's words here in terms of this powerful activity brought to light by the psychology of our day. He says that human beings always repress God's truth because it is contrary to the whole pattern of their life. Human wickedness prevents this truth really reaching them".[70] However, I wonder whether this is convincing in view of vv. 19-21. These verses, as I shall show, point to human beings having a knowledge of God himself. However, vv. 21-32 make it clear that this knowledge of

---

gleichbedeutend der sich selbst erschließenden Wirklichkeit Gottes, kein Abstraktum, sondern das Konkretum Gottes selbst sein wird". He adds, pp. 183-84: "Unheilvoll hat sich jedoch in der gesamten Exegese die griechische und rationalistische Verwendung von 'ἀλήθεια' durchgesetzt. Danach ist 'Wahrheit' ein Wissen von Gott, *cognitio* oder *notitia*, eine Errungenschaft der *mens* und der *ratio*, oder gar eine *facultas* der menschlichen Seele, *lex naturae* und *notitia naturalis*".

[67] Käsemann, *Romans*, p. 80: "The reality of the world and the basic sin of mankind consist in not recognising God in his reality that opens itself to us".

[68] H. Hübner, ἀλήθεια κτλ in *EDNT* 1:59 (57-60), agrees with Bultmann: "ἀλήθεια appears as the disclosed *truth of God*" (Hübner's emphasis). However, I am not so sure that Hübner is right in claiming that "ἀλήθεια almost takes on the sense of δικαιοσύνη θεοῦ". δικαιοσύνη θεοῦ refers to the salvation of God; ἀλήθεια refers to God himself.

[69] J.H. Bavinck, "Human Religion in God's Eyes: A Study of Romans 1:18-32", *SBET* 12.1 (1994) 45-46 (44-52).

[70] Bavinck, "Human Religion", 46. Bavinck goes on to argue that this repression helps explain the nature of the "exchange" (v. 23). Just as repressed feelings manifest themselves in other ways (e.g. slips of the tongue, dreams) so the repression of the truth of God manifests itself in idolatry. "Elements of the truth of God are exiled to the unconscious, to the crypts of human experience. They have not vanished altogether; they are still active and reveal themselves again and again. But they cannot become openly conscious; they appear in disguise. Something else is exchanged or substituted for them. As Calvin said, the human spirit is a factory of idols." For a further discussion of idolatry see chapter 3 below.

God has been lost, not because of some unconscious *repression*, but because of conscious *suppression* of the truth. Therefore I suggest that the translation of the RSV and *BAG* "to suppress" is better.[71]

Human beings therefore suppress the truth as a conscious deliberate act and they suppress it "in unrighteousness" (ἐν ἀδικίᾳ). However, I agree with Kuhlmann in believing that it is a mistake to see the suppression of the truth as originating in immorality.[72] Rather the ἀσέβεια καὶ ἀδικία ἀνθρώπων, upon which God's wrath will come, are both manifest in the suppression of the truth, and conversely this suppression contributes further to the ἀσέβεια καὶ ἀδικία ἀνθρώπων.[73]

2.2 Romans 1.19-20

2.2.1 Romans 1.19

The conjunction διότι introduces the argument of Rom. 1.19-20 which establishes that the truth, that is the "revealed reality" of God, is available to all. διότι does not therefore *directly* give the reason for the revelation of God's wrath. It is rather concerned to establish that all have knowledge of God and so is to be linked to v. 18b.[74]

One of the crucial exegetical questions here is the meaning of τὸ γνωστὸν τοῦ θεοῦ. Two frequent alternatives put forward are "the known

---

[71] See also the magical text in A. Deißmann, *Licht vom Osten*, Tübingen ⁴1923 (¹1908), p. 260: "Κρόνος, ὁ κατέχων τὸν θυμὸν ὅλων τῶν ἀνθρώπων κάτεχε τὸν θυμὸν Ὡρι". Elsewhere in Paul κατέχω can mean "prevent from going away" (Phlm 13), "hold fast" (1 Cor. 11.2; 15.2; 1 Thes. 5.21), "possess" (1 Cor. 7.30; 2 Cor. 6.10) and in 2 Thes. 2.6-7 takes the meaning "restrain". The passive in Rom. 7.6 means "be bound". The verb in Rom. 1.18 does not correspond to any of these meanings elsewhere in the Pauline corpus.

[72] See Zahn, *Römer*, who wishes to see that "die Irreligiosität auf die Immoralität zurückführt". Kuhlmann, *Theologia naturalis*, p. 41 n. 1 rightly comments: "Diese Zerreißung in eine praktische und eine theoretische Seite des menschlichen Verhältnisses zu Gott muß von vornherein vermieden werden, um den ursprünglichen Begriff des *ganzen* Menschen zu erhalten" (Kuhlmann's emphasis).

[73] Kuhlmann, *Theologia naturalis*, p. 40-41.

[74] Schlier, *Römerbrief*, p. 51, believes διότι means "weil es sich um Folgendes handelt".

of God" or "the knowable of God". The word is used only here by Paul. In the rest of the New Testament γνωστός means "known".[75] But in classical Greek and also in LXX it sometimes means "knowable".[76] Such a meaning for γνωστός has been supported in Rom. 1.19[77] and the meaning "known" has been rejected by a number of commentators because, it is argued, the sentence would be a tautology.[78] There is some truth in this, although it must be stressed that although there would be a tautology in the phrase διότι τὸ γνωστὸν τοῦ θεοῦ φανερόν ἐστιν ἐν αὐτοῖς, the addition ὁ θεὸς γὰρ αὐτοῖς ἐφανέρωσεν is by no means superfluous for Paul.[79] Returning to the meaning "knowable", many commentators understand τὸ γνωστὸν τοῦ θεοῦ as a partitive genitive ("what can be known about God"). However, I believe such a partitive understanding of the genitive can be seriously misleading. It implies that knowing God means knowing certain attributes of God. However, as I will argue below, *simply knowing certain attributes of God is as good as knowing nothing about God.* I would rather understand τὸ γνωστὸν τοῦ θεοῦ as "God in his knowability".[80] This parallels "God in his invisibility" (τὰ

---

[75] See Jn 18.15-16; Lk. 2.44; 23.49; Acts 1.19; 2.14; 4.10, 16; 9.42; 13.38; 15.18; 19.17; 28.22, 28.

[76] For this meaning see Plato, *Republic*, 7.517B; Epictetus, *Discourses* 2.20.4; Gen. 2.9 LXX; and possibly Sir. 21.7.

[77] Origen understands γνωστός to mean knowable. Commenting on Rom. 1.19 he writes: *Iam et superius diximus quia notum Dei est hoc quod ex huius mundi consequentia uel rationibus assequi possumus, sicut et ipse apostolus ex consequentibus indicat dicens inuisibilia eius per ea quae facta sunt contemplari* (*Commentaria in epistulam b. Pauli ad Romanos*; see C.P. Hammond Bammel (ed.), *Der Römerbriefkommentar des Origenes: Kritische Ausgabe der Übersetzung Rufins, Buch 1-3*, Freiburg 1990, p. 84; *MPG* 14:863). Many have followed Origen in understanding γνωστός as knowable. So Schlier, for example, translates τὸ γνωστὸν τοῦ θεοῦ as *quod cognoscibile est de deo* (*Römerbrief*, p. 51).

[78] Cranfield, *Romans*, 1:113; Godet, *Romans*, p. 103; Schlier, *Römerbrief*, p. 51. Nevertheless some translations and commentators have taken γνωστός to mean "known". See, e.g., the Vulgate: *quod notum est Dei*.

[79] See the discussion in chapter 3 on the relation of 1.18-32 to Greek Philosophy and Hellenistic Judaism.

[80] See *BA*, p. 328 who take the expression to mean "Gott, soweit er erkennbar ist" or "Gott in seiner Erkennbarkeit". R. Bultmann, γινώσκω κτλ., *TDNT* 1:719 (689-719), actually leaves the question open whether "what may be known of God" is correct or "God in His Knowability" ("Gott in seiner Erkennbarkeit") is correct. In

ἀόρατα αὐτοῦ) of v. 20.[81] I suggest the following translation for Rom.
1.19-20a:

For *God in his knowability* (τὸ γνωστὸν τοῦ θεοῦ) *is manifest* to them, because *God
has revealed himself* to them. 20 For since the creation of the world *God in his
invisibility* (τὰ ἀόρατα αὐτοῦ), namely, his eternal power and deity, has been clearly
perceived in the things that have been made.[82]

---

favour of the latter he cites τὰ κρυπτά τοῦ σκότους (1 Cor. 4.5) and τὸ χρηστὸν τοῦ
θεοῦ (Rom. 2.4). See also his comments on τὰ ἀόρατα αὐτοῦ below (n. 99).

[81] Cf. τὸ χρηστὸν τοῦ θεοῦ which in Rom. 2.4 means "God in his kindness".

[82] Compare K. Barth, *KD* 2.1:131 (*CD* 2.1:119): "Gott ist ihm erkennbar
(wörtlich: Gott ist ihm in seiner Erkennbarkeit offenbar); Gott selbst offenbarte sich
ihm. Denn er, der Unsichtbare (wörtlich: seine Unsichtbarkeit) d.h. seine ewige Kraft
und Gottheit wird seit der Erschaffung der Welt, verständlich in seinen Werken, . . .
". K. Barth, *Der Römerbrief*, München [6]1929, p. 21, gives a slightly different translation of 1.19: "Der Gottesgedanke ist ihnen bekannt, Gott hat ihn ihnen bekannt
gemacht". See also his translation of Rom. 1.21: "Ihrer Kenntnis Gottes zum Trotz
haben sie ihm nicht als Gott Ehre und Dank erwiesen, sondern entleert worden ist ihr
Denken und verfinstert ihr unverständiges Herz". H. Rosin, "To gnoston tou Theou",
ThZ 17 (1961) 164 (161-65), finds Barth's translations attractive in that they avoid the
partitive genitive but is critical in that they bring us near to a tautology. "'Gott ist ihm
in seiner Erkennbarkeit offenbar' kann immer noch so verstanden werden, daß Gott
ihm nur offenbar ist, *sofern* und *soweit* er (überhaupt? allgemein?) erkennbar ist.
Bedeutet es aber, daß Gott *als* der (prinzipiell) Erkennbare ihm offenbar ist, dann
gerät man wieder in die Nähe der gefürchteten 'Tautologie' oder Selbstver-
ständlichkeit und hat zudem keine rechte Erklärung für den folgenden Vers (V. 20)".
On the basis of Gen. 2.9 LXX (τὸ ξύλον τοῦ εἰδέναι γνωστὸν καλοῦ καὶ πονηροῦ
which Rosin translates as "the tree of learning that which is to be known of good and
evil" (cf. *The Septuagint Version of the Old Testament with an English Translation*,
London (n.d.)) he argues that to know good and evil is to distinguish them. This leads
him to his translation of Rom. 1.19 as "Denn das, *woran* sich Gott erkennen läßt, ist
ihnen kund: Gott selbst hat es ihnen kundgetan". Rosin adds: "Woran aber ist Gott zu
erkennen? Woran lassen sich Gott und Nichtgott unterscheiden wie Wahrheit und
Lüge (vgl. V.23-25)? . . . Es sind seine ewige Kraft und Gottheit . . . " (165). In
response to Rosin I would argue that if knowing "good and evil" means distinguishing
between them, little sense is made of the Genesis text (see, for example, C.
Westermann, *Genesis, I. Teilband: Genesis 1-11*, Neukirchen-Vluyn 1974, pp. 328-
33; G. Wenham, *Genesis 1-15*, Waco 1987, pp. 63-64). Further, I defend my translation "God in his knowability" in Rom. 1.19 by pointing to similar expressions like τὸ
χρηστὸν τοῦ θεοῦ ("God in his kindness", Rom. 2.4) and τὰ ἀόρατα αὐτοῦ ("God is
his invisibility", Rom. 1.20).

A further reason for not having a partitive genitive is that Paul develops the thought of v. 19 in v. 20 (and v. 21a) where he speaks of God's being as a whole.[83] Rosin writes:

Mit aller Kraft legt er dar, daß der heidnische Mensch nicht etwas von Gott weiß, sondern *Gott selbst*, Gott ganz, kennt (γνόντες τὸν θεόν, V. 21), weil er Gott tatsächlich kennengelernt, erfahren hat . . .[84]

In the expression φανερόν ἐστιν ἐν αὐτοῖς the preposition ἐν stands for the customary dative.[85] The other possibilities are that God reveals himself "among them" or "in them". The first means that God reveals himself in their midst and the second means that God reveals himself "in them". This second possibility is to be firmly rejected.[86]

This brings me to a discussion of the verb φανερόω. In the above discussion I have translated φανερόω as "reveal". This, however, should not be taken to mean that the verb is synonymous with ἀποκαλύπτω. The verbs are often taken as synonymous in view of the parallelism of 3.21 and 1.17.[87] However, as Bockmuehl has argued, there are some subtle but significant distinctions between the two texts. So in 1.17 the righteousness of God is revealed (ἀποκαλύπτεται) but this revelation

---

[83] Wilckens, *Römer*, 1:105. See R. Bultmann, γινώσκω κτλ., *ThWNT* 1:719 (688-719): "denn auch τὰ ἀόρατα τοῦ θεοῦ in v. 20 bedeutet nicht: 'was an ihm unsichtbar ist', sondern: 'er, der Unsichtbare'" (the translation of this in *TDNT* 1:719 is ambiguous).

[84] Rosin, "To gnoston tou Theou", 162. Although Rosin has some fine insights into Rom. 1.19-20 I do not share all his arguments for the non-partitive understanding of τὸ γνωστὸν τοῦ θεοῦ. So he writes: "Wenn hier wirklich eine gerade Linie von V.19 (γνωστόν) über V.21 (γνόντες) und V.28 (ἐπίγνωσις) zu V.32 (ἐπιγνόντες) führt, dann darf τὸ γνωστὸν τοῦ θεοῦ nicht in partitivem Sinne ('was von Gott erkennbar ist') übersetzt und erklärt werden" ("To gnoston tou Theou", 163). My point is precisely that there is no "gerade Linie". Knowledge of God himself is lost because human beings failed to glorify God (1.21). Knowing τὸ δικαίωμα τοῦ θεοῦ (Rom. 1.32) is merely a remnant of knowledge and and therefore is in fact no knowledge of God himself (just as knowledge of the attributes of God does not amount to a knowledge of God himself). On this crucial point, see the discussion below.

[85] *BDF* 220.1.

[86] Kuhlmann, *Theologia naturalis*, p. 42, argues that God reveals himself. "Und zwar heißt dies nicht, daß in der Seele des Menschen auf magische Weise die Erkenntnis Gottes aufleuchtet".

[87] See R. Bultmann - D. Lührmann, φαίνω κτλ, *ThWNT* 9:1-11; P.-G. Müller, φανερόω, *EDNT* 3:413 (413-14).

occurs "'zeitlos' gegenwärtig" in the gospel; but this gospel presupposes a prior revelation of its content and this is what Rom. 3.21 is concerned with, using the perfect πεφανέρωται.[88] So in 3.21 "haben wir es mit der historischen Offenbarung der Gottesgerechtigkeit im Christusgeschehen der jüngsten Vergangenheit zu tun".[89] Bockmuehl does make some helpful comments as regards the differences in Rom. 1.17 and 3.21, but I believe he has overstated his case in arguing for the empirical nature of the verb φανεροῦν.[90] As I argued in chapter 1, there is an empirical ele-

---

[88] See Cranfield, *Romans*, 1:109.

[89] Bockmuehl, "φανερόω", 96, points to 3.21-26. Note the striking phrase ὃν προέθετο ὁ θεὸς ἱλαστήριον ("whom (referring to Christ) God publicly set forth as a mercy seat") and the use of ἔνδειξις. Bockmuehl argues that νυνὶ δέ (3.21) has temporal as well as theological significance. See also P. Stuhlmacher's translation "Jetzt aber", *Der Brief an die Römer*, Göttingen 1989, p. 54 and Fitzmyer, *Romans*, pp. 341, 343-44.

[90] The problems with Bockmuehl's view that the verb has an objective empirical nature can be seen by considering two points. 1. He argues that in John the verb is not to be equated with γνωρίζω ("φανερόω", 90). But surely Jn 2.11 would support this in that Christ revealed his glory not to everyone, but only to his disciples, for they are the ones who believed in him (καὶ ἐφανέρωσεν τὴν δόξαν αὐτοῦ, καὶ ἐπίστευσαν εἰς αὐτὸν οἱ μαθηταὶ αὐτοῦ). See D.A. Carson, *The Gospel according to John*, Leicester 1991, p. 175: "The glory was not visible to all who had seen the miracle; the glory cannot be identified with the miraculous display . . . The servants saw the sign, but not the glory . . ." As C.K. Barrett, *The Gospel according to John*, London ²1978, (¹1955), p. 193, points out, ἐφανέρωσεν of Jn 2.11 corresponds to ἐθεασάμεθα of Jn 1.14. Bockmuehl gives further support for his view by arguing that the verb as used in Jn 21.1a, b, 14 "mag hier dem emphatischen ὤφθη bei Paulus in 1 Kor 15,3ff entsprechen" (91). This, however, backfires. For the verb ὤφθη as used in 1 Cor. 15 means not an objective appearance but rather an appearance to those whom God has chosen. The verb ὀφθῆναι "appear" is used in the LXX for the appearance of God himself or his angels before men (see P. Stuhlmacher, *Biblische Theologie des Neuen Testaments, Band 1: Grundlegung: Von Jesus zu Paulus*, Göttingen 1992, pp. 172-73). In these instances the concern is not simply with seeing but is bound up with a verbal revelation. See, for example, the ἄγγελος κυρίου in Ex. 3.2, 4ff. Ex. 3.2 runs as follows: "And the angel of the LORD appeared to him in a flame of fire out of the midst of the bush". The Greek aorist passive here (ὤφθη) is equivalent to the niphal form of ראה (וַיֵּרָא) and means "let oneself be seen". וַיֵּרָא מַלְאַךְ יְהוָה אֵלָיו ; ὤφθη δὲ αὐτῷ ἄγγελος κυρίου. I suggest that the expression ὀφθῆναί τινι in 1 Cor. 15 points to the appearance of the risen Jesus to chosen individuals and groups. So if they received an appearance, they would be converted. To return to John, it is true that in Jn 7.4 there is a reference to a "manifestation before all eyes" (Bultmann - Lührmann, φανερόω, 5, with which Bockmuehl, "φανερόω", 93 n. 25, agrees) but

ment in Rom. 3.21-26 in that Paul speaks about the *reconciling act* of Jesus' atoning death whereas in Rom. 1.16-17 he is more concerned with the *reconciling word*. But is Paul really speaking about objective historical events in 3.21-26? Christ is publicly set forward as a ἱλαστήριον for all to see (Rom. 3.25), but did all recognise in Golgotha the presence of God and place of the atonement?[91] This suggests that in Rom. 3.21 Paul is not speaking of a simple historical revelation when he uses φανερόω. Neither does he have a simple empirical revelation in view in Rom. 1.19 in using φανερόω and φανερόν. I suggest that in these texts the verb φανερόω can be translated as "reveal" or "manifest" or "make known". It may well be that there are subtle distinctions between φανερόω and ἀποκαλύπτω. But φανερόω in these texts does not refer to a simple empirical manifestation.[92]

So this knowledge of God is gained not by empirical observation. Knowledge is only gained because God takes the initiative to make himself known. So as Kuhlmann rightly argues, "Gott offenbart sich in der Schöpfung, er schafft das, was ihn erkennen soll, and damit zugleich das, worin er erkannt werden kann: den Kosmos".[93] Further, because Paul most likely had a view of continuous creation, God constantly reveals himself in the cosmos.[94] So revelation of God is not an immediate and

---

this is only because the context makes this clear. So I dispute Bockmuehl's conclusion that the verb refers to "eine konkret-empirische Wahrnehmung" (93). 2. As regards Paul I accept Bockmuehl's point that there can be no simple equation of φανερόω and ἀποκαλύπτω. But again I question his view of a "konkret-empirische Wahrnehmbarkeit" ("φανερόω", 95 in reference to 1.19). Against Bockmuehl, I believe that there are texts in Paul where φανερόω does mean something like γνωρίζω. This can be seen in 2 Cor. 2.14; 4.5 and in the text with which we are concerned, Rom. 1.19.

[91] The ἱλαστήριον was understood in this sense in the Old Testament.

[92] Constrast Bockmuehl, "φανερόω", 95.

[93] Kuhlmann, *Theologia naturalis*, p. 42.

[94] Cf. Kuhlmann, *Theologia naturalis*, p. 42: "Die Offenbarung Gottes steht in der ständigen Erschaffung des Kosmos, in dem der Mensch existiert".

natural empirical issue; rather it is mediated and miraculous. God makes himself known and he takes the initiative.[95]

2.2.2 Romans 1.20

I turn now to Rom. 1.20: τὰ γὰρ ἀόρατα αὐτοῦ ἀπὸ κτίσεως κόσμου τοῖς ποιήμασιν νοούμενα καθορᾶται, ἥ τε ἀΐδιος αὐτοῦ δύναμις καὶ θειότης, εἰς τὸ εἶναι αὐτοὺς ἀναπολογήτους. The conjunction γάρ links v. 19b to v. 20. Before engaging in detailed discussion of some of the terms here, it is necessary to determine the precise structure of v. 20a. Commentators are divided as to whether there is an oxymoron in τὰ . . . ἀόρατα αὐτοῦ . . . καθορᾶται. Kühl, Leenhardt and Cranfield believe Paul is employing a deliberate oxymoron.[96] Fitzmyer believes Paul is playing on two words having the root ὁρᾶν: ἀόρατα and καθορᾶται[97]. I agree with Fitzmyer and see Paul employing a deliberate oxymoron, which, as Kühl writes, finds its resolution in the dativus instrumentalis τοῖς ποιήμασιν and in the participle νοούμενα.[98] So although God's nature is invisible, it is nevertheless perceptible by the νοῦς. But which νοῦς is he thinking of? It is certainly not the ἀδόκιμος νοῦς of Rom. 1.28. Rather, this νοῦς is the one illumined by the pre-existent Christ, the νοῦς which was totally corrupted by the fall, and which is renewed in Christ. The participle νοούμενα of 1.20 therefore has a certain correspondence to the renewed

---

[95] To be fair to Bockmuehl, he does write that God is the one "der diese konkret-empirische Wahrnehmbarkeit verbürgt" (commenting on Rom. 1.19b, "φανερόω", 95). But his view of revelation is nevertheless open to the criticism of Barth, that it is not a mediated revelation. See the discussion in chapter 3 concerning natural revelation and natural theology.

[96] Kühl, *Römer*, p. 50; F.J. Leenhardt, *The Epistle to the Romans* ET, London 1961, p. 62; Cranfield, *Romans*, 1:114. Cf. Pseudo-Aristotle, *De mundo* 399b: καὶ γὰρ ἡ ψυχή, δι᾽ ἣν ζῶμέν τε καὶ οἴκους καὶ πόλεις ἔχομεν, ἀόρατος οὖσα τοῖς ἔργοις αὐτῆς ὁρᾶται ((LCL), 396).

[97] Note that καθορᾶται is a hapax legomenon in the New Testament. The prefix κατα- serves to intensify the verb so giving the meaning "are clearly seen" (Cranfield, *Romans*, 1:115).

[98] Kühl, *Römer*, p. 50: "Das Prädikat καθορᾶται soll, zumal in der verstärkten Form des Komps. (ἀπ. λεγ.) nach Absicht des Apostels als Oxymoron wirken, das in dem Dat. instr. τοῖς ποιήμασιν und in dem Partiz. νοούμενα seine Lösung findet".

νοῦς of Rom. 12.1. The verb νοέω therefore has a meaning which corresponds to the reception of revelation.[99]

Käsemann disputes that Paul is employing an oxymoron. "According to 2 Cor 4:18; 5:7 Paul's theology expressly opposes present 'sight'".[100] However, this objection is somewhat relativised once 1.20 is seen in its context. The possibility of seeing God's invisible nature in creation is lost, for all men failed to give thanks or glorify God (see 1.21-22 and the discussion of these verses below).

I now need to examine the meaning of the whole expression τοῖς ποιήμασιν νοούμενα καθορᾶται. Cranfield writes that "some understand νοούμενα as virtually equivalent to an adverbial expression modifying καθορᾶται (indicating that the seeing referred to is a seeing with the mind's eye) and connect τοῖς ποιήμασιν with the combination νοούμενα καθορᾶται as a whole".[101] Gärtner would seem to take the expression in this way. He argues that the participle νοούμενα is a *participium explicandi causa verbo adiectum*[102] and therefore understands the expression νοούμενα καθορᾶται as "to see with the understanding".[103]

---

[99] See again Kühl, *Römer*, p. 50: "*νοῦν* spricht nur von dem geistigen Erkennen vermöge des *νοῦς*". Cf. Michel, *Römer*, p. 99: "Es ist nicht eine theoretische oder ästhetische Überlegung gemeint, sondern eine Möglichkeit, die Gott selbst schafft (καθορᾶται ist Passiv: 'er läßt sich erschauen'). Was dem natürlichen Auge verborgen ist, kann in einem Erkenntnisvorgang besonderer Art wahrgenommen werden". Contrast Käsemann, *Romans*, p. 41, who believes νοῦς for Paul is the critical evaluative understanding. Käsemann's view is similar to Bultmann's (*Theologie des Neuen Testaments*, p. 212): "Gottes ἀόρατα, sein unsichtbares Wesen, wird seit der Schöpfung der Welt νοούμενα d.h. mit dem Auge des νοῦς, mit dem verstehenden Denken, wahrgenommen (Rm 1,20)".

[100] Käsemann, *Romans*, p. 41.

[101] Cranfield, *Romans*, 1:114.

[102] B. Gärtner, *The Areopagus Speech and Natural Revelation*, Uppsala 1955, p. 136. See *BDF* §416 for the use of the supplementary participle with verbs of perception and cognition.

[103] Gärtner, *Areopagus Speech*, p. 137, translates v. 20 as: "For men see and understand His invisible nature through His works ever since the creation of the world, and with it His everlasting power and divinity". On νοούμενα καθορᾶται, Gärtner writes: "Both the verbs thus describe how, on contemplating God's works, man can grasp enough of His nature to prevent him from the error of identifying any of the created things with the Creator" (*Areopagus Speech*, p. 137). See also Wilckens, *Römer*, 1:105 n. 174, who writes: "νοούμενα gehört zu καθορᾶται und

A second possibility is to see τοῖς ποιήμασιν νοούμενα as a participial clause explaining καθορᾶται. In this case νοούμενα and καθορᾶται can be understood as mental perception (τοῖς ποιήμασιν νοούμενα then meaning "being understood in the things that have been made") or both could refer to physical sight. Cranfield argues that in view of the deliberate oxymoron it is most likely that καθορᾶται and νοούμενα refer to physical sight. So God's invisible nature is seen through his creation.

A third possible interpretation is that given, for example, by Käsemann, "νοούμενα bezieht sich auf ἀόρατα".[104] His translation of 1.20a is: "Denn seit der Weltschöpfung wird er in seiner Unsichtbarkeit erfaßt und an dem Geschaffenen wahrgenommen . . .".[105]

Of these I believe the first is the most likely. The oxymoron, though deliberate, does receive a resolution through the dativus instrumentalis τοῖς ποιήμασιν and in the participle νοούμενα and I suggest that Paul is referring to seeing with the understanding.[106]

This brings me to discuss the expression τὰ . . . ἀόρατα αὐτοῦ. A number of scholars see a reference here to God's invisible attributes, pointing to the plural τὰ . . . ἀόρατα. So we find this in the work of Schjött,[107] Kühl,[108] Michel[109] and Cranfield,[110] and much earlier by Hugh

kennzeichnet dieses als vernünftiges Wahrnehmen, durch welches im Sichtbaren das Unsichtbare geschaut wird".

[104] Käsemann, *Römer*, p. 37 (*Romans*, p. 41).

[105] Käsemann, *Römer*, p. 32.

[106] See Wilckens, *Römer*, 1:105 n. 174: "νοούμενα gehört zu καθορᾶται und kennzeichnet dieses als vernünfiges Wahrnehmen, durch welches im Sichtbaren das Unsichtbare geschaut wird. Dabei wird dem νοῦς durchaus das Vermögen zuge-schrieben, das CorpHerm V 2 so definiert wird: νόησις γὰρ μόνον ὁρᾷ τὸ ἀφανές". Note A.D. Nock and A.-J. Festugière (ed.), *Corpus hermeticum*, 4 vols, Paris 1945-54, 1:61, give the reading μόνη.

[107] Asking what τὰ . . . ἀόρατα αὐτοῦ can mean, P.O. Schjött, "Eine reli-gionsphilosophische Stelle bei Paulus. Röm 1,18-20", *ZNW* 4 (1903) 76 (75-78), writes: "Das Wesen Gottes nicht; denn Wesen ist doch eine Einheit, hier aber heißt es pluralisch τὰ ἀόρατα".

[108] Kühl, *Römer*, p. 50: "τὰ ἀόρατα τοῦ θεοῦ darf nicht übersetzt werden: *etwas von Gottes unsichtbarem Wesen* (JÜLICHER), auch nicht: *was unsichtbar an Gott ist* (LIPSIUS), sondern: *die unsichtbaren Eigenschaften Gottes*".

[109] Michel, *Römer*, p. 99: "τὰ ἀόρατα (Plural!) weist hin auf Gottes unsichtbare Eigenschaften, die nach Paulus durch einen Erkenntnisvorgang (νοούμενα) 'erschaut' oder 'betrachtet' werden können (paradox wirkt der Gegensatz: τὰ ἀόρατα καθορᾶται)".

of St Victor.[111] Reference is also made to 1.20b, where it is argued Paul points to two specific attributes: ἀΐδιος αὐτοῦ δύναμις καὶ θειότης.[112] But a number of scholars believe Paul is in fact referring to the *invisible nature* of God. We find this in the work of Fridrichsen,[113] Kuhlmann,[114] Schlier[115] and Wilckens[116]. In view of what Paul has written in 1.19, I believe it is more likely that Fridrichsen and Schlier are correct. Further, Rom. 1.20b gives an interpretation to τὰ ἀόρατα, not a limitation.[117] In

---

[110] Cranfield, *Romans*, 1:114: "By τὰ . . . ἀόρατα αὐτοῦ are meant God's invisible attributes . . . ".

[111] Hugo of St Victor, *Quaestiones in epistolas Pauli ad Rom* 33 (*MPL* 175:439): "*Quomodo pluraliter dicat, invisibilia Dei, cum Deus sit simplex, et unus, nec aliquid sit in Deo, quod non sit Deus, nec aliquid dicatur hic invisibile Dei, quod non sit Deus? Solutio. Quod unum est et simplex in natura, non ut unum et simplex venit in nostram notitiam, sed ut multa*".

[112] Kühl, *Römer*, p. 50, notes the use of θειότης, which means "*die göttliche Qualität*", and not θεότης, which refers to the "*das göttliche Sein*".

[113] A. Fridrichsen, "Zur Auslegung von Röm 1,19f.", *ZNW* 17 (1916) 160 (159-68), replying to Schjött, writes: "*τὰ ἀόρατα [τοῦ θεοῦ] läßt sich ungezwungen als die Summe des göttlichen Wesens verstehen*" (he compares Col. 1.16, Rom. 5.3, Jn 3.12). "*Und τοῦ θεοῦ braucht nicht ja nicht partitiv zu sein . . . Dem ganzen Ausdruck entspricht, daß Gott ἀόρατος genannt wird Kol 1,15; 1 Tim 1,17. Man muß sich in der Tat fragen, wie anders Paulus den abstrakten Gedanken der Unsichtbarkeit Gottes hätte ausdrücken sollen*".

[114] Kuhlmann, *Theologia naturalis*, p. 41.

[115] On τὰ ἀόρατα αὐτοῦ, Schlier, *Römerbrief*, 52, writes: "Der Plural des Neutrums weist auf die allumfassende Fülle seines Wesens hin".

[116] Wilckens, *Römer*, 1:105, writes that "Paulus in V 20, den Gedanken von V 19 explizierend, von Gottes unsichtbarem Wesen als ganzem sagt . . . ". However, Wilckens' translation does not exactly reflect this interpretation: "Denn seine unsichtbaren (Geheimnisse) sind von der Weltschöpfung her in den (Schöpfungs-)Werken vernünftiger Einsicht durchsichtig" (Wilckens, *Römer*, 1:94).

[117] Käsemann, *Römer*, p. 37, writes: "Gott in seiner Unsichtbarkeit und in der ihn vom kosmischen Sein unterscheidenden θειότης ist ewige, immerwährende Macht". See also the earlier work of Kuhlmann, *Theologia naturalis*, p. 41, who translates 1.20 as: "Kann doch der unsichtbare Gott seit der Weltschöpfung im Geschaffenen deutlich mit der Vernunft gesehen werden, als ewige Macht und Gottheit nämlich". He comments (p. 41 n. 2): "Da τὰ ἀόρατα als ἀΐδιος δύναμις καὶ θειότης definiert werden, muß der Gedanke an bestimmte abgegrenzte Eigenschaften Gottes ausgeschlossen bleiben . . . "

the discussion on natural theology in chapter 3, I will further develop the idea that to know God's attributes alone is to know nothing of God.[118]

In the above discussion it has been taken for granted that ποιήματα refers to the "things that have been made". This, however, has been disputed. Michel argues that ποιήματα refers not to the creation of God (as πλάσματα does in Is. 29.16; Rom. 9.20) but to his works in creation and history.[119] Likewise, M. Barth argues that ποιήματα in the LXX and New Testament denotes "not things or matters . . . but *deeds* or *acts*."[120] Interestingly he points to Is. 29.16 as the exception.[121] Perhaps the crucial issue here is not whether ποιήματα refers to things or acts but rather whether the term can be used for the created order. A text like Ps. 142.5 LXX is of interest here.[122] Ps. 142.5: ἐμνήσθην ἡμερῶν ἀρχαίων καὶ ἐμελέτησα ἐν πᾶσι τοῖς ἔργοις σου, ἐν ποιήμασιν τῶν χειρῶν σου ἐμελέτων. V. 5c probably refers God's acts of creation. The Hebrew is בְּמַעֲשֵׂה יָדֶיךָ and one can compare Ps. 8.4a (כִּי־אֶרְאֶה שָׁמֶיךָ מַעֲשֵׂי אֶצְבְּעֹתֶיךָ; 8.4a LXX: ὅτι ὄψομαι τοὺς οὐρανούς, ἔργα τῶν δακτύλων σου) and Ps. 102.26b (וּמַעֲשֵׂה יָדֶיךָ שָׁמַיִם; Ps. 101.26b LXX: καὶ ἔργα τῶν χειρῶν σού εἰσιν οἱ οὐρανοί) which most certainly refers to God's creation. Further, in the only other occurrence of ποίημα in the New Testament the word refers to God's creative work (Eph. 2.10a: αὐτοῦ γὰρ ἐσμεν ποίημα). Therefore the case against understanding ποιήματα as "things that have

---

[118] Although I do not always agree with Rosin's line of reasoning, he does make this important comment: "Denn wüßte er nur um ewige Kraft und Gottheit als leere Eigenschaften, so wüßte er nicht nur etwas, sondern überhaupt nichts von Gott" (Rosin, "To gnoston tou Theou", 165).

[119] Michel, *Römer*, pp. 99-100. See Ps. Sol. 8.7: Ἀνελογισάμην τὰ κρίματα τοῦ θεοῦ ἀπὸ κτίσεως οὐρανοῦ καὶ γῆς.

[120] M. Barth, "Speaking of Sin", 291. See also Gärtner, *Areopagus Speech*, p. 138, who writes that "neither in New Testament, where it occurs twice, nor in the Septuagint, does the word ποίημα have direct reference to nature, but has a more general one to God's or man's deeds and actions".

[121] Is. 29.16 LXX: οὐχ ὡς ὁ πηλὸς τοῦ κεραμέως λογισθήσεσθε; μὴ ἐρεῖ τὸ πλάσμα τῷ πλάσαντι Οὐ σύ με ἔπλασας; ἢ τὸ ποίημα τῷ ποιήσαντι Οὐ συνετῶς με ἐποίησας; Such parallelism between πλάσμα and ποίημα would seem to destroy part of Michel's argument.

[122] Note the clear allusion to Ps. 142.2 in Rom. 3.20.

been made" is not as strong as may at first appear and indeed the context points to this translation being the most reasonable.[123]

One question which 1.20 raises is how one gains this knowledge of God? The first point to make is that ἀπὸ κτίσεως κόσμου means "since the creation of the world", not "from the created universe", ἀπό therefore being understood in a temporal sense (cf. 2 Cor. 8.10; 9.2) and κτίσις meaning the act of creation.[124] Wilckens writes:

Bei der Erkenntnis Gottes V 20 handelt es sich also nicht um einen *Rückschluß* aus den Werken auf den Künstler, der sie gemacht hat, sondern um das Wahrnehmen Gottes eben *in* seinen Werken, nicht ἐκ τῶν ποιημάτων sondern ἐν τοῖς ποιήμασιν (dativus instrumentalis).[125]

This knowledge therefore does not come about by a *logical deduction* and Paul's argument has nothing to do with an *analogia entis* as one finds in Hellenism.[126] In fact in comparison to Hellenism, Paul says very little in Rom. 1.19-20 about the mechanism of coming to a knowledge of God.[127]

I now turn to the final section of v. 20, the expression εἰς τὸ εἶναι αὐτοὺς ἀναπολογήτους. There is a disagreement as to whether εἰς τὸ εἶναι is final or consecutive.[128] Schlier, for example, takes it as consecu-

---

[123] My position is close to that of Schlier, *Römerbrief*, p. 52: "Τὰ ποιήματα sind hier nicht die Schöpfungstaten Gottes . . . auch nicht das Wirken Gottes in der Geschichte überhaupt . . . sondern die Werke der Schöpfung, die er in der Zeit wirkt. Es sind 'die Werke deiner Hände' von Ps 8,7 oder 'seine Werke' (Ps 102,22), die auch 'sein Werk' (Sir 42,16) heißen, das er ständig vollzieht". He also rightly compares τὰ ποιήματα to 2 Bar. 54.18 ("For his works have not taught you, nor has the artful work of his creation which has existed always persuaded you" and to 1QH 16.8 ("Blessed art Thou, O Lord, Maker [of all things and mighty in] deeds: all things are Thy work (מַעֲשֵׂיךְ הַכּוֹל)!" (G. Vermes, *The Dead Sea Scrolls in English*, Sheffield ³1987, (¹1962), p. 204).

[124] κτίσις can mean "what is created" (cf. Rom. 8.19) and the Vulgate assumes this meaning here (*a creatura mundi*). However, as Cranfield, *Romans*, 1:114, points out, the idea of "from the created universe" has already been expressed by τοῖς ποιήμασιν.

[125] Wilckens, *Römer*, 1:106.

[126] Again see the discussion on natural theology in chapter 3.

[127] See the discussion on natural theology, especially that concerning the differences between Rom. 1.18-32 and Hellenism.

[128] Grammatically εἰς τό with the infinitive can be either final or consecutive (*BDF* 402.2).

tive, for "von einer Absicht Gottes, die Menschen unentschuldbar sein zu lassen, ist im Zusammenhang nicht die Rede".[129] Michel, on the other hand, takes it as final.[130] I can see arguments on both sides. But in view of Paul's predestinarian theology and in view of the parallel between the whole of Rom. 1.18-3.20 and Rom. 11.32a (συνέκλεισεν γὰρ ὁ θεὸς τοὺς πάντας εἰς ἀπείθειαν) I would tend to take εἰς τὸ εἶναι αὐτοὺς ἀναπολογήτους as final.

2.3 Romans 1.21-32

2.3.1 Romans 1.21

Whereas vv. 19-20 (introduced by διότι) establish that the truth is available to all people, vv. 21-32 (also introduced by διότι) establish that people suppress the truth in unrighteousness so developing the idea found in 18b (ἐπὶ πᾶσαν ἀσέβειαν καὶ ἀδικίαν ἀνθρώπων τῶν τὴν ἀλήθειαν ἐν ἀδικίᾳ κατεχόντων). In Rom. 1.21 the following thesis is set forward: διότι γνόντες τὸν θεὸν οὐχ ὡς θεὸν ἐδόξασαν ἢ ηὐχαρίστησαν, ἀλλ' ἐματαιώθησαν ἐν τοῖς διαλογισμοῖς αὐτῶν καὶ ἐσκοτίσθη ἡ ἀσύνετος αὐτῶν καρδία.[131] The participle γνόντες can either be understood conditionally[132] or concessively[133]. The context suggests Paul is most likely using the concessive understanding.

The words γνόντες τὸν θεόν refer back to γνωστόν of v. 19 and, as Kuhlmann argues, "wird als φανερόν interpretiert".[134] The phrase

---

[129] Schlier, *Römerbrief*, p. 54. See also Kuhlmann, *Theologia naturalis*, p. 43 n. 2.

[130] Michel, *Römer*, p. 101 n. 10 considers Luther's translation "also daß sie keine Entschuldigung haben" "sprachlich möglich, aber an dieser Stelle eine nicht sinngemäße Abschwächung".

[131] Eckstein, "Zorn", 88, relates this to ἐν ἀδικίᾳ κατεχόντων.

[132] See the conditional participle in Lk. 9.25; 1 Cor. 11.29. See J.H. Moulton, *A Grammar of New Testament Greek, Volume 1: Prolegomena*, Edinburgh ³1908, p. 230.

[133] See Jas. 3.4; 1 Cor. 9.19. Note especially the rough parallel in Rom. 1.32: τὸ δικαίωμα τοῦ θεοῦ ἐπιγνόντες ("though they know the requirement of the law"). Again see Moulton, *Grammar*, p. 230.

[134] Kuhlmann, *Theologia naturalis*, p. 45.

γνόντες τὸν θεόν has been rather difficult for those who deny a natural theology. Cranfield interprets them as follows:

> They have in fact experienced Him — His Wisdom, power, generosity — in every moment of their existence, though they have not recognised Him. It has been by Him that their lives have been sustained, enriched, bounded. In this limited sense they have known Him all their lives.[135]

The words γνόντες τὸν θεόν of v. 21a are in fact the key problem for anyone who wishes to deny a natural theology in Paul and will be discussed below.[136] Note that γνόντες is in the aorist. There is some controversy concerning the significance of participles and the aorist, but whichever view is adopted it seems clear in this case that Paul is referring to antecedent action.[137] But what sort of antecedent action could this be? There are a number of possible explanations. First, it may be that Paul has in mind the sin of Adam.[138] Secondly, Paul may wish to put over the idea of coming to know God (i.e. the ingressive use).[139] Thirdly, he may

---

[135] Cranfield, *Romans*, 1:116-17.

[136] See chapter 3 (section 4) below.

[137] Porter, *Idioms of the Greek New Testament*, p. 188, puts forward the following generalisation: "If a participle occurs before the finite verb on which it depends (or another verb which forms the governing or head term of the construction), the participle tends to refers to antecedent (preceding) action. If a participle occurs after the finite verb (or other) verb on which it depends, it tends to refer to concurrent (simultaneous) or subsequent (following) action".

[138] See Kühl, *Römer*, p. 52: "Die alte Geschichte vollzieht sich in jeder Generation, und in der gegenwärtigen Generation bei jedem einzelnen Glied der Heidenwelt immer von neuem. Mit den Aoristen aber versetzt der Apostel sich und die Leser zunächst in den Zeitpunkt, in welchem die Menschen einst, bei der Entstehung des Heidentums, und in welchem die Menschen der nachfolgenden Geschlechter bis in die Gegenwart hinein in Gottlosigkeit verfielen".

[139] These first two solutions would assume the participle can indicate the *Aktionsart*. N. Turner (J.H. Moulton), *A Grammar of New Testament Greek, Volume III: Syntax*, Edinburgh 1963, p. 79, points out that the participle "originally had no temporal function but simply indicated the kind of action", but does not seem to commit himself as to whether the participle can point to an *Aktionsart* in the New Testament. But he clearly believes someone like M. Zerwick, *Graecitas Biblica*, Rome ³1955, (¹1944), §184, has gone too far in distinguishing between ὁ ἀκούων (he who hears with lasting effect, Lk. 6.47) and ὁ ἀκούσας (he who hears ineffectively and momentarily, Lk. 6.49) (Turner, *Grammar*, p. 79 n. 3).

simply be wishing to put over the fact that knowing precedes their failure to glorify God.[140] In view of the importance of Adam in Rom. 1.18-32, the first of these is the most probable. Note however, that Paul has not only Adam and his fall in mind, but also Israel and its fall and the fall of every generation.

Now although they knew God, οὐχ ὡς θεὸν ἐδόξασαν ἢ ηὐχαρίστησαν. One of the best treatments of these words I find in Schlier. The first point I wish to take from him is that "give thanks" means something similar to "glorify". "Εὐχαριστεῖν ist absolut zu nehmen. Es meint hier einen δοξάζειν ähnlichen Vorgang".[141] The second point, and this I believe is crucial, is that Paul is not making the point in this verse that men and women, while having a theoretical knowledge of God, failed to acknowledge him, i.e. failed to draw practical consequences from this knowledge of God, failed to "honour him as God or give thanks to him". Such an argument could lead one to conclude that Paul, far from denying a natural theology, is saying that there is a *knowledge* of God but no *acknowledgement* of God. This, I believe, is misrepresentation of Paul's argument. His point rather is that the knowledge of God is only retained and guaranteed if there is subsequent acknowledgement.[142] So human beings

---

[140] See Cranfield, *Romans*, 1:116 n. 4: "The aorist participle is used since their experience of God has necessarily always gone before their failure to recognize its true significance and act accordingly".

[141] H. Schlier, "Die Erkenntnis Gottes nach den Briefen des Apostels Paulus", in *Besinnung auf das Neue Testament: Exegetische Aufsätze und Vorträge II*, Freiburg/Basel/Wien ²1967 (¹1964), 323 n. 11 (319-339).

[142] Schlier, *Römerbrief*, pp. 55-56, writes: "Er hat die Ur- und Grundsünde des Menschen vor Augen, der als geschichtlicher seine Geschöpflichkeit schon preisgegeben hat und nun von daher kommt. Es handelt sich bei Paulus auch nicht darum, daß, wie man manchmal ausgelegt findet, der Mensch aus einem 'theoretischen' Erkennen 'praktische' Konsequenzen zieht. Das γινώσκειν meint vielmehr das ἐν ἐπιγνώσει ἔχειν von 1,28. Das δοξάζειν ἢ εὐχαριστεῖν ist die Weise, wie Gott als der Schöpfer erkannt und in der Erkenntnis gehalten wird. In dem, daß der Mensch Gott sein Ansehen schenkt und ihm dankt, äußert und verwahrt sich das Erkennen Gottes. Das Andenken des wahrnehmenden Denkens, von dem Paulus vorher sprach, versammelt sich in der Andacht der Anerkennung Gottes als des Schöpfers. Diese An-Dacht erweist sich im Danken. Die ursprüngliche Gotteserkenntnis ist letztlich in dem Dank beheimatet, in dem sich das Geschöpf dem Schöpfer ver-dankt. . . . Aber eben diese Gotteserkenntnis, die im δοξάζειν, im Widerspiegeln seiner δόξα, die aus der Schöpfung strahlt, und im εὐχαριστεῖν, im Verdanken, besteht, haben die Heiden

know God but if they do not acknowledge him, this knowledge is lost, both knowledge of God himself and knowledge of his attributes. This is the story we are concerned with. Schlier writes: ". . . das γινώσκειν ist ein ἐν ἐπιγνώσει ἔχειν, damit aber ein γινωσκεῖν, das als solches erst im δοξάζειν ἢ εὐχαριστεῖν vollendet ist".[143]

Paul writes that rather than glorifying God and giving thanks, they became empty in their thoughts (ἀλλ᾽ ἐματαιώθησαν ἐν τοῖς διαλογισμοῖς αὐτῶν)[144]. The use of the verb ματαιόω is significant, being used (with its cognates) in Acts, the Pauline corpus and Catholic epistles.[145] The quotation of Ps. 94.11 in 1 Cor. 3.20 would also seem to form the background for Rom. 1.21 especially in view of διαλογισμός and μάταιος in Ps. 94.11: κύριος γινώσκει τοὺς διαλογισμοὺς τῶν ἀνθρώπων ὅτι εἰσὶν μάταιοι.

The last part of Rom. 1.21 is καὶ ἐσκοτίσθη ἡ ἀσύνετος αὐτῶν καρδία. The καρδία refers to man's inner self and the use of ἀσύνετος suggests Paul is emphasising the intellectual element. The fall of human beings is now clear.

2.3.2 Romans 1.22-31

The ideas set forward in v. 21 are developed in three stages: 1.22-24; 25-27; 28-31. Such a division is given by Klostermann[146], and although adopted by some,[147] goes against most commentators and Greek and

---

nicht durchgehalten.". See also Schlier, "Erkenntnis Gottes", 323: "Die Gotteserkenntnis ist in dem Dank beheimatet, in dem sich das Geschöft Gott ver-dankt". Schlier points out that in German "Dank" is a verbal noun for "denken" (see F. Kluge, *Etymologisches Wörterbuch der deutschen Sprache*, Berlin/New York [22]1989, p. 127; W. Pfeifer, *Etymologisches Wörterbuch des Deutschen*, 3 vols, Berlin 1989, 1:154-55).

[143] Schlier, "Erkenntnis Gottes", 323 n. 12.

[144] Schlatter, *Gottes Gerechtigkeit*, p. 62, understands ἐν as causal.

[145] See E. Tiedtke, *NIDNTT*, 1:551-52 (549-53). The use of μάταιος in Acts 14.15 (Paul's sermon at Lystra) in the context of idolatry is especially interesting. See also Wis. 13.1: Μάταιοι μὲν γὰρ πάντες ἄνθρωποι φύσει, οἷς παρῆν θεοῦ ἀγνωσία καὶ εκ των ὁρωμένων ἀγαθῶν οὐκ ἴσχυσαν εἰδέναι τὸν ὄντα οὔτε τοῖς ἔργοις προσέχοντες ἐπέγνωσαν τὸν τεχνίτην.

[146] Klostermann, "Vergeltung".

English editions.[148] A common division is 24-25; 26-27; 28-31. So the three-fold repetition Διὸ παρέδωκεν αὐτοὺς ὁ θεὸς / διὰ τοῦτο παρέδωκεν αὐτοὺς ὁ θεὸς / παρέδωκεν αὐτοὺς ὁ θεὸς is seen as introducing a new section in each case. However, is such a division convincing? One problem with it is that in such a scheme the οἵτινες of 1.25 is not seen as introducing a new sentence but rather as a connection to 1.24. However, οἵτινες does not have this function in 1.32.[149] Further, there is a much more natural way to understand the passage: in terms of "adäquate Vergeltung". This was first seen by Klostermann. Such a view comes from the Old Testament (see the *ius talionis*)[150] and can be found in Hellenistic Jewish texts (2 Mac. 5.9-10; 9.5-6; 9.18; 13.7-8; Wis. 11.6-8, 15-16; 15.8-16.1; 18.4-5; Philo, *In Flaccum* 170-75[151]), in apocalyptic (Jub. 4.31-32; Test. Naph. 3.2-4[152]), Qumran[153] and Rabbinic texts[154].

---

[147] E.g. J. Jeremias, "Zu Rm 1 ₂₂₋₃₂", *ZNW* 45 (1954) 119-121; Schulz, "Anklage", 161-73; Eckstein, "Zorn", 88. J. Wesley, *The New Testament with Explanatory Notes*, London 1954 (repr.), (¹1754), p. 521, has a similar division. See also W. Popkes, "Zum Aufbau und Charakter von Römer 1.18-32", *NTS* 28 (1982) 499 (490-501), who gives the division v. 21-24, 25-27, 28-31. Note that Popkes has to use vv. 21-24 twice in his analysis of 1.18-32. This is an obvious weakness of his approach.

[148] B.F. Westcott and F.J.A. Hort, *The New Testament in the Original Greek*, London 1956 (repr.), (¹1881), give a space between v. 23 and v. 24. GNT⁴ begins a new paragraph at v. 24. NA²⁶ give spaces between v. 23 and v. 24, v. 25 and v. 26 and between v. 27 and 28.

[149] See Klostermann, "Vergeltung", 2.

[150] Certain texts deal with the human punishment (Gen. 9.6 and the various texts concerned with the *lex talionis* (Ex. 21.24; Lev. 24.20; Dt. 19.21)).

[151] This text from Philo is particularly striking, being a confession put in the mouth of Flaccus, the persecutor of the Jews. See Klostermann, "Vergeltung", 5-6.

[152] Discussed by Jeremias, "Rm 1₂₂₋₃₂", 120. See also the discussion below on Rom. 1.26-27. On my definition of "apocalyptic", see above.

[153] 1QS 4.9-14 is especially interesting for we have here a "Lasterkatalog": "However, to the spirit of deceit belong greed, frailty of hands in the service of justice, irreverence, deceit, pride and haughtiness of heart, dishonesty, trickery, cruelty, 10 much insincerity, impatience, much insanity, impudent enthusiasm, appalling acts performed in a lustful passion, filthy paths for indecent purposes, 11 blasphemous tongue, blindness of eyes, hardness of hearing, stiffness of neck, hardness of heart in order to walk in all the paths of darkness and evil cunning. And the visitation 12 of those who walk in it will be for a glut of punishments at the hands of all the angels of destruction, for eternal damnation for the scorching wrath of the God of revenge, for

The idea is not restricted to Jewish texts. It is found in pagan authors[155] and Christian texts.[156] And so in Rom. 1.22-31 we have a development in

---

permanent error and shame 13 without end with the humiliation of destruction by the fire of the dark regions. And all the ages of their generations they shall spend in bitter weeping and harsh evils in the abysses of darkness until 14 their destruction, without there being a remnant or a survivor among them" (Martínez, *Dead Sea Scrolls*, p. 7).

[154] See Aboth 2.7 where Hillel "saw a skull floating on the face of the water and he said unto it, Because thou drownedst they drowned thee and at the last they that drowned thee shall be drowned" (H. Danby, *The Mishnah*, Oxford 1985 (repr.), ([1]1933), p. 448). Particularly striking is Sot. 1.7-8: "With what measure a man metes it shall be measured to him again: she bedecked herself for transgression — the Almighty brought her to shame; she laid herself bare for transgression — the Almighty likewise laid her bare; she began transgression with the thigh first and afterwards with the belly — therefore the thigh shall suffer first and afterwards the belly. . . 8 Samson went after [the desire of] his eyes — therefore the Philistines put out his eyes . . . Absalom gloried in his hair — therefore he was hanged by his hair" (Danby, *Mishnah*, p. 294). See also W. Bousset and H. Greßmann, *Die Religion des Judentums im späthellenistischen Zeitalter*, Tübingen ³1926, p. 412; E. Schürer, *The History of the Jewish People in the Time of Jesus Christ*, 3 vols, Peabody 1994 (repr.), ([1]1890), 2.2:91-93; G.F. Moore, *Judaism in the First Centuries of the Christian Era*, 3 vols, Cambridge, Mass. 1 1962 (repr.), ([1]1927); 2 1962 (repr.), ([1]1927); 3 1962 (repr.), ([1]1930), 2:248-56; Y. Amir, "Measure for Measure in Talmudic Literature and in the Wisdom of Solomon", in H. Graf Reventlow and Y. Hoffman (ed.), *Justice and Righteousness*, Sheffield 1992, 29-46.

[155] Klostermann, "Vergeltung", 3-4 n. 5, points to Plutarch, *De sera numinis vindicta* 8 (553D) as an example. "Do you not think it better that punishments should take place at a fitting time and in a fitting manner rather than speedily and at once? That Callippus, for example, should have been murdered by his friends with the very dagger with which, a seeming friend, he murdered Dion, and that the bronze statue of Mitys the Argive, who had met his death in a factious quarrel, should in the course of a spectacle in the market-place have fallen on his slayer and killed him?" (*Plutarch's Moralia* (LCL), 7:211-13).

[156] Jeremias, "Zu Rm 1 $_{22-32}$", 119-120, points to the example of Acts 7.41-42. Jeremias says this parallels Rom. 1.22-32 not only in taking the sin of the Golden Calf but also in the use of παρέδωκεν. In addition Eckstein, "Zorn", 87 n. 81, points to the correspondence between the sin (Acts 7.39) and the divine retribution (7.42) (ἀλλὰ ἀπώσαντο καὶ ἐστράφησαν . . . ἔστρεψεν δὲ ὁ θεὸς καὶ παρέδωκεν αὐτοὺς λατρεύειν τῇ στρατιᾷ τοῦ οὐρανοῦ . . .). This retribution takes not only the form of being given over to further idolatry but also to exile in Babylon (see the quotation of Am. 5.17-18 in Acts 7.42-43). The gospels portray Jesus as having an equivocal attitude to such ideas of retribution (Lk. 13.1-5; Jn 9.1-3). Later Christian tradition seems to have adopted some aspects of retribution (e.g. Gregory of Nazianzus, *Orations* 5.2).

three steps (but not necessarily a progression in ἀσέβεια). S. Schulz sees a three-fold "Anklage" and "Vergeltung"[157]:

Accusation: 22 φάσκοντες εἶναι σοφοὶ ἐμωράνθησαν 23 καὶ ἤλλαξαν τὴν δόξαν τοῦ ἀφθάρτου θεοῦ ἐν ὁμοιώματι εἰκόνος φθαρτοῦ ἀνθρώπου καὶ πετεινῶν καὶ τετραπόδων καὶ ἑρπετῶν.

Retribution: 24 Διὸ παρέδωκεν αὐτοὺς ὁ θεὸς ἐν ταῖς ἐπιθυμίαις τῶν καρδιῶν αὐτῶν εἰς ἀκαθαρσίαν τοῦ ἀτιμάζεσθαι τὰ σώματα αὐτῶν ἐν αὐτοῖς·

Accusation: 25 οἵτινες μετήλλαξαν τὴν ἀλήθειαν τοῦ θεοῦ ἐν τῷ ψεύδει καὶ ἐσεβάσθησαν καὶ ἐλάτρευσαν τῇ κτίσει παρὰ τὸν κτίσαντα, ὅς ἐστιν εὐλογητὸς εἰς τοὺς αἰῶνας, ἀμήν.

Retribution: 26 διὰ τοῦτο παρέδωκεν αὐτοὺς ὁ θεὸς εἰς πάθη ἀτιμίας, αἵ τε γὰρ θήλειαι αὐτῶν μετήλλαξαν τὴν φυσικὴν χρῆσιν εἰς τὴν παρὰ φύσιν, 27 ὁμοίως τε καὶ οἱ ἄρσενες ἀφέντες τὴν φυσικὴν χρῆσιν τῆς θηλείας ἐξεκαύθησαν ἐν τῇ ὀρέξει αὐτῶν εἰς ἀλλήλους, ἄρσενες ἐν ἄρσεσιν τὴν ἀσχημοσύνην κατεργαζόμενοι καὶ τὴν ἀντιμισθίαν ἣν ἔδει τῆς πλάνης αὐτῶν ἐν ἑαυτοῖς ἀπολαμβάνοντες.

Accusation: 28a καὶ καθὼς οὐκ ἐδοκίμασαν τὸν θεὸν ἔχειν ἐν ἐπιγνώσει,

Retribution: 28b παρέδωκεν αὐτοὺς ὁ θεὸς εἰς ἀδόκιμον νοῦν, ποιεῖν τὰ μὴ καθήκοντα, 29 πεπληρωμένους πάσῃ ἀδικίᾳ πονηρίᾳ πλεονεξίᾳ κακίᾳ, μεστοὺς φθόνου φόνου ἔριδος δόλου κακοηθείας, ψιθυριστὰς 30 καταλάλους θεοστυγεῖς ὑβριστὰς ὑπερηφάνους ἀλαζόνας, ἐφευρετὰς κακῶν, γονεῦσιν ἀπειθεῖς, 31 ἀσυνέτους ἀσυνθέτους ἀστόργους ἀνελεήμονας·

Interestingly there is a certain word play in that the human sin has a corresponding divine punishment: δόξαν (22) / ἀτιμάζεσθαι (24);

---

[157] Schulz, "Anklage", 166-67.

μετήλλαξαν τὴν ἀλήθειαν τοῦ θεοῦ (25) / μετήλλαξαν τὴν φυσικὴν χρῆσιν εἰς τὴν παρὰ φύσιν (26); οὐκ ἐδοκίμασαν / εἰς ἀδόκιμον νοῦν (28).[158]

What is perhaps not so clear is whether Paul intended an intensification in the sections 22-24 (a), 25-27 (b), 28-32 (c). Some have denied such an intensification[159] whereas others have seen some sort of progression, either a progression from a to b to c[160] or a paralleling of a and b then a progression to c.[161] This last view is I believe correct in view of the giving up to a reprobate mind in v. 28.

2.3.2.1 Romans 1.22-24

We read in 1.22: φάσκοντες εἶναι σοφοὶ ἐμωράνθησαν.[162] This idea is much akin to 1 Cor. 1.18-25. From a Pauline perspective this is the judgement on "Religion". It is a human-made product which, far from bringing human beings to God, actually keeps them away from God.[163] God reveals himself through creation, Christ as the wisdom of God being instrumental in this revelation.[164] But as Paul argues in v. 23, the glory of

---

[158] Cf. M.D. Hooker, "A Further Note on Romans I", *NTS* 13 (1966-67) 182 (181-83).

[159] Klostermann, "Vergeltung", 2, writes: "Eine Entwicklung der ἀσέβεια in klar geschiedenen Stufen ist bei ihm nicht mehr zu finden".

[160] Wesley, *Explanatory Notes*, p. 521, writes: "Here are three degrees of ungodliness and of punishment: the first is described verses 21-24; the second, verses 25-27; the third, in the twenty-eighth and following verses". See also Schulz, "Anklage", 166: "obwohl das Thema der Anklage konstant bleibt, können wir eine deutliche Steigerung bemerken, die in dem 3. Aussagenglied mit dem Lasterkatalog (1.29-31) identisch ist".

[161] Jeremias, "Rm 1 22-32", 120: "Erst beim dritten Ansatz formuliert Paulus den Satz der adäquaten göttlichen talio ganz umfassend: sie verwarfen Gott, darum gab er sie verwerflicher Gesinnung preis".

[162] J. Murray, *The Epistle to the Romans: The English Text with Introduction, Exposition and Notes*, 2 vols, Grand Rapids 1982 (repr.), (1 [1]1959; 2 [1]1965), 1:42, may well be right in suggesting in understanding an instrumental relationship between the participle φάσκοντες and the main verb: "by pretending to be wise they made themselves fools".

[163] For a discussion of "religion", see the discussion in chapter 3 below.

[164] See the discussion in chapter 3 below on "The Question of Natural Revelation and Natural Theology in Paul".

the immortal God is exchanged. Paul goes on to use language of idolatry in this attempt by human beings to bypass God's revelation of himself in Christ and in creation.

Rom. 1.23: καὶ ἤλλαξαν τὴν δόξαν τοῦ ἀφθάρτου θεοῦ ἐν ὁμοιώματι εἰκόνος φθαρτοῦ ἀνθρώπου καὶ πετεινῶν καὶ τετραπόδων καὶ ἑρπετῶν. Rom. 1.23a is not easy to translate. In the Greek Paul seems to be saying two things. First, rather than worshipping God they worshipped images resembling the human and animal form. Secondly, this process entailed exchanging their "image of God" (cf. Gen. 1.26) for the "image of a mortal human being", i.e. Adam[165] and the image of animals. Paul then seems to be indirectly referring to human beings losing the *imago Dei*.[166]

Rom. 1.24: διὸ παρέδωκεν αὐτοὺς ὁ θεὸς ἐν ταῖς ἐπιθυμίαις τῶν καρδιῶν αὐτῶν εἰς ἀκαθαρσίαν τοῦ ἀτιμάζεσθαι τὰ σώματα αὐτῶν ἐν αὐτοῖς. The διό indicates God's retributive response to the sins of 1.22-23. There have been two opposite errors in the understanding of these words. The first is to remove any idea of God's retribution. Such a view was put forward by C.H. Dodd who saw retribution in these verses not as the direct act of God but as the "moral decay of pagan society".[167] The opposite error is to see here the outworking of the ὀργὴ θεοῦ of 1.18.[168] The expression ἐν αὐτοῖς corresponds to ὑφ' ἑαυτῶν.[169]

---

[165] Jervell, *Imago Dei*, p. 323, believes φθαρτὸς ἄνθρωπος must refer to Adam. See also J. Jervell, "Bild Gottes I", *TRE* 6:497 (491-98).

[166] Cf. Rom. 3.23 and Bell, *Provoked to Jealousy*, pp. 196-97. This point will be discussed in more detail in chapter 3 below (see the discussion on Paul's view of the fall).

[167] Dodd, *Romans*, p. 26.

[168] L. Morris, *The Epistle to the Romans*, Leicester 1988, p. 77, admits that 1.18 is eschatological but adds "we should not overlook the other truth that it is also a present reality, as this passage shows (cf. the present tense, *is being revealed*, and vv. 24, 26, 28)".

[169] See R. Hoffmann, in L. Radermacher, *Neutestamentliche Grammatik*, Tübingen ²1925, p. 227 (supplementary note to p. 141), who points out that in the New Testament ὑπό can be replaced by the instrumental ἐν as in Rom. 1.24.

2.3.2.2 Romans 1.25-27

I have argued above for taking v. 25 with v. 26 rather than with v. 24. Οἵτινες then is not to be understood as introducing a relative clause. Such a use is not necessary for the action of v. 24 has already been assigned a cause by the use of διό which looks back to vv. 22 and 23.[170]

Rom. 1.25-27 is a further development of v. 21. These verses also repeat and expand on what has been said in 1.22-24. So the accusation of v. 25a (μετήλλαξαν τὴν ἀλήθειαν τοῦ θεοῦ ἐν τῷ ψεύδει) looks back to v. 21 and repeats the idea of v. 23. Such perversion of the truth according to v. 25b (ἐσεβάσθησαν καὶ ἐλάτρευσαν τῇ κτίσει παρὰ τὸν κτίσαντα) results in the worshipping[171] and serving of the creation rather than the creator (cf. Dt. 4.16-18). Again Paul is putting forward the essence of religion: exchanging the truth of God (i.e. the revealed reality of God)[172] for a lie.

The words διὰ τοῦτο at the beginning of v. 26 link vv. 26-27 back to v. 25 (as διό connected v. 24 to vv. 22-23). So v. 25 puts forward the accusation and vv. 26-27 put forward the corresponding retribution. This consists in being handed over to dishonourable passions (v. 26a: παρέδωκεν αὐτοὺς ὁ θεὸς εἰς πάθη ἀτιμίας) and this is further explained in vv. 26b-27 (note the use of γάρ in v. 26b: αἵ τε γὰρ θήλειαι αὐτῶν μετήλλαξαν τὴν φυσικὴν χρῆσιν εἰς τὴν παρὰ φύσιν).

Note the use of τὴν φυσικὴν χρῆσιν εἰς τὴν παρὰ φύσιν (v. 26) and τὴν φυσικὴν χρῆσιν (v. 27). Cranfield rightly understands φυσικός in Paul to mean "in accordance with the intention of the Creator".[173] Paul does to some extent work with the category of what can be called "natural law".[174]

Although the reference to male homosexuality is clear in Rom. 1.27, some have doubted whether Paul is speaking of female homosexuality in

---

[170] Cranfield, *Romans*, 1:123.

[171] The verb σεβάζεσθαι occurs only here in the New Testament.

[172] See the discussion above on ἀλήθεια in Rom. 1.18.

[173] Although the word φυσικός is found in the LXX only in Wisdom and 3 and 4 Maccabees and was a widely used word in Greek philosophy, it would be mistaken, I believe, to assume that Paul was using the word in a specialist philosophical sense. See the discussion on Rom. 2.14 in chapter 4.

[174] See the discussion in chapter 4 on natural law.

Rom. 1.26. The main reason for this seems to be that lesbianism was rarely discussed in the ancient world and Paul in any case does not explicitly mention sex between women in 1.26.[175] Although 1.27 speaks of male homosexuality, it is argued that a retroactive rhetoric is improbable.[176] Therefore, Miller claims: "The obvious partner for the woman in verse 26 is male and the relationship heterosexual".[177] In this case the word ὁμοίως at the beginning of v. 27 points to non-coital intercourse.[178] This reading is possible especially in view of Test. Naph. 3.1-5:[179] v. 4 refers to the sins of Sodom (homosexual perversion) and v. 5 refers to the Watcher who "departed from nature's order" (heterosexual perversion).[180] However, Paul was a highly creative thinker and although lesbianism was rarely discussed in the ancient world, I suspect that he is in fact referring to female homosexuality in 1.26. As a number of commentators have argued, the use of "female" and "male" rather than "woman" (γυνή) and "man" (ἀνήρ) points to the sexual differentiation[181] and may allude to Gen. 1.27.[182]

It has been questioned whether Paul in fact condemns all male homosexuality in Rom. 1.27. First, there has been an attempt to limit Paul's condemnation to pederasty,[183] a view which is difficult to sustain if

---

[175] J.E. Miller, "The Practices of Romans 1:26: Homosexual or Heterosexual", *NovT* 37 (1995) 8 (1-11).

[176] Miller, "Romans 1:26", 8.

[177] Miller, "Romans 1:26", 8.

[178] M. Stowasser, "Homosexualität und Bibel: Exegetische und hermeneutische Überlegungen zu einem schwierigen Thema", *NTS* 43 (1997) 519 (503-26), writes that the link (ὁμοίως) between v. 26 and v. 27 consists "nicht im Vorgang gleichgeschlechtlicher Liebe, sondern im nicht koitalen Geschlechtsverkehr, der von Frauen in der Antike häufig als Mittel der Empfängnisverhütung praktiziert wurde und dann nur die gleichen Praktiken zuließ, wie Männer miteinander verkehren".

[179] Miller, "Rom. 1:26", 5.

[180] There are also other parallels between Rom. 1.22-27 and Test. Naph. 3.1-5. See the discussion above on "adäquate Vergeltung" and below, chapter 3 section 2, on the relation of Rom. 1.18-32 to apocalyptic.

[181] E.g. Cranfield, *Romans*, 1:125.

[182] According to Michel, *Römer*, p. 105, the order of "female" (1.26) then "male" (1.27) was influenced by Gen. 1.27b: ἄρσεν καὶ θῆλυ ἐποίησεν αὐτούς.

[183] R. Scroggs, *The New Testament and Homosexuality*, Philadephia 1983, pp. 115-18, 130-31.

there is a parallelism between male homosexuality in 1.27 and lesbianism in 1.26. Also, had Paul wished to condemn pederasty alone, he would surely have been more specific.[184] Secondly, it has been argued that Paul condemns only homosexual acts committed by those with a heterosexual orientation, a view which has been well refuted by Hays.[185]

Paul therefore rejects all sexual acts practised between members of the same sex as against nature (παρὰ φύσιν).[186] Paul, in common with the Old Testament and Jewish tradition, considered male homosexual activity a serious perversion, and to this he added lesbianism.[187]

2.3.2.3 Romans 1.28-31

Rom. 1.28a: καὶ καθὼς οὐκ ἐδοκίμασαν τὸν θεὸν ἔχειν ἐν ἐπιγνώσει. These words parallel vv. 22-23 and v. 25 (hence supporting my analysis of vv. 22-31). καθώς has the meaning "since", "because".[188] The word ἐπίγνωσις occurs five times in the authentic Pauline epistles (Rom. 1.28; 3.20; 10.2; Phil. 1.9; Phlm 6).[189] W. Hackenberg claims it is

. . . used consistently in the OT sense, i.e., *knowledge* as recognition of (the will of) God that is effective in the conduct of the one who knows God. . . . Thus Rom 1:28 is not concerned primarily with theoretical knowledge of God . . . but with preserva-

---

[184] See M.D. Smith, "Ancient Bisexuality and the Interpretation of Romans 1:26-27", *JAAR* 64 (1996) 245 (223-56).

[185] See R.B. Hays, "Relations Natural and Unnatural: A Response to John Boswell's Exegesis of Romans 1", *JRE* (1986) 184-215. See also Smith, "Bisexuality", 225.

[186] Cf. K. Hoheisel, "Homosexualität", *RAC* 16:338-39 (289-364).

[187] In the Old Testament female homosexuality is ignored and this is largely continued in later Jewish writing. Miller, "Rom. 1:26", finds lesbianism condemned only in Ps.-Phocylides 190-92. In two texts in the talmud there is simply mild disapproval. See b. Yeb. 76a: "Women who practice lewdness with one another are disqualified from marrying a priest" (cf. b. Shab. 65a).

[188] See Cranfield, *Romans*, 1:127.

[189] The expression ἔχειν ἐν ἐπιγνώσει may be likened to ἐπιγινώσκειν. Schlier, *Römerbrief*, p. 63, compares the expression to ἐν ὀργῇ ἔχειν (meaning "to be angry") of Thucydides, *History of the Peloponnesian War* 2.65.3.

tion or rejection of the correct knowledge of the will of God (ποιεῖν τὰ μὴ καθήκοντα).[190]

Rather more to the point is the view of Schlier.

> Ἐπίγνωσις ist nicht einfach soviel wie γνῶσις, sondern eine Erkenntnis, die zugleich Anerkennung bedeutet oder jedenfalls im Sinn der Erfahrung . . . Der Sache nach ist ἐν ἐπιγνώσει ἔχειν jenes γνῶναι, das sich im δοξάζειν und εὐχαριστεῖν aufhält bzw. in ihm durchhält. Diese Verweigerung der Anerkennung des Schöpfers und die damit gegebene Weltapotheose — denn Gott wird der Mensch nicht los und wenn er ihn nur in der Verkennung hat — ließ die Heiden einem ἀδόκιμος νοῦς von Gott ausgeliefert werden.[191]

Paul makes the point that because they did not see fit to take God into account, God gave them up to a reprobate mind (παρέδωκεν αὐτοὺς ὁ θεὸς εἰς ἀδόκιμον νοῦν), to do the things which should not be done (ποιεῖν τὰ μὴ καθήκοντα, which parallels τοῦ ἀτιμάζεσθαι τὰ σώματα αὐτῶν ἐν αὐτοῖς).

Some have claimed a Stoic influence in view of the use of τὰ μὴ καθήκοντα. However, a number of scholars have rightly been critical of alleged Stoic influence here.[192]

The "Lasterkatalog", Rom. 1.29-31, can be divided as follows (I give v. 28 also so as to make clear the grammatical dependence):

---

[190] W. Hackenberg, ἐπίγνωσις, *EDNT* 2:25.

[191] Schlier, *Römerbrief*, p. 63.

[192] See A. Bonhöffer, *Epiktet und das Neue Testament*, Gießen 1911, pp. 157-58; M. Pohlenz, "Paulus und die Stoa", in K.H. Rengstorf (ed.), *Das Paulusbild in der neueren deutschen Forschung*, Darmstadt 1982, 526 (522-64); A. Vögtle, *Die Tugend- und Lasterkataloge im Neuen Testament*, Münster 1936, pp. 215-17. H. Lietzmann, *An die Römer*, Tübingen ⁵1971, p. 35, rightly argues that the words τὰ μὴ καθήκοντα are "kein Beweiß für stoischen Einfluß". He doubts whether τὰ μὴ καθήκοντα necessarily points to Stoic influence. The Stoa actually use παρὰ τὸ καθῆκον (see Diogenes Laertius 7.108, *SVF* 3:495). But see Epictetus, *Discourses* 3.22.43: "But to desire, or to avoid, or to choose, or to refuse, or to prepare, or to set something before yourself — what man among you can do these things without first conceiving an impression of what is profitable, or what is not fitting (μὴ λαβὼν φαντασίαν λυσιτελοῦς ἢ μὴ καθήκοντος;)" (Epictetus (LCL) 2:147). The expression here is the closest to that found in Rom. 1.28 but is too late to influence Paul. See further the discussion in chapter 3 on the possible Greek influence on Rom. 1.18-32 and the discussion on Rom. 2.14-16 and the excursus on natural law in chapter 4.

28 καὶ καθὼς οὐκ ἐδοκίμασαν τὸν θεὸν ἔχειν ἐν ἐπιγνώσει, παρέδωκεν
αὐτοὺς ὁ θεὸς εἰς ἀδόκιμον νοῦν, ποιεῖν τὰ μὴ καθήκοντα,
29 πεπληρωμένους πάσῃ ἀδικίᾳ πονηρίᾳ πλεονεξίᾳ κακίᾳ,
μεστοὺς φθόνου φόνου ἔριδος δόλου κακοηθείας,
ψιθυριστὰ 30 καταλάλους θεοστυγεῖς ὑβριστὰς ὑπερηφάνους ἀλαζόνας,
ἐφευρετὰς κακῶν, γονεῦσιν ἀπειθεῖς, 31 ἀσυνέτους ἀσυνθέτους
ἀστόργους ἀνελεήμονας·

So there are first four nouns in the dative singular qualified by πάσῃ and
dependent on πεπληρωμένους and in apposition to αὐτούς of v. 28[193];
second, five nouns in the genitive singular dependent on μεστούς and
again in apposition to αὐτούς[194]; third, twelve nouns terms all directly in
apposition to αὐτούς[195].

Such lists of vices (Lasterkataloge) can be found elsewhere in Paul,[196]
in Hellenistic Judaism (Wis. 14.25-26), in apocalyptic (3 Bar. 4.17; 8.5;
13.4; Test. Reub. 3.3-6[197]; Test. Jud. 16.1; 2 En. 10.4-5) and in Qumran
(see 1 QS 4.9-14 quoted above). Such lists of vices were popular among
the Stoics. However, it is unlikely that Paul adopted this directly from the
Stoics. More likely is that Stoicism had influenced Judaism which in turn
influenced Paul. This question will be addressed in the following chapter.

---

[193] Note that all four end in α: ἀδικία, πονηρία, πλεονεξία, κακία.

[194] These words point to lawlessness, as shown by the introductory words φθόνος,
φόνος (Schulz, "Anklage", 167, quoting E. Wibbing, "Die Tugend- und Lasterkatalog im Neuen Testament", Heidelberg Dissertation 1955, pp. 107-8).

[195] First there are four pairs (ψιθυριστὰς - καταλάλους / θεοστυγεῖς - ὑβριστὰς /
ὑπερηφάνους - ἀλαζόνας / ἐφευρετὰς κακῶν - γονεῦσιν ἀπειθεῖς) then four words
beginning with α-privativum (ἀσυνέτου· ἀσυνθέτους ἀστόργους ἀνελεήμονας)
(Schulz, "Anklage", 167, quoting Wibbing, "Die Tugend- und Lasterkatalog", pp.
107-8).

[196] See Rom. 13.13; 1 Cor. 5.10-11; 6.9-10; 2 Cor. 12.20; Gal. 5.19-21. Cf. Eph.
4.31; 5.3-5; Col. 3.5, 8; 1 Tim. 1.9-10; 2 Tim. 3.2-5; Tit. 3.3; 1 Pet. 4.3.

[197] Test. Reub. 3.3-6 mentions seven πνεύματα τῆς πλάνης, spirits of error. On
sevenfold "Lasterkataloge" see E. Kamlah, Die Form der katalogischen Paränese im
Neuen Testament, Tübingen 1964, pp. 121-22; 175.

2.3.3 Romans 1.32

1.32: οἵτινες τὸ δικαίωμα τοῦ θεοῦ ἐπιγνόντες ὅτι οἱ τὰ τοιαῦτα πράσσοντες ἄξιοι θανάτου εἰσίν, οὐ μόνον αὐτὰ ποιοῦσιν ἀλλὰ καὶ συνευδοκοῦσιν τοῖς πράσσουσιν.[198]

The word οἵτινες (cf. 1.25) introduces the conclusion. Just as ἐπίγνωσις was used in 1.28, so here ἐπιγινώσκω is used. Hackenberg argues that it is used, as ἐπίγνωσις is in 1.28, to denote "an obedient recognition of the will of God".[199] I wonder though, whether the use of this word supports such an interpretation.[200] Note that the participle ἐπιγνόντες here has a concessive sense (cf. γνόντες in 1.21). Many believe τὸ δικαίωμα τοῦ θεοῦ refers to the law (cf. 8.4 and the plural in 2.26). Käsemann believes the singular means "die Forderung oder Satzung des Rechtes"[201]. However, a more likely understanding is that the ὅτι is epexegetic[202] (τὸ δικαίωμα τοῦ θεοῦ ἐπιγνόντες ὅτι οἱ τὰ τοιαῦτα πράσσοντες ἄξιοι θανάτου εἰσίν). Schlier writes:

Es ist in diesem Satz nicht davon die Rede, daß die Heiden das Gesetz Gottes als solches erkennen, sondern es ist gesagt, daß sie die göttliche Grundthese der Vergeltung böser Taten erkannt haben.[203]

However, I would wish to qualify Schlier's words by stressing that what is known is simply the principle of retribution. Because knowledge of God has been lost, they no longer know that this is the retribution *of God*.

So although they know of the principle of retribution they nevertheless do such evil things but also approve of those who did such things. 1.32 not only forms a summary to 1.18-31 but also serves as a transition to Romans 2, for here we discover those who rather than approving evil doers, actually judge them.

---

[198] On the textual problems in this verse see Cranfield, *Romans*, 1:133-34.

[199] W. Hackenberg, ἐπιγινώσκω, *EDNT* 2:24 (24-25).

[200] See further the discussion of ἐπίγνωσις in Rom. 3.20 in chapter 6 below.

[201] Käsemann, *Römer*, p. 47.

[202] Schlier, *Römerbrief*, p. 65.

[203] H. Schlier, "Von den Heiden: Römerbrief 1,18-32", in *Die Zeit der Kirche: Exegetische Aufsätze und Vorträge*, Freiburg 1956, 36 (29-37).

Chapter 3

Romans 1.18-32: Issues arising

1. The Relation of Romans 1.18-32 to Greek Philosophy and Hellenistic Judaism

In the exegesis in the last chapter the influence of the Old Testament on Rom. 1.18-32 has, I hope, been clear to see. However, the relationship of Rom. 1.18-32 to Greek philosophy and Hellenistic Judaism is not so clear, especially as regards the issue of natural theology. I therefore now examine this possible relationship paying special attention to natural theology.

At the outset it needs stressing that there may well be Greek philosophical and especially Stoic elements in Paul's argument. The question, however, is whether there has been any *direct* influence or whether such influences have come via Judaism.

W.D. Davies saw Stoic elements in Rom. 1.18-32 (and in Romans 2[1]). But he argued: "the dress in Rom. 1, 2 is Hellenistic but the body Rabbinic".[2] Davies points to the work of Klein.[3] Klein gives an interesting discussion of the Rabbinic idea of ארץ דרך,[4] where ethical norms for all people were to be found[5]; in fact these commandments were a sort of nat-

---

[1] He considered the conscience to be a Stoic idea. See the discussion on Rom. 2.14-16 and the excursus on "Natural Law" in Greek Philosophy in Chapter 4.

[2] W.D. Davies, *Paul and Rabbinic Judaism*, London ²1955, (¹1948), p. 117.

[3] G. Klein, *Der älteste christliche Katechismus und die jüdische Propaganda-literatur*, Berlin 1909. Note, however, that Davies' representation of Klein is not entirely accurate.

[4] Cf. the biblical expression as found in Gen. 6.12: כִּי־הִשְׁחִית כָּל־בָּשָׂר אֶת־דַּרְכּוֹ עַל־הָאָרֶץ.

[5] Klein, *Katechismus*, p. 62. On the two tractates Derek Erets Rabbah and Derek Erets Zutta see S. Safrai (ed.), *The Literature of the Sages. First Part: Oral Tora,*

ural law.[6] Klein believes this idea of דרך ארץ is in the centre of Paul's teaching[7] and argues that the expression μὴ καθήκοντα of Rom. 1.28 "entspricht genau dem Hebräischen שלא כהוגן = ungebührlich, ungeziemend, ein Ausdruck, der in den Derech erez-Gesetzen von der allergrößten Wichtigkeit ist".[8] I am not sure one can be so confident of such a direct Rabbinic influence on Rom. 1.28, but Klein's work does highlight the care which is necessary in positing direct Stoic influence (especially as it is claimed that the term τὰ μὴ καθήκοντα is Stoic).[9]

Schulz argues that along with the Old Testament and apocalyptic, "stoisch-hellenistisch" thought has influenced Rom. 1.18-32.[10] He points to the common vocabulary, i.e., τὰ ἀόρατα αὐτοῦ, νοούμενα καθορᾶται, ἀΐδιος δύναμις, θειότης, ἀφθαρσία, φυσικὴ χρῆσις, νοῦς, τὰ μὴ καθήκοντα. However, in very few cases is there a strong case for Paul taking the particular word directly from pagan-hellenistic tradition. It is more likely that Paul took the words from Hellenistic Judaism or perhaps from popular philosophy (which he learnt through the Hellenistic synagogue). So ἀΐδιος is found as an attribute of God in Wis. 2.23; 7.26 (cf. 4 Mac. 10.15).[11] θειότης is found in Wis. 18.9.[12] τὰ μὴ καθήκοντα is found in Hellenistic Judaism[13]. ἀφθαρσία is found in Wis. 2.23; 6.19 (cf.

Halakha, Mishna, Tosefta, Talmud, External Tractates, Assen/Philadelphia 1987, pp. 379-89.

[6] Klein, *Katechismus*, p. 64.

[7] Klein, *Katechismus*, p. 70.

[8] Klein, *Katechismus*, p. 72. Davies, *Paul*, p. 117 n. 1, points out that the phrase שלא כהוגן is not late as can be seen by Akiba's use of the term in his parable in b. Abod. Zar. 55a.

[9] In fact the usual Stoic term is παρὰ τὸ καθῆκον. See the discussion in chapter 2 above on Rom. 1.28.

[10] Schulz, "Anklage", 162.

[11] Note that ἀΐδιος is also used as an attribute of God in Sib. 5.66, 427, 498. However, this is too late to have influenced Paul directly (book 5 is dated no earlier than 70 AD by J.J. Collins, in Charlesworth, *Pseudepigrapha*, 1:390). The only other use of ἀΐδιος in the New Testament is in Jude 6, where the word is used of "eternal chains", not "God".

[12] Wis. 18.9 speaks of ὁ τῆς θειότητος νόμος. The word is also used in Aristeas 95. Note that θειότης is used only here in the New Testament.

[13] 2 Mac. 6.4; 3 Mac. 4.16. I noted that the usual Stoic term is παρὰ τὸ καθῆκον.

4 Mac. 9.22; 17.12). As regards νοῦς, A. Sand writes that "while νοῦς played a central role in Greek thought . . . its usage in the LXX is greatly diminished".[14] In fact it occurs about 30 times in LXX. In Paul the word is used in various senses (in Rom. 1.28 it means "mind"). Behm believes that in the New Testament

. . . there is no connection with the philosophical or mystico-religious use. νοῦς is not the divine or the divinely related element in man. It is equated neither with the πνεῦμα nor the ψυχή. As in the popular usage of the Greeks the term has no precise meaning . . .[15]

The word ἀόρατος occurs three times in LXX (Gen. 1.2; Is. 45.3; 2 Mac. 9.2) but not in connection with God. It is, however, used in reference to God in Hellenistic Jewish sources.[16] Of the words listed above χρῆσις seems to be the strongest candidate for having a pagan-hellenistic origin. The word is used in LXX, but not in the sense of sexual intercourse (as it is used in Rom. 1.26-27). This sexual meaning is found in Plato, *Laws* 841A (and in Ps.-Plutarch, *Placita philosophorum* 905B, but this is rather too late). I believe that except for the word χρῆσις, Hellenistic Judaism is a more likely source for the words listed. But even the word χρῆσις itself, whilst having a likely pagan origin, probably came to Paul via popular philosophy and the Hellenistic synagogue.[17] It is unlikely that Paul discovered the word whilst reading Plato![18]

---

[14] A. Sand, νοῦς, *EDNT* 2:478 (478-79).

[15] J. Behm and E. Würthwein, νοέω κτλ, *TDNT*, 4:958 (948-1022).

[16] R. Bultmann, "Untersuchungen zum Johannesevangelium", *ZNW* 29 (1930) 187 (169-92), describes ἀόρατος θεός (Col. 1.15; 1 Tim. 1.17; Heb. 11.27) as "hellenistisch" and points to the use of ἀόρατος θεός in Josephus, *Bellum* 7.346 and Aristobulus in Eusebius, *Praeparatio evangelica* 13.12.5 ("Johannesevangelium", 188 n. 2). Note also the use of ἀόρατος with God in the Greek Pseudepigrapha (Life of Adam and Eve (Apocalyse) 35.3; Test. Abr. 9.7; 16.3, 4) and other uses of ἀόρατος (see A.-M. Denis (ed.), *Concordance grecque des Pseudépigraphes d'Ancien Testament*, Louvain-la-Neuve 1987).

[17] Cf. the quotation from Menander, *Thais*, in 1 Cor. 15.33, which Paul also probably came to know through the Hellenistic synagogue.

[18] Cf. M. Hengel, *The Pre-Christian Paul*, London 1991, p. 38, who suggests that "Paul seems to have gone to a good Greek elementary school, which was a *Jewish* school — because the literature from Homer to Euripides used in regular teaching was quite alien to him. The literature that he knows — as is also suggested by his vocabulary — is that of the Septuagint and related religious writings". See again

The relative strength of the pagan influence or Hellenistic Jewish influence can be debated. But what is extremely unlikely is that Paul took these terms directly from philosophical works.[19] As regards Stoicism in particular, it is hard to find direct influence here and some of the terms Paul uses in his argument are quite alien to Stoicism.[20]

Schulz not only appeals to the vocabulary to establish Stoic-hellenistic influence. He points also to "sachliche(n) und gedankliche(n) Beziehungen zu stoischer Terminologie und apologetischen Ausführungen des Diasporajudentums".[21] It is striking to note that although Bultmann sees some Stoic terminology in Rom. 1.19-20, he believes "Paulus rezipiert den griechischen Gedanken nicht".[22] Bornkamm reaches a similar conclusion. Although Bornkamm argues for parallels between Rom. 1.18-32 and Stoicism, he believes that Paul has changed the ideas radically. Bornkamm's work has been especially important and influential that it is worth considering his arguments is some detail.

Bornkamm rightly sees the influence of the Old Testament on Rom. 1.18-32.[23] But he also writes this:

In the presentation of this natural revelation of God, Paul, as is known, shows himself to be influenced in such a striking way by Stoic terminology and apologetic trains of thought, such as are characteristic of Hellenistic Judaism (especially Wisdom of Solomon and Philo), that one must ask the question about literary dependence.[24]

Hengel, *Pre-Christian Paul*, p. 37. "He probably had not read any classical Greek literature worth mentioning apart from the Greek (and Hebrew) Bible and Jewish pseudepigrapha like the Wisdom of Solomon".

[19] Although he may possibly have been influenced by Gentiles he met on his missionary journeys.

[20] For example, Gärtner, *Areopagus Speech*, p. 138 n. 3, writes: "Κτίσις is a word no Stoic could possibly use to describe the regulation of the universe".

[21] Schulz, "Anklage", 162-63.

[22] Bultmann, "Untersuchungen", 188. He also points to Paul's avoidance of the term τεχνίτης for God.

[23] G. Bornkamm, "The Revelation of God's Wrath: Romans 1-3", in *Early Christian Experience* ET, New York 1969, 67 n. 38 (47-70), points to a number of terms many of which have already been discussed above, but we may add the following: "senseless heart" (not "mind" v. 21); "the creator" (not "artificer" as in Wis. 13.1 or "maker" in 13.5); "ungodliness" and "wickedness" (which may refer to the two tablets of the decalogue (see Schlatter, *Gottes Gerechtigkeit*, p. 49)); the Jewish doxology at the end of v. 25.

[24] Bornkamm, "Wrath", 50.

The four sorts of influence he refers to are: 1. "The ingenious construction of the world gives cause for human viewers to ask about their Creator and to infer his divine greatness from the glory of his work". 2. This knowledge of the Creator "does not only represent a theoretical confirmation of the existence of a prime cause but is at the same time a comprehension of the law". 3. Obedience belongs to a right knowledge of God. 4. Closing of oneself to the knowledge of God leads to idolatry. Bornkamm says that these ideas belong to the Hellenistic doctrine of God and are not to be found in Paul.[25] Of these four points I am going to focus on the first.[26]

Bornkamm's first point concerns natural theology. Is it not precisely here that we see the influence of Greek Philosophy? To examine this I now investigate the tradition of natural theology found in the Graeco-Roman world.

I turn first to what could be called teleological arguments, that is arguments from design. This view is found in a number of philosophers. As far as extant fragments are concerned, the first to put forward a teleological argument was Diogenes of Apollonia,[27] although Plutarch says Anaxagoras (who was Diogenes' teacher) was the first of the Greeks.[28] This argument does not appear to be prominent among the pre-Socratics and although in Plato it does play a role,[29] it is not until Aristotle that the

---

[25] Bornkamm, "Wrath", 50.

[26] The other three points will be touched on briefly here. See chapter 4 for a more detailed discussion of points 2 and 3.

[27] A.S. Pease, "Caeli enarrant", *HTR* 34.4 (1941) 164 (163-200). See Fragment B3-5. B5: καὶ μοι δοκεῖ τὸ τὴν νόησιν ἔχον εἶναι ὁ ἀὴρ καλούμενος ὑπὸ τῶν ἀνθρώπων, καὶ ὑπὸ τούτου πάντας καὶ κυβερνᾶσθαι καὶ πάντων κρατεῖν· αὐτὸ γάρ μοι τοῦτο θεὸς δοκεῖ εἶναι καὶ ἐπὶ πᾶν ἀφῖχθαι καὶ πάντα διατιθέναι καὶ ἐν παντὶ ἐνεῖναι (H. Diels and W. Kranz, *Die Fragmente der Vorsokratiker: Band 2*, Dublin/Zürich ¹²1966, (¹1903), p. 61).

[28] Plutarch, *Pericles* 4.4, writes that Anaxagoras was known as Νοῦς, one possible reason for this name being because "he was the first to enthrone in the universe, not Chance, nor yet Necessity, as the source of its orderly arrangement, but Mind (Nous) pure and simple . . ." (Plutarch (LCL), 3:13).

[29] Plato, *Laws* 886A; *Philebus* 28D-E; 30C-D. See also *Timaeus*, 72E-81E for an extended discussion of the design of the human body. Pease, "Caeli enarrant", 168, comments that Timaeus is "our first great cosmology in which design plays a chief rôle". See also Xenophon, *Memorabilia* 1.4.2-19, for Socrates' teleology.

argument is used in some detail.[30] Then in Stoic philosophy the argument reaches its peak.[31] So we find the argument in Zeno,[32] Cleanthes,[33] Chrysippus,[34] and Epictetus.[35] Also the argument from design is employed by Cicero himself[36] and by Seneca[37]. There were, of course,

---

[30] Pease, "Caeli enarrant", 171-72, points out that "In greater fulness than that of Plato's Timaeus, Aristotle, on the basis of his more abundantly collected scientific observations . . . discusses man's physical adaptation to his various needs . . .".

[31] See E. Norden, "Beiträge zur Geschichte der griechischen Philosophie", in A. Fleckeisen (ed.), *Jahrbücher für classische Philologie: Neunzehnter Supplementband*, Leipzig 1893, 435 (365-462).

[32] See Cicero, *De natura deorum* 2.58: ". . . the nature of the world itself, which encloses and contains all things in its embrace, is styled by Zeno not merely 'craftsmanlike' (*artificiosus*) but actually 'a craftsman' (*artifex*), whose foresight plans out the work to serve its use and purpose in every detail" (Cicero (LCL), 19:179).

[33] Cicero, *De natura deorum* 3.13-15, gives four reasons of Cleanthes for believing in gods. First, there is the phenomenon of divination. Second, there is the blessing of a temperate climate and the earth's fertility. Third, there is the awe inspired by lightning, storms, earthquakes etc. But the fourth and "most potent cause of the belief . . . was the uniform motion and revolution of the heavens, and the varied groupings and ordered beauty of the sun, moon and stars, the very sight of which was in itself enough to prove that these things are not the mere effect of chance" (Cicero (LCL), 19:137).

[34] Cicero, quoting Cleanthes, writes (*De natura deorum* 2.16): "'If (he says) there be something in the world that man's mind and human reason, strength and power are incapable of producing, that which produces it must necessarily be superior to man; now the heavenly bodies and all those things that display a never-ending regularity cannot be created by man; therefore that which creates them is superior to man; yet what better name is there for this than 'god'" (Cicero (LCL), 19:139).

[35] Epictetus, *Discourses* 1.6.7-8: "Assuredly from the very structure of all made objects we are accustomed to prove that the work is certainly the product of some artificer (ὅτι τεχνίτου τινὸς πάντως τὸ ἔργον), and has not been contructed at random. 8 Does, then, every such work reveal its artificer (ἐμφαίνει τὸν τεχνίτην), but do visible objects and vision and light not reveal him (τὰ δ' ὁρατὰ καὶ ὅρασις καὶ φῶς οὐκ ἐμφαίνει)?" (Epictetus (LCL), 1:41).

[36] In *De natura deorum* 2.37, Cicero asks a question which appears extremely modern: "At this point must I not marvel that there should be anyone who can persuade himself that there are certain solid and indivisible particles of matter borne along by the force of gravity, and that the fortuituous collision of those particles produces this elaborate and beautiful world?" (Cicero (LCL), 19:213). He goes on to liken such a process to placing letters in a receptacle, shaking them out on the ground and producing the Annals of Ennius. Later Cicero speaks of the "beauty of the creations of divine providence" (2.39) and gives a detailed review of the wonders of nature (2.39-61). It may be said that these passages from Cicero do not reflect his

many objections to such arguments. Lucretius, for example, argued that
the reasoning in teleology is faulty[38] and that the world cannot have been
designed by divine power in view of the many faults.[39]

In addition to these teleological arguments there were cosmological
arguments, although often no clear distinction is made between the two.[40]
For examples of cosmological arguments see Plato[41] and Aristotle[42]. It is
to be stressed that in these arguments, although God may be a first cause,
he fashions the cosmos out of already existing material. *Creatio ex nihilo*
is a distinctively biblical view of creation.[43] In fact Owen goes as far as to

---

own views. However, Pease, "Caeli enarrant", 180, points out that Cicero himself
clearly held to some teleological argument. See *De divinatione* 2.148: "Furthermore,
the celestial order and the beauty of the universe compel me to confess that there is
some excellent and eternal Being, who deserves the respect and homage of men"
(Cicero (LCL), 20:537). See also *De legibus* 1.8.25 (Cicero (LCL), 16:325).

[37] Seneca, *De beneficiis* 4.6.

[38] See Lucretius, *De rerum natura* 4.823-57. Such arguments from design "put
effect for cause and are based on perverted reasoning; since nothing is born in us
simply in order that we may use it, but that which is born creates the use" (Lucretius
(LCL), p. 343).

[39] Lucretius, *De rerum natura* 5.195-323. He points to the vast uninhabitable areas
of the earth, the existence of wild beasts, diseases, and mortality.

[40] See, for example, Plato, *Timaeus* 30A-B.

[41] Plato, *Timaeus* 28C: "And that which has come into existence must necessarily,
as we say, have come into existence by reason of some Cause" (Plato (LCL), 9:51).
He goes on to argue that the architect (ὁ τεκταινόμενος) or constructor (δημιουργός)
in contructing the cosmos fixed his gaze on the Eternal (τὸ ἀΐδιον) (28C-29A). The
argument in Plato, *Laws* 891-99, is somewhat different. Here Plato does not argue for
a δημιουργός as in *Timaeus* but rather for a self-moving soul which manages the
heavens. "Soul (ψυχή) drives all things in Heaven and earth and sea by its own
motions . . ." (*Laws*, 896E, Plato (LCL), 11:341). On the argument in *Laws* 10 see
L.P. Gerson, *God and Greek Philosophy*, London 1990, pp. 71-79.

[42] Aristotle, *Metaphysica* 9.8.1049b24ff (Aristotle, (LCL), 17:457); 12.7.1072aff
(Aristotle, (LCL), 18:145ff).

[43] How early in the biblical tradition this idea developed is, of course, a matter of
debate. Many would see the first idea of creation out of nothing in 2 Mac. 7.28 (cf.
Rom. 4.17; Heb. 11.3) (cf. B.W. Anderson, "Creation", *IDB* 1:728 (725-32)).
However, although creation out of nothing is not explicit in earlier tradition, it is, I
believe, implied in the use of the verb ברא in Gen. 1.

say this: "that the world is related to God as created to Creator was never believed by any Gentile".[44]

I turn now to Hellenistic Judaism. Lindeskog writes: "Man hat den Eindruck, dass der Schöpfungsgedanke eine größere Rolle im hellenistischen Judentum als im hebräischen Alten Testament spielt."[45] Lindeskog makes the point that this change to a greater emphasis on "Ktisiologie" can be found already in the LXX.[46] Perhaps such a ktisiology opens the way for a discussion of "natural theology" as is found in the Wisdom of Solomon.

Many scholars find striking parallels between Wis. 13.1-9 and Rom. 1.19ff.[47] Wis. 13.5: "For from the greatness and beauty of created things comes a corresponding perception of their creator". This may be compared to Rom. 1.20. The writer then goes on to make the point that they did not know God although they should have. Wis. 13.8-9: "Yet again, not even they are to be excused; 9 for if they had the power to know so much that they could investigate the world, how did they fail to find sooner the Lord of these things".[48] This may be compared to Rom. 1.21. Whether these really are parallels will be investigated shortly.

---

[44] Owen, " Natural Revelation", 139.

[45] G. Lindeskog, *Studien zum neutestamentlichen Schöpfungsgedanken*, Uppsala 1952, p. 136. W. Eltester, "Schöpfungsoffenbarung und natürliche Theologie im frühen Christentum", *NTS* 3 (1956-57) 96 n. 1 (93-114), comments: "Dieser Eindruck scheint mir durchaus richtig zu sein und wird sich auch im folgenden noch bestätigen".

[46] Lindeskog, *Schöpfungsgedanke*, p. 136, gives the example of שָׂדִי of Job 8.3 rendered in LXX as ὁ τὰ πάντα ποιήσας and points to the way Greek has a range of terms for "Ktisiologie" such as κτίστης, κτίσις, κτίσμα.

[47] The earliest study on the parallels of which I know is E. Grafe, "Das Verhältniss der paulinischen Schriften zur Sapientia Salomonis", *Theologische Abhandlungen: Carl von Weizsäcker zu seinem siebzigsten Geburtstage gewidmet*, Freiburg 1892, 253-86.

[48] Wis. 13.9: εἰ γὰρ τοσοῦτον ἴσχυσαν εἰδέναι ἵνα δυνωνται στοχάσασθαι τον αἰῶνα, τὸν τούτων δεσπότην πῶς τάχιον οὐχ εὗρον. On αἰών meaning "world" see Ex. 15.18 LXX. H. Sasse, αἰών, αἰώνιος, *TDNT* 1:203 (197-209) points out that "time or course of the world" can easily pass over into that of the "world" itself so that αἰών roughly means κόσμος (cf. 1 Cor. 1.20; 2.6; 3.19).

Going beyond the LXX, Philo of Alexandria has a number of arguments for God's existence based on the natural world.[49] First, there are what could be called teleological arguments: *Legum allegoriae* 3.97-103;[50] *De praemiis et poenis* 41-42;[51] *De specialibus legibus* 1.33ff;[52] 3.187-89.[53] Secondly, there are cosmological arguments: *De fuga et*

---

[49] On Philo's natural theology see especially G. Kuhlmann, *Theologia naturalis bei Philon und bei Paulus*, Gütersloh 1930.

[50] See especially *Legum allegoriae* 3.99, which speaks of "anyone entering this world, as it were some vast house or city, and beholding the sky circling round and embracing within it all things, and planets and fixed stars without any variation moving in rhythmical harmony . . . he will surely argue that these have not been wrought without consummate art, but that the Maker (δημιουργός) of this whole universe was and is God. Those, who thus base their reasoning on what is before their eyes, apprehend God by means of a shadow cast, discerning the Artificer by means of His works (διὰ τῶν ἔργων τὸν τεχνίτης κατανοοῦντες)" (Philo (LCL), 1:367, 369).

[51] See especially *De praemiis et poenis* 42: "Struck with admiration and astonishment they arrived at a conception according with what they beheld, that surely all these beauties and this transcendent order has not come into being automatically but by the handiwork of an architect and world maker (ὑπό τινος δημιουργοῦ κοσμοποιοῦ); also that there must be a providence (ἀναγκαῖον), for it is a law of nature that a maker should take care of what has been made" (Philo (LCL), 8:337).

[52] See *De specialibus legibus* 1.34-35: "So then he who comes to the truly Great City, this world, and beholds hills and plains teeming with animals and plants, the rivers, spring-fed or winter torrents, streaming along, the seas with their expanses, the air with its happily tempered phases, the yearly seasons passing into each other, and then the sun and moon ruling the day and night, and the other heavenly bodies fixed or planetary and the whole firmament revolving in rhythmic order, must he not naturally or rather necessarily gain the conception of the Maker and Father and Ruler also (τοῦ ποιητοῦ καὶ πατρὸς καὶ προσέτι ἡγεμόνος)? For none of the works of human art is self-made, and the highest art and knowledge is shewn in this universe, so that surely it has been wrought by one of excellent knowledge and absolute perfection. In this way we have gained the conception of the existence of God (τοῦτον τὸν τρόπον ἔννοιαν ἐλάβομεν ὑπάρξεως θεοῦ)" (*Philo* (LCL), 7:118-19).

[53] See especially *De specialibus legibus* 3.189, where, after describing the wonders of the heavens, Philo writes: "The mind, having discerned through the faculty of sight what of itself it was not able to apprehend, did not simply stop short at what it saw, but, drawn by its love of knowledge and beauty and charmed by the marvellous spectacle, came to the reasonable conclusion, that all these were not brought together automatically by unreasoning forces, but by the mind of God Who is rightly called their Father and Maker (ἀλλὰ διανοίᾳ θεοῦ, ὃν πατέρα καὶ ποιητὴν ὀνομάζειν θέμις)" (Philo (LCL), 7:595).

inventione 12;[54] *De posteritate Caini* 28;[55] *De mutatione nominum* 54;[56] *Quaestiones et solutiones in Genesin* 2.34[57]; *De decalogo* 52-53[58]; *Quis rerum divinarum heres* 114-16.[59] There are also texts which are neither clearly teleological nor cosmological.[60]

Philo and Josephus share some ideas regarding natural theology. There are some interesting stories regarding Abraham as the one who came to know something of God through the created order.[61] They also share

---

[54] "For the world has come into being, and assuredly it has done so under the hand of some Cause" (Philo (LCL), 5:17).

[55] Philo writes that Dt. 5.31 proves that "that the Existent Being who moves and turns all else is Himself exempt from movement and turning" (Philo (LCL), 2:345).

[56] He writes that Abraham "knew that God stands with place unchanged, yet moves the universal frame of creation, His own motion being the motion of self-extension (not the movement of the legs, for He is not of human form), but a motion whereby He shows His unalterable, unchanging nature" (Philo (LCL), 5:169).

[57] "And this (reason), seeing with a sharp eye both these (celestial phenomena) and through them the higher paradigmatic forms and the cause of all things, immediately apprehends them and genesis and providence, for it reasons that visible nature did not come into being by itself . . . it is necessary that there be some Creator and Father (ποιητήν τινα καὶ πατέρα), a pilot and charioteer, who both begat and wholly preserves and guards the things begotten" (Philo Supplement (LCL), 1:113).

[58] Philo argues that God is "the transcendent source of all that exists" and "the Begetter, the Ruler of the great World-city" (Philo (LCL), 7:33).

[59] Philo argues that "the beginnings of things both material and immaterial are found to be my God only" (Philo (LCL), 4:339).

[60] See, for example, Philo, *De posteritate Caini* 167, where, after discussing the golden calf, writes: "But the Being that in reality is can be perceived and known, not only through the ears, but with the eyes of understanding (ἀλλὰ τοῖς διανοίας ὄμμασιν), from the powers that range the universe, and from the constant and ceaseless motion of His ineffable works" (Philo (LCL) 2:427). To prove that God can be known by "clear intuition" Philo quotes Dt. 32.39: "See, see that I AM" (ἴδετε, ἴδετε, ὅτι ἐγώ εἰμι).

[61] Josephus, *Antiquitates* 1.155 tells of how Abraham was the first to declare that God the creator is one and that the universe is at his command. He explains in 1.156: "This he inferred from the changes to which land and sea are subject, from the course of sun and moon, and from all the celestial phenomena; for, he argued, were these bodies endowed with power, they would have provided for their own regularity, but, since they lacked this last, it was manifest that even those services in which they cooperate for our greater benefit they render not in virtue of their own authority, but through the might of their commanding sovereign, to whom alone it is right to render our homage and thanksgiving" (Josephus (LCL), 4:77, 79). See also Philo, *De virtutibus* 216, who writes this of Abraham: "And therefore, he is the first person

some views which are akin to a "theology of nature". Philo and Josephus believed independently that the menora reflects the seven planets and see it as reflecting the divine order of the heavens.[62] Philo also believed that the two cherubim over the mercy seat represent the two hemispheres, one above the earth and one under it.[63] Further, according to Josephus, the whole tabernacle and the vestments reflect the universe,[64] a view which

---

spoken of as believing in God, since he first grasped a firm and unswerving conception of the truth that there is one Cause (ἓν αἴτιον) above all, and that it provides for the world and all that there is therein" (Philo (LCL), 8:295). The reference is clearly to Gen. 15.6. In the previous verse of Genesis, Abraham is shown the stars. "And he brought him outside and said, 'Look toward heaven, and number the stars, if you are able to number them.' Then he said to him, 'So shall your descendants be'. 6 And he believed the LORD; and he reckoned it to him as righteousness" (Gen. 15.5-6). See also *De mutatione nominum* 54 (quoted above).

[62] See Philo, *Quis rerum divinarum heres* 221-25. Philo thinks the most probable order of the "planets" (λύχνοι) is the sun in the centre with Saturn, Jupiter and Mars "above" and Mercury, Venus and the Moon "below" (compare the structure of the Menora). The same idea is found independently in Josephus, *Antiquitates* 3.144-46. Josephus says the Menora was made up of 70 elements and in 3.182 writes: "By making the candelabrum to consist of seventy portions, he hinted at the ten degree provinces of the planets, and by the seven lamps thereon the course of the planets themselves, for such is their number" (Josephus (LCL), 4:403-5). An analysis of Ex. 25.31ff actually yields 69 elements (*EB(C)* 1:645).

[63] Philo, *Vita Mosis* 2.98. Philo also writes that the two cherubim "are allegorical representations of the two most august and highest potencies of Him that IS, the creative and the kingly. His creative potency is called God, because through it He placed and made and ordered this universe, and the kingly is called Lord, being that with which He governs what has come into being and rules it steadfastly with justice" (2.99, Philo (LCL), 6:497-99). In *De cherubim* 21, Philo writes that the Cherubim of Gen. 3.24 are an "allegorical figure of the revolution of the whole heaven".

[64] Referring to the tabernacle and vestments, Josephus writes: "every one of these objects is intended to recall and represent the universe, as he will find if he will be consent to examine them without prejudice and with understanding. Thus, to take the tabernacle, thirty cubits long, by dividing this into three parts and giving up two of them to the priest, as a place approachable and open to all, Moses signifies the earth and the sea, since these too are accessible to all; but the third portion he reserved for God alone, because heaven also is inaccessible to men. Again by placing upon the table the twelve loaves, he signifies that the year is divided into as many months. . . . The high-priest's tunic likewise signifies the earth, being of linen, and its blue the arch of heaven, while it recalls the lightnings by its pomegranates, the thunder by the sounds of its bells. His upper garment, too, denotes universal nature, which it pleased God to make of four elements. . . . Sun and moon are indicated by the two sardonyxes wherewith he pinned the high-priest's robe. As for the twelve stones,

may well go back to the theology of the Priestly writer and to the Zion traditions in the Old Testament.[65] Such views are more related to a "theology of nature" than to "natural theology" for it is not a question of establishing a knowledge of God in the light of nature but rather a question of establishing a knowledge of nature in the light of God and his revelation to Israel.[66]

There is, therefore, this strong tradition of natural theology in both the Graeco-Roman world and in Hellenistic Judaism.

---

whether one would prefer to read in them the months or the constellations of like number, which the Greeks call the circle of the zodiac, he will not mistake the lawgiver's intention" (*Antiquitates* 3.180-86, Josephus (LCL) 4:403-7).

[65] There are no explicit texts which link the tabernacle and its contents to the structure of the universe but there are a number of hints when one considers the Priestly writing as a whole. So the creation account in Gen. 1.1-2.4a emphasises the establishing of order in terms of space and time. So for space the idea of separation is extremely important (note the importance of separation in the cultic law) and for time the seven day structure is probably meant to give a matrix for the sacrifical cult. Further the movement of the sun and moon is crucial for the cult. See the discussion concerning order in the Priestly writing in P.P. Jensen, *Graded Holiness: A Key to the Priestly Conception of the World*, Sheffield 1992, pp. 216-17. See also J.D. Levenson, *Sinai and Zion: An Entry into the Jewish Bible*, Minneapolis 1985, pp. 89-184. Levenson points out that "Mount Zion is a place of visionary experience" (p. 95), a significant point in view of the predominantly auditory nature of the Sinai revelation. The temple/tabernacle reflects the universe and this is seen for example in the parallelism of the language used for the creation of the cosmos and the contruction of the tabernacle (p. 143). On the creation theology of the Zion symbolism of the Jerusalem cult, see B.C. Ollenburger, *Zion the City of the Great King: A Theological Symbol of the Jerusalem Cult*, Sheffield 1987, especially p. 161. See also the work of B. Janowski on the temple and creation (*Sühne als Heilsgeschehen: Studien zur Sühnetheologie der Priesterschrift und zur Wurzel KPR im Alten Orient und im Alten Testament*, Neukirchen-Vluyn 1982, 309-12; "Tempel und Schöpfung: Schöpfungstheologische Aspekte der priesterschriftlichen Heiligtumskonzeption", *Jahrbuch für Biblische Theologie Band 5: Schöpfung und Neuschöpfung*, Neukirchen-Vluyn 1990, 37-69). Janowski gives some helpful correctives to some of the writing on temple and creation. On the Rabbinic view that the tabernacle/temple reflects the cosmos, see the discussion below (chapter 4).

[66] Cf. G.S. Hendry, *Theology of Nature*, Philadelphia 1980, p. 14. See also the discussion below on Pss. 8, 19, 104. I therefore take "theology of nature" to be an objective genitive, not a subjective genitive.

Turning to Bornkamm's second point, this knowledge about the creator involves a knowledge of the law. This view is to some extent found among the Stoics[67] and can be found in Hellenistic Judaism.[68] There are also some texts in Philo which liken the world to a city implying that God has given certain laws in order that people may lead well ordered lives.[69]

The third point of Bornkamm is that honouring God and obedience belongs to a right knowledge of God. This view was shared by both Greek pagan thought[70] and Hellenistic Judaism[71]. The fourth is that closing of oneself to the knowledge of God leads to idolatry. This again is shared by Greek pagan thought[72] and Hellenistic Judaism[73].

Such then is the possible pagan and Hellenistic Jewish background for Paul's argument in Rom. 1.18-32. I am, however, rather doubtful that much of this tradition has had a direct influence on Paul and it is telling

---

[67] See the discussion of Rom. 2.14-16 and the excursus on "Natural Law" in Greek Philosophy in chapter 4 below.

[68] See Philo, *De opificio mundi* 3: "His exordium, as I have said, is one that excites our admiration in the highest degree. It consists of an account of the creation of the world, implying that the world is in harmony with the Law, and the Law with the world, and that the man who observes the Law is constituted thereby a loyal citizen of the world, regulating his doings by the purpose and will of Nature, in accordance with which the entire world itself also is administered" (Philo (LCL), 1:7). See also *De opificio mundi* 172. However, a text such as Philo, *De praemiis et poenis* 43, quoted by Bornkamm, is not really relevant to *moral* law.

[69] *De specialibus legibus* 1.33-34: "An when he enters a well-ordered city in which the arrangements for civil life are very admirably managed, what else will he suppose but that this city is directed by good rulers? So then he who comes to the truly Great City . . . must he not naturally or rather necessarily gain the conception of the Maker and Father and Ruler also?" (Philo (LCL), 7:119). See further the excursus in chapter 4 on "Natural Law" in Greek Philosophy.

[70] There are some passages of interest in Xenophon, *Memorabilia*. So in 4.6 we read that a pious man worships the gods according to certain laws (4.6.2-4) and behaves well towards other human beings (4.6.5-6). See also 4.3.13 and Marcus Aurelius, *Meditations* 12.28.

[71] See, for example, Philo, *De opificio mundi* 172.

[72] See critique of idols by Empedocles (Fragments 133 and 134) and Varro (see P. Wendland, *Die hellenistisch-römische Kultur in ihren Beziehungen zu Judentum und Christentum: Die urchristlichen Literaturformen*, Tübingen ²1912, pp. 141-42).

[73] See Wisdom of Solomon 13.

that although Bornkamm believes Hellenism has had some influence on Paul, he stresses that Paul has radically changed these views.

I consider first the Wisdom of Solomon. As regards the possible influence of Wisdom, it is necessary to consider the dating. There is no consensus on the dating of Wisdom and dates from 220 BC to 50 AD have been suggested. Although Winston has suggested a late date, believing that the reign of Caligula (37-41 AD) is the most probable time of composition,[74] his arguments are not entirely conclusive[75] and, as I now outline, there are good arguments for an earlier dating. First, I think it likely that Philo knew Wisdom.[76] Secondly, the work was highly esteemed in the second-century Church in both east and west.[77] As well as being quoted by Irenaeus, Tertullian and Clement of Alexandria, it is alluded to by Melito of Sardis (*On Pascha* 24-34)[78] and in the *Teachings*

---

[74] D. Winston, "Solomon, Wisdom of", *ABD* 6:122-23 (120-27).

[75] Winston argues that it is unlikely that Wisdom was written earlier than the Augustan age for there are a number of words or expressions which are not otherwise found before the first century AD. Winston finds 35 such expressions (*Wisdom of Solomon*, New York 1979, p. 22) (see also the earlier work of J.M. Reese, *Hellenistic Influence on the Book of Wisdom and its Consequences*, Rome 1970, pp. 1-25). However, as W. Horbury, "The Christian use and the Jewish origins of the Wisdom of Solomon", in J. Day, R.P. Gordon and H.G.M. Williamson (ed.), *Wisdom in ancient Israel: Essays in honour of J.A. Emerton*, Cambridge 1995, 183 (182-96), points out, there is not a large amount of first century BC Greek literature. Winston finds a pointer to the reign of Caligula in Wis. 5.17-23, where the destruction of the wicked is described. This could point to Caligula. However, Horbury's view ("Wisdom", 196) seems equally if not more plausible. He believes that Wis. 1-10 reflects "circumstances in which the 'Epicureanism' represented in Ecclesiastes, Ecclesiasticus and many Jewish epitaphs seemed influential — perhaps near the beginning of the first century BC, when Alexander Jannaeus reigned in Judaea and repressed the Pharisees". Also, the anti-gentile polemic of Wis. 11-19 "suits needs continually present among the Jews of Egypt".

[76] See J. Laporte, "Philo in the Tradition of Wisdom", in R.L. Wilken (ed.), *Aspects of Wisdom in Judaism and Early Christianity*, Notre Dame/London 1975, 105-6 (103-41).

[77] See Horbury, "Christian Use", 184-85; M. Gilbert, "Wisdom Literature", in M.E. Stone (ed.), *Jewish Writings of the the Second Temple Period*, Assen/Philadelphia 1984, 312-13 (283-324).

[78] See S.G. Hall, *Melito of Sardis: On Pascha and fragments*, Oxford 1979, pp. 12-17.

of Silvanus, a non-Gnostic Christian writing from Nag Hammadi.[79] The Old Latin version is probably second century[80] and the book of Wisdom is mentioned in the Muratorian Canon. Such widespread Christian use is difficult to account for if Wisdom is given a late dating. Thirdly, it is likely that Clement of Rome quotes Wisdom.[81] Fourthly and particularly, there are echoes of Wisdom in Paul and in other New Testament writers.[82] It is therefore highly likely that Paul knew this work and that he was influenced by it. But in what sense was he influenced? As I will argue below, the personified figure of wisdom did influence his Christology. As regards natural revelation and natural theology, he was to some extent influenced by Wisdom but there are some significant differences.[83] So in Rom. 1.18-32, we see that knowledge of God appears to be open to all.[84] This, incidentally, is a striking point, especially in view of Paul's predestinarian theology. And because this knowledge is open to all, and because no one has given thanks, all are guilty. The idea in Wis. 13.6-7, however, is rather different. There is some uncertainty as to whether the Gentiles are guilty.

> Yet these men are little to be blamed, for perhaps they go astray while seeking God and desiring to find him. 7 For as they live among his works they keep searching, and they trust in what they see, because the things that are seen are beautiful.

Despite the fact that the writer goes on in 13.8 to say "they are not to be excused", it seems that their not finding God is an *error*. Paul has a quite different approach. The problem with human kind is not one of ignorance

---

[79] See J.M. Robinson (ed.), *The Nag Hammadi Library in English*, Leiden/New York/København/Köln ³1988, (¹1977), p. 393 (compare 112.37-113.7 with Wis. 7.25-26).

[80] See Gilbert, "Wisdom Literature", 313, who pointing to D. de Bruyne, "Étude sur le texte latin de la Sagesse", *RBén* 41 (1929) 101-33, writes that it probably arose in Christian Africa between 150 and 200 AD.

[81] See the quotation of Wis. 2.24 in 1 Clem. 3.4 and Wis. 12.12 in 27.5 (see J.B. Lightfoot, *The Apostolic Fathers*, 5 vols, Peabody 1989 (repr.), (¹1889-90), 2:21 n. 15; 91 n. 11).

[82] See for example the *loci citati vel allegati* in NA²⁶, pp. 772-73.

[83] But I would not go so far as Feine, *Theologie des Neuen Testaments*, p. 187, when he writes: "Paulus mag dies jüdische Apokryphon gekannt haben, von besonderem Einfluß auf ihn war es nicht".

[84] Bornkamm, "Wrath", 55.

but of blatant sinning "with a high hand".[85] However, it does need stressing that in Wis. 13.1-9, the focus is on heavenly bodies. Much stronger condemnation is reserved for those who worship images made of gold, silver and wood.[86]

Turning to Philo we see an even greater difference. One striking difference is their respective views on knowledge of God and praising God. Philo, like Paul, does see a link between knowing God and giving thanks. But for Philo, praise is the "last attainable step to which man can raise himself"[87]. So the one who praises God is the one who has succeeded in going beyond the things one sees[88] and in praising is taken out of himself.[89] For Paul, however, "giving thanks" and "glorifying" means the "acceptance of creaturely existence in obedient, thankful subjection under the creator".[90] As Schlier has argued, it is only by praising that the knowl-

---

[85] See also Godet, *Romans*, p. 106: "But what a difference between the tame and superficial explanation of idolatry, which the Alexandrian author gives to his readers, and the profound psychological analysis contained in the preceding verses of St. Paul! The comparison brings out exactly the difference between the penetration of the author enlightened from above, and that of the ordinary Jew seeking to reconstruct the great historic fact of idolatry by his own powers". Although some may be unhappy with his denigration of Wisdom, he does point to the difference in atmosphere of the two works, although perhaps Paul's great contribution is not a "psychological analysis" but rather a theological analysis.

[86] Winston, *Wisdom*, p. 7. I am grateful to Prof. Brendan Byrne for originally alerting me to this distinction. See B.J. Byrne, *Romans*, Collegeville, Minnesota 1996, pp. 64-65.

[87] Bornkamm, "Wrath", 56.

[88] See Philo, *De congressu quaerendae eruditionis gratia* 103-105, who referring to the priests says: "they are commanded to offer always the tenth of the ephah of fine flour (Lev. vi.20), for they have learned to rise above the ninth, the seeming deity, the world of sense, and to worship Him who is in very truth God, who stands alone as the tenth. For to the world belong nine parts, eight in heaven, one of the stars which wander not and seven of those that wander . . . Now the mass of men pay honour to these nine parts and to the world which is formed from them, but he that has reached perfection honours Him that is above the nine, even their maker God, who is the tenth" (Philo (LCL), 4:509, 511).

[89] See *Legum allegoriae* 1.82: "For indeed the very word denoting confession (of praise) vividly portrays the acknowledgement that takes a man out of himself" (Philo (LCL), 1:201).

[90] Bornkamm, "Wrath", 57.

edge of God is retained. Praise belongs to the very beginning, not to the goal.

I am also sceptical about the influence of Greek Philosophy. Many have seen some Stoic influence in Paul's argument in Rom. 1.18-32 (and in 2.14-16). Bornkamm has by no means established a direct influence of Stoicism.[91] All the influences he refers to could have been obtained from Hellenistic or Palestinian Judaism.[92] But although I disagree with Bornkamm on the influence of Stoicism, he does rightly draw attention to the differences between Paul and Stoicism and other non-Christian philosophy.[93]

The major differences between Rom. 1.18-32 and "Hellenism" on the issue of natural knowledge of God can be summarised as follows.

1. Hellenism is apologetic; Rom. 1.18-32 is an accusation. The Greek view and Hellenistic Jewish view is that idolatry and immorality are the result of a deficient knowledge of God.[94] For Paul, however, knowledge does not necessarily lead to a good life. For Bornkamm, Rom. 1.18-3.20 is an accusation and not an apology, so differing from the parallel literature.[95] So it is not the ignorance of God but the knowledge of God which

---

[91] See Eltester, "Schöpfungsoffenbarung", 98, who, although arguing that Paul touches on Stoic philosophy, suggests that this Stoic influence came indirectly via Hellenistic Judaism.

[92] Concerning some of the influences of Stoicism on Palestinian Judaism, see the excursus in chapter 4 below on "'Natural Law' in Judaism".

[93] Bornkamm, "Wrath", 56, writes: "Thus Paul frees the concepts and arguments that he takes from contemporary non-Christian philosophy and theology from the presuppositions of Greek thought, and the sense in which he uses them becomes entirely different. The knowledge of God as question and accessible possibility does not concern him. What concerns him, rather, is the question whether this knowledge is personal (1.28), whether the truth of God remains truth and its power is acknowledged (1.18, 25). Thus what concerns him in Rom. 1.18ff has nothing to do with the disclosure of the divine being, but with the uncovering of human existence. . . Paul's sentence, 'knowing God . . . they became futile in their thinking,' appears to be contradictory. . . . And is it not therefore more appropriate to say with Wisdom (13.1): 'For all men who were ignorant of God were foolish by nature'? However, Paul abides by the 'knowledge of God' because it is not nullified even in the conceit and vanity of men and man has not ceased to be God's creature".

[94] Bornkamm, "Wrath", 53, writes: "Thus, the goal of philosophical reflection and religious teaching is to lead man out of the fog of this ignorance back into the right knowledge of the divine world and of himself".

is the sign of the ungodly world. Bornkamm writes that Rom. 1.18ff is not an

. . . apologetic and pedagogical discussion, because *the intention of the Apostle is not to infer God's being from the world, but to uncover the being of the world from God's revelation; not to prove the revelation of God before the judgement of the world, but to unveil the judgement of God over the world revealed in the law.*[96]

I would, however, disagree with Bornkamm on one important issue. He assumes that the knowledge of God is a present knowledge for it is the "present basis for the inexcusability of man (v. 20)."[97]

2. Hellenism discusses how knowledge of God comes about. Paul does not discuss this, although some hints are given in Rom. 1.20. In the philosophical-religious environment it is a central question and the "analogy of being" is used.[98] Paul does not employ such comparisons or

---

[95] Although Bornkamm may have overstated the differences in that there is some element of accusation in Wis. 13 (see v. 8: πάλιν δ' οὐδ' αὐτοὶ συγγνωστοί), his general conclusion is correct: "The missionary-apologetic sermon of Hellenistic and Jewish character aims at awakening the knowledge of God from a look at the world, for in this knowledge man finds his destiny. Therefore, it seeks to displace 'ignorance' and to disclose to its hearers the nature and rule of the deity on the basis of man's concern and of what he basically already knows. . . . So the thoroughgoing presupposition in the Gentile and Hellenistic doctrine of God is this, that the knowledge of God, because it stands in agreement with the reasonable understanding of the world open to every man, presents an open possibility from which no one is excluded" (Bornkamm, "Wrath", 54). Cf. E. Fascher, "Deus invisibilis: Eine Studie zur biblischen Gottesvorstellung", *MThS* (1931) 71 (41-77).

[96] Bornkamm, "Wrath", 59 (his emphasis).

[97] Bornkamm, "Wrath", 54. Cf. the view of Althaus, *Die christliche Wahrheit*, p. 38 (quoted below). It is interesting to note that Bornkamm's article originally appeared in 1935 (*ZNW* 34 (1935) 239-62) in the context of the controversy between the "German Christians" and the "Confessing Church". G. Theißen, "Theologie und Exegese in den neutestamentlichen Arbeiten von Günther Bornkamm", *EvTh* 51 (1991) 316 (308-22), points out: "Gegen die sublimere schöpfungstheologische Paulusinterpretation macht er (Bornkamm) geltend, die *theologia naturalis* des Paulus diene einzig und allein eben dieser Konfrontation des Menschen mit seinem Richter. . . Die 'natürliche Theologie' sei ein Argument, um alle Menschen als Sünder zu überführen, nicht aber, um eine Schöpfungsoffenbarung oder einen Volksnomos neben der Christusoffenbarung einzuführen". This is also relevant for Bornkamm's work on Rom. 2.14-16.

[98] Wis. 13.3-5: "If through delight in the beauty of these things (i.e. fire, wind, swift air, circle of the stars, turbulent water, luminaries of heaven) men assumed them to be gods, let them know how much better than these is their Lord, for the author of

chains of reasoning as one finds in Philo[99] and any teleological or cosmological arguments are alien to him.[100] Creation for Paul does reveal God but only because God has taken a special initiative to reveal himself through it. But the world does not reveal God on the basis of the world being God's image.[101] As Bornkamm correctly argues, the addition ὁ θεὸς γὰρ αὐτοῖς ἐφανέρωσεν (Rom. 1.19b) "tautological from the standpoint of a Greek understanding of the world, is in no way superfluous for Paul"[102].

---

beauty created them. 4 And if men were amazed at their power and working, let them perceive from them how much more powerful is he who formed them. 5 For from the greatness and beauty of created things comes a corresponding perception of their creator". See also Pseudo-Aristotle, *De mundo* 399b: "This is what we must also believe about God, who is mightiest in power, outstanding in beauty, immortal in life, and supreme in excellence, because though he is invisible to every mortal thing he is seen through his deeds" (D.J. Furley, *Aristotle: On the Cosmos* (LCL), London/Cambridge Mass. 1955, pp. 397-99).

[99] In *De praemiis et poenis* 43, Philo speaks of those "truly admirable persons" who have "advanced from down to up by a sort of heavenly ladder (κάτωθεν ἄνω προῆλθον οἷα διά οὐρανίου κλίμακος) and by reason and reflection happily inferred the Creator from His works (ἀπὸ τῶν ἐργῶν εἰκότι λογισμῷ στοχασάμενοι τὸν δημιουργόν)" (Philo (LCL), 8:337).

[100] Davies, *Paul*, p. 116, puts forward a questionable parallel between Rom. 1.18ff and Philo, *De specialibus legibus* 1.34ff, which is a sort of teleological argument for the existence of God (*De specialibus legibus* 1.34-35 is quoted above in the section on Philo's teleological arguments).

[101] Bornkamm, "Wrath" 55, 67 n. 36. See H. Kleinknecht, in G. Kittel, H. Kleinknecht, G. von Rad, εἰκών *TDNT* 2:389 (381-397). They point to the close of Plato's *Timaeus* (92C), where the cosmos is described as εἰκὼν τοῦ νοητοῦ, and point out that the concept of images is important in the Hermetic literature, where the world is seen as the first image and man the second image of God (or image of the cosmos). πρῶτος γὰρ πάντων ὄντως καὶ ἀίδιος καὶ ἀγέννητος καὶ δημιουργὸς τῶν ὅλων θεός· δεύτερος δὲ ὁ κατ᾽ εἰκόνα αὐτοῦ ὑπ᾽ αὐτοῦ γενόμενος καὶ ὑπ᾽ αὐτοῦ συνεχόμενος καὶ τρεφόμενος καὶ ἀθανατιζόμενος, ὡς ὑπὸ ἀιδίου πατρὸς, ἀείζωον ὡς ἀθάνατος. . . . τὸ δὲ τρίτον ζῷον, ὁ ἄνθρωπος, κατ᾽ εἰκόνα τοῦ κόσμου γενόμενος . . . (*Corpus hermeticum* 8.2, 5, Nock and Festugière (ed.), *Corpus hermeticum*, 1:87). Kleinknecht writes: "God holds the world together, and the world man. Here, then, we have the basic thought of the harmony which is established by the συμπάθεια τῶν ὅλων of the Stoa".

[102] Bornkamm, "Wrath", 55.

3. Hellenism has an impersonal view of God. Paul's view is thoroughly personal. So in the pagan sources there is a rejection of personal conceptions of deity from Xenophanes onwards[103] and this is often manifest in the fact that such a god has many names or no names.[104] Such a view of God has certainly influenced Hellenistic Judaism[105]. It is striking that in the Hellenistic texts discussed above regarding natural knowledge of God, knowing God is less personal than Paul's conception and in fact less personal than the view we find in the Old Testament. This shift from the Old Testament view may be seen clearly in a text such as Philo, *De virtutibus* 215-16 (quoted above). This represents a serious shift from the Old Testament view of knowledge of God as personal. Paul, however, has a thoroughly personal view of God, even in Rom. 1.18-32.[106] Paul, I believe, is more faithful to the Old Testament tradition (found say in the Patriarchal narratives) than the Hellenistic Jewish texts are. Weber, however, puts forward a different perspective. Pointing to Rom. 1.19-21, he writes: "Die biblische Urgeschichte erklärt die Gotteserkenntnis der Urväter ganz anders, als aus der fortlaufenden Naturoffenbarung Gottes".[107] Weber argues that Paul's approach seems much more modern

---

[103] Owen, "Natural Revelation", 140. He points to Euripides, *Daughters of Troy* 885-87, where Hecuba says Zeus is δυστόπαστος εἰδέναι. Perhaps he is ἀνάγκη φύσεος or νοῦς βροτῶν. Zeus "becomes a wholly impersonal, wholly immanent being". See also Seneca, *Naturales quaestiones* 2.45 (quoted below).

[104] See the discussion below on theocrasy.

[105] Cf. E.D. Schmitz, "Knowledge", *NIDNTT* 2:396 (390-406), who points out that the "confrontation between Hellenistic Judaism and polytheism led to the development of a semi-dogmatic concept of the knowledge of God. The knowledge of God meant above all knowing that there was one God, and combatting the claims of heathen deities to be gods". See, for example, the Letter of Jeremiah. On the issue of the names of God, see Wis. 13.1-5, which refers to God as the existent one (ὁ ὤν, 13.1), the craftsman (τεχνίτης, 13.1) and the first cause (ὁ γενεσιάρχης, 13.3). Although there are many names for God in the Old Testament, they are not of this impersonal nature. See also Aristeas 16: "These people worship God the overseer and creator of all, whom all men worship including ourselves, O King, except that we have a different name. Their name for him is Zeus and Jove".

[106] I question Owen's point that "the divine *mysterium* of Rom. i.19-20 does not have any personal characteristics" ("Natural Revelation", 139). See the discussion below on the Christological reference in these verses.

[107] Weber, *Missionspraxis*, p. 28.

than the "Bericht der Genesis mit ihren naiven Erzählungen von persönlich-sinnlichen Verkehr Gottes mit den ersten Menschen".[108] However, Weber I believe is guilty of a misreading of Rom 1.18ff. He has perhaps assumed that knowledge of God is "automatic", knowledge about God which is based simply on observing the created order. However, as I have argued in the exegesis in chapter 2, Rom. 1.19-20 suggests something different: God reveals *himself* to humankind.

I conclude that there is no clear evidence for a direct influence of Greek philosophical works on Paul's argument (although I would not rule out the possibility that Paul may have been influenced by the philosophical outlook of Gentiles he encountered in his mission). Nor indeed do I believe that very hellenised authors like Philo had direct influence upon Paul. But a work such as Wisdom of Solomon may well have been known to Paul and it is probable that certain themes there influenced his thinking. As I argue below, the figure of wisdom probably influenced his Christology. But on the theme of natural theology we have seen that Paul's approach is somewhat different to that found in Wisdom of Solomon. The conclusion I reach regarding the lack of direct Hellenistic influence on Paul coheres with what we can construct of Paul's education. He was educated in Jerusalem at the feet of Gamaliel (Acts 22.3).[109] Any Greek philosophical influences would have come, I believe, mainly through Palestinian Judaism or the Hellenistic synagogue.

2. The Relation of Romans 1.18-32 to Apocalyptic

In the exegesis of Rom. 1.18-32 I have pointed to the Old Testament background. In particular, there are a number of similarities with Jewish apocalyptic. The idea in Rom. 1.18 of the wrath of God being revealed

---

[108] Weber, *Missionspraxis*, p. 28.

[109] For a defence of the tradition in Acts 22.3, see Bell, *Provoked to Jealousy*, pp. 290-95.

upon ungodliness and wickedness is similar to that in 1 En. 91.7-9.[110] Also Rom. 1.19-23 shares ideas with apocalyptic.[111] One can point to Test. Naph. 3.1-5;[112] 1 En. 91.4-6; 99.1-2;[113] Sib. 3.6-45. Note also that Paul is influenced by the apocalyptic idea of the world coming to an end.[114]

Especially interesting are three texts related to the question of natural revelation. First, 1 En. 36.3-4. This is in the context of Enoch's third journey. In his journey to the South, Enoch goes "to the extreme ends of the earth" (36.1) and from there goes "in the direction of the extreme ends of the heaven" (36.2) and sees there the gates of heaven. 1 En. 36.3-4 is as follows:

---

[110] 1 En. 91.7-9: "When sin, oppression, blasphemy, and injustice increase, crime, iniquity, and uncleanliness shall be committed and increase (likewise). Then a great plague shall take place from heaven upon all these; the holy Lord shall emerge with wrath and plague in order that he may execute judgement upon the earth. 8 In those days, injustice shall be cut off from its (sources of succulent) fountain and from its roots—(likewise) oppression together with deceit; they shall be destroyed from underneath heaven. 9 All that which is (common) with the heathen shall be surrendered; the towers shall be inflamed with fire, and be removed from the whole earth. They shall be thrown into the judgement of fire, and perish in wrath and in the force of the eternal judgment" (translation of E. Isaac, in Charlesworth, *Pseudepigrapha*, 1:72).

[111] Schulz, "Anklage", 165.

[112] See especially Test. Naph. 3.2-4: "Sun, moon, and stars do not alter their order (οὐκ ἀλλοιοῦσι τάξιν αὐτῶν), thus you should not alter the Law of God by the disorder of your actions (οὕτως καὶ ὑμεῖς μὴ ἀλλοιώσητε νόμον θεοῦ ἐν ἀταξίᾳ πράξεων ὑμῶν). 3 The gentiles, because they wandered astray and forsook the Lord, have changed the order (ἠλλοίωσαν ταξιν αὐτῶν), and have devoted themselves to stones and sticks, patterning themselves after wandering spirits. 4 But you, my children, shall not be like that: discern the Lord who made all things, so that you do not become like Sodom, which departed from the order of nature (ἥτις ἐνήλλαξε τάξιν φύσεως αὐτῆς)" (translation of H.C. Kee, in Charlesworth, *Pseudepigrapha*, 1:812)." This text has also been mentioned above concerning retribution. Note the common ideas in Rom. 1.22-24, 25-27: idolatry leads to sexual perversion.

[113] 1 En. 99.1-2: "Woe unto you who cause wickedness! Who glorify and honor false words, you are lost, and you have no life of good things; woe unto you who alter the words of truth and pervert the eternal law! They reckon themselves not guilty of sin, they shall be trampled on upon the earth" (Isaac, in Charlesworth, *Pseudepigrapha*, 1:79).

[114] Eltester, "Schöpfungsoffenbarung", 98.

Through one of these small gates pass the stars of heaven and travel westward on the path which is shown to them. I blessed — and I shall always bless — the Lord of Glory, who performed great and blessed miracles in order that he may manifest his great deeds to his angels, the winds, and to the peoples so that they might praise the effect of all his creation — *so that they might see the effect of his power and praise him in respect to the great work of his hands and bless him forever.*[115]

The second text is 2 Bar. 54.17-18:

But now, turn yourselves to destruction, you unrighteous ones who are living now, for you will be visited suddenly, since you have once rejected the understanding of the Most High. 18 For his works have not taught you, nor has the artful work of his creation which has existed always persuaded you.[116]

The third text is Test. Moses 1.12-13:

He created the world on behalf of his people, but he did not make this purpose of creation openly known from the beginning of the world so that the nations might be found guilty, indeed that they might abjectly declare themselves guilty by their own (mistaken) discussions (of creation's purpose).[117]

Therefore apocalyptic serves as an important background to Paul's thought in Rom. 1.18-32.[118] However, he does differ from apocalyptic in two distinct ways. First, apocalyptic assumes that there are some righteous people among the Jews. Paul argues in Rom. 1.18-3.20 that all human beings are guilty. Second, apocalyptic believes the law is a means of hope. For Paul, however, the law gives no hope. The only hope is through the gospel.

---

[115] Isaac, in Charlesworth, *Pseudepigrapha*, 1:29 (my emphasis).

[116] Translation of A.F.J. Klijn, in Charlesworth, *Pseudepigrapha*, 1:640. Following from this is a text which is especially interesting in relation to Adam and his effects on subsequent generations. 2 Bar. 54.19: "Adam is, therefore, not the cause, except only for himself, but each of us has become our own Adam". Compare Rom. 1.18-32; 5.12-21; 7.7-25, where Adam's sin has a profound effect on subsequent generations. See also the discussion below on Jewish views of the fall and Paul's view of the fall.

[117] Translation of J. Priest, in Charlesworth, *Pseudepigrapha*, 1:927.

[118] On Paul and apocalyptic, see Bell, *Provoked to Jealousy*, pp. 288-90.

3. The Relation of Romans 1.18-32 to Wisdom Literature

I have already considered some aspects of the relation of Paul's thought to the Wisdom of Solomon, concluding that this work may have exerted some influence on Paul as regards natural revelation and natural theology. But there is of course a long wisdom tradition which sought for "order" in the world.[119] Such order embraced both nature and history, two categories which for us may appear very different, but which for the wisdom school were very much related. As Hermisson points out, "'nature wisdom' and 'culture wisdom' are not as far apart as it may seem at first".[120] This all-embracing character of wisdom is an appropriate nature background for Paul's thought in that he brings together "nature" and "culture" in Rom. 1.18-32 and in 2.14-16. Focusing on nature, it was Zimmerli who first stressed wisdom as creation theology.[121] The wisdom tradition extends beyond the so-called wisdom literature, including, significantly, Ps. 104[122] and Ps. 19.[123]

---

[119] See H. Gese, *Lehre und Wirklichkeit in der alten Weisheit*, Tübingen 1958, pp. 33-44ff, 65ff; R.E. Murphy, "Wisdom in the OT", *ABD* 922 (920-31); R.E. Murphy, "Wisdom — Theses and Hypotheses", in J.G. Gammie et al. (ed.), *Israelite Wisdom: Theological and Literary Essays in Honor of Samuel Terrien*, Missoula 1978, 35-36 (35-42). However, Murphy, speaks of placing wisdom in the "straitjacket of 'order'" in his later work (see "The personification of Wisdom", in J. Day, R.P. Gordon and H.G.M. Williamson (ed.), *Wisdom in ancient Israel: Essays in honour of J.A. Emerton, Cambridge 1995, 233 (222-33)*).

[120] H.-J. Hermisson, "Observations on the Creation Theology in Wisdom", in J.G. Gammie et al. (ed.), *Israelite Wisdom: Theological and Literary Essays in Honor of Samuel Terrien*, Missoula 1978, 44 (43-57).

[121] W. Zimmerli, "Ort und Grenze der Weisheit im Rahmen der alttestamentlichen Theologie", in *Gottes Offenbarung: Gesammelte Aufsätze zum Alten Testament*, München 1963, 300-315 (= "The Place and Limit of the Wisdom in the Framework of Old Testament Theology", *SJT* 17 (1964) 146-58).

[122] Hermisson, "Creation Theology", 47-49. The wisdom tradition is found not only in v. 24 ("O LORD, how manifold are thy works! In wisdom hast thou made them all; the earth is full of thy creatures") but also in its interest in cosmology (vv. 2, 5), the natural world (vv. 6-9) and natural history (vv. 17-18, 21-22; cf. 1 Kgs 4.33). Hermisson compares Ps. 74 to Eccl. 3.11a ("He has made everything beautiful in its time") and Prov. 16.4a ("The LORD has made everything for its purpose").

[123] H. Gese, "Die Einheit von Psalm 19", in *Alttestamentliche Studien*, Tübingen 1991, 146 (139-48) writes: "Der Grundgedanke der Komposition von Ps 19, die Entsprechung der in der Schöpfung logoshaft wirkenden Schöpferherrlichkeit, des

Highly significant for Rom. 1.18-32 are texts which personify wisdom, and I will consider three such texts: Prov. 8.22-31; Sir. 24; Wis. 7.21-8.1.[124]

So first, I consider Prov. 8.22-31. There has been some controversy whether wisdom in this text participates in the creation of the world.[125] Much of the discussion centres around the meaning of the word אָמוֹן in Prov. 8.30.[126] This has been understood by many to mean "masterworkman"[127] and such an understanding could be supported by tradition in that LXX has ἁρμόζουσα,[128] the Vulgate has *componens*

Schöpfungs-Logos, und der Offenbarungs-Tora, die, hier ganz weisheitlich beschrieben, von der weisheitlichen Erkenntnis nicht grundsätzlich geschieden werden kann, läßt sich in der Entwicklung von Hi 28 über Prov 8 zu Sir 24 verfolgen".

[124] There are, of course, other texts where wisdom is personified such as Sir. 1.1-10; 4.11-19; 6.18-31; 14.20-15.8; 51.13-30; Bar. 3.9-4.4. Although Job 28 anticipates many of the ideas found in Prov. 8 and Sir. 24, wisdom is not explicitly personified in this text (cf. G. von Rad, *Wisdom in Israel* ET, London 1972, p. 148). However, some do seem to think wisdom here is personified (see, for example, N.C. Habel, *The Book of Job*, London 1985, pp. 388-401). If the "deep", "sea" (28.14), "Abaddon" and "death" (28.22) are personified, perhaps wisdom also could be personified.

[125] B. Gemser, *Sprüche Salomos*, Tübingen 1937, pp. 38-39 writes: "Aber die Meinung vieler Erklärer, daß der Weisheit hier ein tätiger Anteil an der Schöpfung zugeschrieben wird, trifft doch nicht das Richtige. Vielmehr ist Jahwe der Schöpfer. Von der Weisheit wird nur gesagt, daß sie der Schöpfung beigewohnt hat, nicht als Helferin, sondern wie ein Kind, das in der Werkstatt seines Vaters spielt". He is therefore critical of Bousset-Greßmann, *Religion des Judentums*, pp. 342-57, for seeking here the beginning of the Jewish-Hellenistic idea of intermediaries ("Hypostasen"). Gemser is supported by McKane, *Proverbs*, p. 357. See also H. Gese, "Die Weisheit, der Menschensohn und die Ursprünge der Christologie als konsequente Entfaltung der biblischen Theologie", in *Alttestamentliche Studien*, Tübingen 1991, 225-26 (218-48).

[126] See the recent short survey by M.V. Fox, "'Amon Again", *JBL* 115 (1996) 699-702 and the more detailed survey and discussion of H.-P. Rüger, "'Amôn — Pflegekind. Zur Auslegungsgeschichte von Prv 8:30a", in *Übersetzung und Deutung: Festschrift A.R. Hulst*, Nijkerk 1977, 154-63.

[127] See, for example, H. Ringgren in H. Ringgren, W. Zimmerli, O. Kaiser, *Sprüche/Prediger/Das Hohe Lied/Klagelieder/Das Buch Esther*, Göttingen 1962, p. 39, who translates v. 30a as "da war ich ihm zur Seite als Werkmeisterin"; see also *BDB*, p. 54.

[128] The verb ἁρμόζω can mean "to adapt" or "to suit" (see *LEHC*). The phrase ἤμην παρ᾽ αὐτῷ ἁρμόζουσα could then mean "I was by him suiting myself to him" or "I was by him arranging all things" (see *The Septuagint Version of the Old Testament*

("composing") and the Syriac has mtqn' hwyt ("I was establishing"). However, other proposals have been put forward, the most convincing being that אָמוֹן ("pet, darling, nursling") should be read.[129] But whatever the original reading, for Paul the reference was probably to the "masterworkman". This was not only because of the Septuagintal ἁρμόζουσα but also because he may have read it in the light of Wis. 7.21 and 8.6, where wisdom is called a τεχνῖτις ("fashioner").

The second text is Sirach 24, which is a development of the view of Prov. 8.22-31. In the remarkable poem of Sir. 24.3-22, wisdom tells of her divine origin (v. 3), that she is in the whole world (vv. 4-5) but that at the command of the Creator made her dwelling in Jacob (v. 8). She ministered before God in the tabernacle, and "was established in Zion".[130] Having taken root in Israel (v. 12), wisdom grew like a tree (vv. 13-17) and offers an invitation to eat of her fruit (vv. 19-22). The poem finishes: "Whoever obeys me will not be put to shame, and those who work with my help will not sin" (24.22). Then comes the crucial identification of wisdom with torah. "All this is the book of the covenant of the Most High

---

with an English Translation, London (n.d.), p. 795). Or another possibility is: "I was in harmonious community with him" (Hengel, *Judaism and Hellenism*, 2:104 n. 358). On the Septuagintal translation of Prov. 8.22-31 and the influence of Greek philosophy, see Hengel, *Judaism and Hellenism*, 1:162-63, who refers to G. Gerleman, "The Septuagint Proverbs as a Hellenistic Document", *OTS* 8 (1950) 15-27.

[129] See C.H. Toy, *A Critical and Exegetical Commentary on the Book of Proverbs*, Edinburgh 1899, pp. 177-78; McKane, *Proverbs*, p. 357; von Rad, *Wisdom*, p. 132. Such a view is supported by Aquila's τιθηνουμένη ("nursed"). R.N. Whybray, *Proverbs*, Grand Rapids 1994, pp. 134-35, finds the argument for the translation "nursling" weak and adopts the suggestion of O. Keel that אָמוֹן does not refer to wisdom at all but to Yahweh as creator. I mention just two further views. R.B.Y. Scott, "Wisdom in Creation: The 'Āmôn of Proverbs VIII 30", *VT* 10 (1960) 222 (213-23), argues for the form 'ōmēn meaning "binding, uniting". O. Plöger, *Sprüche Salomos*, Neukirchen-Vluyn 1984, argues that in view of the references to time at the end of second and third members of Prov. 8.30, the word אָמוֹן standing at the end of the first member could be an adverb of time meaning "beständig".

[130] H. Gese, "Ursprünge der Christologie", 228, writes that Sir. 24.9-12 makes clear "daß die Weisheit die göttliche Schekina auf dem Zion ist, nach der Darstellung der Priesterschrift die Stiftshütte des Wüstenheiligtums, die zum Zionstempel wird, d.h. der Kult, wie er als Sinaioffenbarung das Zentrum der Tora bildet".

God, the law which Moses commanded us as an inheritance for the congregation of Jacob".[131] The writer here seems to have a dual view of the law: the commandments given to Israel and the five books of Moses.[132] The identity of law and wisdom is found in earlier literature but finds its first clear expression here. It is also found later in Rabbinic literature.[133] Sir. 24 is not only important for Paul's Christology but also for his argument in Rom. 1.18-32 and 2.14-16.[134]

The last text is Wis. 7.21-8.1. Here, as we have seen, wisdom is the πάντων τεχνῖτις ("fashioner of all things"), and it is she who taught Solomon (7.22a). We read that in her

22 there is a spirit that is intelligent, holy, unique, manifold, subtle, mobile, clear, unpolluted, distinct, invulnerable, loving the good, keen, irresistible, 23 beneficient, humane, steadfast, sure, free from anxiety, all-powerful, overseeing all, and penetrating through all spirits that are intelligent and pure and most subtle. 24 For wisdom is more modile than any motion; because of her pureness she pervades and penetrates all things. 25 For she is a breath of the power of God (ἀτμὶς γάρ ἐστιν τῆς τοῦ θεοῦ δυνάμεως), and a pure emanation of the glory of the Almighty (καὶ ἀπόρροια τῆς τοῦ παντοκράτορος δόξης εἰλικρινής); therefore nothing defiled gains entrance into her. 26 For she is a reflection of eternal light (ἀπαύγασμα γάρ ἐστιν φωτὸς ἀιδίου), a spotless mirror of the working of God (καὶ ἔσοπτρον ἀκλίδωτον τῆς τοῦ θεοῦ ἐνεργείας), and an image of his goodness (καὶ εἰκὼν τῆς ἀγαθότητος αὐτοῦ). 27 Though she is but one, she can do all things, and while remaining in herself, she renews all things; in every generation she passes into holy souls and makes them friends of God, and prophets; 28 for God loves nothing so much as the man who lives with wisdom. 29 For she is more beautiful than the sun, and excels every constellation of the stars. Compared with the light she is found to be superior, 30 for it is succeeded by the night, but against wisdom evil does not prevail. 8.1 She reaches mightily from one end of the earth to the other, and she orders all things well.

These texts (Prov. 8.22-31; Sir. 24; Wis. 7.21-8.1) are well known for forming the basis of the various wisdom Christologies in the New Testament.[135] Less well known, however, is their possible influence on Paul's

---

[131] See also Sir. 15.1; 17.11; 19.20; 21.11.

[132] Murphy, "Personification of Wisdom", 227, writes: "Since Ben Sira speaks of the 'book of the covenant of the Most High', it seems likely that he has in mind the whole Torah or Pentateuch". That may be so, but the phrase "the law which Moses commanded us" (cf. Dt. 33.4), points specifically to the commandments.

[133] See Moore, *Judaism*, 1:265.

[134] See chapter 4 below.

[135] See, for example, Heb. 1.3; Col. 1.15; 2 Cor. 4.4. In fact Gese, "Ursprünge der Christologie", 233, makes the point that in the Similitudes of Enoch (which he

argument in Rom. 1.18-32 (and Rom. 2.14-16).[136] The main points of influence are: 1. wisdom was very important in relating the way God (who transcends the universe) actually works in it;[137] 2. wisdom is crucial in the realm of revelation;[138] 3. wisdom is related to issues of both cosmology and personal conduct;[139] 4. wisdom as personified and pre-existent, forms an important background to Paul's wisdom Christology.[140]

To summarise so far, I believe the most important influences on Paul in Rom. 1.18-32 are apocalyptic and wisdom traditions.[141] Secular Greek philosophy seems to have played little if any direct influence, although Paul may have been influenced by some parts of "Hellenistic Judaism".[142]

---

dates to the period just before the New Testament) there is the influence of wisdom on the Son of Man tradition.

[136] Cf. E.J. Schnabel, "Wisdom", in G.F. Hawthorne - R.P. Martin - D.G. Reid (ed.), *Dictionary of Paul and his Letters*, Leicester 1993, 968 (967-73).

[137] Cf. Murphy, "Personification", 232, who writes that personified wisdom "is simply unequalled in the entire Old Testament. . . . She is born of God, and that brings a sense of the divine presence and closeness to *all* of creation that is simply unequalled. She is not an intermediary. Such a role would make of the Lord a kind of absentee landlord. Far from this is the intimate association between Lord/Wisdom in the experience of human beings, as described by the sages. There is the curious and admirable mixture of what we today call transcendence and immanence".

[138] See, for example, Sir. 1.9-10. See also the discussion in Gese, "Ursprünge der Christologie", 227-28.

[139] This is seen not only in texts like Sir. 24 but also in Ps. 19 (see below).

[140] On Wisdom Christologies, see, for example, E.J. Schnabel, *Law and Wisdom from Ben Sira to Paul*, Tübingen 1985, pp. 236-64.

[141] Note that Apocalyptic tradition has, according to Gese, a "weisheitlicher Charakter" ("Ursprünge der Christologie", 231). But he also rightly believes von Rad has gone too far in classifying Apocalyptic literature as Wisdom literature. As an example of the intersection of wisdom and apocalyptic, see 1 En. 42.1-2, which, as Gese, "Ursprünge der Christologie", 231, points out, is a development of the picture in Sir. 24: "Wisdom could not find a place in which she could dwell; but a place was found (for her) in the heavens. 2 Then Wisdom went out to dwell with the children of the people, but she found no dwelling place. (So) Wisdom returned to her place and she settled permanently among the angels" (translation of E. Isaac, in Charlesworth, *Pseudepigrapha*, 1:33).

[142] Cf. T. Schmeller, "Stoics, Stoicism", *ABD* 6:213 (210-14).

4. The Question of Natural Revelation and Natural Theology in Paul

The issue of natural revelation and natural theology has been discussed to some extent in the above two sections. Now I focus on Paul's own view.[143]

During this study it will become clear that Rom. 1.18-3.20 is to be understood as a "history of Damnation" (*Verdammnisgeschichte*) and, as I have already argued, the first section, Rom. 1.18-32, is an accusation of humankind. In order to demonstrate that Jew and Gentile are without excuse (ἀναπολόγητος, 1.20) Paul has to argue that God's "invisible nature . . . has been clearly perceived in the things that have been made (τοῖς ποιήμασιν)". Such knowledge is not an innate knowledge in humankind[144]; neither is it reached by a process of deduction or by means of a "heavenly ladder"[145]; rather it is revealed by God (1.19b). And this knowledge is of God himself; it is not simply knowledge of his attributes.[146]

---

[143] I should perhaps add here that I use the term "natural revelation" rather than "general revelation" to stress that I am only considering revelation of God through the natural world (as in Rom. 1.19-21).

[144] See Barth, "Speaking of Sin", 291.

[145] Cf. Philo, *De praemiis et poenis* 43 (quoted in section 1 above).

[146] As we have seen, a number of commentators seem to assume on the basis of Rom. 1.19-20a that only certain attributes of God are revealed. The RSV may give this impression also: "For what can be known about God is plain to them, because God has shown it to them. 20 Ever since the creation of the world his invisible nature, namely, his eternal power and deity, has been clearly perceived in the things that have been made." I would alter the RSV in the following way: "For *God in his knowability* (τὸ γνωστὸν τοῦ θεοῦ) *is manifest* to them, because *God has revealed himself* to them. 20 For since the creation of the world *God in his invisibility* (τὰ ἀόρατα αὐτοῦ), namely, his eternal power and deity, has been clearly perceived in the things that have been made" (cf. Barth, *CD* 2.1:119). In the exegesis of Rom. 1.19, it was argued that the genitive τὸ γνωστὸν τοῦ θεοῦ is not to be understood in a partitive sense ("things which can be known of God"). Rather it means "God in his knowability" which parallels "God is his invisibility" (τὰ ἀόρατα αὐτοῦ) of v. 20. But note that even some of those who oppose the partitive understanding of τὸ γνωστὸν τοῦ θεοῦ seem to reduce the knowledge of God to his attributes. So M. Barth, "Speaking of Sin", 291, is right to say: "*To gnoston* in v. 19 is explained by vv. 21, 28, 32 not as a knowable *part* of God (Calvin: his being creator, not His virtues; St. Thomas: His existence, not His mysteries)" but wrong to continue "but as

If the knowledge revealed is that of God himself, one would assume that for Paul, it is not only "God the Father" who is revealed but also "God the Son". Although this point is accepted by very few commentators I believe it must belong to the logic of Paul's theology. If Paul believed that Christ was fully God[147] and that he was instrumental in the creation of the world (1 Cor. 8.6),[148] it seems only natural to conclude that the "pre-existent" Christ is also revealed in creation.[149] H. Schulte, following a suggestion of J. Schniewind, writes "daß auch in Röm. 1,18ff. mit 'ἀλήθεια, θειότης, δόξα, νοῦς' ein christologischer Bezug durchschimmert".[150] In fact as the wisdom of God (cf. 1 Cor. 1.30)

---

knowledge of His 'power and divinity' (v. 21) or of His decree (His righteous will, legal order, righteousness v. 32)." It is instructive to compare Barth, *CD* 2.1:53-55. See, for example, *CD* 2.1:51, where he writes that "the idea of impartation must not be taken to mean that in His revelation God gives Himself to be known by us only in part, so that we still have to await the revelation of another God in another and higher order, or the revelation of the same God in a different form".

[147] Paul believed Christ shared the very nature of God (Phil. 2.6). Any Pauline texts which point to a subordination of Christ refer to his submission to the Father (1 Cor. 11.3; 15.28), i.e. they refer to Christ's *function*, not his *ontology*.

[148] 1 Cor. 8.6: "yet for us there is one God, the Father, from whom are all things and for whom we exist, and one Lord, Jesus Christ, through whom are all things and through whom we exist".

[149] It is perhaps worth mentioning at this point that the *Extra Calvinisticum* whereby after the incarnation the λόγος by whom all things were made continues to be present and active beyond the flesh is quite foreign to Paul's thought. I believe Lutheran theologians have been faithful to Paul (and the New Testament as a whole) in rejecting such an idea. See J.T. Mueller, *Christian Dogmatics*, St. Louis 1934, p. 280, and W. Elert, *Der christliche Glaube*, Erlangen ⁶1988, (¹1940), p. 312. I hope to pursue this in more detail in a future study on atonement and Christology.

[150] H. Schulte, *Der Begriff der Offenbarung im Neuen Testament*, München 1949, p. 26. See also Lackmann, *Geheimnis der Schöpfung*, p. 192, who writes "daß jene von den Heiden erfahrene 'ἀΐδιος δύναμις' und 'θειότης' eine Begegnung mit dem Geheimnis des *VERBUM aeternum*, ja der ganzen heiligen Trinität sei. (Römer 11,36)". Although Paul had no developed idea of a "Trinity", Lackmann's words do seem to sum up what Paul believed about the revelation of God in creation. Such a suggestion can be given some weight by pointing to Paul's wisdom Christology. See, for example, Wis. 7.25b (καὶ ἀπόρροια τῆς τοῦ παντοκράτορος δόξης εἰλικρινής) and 7.26a (ἀπαύγασμα γάρ ἐστιν φωτὸς ἀιδίου).

Christ plays a crucial role in this revelation.[151] Christ is both the *object* of natural revelation and the *means* of revelation. One therefore misunderstands Paul if one believes that Christ came in first with the justification of the ungodly (e.g. Rom. 3.21-26).[152]

So God has revealed himself in creation and there is no problem in speaking of a "natural revelation" in Rom. 1.18ff provided one bears in mind that Christ is also revealed.

The question of a "natural theology", however, is more complex. It is important to stress that the traditional form of natural theology whereby one tries to argue for the existence of God (e.g. cosmological argument, teleological argument) is alien to Paul's thought. So Boylan's comment on Rom. 1.20 that Paul possibly "has in view a process of inference, like the argument from Causality (the Cosmological Argument)" is wide of the mark.[153] Also I have already argued that the natural theology of Philo is completely different to Paul's view in Rom. 1.18ff. Is it meaningful then to discuss what Paul felt about natural theology? I believe it is meaningful

---

[151] In the Old Testament and later Jewish literature, "wisdom" is especially important in God's activity in the world, for she links God's transcendence with his immanence (see Prov. 8.22-31; Wis. 7.22-8.1; Sir. 1.1-10). For wisdom's role in revelation see, for example, Sir. 1.9-10: "The Lord himself created wisdom; he saw her and apportioned her, he poured her out upon all his works. 10 She dwells with all flesh according to his gift, and he supplied her to those tho love him". Interestingly, wisdom also became associated with the Jewish law in the intertestamental writings (see Sir. 24). It is also widely recognized that Paul had a "wisdom Christology". For further discussion of the role of wisdom, see above and the discussion in chapter 4 below. H. Ott, "Röm 1,19ff als dogmatisches Problem", *TZ* 15 (1959) 47-49 (40-50) also stresses Christ's role in natural revelation. So he writes: "*In Jesus Christus wird Gott als der erkannt, der in den Werken Seiner Schöpfung immer schon offenbar gewesen ist*" (Ott's emphasis). But he has not made the link to the Old Testament wisdom tradition.

[152] One may add the important point of G.B. Caird, *The Language and Imagery of the Bible*, London, 1980, p. 51, that it is the contention of the writers of the New Testament "that with the coming of Jesus the whole situation of mankind has so altered as to change the semantic content of the word 'God'". Cf. N.T. Wright, *The New Testament and the People of God*, London 1992, p. 475; *The Climax of the Covenant: Christ and the Law in Pauline Theology*, Edinburgh 1991, pp. 266-67.

[153] Boylan, *Romans*, p. 20.

provided one defines "natural theology" in the widest possible sense. I take the term to mean knowledge of God gained from the creation *independent of God's special revelation to Israel and independent of the gospel* (but not necessarily *independent of Christ*).[154] Further, I believe Rom. 1.18ff does actually say something about natural theology.[155]

What then are we to say to natural theology in Rom. 1.18ff? First, Paul does speak of knowledge of God in Rom. 1.19-20. God has revealed himself (v. 19b) and his invisible nature has been clearly perceived in the things that have been made (v. 20). Further, he speaks of "knowing God" (v. 21a). But Paul goes on to say human beings "became futile in their thinking and their senseless minds were darkened" (v. 21b). "Claiming to be wise, they became fools" (v. 22). "And because they did not see fit to have God in their knowledge, God gave them up to a base mind and to do what is improper" (v. 28, my translation). This then is the story which concerns us. A story of men and women moving from a position of knowledge to a position of ignorance. But what exactly is happening here? Let us consider v. 21: "for although they knew God they did not honour him as God or give thanks to him, but they became futile in their thinking and their senseless minds were darkened". Paul is not saying that men and women, while having a theoretical knowledge of God, failed to acknowledge him, i.e. failed to draw practical consequences from this knowledge of God, failed to "honour him as God or give thanks to him". Such an argument could lead one to conclude that Paul, far from denying a natural theology, is saying that there is a *knowledge* of God but no *acknowledgement* of God. This, I believe, is a misrepresentation of Paul's

---

[154] Many definitions in Christian theology speak of natural theology as knowledge of God independent of Christ. Cf. Barth's definition: "Natural theology is the doctrine of a union of man with God existing outside God's revelation in Jesus Christ" (*CD* 2.1:168). If this definition is taken I would have to rule out natural theology almost from the start as far discussion of Paul is concerned.

[155] I say this because some imply the verses have little to do with natural theology. See C.K. Barrett, *A Commentary on the Epistle to the Romans*, London ²1991, (¹1957), p. 35, who, commenting on Rom. 1.19, writes: "It is not Paul's intention in this and the following verse to establish a natural theology; nor does he create one unintentionally. He is concerned with the moral principles of God's judgement . . .".

argument. His point is that the knowledge of God is only retained and guaranteed if there is subsequent acknowledgement.[156] Because men and women failed to honour God and give him thanks, they lost their knowledge of God (see Rom. 1.21-23, 28). The knowledge which was lost was both knowledge of God himself and knowledge of his attributes.[157] Paul then is referring to a fall from knowledge, to lack of acknowledgement, to total ignorance of God.

When Paul speaks of this "fall", to what is he referring? Is he referring to the "fall of Adam", the "fall of Israel" or the "fall of every generation"? I argued in chapter 2 above that Paul refers to all three.[158] First, there are several allusions to the fall of Adam (and Eve) in this passage.[159] Secondly, there are clear allusions to the fall of Israel, in particular the episode of the golden calf.[160] Thirdly, Paul in some sense believes this "fall" relates to his present generation and presumably to every previous generation. Further, although it may appear he is referring to wickedness characteristic of Gentiles (and the Jewish reader probably read it so),[161] Paul is most likely castigating both Jews and Gentiles.[162] So

---

[156] See Schlier, "Von den Heiden", 31: "Die Erkenntnis Gottes hält stand nur in der Anerkennung Gottes als des Schöpfers. Die Anerkennung Gottes als des Schöpfers vollzieht sich in seinem Lobpreis und in Dank gegen ihn" (Cf. *Römerbrief*, p. 55). In view of the importance of wisdom in discerning God in creation, see Wis. 6.16: ". . . she goes about seeking those worthy of her, and she graciously appears to them in their paths, and meets them in every thought"; compare Wis. 1.4: ". . . wisdom will not enter a deceitful soul, nor dwell in a body enslaved to sin".

[157] The fact that knowledge of God's attributes is lost is suggested by Rom. 1.22-23: "Claiming to be wise, they became fools, 23 and exchanged the glory of the immortal God for images resembling mortal man or birds or animals or reptiles".

[158] See the end of the introductory section to that chapter.

[159] The allusion to Gen. 1.26a in Rom. 1.23 was noted and the common element in Paul and Judaism that the fall involved sexual immorality.

[160] It was noted in the exegesis that Rom. 1.23 recalls Ps. 106.20: "They exchanged the glory of God for the image of an ox that eats grass" and Jer. 2.11: "Has a nation changed its gods, even though they are no gods? But my people have changed their glory for that which does not profit".

[161] See especially Rom. 2.17ff, where Paul turns on the Jew who thinks Paul's comments in 1.18-32 are relevant to Gentiles only.

[162] It would be difficult to exclude a reference to Jews in Rom. 1.18-32 if Paul alludes to both the fall of Adam and the fall of Israel.

this fall from "knowing God" to "suppressing the truth" to becoming "futile in their thinking" seems to relate in some way to every generation of Jews and Gentiles[163] and means they are without excuse (ἀναπολόγητος, v. 20).

We have here then a movement of thought from knowledge of God to ignorance. One of the main errors committed by those who find a "natural theology" in Rom. 1.18-32 is that they read off an idea from the first point in the story. Such a use of the text is, I believe, misguided.[164] That this approach is mistaken should be clear by an examination of a parallel text, 1 Cor. 1.18ff, which is almost an earlier version of his argument. In fact the whole passage 1 Cor. 1.18ff parallels Rom. 1.16ff in a number of respects.[165] Especially important is 1 Cor. 1.21: ἐπειδὴ γὰρ ἐν τῇ σοφίᾳ τοῦ θεοῦ οὐκ ἔγνω ὁ κόσμος διὰ τῆς σοφίας τὸν θεόν, εὐδόκησεν ὁ θεὸς διὰ τῆς μωρίας τοῦ κηρύγματος σῶσαι τοὺς πιστεύοντας. So "in the wisdom of God (ἐν τῇ σοφίᾳ τοῦ θεοῦ), the world did not know God through wisdom". The preposition ἐν (ἐν τῇ σοφίᾳ τοῦ θεοῦ) is best understood spatially: in the midst of wisdom.[166] In a discussion of the per-

---

[163] See pp. 97-98 below for further clarification on how the "fall" relates to every generation.

[164] One may compare making theological statements of Israel by reading off from Rom. 9.27 that "only a remnant of them will be saved" without going on to 11.26 that "all Israel will be saved" (see Bell, *Provoked to Jealousy*, pp. 139-40). See also the mistake of believing there are pious Gentiles who keep the law in Rom. 2.14-15 without going on to consider Rom. 3.9-20, which makes it quite clear there are no pious Gentiles.

[165] E. Jüngel, *Paulus und Jesus*, Tübingen ⁶1986, (¹1962), p. 31, writes: "Die Parallelität der theologischen Gedankenführung in Rm 1 und 1. Kor 1 ist offensichtlich". In addition to the parallel between 1 Cor. 1.21 and Rom. 1.18ff, note also the following: 1 Cor. 1.18 speaks of λόγος τοῦ σταυροῦ: τοῖς δὲ σῳζομένοις ἡμῖν δύναμις θεοῦ ἐστιν; Rom. 1.16 speaks of εὐαγγέλιον: δύναμις γὰρ θεοῦ ἐστιν εἰς σωτηρίαν παντὶ τῷ πιστεύοντι. Both speak of the power of God for salvation. Also the content of both λόγος τοῦ σταυροῦ and εὐαγγέλιον is the same: the δικαιοσύνη θεοῦ (Jüngel, *Paulus und Jesus*, p. 30). One of the differences is "daß Paulus in 1. Kor 1,18ff. nebeneinander in dialektischer Antithetik erörtert, was er in Rm 1,16ff. nacheinander entfaltet . . ." (*Paulus und Jesus*, p. 31).

[166] See the comment and translation of H. Schlier, "Kerygma und Sophia - Zur neutestamentlichen Grundlegung des Dogmas", *Die Zeit der Kirche*, Freiburg, 210 (206-232): "Gott hat deshalb die Weisheit und das Erkennen 'töricht' gemacht, weil 'die Welt inmitten der Weisheit Gottes Gott nicht auf dem Wege der Weisheit erkannte'". Cf. G. Bornkamm, "Glaube und Vernunft bei Paulus", in *Studien zu*

son's perception of God through the creation, wisdom would seem to be
the obvious category to use.[167] Although Paul does not explicitly mention
σοφία in the section Rom. 1.18-32[168], he does write in 1.22: φάσκοντες
εἶναι σοφοὶ ἐμωράνθησαν. Also wisdom is one of the key ideas in 1 Cor.
1.18ff and a number of scholars have rightly pointed to the parallels
between Rom. 1.18ff and 1 Cor. 1.18ff, giving some confirmation to the
view that Paul is using categories of wisdom in Rom. 1.18ff.[169] One of

---

Antike und Urchristentum: Gesammelte Aufsätze Band II, München 1970, 120-21
(119-37); U. Wilckens, *Weisheit und Torheit: Eine exegetisch-religionsgeschichtliche
Untersuchung zu 1. Kor. 1 und 2*, Tübingen 1959, p. 33. H. Conzelmann, *Der erste
Brief an die Korinther*, Göttingen ²1981, (¹1969), p. 64, writes that it is unlikely to
mean in the period of wisdom, i.e. before the fall (i.e. ἐν is temporal). This seems
reasonable since it is doubtful that Paul envisaged a period of original innocence
before the fall. See also H. Conzelmann, *Grundriß der Theologie des Neuen Testaments*, Tübingen ⁴1987 (revised by A. Lindemann), (¹1967), p. 272, where on Rom.
1.18 he writes: "Zielpunkt der Ausführungen des Paulus ist die Feststellung, daß die
Menschen diese ihre Möglichkeit, durch die sie wirklich Menschen geblieben wären,
nicht verwirklichten. Das ist ein Urteil, das Paulus nicht an der Heilsgeschichte oder
am Mythos vom Sündenfall abliest, sondern das er unmittelbar aus seinem Offen-
barungsbegriff gewinnt". Other possible understandings of ἐν in 1 Cor. 1.21 are
causal (Lightfoot, *Notes*, p. 161: "owing to the wise dispensation of God") and ἐν as
quasi-instrumental (see J. Héring, *The First Epistle of Saint Paul to the Corinthians*
ET, London 1962, p. 8: "For the world did not recognize God by the divine wisdom
(displayed in creation) . . . "; cf. W.G. Kümmel in H. Lietzmann and W.G.
Kümmel, *An die Korinther I/II*, Tübingen ⁵1969, p. 169). On the various interpretations see A.J.M. Wedderburn, "ἐν τῇ σοφίᾳ τοῦ θεοῦ — 1 Kor 1 ₂₁", *ZNW* 64 (1973)
132-34. Wedderburn himself prefers "in God's wisdom" in the sense of "the wise
God saw fit that the world of men should not come to know him through its own wisdom" ("1 Kor 1 ₂₁", 133-34; cf. G. Fee, *The First Epistle to the Corinthians*, Grand
Rapids 1987, pp. 72-73). As far as the spatial understanding is concerned, he is critical of Wilckens' particular version of it but gives no compelling reason why an
understanding such as Schlier's should not be adopted.

[167] Commenting on 1 Cor. 1.21, Schlier, "Kerygma und Sophia", 210, says this of
wisdom: "Die Weisheit ist nämlich hier zunächst die ursprüngliche Weise, in der sich
Gott dem Geschöpf eröffnet und das Geschöpf seines Schöpfers innewird". See also
n. 151 above.

[168] In fact the term σοφία only occurs at Rom. 11.33 in the letter. But note its
proximity to 11.36 (which in turn reflects the language of 1 Cor. 8.6).

[169] Schlier, for example, has pointed to the parallels between Rom. 1.18ff and 1
Cor. 1.18ff. He writes concerning 1 Cor. 1.21 ("Kerygma und Sophia", 210):
"Erkennen ist hier nichts anderes als ein verstehendes Inne-werden Gottes durch die
lichte Weisung des Seienden aus dem Sein selbst. Weisheit ist das durch die

the key points in Romans 1, as in 1 Corinthians 1, is that God cannot be known through human wisdom.

In the light of this story of "the fall" in Rom. 1.18-32, a story in which the human being moves from knowledge of God to ignorance, what are we to conclude about Paul's view of natural theology? I suggest that rather than "reading off" from the beginning (e.g. "knowing God" v. 21) it is more appropriate and more fitting for Paul's whole theology to conclude that there is no natural knowledge of God, even though God through his wisdom is revealing himself in creation.[170] But can one at least say that human beings at some point have some knowledge of God through the creation? Do not the words "knowing God" (γνόντες τὸν θεόν, Rom. 1.21) demand this (not to mention the whole of v. 20)? So if Adam was in a state of knowing God before his fall, and if Israel was in the state of knowing God before the golden calf incident, does not every human being also have some natural knowledge of God at some point even though he represses this truth and falls away from this truth? I believe the answer has to be "No". I do not believe Paul intended Rom. 1.18-32 to be historicised in such a fashion, i.e. I do not think he believed that in each generation there is actually a point of "innocence" at which human beings "know God" after which they fall into ignorance. For the "fall" of the human being is not so much in his own history but rather in the history of Adam (cf. Rom. 5.12-21; 7.7-12).[171] According to Paul,

---

Anweisung Gottes in der Schöpfung auf ihn Angewiesensein des Geschöpfes. Dem-gegenüber, meint der Apostel, ist die Situation des Menschen und mit ihm der Welt, so wie sie in der Geschichte vorkommen, diese: der Mensch läßt sich in seinem Erkennen vorgängig nicht mehr aus dem Seienden von Gott auf Gott verweisen, sondern er läßt sich nur noch von dem Seienden auf das Seiende verweisen. Er vollzieht nämlich, wie Röm. 1,21f. zeigt, in und unter seinem Erkennen nicht mehr die Anerkennung Gottes als des Schöpfers."

[170] I may be criticised for "reading off" from the end of the story. However, when such stories occur in Paul, the emphasis does seem to be on the end result. So concerning Israel's salvation Rom. 11.26 is more significant than Rom. 9.27 and concerning salvation by works Rom. 3.20 is more significant than Rom. 2.12-16. See the discussion in the following chapters.

[171] I do not have space here to engage in a detailed discussion of Rom. 5.12. I would simply support commentators like F.F. Bruce, *The Epistle of Paul to the Romans*, London 1963, pp. 129-30, and Cranfield, *Romans*, 1:277-78, who, while understanding ἐφ᾿ ᾧ as "because" nevertheless support Augustine's theological inter-

Adam may have had some form of original innocence; the rest of humankind, however, did not. Human beings in their own history find themselves already fallen.[172] Paul's view is therefore radically different to that of Philo.[173]

The conclusion that Paul denied the present actuality of a natural theology in Rom. 1.18-32 coheres with other Pauline texts. There are two texts which state that non-Christian Gentiles have no knowledge of God. First, see Gal. 4.8-9:

Formerly, when you did not know God, you were in bondage to beings that by nature are no gods; 9 but now that you have come to know God, or rather to be known by God, how can you turn back again to the weak and beggarly elemental spirits, whose slaves you want to be once more?

Secondly, see 1 Thes. 4.4-5:

. . . that each of you know how to take a wife for himself in holiness and honour 5 not in the passion of lust like heathen who do not know God.

But especially important is 1 Cor. 1.21, a text which has already been discussed:

For since, in the wisdom of God, the world did not know God through wisdom, it pleased God through the folly of what we preach to save those who believe.

This conclusion I reach concerning Paul's natural theology is also confirmed by Paul's use of Ps. 19.4 (18.5) in Rom. 10.18. This is perhaps

---

pretation. So participating in Adam's sin parallels participating in Christ's death and resurrection. See 1 Cor. 5.22, 2 Cor. 5.14, 17 as well as Rom. 5.18-19.

[172] See G. Eichholz, *Die Theologie des Paulus in Umriß*, Neukirchen-Vluyn ⁵1985, (¹1972), p. 76: "Nach Röm 5,12-21 sind wir *immer schon Adam*, dessen Signum Ungehorsam ist" (Eichholz' emphasis).

[173] Kuhlmann, *Theologia naturalis*, p. 50, writes: "Philon interpretiert die menschliche Existenz in ihrer Individuation, die Ausdehnung zwischen Geburt und Tod, als ständige Entscheidung für oder wider Gott. . . . Nach Paulus hat der Mensch seine wirkliche Geschöpflichkeit immer schon und endgültig aufgegeben und damit den wirklichen Gott unwiederbringlich aus den Augen verloren . . ." See also his comments on p. 52, again contrasting Philo and Paul: "Für Philon ist Gott aus dem Kosmos erkennbar. . . Für Paulus hat der Kosmos diese Offenbarungsqualität nicht mehr. Er 'hat' sie nur als schlechthin verlorene Wirklichkeit".

the clearest of all Old Testament passages about the heavens telling the glory of God. Paul, however, applies the verse not to the heavens but to the gospel.[174]

Not only does the view that Paul denied the actuality of a natural theology cohere with his other letters; it also coheres with the Paul we know from the Acts of the Apostles. I dispute the commonly held view that Paul's speeches in Acts 14.15-17 and 17.22-31 support a natural theology. Both texts from Acts stress the ignorance of the people.[175] I also believe my conclusion about Paul's natural theology seems reasonable in view of Paul's Jewish background. There was very little in Jewish literature about a revelation to Gentiles independent of God's revelation to Israel.[176] Paul the Christian had a much more pessimistic anthropology

---

[174] See my discussion of Rom. 10.18 in *Provoked to Jealousy*, pp. 93-95.

[175] See Acts 14.16; 17.23: "What therefore you worship in ignorance" (a preferable translation to that of the RSV "What therefore you worship as unknown"). Also, although God may not have left himself without witness (14.17; 17.24-29) there is in fact no natural knowledge of God. In Acts 14.12 the crowd believe that Barnabas was Zeus, and Paul Hermes! In Acts 17.16 we read that the city of Athens was full of idols! In Acts 14.15 Paul calls on his hearers to "turn from these vain things to a living God" and in Acts 17.30 "to repent". Far from being a preparation for faith, the two texts in Acts point to the contrary. Any natural knowledge they had of God was in fact no knowledge (cf. S.R. Spencer, "Is Natural Theology Biblical", *GTJ* 9 (1988) 63-67 (59-72)). Therefore I conclude that although the emphasis in Acts and in Rom. 1.18-32 may be different, they actually cohere (see R. Pesch, *Die Apostelgeschichte*, 2 vols, Zürich/Einsiedeln/Köln/Neukirchen-Vluyn 1986, 2:142). For a bringing together of Rom. 1.18-32 and Acts 17, see Wilckens, *Römer*, 1:115; F.F. Bruce, "Is the Paul of Acts the Real Paul", *BJRL* 58 (1975-76) 282-305 (responding to Vielhauer, "On the 'Paulinism' of Acts", 33-50); D. Wenham, "The Paulinism of Acts again: two historical clues in 1 Thessalonians", *Themelios* 13 (1988) 53-55. I give qualified support to Bruce in *Provoked to Jealousy*, pp. 292-93 (n. 20).

[176] H. Bietenhard argues that it would be strange if Paul were to teach a natural theology (for the Gentiles) for it was certainly not taught in Rabbinic Judaism nor in Hellenistic Judaism. The clearest parallel to Romans 1 is the book of Wisdom. Bietenhard, "Natürliche Gotteserkenntnis der Heiden", *ThZ* 12 (1956) 187 (275-88), argues: "nach dieser Schrift offenbart sich Gott in seinen Werken; man könnte und sollte grundsätzlich aus der Natur auf ihren Schöpfer und Herrn schließen können. Aber faktisch wird diese Möglichkeit nie und nirgends realisiert: Der Mensch außerhalb des Judentums kommt nicht dazu, seinen Sinn über die Kreatur und Kreaturvergötterung hinaus zu erheben". Bietenhard does point to the story where Abraham deduces God's existence from the created order (Apocalypse of Abraham 7.1-11) but makes the valid point that the only thing Abraham is able to deduce is that there is one God. Abraham

than all strands of Judaism and it would therefore be logical for him to have an even more negative view of the Gentiles' ability to know God through the created order. Further, Paul's idea of the impossibility of a natural theology extends to the Jews also.[177] This may seem odd in view of the various nature Psalms in the Old Testament (Pss. 8, 19, 104) and the wisdom literature. However, these texts are all written from the perspective of faith and although Ps. 19.1-4 may be described as natural theology (again from the perspective of faith)[178] Pss. 8 and 104 are concerned with a "theology of nature", not "natural theology".[179] And for Paul, if any "Old Testament Saint" really knew God (e.g. Abraham, David), he was known only through Jesus Christ.[180]

To return to Rom. 1.18-32, knowledge of God is in fact lost because people failed to acknowledge God. "Claiming to be wise, they became fools" (v. 22). If "natural theology" for those in Adam leads anywhere, it is to idolatry, making a god in the image of a human being.[181] According to Paul, idolatry is the inevitable result of natural theology.[182]

---

must ask for revelation (7.12) and God does in fact reveal himself (Apocalypse of Abraham 8ff). Compare also Josephus (*Antiquitates* 1.155-56) which says Abraham was the first to declare that God the creator is one and that the universe is at his command, inferring this "from the changes to which land and sea are subject, from the course of sun and moon, and from all the celestial phenomena" (LCL 4:77, 79). In these stories Abraham is effectively a "Gentile". Abraham then is to some extent an exception but nevertheless I think that Bietenhard's point that a natural theology for the Gentiles is not taught in Judaism is largely correct.

[177] This, of course, has to be said if Rom. 1.18-32 refers to Jews as well as Gentiles. Note that Bietenhard, "Gottes Erkenntnis", believes the reference in 1.18-32 is to Gentiles only.

[178] Also I noted above how Paul applies Ps. 19.4 in Rom. 10.18.

[179] Cf. H. Dembowski's understanding of a theology of nature: "Ziel solcher Theologie der Natur ist es nicht, Gott in oder aus der Natur zu erkennen. Ihr Ziel ist vielmehr, Natur heilsam wahrzunehmen" ("Natürliche Theologie - Theologie der Natur", *EvTh* 45 (1985) 244 (224-48)).

[180] For further details on these points, see the systematic discussion below.

[181] See the exegesis of Rom. 1.22-23 above and the excursus below on Paul's view of the fall. It was noted that Rom. 1.23 is saying two things. First, rather than worshipping God they worshipped images resembling the human form etc. Second, this process entailed exchanging their "image of God" (cf. Gen. 1.26) for the "image of mortal man", i.e. Adam, and even for the image of animals.

[182] Cf. Kuhlmann, *Theologia naturalis*, p. 140.

If I am to follow Paul in rejecting natural theology, three possible theological objections could be raised. First, if there is no knowledge of God from the created order, how can humankind be guilty for not believing in God? Secondly, if there is no natural knowledge of God how does one recognise God when he reveals himself in the gospel?[183] Thirdly, if there exists some knowledge of God's law (Rom. 1.32; 2.14-16), does this not imply knowledge of God himself? The first objection betrays a misunderstanding of Paul's theology. In order to show humankind to be guilty, he simply has to show that God has revealed himself in creation such that humankind has the possibility of knowing God, even though this possibility is not realised because all are in Adam.[184] The second point can be answered by saying that the revelation through the gospel contains within itself the new categories required for knowing God. When the gospel is heard it is not a case of recognising a God of whom one had some previous vague knowledge; it is a case of coming to know God for the very first time. Indeed one can say that any so-called natural knowledge of God, far from being a preparation for faith in Christ, is a definite obstacle.[185] As regards the third point one may say that although the natural man knows of God's *law* he does not understand it as being *God's* law. In fact in ancient Judaism it is striking that although the Gentiles have virtually no natural knowledge of God, some knowledge of good and evil is assumed among the Gentiles.[186]

---

[183] These two points arise in P. Althaus' discussion of Ur-Offenbarung ("Ur-Offenbarung", *Luthertum* 46 (1935) 12 (4-24): "Der Mensch ist mit seiner Entscheidung gegen Christus unentschuldbar, weil er kraft der Ur-Offenbarung weiß, vor wem er steht, wenn er vor Christus steht. Er weiß um Gottes Wirklichkeit in Christus nicht erst dadurch, daß der Heilige Geist ihm den Glauben schenkt. Er weiß als Mensch so viel von Gott, daß er Gott in Jesus Christus 'wiedererkennen' müßte".

[184] This in fact parallels the case of Israel being guilty for not believing the gospel even though God has hardened them (Rom. 11.1-10; cf. 9.6-29).

[185] See E. Schlink "Die Offenbarung Gottes in seinen Werken und die Ablehnung der natürlichen Theologie", *ThBl* 20 (1941) 9 (1-14): "Die natürliche Gotteserkenntnis steht in praxi immer gegen das verkündigte Evangelium, sie ist nicht Vorstufe, sondern Feind des Wortes Gottes, nicht Vorbereitung auf den Glauben, sondern Irrglauben".

[186] I would wish to qualify what Bietenhard says about the Gentiles' knowledge of God and their knowledge of moral laws. See Bietenhard, "Natürliche Gotteserkenntnis", 288: "Auch alle Erkenntnis von Recht und Gerechtigkeit, von

The central theological conclusion of this section is that although God reveals himself in creation, human beings are blind to this revelation for they find themselves "in Adam". In this sense a "natural theology" is excluded. But what of those "in Christ"? Paul gives no answer. But it would seem reasonable to assume that if our being in Adam is the reason for not knowing God through creation, then once we are "in Christ" the possibility may exist for a natural theology. This brings me to a discussion of the systematic theological implications of this exegetical-theological inquiry.

5. Natural Revelation and Natural Theology: Systematic Discussion

In this section I ask what implications Rom. 1.18-32 has for the systematic theological discussion regarding natural revelation and natural theology. I should first explain why I am including such a section in a "Wissenschaftliche Untersuchung zum Neuen Testament". First, the New

---

Ordnung und Sitte in der Welt geht auf geschichtliche Offenbarung Gottes an die Menschen zurück". I largely agree with him that in Judaism Gentiles have no natural knowledge of God but I disagree with him when he asserts that Gentiles have no natural knowledge of good and evil independent of the revelation given to Israel. First, does not a text like Test. Jud. 20 point to some kind of natural law? Second, does not the ontological view of the Torah which developed during the period of the hellenisation of Judaism when the cosmic function of Wisdom was passed on to the Torah (see Sir. 24) form some basis for a knowledge of good and evil independent of the special revelation given to Israel? That Paul did have a view that the Gentiles have some natural knowledge of good and evil is clear from Rom. 2.14-16. It may be objected that some of this natural law given to Gentiles may include laws concerning God (e.g. laws forbidding idolatry) and so a division between "natural theology" and "natural law" is invalid. I would respond in three ways. First, Gentiles do not *do all the law* and this may suggest that they do not *know all the law*. Secondly, in view of Paul's views about Gentiles, it is precisely in matters concerning attitudes to God that they are likely to be ignorant. Thirdly, although knowledge of law can be broken down into individual commandments, knowledge of God cannot be broken down in an analogous way. Knowledge of God cannot be broken down by listing his attributes (see the discussion above).

Testament has been studied by systematic theologians in relation to the question of natural theology, and in fact Rom. 1.19-21 has been one of the key texts. Secondly, it is unwise to divorce the study of Rom. 1.18-32 from the systematic discussion. In fact, I believe the ultimate aim of New Testament scholarship should be to relate it to theological questions. One can, of course, approach the New Testament from a variety of perspectives (linguistic, historical, even sociological), but if one never arrives at questions of theology itself, I believe one has missed the whole point of studying the New Testament.

Rom. 1.18-3.20 has often been taken to support a natural theology. So appeal has been made to Rom. 1.20[187] and other verses.[188] Barth, however, has been critical of such a use of this passage.[189] He writes:

Let us admit at once: if 1.19-21 had come to us by themselves, say as fragments of an unknown text by an unknown author, then one might possibly conjecture that all these words referred to the existence of a 'natural' knowledge of God by the Gentiles, prior to and independent of God's revelation in Jesus Christ.[190]

---

[187] I give just four examples of the use of Rom. 1.20: 1. Thomas Aquinas, *Summa theologiae* 1a.2.2: "*invisibilia Dei per ea quae facta sunt intellecta conspiciuntur. Sed hoc non esset nisi per ea quae facta sunt posset demonstrari Deum esse, primum enim quod oportet intelligi de aliquo est an sit*" (*Summa Theologiae: Latin Text and English Translation, Introductions, Notes, Appendices and Glossaries: Volume 2 (1a.2-11)*, London 1964, p. 8); 2. Luther, Commentary on Galatians: "*Omnes homines naturaliter habent illam generalem cognitionem, quod sit Deus, Iuxta illud Ro. 1.: 'Quatenus Deus cognosci potest, notus est illis. Invisibilia enim eius' etc.*" (*In epistolam S. Pauli ad Galatas Commentarius ex praelectione D. Martini Lutheri collectus*, in *WA* 40.1:607); 3. the third sitting of the first vatican council: "*Eadem sancta mater Ecclesia tenet et docet, Deum, rerum omnium principium et finem, naturali humanae rationis lumine e rebus creatis certo cognosci posse; 'invisibilia enim ipsius, a creatura mundi, per ea quae facta sunt, intellecta, conspiciuntur'*" (Denzinger, 3004 (1785)). 4. Locke quotes 1.20 in Essay, 4.10.7: "For I judge it as certain and clear a Truth, as can any where be delivered, That 'the invisible Things of GOD are clearly seen from the Creation of the World, being understood by the Things that are made, even his Eternal Power, and God-head'" (J. Locke, *An Essay Concerning Human Understanding*, ed. by P.H. Nidditch, Oxford 1975, p. 622).

[188] So Locke in his paraphrase of 1.18 refers to men "who live not up to the light that god had given them" (*A Paraphrase and Notes on the Epistles of St Paul*, ed. by A.W. Wainwright, 2 vols, Oxford 1987, 2:494).

[189] See Barth *A Shorter Commentary on Romans* ET, London 1959, pp. 26-31; *CD* 1.2:306-7; *CD* 2.1:119-21.

[190] Barth, *Shorter Commentary*, p. 26. See also *CD* 2.1:119 (*KD* 2.1:131) and *CD*

Interestingly Barth used similar logic when discussing the Psalms. Barth in fact was not concerned to show there was no natural theology in the bible or that there were no sections which focus on natural theology, "only that the interpretative process as a whole apparent in the Old Testament text shows no consistent interest in maintaining the independent significance of such units".[191]

In Germany this century the debate about natural theology was often in the context of National Socialism[192] and some have stressed that this situation largely accounts for Barth's negative approach to it.[193] The first article of the Barmen declaration is well known. First Jn 14.6 and Jn 10.1, 9 are quoted and then there is the comment:

Jesus Christ, as he is testified to us in the Holy Scripture, is the one Word of God, whom we are to hear, whom we are to trust and obey in life and in death. We repudiate the false teaching that the church can and must recognize yet other happenings and powers, images and truths as divine revelation alongside this one word of God, as a source of her preaching.[194]

1.2:306-7 (*KD* 1.2:334-35). For a helpful explanation as to why Barth opposed natural theology see T.F. Torrance, *The Ground and Grammar of Theology*, Charlottesville 1980, pp. 89-90: "So far as scientific method in concerned, Barth demands a rigorous mode of inquiry in which form and content, method and subject-matter are inseparably joined together, and he rejects any notion that we can establish how we know apart from our actual knowledge and its material content". See below for further comment concerning Torrance on Barth.

[191] M. Howey, "A Study in the Theological Exegesis of Karl Barth", Nottingham M.Th. thesis 1996, p. 27, responding to J. Barr's point in *Biblical Faith and Natural Theology*, Oxford 1993, pp. 88-89: "Nobody is trying to prove that there is nothing but natural theology in the Bible. There are, however, units, substantial literary units, complete speeches, complete poems, even if only a few of them, which meditate mainly or even solely on natural theology".

[192] Barr, *Natural Theology*, p. 11, writes that "it was thus the rise of German totalitarianism, whether rightly interpreted or not, that brought the issue of natural theology into an absolutely central position".

[193] Again, see Barr, *Natural Theology*, p. 11, who writes that "the conceptuality of Barthian theology was resolutely clamped upon the picture of the political conflict in Germany". Barr, incidentally, believes the association of National Socialism and Natural Theology was mistaken. He points out that "foreign Church opinion, outside Germany, was almost total in its opposition to the Church policy of the German government, but actually supported some natural theology of creation and was against the total rejection of the same by the Confessing Church" (*Natural Theology*, p. 12).

[194] "Jesus Christus, wie er uns in der heiligen Schrift bezeugt wird, ist das eine

Later Barth wrote that this declaration and the concluding article (which acknowledges this to be the indispensable theological foundation for the German Evangelical Church), "contained in itself a purifying of the Church not only from the concretely new point at issue, but from all natural theology".[195]

A theologian at the other end of the spectrum was Paul Althaus.[196] He had an important place for natural theology.[197] Althaus' idea of "Ur-Offenbarung" is very much based on Romans 1-2. He finds Barth's exegesis inconsistent and artificial and is critical of those who wish to find a revelation only in the past. Pointing to the present in Rom. 1.19-20 he argues:

Die Kundgebung Gottes ist also nicht eine einmalige, der Vergangenheit, dem Urstande angehörige, sondern eine andauernde, gegenwärtige, auch an den sündigen Menschen, an alle Geschlechter ergehende.[198]

Wort Gottes, das wir zu hören, dem wir im Leben und im Sterben zu vertrauen und zu gehorchen haben. Wir verwerfen die falsche Lehre, als könne und müsse die Kirche als Quelle ihrer Verkündigung außer und neben diesem einen Worte Gottes auch noch andere Ereignisse und Mächte, Gestalten und Wahrheiten als Gottes Offenbarung anerkennen" (taken from K. Scholder, *The Churches and the Third Reich, Vol. 2* ET, London 1988, pp. 148-49).

[195] Barth, *CD* 2.1:175. It is worth pointing out here that contrary to what Brunner believed, Barth did not radically change his mind on the issue of natural theology. See A. Szekeres, "Karl Barth und die natürliche Theologie", *EvTh* 24 (1964) 236-41 (229-42).

[196] It may seem more appropriate to take the example of E. Brunner in view of his famous disagreement with Barth over natural theology. However, in taking Althaus, some of the issues regarding natural theology are put into sharper focus. Further, Althaus is interesting in being at home in both the fields of New Testament and Systematic theology.

[197] It has often been said that Althaus had sympathy for the "German Christians". However, although Althaus wrote (with Werner Elert) the "Ansbacher Ratschlag" (questioning the Barmen declaration) and the "Erlanger Gutachten" (attempting to give a theological justification for not allowing those of Jewish descent to assume Church office), he also wrote against the "German Christians" (K. Beyschlag, *Die Erlanger Theologie*, Erlangen 1993, p. 166 n. 323). See also M. Meiser, *Paul Althaus als Neutestamentler: Eine Untersuchung der Werke, Briefe, unveröffentlichten Manuskripte und Randbemerkungen*, Stuttgart 1993 and my review in *SEÅ* 61 (1996) 53-55.

[198] Althaus, *Die christliche Wahrheit*, p. 38.

Althaus certainly felt he had Christian tradition behind him. He argued that this "Ur-Offenbarung" is found in scripture (Romans 1-2), among the reformers, and in protestant orthodoxy. The war against natural revelation he argues started with A. Ritschl and the main reason for this was his neo-Kantianism.[199]

Die Natur war seit Kant und durch die Naturwissenschaft des 19. Jahrhundert entgottet — wer hätte noch Mut gehabt zu einer Theologie der Natur auf Grund von Röm. 1,20? . . . Nicht der Eifer für die Ehre Christi, sondern die Geisteslage, nicht das theologische Thema, sondern die philosophische, weltanschauliche Haltung trieb zur Verneinung der Ur-Offenbarung.[200]

One of the key reasons for holding to an Ur-Offenbarung for Althaus is that people are thereby shown to be guilty.[201] This revelation cannot be cast back in the past. "Unsere Sünde gegen Gott ist nicht nur die Wirkung von Adams Sünde, sondern auch die Wirklichkeit der Sünde Adams, d.h. sie geschieht wie Adams Sünde angesichts von gegenwärtiger Ur-Offenbarung".[202] To the charge that Ur-Offenbarung weakens the view that man is through and through a sinner Althaus says that it is exactly the other way round: "Daß der Mensch durch und durch Sünder ist, gilt nur, weil er durch die Ur-Offenbarung von Gott weiß und ständig auf ihn bezogen ist."[203] Althaus has a fair point and, as he recognises, it forms a key part in Paul's argument in Rom. 1.18-3.20; i.e. men and women sin with a "high hand".[204] However, I am not so sure that we can read off from this the view that man actually possessed knowledge of God. As I have suggested, there is only a residue of knowledge, i.e. some knowledge of the law (2.14-16) and some knowledge of a principle of retribu-

---

[199] Althaus, "Ur-Offenbarung", 4. Actually there is a debate whether Ritschl was in fact a "neo-Kantian". See J. Richmond, *Ritschl: A Reappraisal*, London 1978, pp. 21-22. He argues the "neo-Kantianism as a coherent movement was impossibly late to have exerted much influence on Ritschl in the crucial period of 1864-74" (p. 21). "Ritschl *did not at all* (prior to the production of his theological constructions) take over any abstract conceptual or epistemological schema from any philosophial school whatever" (p. 22, Richmond's emphasis). Rather Ritschl was a "philosophical theologian" (p. 22).

[200] Althaus, "Ur-Offenbarung", 4.

[201] Althaus, "Ur-Offenbarung", 10.

[202] Althaus, "Ur-Offenbarung", 10.

[203] Althaus, "Ur-Offenbarung", 11.

[204] See Bell, "Sin Offerings", 56-58.

tion (1.32), which, as I have argued, adds up to no knowledge of God. I would therefore disagree with the way Althaus relates the Ur-Offenbarung to *justitia civilis*: "Die Ur-Offenbarung begründet das Wissen der Menschen um Gottes Gesetz".[205] As far as law is concerned they simply know God's *law*, not *God's* law.

When it comes to hearing the gospel of Christ, Althaus speaks of "wiedererkennen".

Weil jeder Mensch durch Gottes ursprüngliche Bekundung an seinen Geist und sein Gewissen um Gott weiß, kann er auch für Christus nicht blind sein. Er muß die Göttlichkeit seines Wortes erkennen, weil er Gottes Stimme schon einmal gehört hat. Er muß vernehmen, daß durch Jesus das Wort weiter gesprochen wird, das Gott zu sprechen schon angehoben hat; daß es bei Jesus um das Gleiche geht wie in dem Bewußtsein um Gott, das jedem Menschen mit seiner Existenz gegeben ist: um die Bindung an den Schöpfer, um die Beugung unter ihn, um die Verantwortlichkeit und Schuld. Er muß merken, daß das Evangelium die Züge des Wortes trägt, das er immer schon von Gott gehört hat. Die Menschen müssen in diesem Sinne Gott in Jesus *wiedererkennen*.[206]

I wonder though whether such a view coheres with Paul's theology? At best it could apply to Jews. Jews are in a covenant relationship with God (Rom. 9.4-5) and are God's people. And when a Jew converts (2 Cor. 3.16), or when Israel comes to faith in Christ at the parousia (Rom. 11.26), it may be possible to speak of "wiederkennen". But such a view seems highly implausible for Gentiles. Paul says explicitly that Gentiles who are not Christian do not know God (Gal. 4.8; 1 Thes. 4.5). Here

---

[205] Althaus, "Ur-Offenbarung", 13.

[206] Althaus, *Die christliche Wahrheit*, p. 43 (Althaus' emphasis). Cf. "Ur-Offenbarung", 12, quoted above. Althaus, "Ur-Offenbarung", 12, adds that Lutheranism is different to Calvinism on this point: "Das Luthertum hat immer stark die Verantwortung angesichts der Gegenwart Gottes und die wirkliche Schuld des Unglaubens betont" (12). On Luther's own view see P. Althaus, *Die Theologie Martin Luthers*, Gütersloh ⁶1983 (¹1962), pp. 27-30. See especially his comments on Rom. 1.19: *Quia, omnes, qui idola constituerunt et coluerunt et deos vel Deum appellauerunt, item immortalem esse Deum i.e. sempiternum, item potentem et adiuuare valentem, certe ostenderunt se notionem diuinitatis in corde habuisse. Nam Quo pacto possent Simulachrum vel aliam creaturam Deum appellare vel ei similem credere, Si nihil, quid esset Deus et quid ad eum pertineret facere, nossent?* (WA 56.176.29-34). See also P.S. Watson, *Let God be God: An Interpretation of the Theology of Martin Luther*, London 1947, pp. 76-81.

Althaus makes a distinction between two sorts of knowing. "Sie kannten und kennen Gott, sofern er sich ihnen fortdauernd kundtut (Röm. 1,21). Aber weil sie mit dieser Erkenntnis keinen Ernst machen, Gott nicht in Dank und Anbetung anerkennen, erkennen sie ihn tatsächlich nicht."[207] I am not sure this is a helpful distinction.[208]

Such are the views of Barth and Althaus. My approach to Rom. 1.18-32 can be seen as a fight on two fronts, namely against Althaus and against Barth. Against Barth I have argued that there is a revelation of God in nature and this revelation involves Christ. Against Althaus I have argued that this revelation of God includes revelation of Jesus Christ but that there is actually no natural theology for those in Adam.

In order to highlight possible problems with an approach such as that of Althaus, I now consider two consequences of a natural theology: natural religion and theocrasy (the combining of different gods into one deity). So first I take the question of natural religion. Any natural religion will inevitably involve idolatry. This is clearly portrayed in Rom. 1.18-32. Natural religion is a human attempt to reach God and comes into effect as men and women suppress the truth.[209] Barth speaks of "the criminal arrogance of religion".[210] He writes:

---

[207] Althaus, *Die christliche Wahrheit*, p. 136. Cf. Althaus, *Der Brief an die Römer*, Göttingen [10]1966, p. 21.

[208] The same sort of distinction has been made as regards the problem of knowing/understanding the gospel in Rom. 10.19 and not knowing the righteousness of God in Rom. 10.3. So Althaus, *Römer*, p. 107, writes on 10.3: "Israel weiß davon (s. v. 19), aber hat diese Gerechtigkeit — wie einst Paulus selber (Phil. 3,4ff.) — verkannt, nicht gewürdigt". This problem however only arises if the question in Rom. 10.19 is taken to mean "did Israel not know/understand the gospel" (i.e. reading εὐαγγέλιον as the object to the question ἀλλὰ λέγω, μὴ Ἰσραὴλ οὐκ ἔγνω;). The problem of reconciling 10.19 with 10.3 disappears if the question is taken to be "did Israel not know that God's purposes for salvation were universal, as Ps. 19.4 suggests?" See Bell, *Provoked to Jealousy*, pp. 101-2.

[209] Schlatter, *Gottes Gerechtigkeit*, 64: "Hielt Paulus die Religion für die Tat der Menschheit, die sie schuldig macht? Ja; denn ihre Religion ist ihr Kampf gegen die Wahrheit, ihr Streit gegen Gott. Hielt er die Religion für ihre Strafe, für ein bitteres Verhängnis, das sie leiden muß? Ja. Denn sie knechtet zwangsweise die Völker und versenkt sie in den Wahn. Göttliches Wirken und menschliches Wollen sind in dem, was geschieht, untrennbar vereint." Cf. H. Schlier, "Über die Erkenntnis Gottes bei den Heiden (Nach dem Neuen Testament)", *EvTh* 2 (1935) 22 (9-26).

[210] Barth, *Romans*, p. 37.

Revelation does not link up with a human religion which is already present and practised. It contradicts it, just as religion previously contradicted revelation. It displaces it, just as religion previously displaced revelation; just as faith cannot link up with a mistaken faith, but must contradict and displace it as unbelief, as an act of contradiction.[211]

As far as Rom 1.18-3.20 is concerned, one can say with M. Barth: "Man's religion is thus condemned and punished because it is 'suppression of (God's v. 25) truth by unrighteousness' (1.18)."[212] But what of the God who reveals himself in Rom. 1.20? I take Althaus' point that such a God is not an idol.[213] But he is precisely not an idol because he is the trinitarian God. I would suggest though that the "god" which Althaus speaks of in his teaching on "Ur-Offenbarung" ("die Macht", "die Schicksalsmacht" and "ein Herr" etc)[214] is more like an idol even though Althaus later relates this god to the one true God.

The second consequence of natural theology can be theocrasy. I begin by considering the question of the names of God. A natural theology would suggest, on the one hand, a god without a name. For if this god is perceived through the created order, one comes to know only his existence, not his name. But, on the other hand, this god may be equated to other gods which are given one name by one group and another by another group. Because this god of the different groups is equated, he ends up having many names. Hengel writes that "theocrasy", the combining of different gods in one deity, "regards the names that have been given to them in history as 'noise and smoke'" and Hengel traces this back to Zeno: "There exists one God and spirit and fate and Zeus, who is also named with many other names".[215] Hengel comments: "The universal religious attitude of learned men which developed in the Hel-

---

[211] Barth, *CD* 1.2:303.

[212] M. Barth, "Sin", 291.

[213] Althaus, *Die christliche Wahrheit*, 1:59.

[214] See below for further discussion.

[215] See Diogenes Laertius 7.135 (*SVF* 1:102): ἕν τε εἶναι θεὸν καὶ νοῦν καὶ εἱμαρμένην καὶ Δία πολλαῖς τε ἑτέραις ὀνομασίαις προσονομάζεσθαι.

lenistic period through '*theocrasy*' regarded *the different religions as in the end only manifestations of the one deity*".[216] Such "theocrasy" is found in Terentius Varro, who claimed Iao (the Jewish divine name) and Jupiter formed one deity.[217] Seneca also believed that any name is suitable for Jupiter.[218] In fact it seems the idea of theocrasy, which originated with the Stoics, became a widely known view in antiquity.[219] See also *Corpus hermeticum* 5.10[220] and Celsus in *Contra Celsum* 1.24 and 5.41.[221] Such a

---

[216] M. Hengel, *Judaism and Hellenism* ET, London 1974, 1:261 (Hengel's emphasis).

[217] See Hengel, *Judaism and Hellenism*, 1:262. Hengel (1:260) believes Varro knew of the name Iao from Posidonius.

[218] He calls Jupiter "the controller and guardian of the universe, the mind and spirit of the world, lord and artificer of this creation. Any name for him is suitable. You wish to call him Fate (*fatum*)? You will not be wrong. It is he on whom all things depend, the cause of causes. You wish to call him Providence (*providentiam*)? You will still be right. It is by his planning that provision is made for this universe so that it may proceed without stumbling and fulfil its appropriate function. You wish to call him Nature (*naturam*)? You will not be mistaken. It is he from whom all things are naturally born, and we have life from his breath. You wish to call him the Universe (*mundum*)? You will not be wrong. He himself is all that you see, infused throughout all his parts, sustaining both himself and his own" (*Naturales quaestiones* 2.45, Seneca (LCL), 7:172-73).

[219] Hengel, *Judaism and Hellenism*, 1:262; M.P. Nilsson, "The High God and the Mediator", *HTR* 56 (1963) 108-9 (101-20). Nilsson and Hengel point to the scholiast Servius. In *Ad Georgica* 1.5, Servius writes: *Stoici dicunt non esse nisi unum deum et unam eandemque esse potestatem, quae pro ratione officiorum variis nominibus appellatur: unde eundem Solem, eundem Liberum, eundem Apollinem vocant; item (eandem) Lunam, eandem Dianam, eandem Cererem, eandem Junonem, eandem Proserpinam dicunt.* Then in *Ad Aeneidem*, 4.638, we read: *et sciendum Stoicos dicere unum esse deum, cui nomina variantur pro actibus et officiis.* Both texts are quoted in Nilsson, "High God", 108-9.

[220] "For all are He and He is all. And for this cause He has all names, because they are of one Father. And for this cause he has himself no name, because He is Father of all" (adapted from the translation in Bornkamm, "Wrath", 50-51). The Greek is: πάντα γὰρ ἃ ἔστι καὶ οὗτός ἐστι, καὶ διὰ τοῦτο ὀνόματα ἔχει ἅπαντα, ὅτι ἑνός ἐστι πατρός, καὶ διὰ τοῦτο αὐτὸς ὄνομα οὐκ ἔχει, ὅτι πάντων ἐστὶ πατήρ (Nock and Festugière, *Corpus hermeticum*, 1:64).

[221] Celsus says "it makes no difference whether one calls the supreme God by the name used among the Greeks, or by that, for example, used among Indians, or by that among the Egyptians" (*Contra Celsum* 1.24, in H. Chadwick (ed.), *Origen: Contra Celsum*, Cambridge 1965 (repr.), (¹1953), p. 23). See also 5.41: "I think, therefore, that it makes no difference whether we call Zeus the Most High, or Zen, or Adonai,

view also influenced Judaism as has been seen in Aristeas 15-16.[222] Aristobulus also equated the God of Judaism with the God of the philosophers[223] and Josephus developed the view that Greek philosophical ideas of God actually came from Moses,[224] a view which goes back to Aristobulus.[225] One can compare the modern view that Christians and Muslims worship the same god.[226] I believe such a view cannot be sustained on the basis of Paul's theology. According to Paul, all religions except Christianity and Judaism refer to a deity which is something other than the one true God. Christians and Jews may have wrong ideas about

---

or Sabaoth, or Amoun like the Egyptians, or Papaeus like the Scythians" (p. 297). In 1.24 Origen says that "a profound and obscure question is raised by this subject" and puts forward three theories: that of Aristotle (names being given by arbitrary determination), that of the Stoics (names being imitations of the things described) and that of Epicurus (names being given by nature, but still being essentially arbitrary).

[222] Aristeas 16 was quoted above.

[223] See Eusebius, *Praeparatio evangelica* 13.12.7-8 (see K. Mras, *Eusebius Werke, Bd. 8: Die Praeparatio Evangelica* (GCS), 2 vols, Berlin 1954-56, 2:195).

[224] See *Contra Apionem* 2.168: "That the wisest of the Greeks learnt to adopt these conceptions of God from principles with which Moses supplied them, I am not now concerned to urge; but they have borne abundant witness to the excellence of these doctrines, and to their consonance with the nature and majesty of God. In fact, Pythagoras, Anaxagoras, Plato, the Stoics who succeeded him, and indeed nearly all the philosophers appear to have held similar views concerning the nature of God" (Josephus (LCL), 1:359-61).

[225] See Eusebius, *Praeparatio evangelica* 13.12.1-2 (K. Mras, *Die Praeparatio Evangelica*, 2:190-91).

[226] Such a view can be found not only in works like that of H. Küng, *Christianity and the World Religions* ET, London 1987, p. 129, but also in the mainstream of theological thinking. See, for example, *Lumen gentium* (from the fifth sitting of the Second Vatican Council, November 1964) (Denzinger 4140). This refers to Muslims *qui fidem Abrahae se tenere profitentes, nobiscum Deum adorant unicum, misericordem*. On Roman Catholic attitudes to other religions see D. Wright, "The Watershed of Vatican II: Catholic Attitudes Towards Other Religions", in A.D. Clarke and B.W. Winter (ed.), *One God, One Lord in a World of Religious Pluralism*, Cambridge 1991, 153-71. See also J. Neusner, *Jews and Christians*, London 1991, p. 121, who writes that Jews and Christians "really do worship one God, who is the same God, and who is the only God, we and the Muslims with us". I would agree with Neusner that Jews and Christians worship the same God, for both Jews and Christians are his covenant people. However, Jews have the wrong conception of this God they worship, for they deny the divinity of Christ.

the one true God, but they and only they are referring to this one reality.[227] Outside these covenant peoples, all speech about "God" refers to something other than the true God.

Returning to ancient Judaism, it must be stressed that although there was some theocrasy, most Jews, even in the diaspora, refused a transference of non-Jewish divine names. Because the name Yahweh-Iao was suppressed and because the names κύριος and θεός have no specific religious significance, the view then emerged in the Greek world that the God of the Jews was nameless.[228] As Hengel says, Jews then "made a virtue out of necessity and argued that the true God had to be nameless".[229]

If most Jews resisted a theocrasy, it is not surprising that the idea cannot be found anywhere in the New Testament. Although Althaus obviously does not engage in blatant theocrasy, there is a rather sinister idea in his teaching on "Ur-Offenbarung" that one can be aware that there is a "god" but not know who he is. So he speaks of being conscious that we are "in den Händen der Schicksalsmacht, die unser von außen und von innen ganz mächtig ist, unentrinnbar, allgegenwärtig".[230] He goes on to speak of "die Macht", "die Schicksalsmacht" and "ein Herr". "Wir sind in den Händen eines Herrn über uns".[231] This idea, as Berkouwer writes,

---

[227] In this discussion, it is essential to make a clear distinction between reference and description. Although Christian and Jewish *descriptions* of God may differ, the *reference* is the same. For example, in Rom. 10.2 Paul does not dispute that Jews worship the same God as Christians do. Pagans on the other hand have a completely different reference when they speak of "god". In fact Paul argues in 1 Cor. 10.19-20 that pagans sacrifice not to a "god" but to a demons (see, for example, the comments of F. Lang, *Die Briefe an die Korinther*, Göttingen 1986, p. 128, and W. Schrage, *Der erste Brief an die Korinther: 2. Teilband 1Kor 6,12-11,16*, Solothurn/ Düsseldorf/Neukirchen-Vluyn 1995, p. 444). Paul seems to be saying that as far as pagan gods are concerned, the *reference* as well as the *description* are quite different. A somewhat different approach is taken by N.T. Wright. He writes: "The New Testament writers claim that, though there is only one god, all human beings of themselves cherish wrong ideas *about* this one god" (*The New Testament and the People of God*, p. 475, Wright's emphasis). See, however, his important qualification: "In worshipping the god thus wrongly conceived, they worship an idol".

[228] See Hengel, *Judaism and Hellenism*, 1:266-67.

[229] Hengel, *Judaism and Hellenism*, 1:267.

[230] Althaus, *Die christliche Wahrheit*, 1:65.

[231] Althaus, *Die christliche Wahrheit*, 1:66.

"displays the heart of Althaus' natural theology".[232] To some extent, Althaus can therefore agree with Schleiermacher's idea of the "schlechthinnige Abhängigkeitsgefühl".[233]

Although Althaus' idea of "Ur-Offenbarung" does not correspond to the tradition of rational natural theology[234] I would maintain that his Ur-Offenbarung is not in keeping with Pauline theology and corresponds to little of what is in the bible. The rational natural theology is even more alien to biblical thought, having its origins in pagan Greek/Roman thought. What is particularly striking is the way in which classical natural theology has argued "from below to above" almost as pagan Greek philosophy did.

However, Barr adopts a very different position, arguing that natural theology itself is to be found in both the Old and New Testaments. Although there may be some natural theology in Ps. 19.1-4 (but from the perspective of faith), Psalms 8 and 104 are, as I argued above, theologies of nature, not natural theologies. The same can be said for the wisdom literature. This literature was written by those who already had faith in the God of Israel. Barr, however, makes the point that much of the Old Testament uses material which was "common ground to large populations, even though these populations had very different religious systems".[235] Barr concedes: "The Bible, perhaps, *made* this material *into* revelation, it became revelatory in its biblical form and in relation to other biblical elements". But he adds that the "building blocks still came

---

[232] G.C. Berkouwer, *General Revelation* ET, Grand Rapids 1955, p. 49.

[233] Althaus, *Die christliche Wahrheit*, 1:66, writes: "Schleiermacher hat also durchaus recht, wenn er auf das Bewußtsein der schlechthinnigen Abhängigkeit hinweist, es mit dem Bewußtsein Gottes gleichsetzt und hierin die Gegenwart Gottes in der menschlichen Existenz findet (Der christliche Glaube, § 4). Sein Fehler ist nur: er findet die Selbstbezeugung Gottes allein in dem Abhängigkeitsgefühl. Er schweigt z.B. von der Erfahrung eines unbedingten Anspruchs". Note also the striking comment: "Die Theologie muß also als Anthropologie einsetzen" (*Die christliche Wahrheit*, 1:64).

[234] In fact he criticised Barth for confusing the two. See Althaus, *Die christliche Wahrheit*, 1:58: "Barth vereinerleit und verwechselt ständig die Frage der Ur-offenbarung und die Behauptung einer rationalen natürlichen Theologie".

[235] Barr, *Natural Theology*, pp. 97-98.

out of something that was close to the operation of natural theology".[236]
However, I maintain in response that whether elements from other traditions are taken up, changed or unchanged, depends on God himself. I
therefore question whether there is natural theology in the Old Testament.
Likewise I find no natural theology in the New Testament. The only texts
which could point to this are Rom. 1 and Acts 17, but in neither of these
texts, as I have argued, is there natural theology.[237]

Some of my conclusions regarding natural theology and natural revelation may sound "Barthian". Although I am indebted to some of Barth's
views on revelation, my position differs from Barth in three crucial
respects. First, Barth failed to find the dynamic of thought in Rom. 1.18-
32 and his exegesis is sometimes strained.[238] Secondly he did not, as far
as I know, explicitly set forth Christ's role in natural revelation.[239]

---

[236] Barr, *Natural Theology*, p. 98.

[237] Having mentioned Barr I should say that I am concerned not only about some of
his points of exegesis but also about his criticism of Barth. His misunderstandings
have been pointed out by Anthony Thiselton in his review article "Barr on Barth and
Natural Theology: A Plea for Hermeneutics in Historical Theology", *SJT* 47 (1994)
519-28, and by my student Matthew Howey, who has focused on Barr's misunderstandings of Barth's view of scripture. He shows that whereas Barr sees Barth as
using "Word of God" and "revelation" as interchangeable (Barr, *Natural Theology*,
p. 195, says "in Barth's theology the Bible was subsumed as one of the three forms of
revelation, three forms of the Word of God which comes to humanity"), Barth himself saw the bible as the "witness of divine revelation" (e.g. *CD* 1.2:479). "The Bible
is the concrete means by which the Church collects God's past revelation, is called to
expectation of His future revelation, and is thus summoned and guided to proclamation and empowered for it. The Bible, then, is not in itself and as such God's past
revelation, just as Church proclamation is not in itself and as such the expected future
revelation. The Bible, speaking to us and heard by us as God's Word, bears witness
to past revelation" (*CD* 1.1:111). Jesus Christ alone, the "Word of God revealed"
and God's saving act in him, is revelation (*CD* 1.1:119).

[238] Although I agree with Barth on Rom. 1.19-20, the critique of Lackmann,
Geheimnis der Schöpfung, p. 182, is to some extent justified: "Diese Auslegung
Barths ist eine für sein Denken theologisch folgerichtige Konstruktion, aber sie ist
keine Wiedergabe dessen, was bei Paulus steht".

[239] This omission is curious in view of his Christocentric theology. Note that Barth
does speak of some sort of natural revelation. "The world which has always been
around them, has always been God's work and as such God's witness to himself.
Objectively the Gentiles have always had the opportunity of knowing God, his
invisible being, his eternal power and godhead" (Barth, *Shorter Commentary*, p. 28).
C. Brown, *Karl Barth and the Christian Message*, London 1967, p. 98 n. 4, does

Thirdly, he did not, as I do, make a clear distinction between natural revelation and natural theology. These three points are in fact intimately related as I now show.

On the third point, it is well known that Barth did not make a distinction between natural revelation and natural theology and because there could be no natural theology there could also be no natural revelation. Barth made the important point that revelation brings with it the capacity to understand. I believe this is the case when someone comes to know God, and this is one reason why I am unhappy with Althaus' view of "wiedererkennen". But could there not be revelation which falls on deaf ears and blind eyes? According to Paul, when the gospel is preached, God gives the capacity to some people to understand the gospel. But when it comes to natural revelation as in Rom. 1.18ff, it seems that those in Adam are given no capacity for the reception of this revelation. It is rather like speaking to someone who is deaf, or showing a picture to someone who is blind. In such a circumstance, it may be asked whether it makes any sense to speak of "revelation". Usually it does not make sense to do so. But there are two ways of getting round this problem. First, one could write a story whereby someone saw a picture which was drawn for him, but subsequently went blind. Or one could speak of showing a picture to a number of people, some of whom could see and some of whom were blind. The first way is the sort of thing happening in Rom. 1.18-32. There is revelation which results in human beings knowing God; but human beings "became futile in their thinking and their senseless minds were darkened" (Rom. 1.21). The second scenario is found in the preaching of the gospel whereby some believe and other do not. In both cases one can speak of revelation, even though for some (or even all) there is no reception of revelation.[240]

---

point out though that "Barth insists that this revelation of God in nature should be viewed in the context of the covenant of grace in Christ" (see *CD* 2.1:112ff; 3.1:97, 232). Ott, "Röm 1,19ff als dogmatisches Problem", 47, seems to find this view implicit in Barth. On Ott's own view of Christ's role in natural revelation, see above.

[240] One way of dealing with revelation which is not received is to speak of incomplete revelation. Cf. W. Temple, *Nature, Man and God*, London 1964, p. 318: "But we have to add that though the revelation is chiefly given in objective fact, yet it becomes effectively revelatory only when that fact is apprehended by a mind qualified to appreciate it". I find this more nuanced than the words of J. Baillie, *The Idea of*

So the distinction between natural revelation and natural theology is achieved in Rom. 1.18-32 by the writing of a story, and, significantly, this is precisely what Barth failed to pick up. I hope it is now clear how the dynamic of the text and the ability to distinguish between natural revelation and natural theology are related.

Also related is the way in which Christ is revealed in the natural order. Christ, as the wisdom of God, plays a crucial role in this revelation. Because I stress Christ's role here, one of the central objections of Barth (and of Barthians) to natural revelation and natural theology is irrelevant. So Barth writes: "By way of natural theology, apart from the Bible and the Church, there can be attained only abstract impartations concerning God's existence as the Supreme Being and Ruler of all things, and man's responsibility towards Him".[241] A good summary of Barth's objection to natural theology is put forward by Torrance:

So far as theological content is concerned, Barth's argument runs like this. If the God whom we have actually come to know through Jesus Christ really *is* Father, Son, and Holy Spirit in his own eternal and undivided Being, then what are we to make of an independent natural theology that terminates, not upon the Being of the Triune God— but upon some Being of God in general? . . . If really to know God through his saving activity in our world is to know him as Triune, then the doctrine of the Trinity belongs to the very groundwork of knowledge of God from the very start, which calls in question any doctrine of God as the One God gained apart from his trinitarian activity—but that is the kind of knowledge of God that is yielded in natural theology of the traditional kind.[242]

As regards traditional natural theology I agree. But there is another possible natural theology: knowing the *triune God* from the created order and to such a natural theology Barth's critique as put forward by Torrance is irrelevant. If there were no fall it would be possible to know God, Father, Son and Holy Spirit, through the created order.[243] Such a natural theology

---

Revelation in Recent Thought, New York 1956, p. 64, who writes: "We must therefore say that the receiving is as necessary to a completed act of revelation as the giving".

[241] Barth, *CD* 4.3.1:117.

[242] Torrance, *The Ground and Grammar of Theology*, p. 89.

[243] This is not speculating beyond the limits of revelation, for in the beginning of Paul's argument (Rom. 1.19-21a) no "fall" is assumed. He works on the premise that men and women could have known God from the created order through natural revelation. Only in Rom. 1.21bff does the fall of human kind enter the argument.

could also be exempt from Hunsinger's critique. He believes that the central motifs in Barth's theology are "actualism", "particularism" and "objectivism".[244] Hunsinger writes:

Natural theology, it might be said, is presented as a theology that violates the essential precepts of objectivism, actualism, and particularism. Not mediated, not miraculous, and not unique in kind is the way our access to God appears, from the standpoint of natural theology.[245]

In natural theology access to God is therefore immediate, natural and general rather than mediated, miraculous and unique. But a natural theology, as may have been possible if were no fall, could be immune from these criticisms.[246]

If a natural theology would have been possible had there been no fall, what about those "in Christ"? I believe it is possible to have a "natural theology" for Christians. I am not thinking of the sort of "Christian natural theology" which Barth opposed,[247] but rather that Christians see some-

---

[244] "Actualism" means that "our relationship to God is . . . an event. It is not possessed once and for all, but is continually established anew by the ongoing activity of grace" (G. Hunsinger, *How to Read Karl Barth: The Shape of his Theology*, Oxford 1991, p. 31). As far as particularism is concerned, "Barth's theology makes a concerted attempt always to move from the particular to the general rather than from the general to the particular" (Hunsinger, *Barth*, p. 32). "Objectivism" means that "knowledge of God as confessed by faith is objective in the sense that its basis lies not in human subjectivity but in God" (Hunsinger, *Barth*, p. 35). It therefore means that "truth is always conceived as 'mediated'. Truth is not immediately apprehensible in matters of revelation and salvation; it is not accessible to us on the basis of general considerations or by our own innate powers of cognition and perception" (Hunsinger, *Barth*, p. 76).

[245] Hunsinger, *Barth*, p. 96.

[246] Cf. the important words of C. Link, *Die Welt als Gleichnis: Studien zum Problem der natürlichen Theologie*, München 1976, p. 302 (although relating to a somewhat different context): "Die Welt is kein Gleichnis des Himmelreichs, sie kann es nur werden". Such an approach to natural theology could avoid the problems Hunsinger outlines.

[247] See *CD* 2.1:135. The sort of thing Barth was against is neatly summed up by Thiselton: "I have only to open my Bible or attend a church service, and divine communication is guaranteed" ("Barr on Barth", 526).

thing of God in the created order. Luther speaks of creation as God's mask: " . . every creature is His Mask".[248] He writes: "All created ordinances are masks or allegories wherewith God depicts His theology; they are meant, as it were, to contain Christ".[249] Perhaps Christians can perceive God, Father, Son and Holy Spirit in creation, so being able to develop a "natural theology" from the perspective of faith in Christ.[250]

The view one takes on natural theology is very much related to the question of the "fall". It is to this theme that I now turn.

6.   Jewish Views of the Fall

The "fall" is clearly an important issue in Rom. 1.18-32 and in fact in the whole section 1.18-3.20. I consider first Jewish views and then Paul's own view.

There has been some disagreement whether the fall of Adam resulted in the loss of the image of God. A number argue for it not being lost through Adam's fall.[251] So it is often pointed out that several things were lost but the image of God was not one of them.[252] Gen. R. 12.6 mentions six things which Adam lost: "his lustre, his immortality (lit. 'life'), his

---

[248] Watson, *Let God be God*, p. 79. See *WA* 40.1.174.3: "*Ideo universa creatura eius est larva*".

[249] Watson, *Let God be God*, p. 79. See *WA* 40.1.463.9-464.2: "*Omnes ordinationes creatae sunt dei larvae, allegoriae, quibus rethorice pinget suam theologiam*: sol als *Christum* in sich fassen". Watson rightly comments that they contain Christ for there is no other God: "Er heisst Jesus Christ, Der Herr Zebaoth, Und ist kein andrer Gott" (Ein' feste Burg). Cf. my comments above on Christ being revealed in creation.

[250] Very briefly I believe it is possible to perceive something new of God through a "Christian natural theology", although the things discovered may be new in degree and not in kind. Ps. 104 may tell us about God's ordering of creation. But perhaps a Christian Particle Physicist or Micro-biologist may see something even more profound in investigating the subtlety of God's ordering of creation. Again, this is material for a further study.

[251] G. Kittel, in G. Kittel, G. von Rad and H. Kleinknecht, εἰκών *TDNT* 2:393 (381-97) (*ThWNT* 2:391); F.R. Tennant, *The Sources of the Doctrines of the Fall and Original Sin*, Cambridge 1903, p. 149; Moore, *Judaism*, 1:479.

[252] Kittel, εἰκών, *TDNT* 2:393; Moore, *Judaism*, 1:479 n. 2.

height, the fruit of the earth, the fruit of trees, and the luminaries".[253] But Jervell believes the image of God was in fact lost through Adam's fall. He argues that among the six things lost there are things which are related to the image of God.[254] So Adam lost his "lustre" (זִיו), his immortality (חַיִּי), and his stature (קוֹמָה), all of which were, according to Jervell, related to his image of God. Also Jervell points to texts which show that after the expulsion from the Garden of Eden, Adam produced evil spirits, demons and ghosts. See, for example, the tradition of R. Jeremiah b. Eleazar (b. Erub. 18b):

In all those years during which Adam was under the ban he begot ghosts and male demons and female demons, for it is said in Scripture, 'And Adam lived a hundred and thirty years and begot a son in his own likeness, after his own image', from which it follows that until that time he did not beget after his image.

Such a text, Jervell argues, suggests that ". . . Adam seine Gottgleichheit verlor, sie aber mit der Buße wiederbekam".[255] See also Gen. R. 24.6, where it is added that four things changed in the days of Enosh: "The mountains became [barren] rocks, the dead began to feel [the worms], men's faces became ape-like, and they became vulnerable to demons".

Kittel does not dispute that there are texts which speak of the image of God in humans being lost but disputes whether this has anything to do with Adam's specific sin.[256] Furthermore, Moore makes the point that although "Jewish imagination, increasingly in later times, invested Adam before the fall with many extraordinary physical qualities . . . he was not conceived as being mentally and morally otherwise constituted than his posterity".[257] Also, as I shall later argue, there is no indication that Adam and his posterity lost free will. One reason Jervell comes to the conclusion he does is that in his discussion of the "verlorene Gottesebenbildlichkeit" he focuses on the "spekulativ-protologische Auslegung" of Gen. 1.26-27. However, if one were to give full weight to the "ethisch-

---

[253] Soncino, p. 91.

[254] Jervell, *Imago Dei*, p. 113 (cf. pp. 99-104).

[255] Jervell, *Imago Dei*, p. 113.

[256] Kittel, εἰκών, 393, points to b. M. Kat. 15a-15b. "Bar Ḳappara taught: '[God says], 'I have set the likeness of mine image on them and through their sins have I upset it'".

[257] Moore, *Judaism*, 1:479.

anthropologische Auslegung" a somewhat different picture may emerge. So taking texts such as Aboth 3.14 (3.15)[258] and Mek. Ex. Baḥodesh 8[259] one gains the impression that the image of God in the Israelite (and the non-Israelite) still to some extent remains.[260]

An interesting Jewish background to the fall in Rom. 1.18-32 is the Rabbinic legend of the serpent tempting Eve in terms of unchastity[261] and

---

[258] Aboth 3.14 (3.15): "He (R. Akiba) used to say: Beloved is man for he was created in the image [of God]; still greater was the love in that it was made known to him that he was created in the image of God, as it is written, 'For in the image of God made he man' (Gen. 9.6)" (Danby, *Mishnah*, p. 452).

[259] Mek. Ex. Baḥodesh 8: "How then are the Ten Commandments arranged? Five on the one tablet and five on the other. On the one tablet was written: 'I am the Lord thy God.' And opposite it on the other tablet was written: 'Thou shalt not murder.' This tells that if one sheds blood it is accounted to him as though he diminished the divine image (דמות). To give a parable: A king of flesh and blood entered a province and the people set up portraits, broke his images, and defaced his coins, thus diminishing the likeness of the king. So also if one sheds blood it is accounted to him as though he had diminished the divine image. For it is said: 'Whoso sheddeth man's blood . . . for in the image of God made He man' (Gen. 9.6)" (Lauterbach, *Mekhilta*, 2:262; for a helpful discussion of this passage, see F. Avemarie, *Tora und Leben: Untersuchungen zur Heilsbedeutung der Tora in der frühen rabbinischen Literatur*, Tübingen 1996, pp. 93-96). Here, as earlier in Baḥodesh 8 (Lauterbach, *Mekhilta*, 2:260), the sixth commandment is related to Gen. 9.6. Note that according to this text, the image is related to the issue of human worth. A similar view of the image is put forward in Gen. R. 8.12 (on Gen. 1.28): "'And have dominion (*redu*) over the fish of the sea (1.28). R. Ḥanina said: if he merits it, [God says,] '*uredu*' (have dominion); while if he does not merit, [God says,] '*yerdu*' (let them descend). R. Jacob of Kefar Ḥanan said: of him who is in our image and likeness [I say] '*uredu*' (and have dominion); but of him who is not in our image and likeness [I say] '*yerdu*' (let them descend)" (Soncino, 1:62).

[260] See E. Larsson, *Christus als Vorbild: Eine Untersuchung zu den paulinischen Tauf- und Eikontexten*, Uppsala 1962, p. 144, who believes that the image of God in Adam is not totally lost as a result of his fall. "Wir haben es also mit Vorstellungen über eine gewaltig verminderte, aber nicht ganz zerstörte Gottesebenbildlichkeit zu tun". See also *Christus als Vorbild*, p. 165: "Der Mensch an sich — als physisch-psychisches Wesen — ist Gottes Ebenbild". Larsson also makes the point that this is true for the non-Israelite too.

[261] See b. Sot. 9b; Gen. R. 18.6; 20.11; 22.2; b. Shab. 146a: "For when the serpent came upon Eve he injected a lust into her" (cf. b. Abod. Zar. 22b). b. Yeb. 103b: "For R. Joḥanan stated: When the serpent copulated with Eve, he infused her with lust".

Adam and Eve having unnatural intercourse with demons.[262] The tradition may well go back to the first century AD.[263] Traditions of Satan corrupting Eve are occasionally found in the Pseudepigrapha.[264] This clearly has parallels with Rom. 1.23-27. A further point is that Rabbinic sources speak of Adam's fall in terms of idolatry and sexual immorality both of which are relevant to Rom. 1.18ff. In fact the main tradition was that six commandments were given to Adam: concerning idolatry, blasphemy, cursing judges, shedding of blood (i.e. murder), sexual immorality and robbery.[265] But R. Judah said "Adam was prohibited idolatry only".[266]

As we have seen in chapter 2, Wedderburn has questioned aspects of the Adam background to Rom. 1.18ff.

Adam in Genesis only turns away from God after his sin and only then is he barred from God's presence (Gen. 3:8, 23f.); in Romans man turns away from God and only then does he fall into idolatry (1:21-5). More seriously, the attempt to see in Rom. 1 allusions to the sexual seduction of Eve by the serpent as it is found in some Jewish traditions stumbles against the fact that sexual perversions are a further development of man's decline and not its cause.[267]

Wedderburn is clearly right in pointing to these differences. However, I do not think the differences are so significant and can be accounted for by saying that Paul's interest seems to be on *losing the knowledge of God* whereas in Genesis (and Jewish tradition) it is a matter of sin and certain consequences, the knowledge of God being retained after the "fall". This theological interest of Paul therefore accounts for the difference between Gen. 1-3 and Rom. 1. Gen. 1-3 formed a background for Paul's argument, taking certain elements from Genesis and changing them in view of his theological interests.

What is particularly important for texts like Rom. 1.23 is that Jewish tradition frequently associated Adam's fall with the golden calf episode.

---

[262] Gen. R. 20.11; 24.6.

[263] See H. St John Thackeray, *The Relation of St Paul to Contemporary Jewish Thought*, London 1900, pp. 50-52; Tennant, *Fall and Original Sin*, pp. 152-60 (mentioned by Hooker, "Adam", 302 n. 2).

[264] 2 En. 31.6; Apocalypse of Abraham 23.

[265] See Gen. R. 16.6. Slightly different laws are given by R. Joḥanan in b. Sanh. 56b: "social laws" (i.e. establishing courts of justice); blasphemy; idolatry; bloodshed; adultery; robbery.

[266] b. Sanh. 56b.

In order to perceive this connection it has first to be noted that Moses and the exodus generation are given an exalted status. So Pseudo-Philo 12.1 speaks of Moses' glory as does Dt. R. 11.3 (which affirms that Moses is superior to Adam). Lev. R. 11.3 refers to Israelites flying[268] and having godlike qualities.[269] Moses and Israel are therefore given a highly exalted status. This, however, is destroyed by the golden calf episode. As a result of this act of idolatry, death comes into the world.[270] Some texts even talk about future generations being punished as a result of the golden calf incident.[271] However, it needs stressing that the idea of a doctrine of "Original Sin" is not to be found in Jewish texts.

In this connection it is necessary to say something about the evil inclination (יצר הרע) and the good inclination (יצר הטוב).[272] The term יצר in the

---

[267] Wedderburn, "Adam", 415-16.

[268] Although Ex. 19.4 ("and how I bore you on eagles wings") is not quoted, it almost certainly forms the background for this part of Lev. R. 11.3.

[269] Note that here (as in Dt. R. 7.12) Ps. 82.6 is quoted ("You are gods, sons of the Most High, all of you") ("I said: Ye are godlike beings") but 82.7 is not quoted ("nevertheless, you shall die like men, and fall like a prince") although this verse is quoted in other texts (see Mek. Ex. Baḥodesh 9, quoted below).

[270] Ex. R. 32.1: "Had Israel waited for Moses and not perpetrated that act, there would have been no exile, neither would the Angel of Death have had any power over them. . . . As soon, however, as they said, 'This is thy god, O Israel' (Ex. 32.4), death came upon them. God said: 'You have followed the course of Adam who did not withstand his trials for more than three hours, and at nine hours death was decreed upon him." (Soncino, p. 404). See also Ex. R. 32.7; Lev. R. 11.3; Num. R. 16.24. Mek. Ex. Baḥodesh 9 (Lauterbach, *Mekilta*, 2:271-72): "If it were possible to do away with the Angel of Death I would. But the decree has long ago been decreed. R. Jose says: It was upon this condition that the Israelites stood up before mount Sinai, on condition that the Angel of Death should have no power over them. For it is said: 'I said: Ye are godlike beings,' etc. (Ps. 82.6). But you corrupted your conduct. 'Surely ye shall die like men' (Ps. 82.7)".

[271] b. Sanh. 102a: "R. Isaac said: No retribution whatsoever comes upon the world which does not contain a slight fraction of the first calf". Cf. Ex. R. 43.2; Eccl. R. 9.11.1; Lam. R. 2.1.3. This last text says that according to R. Ishmael b. Naḥmani and R. Joḥanan, the consequences of the sin of the golden calf lasted until the destruction of the Temple. See also Jervell, *Imago Dei*, p. 321.

[272] On this see Billerbeck, *Kommentar*, 4.2:466-83; S. Schechter, *Aspects of Rabbinic Theology*, New York ²1961, (¹1909), pp. 242-92; E.E. Urbach, *The Sages - Their Concepts and Beliefs* ET, Cambridge/London ²1979, (¹1975), pp. 471-83.

Hebrew Bible can mean "vessel" (Is. 29.16) or "that which is formed in the mind, imagination, purpose" (Gen. 6.5; 8.21; Dt. 31.21; 1 Chr. 28.9; 29.18; Is. 26.3). In Sir. 15.14 it means "natural inclination" in the specific sense of free will.[273] The idea of two inclinations is found in Test. Ash. 1.3-9, which speaks of the two inclinations (δύο διαβούλια).[274] The stereotyped terms יצר הרע and יצר הטוב were Rabbinic, יצר הרע being older than יצר הטוב, the latter first occurring most likely in R. Jose the Galilaean (early second century).[275] According to Tennant, the talmudic literature "insists on a man's capacity to control his evil inclination, mighty as it is" and there is "no hint that his free-will is diminished in consequence of the sin of his first parents".[276] Further, the evil inclination, although implanted in Adam, is not a consequence of Adam's sin.[277] The evil inclination was the cause of Adam's sin and in fact in some texts is personified.[278] This evil inclination then can rule over everyone. It was, however, possible to resist the evil inclination through the torah. So in b. Bab. Bat. 16a we read: "If God created the evil inclination, He also created the Torah as its antidote (lit. spices)" (ברא הקדוש ברוך הוא יצר הרע ברא לו תורה תבלין).[279] See also Sifre Dt. 45:

---

[273] See P.W. Skehan and A.A. Di Lella, *The Wisdom of Ben Sira*, New York 1986, p. 272.

[274] T. Ash. 1.3-9: δύο ὁδοὺς ἔδωκεν ὁ θεὸς τοῖς υἱοῖς τῶν ἀνθρώπων καὶ δύο διαβούλια καὶ δύο πράξεις καὶ δύο τρόπους καὶ δύο τέλη. 4 διὰ τοῦτο πάντα δύο εἰσίν, ἓν κατέναντι τοῦ ἑνός. 5 ὁδοὶ δύο, καλοῦ καὶ κακοῦ· ἐν οἷς εἰσι τὰ δύο διαβούλια ἐν στέρνοις ἡμῶν διακρίνοντα αὐτάς. 6 ἐὰν οὖν ἡ ψυχὴ θέλῃ ἐν καλῷ, πᾶσα πρᾶξις αὐτῆς ἐστιν ἐν δικαιοσύνῃ, κἂν ἁμάρτῃ, εὐθὺς μετανοεῖ. 7 δίκαια γὰρ λογιζόμενος καὶ ἀπορρίπτων τὴν πονηρίαν ἀνατρέπει εὐθὺς τὸ κακὸν καὶ ἐκριζοῖ τὴν ἁμαρτίαν. 8 ἐὰν δὲ ἐν πονηρῷ κλίνῃ τὸ διαβούλιον, πᾶσα πρᾶξις αὐτῆς ἐστιν ἐν πονηρίᾳ, καὶ ἀπωθούμενος τὸ ἀγαθὸν προσλαμβάνει τὸ κακὸν καὶ κυριευθεὶς ὑπὸ τοῦ Βελιάρ, κἂν ἀγαθὸν πράξῃ, ἐν πονηρίᾳ αὐτὸ μεταστρέφει. 9 ὅταν γὰρ ἐνάρξηται ὡς ἀγαθὸν ποιῶν, τὸ τέλος τῆς πράξεως αὐτοῦ εἰς κακὸν ποιεῖν ἀνελαύνει· ἐπειδὴ ὁ θησαυρὸς τοῦ διαβουλίου ἰοῦ πονηροῦ πνεύματος πεπλήρωται.

[275] Tennant, *Fall and Original Sin*, p. 170.

[276] Tennant, *Fall and Original Sin*, p. 175.

[277] Tennant, *Fall and Original Sin*, p. 171.

[278] Note that in b. Bab. Bat. 16a, the evil inclination is identified with Satan. "Resh Lakish said: Satan, the evil prompter, and the Angel of Death are one" (אמר ר"ל הוא שטן הוא יצר הרע הוא מלאך המות).

[279] Cf. b. Shab. 146a: "For when the serpent came upon Eve he injected a lust (זוהמא) into her". But the text continues: "as for the Israelites who stood at Mount

Thus also the Holy One, blessed be He, said to Israel, 'My children, I created an Inclination to evil in you . . . busy yourselves with words of torah, and the Inclination to Evil will not rule over you; but if you abandon the words of Torah, it will gain mastery over you . . ..[280]

The torah also acted as an antidote for proselytes.[281] It was also possible to overcome the power of the evil inclination by means of the good inclination.[282] According to Aboth Rabbi Nathan 16, the "evil inclination is senior to the good inclination by thirteen years". So the general view was that the evil inclination ruled from the earliest childhood[283] and then at 13 the good inclination came into operation. Note also that the power of the evil inclination is related to the 248 members of the body. See Aboth R. Nathan 16.2:

When a man's passions are stirred and he is about to commit an act of lewdness, all his limbs are ready to obey him, because the evil inclination is king over the two hundred and forty-eight limbs of man. On the other hand, when a man is about to perform an act of piety, all his limbs become sluggish, because the evil inclination which is within him bears sway over the two hundred and forty-eight limbs of his body, whereas the good inclination is like one who is confined in prison, as it is stated, 'For out of prison he came forth to be king' (Eccl. 4.14), which verse had been interpreted as referring to the good inclination.

Sinai, their lustfulness departed" (cf. b. Yeb. 103b; b. Abod. Zar. 22b). For idolaters, however, their lust does not depart.

[280] R. Hammer, (ed.), *Sifre: A Tannaitic Commentary on the Book of Deuteronomy*, New Haven/London 1986, p. 97. See the discussion of this passage in Avemarie, *Torah und Leben*, pp. 121-23. See also his discussion of the restraining of the evil inclination in *Torah und Leben*, pp. 117-33.

[281] In b. Shab. 146a R. Ashi said: "Though they (proselytes) were not present, their guiding stars were present, as it is written, 'Neither with you only do I make this covenant and this oath, but with him that standeth here with us this day before the Lord our God, and also with him that is not here with us this day' (Dt. 29.14-15)".

[282] b. Ber. 5a: "So R. Levi b. Ḥama says in the name of R. Simeon b. Lakish: 'A man should always incite the good impulse to fight against the evil impulse. . . . If he subdues it, well and good. If not, let him study the Torah. . . . If he subdues it, well and good. If not let him recite the Shema' . . . If he subdues it, well and good. If not, let him remind himself of the day of death".

[283] For the texts, see Billerbeck, *Kommentar*, 4.2:471-72.

Although the evil inclination can act as a "king" over the human being, this is by no means inevitable. So the evil inclination is not related to the idea in Paul of "original sin". Further, according to Rabbinic thinking, free will was not lost as a result of the fall. The consequences of the fall were death and the loss of certain supernatural characteristics. The nearest possible parallel to "original sin" is the legend of Eve being infected with lust by Satan.[284] But this idea does not seem to have served the purpose of explaining universal sinfulness.[285]

Note also that although for the author of 2 Baruch, Adam's sin had serious consequences,[286] the view of "original sin" is denied in 2 Bar. 54.15:

> For, although Adam sinned first and has brought death upon all who were not in his own time, yet each of them who has been born from him has prepared for himself the coming torment. . . . 19 Adam is, therefore, not the cause, except only for himself, but each of us had become his own Adam.[287]

A likely explanation for this trend in Judaism to stress free will is that God was becoming increasingly transcendent and impersonal, so the actions of human beings were ascribed precisely to human beings. This then gives rise to an absolute view of the human free will as is found in apocalyptic and Rabbinic Judaism.[288]

7. Paul's View of the Fall

Rom. 1.18-32 clearly refers to some sort of "fall". But as noted in chapter 2 and in the excursus on natural theology, it is not immediately clear whether Paul speaks of Adam and Eve or every generation. Weber notes "daß die Aussagen, die der Behauptung eines ursprünglichen Wahrheitsbesitzes der Menschheit zur Begründung dienen, präsentisch

---

[284] See the texts in n. 261 above.

[285] Tennant, *Fall and Original Sin*, p. 176.

[286] See J.R. Levison, *Portraits of Adam in Early Judaism*, Sheffield 1988, pp. 129-44, 157-58, for a discussion of the effects of Adam's sin on subsequent generations in 2 Baruch.

[287] Klijn, in Charlesworth, *Pseudepigrapha*, 1:640.

[288] Cf. D. Carson, *Divine Sovereignty and Human Responsibility*, London 1981, p. 74.

gefaßt sind".[289] This present tense has been interpreted in a number of ways. So Schlatter sees a constant repetition of the Fall.[290] Bernhard Weiß sees the fall of the Gentiles as something complete, but that vv. 19-20 show that every revelation makes humankind inexcusable.[291] Weber's own conclusion is that the verses only make sense if seen in the light of Paul's mission to Gentiles.[292] The view of Owen is that "Gentiles did not turn to idolatry after rejecting a prior non-idolatrous revelation: they were born into idolatry which was the established norm of worship".[293] He goes on to say "that every idolater at *some* time, or times, has a measure of insight into God's θειότης, and that every idolator (sic), instead of letting the insight grow, suppresses it".[294] I do not think any of these views do justice to Paul's view of the fall in Rom. 1.18-32. The view I have

---

[289] Weber, *Missionspraxis*, p. 26.

[290] Schlatter, *Gottes Gerechtigkeit*, p. 61, points out that there is no subject change from Rom. 1.18 to 1.19-20: "Vom Menschen spricht er, wie er immer war und überall ist. Sie suchten alle ihre eigene Ehre, priesen sich selber, und eigneten sich die göttlichen Gaben an, als wäre Gott schuldig, sie zu begaben. Er denkt nicht nur an die jetzt Lebenden, sondern schaut sie als Glieder der Menschheit, die ihr Denken und Handeln vom gemeinsamen Leben empfangen, formt aber nicht ein Gesichtsbild, das den jetzt vorhandenen Zustand durch das erklären möchte, was einst geschehen ist".

[291] B. Weiß, *Römer*, p. 82 n. 2: "Allerdings setzt der Apostel V.19f. voraus, dass sich jene Selbstoffenbarung Gottes immer noch vollzieht und immer noch die Menschen unentschuldbar macht; aber die folgenden Aoriste . . . zeigen doch, dass er den Abfall der Menschheit von der ihr gewährten Gotteserkenntniss als eine abgeschlossene Thatsache betrachtet und so wirklich den Abfall des Heidenthums von dem ursprünglichen Monotheismus beschreibt, wenn auch derselbe sich immer noch aufs Neue wiederholt". See also Pfleiderer, *Urchristentum*, 1:211: "Vorausgesetzt ist also dabei eine ursprüngliche wahre Gotteserkenntnis auf Grund der natürlichen Offenbarung. . . . Und weil diese Offenbarung Gottes in der Natur immer die gleiche ist, so besteht also auch die Möglichkeit einer natürlichen Gotteserkenntnis noch immer wie zu Anfang".

[292] Weber argues, as we have seen in chapter 2, that there can be no doubt "daß Paulus in unserm Abschnitt zu der Behauptung einer ursprünglichen reinen Gotteserkenntnis gelangt von der Gegenwart des natürlichen religiösen Bewußtseins aus". He concludes that the basis for this lies "in der Missionswirksamkeit Pauli, von der wir Röm. 1,18ff. einen wichtigen Niederschlag haben".

[293] Owen, "Natural Revelation", 141.

[294] Owen, "Natural Revelation", 141-42.

argued for in chapter 2 and in the excursus on natural theology is that Paul refers to the fall of Adam, to Israel and to every generation.[295]

Especially important for the discussion of Paul's view of the fall is Rom. 1.23: καὶ ἤλλαξαν τὴν δόξαν τοῦ ἀφθάρτου θεοῦ ἐν ὁμοιώματι εἰκόνος φθαρτοῦ ἀνθρώπου καὶ πετεινῶν καὶ τετραπόδων καὶ ἑρπετῶν. A key issue here is whether Paul is talking of a change in the object of man's worship or a change in man's nature?[296] Most commentators seem to take the former. Paul, it is argued, is simply referring to a change in the object of man's worship. Further, Paul is referring to Gentile idolatry, i.e. Gentiles worshipping "images resembling mortal man or birds or animals or reptiles". So Cranfield and Michel believe the word ὁμοίωμα has the sense of "likeness" as in Ps. 105.20 and Dt. 4.16-18, while εἰκών denotes the actual "form" ("Gestalt") of the man or animal.[297] Barrett translates the phrase ὁμοιώματι εἰκόνος as "mere shadowy image".[298] However, Jervell is critical of such approaches. He argues that idolatry in the form of veneration of images was not typical for Gentiles of this time[299] and in fact the reference to worshipping animals could only be relevant to the Egyptians.[300] He and some other scholars believe that the key to understanding the verse is to see an allusion to Gen. 1.26-27.[301] Jervell's own approach is as follows. He believes that Paul is not actually referring to idols in Rom. 1.23. He argues that the φθαρτὸς ἄνθρωπος

---

[295] See the discussion of natural theology in the excursus above. Note also Hooker's criticism of Owen's approach ("Adam", 298-99).

[296] See Wedderburn, "Adam", 417.

[297] Cranfield, *Romans*, 1:120; Michel, *Römer*, p. 103.

[298] Barrett, *Romans*, p. 37.

[299] Jervell, *Imago Dei*, p. 322 n. 501, writes: "Die Idolatrie, als Bilderverehrung verstanden, ist nicht typisch für jene Zeit".

[300] A number of commentators do in fact believe the reference is to Egyptian idolatry. Michel, *Römer*, p. 103, writes: "Man könnte etwa an Falke und Ibis, an Krokodil und Schlange denken, die in Ägypten verehrt werden". Likewise, Käsemann, *Romans*, pp. 45-46, thinks the reference is to Egyptian idols and is critical of much of Jervell's argument at this point.

[301] See N. Hyldahl, "A Reminiscence of the Old Testament at Romans i.23", *NTS* 2 (1955-56) 288 (285-88), believes that in Rom. 1.23, Gen. 1.26ff is of more importance than Dt. 4.15-18. See also Hooker, "Adam", 300, who stresses the link between Rom. 1.18-32 and the creation story.

must be Adam and Paul is speaking of humans being copies of Adam.[302] In Ancient Judaism it was also assumed that the Israelite was a copy of Adam but this was positively understood. But for Paul, to be in Adam's image was to be in εἰκὼν τοῦ χοϊκοῦ (ἀνθρώπου).[303] But not only have people taken on the image of mortal man; they have also taken on the image of birds, four footed creatures and reptiles.[304]

Although Jervell has some insights, I am not convinced that there is no reference to idolatry in Rom. 1.23. First, the allusion to Ps. 106.20 suggests idolatry.[305] Secondly, Jervell seems to have overstated his case in arguing that veneration of images was not typical of Gentiles at this time. He refers to Norden[306] and Wendland[307]. However, both these authors

---

[302] Jervell, *Imago Dei*, p. 321, says Rom. 1.23 alludes to Gen. 1.26-27 and Ps. 106.20. Rabbis made a distinction between דיוקונא and דמות to distinguish between "Vorbild" and "Abbild". דיוקונא is a loan word from Greek εἰκών (for the various forms see S. Krauß, *Griechische und lateinische Lehnwörter im Talmud, Midrasch und Targum*, 2 vols, Berlin 1898-99, 2:40-41). J. Levy, *Wörterbuch über die Talmudim und Midraschim*, 4 vols, Darmstadt 1963, 1:394, thinks it is combination of δύο and εἰκών and Jervell, *Imago Dei*, p. 97 n. 101, supports this in view of b. Bab. Bat. 58a (נסתכלת בדמות דיוקני בדיוקני עצמה אל תסתכל), "Thou hast beholden the likeness of my likeness, my likeness itself thou mayest not behold" (Soncino)) and b. Hul. 91b. דמותא on the other hand corresponds to ὁμοίωμα. Ancient Judaism linked creation and Exodus such that just as Adam lost his glory, so Israel lost her glory too. See the excursus above on Jewish views of the fall.

[303] 1 Cor. 15.49: καὶ καθὼς ἐφορέσαμεν τὴν εἰκόνα τοῦ χοϊκοῦ, φορέσομεν καὶ τὴν εἰκόνα τοῦ ἐπουρανίου. Adam, therefore, is associated with φθορά (cf. 15.42b, 53, 54). Cf. φθαρτὸς ἄνθρωπος, Rom. 1.23.

[304] This would seem to be the logic of Rom. 1.23. Compare the Jewish tradition that after the fall man looked like an animal. See especially Mek. Ex. Beshallaḥ 7.78-84 and its reference to Ps. 106.20: "R. Pappias also expounded: 'Thus they exchanged their glory for the likeness of an ox that eateth grass' (Ps. 106.20). . . Nothing is more disgusting and repulsive than an ox when he is grazing" (Lauterbach, *Mekilta*, 1:248-49). Also the animals were no longer subject to man; man was on the same level and began to worship animals.

[305] Note also the references to animal worship in Ezek. 8.10 and the important role the serpent takes, especially the brazen serpent. On the question of animal worship in the Old Testament see J.F. McCurdy, "Animal Worship", *JE* 1:604-6, and "Brazen Serpent", *JE* 3:358-59.

[306] E. Norden, *Agnostos Theos: Untersuchungen zur Formengeschichte religiöser Rede*, Stuttgart ⁴1956, (¹1912), pp. 128ff.

[307] Wendland, *Die hellenistisch-römische Kultur*, pp. 244-45.

point not to the actual situation in the Graeco-Romans world but rather to the philosophical and semi-philosophical literary traditions.[308] Veneration of images seems to be more widespread than Jervell allows.[309] Thirdly, and this seems to be an especially important point, it may be that there were some Gentiles who did not engage in veneration of images. But if Paul is to put over in the clearest way that any worship of God outside of his revelation of himself is idolatry, then the best way of putting it over is

---

[308] Wendland makes the point that Paul has given "eine stark schematische Zeichnung, die sich im einzelnen in den Formen der jüdischen Apologetik bewegt" (*Die hellenistisch-römische Kultur*, p. 245). Also Norden points to the tradition among pagans of a "religiöse(n) Propagandarede" (*Agnostos Theos*, p. 129). He writes: "Aufforderung zur Erkenntnis Gottes als eines menschenunänhlichen, geistigen Wesens und zu der dadurch bedingten Sinnesänderung, Prädikation dieses Gottes und die rechte Art seiner Verehrung (nicht blutige Opfer, sondern im Geiste), ewiges Leben und Seligkeit als Lohn solcher Erkenntnis: das waren die festen Punkte des schematischen Aufbaus. Dieser Typus war nicht auf die Predigten altchristlicher Missionare (katholischer wie häretischer) beschränkt, sondern wir fanden ihn auch in einem von einem Juden verfaßten pseudoheraklitischen Briefe, in hermetischen Traktaten, in Dialexeis von pythagoreischen und stoischen Wanderrednern, wie Apollonios von Tyana, ja wir konnten ihn . . . auch für Lucretius und (vor allem aus Ciceros Somnium) auch für Poseidonius . . . erweisen" (*Agnostos Theos*, pp. 129-30). He goes on to refer to Greek pagan writers like Empedocles, who writes that we cannot see or feel God (Fragment 133) and that he is not like human beings but is a spirit (Fragment 134) (see H. Diels and W. Kranz, *Die Fragmente der Vorsokratiker: Band 1*, Berlin ⁶1951, (¹1903), pp. 365-66). So Norden's point is that Jews and Christians were not alone in condemning idolatry. But this hardly supports Jervell's point that worship of images was not typical for Gentiles.

[309] The veneration of animal images was not confined to Egypt. The use of animals could be extended to Assyria (Lightfoot, *Notes*, p. 253) and possibly to the Asclepius cult (Asclepius using the image of the snake (*KP*, 1:643-48)) and the Roman household *genius* whose image was a house-snake (see A. Kamm, *The Romans*, London 1995, pp. 87-88). As regards the worship of the human form, Fitzmyer, *Romans*, p. 283, points to pagan gods being found in human form as statues and reliefs in ancient Syria, Mesopotamia, Anatolia and Egypt (see *ANEP*, 464-573, 822-37, pp. 160-91, 352-53). Note that although J. Gray writes that "Higher thought in the Greco-Roman world had really outgrown idolatry and the old cults of Greece and Rome" (Gray, "Idolatry", *IDB*, 2:678 (675-78)), use of images at the popular level was still widespread in the world Paul knew (and used in mystery religions). The Lucan Paul finds that Athens is full of idols (Acts 17.16). On the many idols in Athens, see Livy, *Ab urbe condita libri* 45.27.11 and Pausanias, *Description of Greece* 1.17.1. Note that although the mystery religions had some popularity, images were still used here.

to write of human beings worshipping idols.[310] So I do not wish to exclude a reference to idolatry in Rom. 1.23. But Jervell does, I believe, have compelling arguments for allusions to Gen. 1.26-27 and I think he is right to see a reference to the change in the image of man in Rom. 1.23. Is it not possible to combine these two ideas of idolatry and the change in the image of man? I believe it is. Wedderburn points out that according to the Old Testament and Paul a man becomes like that which he worships. There may be a tranformation of the person as in 2 Cor. 3.18 (ἡμεῖς δὲ πάντες ἀνακεκαλυμμένῳ προσώπῳ τὴν δόξαν κυρίου κατοπτριζόμενοι τὴν αὐτὴν εἰκόνα μεταμορφούμεθα ἀπὸ δόξης εἰς δόξαν καθάπερ ἀπὸ κυρίου πνεύματος). But there may also be a debasing as in Rom. 1.23.[311] As I wrote in the exegesis of Rom. 1.23, Paul is saying two related things. First, rather than worshipping God the creator, they have worshipped images resembling the human and animal form. Second, this process entails exchanging their "image of God" for the "image of mortal man", i.e. Adam, and also the image of beasts.

This brings me on to the issue of the loss of the image of God.[312] This is hinted at in Rom. 1.23 and is made more explicit in Rom. 3.23 and in the fact that only Jesus has the image of God (2 Cor. 4.4), believers being

---

[310] So in Greek religion where a god may be worshipped without an image, it may not be immediately apparent that idolatry is going on. Likewise today, it may be not immediately apparent that worship of certain deities (even if there is no image of them) is idolatry. Note also the comments of J. Gray, "Idol", *IDB* 2:675 (673-75), who points out that in the NT "references to idols . . . are generally not specifically to images but to the worship of alien gods in which the idol in the Greco-Roman age might signify much or little". See, for example, Paul's language in 1 Thes. 1.9b were he speaks of πῶς ἐπεστρέψατε πρὸς τὸν θεὸν ἀπὸ τῶν εἰδώλων δουλεύειν θεῷ ζῶντι καὶ ἀληθινῷ. The key idea is surely that the Thessalonians had worshipped *foreign deities*, not necessarily that they had worshipped *images*. See also C.A. Wanamaker, *Commentary on 1 & 2 Thessalonians*, Grand Rapids 1990, p. 86: "The word 'idols' has symbolic significance here because it embraces the totality of the religious experience of his readers (and by implication their social existence) before their conversion".

[311] Note also Jer. 2.5b alluded to in Rom. 1.21: καὶ ἐπορεύθησαν ὀπίσω τῶν ματαίων καὶ ἐματαιώθησαν ("and went after worthlessness (vanities) and became worthless (vain)"). Exactly the same expression (in LXX and MT) occurs in 2 Kgs 17.15. The Hebrew is: וַיֵּלְכוּ אַחֲרֵי הַהֶבֶל וַיֶּהְבָּלוּ.

[312] See Bell, *Provoked to Jealousy*, pp. 196-97.

conformed to this image (Rom. 8.29). Because these texts lie outside of my main interest here, Rom. 1.18-3.20, I will not discuss them in any detail. But this radical idea has obvious implications for the question of natural theology.

In view of this, it should be clear that Paul has a radical view of the fall. In fact his anthropology is the most pessimistic of the New Testament writers.[313] But Paul believes that not only are the Gentiles like beasts; Jews also have become like animals.[314] It is then hardly surprising that Paul denies the actuality of "natural theology" and, as we shall see in the subsequent chapters, any justification by works.

---

[313] He is also certainly more pessimistic than Rabbinic anthropology. Although there are Rabbinic sources which are extremely negative towards the Gentiles, these have nothing to do with anthropological pessimism but are basically xenophobic texts. See the texts quoted in Billerbeck, *Kommentar*, 1:360 (e.g. Mek. Ex. Beshallah 2 (on 14.7): "R. Simon the son of Yohai said: 'The nicest among the idolaters (lit. Gentiles, גוים),—kill'" (Lauterback, *Mekilta*, 1:201); b. Bab. Met. 114b: "R. Simeon b. Yohai said: The graves of Gentiles do not defile, for it is written, 'And ye my flock, the flock of my pastures' (Ezek. 34.31), are men; only ye are designated 'men'". This is followed by the following striking words which, for some reason, have not been translated in the Soncino edition (but is given by Billerbeck): "But the worshippers of stars are not called men"; b. Yeb. 60b-61a: "And so did R. Simeon b. Yohai state [61a] that the graves of idolaters do not impart levitical uncleannes by an 'ohel', for it is said, 'And ye My sheep the sheep of My pasture, are men'; you are called 'men' but the idolaters are not called men". See also Billerbeck, *Kommentar*, 4:722 (again a quotation from b. Yeb. 60b and 4:1067 (Pes. R. 10.5: "R. Levi said . . . What a number of nations in the world! What a vast number of nations which He does not trouble Himself about" (W.G. Braude (ed.), *Pesikta Rabbati*, 2 vols, New Haven/London 1968. 1:177)). Note also that there are Rabbinic texts which affirm that Gentiles have the image of God. See also the idea that the Gentile who studies the Torah is as a High Priest (see b. Sanh. 105a; b. Abod. Zar. 3a; b. Bab. Kam. 38ab).

[314] It needs stressing, however, that Israel remains the covenant people of God. One of the paradoxes in Romans is that Jews have lost the image of God (which also entails losing the glory of God). But in another sense Israel still retain the glory (Rom. 9.4-5). This, however, is not a glory which is inherent in Israel. This may answer B.J. Byrne's point in a review of my work *Provoked to Jealousy*, who writes that "it seems inconsistent to hold that Israel has lost God's 'image' . . . but nonetheless retains the 'glory'" (*JTS* 46 (1995) 278 (277-79)).

Chapter 4

Romans 2.1-16: Judgement According to Works

1. The Problem of Romans 2

A number of recent works have viewed Romans 2 as a stumbling block for Luther's interpretation of Paul.[1] Rom. 3.28 says a man is justified by faith apart from works of law. But does not Romans 2 teach a justification according to works? See, for example, Rom. 2.6 (ὅς ἀποδώσει ἑκάστῳ κατὰ τὰ ἔργου αὐτοῦ, a quotation probably from Ps. 61.13 LXX which Paul appears to affirm) and Rom. 2.13 (οὐ γὰρ οἱ ἀκροαταὶ νόμου δίκαιοι παρὰ τῷ θεῷ, ἀλλ᾽ οἱ ποιηταὶ νόμου δικαιωθήσονται). Is not justification "to the doers"?[2]

There have been a variety of ways of interpreting Romans 2.[3] The following list is a representative sample.

1. J.C. O'Neill regards the entire chapter as an interpolation.[4] There is, however, no textual evidence to support this view.

2. The Tübingen school understood the chapter to be directed against Jewish Christians.[5] Such a view is of course linked to the view that Paul

---

[1] See, for example, F. Watson, *Paul, Judaism and the Gentiles*, Cambridge 1986, chapter 6.

[2] Snodgrass, "Romans 2".

[3] Note that although I am taking the units to be Rom. 2.1-16, then Rom. 2.17-3.8, many commentators have taken the unit to be Rom. 2.1-29. Therefore in the following pages I am considering the various approaches to Romans 2 as a whole, even though I do not agree with the implied analysis.

[4] J.C. O'Neill, *Paul's Letter to the Romans*, Harmondsworth 1975, pp. 40, 53, 264-65.

[5] Weber, *Missionspraxis*, p. 21, points to the related work of R.A. Lipsius, "Der Brief an die Römer", in H.J. Holtzmann (ed.), *Handkommentar zum Neuen Testament*, 3 vols, Freiburg/Leipzig ²1892-93, 2.2:70-206. See Lipsius, "Römer", 81 (quoted in Weber p. 23): "Daß der Besitz des Gesetzes, der Beschneidung, der Verheißungen Gottes für sich allein dem Volke nichts hilft, muß auch der Judenchrist

is attacking Jewish Christians. This is extremely unlikely. Romans is addressed to a predominently Gentile Christian Church and Paul in Romans 14 stresses that understanding should be shown to Jewish Christians (who largely correspond to the "weak").[6]

3. O. Pfleiderer understands judgement according to works in Romans 2 (and in other Pauline texts) as Jewish thinking from Paul's past where judgement according to works played a central part.[7] However, Romans 2 itself suggests that Paul has integrated judgement according to works into his theology. See, for example, Rom. 2.16 where such judgement is through Jesus Christ according to the gospel entrusted to Paul.

4. H. Räisänen and E.P. Sanders argue that Romans 2 is a contradiction in Paul's theology which must be allowed to stand.[8] I believe there are some contradictions *between* Paul's letters and this, I believe, is usually owing to a development in Paul's thinking.[9] However, within a particular letter Paul's theology is generally coherent.[10] I hope to show that Romans 2 does not contradict the rest of Paul's theology.

---

anerkennen, ebenso wie er die Tatsache einräumen muß, daß keiner das Gesetz wirklich erfüllt, der Besitz des Gesetzes also die Übertreter ihrer Schuld und Straffälligkeit vor Gott überführt". See also H. Lüdemann, *Die Anthropologie des Apostels Paulus und ihre Stellung innerhalb seiner Heilslehre*, Kiel 1872, pp. 203, 206.

[6] See Bell, *Provoked to Jealousy*, pp. 64-78.

[7] O. Pfleiderer, *Der Paulinismus: Ein Beitrag zur Geschichte der urchristlichen Theologie*, Leipzig ²1890, p. 280-82. Pfleiderer further writes: "Dass diese Erwartung eines nach den einzelnen Werken vergeltenden Gerichts einer andersartigen Gedankenreihe entstammt als die Lehre von der Rechtfertigung aus Gnaden und mit dieser nicht unmittelbar zu vereinigen ist, das dürfte sich schwerlich bestreiten lassen" (*Urchristentum*, 1:258). See also P. Feine, *Das gesetzesfreie Evangelium des Paulus*, Leipzig 1899, p. 73; W. Wrede, *Paulus*, Halle 1904, p. 81 (= K.H. Rengstorf, *Das Paulusbild in der neueren deutschen Forschung*, Darmstadt 1982, 76 (1-97)); H. Weinel, *Biblische Theologie des Neuen Testaments*, 2 vols, Tübingen ³1920-21, 1:266, 2:409; H.J. Holtzmann, *Lehrbuch der Neutestamentlichen Theologie*, 2 vols, Tübingen ²1911 (ed. by A. Jülicher and W. Bauer), 2:224.

[8] See H. Räisänen, *Paul and the Law*, Tübingen 1983, pp. 101-7; E.P. Sanders, *Paul, the Law and the Jewish People*, Philadelphia 1983, pp. 123-36.

[9] A classic example is his view on Israel in 1 Thes. 2.16 and Rom. 11.26. See my discussion of these passages in *Provoked to Jealousy*, pp. 136-40, 331-32.

[10] In fact in my studies on Paul so far, I have been struck by the remarkable coherence of his theology. I wish to defend this position in future studies on Paul's christology and view of the atonement.

5. Lietzmann believes that Paul is speaking hypothetically. "In V.5-12 argumentiert Pls noch immer vom vorevangelischen Standpunkt aus, der keine Glaubensgerechtigkeit kennt und ein Urteil auf Grund der eigenen Leistungen erwartet. Da er in diesem Zusammenhang aber die Idee der Werkgerechtigkeit gerade ad adsurdum führen will, so müssen streng logisch diese ganzen Erörterungen als hypothetisch bezeichnet werden: es würde so kommen, wenn 1) das Evangelium nicht wäre und 2) die Erfüllung des Gesetzes möglich wäre."[11] Although Rom. 2.16 could pose a problem for Lietzmann's view (i.e. God will judge the secrets of men through Jesus Christ according to the gospel entrusted to Paul)[12] his understanding of Romans 2 deserves special consideration.

6. E. Weber, as we have seen already, relates Romans 1-3 to missionary preaching and sees the declaration of guilt as the necessary precondition of the justification of the ungodly.[13] Again there is something

---

[11] Lietzmann, *Römer*, pp. 39-40. See also B. Weiß, *Römer*, p. 107: "Da der Apostel immer noch in der Darlegung begriffen ist, wie allein das Evangelium mit seiner Offenbarung einer gottgeschenkten Gerechtigkeit vom Zorne Gottes und dem ewigen Verderben erretten kann (1_{16}f.), so handelt es sich hier zunächst zweifellos um die Urnorm der göttlichen Gerechtigkeit, d.h. darum, wie sich das Schicksal der Menschen gestalten würde, wenn es kein Evangelium gäbe". J. Weiß seemed to share this view also. Commenting on Rom. 2.3-11, he writes (*Urchristentum*, Göttingen 1917, p. 420): "Freilich könnte man sagen: in diesem Abschnitt erörtert Paulus das Loos der Menschheit, wie es sein würde, wenn nicht durch das Evangelium ein neuer Weg zum Heil (1,17; 3,21) dargeboten wäre; und für die Christen, die auf dem Boden des neuen Heils stehen, die ja schon durchs Gericht hindurchgegangen sind, insofern, als sie die Gerechtsprechung bereits empfangen haben (Röm. 5,1), treffe dies alles nicht mehr zu, vor allem nicht der Grundsatz, daß Gott 'jedem nach seinen Werken vergelten werde' — denn die Werke als Maßstab des Gerichts sollen ja nunmehr ausgeschaltet sein (Röm. 3,28 χωρὶς ἔργων) — es soll ja das Heil lediglich auf den Glauben hin verliehen werden". See also Wetter, *Vergeltungsgedanke*, p. 97.

[12] Concerning the expression εὐαγγέλιόν μου Lietzmann, *Römer*, p. 43, writes: "Mir scheint — bessere Einsicht vorbehalten —, daß Paulus hier unter εὐαγγέλιόν μου nicht speziell die Heilslehre vom Glauben verstanden wissen will, von der er den Römern ja noch nichts gesagt hat, sondern seine Gesamtverkündigung meint, deren ersten Teil 'vom Zorne Gottes und dem Gericht nach den Taten' er jetzt noch vorträgt". It will become clear in my discussion of 2.16 why I am not quite in agreement with Lietzmann's understanding of εὐαγγέλιόν μου.

[13] Weber, *Missionspraxis*, p. 47: "Die Sätze des Apostels haben ihre gewiesene Stelle in der Missionsrede, die mit dem Ernste des streng nach der höchsten Norm verfahrenden Gerichts erst die Gewissen erwecken musste." Cf. P. Wernle, *Der Christ und die Sünde bei Paulus*, Freiburg/Leipzig 1897, p. 99: "Aus der

important in this view.[14] There is certainly a movement of thought from 1.18 to 3.20 and then from 3.20 to 3.21.

7. Related to view 6. are the views of Bultmann[15] and Braun,[16] who rightly emphasise God's role as judge and the dialectical nature of Rom. 1-3.

8. Cranfield believes that Paul is speaking of Gentile Christians who fulfil the law through faith in Christ.[17] There are numerous problems with this view as I hope will become clear in the exegesis of 2.14-16.

9. Related to the previous approach is that of L. Mattern.[18] Although in the exegesis of Romans 2 she does not believe Paul is explicitly speaking of Gentile Christians,[19] her approach to Romans 2 is very similar. She concludes that if her interpretation is correct

. . . dann ist das Rö 2,5ff. geschilderte Gericht nicht nur für Heiden und Juden, sondern auch für Christen gültig - und zwar nicht nur als Hintergrund der Gnadenpredigt. Die Scheidung der Menschheit durch das Gericht ist dann identisch mit der Scheidung von Christen und Nichtchristen.[20]

Gerichtspredigt folgt die Notwendigkeit der Offenbarung der Gnade Gottes (γὰρ 1,18). Die Gerichtspredigt hat nur diesen Zweck; sie will nicht bessern, sondern gläubig machen".

[14] See the discussion of Weber in chapter 2 above.

[15] R. Bultmann, "Die Bedeutung des geschichtlichen Jesus für die Theologie des Paulus", in *Glauben und Verstehen: Gesammelte Aufsätze, Bd 1*, Tübingen ⁹1993, (¹1933), 195 (188-213): "In der Tat beruht der Unterbau des Römerbriefes, nämlich 1,18-3,20, in der Fixierung des Gottesgedankens, daß Gott der Richter ist, der das gute Werk vom Menschen fordert. Und die Glaubenspredigt bringt nicht einen neuen Gottesbegriff, des Inhalts, daß Gott nicht der Richter, sondern nur der Gnädige sei. Vielmehr sind nach Paulus Glaube und Gnade nur auf Grund des festgehaltenen Gottesgedankens, daß Gott der Richter ist, zu verstehen. Deshalb kann Paulus ja sogar die Christen auf diesen Richter-Gott und sein nach den Werken sich vollziehendes Gericht verweisen".

[16] H. Braun, *Gerichtsgedanke und Rechtfertigungslehre bei Paulus*, Leipzig 1930, p. 38: "Paulus redet vom Gericht so, daß des Gerichtes Tatsächlichkeit den Hintergrund der Gnadenpredigt bildet".

[17] See especially Rom. 2.14-16; 2.25-29 (Cranfield, *Romans*, 1:152-62).

[18] L. Mattern, *Das Verständnis des Gerichtes bei Paulus*, Zürich 1966.

[19] See Mattern, *Verständnis*, pp. 137-38 n. 377.

[20] Mattern, *Verständnis*, p. 137.

I believe there are a number of problems with such an approach. First, I believe she ignores the turning point in Paul's argument at 3.21. Second, she adopts a reformed view that works are the sign of election.[21]

Von einem eigentlichen *Gericht* über Christen aber spricht Paulus hier nicht; Rö 2 prüft nur, ob der Glaube wirklich Glaube und nicht vielmehr fromme Illusion ist.[22]

Is not the *ultimate* sign of election for Paul confession of faith?[23] I will return to this question in the final chapter.

10. Snodgrass argues that Romans 2 is an integral part of Paul's theology describing the circumstances before the coming of the gospel. He stresses, however, that the gospel did not reverse or negate "the basic structure of what precedes".[24] The basic problem of Snodgrass' approach is that he fails to understand the theme of 1.18-3.20 (see the discussion of the theme of 1.18-3.20 in chapter 1 above).

I believe a number of these approaches have important insights. My own approach is that Romans 2 describes an actual judgement (through Jesus Christ according to the gospel entrusted to Paul). Although the judgement of Romans 2 is a judgement which according to Paul will actually take place, there are nevertheless two hypothetical elements in the argument. First, it is assumed that there are some pious Gentiles (2.14-16, 25-29) and Jews (2.7-10). Second, nothing is said in the section 1.18-3.20 that Christians will be saved from this judgement.

In the exegesis of Romans 2 it is essential to keep in mind the theme of 1.18-3.20. I turn now to a study of Rom. 2.1-16.

---

[21] On this issue see the discussion "Romans 2 and the Question of Christian Obedience" in the concluding chapter below.

[22] Mattern, *Verständnis*, p. 138.

[23] Rom. 10.9 immediately comes to mind. See also 1 Thes. 5.9-10 and the article of M. Lautenschlager, "Εἴτε γρηγορῶμεν εἴτε καθεύδωμεν: Zum Verhältnis von Heiligung und Heil in 1 Thess 5,10", *ZNW* 81 (1990) 39-59.

[24] Snodgrass, "Romans 2", 81.

2. Introduction to Romans 2.1-16

In the previous chapter I claimed that the theme of 1.18-3.20 was: "All, Jews and Gentiles, will be condemned on the day of judgement thereby demonstrating the necessity of the revelation of the righteousness of God from faith to faith". Having demonstrated in 1.19-32 that human beings suppress the truth in unrighteousness Paul argues in Rom. 2.1-16 that all will be judged according to their works and not even the one who thinks he is righteous has an excuse before God's judgement.

But who is addressed in 2.1 and the subsequent 15 verses? A common view is that Paul turns to the Jew in 2.1: Διὸ ἀναπολόγητος εἶ, ὦ ἄνθρωπε πᾶς ὁ κρίνων· ἐν ᾧ γὰρ κρίνεις τὸν ἕτερον, σεαυτὸν κατακρίνεις, τὰ γὰρ αὐτὰ πράσσεις ὁ κρίνων. It is argued that as in Am. 1.3-2.3 Paul has first addressed the Gentiles (Rom. 1.18-32). Paul has described the ways in which the Gentiles have suppressed the truth.[25] Then in 2.1[26] he turns to the Jew to show he is just as guilty.[27] Although Paul does not explicitly refer to the Jew until 2.17 it is argued that in 2.1 he already has the Jew alone in mind. An alternative view is that Rom. 2.1-16 addresses both Jews and Gentiles and that the Jew is not singled out until 2.17.[28] I consider this second view to be the most probable. The

---

[25] Cf. Am. 1.3:

כֹּה אָמַר יְהוָה
עַל־שְׁלֹשָׁה פִּשְׁעֵי דַמֶּשֶׂק וְעַל־אַרְבָּעָה לֹא אֲשִׁיבֶנּוּ
עַל־דּוּשָׁם בַּחֲרֻצוֹת הַבַּרְזֶל אֶת־הַגִּלְעָד:

[26] Cf. Am. 2.4:

כֹּה אָמַר יְהוָה
עַל־שְׁלֹשָׁה פִּשְׁעֵי יְהוּדָה וְעַל־אַרְבָּעָה לֹא אֲשִׁיבֶנּוּ
עַל־מָאֳסָם אֶת־תּוֹרַת יְהוָה וְחֻקָּיו לֹא שָׁמָרוּ
וַיַּתְעוּם כִּזְבֵיהֶם אֲשֶׁר־הָלְכוּ אֲבוֹתָם אַחֲרֵיהֶם:

[27] See Dodd, *Romans*, p. 30 (2.1-3.20 entitled "Sin and Retribution in the Jewish World"); Boylan, *Romans*, p. 33; Schlier, *Römerbrief*, p. 66 (2.1-3.20 entitled "Gottes Gericht über die Juden"); Nygren, *Romans*, p. 113.

[28] See Leenhardt, *Romans*, p. 74. Note that although Michel, *Römer*, p. 113, believes that Paul refers to the "'Mensch' schlechthin" in 2.1, he then writes: "Wenn Paulus sich an jeden, der 'richtet', wendet (κρίνειν heißt 'richten' im aburteilenden Sinn), dann denkt er vor allem an das jüdische Selbstbewußtsein, das sich jede Gleichstellung mit dem Heiden in der Schuldfrage verbittet".

language of 2.1-16 appears quite general. Paul addresses his hearer as ὦ ἄνθρωπε (vv. 1, 3) which specifies neither Jew nor Gentile. Also, if 2.1ff were to concern just the Jew, the argument in 2.17ff, where the Jew is specifically mentioned, would seem to duplicate Paul's argument in 2.1ff. In 2.1ff Paul is referring to any person who thinks he is doing the right. In the discussion on the addressees in Rom. 1.18-32 I argued that the force of διό in Rom. 2.1 is not rhetorical but is to be understood in its full consecutive sense. The logic of the section then is that Rom. 1.18-32, which concerns the sin of Jew and Gentile, is continued in Rom. 2.1ff by addressing those self-righteous Jews and Gentiles, who believe the comments of Rom. 1.18-32 do not apply to them. We see again that the ideas of Rom. 1.18 are developed in Rom. 1.19-2.16.[29]

There are two possible objections to the view that 2.1ff concerns Jews and Gentiles. First, it could be said that Rom. 2.17 seems to assume Paul has already been addressing the Jew. But this problem can be overcome by saying that 2.1-16 is about the Gentile *and the Jew*. A second objection is that the comments in Rom. 2.4-5 appear to refer to God's covenant relationship with Israel. Is it not precisely Israel who God wishes to lead to repentance? The answer, perhaps surprisingly, is no. This should be absolutely clear by the reference in both verses 9 and 10 "to the Jew first and to the Greek".

3. Romans 2.1-4: The Self-Righteous Judge

The διό of 2.1 refers back to the whole section 1.18-32.[30] Paul refers to every self-righteous person who agrees with the charges brought against

---

[29] See chapter 2 section 2 above.

[30] The particle διό is not a "farblose Übergangspartikel" as Lietzmann, *Römer*, p. 39, suggests. Further, it is not necessary to explain v.1 as a gloss (R. Bultmann, "Glossen im Römerbrief", in *Exegetica: Aufsätze zur Erforschung des Neuen Testaments*, Tübingen 1967, 281 (278-84), who argues that v.1 originally stood after v.3). There are no text critical reasons for such a suggestion. As Wilckens, *Römer*, 1:123, has pointed out, v. 3 assumes v. 1 and διό "muß auf 1,18-32 insgesamt zurückbezogen sein". It is true that there is a break in the train of thought from 1.32 to 2.1 and Bultmann's solution makes a smoother argument. However, as G. Bornkamm, "Gesetz und Natur: Röm 2₁₄₋₁₆", in *Studien zu Antike und Urchristentum*, München 1970, 95 n. 4 (93-118) argues: "Doch scheint mir der Bruch dieses

those of 1.18-32. Paul uses the second person singular which, as Cranfield points out, is characteristic of, but not peculiar to, the Hellenistic diatribe and is here used for the sake of vividness.[31] Having demonstrated that blatant sinners are guilty before God, Paul argues in 2.1 that the self-righteous Jew and Gentile is without excuse also, for in judging others he condemns himself (cf. 2 Sam. 12.7: "You are the man"). In v. 2 Paul puts forward the common ground between himself and the representative self-righteous judge:[32] οἴδαμεν δὲ ὅτι τὸ κρίμα τοῦ θεοῦ ἐστιν κατὰ ἀλήθειαν ἐπὶ τοὺς τὰ τοιαῦτα πράσσοντας. The idea here is remarkably similar to that in Mt. 7.1-2 and may point to common tradition.[33] Rom. 2.3 is then closely connected to 2.1-2 (λογίζῃ δὲ τοῦτο, ὦ ἄνθρωπε ὁ κρίνων τοὺς τὰ τοιαῦτα πράσσοντας καὶ ποιῶν αὐτά, ὅτι σὺ ἐκφεύξῃ τὸ κρίμα τοῦ θεοῦ;).[34] In vv. 1-3 Paul is attacking the self-righteous person

---

Gedankengangs gerade zu Absicht und Stil der Sätze zu gehören". Lagrange, *Romains*, p. 42, rightly remarks: "Il est certain que le début du chap. II est fort abrupt. Mais le hiatus entre I,32 et II,1 s'explique précisément parce que Paul passe d'un sujet à un autre". A. Fridrichsen's suggested reading of δίς instead of δίο seems unnecessary ("Der wahre Jude und sein Lob", *Symbolae Arctoae* 1 (1927) 40 (39-49)) so giving the translation "*Doppelt* unentschuldbar bist du, o Mensch . . .!" I believe δίο refers back to the whole section 1.18-32. Less likely is the view of Pohlenz, "Paulus und die Stoa", 527, who writes that when Paul uses διό in Rom. 2.1 "knüpft er an die Worte τὸ δικαίωμα τοῦ θεοῦ ἐπιγνόντες (1₃₂) an, die freilich dem Gedanken von 2₁₄ vorgreifen". As pointed out above διό has full consecutive force.

[31] Cranfield, *Romans*, 1:142.

[32] Cf. Cranfield, *Romans*, 1:143 (against Dodd, *Romans*, p. 32).

[33] Berger, *Exegese*, p. 227.

[34] It has been argued that this may echo Wis. 15.2a: καὶ γὰρ ἐὰν ἁμάρτωμεν, σοί ἐσμεν, εἰδότες σου τὸ κράτος. However, the parallel breaks down to some extent when Wis. 15.2b is also considered: οὐχ ἁμαρτησόμεθα δέ, εἰδότες ὅτι σοὶ λελογίσμεθα. One problem of A. Nygren's discussion of the parallels between Rom. 2.1-6 and Wis. 11-15 (*Romans*, pp. 113-17) is that he assumes that the righteous = "Israel" and the unrighteous = "Gentiles" in the book of Wisdom and that he assumes Rom. 2.1ff concerns only the Jew. However, in Wis. 1-5 apostate Jews also belong to the ungodly (see Wis. 1.16-2.20 and G. Siegfried, "Wisdom, Book of", *HDB*, 4:929 (928-31)). In fact the conclusion of J.P. Weisengoff, "The Impious of Wisdom 2", *CBQ* 11 (1949) 64-65 (40-65), is that the "view according to which the 'impious' are identified primarily with apostate Jews but with their pagan associates not excluded, rests on solid foundations".

(cf. Jesus' attack on the Pharisees in Mt. 23.1-36), arguing that although he may think he is righteous, he is in fact no better than those described in 1.18-32.[35] In 2.4 Paul brings in another argument: ἢ τοῦ πλούτου τῆς χρηστότητος αὐτοῦ καὶ τῆς ἀνοχῆς καὶ τῆς μακροθυμίας καταφρονεῖς, ἀγνοῶν ὅτι τὸ χρηστὸν τοῦ θεοῦ εἰς μετάνοιάν σε ἄγει;[36] Related to this self-righteousness attitude is the assumption that one will be exempt from the judgement of God.

It is striking to compare 1.32 to 2.1-3. In 1.32 people do things they know to be wrong and approve of others who do them; in 2.1-3 people do what they know to be wrong and condemn others.[37]

4. Romans 2.5-6: The Coming Wrath

In 2.5 Paul warns that on account of the hardness and unrepentant heart (κατὰ δὲ τὴν σκληρότητά σου καὶ ἀμετανόητον καρδίαν) the addressee is storing up wrath in the day of wrath when God's righteous judgement will be revealed. Paul clearly shares the view of the apocalypses that there is a chance of repentance but only up until the eschatological judgement.[38] This then raises the interesting question whether Paul believed that perfect obedience of the law[39] was necessary for acquittal at the final judgement. This issue will arise in the discussion of Rom. 2.12-13 and will be addressed again in the concluding chapter. V. 6 clearly shows that Paul is working with an assumption of judgement according to works which

---

[35] Note that Lightfoot, *Notes*, p. 258, believes the parable of the Pharisee and the Publican "is the best commentary on this whole section" (2.1-29). However, one does not necessarily have to support Lightfoot in the belief that the Jew is addressed in 2.1ff. Leenhardt, *Romans*, p. 74, writes that "the Pharisee is always present in each one of us". Note also that G. Meyer, *Der Römerbrief*, Gütersloh 1913, p. 32, entitles the section 2.1-11 "Selbstgerechtigkeit".

[36] Again, compare Wis. 15, this time v.1 (Σὺ δέ, ὁ θεὸς ἡμῶν, χρηστὸς καὶ ἀληθής, μακρόθυμος καὶ ἐλέει διοικῶν τὰ πάντα).

[37] J.R.W. Stott, *Romans*, Leicester 1994, p. 81.

[38] See 2 Bar. 85.12; 1 En. 50.4.

[39] Although Paul does not mention the law in Rom. 2.1-11, it becomes clear in 2.12-16 that obedience is to be measured according to whether the law is kept.

implies a justification according to works (cf. 2.13). Paul is quoting from Ps. 61.13 LXX (or possibly from Prov. 24.12).[40]

5. Romans 2.7-11: Two Possible Outcomes

Rom. 2.7-11 picks up the idea of ἑκάστῳ in v. 6. There is a remarkable double chiasmus in vv. 7-10. First v. 7 corresponds to v. 10 in speaking of the reward (+) and v. 8 corresponds to v. 9 in speaking of the punishment (-). Then 7a and 10b refer to human action (h) and 7b and 10a God's reaction (r) and then 8a and 9b refer to human action (h) and 8b and 9a to God's reaction (r). We end up with the following pattern: + h + r (v. 7); - h - r (v. 8); - r - h (v. 9); + r + h (v. 10).[41] The function of this chiasmus is simply to stress the two possible outcomes of judgement according to works.[42]

---

[40] See also other Old Testament texts such as Jer. 17.10. R. Heiligenthal, *Werke als Zeichen*, Tübingen 1983, pp. 172-74, gives a list of parallels from the Pseudepigrapha and early Christian literature. He concludes: "Aufgrund dieser ausgeprägten semantischen Stabilität erscheint ein direktes Zitat aus Ψ 61,13 durch Paulus unwahrscheinlich. Wahrscheinlicher ist, daß Paulus innerhalb einer breiten Überlieferungstradition der Vergeltungsaussagen steht". If the quotation is from Ps. 61.13 LXX, Paul has clearly changed the idea of the righteous Psalmist being vindicated through judgement on his enemies (ὅτι τὸ κράτος τοῦ θεοῦ, καὶ σοί, κύριε, τὸ ἔλεος, ὅτι σὺ ἀποδώσεις ἑκάστῳ κατὰ τὰ ἔργα αὐτοῦ) to the idea of the threat of judgement against every Jew and Gentile.

[41] See O. Kuss, *Der Römerbrief*, Regensburg 1:1957; 2:1959; 3:1978, 1:65. See also the earlier work of E. von Dobschütz, "Zum Wortschatz und Stil des Römerbriefs", *ZNW* 33 (1934) 60 (51-66), and J. Jeremias "Chiasmus in den Paulusbriefen", *ZNW* 49 (1958) 149 (145-56).

[42] E. Jüngel, "Ein paulinischer Chiasmus; Zum Verständnis der Vorstellung vom Gericht nach den Werken in Röm 2,2-11", *Unterwegs zur Sache: Theologische Bemerkungen*, München ²1988, (¹1972), 173-78, makes a number of incisive comments regarding the relationship of judgement according to works and justification by faith. However, I believe he is reading too much into the chiasmus here when he sees Paul speaking of judgement under law in vv. 7-8 but under grace in vv. 9-10. See his conclusion, "Chiasmus", 178: "Der formale doppelte Chiasmus in der Rede vom Gericht nach den Werken in Röm 2,7-10 ist also sachlich bedingt durch den theologischen 'Chiasmus' von Gesetz und Evangelium, der die ganze Erörterung seit Röm 1,16f bis Röm 3,21ff hin bestimmt. Es gibt wohl keinen sinnvolleren Chiasmus, dessen formale Eigenart — Umkehrung durch Überkreuzung — hier die Sache selbst zur Sprache bringt: das Kreuz als Kehre".

What does Paul mean by ἔργον ἀγαθόν in 2.7? Does he mean a fulfilling of the law or a life as an expression of faith? Cranfield prefers the latter and points out that Paul speaks not of *deserving* but *seeking* glory, honour and immortality.[43] Travis also believes Paul is referring to the Christian. He points to the use of the singular ἔργον (v. 7), τὸ ἀγαθόν (v. 10) and conversely τὸ κακόν in v. 9. Paul is then concerned with "the summary of a person's character, a description of the direction of his life".[44] Further, terms like τὸ ἀγαθόν and τὸ κακόν are "*religious* terms, not merely ethical ones".[45] But it is mistake to go from there to argue that as only Christians are those who can "do good", Paul must be referring to Christians here. I can see nothing in the text to suggest Paul is speaking of the outworking of Christian faith. He must, I believe, be referring to fulfilling the law. This is suggested by the following verses, 2.12-16, which will be studied in some detail in the next two sections.

In 2.8 we have the combination of words ὀργὴ καὶ θυμός which is probably taken from the Old Testament.[46] Such Old Testament texts which use this combination certainly suggest God's wrath is an emotion of God.[47] In the NT ὀργή is nearly always used. Hollander writes that "While in the LXX the original distinction between θυμός as emotion and ὀργή as expression of emotion is almost totally lost, in later Judaism and in the NT an undeniable hesitation exists in associating θυμός — contrary to ὀργή — with God (in the NT only in Rom 2:8 and in Revelation), probably because of the primarily emotional connotations of the word θυμός".[48] His judgement seems sound. The word θυμός is avoided in con-

---

[43] So Cranfield, *Romans*, 1:147, writes that the most likely reference of ἔργον ἀγαθόν is "to goodness of life, not however as meriting God's favour but as the expression of faith".

[44] S.H. Travis, *Christ and the Judgment of God*, Basingstoke 1986, p. 59.

[45] Travis, *Judgment*, p. 60.

[46] See Dt. 9.19a: καὶ ἔκφοβός εἰμι διὰ τὴν ὀργὴν καὶ τὸν θυμόν, ὅτι παρωξύνθη κύριος ἐφ᾽ ὑμῖν ἐξολεθρεῦσαι ὑμᾶς· Cf. Ps. 2.5; Hos. 13.11.

[47] Wetter, *Vergeltungsgedanke*, p. 16, points out that in LXX ὀργή translates 15 Hebrew words and θυμός more than 20 words. It is striking to see the range of Hebrew words used for anger (see E. Hatch and H.A. Redpath, *A Concordance to the Septuagint*, 2 vols, Grand Rapids 1983 (repr.), (¹1897)).

[48] H.W. Hollander, θυμός, *EDNT*, 2:160 (159-60). Contrast F. Büschel, θυμός κτλ, *TDNT* 3:168 (167-72), who writes that "there is no material difference" between ὀργή and θυμός in the New Testament.

nection with God by both Philo and Josephus[49] and, as Hollander notes, outside Revelation Rom. 2.8 is the only place in the NT where θυμός is used of the wrath of God. Elsewhere in Paul the use of θυμός (for people) is included in catalogues of vices (2 Cor. 12.20; Gal. 5.20; cf. Eph. 4.31; Col. 3.8). I conclude that in Rom. 2.8 θυμός probably does signify an emotion of God (cf. his jealousy). However, this is the *only instance* in the letters of Paul where God's wrath is expressed as an emotion and it is unwise, as Godet has done, to use this use of θυμός to bolster an argument that God's wrath is a feeling.[50]

In vv. 9-10 there is a basic repetition of vv. 7-8 but in the reverse order. In v. 9 two new words in Romans describing the fate of sinners are used: θλῖψις καὶ στενοχωρία. Although they are used in the LXX, they refer there to punishment experienced in this life.[51] Paul applies the words in v. 9 to the eschaton. Such anguish and distress will come ἐπὶ πᾶσαν ψυχὴν ἀνθρώπου τοῦ κατεργαζομένου τὸ κακόν, Ἰουδαίου τε πρῶτον καὶ Ἕλληνος. Note also the mention in v. 10 of παντὶ τῷ ἐργαζομένῳ τὸ ἀγαθόν, Ἰουδαίῳ τε πρῶτον καὶ Ἕλληνι. Paul then appropriately finishes this section by concluding that there is no partiality in God.[52] This theme is obviously important but it would be a mistake to see it as the main governing principle in this section of Romans. Bassler goes to the extreme of saying "Rom. 2:11 emerges clearly as the pivotal point in the argument, summarizing 1:16-2.10 and introducing 2:12-29".[53] Apart

---

[49] See Hanson, *Wrath*, pp. 57, 65, 87.

[50] See Godet, *Romans*, p. 102, who writes: "Ritschl will not recognize an inward *feeling* in the wrath of God, but merely an outward *act*, a *judgment*. But why in this case does Paul use the word *wrath*, to which he even adds, ii.8, the term θυμός, *indignation*, which denotes the *feeling* at its deepest?" On the issue of the wrath of God see the discussion in chapter 2 on Rom. 1.18.

[51] See the use of this pair of words in Dt. 28.53, 55, 57; Is. 8.22; 30.6.

[52] The word προσωπολημψία is based on the septuagintal πρόσωπον λαμβάνειν (Hebrew פָּנִים נָשָׂא). A number of texts in the Old Testament make it clear that God shows no favouritism (e.g. Dt. 10.17; 2 Kgs 3.14; Ps. 82.2 (81.2); see also Sir. 35.12-13; Ps. Sol. 2.18). Paul therefore applies this idea to the specific issue of Jews and Gentiles.

[53] Bassler, "Divine Impartiality", 45.

from some of her questionable analysis of the text,[54] I do not believe impartiality is the main theme in Rom. 1-4; as I argued in chapter 1, divine impartiality is logically dependent on justification.

6. Romans 2.12-13: Justification by Doing the Law

Rom. 2.12-16 forms a unit[55] and I begin by considering 2.12-13. Paul relates the judgement according to works to the question of the possession and doing of the law. Paul asserts in vv. 12-13 that future justification (i.e. acquittal at the final judgement) is not according to whether one possesses the law or not. Even the Jew who sins will be judged through the law. Justification does not depend on whether one *possesses* the law but on whether one *does* the law (οὐ γὰρ οἱ ἀκροαταὶ νόμου δίκαιοι παρὰ [τῷ] θεῷ, ἀλλ' οἱ ποιηταὶ νόμου δικαιωθήσονται, Rom. 2.13).[56] Further, doing the law involves a complete obedience. V. 12 asserts that anyone

---

[54] See for example the analysis of 1.16-2.10 as a unit and the proposed ring structure of these verses ("Divine Impartiality", 47). There are a number of problems with such an analysis, one of which is confusing the σωτηρία through the gospel of 1.16 with the promise of δόξα καὶ τιμὴ καὶ εἰρήνη to those who work the good of 2.10. I believe the suggestion I made above that the unit is 1.18-2.16 (and 1.18-3.20) is more convincing.

[55] This goes against the judgement of Pohlenz, "Paulus und die Stoa", 528, who views vv. 11-14 as a chain: "Die vier Sätze in v. 11-14 werden alle durch γὰρ eingeleitet; sie sind also die Glieder einer Kette, von denen eins immer durch das folgende begründet oder erläutert wird". He adds: "Der ganze Gedankengang bringt aber die Ausführung der These von 2₆ ἀποδώσει ἑκάστῳ κατὰ τὰ ἔργα αὐτοῦ mit spezieller Aufteilung auf die Juden und Heiden, die durch den Begriff des Gesetzes nötig wird". Note also that Luther in the 1546 German bible takes 2.11 with 2.12-16 and not with 2.5-10. I believe that 2.11 belongs more to 2.7-10 especially in view of the theme of the impartiality of God (compare Ἰουδαίῳ τε πρῶτον καὶ Ἕλληνι (2.10b) with οὐ γάρ ἐστιν προσωπολημψία παρὰ τῷ θεῷ (2.11)). Note also that 2.6 and 2.11 bracket the complex chiasmus in 2.7-10.

[56] Paul is not attacking a Jewish view that studying is more important than doing the torah (as Dodd, *Romans*, pp. 34-35 suggests). The whole idea of studying the law was in fact to do it. To the question whether studying or practice is more important, R. Akiba said "Study is greater, for it leads to practice" (b. Kid. 40b, Soncino, p. 202). See also Hengel, *Judaism and Hellenism*, 1:173: ". . . only on the basis of constant study (of the Torah) was it possible to observe the commandments correctly".

who sins, Jew or Gentile, will be condemned. In v. 13 the expression οἱ ποιηταὶ νόμου refers to those who keep the whole law.[57] Doers of the law are, to use the language of the Isaiah Targum, those who do not sin (7.3; 10.21-22) and so are "righteous people which have kept the law with a perfect heart" (26.2).[58] The demand for a perfect obedience in v. 13 corresponds exactly to Gal. 3.10[59] and Gal. 5.3[60]. One should add, though, that such perfect obedience in Romans 2, as in the Isaiah Targum, does include an element of repentance.[61]

7. Romans 2.14-16: Gentiles Judged according to their Law

Rom. 2.14-16 is especially difficult and will be tackled by asking six questions: 1. What is Paul trying to prove? 2. Is Paul referring to the present, the future, or both in these verses? 3. What is the relationship of 15b to 15c? 4. Who are the ἔθνη of 2.14? 5. What is the law which the Gentiles do? 6. What is the nature of the judgement in 2.16?

---

[57] Cf. F. Flückiger, "Die Werke des Gesetzes bei den Heiden (nach Rom. 2,14ff.)", *ThZ* 8 (1952) 28 (17-42): "Nur die Täter des Gesetzes werden gerechtgesprochen, womit nur das ganze Werk gemeint sein kann. Den gleichen Sinn hat auch das singularische τὸ ἔργον τοῦ νόμου in Vers 15. Ein bloß gelegentlicher Gehorsam ist eigentlich Ungehorsam und könnte unmöglich 'das Werk des Gesetzes' heißen". For the idea of doing the whole law see 4Q470 (לעשות ולהעשות את כל התורה) (referring to Zedekiah (see E. Larsson, L.H. Schiffman, J. Strugnell, "4Q470, Preliminary Publication of a Fragment Mentioning Zedekiah", *RevQ* 63.16 (1994) 335-36 (335-49))) and 4Q174 4.2 (4QFlor 2.2) (ועשו את כול התורה). I am grateful to Dr P.M. Casey for bringing these texts to my attention.

[58] Hofius, "Rechtfertigung des Gottlosen", 127 nn. 32, 33. The expression οἱ ποιηταὶ νόμου (which occurs only in 1 Mac. 2.67 in LXX) is equivalent to the Aramaic עבדי אוריתא (Targ. Is. 4.2; 5.20; 9.6; 13.12; 31.9; 42.21; 53.10) and the Hebrew עושי התורה (1QpHab 7.11; 8.1; 12.4-5).

[59] Gal. 3.10: ὅσοι γὰρ ἐξ ἔργων νόμου εἰσίν, ὑπὸ κατάραν εἰσίν· γέγραπται γὰρ ὅτι Ἐπικατάρατος πᾶς ὃς οὐκ ἐμμένει πᾶσιν τοῖς γεγραμμένοις ἐν τῷ βιβλίῳ τοῦ νόμου τοῦ ποιῆσαι αὐτά. The quotation is from Dt. 27.26 (cf. Dt. 28.58).

[60] Gal. 5.3: μαρτύρομαι δὲ πάλιν παντὶ ἀνθρώπῳ περιτεμνομένῳ ὅτι ὀφειλέτης ἐστὶν ὅλον τὸν νόμον ποιῆσαι.

[61] Repentance, as we have seen, is briefly mentioned in Rom. 2.4. See also Targ. Is. 7.3 (and 10.21-22) which together with "the remnant that have not sinned" (שאר דלא חטו) mentions "they that have turned from sin" (דתבו מחטאה). This is discussed further in the conclusion to this chapter below.

1. So first, what is Paul trying to prove? According to Bultmann,

... V. 14 und V. 15 gehören zusammen als der Beweis dafür, daß Gottes Gericht dereinst mit vollem Recht auch über diejenigen ergehen wird, die ἀνόμως (dh ohne das Mosegesetz) gesündigt haben.[62]

In view of 2.12-13 there is certainly something in this. Also Paul has to show that the Gentiles have their own law by which they will be judged.[63] Although he has already shown in 1.18-32 that the Gentiles deserve death, he has not explicitly explained the criteria by which the Gentiles will be judged. In fact ἀνόμως in 2.12 is used in a relative sense for in vv. 14-15 Paul argues that Gentiles do in fact have a law and vv. 14-15 act as a correction to v. 12.[64] That Paul is concerned with the condemnation (or possible acquittal) of the Gentiles is also suggested by 2.15-16 (οἵτινες ἐνδείκνυνται τὸ ἔργον τοῦ νόμου γραπτὸν ἐν ταῖς καρδίαις αὐτῶν, συμμαρτυρούσης αὐτῶν τῆς συνειδήσεως καὶ μεταξὺ ἀλλήλων τῶν λογισμῶν κατηγορούντων ἢ καὶ ἀπολογουμένων, ἐν ἡμέρᾳ ὅτε κρίνει ὁ θεὸς τὰ κρυπτὰ τῶν ἀνθρώπων κατὰ τὸ εὐαγγέλιόν μου διὰ Χριστοῦ Ἰησοῦ). Eckstein rejects this, believing that Paul is concerned with the "Tun" in 2.14-15 and not with the "Verurteilung".[65] Although I am indebted to Eckstein's fine study, I find this particular point unsatisfactory, for v. 15 (and v. 16) are clearly concerned with the possible condemnation of the Gentiles.

Therefore I believe Paul is establishing in vv. 14-16 that Gentiles also have a law by which they will be judged and this judgement will be through Jesus Christ. The law will condemn those Gentiles who are not "doers of the law".[66]

---

[62] Bultmann, "Glossen", 282. Bultmann, as we shall see, regards 2.16 as a gloss.

[63] Althaus, *Römer*, p. 25, argues that the issue in 2.14 is: "Aber kann der Heide je 'Täter des Gesetzes' sein? Fehlt ihm nicht dazu eben das Gesetz?" This question would naturally arise in view of v. 13 (οὐ γὰρ οἱ ἀκροαταὶ νόμου δίκαιοι παρὰ [τῷ] θεῷ, ἀλλ᾽ οἱ ποιηταὶ νόμου δικαιωθήσονται). Lietzmann, *Römer*, p. 41, has a similar view. He suggests that vv. 14-15 show "Nichts anders, als daß die Heiden das Gesetz kennen".

[64] Bornkamm, "Gesetz und Natur", 100; Jüngel, *Paulus und Jesus*, p. 27.

[65] H.-J. Eckstein, *Der Begriff Syneidesis bei Paulus*, Tübingen 1983, p. 145.

[66] E. Jüngel, "Das Gesetz zwischen Adam und Christus", in *Unterwegs zur Sache*, München ²1988, (¹1972), 155 (145-72), writes: "Allein in der Bezogenheit auf den

2. I turn now to the question of present and future in these verses. Commenting on 2.14-16 Eichholz writes

Das besondere Problem unserer Verse besteht in der Frage, wie sich die *präsentischen und futurischen Aussagen* in ihnen miteinander verbinden lassen.[67]

I consider five possibilities:

i. The first is to take vv. 14-15 as present and v. 16 as future. If this is done the move to v. 16 is extremely hard and it is then necessary to insert something. Althaus inserts the words "wie sich zeigen wird" between 2.15 and 2.16.[68] Pohlenz[69] suggests inserting something with the sense καὶ δικαιωθήσονται (in view of 3.9-20 perhaps καὶ κατακριθήσονται would be more appropriate!). The other possibility is to view vv. 14-15 as a parenthesis and link v. 16 back to v. 13.[70] This, however, would seem rather clumsy and is to be rejected.[71]

ii. The second solution is to take vv. 14-15 and v. 16 as future.[72] In this case the problem in relating the two is eased. However, it seems very unlikely that Paul is referring to the future in v. 14 (see below).

iii. The third solution is to take v. 14 as present but then understand ἐνδείκνυνται in v. 15 as a future present and relate this to ἐν ἡμέρᾳ ὅτε in v. 16. This means that vv. 15-16 are taken as future.

iv. The fourth solution is to take vv. 14-15 and 16 as both referring to the present.[73] However, I believe that v. 16 clearly points to the final judgement (see below).

v. The fifth solution is that vv. 14-15b are present and vv. 15c-16 future. The future understanding then comes with καὶ μεταξὺ ἀλλήλων

Nomos wird der Mensch als Sünder anklagbar. Deshalb mußte die Geltung des Gesetzes *für alle* Menschen erwiesen werden" (Jüngel's emphasis).

[67] Eichholz, *Theologie des Paulus*, p. 92 (Eichholz' emphasis).

[68] Althaus, *Römer*, p. 20. See also: Kuss, *Römerbrief*, 1:68, who inserts "das wird sich alles einmal erweisen"; Michel, *Römer*, p. 126, who translates 2.16 as "dieser verborgene Tatbestand wird am Tage des Gerichts aufgedeckt, nämlich dann, wenn Gott die Verborgenheit der Menschen richten wird, wie ich es in meinem Evangelium durch Jesus Christus verkündige"; Schlier, *Römerbrief*, p. 81.

[69] Pohlenz, "Paulus und die Stoa", 535.

[70] See, for example, J. Ziesler, *Paul's letter to the Romans*, London 1989, p. 88.

[71] Pohlenz, "Paulus und die Stoa", 534.

[72] This seems to be the solution of Eichholz, *Theologie des Paulus*, pp. 92-93.

[73] B. Reicke, "Syneidesis in Röm. 2,15", *ThZ* 12 (1956) 161 (157-61).

τῶν λογισμῶν κατηγορούντων ἢ καὶ ἀπολογουμένων . . . (these genitive absolutes are then related to κρίνει of v. 16 rather than to ἐνδείκνυνται of v. 15).[74]

Of these possibilities I believe (v) is the strongest. One reason is that v. 15c is best related to v. 16 rather than to v. 15b (see the next section) thereby forming a smooth transition between v. 15 and v. 16. I will now discuss the time aspect of the three verses in the order v. 14, v. 16 and v. 15 (v. 15 being the most difficult).

I believe that 2.14 must refer to the present. This is clear from the very first word, ὅταν. One possible meaning is "wenn einmal",[75] and Godet understands ὅταν to mean "when it happens that", commenting: "These are sporadic cases, happy eventualities".[76] More likely though is the view of Bauer-Aland (col. 1190), that ὅταν with the subjunctive means "dann, wann, wenn", "wobei ὅταν in seiner Bedeutung oft nahe an ἐάν heranrückt, indem die Zeitangabe zugleich die Bedingung bezeichnet, unter der die Handlung des Hauptsatzes stattfindet". γάρ in 2.14 probably means "for" rather than "namely"[77] and in view of the doubt expressed whether Gentiles are "doers of the law" (see κατηγορούντων ἢ καὶ ἀπολογουμένων in v. 15c) this conjunction probably links v. 14 to both vv. 12 and 13.

As regards v. 16 it is most natural to take this as a reference to the final day of judgement. It is on this day that God will judge the secrets of men through Jesus Christ according to Paul's gospel. Although in Nestle the verb has a present form κρίνει (a future accentuation κρινεῖ is also possible) I believe the verb has a future meaning.[78] The judgement just a few verses earlier is also future (2.12-13) as is also the case in 2.5.

---

[74] See the NRSV of vv. 15-16: "They show that what the law requires is written on their hearts, to which their own conscience also bears witness; and their conflicting thoughts will accuse or perhaps excuse them 16 on the day when, according to my gospel, God, through Jesus Christ, will judge the secret thoughts of all".

[75] R. Steinmetz, *Das Gewissen bei Paulus*, Berlin 1911, p. 24.

[76] Godet, *Romans*, p. 123.

[77] H. Menge, *Die Heilige Schrift*, Stuttgart 1949, translates γάρ with "nämlich".

[78] Reicke, "Syneidesis", 161, believes the reference in 2.16 is to the missionary preaching. He rejects a reference to the final judgement because of the present form of the verb κρίνει but does not even consider the possibility of a future present. Concerning 2.14-16 he writes: "Sprachlich und sachlich gut begreiflich aber wird der

The major difficulty arises in 2.15. The understanding of the present and future here depends on how the structure of the verse is understood. This is discussed in the next section and I anticipate some of the conclusions of that section. 2.15a is most likely present as is 2.15b which is dependent upon 15a. 15c, however, can be related either to 15ab or 16. If it is related to the future judgement of v. 16 it provides an excellent bridge between 15ab and 16.

I now turn to the relationship of 15b to 15c.

3. Rom. 2.15 can be set out as follows:

(a) οἵτινες ἐνδείκνυνται

τὸ ἔργον τοῦ νόμου γραπτὸν ἐν ταῖς καρδίαις αὐτῶν,

(b) συμμαρτυρούσης αὐτῶν τῆς συνειδήσεως

(c) καὶ μεταξὺ ἀλλήλων τῶν λογισμῶν κατηγορούντων ἢ καὶ ἀπολογουμένων,

The terms ἐνδείκνυνται and συμμαρτυρούσης are to be understood in a forensic sense. In v. 15a Paul speaks of the witness of the Gentiles themselves who have the "work of the law" written on their hearts. Then in v. 15bc there are genitive absolutes and they can be related in a number of different ways.

i. One possibility is to take the first καί in v. 15c as epexegetic. Rom. 2.15c would then explain how the conscience works.[79] The problem with such a solution is that for Paul the conscience does not seem to consist of conflicting thoughts.

ii. A second way of understanding the καί in v. 15c is to take v. 15c in coordination with v. 15b, καί linking two genitive absolutes in a chiastic

---

Satz, wenn man an den Zeitpunkt der Bekehrung der Heiden durch die paulinische Predigt denkt ('Tag' steht ja in der Bibel oft für 'Zeitpunkt'). Dann gewinnt der Ausdruck 'nach meinem Evangelium' einen vollen Sinn". I will return to Reicke's understanding in point 3.iv below. As far as the Versions are concerned, there are various interpretations of κρίνει: the Vulgate has a future (*in die cum iudicabit Deus . . .*), the Old Latin has a perfect (*in die cum iudicavit deus . . .*), and the Peshitta has a present participle (d'n).

[79] J. Stelzenberger, *Syneidesis im Neuen Testament*, Paderborn 1961, pp. 80-81, commenting on v. 15c writes: "Hier wird eine Umschreibung der Funktion des Gewissens gegeben". See also H. Ridderbos, *Paul: An Outline of His Theology* ET, London 1977, p. 288.

arrangement, the participles in v. 15c being understood in a predicative sense. Eichholz, who adopts this, translates Rom. 2.15 as follows: "Sie weisen nach, daß das von der Tora geforderte Werk ihnen ins Herz geschrieben ist, wobei ihr Gewissen (Bewußtsein) Zeugnis ablegt und (ihre) Gedanken einander verklagen oder auch verteidigen".[80] Eckstein[81] rejects this as it wrongly understands the conscience as "Bezeugen" and not as "Bestätigung".[82]

iii. A third way is to take v. 15c again in coordination with v. 15b but being dependent on the participle συμμαρτυρούσης of v. 15b, the participles in v. 15c being understood as attributive. This is Eckstein's solution and he gives the translation ". . . Mitzeuge dafür sind ihr Gewissen und die Gedanken, die sich untereinander verklagen und entschuldigen".[83]

---

[80] Eichholz, *Theologie des Paulus*, 86.

[81] Eckstein, *Syneidesis*, p. 166.

[82] I believe that Eckstein is correct in understanding the συνείδησις as a "Bestätigung". See also Schlatter, *Gottes Gerechtigkeit*, pp. 92-93. Commenting on 2.15 and the parallel in 9.1 (συμμαρτυρούσης μοι τῆς συνειδήσεώς μου) he writes: "Hier entsteht kein Zweifel darüber, wessen Aussage durch das Gewissen bestätigt werde. Neben dem redenden Ich steht die συνείδησις als eine selbständige Größe, die sich nicht durch den Redenden beeinflußen läßt, und aus dem Verhältnis, in dem die Aussage des Gewissens zur Angabe des Sprechenden steht, ergibt sich die Wahrheit oder Unwahrheit seines Worts und das Recht oder Unrecht seines Anspruchs. Durch das göttliche Wirken wird die göttliche Schrift in das Herz des Menschen gelegt und erweckt sein Denken, Wollen und Handeln. Dieses geschieht aber im Licht des Bewußtseins; es wird von der συνείδησις wahrgenommen, gemessen und als richtig anerkannt, und dieses Wissen und Werten erhält sich unabhängig vom Willen des Menschen". Concerning the verb συμμαρτυρεῖν H. Strathmann, μάρτυς κτλ, *ThWNT* 4:515 (477-520) writes: "Es bedeutet zunächst '*mitbezeugen*, als Zeuge neben einem oder mehreren Zeugen etwas bezeugen oder bestätigen" (referring to *BGU* I.86, 40ff). For the meaning "bestätigen" see also H. Cremer, *Biblisch-Theologisches Wörterbuch des neutestamentlichen Griechisch* (bearb. von J. Kögel), Gotha [11]1923, pp. 720-21, and Bauer-Aland, col. 1553.

[83] Eckstein, *Syneidesis*, p. 166. Wilckens and Althaus analyse 15bc in a similar way: ". . ., wobei Zeugnis gibt ihr Gewissen und die gegenseitig einander anklagenden oder auch verteidigenden Gedanken" (Wilckens, *Römer*, 1:131); ". . . wovon auch ihr Gewissen Zeugnis ablegt und die Gedanken, die im Verkehr miteinander anklagen oder auch entschuldigen" (Althaus, *Römer*, p. 24).

iv. B. Reicke[84] takes τῶν λογισμῶν in v. 15c as an objective genitive to συνειδήσεως in v. 15b and understands συνείδησις as "Gefühl".[85] He then puts forward the interesting but I believe unconvincing translation of 15bc: ". . . was ihr Gefühl — auch untereinander — für die anklagenden, oder auch verteidigenden, Gedanken bestätigt".[86]

v. A fifth possibility is to take v. 15c with 16. The genitive absolutes of v. 15c (καὶ μεταξὺ ἀλλήλων τῶν λογισμῶν κατηγορούντων ἢ καὶ ἀπολογουμένων) are then related to the main verb in v. 16, κρίνει. If κρίνει is understood as a future, the accusing and excusing are also seen as future.[87] There is much to commend such a solution. It makes sense of the present and future in vv. 14-16, and provides a smooth transition between v. 15 and v. 16.

Of these various possibilities solutions (iii) and (v) are probably the best. If (iii) is adopted, we have three witnesses (cf. Dt. 19.15).[88] First, the Gentiles show the work of the law written on their heart. Second, there is the confirmation of the conscience. Then third the confirmation of the accusing or perhaps excusing thoughts.[89] However, I argued in section 2. that if solution (v) is adopted the transition from v. 15 to v. 16 is made smooth and coherent. I therefore opt for solution (v).

4. The fourth question concerns the identity of the ἔθνη of Rom. 2.14. A number of commentators suggest that they are Gentile Christians.[90]

---

[84] Reicke, "Syneidesis", 159.

[85] συνείδησις with an objective genitive then meaning "feeling for something".

[86] Reicke, "Syneidesis", 160. Erasmus (in R.D. Sider (ed.), *Annotations on Romans* (Collected Works of Erasmus 56), Toronto 1994, pp. 82-83) was critical of those who, on the basis of the Vulgate, related the genitive *cogitationum* to the preceding *conscientia* (the Vulgate of 2.15 is: *qui ostendunt opus legis scriptum in cordibus suis testimonium reddente illis conscientia ipsorum et inter se invicem cogitationum accusantium aut etiam defendentium*).

[87] Cf. NRSV.

[88] Kühl, *Römer*, p. 81; Lietzmann, *Römer*, p. 41; Bornkamm, "Gesetz und Natur", 111; Wilckens, *Römer*, 1:137.

[89] μεταξὺ ἀλλήλων is not to be understood in antithesis to the inner thoughts of v. 15ab (contra Schlatter, *Gerechtigkeit*, p. 93; Althaus, *Römer*, p. 22). Paul means here the thoughts of the individual person about himself, not thoughts between people.

[90] Reicke, "Syneidesis", and "Natürliche Theologie nach Paulus", *SEÅ* 22/23 (1957/58) 166 (154-67) has a related understanding. He believes Paul is speaking of the conversion of Gentiles. Concerning Rom. 2.15b, he writes: "Man möge einfach

Such an interpretation goes back to Ambrosiaster[91] and Augustine[92] and is defended by a number of scholars this century.[93] Cranfield connects φύσει with the preceding words and takes ἔθνη τὰ μὴ νόμον ἔχοντα φύσει to mean "Gentiles which do not possess the law by nature, i.e. by virtue of their birth".[94] An argument used to support the idea that Paul is referring to Gentile Christians is the use of γραπτὸν ἐν ταῖς καρδίαις αὐτῶν. Cranfield believes Paul has Jer. 31.33 deliberately in mind. He points to the verbal similarity (Jer. 38.33 LXX: δώσω νόμους μου εἰς τὴν διάνοιαν αὐτῶν καὶ ἐπὶ καρδίας αὐτῶν γράψω αὐτούς) and to the fact that Paul refers to this passage elsewhere (Cranfield mentions 1 Cor. 11.25; 2 Cor. 3.2, 3, 6, 14; 6.16).

There are five basic problems in taking ἔθνη to refer to Gentile Christians in Rom. 2.14. 1. The description ἀνόμως and τὰ μὴ νόμον ἔχοντα is impossible for Gentile Christians who are μὴ ὢν ἄνομος θεοῦ ἀλλ᾽ ἔννομος χριστοῦ (1 Cor. 9.21).[95] 2. Paul certainly could use ἔθνη to refer to Gentile Christians as opposed to Jews.[96] But in Romans 2 Paul contrasts Jews and Gentiles, not Jews and Gentile Christians (see Rom. 2.9-10; 2.12; 2.25-29). 3. The formulation or the idea that Gentile Christians fulfil the law φύσει[97] does not sound at all Pauline. 4. Paul is

---

an die Argumente, die Paulus in seiner Missionspredigt gegen die Heiden anführt, denken" ("Syneidesis", 160).

[91] Ambrosiaster, *In epistolam ad Romanos*, CSEL 81.1:74-75.

[92] Augustine, *Contra Iulianum* 4.3.23-25 (*MPL* 44.750); *De spiritu et littera* 26.43-28.49 (*CSEL* 60.196-204).

[93] Barth, *Shorter Commentary*, p. 36; *KD* I/2, ⁵1960, p. 332 (contrast Barth's earlier view in *Epistle to the Romans*, pp. 65-66); Flückiger, "Die Werke des Gesetzes bei den Heiden", 17-42; M. Barth, "Speaking of Sin", 292; W. Mundle, "Zur Auslegung von Röm 2,13ff.", *ThBl* 13 (1934) 249-56; Cranfield, *Romans*, 1:156.

[94] Cf. J.A. Bengel, *Gnomon novi testamenti*, Berlin 1855 (repr. of ³1773), p. 348.

[95] See Zahn, *Römer*, p. 122.

[96] See Rom. 11.13. Bornkamm, "Gesetz und Natur", 109 n. 39 is therefore not correct to argue that Paul uses ἔθνη in the antitheses Gentiles/Jews, Gentiles/Christians, Gentile Christians/Jewish Christians but never in the antithesis Jews/Gentile Christians. Bornkamm claims that in Rom. 11.13 "Paulus redet von Heiden im Gegensatz zu Juden". This is not the case: he uses ἔθνη of Gentile Christians as opposed to Jews.

[97] I believe φύσει modifies what follows (contra Bengel and Cranfield). If φύσει modified the preceding phrase (τὰ μὴ νόμον ἔχοντα) Paul would have inserted φύσει

not concerned with Christians in Rom. 1.18-3.20. Although the righteousness of God revealed in the gospel has already been mentioned (1.16-17)
it is not taken up again until 3.21. 5. In Hellenistic Judaism the Jeremiah
passage is never used in the apologetic sense of νόμος ἄγραφος.[98] In
view of these arguments it is better to understand the ἔθνη as non-
Christian Gentiles.

5. The next issue is what is the law of the Gentiles, i.e. the law
referred to in τὰ τοῦ νόμου (2.14) and τὸ ἔργον τοῦ νόμου (2.15) (see also
the expression ἑαυτοῖς εἰσιν νόμος (2.14)), and what precisely is the relation of this law to the Torah of the Jews? Is it "qualitatively the same law
as that which had been given to the Jews"[99] or is it just an "Analogie"[100]?
Or is Paul thinking of "natural law"?[101] Related to this is the possibility
that Paul was influenced by Greek philosophy, especially Stoicism. Or is
this law "nur durch logischen Rückschluß aus den konkreten Taten
verifizierbar"?[102]

To some extent the law of the Gentiles can be logically derived from
their deeds for, as Lietzmann points out, Gentiles could fulfil *some* of the
laws.[103] Further, one can say that the law of the Gentiles is not dependent
on Jewish tradition (ἑαυτοῖς, 2.14b) and is not written except ἐν ταῖς
καρδίαις (2.15a). The law Paul refers to in 2.14-15 is not the body of
commandments given to Moses; neither is it some core of the law such as

---

within this participial phrase (Fitzmyer, *Romans*, p. 310). See the use of φύσει in
Rom. 2.27 and Gal. 2.15.

[98] This point is made by Wilckens, *Römer*, 1:134-35, who also points to a private
communication from M. Hengel.

[99] Ridderbos, *Paul*, p. 106.

[100] Michel, *Römer*, p. 123: "Grundsätzlich geht er von der Gültigkeit des mosaischen Gesetzes aus, und das den Heiden verpflichtende Gebot Gottes ist ein *Analogon*
zum mosaischen Gesetz" (Michel's emphasis). Käsemann, *Römer*, pp. 59-60: "Alles
kommt ihm darauf an, daß auch die Heiden den transzendenten Anspruch des
göttlichen Willens erfahren und sich darin — weder 'das' noch 'ein' — Gesetz werden. Damit stehen sie zwar nicht in Identität, jedoch in gewisser Analogie (Michel) zu
den Juden".

[101] See S. Lyonnet, "Lex naturalis et iustificatio Gentilium", *Verbum Dei* 41
(1963) 238-42.

[102] Eckstein, *Syneidesis*, p. 154.

[103] Lietzmann, *Römer*, p. 40.

the decalogue.[104] He does not directly relate this law of the Gentiles to the creation (cf. 1.20[105]); neither does he relate it to the time of Adam nor to the time of Noah. What sort of law is Paul then thinking of? First, the law Paul refers to is clearly an "unwritten law".[106] M. Hengel points out that the idea of the torah being written into man is found from the time of the tannaim.[107] Although written after 70 AD, 2 Bar. 57.2 is especially inter-

---

[104] Pohlenz, "Paulus und die Stoa", 531, is therefore wrong when he claims Paul is thinking "an die sittlichen Grundgedanken, wie sie etwa im Dekalog zusammengefaßt sind". Cf. A. Jülicher, "Der Brief an die Römer", in W. Bousset and W. Heitmüller (ed.), *Die Schriften des Neuen Testaments*, 4 vols, Göttingen ³1917, 3:240 (223-335). Käsemann, *Römer*, p. 59, rightly says that "der Apostel hat die Tora nicht auf das Sittengesetz beschränkt . . .".

[105] Pohlenz, "Paulus und die Stoa", 531, correctly argues: "Er kennt nur *ein* Gesetz, das von Gott gegebene. Er erkennt an, daß es auch Heiden gibt, die seine Anforderungen — innerhalb der menschlichen Grenzen — erfüllen; aber das tun sie nicht, weil ein aus der Natur stammendes Vernunftgesetz ihnen vorschreibt, was sie zu tun und zu lassen haben, sondern weil sich auch ihnen Gott geoffenbart hat. Wie Gott allen Menschen einen natürlichen Weg eröffnet hat, um ihn aus seinen Werken zu erkennen, so hat er ihnen auch seinen Willen ins Herz geschrieben, so daß sie auch ohne schriftlich niedergelegte Offenbarung φύσει das Gute tun können". See also his words: "Eine selbständige 'Natur' neben Gott gibt es nicht" ("Paulus und die Stoa", 531).

[106] On this term see H. Kleinknecht in H. Kleinknecht and W. Gutbrod, νόμος κτλ *TDNT* 4:1027-28 (1022-91), and I. Heinemann, "Die Lehre vom ungeschriebenen Gesetz im jüdischen Schrifttum", *HUCA* 4 (1927) 149-71. Heinemann makes the important point that in the Greek idea of νόμος ἄγραφος, the point is not that such a law is not *written* but that it is not *given*. So in Sophocles' *Antigone* both the law of King Creon and the law which Antigone appeals to are unwritten; but whereas King Creon's laws were *given*, Antigone's was not ("Lehre", 149-50). In reply to Creon's question "And yet you dared to trangress these laws?", Antigone replies: "Yes, for it was not Zeus who made this proclamation, nor was it Justice who lives with the gods below that established such laws among men, nor did I think your proclamation strong enough to have power to overrule, mortal as they were, the unwritten and unfailing ordinances of the gods (ἄγραπτα κἀσφαλῆ θεῶν νόμιμα)" (Sophocles, *Antigone* 449-55, in H. Lloyd-Jones, *Sophocles* (LCL), 2:42-45). It is clear that this distinction between "unwritten law" and "written law" does not correspond to the Jewish idea of oral and written law. In the following discussion I use the term νόμος ἄγραφος primarily in its Greek sense and not in the Rabbinic sense of תורה שבעל פה. This Greek sense of the term is related to the idea of natural law and came to influence some Jewish concepts. See below the excurses on natural law.

[107] Hengel, *Judaism and Hellenism*, 1:173 (*Judentum und Hellenismus*, pp. 315-16). Hengel refers to Targ. Yer. I to Gen. 1.27 which says that God made man with 248 members and 365 veins; this corresponds to the 248 commandments and 365

esting for Rom. 2.14-16[108] in that it relates "the unwritten law"[109], "the works of the commandments"[110] and "the coming judgement"[111]:

For at that time *the unwritten law* (l' ktb' nmws') was in force among them (i.e. Abraham, Isaac, Jacob), and *the works of the commandments* ('bd' dpwqdn') were accomplished at that time, and the belief in *the coming judgement* (dyn' d'tyd) was brought about, and the hope of the world which will be renewed was built at that time, and the promise of the life that will come later was planted.[112]

Note also that according to Philo, *De Abrahamo* 275-76, Abraham did the divine law and commands. He did them "not taught by written words, but unwritten nature gave him the zeal to follow where wholesome and untainted impulse led him." (οὐ γράμμασιν ἀναδιδαχθείς, ἀλλ' ἀγράφῳ τῇ φύσει σπουδάσας ὑγιαινούσαις καὶ ἀνόσοις ὁρμαῖς ἐπακολουθῆσαι).[113] Also a striking parallel to Rom. 2.14-16 can be found in Test. Jud. 20.[114] This text is of special interest because whereas the texts

---

prohibitions in the Torah. בצילמא אלקים ברא יתיה במאתן וארבעין ותמני איברין בתלת מאה ושיתין וחמשא גידין. Although the text gives 665, one should read בשית instead of בתלת (see M. Ginsburger, *Pseudo-Jonathan (Thargum Jonathan ben Usiël zum Pentateuch)*, Berlin 1903, p. 3 n. 4). The dating of this text is extremely difficult. For a discussion of this dating and the date of the tradition concerning the 613 commandments, see the excursus below, where I suggest that a date in the time of the tannaim is possible but a date in the time of the amoraim is more probable.

[108] See Stuhlmacher, *Römer*, p. 41.

[109] Syriac: l' ktb' nmws'; possible Greek and Hebrew equivalents are ὁ νόμος ὁ μὴ γεγραμμένος and הַתּוֹרָה אֲשֶׁר לֹא כְּתוּבָה הִיא. According to A.F.J. Klijn, 2 Baruch was originally written in Hebrew and was later translated into Greek and the Greek in turn was translated into Syriac (Charlesworth, *Pseudepigrapha*, 1:616).

[110] Syriac: 'bd' dpwqdn'. This probably corresponds to Aramaic: עוּבְדֵי מִצְוָותָא; Greek: ἔργα ἐντολῶν; cf. ἔργα νόμου; Hebrew: מַעֲשֵׂי מִצְוֹת.

[111] Syriac: dyn' d'tyd; Greek ἡ μελλούση κρίσις; Hebrew: הַדִּין הַבָּא.

[112] Translation of A.F.J. Klijn, in Charlesworth, *Pseudepigrapha*, 1:641.

[113] *Philo* (LCL), 6:134-135. Further, Philo says (*De Abrahamo* 276) Abraham was "himself a law and an unwritten statute" (νόμος αὐτὸς ὢν καὶ θεσμὸς ἄγραφος). Note the reference to νόμοι ἄγραφοι (*De decalogo* 1) and what Philo says of those before Moses: "These are such men as lived good an blameless lives, whose virtues stand permanently recorded in the most holy scrptures . . . for in these men we have laws endowed with life and reason (ἔμψυχοι καὶ λογικοὶ νόμοι)" (*De Abrahamo* 4-5, Philo (LCL) 6:7). See also Schürer, *A History of the Jewish People in the Time of Jesus Christ*, 2.3:338-341.

[114] This is referred to in Michel, *Römer*, 120, n. 28 and Stuhlmacher, *Römer*, p. 41.

from 2 Baruch and Philo refer to the Patriarchs, this text includes the Gentiles. I have devoted an excursus below to Test. Jud. 20 as a background for Rom. 2.14-16. Another factor to bear in mind is the tradition that the Torah was offered to all the nations but only Israel accepted it.[115]

In view of this rich Jewish background it seems quite unnecessary to posit a direct pagan influence. Many have found parallels with pagan philosophy,[116] particularly Stoicism, especially in view of Paul's use of φύσις in 2.14.[117] It may be the case that Paul was to some extent influenced by popular philosophy which he most likely learnt through the Hellenistic synagogue[118]. However, when we look at Paul's own use of φύσις, it is clear that the word has no specific philosophical content (Gal. 2.15; Rom. 2.27; Gal. 4.8) and the likelihood that Paul derived his view of law in Rom. 2.14-15 directly from Stoicism is slim.[119] I believe the background for Paul's thought concerning the law in Rom. 2.14-15 is to be found in Palestinian Judaism which, as Hengel has conclusively shown, had undergone a process of hellenisation during the Hellenistic era. During this time of hellenisation an ontological view of the Torah developed and the cosmic function of wisdom was passed on to the law.[120] So in Paul's time it is most likely that the Torah was viewed as pre-existent and as involved in the creation of the world.[121] Paul's thought on the law had of course undergone a radical change after his conversion but

---

[115] Again this is discussed in the excursus below: "Rabbinic Views of the Law Revealed to the Gentiles".

[116] For example, one could point to Cicero, *De legibus* 1.6.18: . . . *lex est ratio summa insita in natura, quae iubet ea, quae facienda sunt, prohibetque contraria. eadem ratio cum est in hominis mente confirmata et confecta, lex est.*

[117] Dodd, *Romans*, p. 36, claimed that Paul argued "exactly like a stoic" here. Dodd is supported by Davies, *Paul*, p. 116.

[118] Cf. Hengel, *Pre-Christian Paul*, pp. 2-3.

[119] See further the discussion below in the excursus on "'Natural Law' in Greek Philosophy".

[120] Hengel, *Judaism and Hellenism*, 1:171-72 (*Judentum und Hellenismus*, pp. 309-310).

[121] I qualify with "most likely" because all the texts that speak explicitly of this are later than Paul (e.g. Aboth 3.15; Sifre Dt. 37).

it is likely that some elements of the cosmic dimension of the law remained. In Galatians Paul obviously wished to downplay some aspects of the law stressing that it came 430 years after the promise to Abraham (Gal. 3.17). But in Romans Paul was not facing the Judaisers and felt able to say that the law was there at the time of Adam.[122] I suggest that on one level Paul considered God's law almost as a metaphysical entity. This is not so impossible as may first appear when one considers the ontological view of the law in Judaism. As God's word it is *manifest* for Jews through the 613 commandments, the core of which was written on the two tablets. For Gentiles it is written on their hearts.[123] Because all are in Adam (Rom. 5.12ff) this word of God is a condemning word (2 Cor. 3) and condemns not only Jews but Gentiles also.[124] Although the Gentiles do not have the "law" as manifest in the 613 commandments they do have the demand of the law (τὸ ἔργον τοῦ νόμου) written on their hearts. I believe Schlatter is right to see the activity of God in this writing. "Geschrieben hat Gott in ihren Herzen; darum sind sie sich das Gesetz. Die Schrift in den Herzen ist das Gegenstück zur Schrift auf den Tafeln."[125] God's condemning word comes then through the law and it condemns Gentiles as well as Jews.[126]

---

[122] I take Rom. 7.7-13 to refer to the story of Adam. This law was obviously not in the form it was given to Moses.

[123] Cf. Bornkamm, "Gesetz und Natur", 101: "Νόμος meint also das eine und gleiche Gottesgesetz, das Juden und Heiden nur in verschiedener Weise gegeben ist". I have therefore slightly qualified Pohlenz' point ("Paulus und die Stoa", 530, quoted above n. 105) that Paul knows only of a law given to Jews.

[124] There is a rough parallel with Paul's view of the gospel. This is God's own word (cf. Hofius, "Wort Gottes", 150-51) but is manifest in, but not identified with, the apostolic preaching and apostolic writings. So just as the gospel is God's life giving word for both Jews and Gentiles, the law is God's condemning word for both Jews and Gentiles.

[125] Schlatter, *Gottes Gerechtigkeit*, p. 91.

[126] Concerning the Gentile and the unwritten law, Käsemann, *Römer*, p. 60, writes: "Sie können dem so wenig entfliehen wie sich selbst. Die Ausdrucksweise verfolgt also das gleiche Ziel wie die Anschauung vom νόμος ἄγραφος, nämlich den Menschen auf das ihn unbedingt Verpflichtende zu stellen". Similar is the view of Eichholz, *Theologie des Paulus*, pp. 92-93: "Paulus sähe den Menschen der Völkerwelt bei einem Wissen um das, was die Tora fordert, behaftet, auch wenn er die Tora nicht hat. Daß er behaftet ist, wird er selbst nicht bestreiten, wenn er am Jüngsten Tag vor Jesus Christus steht."

Note that this condemnation does *not* come through the conscience. I believe M. Thrall is incorrect to argue that Paul "had come to regard the conscience as performing in the Gentile world roughly the same function as was performed by the Law amongst the Jews".[127] She argues that Paul began "to equate conscience and the Law" because in Greek thought the conscience was spoken of metaphorically as a prosecutor, judge, stern accuser etc. The conscience is then "an agent of condemnation".[128] However, as Eckstein has shown, the conscience does not have this condemning function for Paul.[129]

I now wish to focus on the precise expressions used in relation to the law of the Gentiles. In v. 14 we have τὰ τοῦ νόμου ποιῶσιν. Walker has a special understanding of this. He translates τὰ τοῦ νόμου literally as "das

---

[127] M. Thrall, "The Pauline Use of ΣΥΝΕΙΔΗΣΙΣ", *NTS* 14 (1967-68) 124 (118-25).

[128] Cf. Fascher, "Deus invisibilis", 73, who writes that there is no excuse for the ἄνομοι "denn ihnen hat Gott das anklagende und richtende Gewissen gegeben (Röm. 2,15)".

[129] Eckstein, *Syneidesis*, p. 177, correctly points out that when Paul assumes the Gentiles know God and τὸ δικαίωμα τοῦ θεοῦ, then this knowledge or their "schuldiges Nichtwissen" is assigned to the νοῦς or καρδία (Rom. 1.20, 21, 28). "So ist also der νοῦς bzw. die καρδία und nicht die Syneidesis für das Wissen der 'bestehenden Forderung', das 'Wissen um Gut und Böse und um das diesem entsprechende Verhalten in Einem' zuständig" (*Syneidesis*, p. 177, quoting Bultmann, *Theologie des Neuen Testaments*, p. 217). Concerning the νοῦς, Eckstein, p. 177, writes: "Er ist die Instanz, die fragt: Was ist meine Pflicht, was ist gut, wie kann ich das Gute in einer bestimmten Situation anwenden, kurz, wie soll ich mich verhalten?" On the other hand, the "Instanz der Syneidesis" has the task "das Denken, Wollen, Reden und Handeln des Menschen auf die Übereinstimmung mit den bewußt oder unbewußt akzeptierten Normen des νοῦς zu überprüfen und das Ergebnis dem Menschen bestätigend oder anklagend zu bezeugen. Ist das νοῦς mit seinem δοκιμάζειν auf das Objekt des zu Tuenden ausgerichtet, so ist die Syneidesis mit ihrem δοκιμάζειν reflexiv auf das handelnde Subjekt in seinem Tun bezogen und fragt: Tust Du das, was Du als das Gute ansiehst, stimmt Dein Verhalten mit Deiner Entscheidung überein?" Eckstein, *Syneidesis*, p. 178, rightly argues that Paul's concept of συνείδησις does not correspond to Philo's concept of συνειδός which has the function of an accuser (contrast Thrall, "ΣΥΝΕΙΔΗΣΙΣ", 124). "Für Paulus vermittelt die Syneidesis als in diesem Sinne neutrale Instanz sowohl positive wie negative Beurteilungen und wird wohl auch aus diesem Grunde nicht im Zusammenhang der Anklage von Röm 1,18-3,20 als theologischer Begriff zum Schulderweis eingeführt."

des Gesetzes".[130] In view of Rom. 1.18-32 he then argues: "Indem die Heiden also faktisch sündigen, kann von ihnen gesagt werden, daß sie tun das des Gesetzes ist".[131] He continues: "Im Rahmen des Römerbriefes kann diese Aussage nicht überraschen; hier ist die Sünde ja die essentielle Eigenheit des Gesetzes (Röm. 4,15; 5,20; 7,7b; 7,8b; 8,2 νόμος τῆς ἁμαρτίας; vgl. Gal. 3,19; 1 Kor. 15,56)".[132] The problem with such a solution is that it ignores what Paul in 2.25-29 is saying, something which bears many resemblances to 2.14-15. I suggest that the expression ἔθνη . . . τὰ τοῦ νόμου ποιῶσιν means ἔθνη . . . τὰ δικαιώματα τοῦ νόμου ποιῶσιν[133] and is parallel to ἡ ἀκροβυστία τὰ δικαιώματα τοῦ νόμου φυλάσσῃ (2.26) and ἡ ἐκ φύσεως ἀκροβυστία τὸν νόμον τελοῦσα (2.27).

The other important expression regarding the law of the Gentiles is τὸ ἔργον τοῦ νόμου (2.15) which I believe means the work which the law requires in the sense of מִצְוָה/מִצְוֹת.[134] Normally the plural without articles (ἔργα νόμου) is used and means the works as actually performed.[135] Cranfield believes the singular is used here to bring out the essential unity of the law.[136]

6. The final question is what is the nature of the judgement in 2.16? This verse was considered such a problem that some suggested it was a gloss.[137] Note also that Moffatt moved 2.16 to give the sequence 12, 13, 16, 14, 15,[138] a suggestion which Dodd[139] adopted.

---

[130] R. Walker, "Die Heiden und das Gericht: Zur Auslegung von Römer 2,12-16", *EvTh* 20 (1960) 305 (302-14).

[131] Walker, "Heiden", 305. He adds: "Im Blick auf den wörtlichen Sinn von τὰ τοῦ νόμου (das des Gesetzes = das dem Gesetz Zugehörige) und angesichts der Aussagen von 1,18-32 (vgl. 3,9ff.) ist es unmöglich, anzunehmen, Paulus rede hier von einer Erfüllung der Forderung des Gesetzes, von einem Tun des Gesetzes seitens der Heiden" ("Heiden", 305 n. 9).

[132] Walker, "Heiden", 305.

[133] The other possible way to understand τὰ τοῦ νόμου is as τὰ ῥήματα τοῦ νόμου (see Dt. 28.58; 29.28; 31.9; Jos. 9.4 (B)) or τὰ ἔργα τοῦ νόμου.

[134] Cf. Billerbeck, *Kommentar*, 3:161.

[135] Rom. 3.20, 28; Gal. 2.16; 3.2, 5, 10.

[136] Cranfield, *Romans*, 1:158.

[137] See especially Bultmann, "Glossen", 282-83. Bultmann found problems with the use of the expression κατὰ τὸ εὐαγγέλιόν μου and with what he thought was an abrupt switch to the future in v. 16 and concluded that 2.16 was "ein Fremdkörper im Text", based on 1 Cor. 4.5.

One of the main problems here is the expression κατὰ τὸ εὐαγγέλιόν μου. I take εὐαγγέλιον to mean gospel in the sense of the reconciling word of God and τὸ εὐαγγέλιόν μου to mean the gospel entrusted to Paul.[140] In view of the word order it is natural to take κατὰ τὸ εὐαγγέλιόν μου with διὰ Χριστοῦ Ἰησοῦ or more precisely to take κρίνει with διὰ Χριστοῦ Ἰησοῦ with κατὰ τὸ εὐαγγέλιόν μου making it clear that judgement is through Jesus Christ. As Moo puts it: "It is through Christ Jesus that God judges, as my gospel teaches".[141] This makes perfect sense.[142] That the gospel has something to do with judgement is not so strange as may first appear. Rom. 1.16-17, setting out the righteousness of God which is revealed in the gospel, is followed in 1.18 by the revelation of the eschatological wrath of God. The section beginning 1.18 depicts man "in the light of the cross of Christ".[143] Further, as I will emphasise later, Paul's portrayal of sinful humanity in Rom. 1.18-3.20 is not based on empirical evidence. It is rather, as Oltmanns stresses, "eine Glaubenstatsache". Paul puts himself "in die Lage des unerlösten Menschen, die er von dem Evangelium aus erst recht erfassen kann".[144]

---

[138] J. Moffatt, *The New Testament: A New Translation*, London 1913.

[139] Dodd, *Romans*, p. 35.

[140] Hofius, "Wort Gottes", 152 n. 28. Some believe the reference is to the whole message of Paul. See Lietzmann, *Römer*, on 1.16, quoted in Flückiger, "Werke", 37. Lietzmann believes that Paul does not mean "speziell die Heilslehre vom Glauben" but rather "seine Gesamtverkündigung".

[141] Moo, *Romans*, p. 155.

[142] The idea of delegated judgement is also found in 1 En. 45.3 ("On that day Mine Elect One shall sit on the throne of glory / And shall try their works, / And their places of rest shall be innumerable" (Charles' translation). Taking 2.12-16 together, I believe it is now clear that the standard by which Jews and Gentiles will be judged is whether they have kept the law.

[143] Cranfield, *Romans*, 1:104. Note that Cranfield entitles the section 1.18-3.20 "In the light of the gospel there is no question of men's being righteous before God otherwise than by faith". However, I am not in agreement with Cranfield that 1.18 concerns the wrath of God shown in the "on-going proclamation of the gospel" and basic to this is "the prior revelation of the wrath of God in the gospel events" (*Romans*, 1:109-10).

[144] K. Oltmanns, "Das Verhältnis von Röm 1,18-3,20 zu Röm 3,21ff.", *ThBl* 8 (1929) 114 (110-116). Oltmanns has been sharply criticised by Kuhlmann, *Theologia Naturalis*, pp. 48-49 (n. 1). Kuhlmann argues: "'Die Sündigkeit des Menschen' ist keineswegs 'eine Glaubenstatsache', sondern der tatsächliche Bestand des men-

In this connection it is interesting to note that although the law brings about an objective knowledge of sin (διὰ γὰρ νόμου ἐπίγνωσις ἁμαρτίας Rom. 3.20) it is the gospel which actually reveals a full knowledge of sin to the individual. This is suggested by the conversion of Paul. Paul the Pharisee clearly considered himself a successful Jew (Phil. 3.5-6). But although he knew of the sinfulness of man (e.g. Ps. 51) it was only in the light of the gospel that Paul fully realised the wretchedness of the human situation and his own sinfulness.[145] As Oltmanns rightly observes:

> Aber auch nur der, der weiß, daß ihm vergeben ist, kann auch die ganze Hoffnungslosigkeit der Sünde einsehen; der Mensch, der unter der ὀργή (dem Zorn) steht, weiß von seiner verzweifelten Lage selbst nicht, and wenn er sie ahnt, so muß er doch immer davon wegsehen, wenn er sich nicht selbst aufgeben will.[146]

Therefore in Rom. 2.16 it is the gospel which reveals sin to be sin. It is on the last day that the Gentile will have a knowledge of his sin. On that day, when God judges the secrets of men through Jesus Christ according to the gospel, the Gentiles will show the work of the law, i.e. the demand of the law, written on their hearts. Their consciences and their accusing (and perhaps excusing) thoughts will confirm this and it will be clear that they are without excuse.

Having studied Rom. 2.12-16 one would assume that Paul does support a justification by works (2.12-13) and seems to assume the existence of Gentiles who do the ordinances of the law and so gain acquittal when Jesus comes to judge the secrets of men (2.14-16). Does it not seem that there is a way of salvation for pious Jews and pious Gentiles other than

---

schlichen Daseins, das unabhängig davon existiert, ob es in diesem seinem sündigen Bestande von ihm selbst erkannt wird oder nicht. . . . Die Erkenntnis der Sünde bleibt gerade auf Grund ihres existentiellen Charakters in der Sünde. Die existentielle Sündenerkenntnis ist demnach nicht das Erzeugnis des Glaubens, sondern nur die Vollständigkeit der sündigen Existenz im Vollzuge ihres Sichselbstbewußtwerdens". To some extent Paul did not need faith in Christ to see the sinfulness of human beings. But I believe he could only put forward his radically pessimistic view in the light of faith in Christ. See further the discussion of Rom. 3.20 in chapter 6 below.

[145] Only Paul the Christian could write Rom. 7.14-25 which I understand to be a description of the pre-Christian Paul through Christian spectacles.

[146] Oltmanns, "Verhältnis", 114.

through faith in Christ? I return to this question in the concluding chapter. However, I now sketch the solution I reach there.

The conclusion that there is a way of salvation other than through faith in Christ can only be held if the context of our verses is ignored. I believe Rom. 2.12-16 (and in fact the whole of Romans 2) only makes sense if it is seen as part of the argument of 1.18-3.20 where Paul is establishing that Jews and Gentiles are heading for condemnation on the day of judgement. In 3.9-20 it becomes clear that no one will be acquitted through works of law: both Jew and Gentile are under the power of sin (3.9) as scripture makes clear (3.10-18). On reading 3.9-20 one must conclude that the pious Jews and pious Gentiles of Rom. 2.12-16 *do not exist.*[147] Paul's argument comes to a climax in 3.20 where he concludes that there will be no acquittal at the final judgement on the basis of observing the law — in fact the law reveals sin to be sin (διότι ἐξ ἔργων νόμου οὐ δικαιωθήσεται πᾶσα σὰρξ ἐνώπιον αὐτοῦ, διὰ γὰρ νόμου ἐπίγνωσις ἁμαρτίας). In 1.18-3.20 Paul has thereby demonstrated the necessity of the revelation of the righteousness of God from faith to faith.

8.   Excursus on Testament of Judah 20 as a Background for Romans 2.14-16

The similarities between Test. Jud. 20 and Rom. 2.14-16 are so strong that, on first impression, one wonders whether there is a Christian interpolation here. However, I can see no clear evidence for this.[148] According to Charles, the original language of the Testaments was Hebrew.[149] One

---

[147] The same can be said for those of vv. 6-11 and 27-29.

[148] R.H. Charles finds no interpolation here. However, J. Becker, *Untersuchungen zur Entstehungsgeschichte der Testamente der Zwölf Patriarchen*, Leiden 1970, p. 315, describes Test. Jud. 20 as a "'dogmatische' Belehrung über die zwei Geister" and writes: "Die Ausführungen sind unter stark psychologischem Interesse geschrieben und haben darin im Grundstock des TJud keine Entsprechung". Becker's point is questioned by J.H. Ulrichsen, *Die Grundschrift der Testamente der Zwölf Patriarchen*, Uppsala 1991, pp. 170-71, who writes that Test. Jud. 20 is related to other original parts of Test 12, especially Test. Asher. The view of M. de Jonge, that the Testaments are Christian (*The Testaments of the Twelve Patriarchs: A Study of Their Text, Composition, and Origin*, Leiden 1953), has not been widely accepted.

[149] Charles, *Apocrypha and Pseudepigrapha*, 2:287.

reason for believing this is that the idiom of the Greek is often Hebraic and foreign to the Greek language. An example occurring in Test. Jud. 20 is the expression ἐν στήθει ὀστέων αὐτοῦ which, although unintelligible in Greek, in Hebrew makes perfect sense, namely בְּלֵב עַצְמוֹ "in his very heart".[150] However, H.C. Kee argues that semitisms in the Testaments of the Twelve Patriarchs could come from LXX. "The peculiarities of the document can be accounted for fully if we assume that it was written originally in Greek, with Hebrew and Aramaic testaments serving as models and perhaps to a very limited extent as sources for detail."[151] Perhaps some of the Semitisms could be accounted for in this way. However, it cannot account for the expression ἐν στήθει ὀστέων αὐτοῦ.[152]

The following parallels to Rom. 2.14-16 can be found in Test. Jud. 20:[153]

a. The idea of certain things being written on the heart. 20.3: καίγε τὰ τῆς ἀληθείας καὶ τὰ τῆς πλάνης γέγραπται ἐπὶ τὸ στῆθος τοῦ ἀνθρώπου. καὶ ἓν ἕκαστον αὐτῶν γνωρίζει κύριος. Cf. τὸ ἔργον τοῦ νόμου γραπτὸν ἐν ταῖς καρδίαις αὐτῶν (Rom. 2.15). However, whereas the "work of the law" is written on the heart in Rom. 2.15, in Test. Jud. it is the "things of truth and things of error"[154]. Note that this reflects the language of Prov. 3.3 MT[155] and Jer. 31.33[156]. In Test. Jud. 20.3-4

---

[150] Charles, *Apocrypha and Pseudepigrapha*, 2:287.

[151] Kee, in Charlesworth, *Pseudepigrapha*, 1:777.

[152] For example, in Ezek. 40.1 בְּעֶצֶם הַיּוֹם הַזֶּה is rendered ἐν τῇ ἡμέρᾳ ἐκείνῃ and in Gen. 7.13 the same Hebrew expression is rendered ἐν τῇ ἡμέρᾳ ταύτῃ and in Gen. 17.23, 26 by ἐν τῷ καιρῷ τῆς ἡμέρας ἐκείνης. In fact there is no case in LXX where the Greek ὀστέον is used to render the Hebrew עֶצֶם in the sense of "self" (usually "this selfsame day") (see Ex. 12.17, 41, 51; Lev. 23.21, 28, 29, 30; Dt. 32.48; Jos. 5.11; Ezek. 2.2; Lev. 23.14; Jos. 10.17).

[153] I have used the Greek text of M. de Jonge (ed.), *The Testaments of the Twelve Patriarchs: A Critical Edition of the Greek Text*, Leiden 1978.

[154] Note that the things written on the heart are not what God *wishes them to do* but *what they have in fact done*. There is, therefore, no parallel with Ezek. 20.25, where bad statutes are given as a judgement.

[155] MT: חֶסֶד וֶאֱמֶת אַל־יַעַזְבֻךָ קָשְׁרֵם עַל־גַּרְגְּרוֹתֶיךָ כָּתְבֵם עַל־לוּחַ לִבֶּךָ

The LXX of 3.3b is somewhat different: ἐλεημοσύναι καὶ πίστεις μὴ ἐκλιπέτωσάν σε, ἄφαψαι δὲ αὐτὰς ἐπὶ σῷ τραχήλῳ, καὶ εὑρήσεις χάριν (3.3).

[156] 31.33 MT: כִּי זֹאת הַבְּרִית אֲשֶׁר אֶכְרֹת אֶת־בֵּית יִשְׂרָאֵל אַחֲרֵי הַיָּמִים הָהֵם נְאֻם־יְהוָה נָתַתִּי אֶת־תּוֹרָתִי בְּקִרְבָּם וְעַל־לִבָּם אֶכְתֲּבֶנָּה וְהָיִיתִי לָהֶם לֵאלֹהִים וְהֵמָּה יִהְיוּ־לִי לְעָם:

στῆθος renders לֵב as in Ex. 28.29, 30. Note also Test. Jud. 20.4b: ὅτι ἐν στήθει ὀστέων αὐτοῦ ἐγγέγραπται ἐνώπιον κυρίου.

b. Conscience (συνείδησις) (cf. Rom. 2.15) occurs in 20.2 (h): καὶ μέσον ἐστὶ συνειδήσεωσ (c: μέσον ἐστὶ τῆς συνηδήσεως; de Jonge: καὶ μέσον ἐστὶ τὸ τῆς συνέσεως τοῦ νοός). However, note that R.H. Charles believes that the α family of texts (which includes h and c) is defective and corrupt in vv. 2-4[157]. συνείδησις is also used in Test. Reub. 4.3. Note also that the function of the conscience is assigned to the καρδία in 20.5[158]: καὶ τὸ πνεῦμα τῆς ἀληθείας μαρτυρεῖ πάντα καὶ κατηγορεῖ πάντων, καὶ ἐμπεπύρισται ὁ ἁμαρτήσας ἐκ τῆς ἰδίας καρδίας, καὶ ἆραι πρόσωπον οὐ δύναται πρὸς τὸν κριτήν.

c. The secrets of men being exposed occurs in Test. Jud. 20.4: καὶ οὐκ ἐστὶ καιρὸς ἐν ᾧ δυνήσεται λαθεῖν ἀνθρώπων ἔργα, ὅτι ἐν στήθει ὀστέων αὐτοῦ ἐγγέγραπται ἐνώπιον κυρίου. Cf. Rom. 2.16.

d. The theme of judgement occurs in 20.5 (quoted above under 2.). Again, cf. Rom. 2.16.

These parallels again suggest that Paul's thinking in Rom. 2.14-16 is thoroughly Jewish.

9. Excursus on Rabbinic Views of the Law Revealed to the Gentiles

In view of Rom. 2.14-16 it is of interest to pursue the Rabbinic idea of the law revealed to the Gentiles.

There was a Rabbinic idea that the law was offered to all the nations but only Israel accepted it. This is found in both schools of Ishmael and

---

38.33 LXX: ὅτι αὕτη ἡ διαθήκη, ἣν διαθήσομαι τῷ οἴκῳ Ισραηλ μετὰ τὰς ἡμέρας ἐκείνας, φησὶν κύριος Διδοὺς· δώσω νόμους μου εἰς τὴν διάνοιαν αὐτῶν καὶ ἐπὶ καρδίας αὐτῶν γράψω αὐτούς· καὶ ἔσομαι αὐτοῖς εἰς θεόν, καὶ αὐτοὶ ἔσονταί μοι εἰς λαόν·

[157] R.H. Charles, *The Greek Versions of the Testaments of the Twelve Patriarchs*, Oxford 1908, p. 95. See also de Jonge *Testaments*, p. 73.

[158] See Eckstein, *Syneidesis*, p. 119; C. Maurer, σύνοιδα κτλ, *ThWNT* 7:909 (897-918).

Akiba in the second century and is part of common earlier tradition. So the law was not given in secret. It was given in a public place, in the desert (Ex. 19.1), not in the land of Israel.[159] It was revealed in broad daylight[160] with thunder and lightning[161] with a loud voice[162]. It was revealed at Sinai not in one language but in four: Hebrew, Latin, Arabic and Aramaic.[163] However, on the basis of Gen. 10 there were 70 nations and there is the tradition that the law was heard in 70 languages at once.[164] There was then the tradition that Moses in the plains of Moab interpreted the law in 70 languages and again the tradition that the law

---

[159] Mek. Ex. Baḥodesh 1: "The Torah was given in public, openly in a free place. For had the Torah been given in the land of Israel, the Israelites could have said to the nations of the world: You have no share in it. But now that it was given in the wilderness publicly and openly in a place that is free for all, everyone wishing to accept it could come and accept it" (Lauterbach, *Mekilta*, 2:198). Note that such a text completely contradicts the idea of Israel's national righteousness and some of the ideas of the new perspective. First, it shows that Rabbinic Judaism had a weak view of election (i.e. it was up to Israel to accept the torah). Second, it shows that the torah was available for Gentiles also.

[160] "One might suppose that it was given at night, but Scripture says: 'And it came to pass on the third day when it was morning' (v. 16)" (Mek. Baḥodesh 1, Lauterbach, *Mekilta*, 2:198). "Did I not give it in broad daylight?" (Mek. Baḥodesh 1, Lauterbach, *Mekilta*, 2:199).

[161] "One might suppose that it was given in silence, but Scripture says: 'When there were thunders and lightning'" (Mek. Baḥodesh 1, Lauterbach, *Mekilta*, 2:198).

[162] "One might suppose that they could not hear the voice, but Scripture says: 'The voice of the Lord in powerful, the voice of the Lord is full of majesty,' (Ps. 29.4)" (Mek. Ex. Baḥodesh 1, Lauterbach, *Mekilta*, 1:198).

[163] See Sifre Dt. 343 (on Dt. 33.2): "when God revealed Himself to give the Torah to Israel, He spoke to them not in one language but in four languages, as it is said, 'And He said: The Lord came from Sinai' — this refers to the Hebrew language — 'and rose from Seir unto them' — this refers to the Romans language — 'He shined forth from Mount Paran' — this refers to the Arabic lanuage — 'and He came from the Myriads of Kodesh' — this refers to the Aramaic language" (Hammer, *Sifre*, p. 352). Seir (i.e. Edom) is regularly used as an alias for Rome.

[164] See b. Shab. 88b: "Every single word that went forth from the Omnipotent was split up into seventy languages (so R. Joḥanan). The School of R. Ishmael taught: 'And like a hammer that breaketh the rock in pieces'; just as a hammer is divided into many sparks, so every single word that went forth from the Holy One, blessed be He, split up into seventy languages".

was inscribed on the altar of Mount Ebal and the nations sent their scribes to copy it in 70 different languages.[165]

However, although the Torah was offered to all nations, they all rejected the offer. So we read in Sifre Dt. 343:

> He went first to the children of Esau and asked them, 'Will you accept the Torah?' They replied, 'What is written in it?' He said to them 'Thou shalt not murder' (Ex. 20.13). They replied that this is the very essence of these people, that their forefather was a murderer, as it is said, 'But the hands are the hands of Esau' (Gen. 27.22), and, 'By thy sword shalt thou live' (Gen. 27.40).[166]

Similarly the Torah was offered to the Ammonites (who are murderers), the Moabites and Ammonites (who are adulterers) and the Ishmaelites (who are stealers).[167] The Torah was offered to every nation but they all refused. They were not even able to keep the seven commandments of Noah.[168]

There are three important theological themes which I want to highlight in this tradition of the law being offered to all nations. First, it puts the election of Israel into a new light. The view of election here is really that of synergism: only Israel decided to accept the torah.[169] It is also striking how some Rabbis were open to the acceptance of Gentiles.[170] Secondly,

---

[165] See Moore, *Judaism*, 1:278.

[166] Hammer, *Sifre*, p. 352.

[167] Sifre Dt. 343 (Cf. Mek. Ex. Baḥodesh 5 (Lauterbach, *Mekilta*, 2:234-35)). See also Moore, *Judaism*, 3:87.

[168] Mek. Ex. Baḥodesh 5: "R. Simon b. Eleazar says: If the sons of Noah could not endure the seven commandments enjoined upon them, how much less could they have endured all the commandments of the Torah!" (Lauterbach, *Mekilta*, 2:235-36). Cf. Sifre Dt. 343 (Hammer, *Sifre*, p. 353).

[169] I discuss this briefly in *Provoked to Jealousy*, p. 191-93.

[170] One of the most striking texts here is Sg of Sgs R. 5.16.5, where Lev. 20.26 is commented upon. "It is written, 'And I have set you apart from the peoples' (Lev. 20.26). Had it said, 'I have set the peoples apart from you', there would have been no hope for the enemies of Israel. . . . For a man who picks the bad out from the good, once he has put the bad aside, does not sift any more. But he who sifts the good from the bad goes and sifts again. So had it .been said, 'I have set the nations apart from you', there would have been no hope for the enemies of Israel; but it is said, 'And I have set you apart from the peoples', to be attached to Me and My name for ever. R. Aḥa said: From this we learn that the Holy One, blessed be He, told the nations that they should repent, so that He might bring them under His wings" (Soncino, pp. 254-55).

the law was offered to all the nations in order to show that they are without excuse.[171] This is seen in Mek. Ex. Baḥodesh 5: "And it was for the following reason that the nations of the world were asked to accept the Torah: In order that they should have no excuse for saying: Had we been asked we would have accepted it".[172] Thirdly, the fact that the torah was offered to all nations underlines the universal nature of the law. The puzzle, though, is how is it that the commands of the torah do not correspond to the unwritten law of the Gentiles. Sometimes this unwritten law was seen as corresponding to the seven commands given to Noah.[173] But although the Gentiles have far fewer commands than the Gentiles, the fact that the torah is a universal law does explain why the Rabbis bothered at all to consider the law for Gentiles.[174] This brings me on the question of the relationship between torah and creation.

The specific text Targ. Yer. I Gen. 1.27 has been mentioned earlier in the exegesis of Rom. 2.14-16. According to this text God made man with 248 members and 365 veins corresponding to the 248 commandments and 365 prohibitions in the Torah (for the dating of this text see the following excursus). One of the ideas behind this is that if the law was involved in the creation of the world, the world, it would appear, could reflect aspects of the torah. The possibility would then exist for the law to become a universal law. Jervell, however, argues that the Rabbis did not see Torah as a "Weltgesetz".[175] He points out that the Rabbis understood the image of God in terms of the sign of the covenant, circumcision. So according to Aboth R. Nathan 2 (18b (2)), Adam "came into the world circumcised, for it is stated, 'And God created man in His own

---

[171] Cf. Paul's stress on the Gentiles' ἀναπολόγητος in Rom. 1.20 and 2.1.

[172] Lauterbach, *Mekilta*, 2:234 (on Ex. 20.2).

[173] Cf. b. Bab. Kam. 38a; b. Abod. Zar. 2b-3a. The seven commandments are listed in b. Sanh. 56a: "Our Rabbis taught: Seven precepts were the sons of Noah commanded: social laws; to refrain from blasphemy; idolatry; adultery; bloodshed; robbery; and eating flesh cut from a living animal". R. Ḥanania b. Gamaliel added partaking of blood from a living animal; R. Ḥidka added emasculation; R. Simeon added sorcery (b. Sanh. 56b).

[174] I am grateful to Dr F. Avemarie for this insight.

[175] Jervell, *Imago Dei*, p. 81.

image'".[176] Seth also was born circumcised (Gen 5.3 being quoted: ויולד
בדמותו כצלמו) as was Noah, Shem, Jacob, Joseph, Reuben, Moses,
Balaam, Samuel, David, Jeremiah, Zerubbabel and Job. Therefore,
according to Jervell, Gen. 1.26-27 was understood as the creating of the
Israelite.[177] But I have already indicated that Jervell's understanding of
the *imago dei* is too narrow.[178] Among the texts Jervell points to for support are Sanh. 4.5 and b. Bab. Met. 114b. But both texts could be
understood in a sense which would not support Jervell's contention that
only the Israelite had the image of God.[179] There are also texts which

---

[176] The quotation from Gen. 1.27 probably implies perfection. See the previous
section (2.5), where it is said Job was born circumcised in view of his being "a
whole-hearted and an upright man" (Job 1.8).

[177] Jervell, *Imago Dei*, pp. 81-82.

[178] See the discussion of Jewish views of the fall in chapter 3 above.

[179] See Sanh. 4.5: "Therefore but a single man was created in the world, to teach
that if any man has caused a single soul to perish from Israel Scripture imputes it to
him as though he had caused a whole world to perish; and if any man saves alive a
single soul from Israel Scripture imputes it to him as though he had saved alive a
whole world". The words "from Israel" are missing from some manuscripts. Jervell
claims they are missing probably because the equation of Israelite with man was
obvious (Jervell, *Imago Dei*, p. 82 n. 46). But was it so obvious? A little later in
Sanh. 4.5 we read that "the King of kings, the Holy One, blessed is he, has stamped
every man with the seal of the first man" and this means "every one must say, For
my sake was the world created". Moore, *Judaism*, 1:445, believes that the words
"from Israel" are a later interpolation. For the view that the non-Israelite was considered not to be a human being, Jervell, *Imago Dei*, p. 82, points to b. Bab. M.
114b: "R. Simeon b. Yohai said: The graves of Gentiles do not defile, for it is written, 'And ye my flock, the flock of my pastures, are men' (Ezek. 43.31); only ye are
designated 'men'." (Note that Ezek. 43.31 is used to make the same point in b. Ker.
6b: "Ye are called 'adam' but heathens are not called 'adam'"). However, the
explanation given in the footnote of the Soncino edition that the text in b. Bab. Met.
114b is saying Gentiles are "inhuman" (R. Simeon was persecuted by Romans) seems
more plausible. See also my comment in chapter 3 above that this text like certain
other negative texts about the Gentiles is motivated by xenophobia. Jervell also supports his view by referring to the idea of converts to Judaism becoming like a new
creation (b. Yeb. 22a: "one who has become a proselyte is like a child newly born"
(וגר שנתגייר כקטן שנולד דמי)). But the idea of being a new creation does not necessarily mean that the Gentile was not a human being before becoming a proselyte. The
image of new creation may be simply to do with his new legal status and that all
previous family ties are severed (see note a10 of b. Yeb. 22a in the Soncino edition).
However, having said that, there may be an idea that only the Israelite is a human
being in the full sense of the word. This may be hinted at in a text such as Gen. R.

show that special consideration must be shown to the Gentile in order that God's name be not profaned.[180] The upshot of all this is that one cannot easily deny the idea of the law being a universal law. Further the idea of the torah being such a universal law finds support in the link between law and creation as found in Targ. Yer. I Gen. 1.27.[181] This is confirmed by the other ways in which torah and creation are linked in Rabbinic literature. God, as we have seen, created the world through the torah. So in Aboth 3.15 the torah is referred to as the "precious instrument through which the world was created" (כְּלִי חֶמְדָּה שֶׁבּוֹ נִבְרָא הָעוֹלָם).[182] Therefore in Rabbinic Judaism, as well as in wisdom literature and in "Hellenistic Judaism", the torah was seen as a "Weltgesetz", valid in different ways for Gentiles and Jews.[183] Such ideas about law therefore form an important background to Paul's argument in Rom. 2.14-16.

10. Excursus on the Dating of the Tradition in Targum Yerushalmi I Genesis 1.27

As noted above, Targ. Yer. I to Gen. 1.27 says that God made man with 248 members and 365 veins corresponding to the 248 commandments and 365 prohibitions in the Torah. בצילמא אלקים ברא יתיה במאתן וארבעין ותמני איברין בתלת מאה ושיתין וחמשא גידין. The dating of this text is extremely difficult. It can be approached in two ways: first, by asking the dating of Targ. Yer. I itself; secondly, by asking when the tradition arose concerning the 613 commandments (with its division into 248 positive and 365 negative commandments).

The final form of Targ. Yer. I must be given a post-Islamic date in view of the mention of the names of the wife and daughter of

---

39.14: ". . . he who brings a Gentile near [to God] is as though he created him".

[180] See Urbach, *Sages*, 1:358-59. See, for example, b. Bab. Kam. 113a.

[181] Such a view is admittedly rare but nevertheless highly significant. Jervell, *Imago Dei*, p. 80, believes it is rare because of the fear that the torah could be seen as creator and therefore as God.

[182] See also Sifre Dt. 37.

[183] See the excursus below on "'Natural Law' in Judaism" and the discussion in chapter 3 on the wisdom tradition behind Rom. 1.18-32.

Mohammed. However, the Targum most likely contains much older tradition.[184] It is therefore necessary to develop some methodology to help in the dating of this earlier material. One of the issues is the relationship between the different Targumim. So Paul Kahle argued that Onkelos was a wholly Babylonian product whereas the Palestinian Targumim represent an earlier Targum current in Palestine in pre-mishnaic times, even pre-Christian times. The Kahle school has been criticised by A.D. York who, whilst not denying the existence of old traditions in Palestinian Targumim, is critical of Kahle's strict dichotomy between Palestinian Targumim and Babylonian Targumim (Onkelos and Jonathan) and the pre-dating of the Palestinian Targum.[185] S.A. Kaufman has developed some methodological principles for dating Targumic material,[186] but one of the problems with his approach is that he assumes an original "Palestinian Targum" from which the other Palestinian Targumim developed.[187]

---

[184] R. Hayward, "The Date of Targum Pseudo-Jonathan: Some Comments", *JJS* 60 (1989) 7-30, argues that as far as the targum to Gen. 27 is concerned, there is no firm evidence for a post-Islamic dating. Unfortunately, he jumps to the conclusion that "it cannot simply be maintained that a late, post-Islamic date for Ps-Jon is one of the assured results of modern scholarship" ("Targum Pseudo-Jonathan", 30). As A. Shinan, "Dating Targum Pseudo-Jonathan: Some More Comments", *JJS* 61 (1990) 60 (57-61), comments, such a conclusion is hard to justify for allusions to Islam and anti-Islamic polemic are not in Gen. 27 but in its treatment of Hagar and Ishmael. As regards older tradition in Palestinian Targumim, the revised Schürer gives the following rule of thumb: "unless there is specific proof to the contrary, the haggadah of the Palestinian Targums is likely to be Tannaitic and to antedate the outbreak of the Second Jewish Revolt in A.D. 132" (*History of the Jewish People*, 1:105).

[185] A.D. York, "The Dating of the Targumic Literature", *JSJ* 5 (1971) 59 (49-62).

[186] See S.A. Kaufman, "On Methodology in the Study of the Targums and their Chronology", *JSNT* 23 (1985) 117-24, and "Dating the Language of the Palestinian Targums and their Use in the Study of First Century CE Texts", in D.R.G. Beattie and M.J. McNamara (ed.), *The Aramaic Bible: Targums in their Historical Context*, Sheffield 1994, 118-141. In the latter article Kaufman writes that when "Pseudo-Jonathan is not simply copying Onqelos and its language or the Palestinian Targum and its language, or lifting a phrase straight out of one of its midrashic sources, it does have its own distinctive language — its own grammar and its own lexicon" (124). In this case the language is an authentic Aramaic dialect which he calls Late Jewish Literary Aramaic. One could argues that such is the case in Targ. Yer. I Gen. 1.27.

[187] Kaufman, "Dating", 130, speaks of "a proto-targum from which the Palestinian

I turn now to the second issue which may help in dating the tradition in Targ. Yer. I Gen. 1.27: the dating of the tradition of the 613 commandments. This has often been taken to occur in the time of the Tannaim. So A.H. Rabbinowitz seems to assume a tannaitic origin and believes that it was in the school of R. Akiba that this tradition crystallised.[188] He refers to Sifre Dt. 76 where he says 365 prohibitions are mentioned. This, however, is probably an interpolation.[189] Likewise in Mek. de R. Ishmael (which Rabbinowitz also refers to), there is an interpolation. "Now it is surely an argument from minor to major: If they (the Gentiles) failed to observe the seven precepts enjoined upon the Children of Noah, how much less (would they be able to keep) the six hundred and thirteen commandments". But the reading should be "how much less all the commandments of the Torah".[190] However, Sifre Dt. 76 is one of the earliest tradi-

---

Targum and Targum Onqelos are separately descended". This view is found among other scholars. See the "geneological relationships between the recensions and manuscripts of the pentateuchal targumim" given by P.S. Alexander, "Jewish Aramaic Translations of Hebrew Scriptures", in M.J. Mulder (ed.), *Mikra: Text, Translation, Reading and Interpretation of the Hebrew Bible in Ancient Judaism and Early Christianity*, Assen/Philadelphia 1987, 244 (fig. 1) (217-253). My problem with this view is that if targumim began as an Aramaic translation/paraphrase of the Hebrew bible for use in synagogue worship, it seems unlikely that there would be an original "proto-targum". See also U. Gleßmer, *Einleitung in die Targume zum Pentateuch*, Tübingen 1995, p. 94, who criticises Alexander for not taking more account of the liturgical use of targumim. On the other hand one has to reckon with the fact that a "the Targum at the oral stage was never a haphazard, random, extemporaneous translation but rather it was a fixed, traditional, authorized version which was memorized and recited" (E.G. Clarke, "The Bible and Translation: The Targums", in B.H. McLean (ed.), *Origins and Method: Towards a New Understanding of Judaism and Christianity*, Sheffield 1993, 389 (380-93). See also Alexander, "Jewish Aramaic Translations", 238-39. Nevertheless if one takes the liturgical use of targumim seriously, one has to realise the possibility that the many original targumic texts later became standardised into those we now know (e.g. Targ. Yer. I, II and Neofiti).

[188] A.H. Rabbinowitz, "The 613 Commandments", *EJud* 5:760-61 (760-83).

[189] Urbach, *Sages*, pp. 836-37 (n. 1) points to Finkelstein's edition, where it is said that in MSS. א and ה the text has "the three hundred positive precepts in the Torah". This is perhaps meant to be a round number.

[190] See Urbach, *Sages*, p. 343 and Mek. Ex. Baḥodesh 5 (Lauterbach, *Mekilta* 2:236 (also quoted above)).

tions about the number of positive commandments and 300 is probably given as a round number. The earliest tradition which refers to 365 prohibitions and 248 positive commandments is probably that going back to R. Simlai, a Palestinian teacher of the second generation of the Amoraim.[191]

The earliest tradition of there being 248 members of the body is possibly Ohol. 1.8 (cf. b. Bek. 45a). On 248 commandments see y. Ber. 8b (4.4):

Herr der Welt, ich habe (in Gedanken) die 248 Glieder, die du mir gabst, geprüft und habe kein einziges Glied gefunden, von dem man sagen könnte, daß ich dich damit erzürnte, dann (habe ich doch) erst recht Anspruch darauf, am Leben erhalten zu bleiben.[192]

My conclusion then is that the tradition in Targ. Yer. I Gen. 1.27 probably comes from the period of the Amoraim.[193] There is, however, a possibility of it coming from the Tannaim. In that case it would be the earliest extant witness for there being 613 commandments in the Torah.

---

[191] See b. Mak. 23b: "R. Simlai when preaching said: Six hundred and thirteen precepts were communicated to Moses, three hundred and sixty-five negative precepts, corresponding to the number of solar days [in the year], and two hundred and forty-eight positive precepts, corresponding to the number of the members of man's body". The text continues (b. Mak. 24a) by giving the view of R. Hamnuna (third generation of Amoraim) that the number 613 is reached by taking the letter value of תורה (400 + 6 + 200 + 5 = 611) and adding the two commandments of the decalogue heard from the mouth of God ("I am"; "Thou shalt have no [other Gods]"). Note the parallel in Ex. R. 33.7 (although R. Hamnuna is not mentioned). A different method of arriving at 613 commandments is used in Num. R. 13.15-16; 18.21. Here it is said that there are 613 letters in the tables of the ten commandments (from אנכי (Ex. 20.2) to לרעך (Ex. 20.16)). In addition Num. R. 13.15-16 argues from the word קטרת (incense, Num. 7.20) that if ק, the fourth letter from the end of the alphabet is replaced by ד, the fourth letter from the beginning (a method of interchange called athbash), one arrives at דטרת which has a numerical value of 4 + 9 + 200 + 400 = 613, hence the number of commandments. Urbach, *Sages*, p. 343, writes that there is no evidence of an attempt to count the actual precepts in the Talmudic era and that the enumerators of the commandments from the compilers of Halakhot Gedolot onwards encountered many difficulties.

[192] Translation of C. Horowitz, *Der Jerusalemer Talmud in deutscher Übersetzung. Band I: Berakhoth*, Tübingen 1975, p. 131.

[193] Cf. Urbach, *Sages*, p. 343, and Avemarie, *Tora und Leben*, p. 51 n. 9.

11. Excursus on "Natural Law" in Greek Philosophy

In view of Rom. 1.18ff and Rom. 2.14-16, the issue of "natural law" is of some importance for Paul's argument. This excursus focuses on Greek Philosophy and then in the next excursus I consider Judaism.

In chapter 3 I considered briefly the relation of God to law. There certainly are Greek texts which relate God to law. See Cleanthes, *Hymn to Zeus* 1-2: "Greetings, most glorious of the immortals, of many names, almighty Zeus, ruler of nature, you who govern the universe according to law".[194] Note also that the world is likened to a "city", i.e. it is ruled by law,[195] an idea also found in Philo.[196] Further, one can say that Zeus is the directing logos and soul of the whole.[197] The deity itself is therefore the common law.[198] Also there are texts which make a link between God

---

[194] Translation taken from Bornkamm, "Wrath", 51. For the Greek see *SVF* 1:537: Κύδιστ᾽ ἀθανάτων, πολυώνυμε, παγκρατὲς αἰεί, Ζεῦ, φύσεως ἀρχηγέ, νόμου μέτα πάντα κυβερνῶν.

[195] See especially the texts in *SVF* 3:327-39. See, for example, Dio Chrysostom Or. 36 § 20: τὴν πόλιν φασὶν εἶναι πλῆθος ἀνθρώπων ἐν ταὐτῷ κατοικούντων ὑπὸ νόμου διοικούμενον (*SVF* 3:329). Text 327 is from Clement of Alexandria (*Stromata* 4.26) and text 328 from Stobaeus (*Eclogae* 2.7). See Cicero, *De natura deorum* 2.62: "For the world is as it were the common dwelling-place of gods and men, or the city that belongs to both; for they also have the use of reason and live by justice and by law" (Cicero (LCL), 19:273).

[196] See chapter 3 above. I add the text *De somniis* 2.245-49. In a discussion of Ps. 46.4 (Ps. 45.5 LXX) (Philo's version is τὸ ὅρμημα τοῦ ποταμοῦ εὐφραίνει τὴν πόλιν τοῦ θεοῦ ("the strong current of the river makes glad the city of God")) Philo argues this cannot refer to Jerusalem but refers to the universe (κόσμος). "It is perfectly true that the impetuous rush of the divine word (θείου λόγου) borne along (swiftly) and ceaselessly with its strong and ordered current does overflow and gladden the whole universe through and through" (2.247, Philo (LCL), 5:555-57). Also, the word πόλις can be used for the "soul of the Sage, in which God is said to walk as in a city" (2.248) as in Lev. 26.12. So "when the happy soul holds out the sacred goblet of its own reason, who is it that pours into it the holy cupfuls of true gladness, but the Word, the Cup-bearer of God and Master of the feast, who is also none other than the draught which he pours . . ?" (2.249, Philo (LCL), 5:555). Note the constant relation of the ordering of the universe and the ordering of moral life, here through the activity of the λόγος.

[197] See Philodemus, *De pietate* 11, who quotes Chrysippus, said who said Zeus was τὸν ἄπαντ(α διοικοῦ)ντα λόγον κ(αὶ τὴν) τοῦ ὅλου ψυχή(ν . .) (*SVF* 2:1076).

[198] See Diogenes Laertius 7.88 (*SVF* 1:162): ὁ νόμος ὁ κοινός, ὅσπερ ἐστὶν ὁ ὀρθὸς

and law by saying man shares something of the deity: "For we Thine off-spring are, and all created things that live and move on earth receive from Thee the image of the One".[199] Then there is the idea in Plutarch, where a link is made between the universe being "a most holy temple and most worthy of a god" and having a life "full of tranquillity and joy, and not in the manner of the vulgar . . . ".[200] Does not this give a background to Rom. 2.14-16 (as well as Rom 1.18ff)? To be even more specific, there is the tradition especially in Stoicism of the relation between law and nature. So Cicero gives the view that there is a link between law and nature in that there is one law given by God for all nations and all times and those who are disobedient will bear its penalties.[201]

Although there are some parallels here with Rom. 2.14-16 one has to bear in mind that parallels do not necessarily point to dependence.[202] Further, the parallels are not strong and there are some significant dif ferences.

First, I consider the specific issue of law and nature. For the Greeks, nature was the more important category and law was an arbitrary subjec-tive judgement. For Rom. 2.14-16, however, νόμος is central and φύσις is a subsidiary theme.[203]

λόγος, διὰ πάντων ἐρχόμενος, ὁ αὐτὸς ὢν τῷ Διΐ, καθηγεμόνι τούτῳ τῆς τῶν ὄντων διοικήσεως ὄντι.

[199] Cleanthes, *Hymn to Zeus* 4-5 (translation taken from Bornkamm, "Wrath", 52). For the Greek see SVF 1:537: ἐκ σοῦ γὰρ γένος εἴσ' ἤχου μίμημα λαχόντες μοῦνοι, ὅσα ζώει τε καὶ ἔρπει θνήτ' ἐπὶ γαῖαν. Note the word for image is μίμημα, not εἰκών or ὁμοίωμα.

[200] *De tranquillitate animi* 20 (477C-D) (Plutarch, (LCL), 6:239).

[201] Cicero, *De re publica* 3.33: "True law is right reason in agreement with nature (*Est quidem vera lex recta ratio naturae congruens*); it is of universal application, unchanging and everlasting; it summons to duty by its commands, and averts from wrongdoing by its prohibitions. . . . And there will not be different laws at Rome and at Athens, or different laws now and in the future, but one eternal and unchangeable law will be valid for all nations and all times, and there will be one master and ruler, that is, God, over us all, for he is the author of this law, its promulgator, and its enforcing judge. Whoever is disobedient is fleeing from himself and denying his human nature, and by reason of this very fact he will suffer the worst penalties, even if he escapes what is commonly considered punishment" (Cicero (LCL), 16:211).

[202] A point well made by S. Sandmel, "Parallelomania", *JBL* 81 (1962) 1-13, in reference to the way New Testament scholars use Rabbinic material.

[203] See Pohlenz, "Paulus und die Stoa", 529-30: "Für die Griechen war die Physis von vornherein die höchste Instanz auch in sittlichen Fragen, und ihr gegenüber

A second area in which scholars have seen a Greek pagan influence, and particularly a Stoic influence, is the question of conscience. Concerning συνείδησις A. Bonhöffer writes that it "spielt . . . in der Stoa gar keine nennenswerte Rolle".[204] It only occurs in Epictetus once and that is probably not genuine.[205] In any case Epictetus was born about the time Paul was writing Romans[206]. Pierce points out that Chrysippus predicates συνείδησις of every living creature.[207] However, it is not exclusive to man and has no moral connotation[208]. Marcus Aurelius, *Meditations* 6.30 once uses the term εὐσυνείδητος ("with a good conscience") but he is too late to throw any light on Paul.

Therefore, despite a recent attempt to read Rom. 2.14-16 in the light of Stoicism,[209] Paul appears *not* to be influenced directly by Stoicism in Rom. 2.14-16.[210] Neither is pagan Greek philosophy the key to the passage. I would therefore question Bornkamm's assertion that the passage

---

wurde der Nomos zur willkürlichen subjektiven Menschenschätzung, die nur relative Verbindlichkeit gewann, wenn sie sich bei einem Volke durchsetzte. Von diesen einzelnen Nomoi schieden dann freilich die Stoiker den die ganze Menschheit umfassenden und verpflichtenden Nomos, das Vernunftgesetz; aber seine bindende Kraft hatte dieses nur, weil es sich auf die Physis gründete, die also den höchsten Platz behauptete. Bei Paulus dagegen wurde dieser gerade von dem Nomos eingenommen; denn er kannte nur das eine von Gott gegebene und seinem jüdischen Volke geoffenbarte Gesetz, neben dem es keine andere Autorität in sittlichen Fragen geben konnte, am wenigsten in einer von Gott unabhängigen Natur".

[204] Bonhöffer, *Epiktet und das Neue Testament*, p. 156.

[205] Schweighäuser, Fr. 97 (see also C.A. Pierce, *Conscience in the New Testament*, London 1955, p. 15). See Epictetus, *Discourses* 3.22.94 (LCL, 2:165) for the use of τὸ συνειδός. But Bonhöffer points out that here τὸ συνειδός means selfconsciousness and has no ethical meaning (see also Eckstein, *Syneidesis*, p. 65): τῷ δὲ Κυνικῷ ἀντὶ τῶν ὅπλων καὶ τῶν δορυφόρων τὸ συνειδὸς τὴν ἐξουσίαν ταύτην παραδίδωσιν.

[206] His dates, according to *KP*, 2:313, are 55-135 AD.

[207] Pierce, *Conscience*, p. 14.

[208] See *SVF* 3:178 (Diogenes Laertius 7.85).

[209] J.W. Martens, "Romans 2.14-16: A Stoic Reading", *NTS* 40 (1994) 55-67.

[210] On Rom. 1.28 (τὰ μὴ καθήκοντα) see Martens' admission that Paul is not using the exact Stoic term (this would be παρὰ τὸ καθῆκον, see Bonhöffer, *Epiktet und das Neue Testament*, pp. 157-58, and Pohlenz, "Paulus und die Stoa", 526).

2.14-16 is "allein aus griechischen Denken verständlich"[211]. Judaism provides a much more satisfactory background and it is to the issue of "natural law" in Judaism that I now turn.

12. Excursus on "Natural Law" in Judaism

As I have already pointed out in the exegesis of Rom. 2.14-16, one of the key Jewish ideas behind these verses is the relation of wisdom and law. The two began to be related as early as Dt. 4.6 and further developed in Psalms 1 and 119.[212] So in Ps. 119 there is some sort of natural law.[213] In Ps. 119.89-90 we read: "For ever, O Lord, thy word is firmly fixed in the heavens. Thy faithfulness endures to all generations; thou hast established the earth, and it stands fast".[214] Such a text may well have influenced Paul's thinking in Rom. 2.14-16. But more important is the later development of this where there is a complete identification of torah and wisdom. This, as Hengel has argued, came about because of the encounter with Hellenistic thought. So the view in Stoicism of the relation between law and nature influenced the view found in Ben Sirach concerning the link between law and wisdom, whereby wisdom is seen as a "kind of '*world reason*' emanating from God, which filled and permeated the whole creation and finds the culmination of its task in making man a rational being".[215] Wisdom in Ben Sirach was therefore similar to the Stoic logos.[216] Ben Sirach has probably been influenced by Stoicism here.

---

[211] Bornkamm, "Gesetz und Natur", 104.

[212] Hengel, *Judaism and Hellenism*, p. 161. See also chapter 3 above.

[213] Barr, *Natural Theology*, pp. 89-90, stresses the role of natural law in Ps. 119 but, I believe, makes the mistake of thinking this supports "natural theology". I hope I have made it clear in chapter 3 why "natural law" does not necessarily support "natural theology".

[214] J.D. Levenson, "The Sources of the Torah: Psalm 119 and the Modes of Revelation in Second Temple Judaism", in P.D. Miller, P.D. Hanson and S.D. McBride (ed.), *Ancient Israelite Religion*, Philadelphia 1987, 569 (559-74), referred to in Barr, *Natural Theology*, p. 90, writes that "the commandments that the psalmist practices, even those which may be Pentateuchal, constitute a kind of revealed natural law".

[215] Hengel, *Judaism and Hellenism*, 1:159. Hengel points to Sir. 1.9-10, 19.

[216] See Diogenes Laertius 7.88 and Cicero, *De re publica* 3.33 (quoted above).

Further, Stoic thought may well have exerted an influence on Ben Sirach in that the logos not only ordered the universe (in a deterministic way) but also directed the ways of men and women who were responsible human agents.[217] Also, Hellenism influenced Judaism in that certain Greek views were found unacceptable and therefore forced parts of Judaism to renounce certain ideas and develop their own. So in the conflict with Hellenism, if Greeks had their "wisdom", the Jews could counteract this by saying they also had a "wisdom" which was "torah".[218] Also Ben Sirach's stress on free will (15.11-17) may be a rejection of the determinism found in Koheleth, in Wisdom schools and in determinist astrology which were in turn influenced by Hellenism.[219]

I believe the ontological view of the Torah which developed during the time of hellenisation, where the cosmic function of Wisdom was passed on to the law, is important for Rom. 2.14-16. There is therefore Hellenistic influence on Paul, but little direct influence. Also there are certain Jewish texts referring to a sort of natural law which, while not perhaps directly influencing Paul, do show that Jews where saying roughly similar things. So there are the texts already mentioned: Test. Jud. 20, 2 Bar. 57.2, and Philo, *De Abrahamo* 175-76. Further, there are texts which relate law to creation, which is of interest in view of Rom. 1.18-32. So this is found for example in Philo[220] and 4 Maccabees.[221] Again it is unlikely that these authors directly influenced Paul. Paul the Pharisee

---

[217] Cf. Diogenes Laertius 7.87 (*SVF* 1:552).

[218] Hengel, *Judaism and Hellenism*, 1:162, in agreement with J. Fichtner, *Die altorientalische Weisheit in ihrer israelitisch-jüdischen Ausprägung*, Gießen, 1933, pp. 127-28.

[219] Hengel, *Judaism and Hellenism*, 1:140.

[220] See *De vita Mosis* 2.51, where Philo writes that Moses "inserted the story of the genesis of the 'Great City', holding that the laws were the most faithful picture of the world-polity" (Philo (LCL), 6:475). See also *De specialibus legibus* 2.13: "what else are laws and statutes but the sacred word of Nature" (Philo (LCL), 7:315).

[221] 4 Mac. 5.25: "Therefore we do not eat defiling food; for since we believe that the law was established by God, we know that in the nature of things the Creator of the world in giving us the law has shown sympathy toward us". This text is interesting not so much in that it points to a νόμος ἄγραφος as Käsemann, *Römer*, p. 59, believes (this point is debatable), but because it relates the Jewish law (including the ceremonial law!) to God's will in creation.

would probably find Philo's Alexandrian theology alien or even heretical. As far as 4 Maccabees is concerned, although it was later part of the Septuagint, it was probably written too late to have influenced Paul.[222] But nevertheless, these texts show that Jews around Paul's time were perhaps thinking similar things about natural law.

Hellenism not only affected the so-called "Hellenistic Judaism"; it also influenced "Palestinian Judaism". So the idea found in Targ. Yer. I Gen. 1.27 may have been influenced by Greek thought.[223] The idea that the created human being reflects the torah is similar to the Greek view that there is a link between natural theology (especially the teleological argument) and natural law; in fact in the teleological arguments much was made of the structure of the human being.[224] It is also possible and perhaps probable that Greek idea of $\nu\acute{o}\mu o\varsigma$ $\check{\alpha}\gamma\rho\alpha\phi o\varsigma$ influenced texts such as 2 Bar. 57.2.[225]

One Jewish idea which may possibly have influenced Paul's argument concerning natural law (and theology of nature) is the understanding of the temple/tabernacle. Admittedly Paul does not mention the temple in Rom. 1.18-3.20 but the Jewish understanding of it does bring together a remarkably wide spectrum of issues which were of interest for Paul. First, the temple or tabernacle and its contents were seen to reflect the universe. This view was found in Philo and Josephus, and as I argued in chapter 3 above, may well go back to the Priestly writer. The view can

---

[222] G.W.E. Nickelsburg, *Jewish Literature between the Bible and the Mishnah: A Historical and Literary Introduction*, Philadelphia 1981, p. 226, suggests a date of 40 AD, the book being written in response to Caligula's attempt to erect his statue in the Temple. This dating was earlier suggested by M. Hadas, *The Third and Fourth Books of Maccabees*, New York 1953, pp. 95-96.

[223] For other ways in which Greek thought influenced Rabbinic anthropology, see R. Meyer, *Hellenistisches in der rabbinischen Anthropologie: Rabbinische Vorstellungen vom Werden des Menschen* Stuttgart 1937.

[224] See Pease, "Caeli enarrant", 171-72, and the references to Aristotle's discussion of the parts of the human body. It is interesting to compare the "anthropic principle", much discussed in the present science-theology debate. This principle points to the fine-tuning in the forces of nature and in the initial conditions of the universe which allows the evolution of human life. See, for example, J.D. Barrow and F.J. Tipler, *The Anthropic Cosmological Principle*, Oxford 1986.

[225] Heinemann, "Lehre", 164-65.

also be found in a variety of Rabbinic texts.[226] In fact the Rabbis believed that the contruction of the earth began with the foundation stone of the temple, the Eben Shetiyah.[227] The earth is said to have stood firm once the sanctuary was built.[228] The tabernacle and its separate parts correspond to the six days of creation. The two tables in the ark correspond to the heaven and earth created on the first day; the curtain dividing the holy from the holy of holies corresponds to the firmament created on the second day; the laver corresponds to the great sea created on the third day and likewise the bread of the presence corresponds to the plant kingdom created on the third day to nourish man; the candlestick corresponds to the two luminous bodies, the sun and the moon and the seven branches of the candlestick correspond to the seven planets created on the fourth day; the cherubim correspond to the birds created on the fifth day; man created on the sixth day does not correspond to any particular part of the tabernacle but was appointed to minister in it.[229] Such views cohere rather well with Paul's theology of nature. Secondly, the tabernacle/temple was a reflection of the human body.[230] The concept of the temple may then be a way of relating natural law and natural theology. It is also significant that the early Christian tradition associated Christ, the Christian and the Church with the temple[231] and Paul in Rom. 3.25 relates Christ to the

---

[226] See, for example, B. Ego, *Im Himmel wie auf Erden: Studien zum Verhältnis von himmlischer und irdischer Welt im rabbinischen Judentum*, Tübingen 1989, pp. 21-22, 42-43, who discusses the temple as a microcomos and an *imago mundi*.

[227] L. Ginzberg, *The Legends of the Jews* ET, 7 vols, Philadelphia 1909-38, 1:12. For the sources see *Legends*, 5:14-16 (n. 39). See, for example, b. Yoma 54b: "AND IT WAS CALLED SHETIYAH: A Tanna taught: [It was so called] because from it the world was founded. We were taught in accord with the view that the world was started [created] from Zion on". The Ark of the covenant is said to stand on this foundation stone. See t. Yoma 3.6, quoted in Billerbeck, *Kommentar*, 3:170 (b): "Ein Stein war dort (im Allerheiligsten) seit den Tagen der früheren Propheten, u. er wurde Grundstein שתייה genannt, u. seine Höhe betrug von der Erde an 3 Fingerbreiten, denn anfänglich befand sich dort auf ihm die Lade (daher der Name 'Grundstein')".

[228] Ginzberg, *Legends*, 3:150. See also *Legends*, 6:62 n. 320.

[229] Ginzberg, *Legends*, 3:151. For the texts see *Legends*, 6:62-63 (n. 321).

[230] See Jensen, *Holiness*, p. 98. See also Ginzberg, *Legends*, 6:62-63 (n. 321).

[231] For Christ see Jn 2.21 ("he spoke of the temple of his body", cf. 2.19) and 1.14 (Jesus as tabernacle). There is disagreement on Mk 14.58 (Mt. 26.61). R. Pesch, *Das Markusevangelium*, 2 vols, Freiburg/Basel/Wien 1 ⁵1989, (¹1976); 2

ἱλαστήριον.[232] This view is speculative, but I offer it as one possible way of explaining some of Paul's thought on natural law (and theology of nature).

In this connection it is instructive to compare the role of "natural law" in Rom. 1.18-32 and that in Rom. 2.14-16. In the former passage, law and creation are clearly linked, the background to this being the Jewish link between creation and law. It is important to recognise that this law which is related to creation is also related to the law revealed to Israel. So Jervell makes the point that Paul does not have a natural revelation in 1.18-32 which stands in contrast to the revelation of law of the Jews.[233] 1.18-32 speaks of the revelation of the law, "aber von dieser doch so, wie sie in den Schöpfungswerken und in den Taten Gottes in der Geschichte and Natur zum Ausdruck kommt".[234] However, I differ from Jervell in emphasising that God himself is revealed in Rom. 1.19-21a. This knowledge is lost but the remnant of the knowledge is knowledge of the law. In Rom. 2.14-16, Paul does not directly relate the law which the Gentiles do to creation. But, as I argued in the exegesis of this passage, there is an indirect link, for Paul has in mind the torah ontology found in the wisdom

---

[4]1991, ([1]1977), 2:434, believes Jesus is simply speaking of the destruction of the Jerusalem temple and the building of the messianic temple. Contrast the view of W. Lane, *The Gospel according to Mark*, Grand Rapids 1974, p. 534, who understands Mk 14.58 in the light of Jn 2.19. For the believer as a temple see 1 Cor. 6.19 and for the body of Christians as a temple see 1 Cor. 3.16-17. See also the view of the Church as a temple in Eph. 2.19-21.

[232] The mercy seat was the most important part of the ark which according to Rabbinic tradition was built upon the foundation stone (see above).

[233] Jervell, *Imago Dei*, p. 325, points to Test. Naph. 3.4: "In the firmament, in the earth, and in the sea, in all the product of his workmanship discern the Lord who made all things, so that you do not become like Sodom, which departed from the order (τάξις) of nature.

[234] Jervell, *Imago Dei*, p. 318. See also Moore, *Judaism*, 1:276-77, who points to the law being the focus of the revelation of God and if the fortunes of nations (and destiny after death) depend on keeping the law, does it not seem unjust that they know nothing of it. And so the tradition developed that the law must have been revealed to Gentiles also (p. 277), "not alone the rudimentary law given to Adam and repeated to Noah, but the law in its Sinaitic completeness" (p. 277). On the revelation of the law to the nations see the excursus "Rabbinic view of the Law revealed to the Gentiles" and the excursus below "Tradition of righteous Gentiles in Judaism".

tradition and in Rabbinic Judaism. And so in this passage Paul refers to the law which has been revealed to Jews and Gentiles in different ways.[235]

Again the overwhelming impression is that Paul was primarily influenced in both Rom. 1.18-32 and 2.14-16 by Jewish thought; further, any Hellenistic influences appear to have come via Judaism.

13. Excursus on the Tradition of Righteous Gentiles in Judaism

Although the general view in Judaism was that the Gentiles form a *massa perditionis*, there are occasional texts which point to Gentiles being saved. This again is of interest in view of Rom. 2.12-16.

The first text I wish to consider in b. Sanh. 105a. The translation given in the Soncino edition is as follows:

Now only Balaam will not enter [the future world], but other [heathens] will enter. On whose authority is the Mishnah [taught]? — On R. Joshua's. For it has been taught: R. Eliezer said, 'The wicked shall be turned into hell, and all the nations that forget God' (Ps. 9.17). 'The wicked shall be turned into hell' — this refers to trans-gressors among Israel; 'and all the nations that forget God' — to transgressors among the heathen. This is R. Eliezer's view. But R. Joshua said to him: Is it stated, and [those] *among* all the nations? Surely 'all the nations that forget God' is written! But [interpret thus]: 'The wicked shall be turned into hell', and who are they? — 'all the nations that forget God'.

Such a text based on the Vilna edition gives the impression that Eliezer is lenient but Joshua is strict.[236] However, on text critical considerations it seems clear that it was Joshua who was the more lenient. The key point is that the word פשעי is missing in Ms. Florence and Karlsruhe.[237] So Eliezer's view is "'The wicked shall be turned into hell' — this refers to

---

[235] See the quotation from Pohlenz, "Paulus und die Stoa", 531, quoted above, n. 105. Note, that Rom. 2.14-15 has been a key text in the catholic discussion of natural law. See, for example, A. Scharnagl, "Naturrecht", *LThK*[1] 7:453 (453-55), and A. Eberle, "Naturgesetz", *LThK*[1] 7:451 (451-53).

[236] This is assumed by B. Salomonsen, *Die Tosephta. Seder IV: Nezikin 3: San-hedrin - Makkot*, Stuttgart/Berlin/Köln/Mainz 1976, p. 203 n. 15: "Nach b Sanh 105a vertritt R. Eli'ezer die mildere Ansicht", who it appears had only the Vilna edition to hand.

[237] See R.N.N. Rabbinovicz, *Sefer dikdukei sofrim. Variae Lectiones in Mischnam et in Talmud Babylonicum*, 16 vols, Munich/Mainz/Przemysl 1866-97, 11:324.

transgressors among Israel; 'and all the nations that forget God' — to the heathen". Further Yalqut Shimoni[238] gives: ישובו רשעים לשאול' אלו פושעי ישר'. כל גוים שכחי אלהים אלו אומות העולם.

That it was Eliezer who was strict and Joshua lenient is confirmed by t. Sanh. 13.2.

> R. Eliezer says, 'None of the gentiles has a portion in the world to come as it is said, 'The wicked shall return to Sheol, all the gentiles who forget God' (Ps. 9.17). 'The wicked return to Sheol — these are the wicked Israelites'. [Supply: 'And all the gentiles who forget God — these are the nations']. Said to him R. Joshua, 'If it had been written, 'the wicked shall return to Sheol — all the gentiles', and then said nothing further, I should have maintained as you do. Now that it is in fact written, 'All the gentiles who forget God', it indicates that there also are righteous people among the nations of the world, who do have a portion in the world to come'."[239]

Therefore it was R. Joshua who was lenient, not R. Eliezer.

There was also the tradition that Gentiles who obey the commandments share its promises.

> R. Meir used to say, Whence do we know that even a heathen who studies the Torah is as a High Priest? From the verse, '[Ye shall therefore keep my statutes, and my judgements:] which, if man do, he shall live in them' (Lev. 18.5). Priests, Levites, and Israelites are not mentioned, but 'men': hence thou mayest learn that even a heathen who studies the Torah is as a High Priest! — That refers to their own seven laws.[240]

14. Conclusions

In view of the above analysis I conclude that the main purpose of Rom. 2.1-16 is to establish that both Jew and Gentile will be judged according to works, the standard by which they are judged being the law. Further, Rom. 2.12-13 makes it quite plain that a complete obedience to the law is

---

[238] See A. Hyman and J. Shiloni (ed.), *Yalqut Shim'oni: Bemidbar*, Jerusalem 1986, p. 472.

[239] J. Neusner, *The Tosefta: Neziqin*, New York 1981, p. 238.

[240] b. Sanh. 105a (cf. b. Abod. Zar. 3a; b. Bab. Kam. 38a). There is also a discussion in Sifra on Lev. 18.5 in the name of R. Jeremiah. Note, however, the opposite view of R. Johanan in b. Sanh. 105a: "A heathen who studies the Torah deserves death".

necessary in order to be acquitted at the final judgement. But what about repentance (Rom. 2.4)? Does not this assume that perfect obedience is not in fact required? The answer, perhaps surprisingly, is no. Repentance in Judaism in Paul's time was very often seen as a "work".[241] Therefore repentance itself could be seen as belonging to the category "works". Therefore strange as it may seem, "perfect obedience" could include an element of repentance. However, it seems that such repentance seemed to play at most a minor part in Paul's consideration of the final judgement. In this sense Paul shared the view of the apocalypses, where "Die Umkehr nimmt . . . einen sehr begrenzten Raum ein".[242]

In view of this theology of justification by works, the most important question is how and whether this view can be reconciled to Paul's theology elsewhere of justification *sola fide*, *sola gratia*. This issue will be addressed in the final chapter.

---

[241] See R.H. Bell, "Teshubah: The Idea of Repentance in Ancient Judaism", *JPJ* 5 (1995) 42-45.

[242] E. Sjöberg, *Gott und die Sünder im palästinischen Judentum*, Stuttgart/Berlin 1938, p. 250. There are a number of texts where repentance is discussed (see, e.g., Jub. 1.23, quoted in the previous note). However, it must be said that "der positive Wunsch Gottes, daß die Sünder, statt dem endgültigen Gericht zu verfallen, durch die Umkehr gerettet werden, sehr wenig zum Ausdruck kommt" (Sjöberg, *Gott und die Sünder*, p. 215). Sjöberg, commenting on 1 En. 91-105, writes (p. 251 n. 4): "Hier finden wir Mahnungen an die Gerechten, an Gott festzuhalten, weiterhin auf dem Wege der Gerechtigkeit zu gehen und sich vor jeder Sünde zu hüten (I Hen. 91,3f.19; 94,1.3f; 104,6 und öfters). Die Sünder dagegen werden nur mit Droh- und Weherufen angeredet (I Hen. 94,6-11; 95,4-7; 96,4-8; 97,2-10; 98,1-100,4; 100,7-9; 102,1-3.9-11; 103,5-8). Die einzige Ausnahme ist I Hen. 104,9, wo wirklich die Sünder zum Aufgeben ihrer törichten Gottlosigkeit ermahnt werden. Aber auch hier ist diese Mahnung sehr wenig betont. Dem Verfasser liegt vielmehr daran, die Torheit der Sünder darzustellen, als daran, sie von ihrer Torheit zu bekehren". This last sentence could be applied to Paul's warning in Rom. 2.4. As far as rabbinic Judaism was concerned, there was more room for repentance. But even here repentance is not possible for everyone. For example, there was no forgiveness for leading many to sin (Aboth 5.18) or for profaning the divine name (Sifre Dt. 328 (on Dt. 32.38)). That Paul regarded perfect obedience as necessary suggests that he belonged to the "right wing" of the rabbinic spectrum. Cf. Gamaliel II who wept when he came to the end of the 13 requirements of Ezek. 18.5-9. "Only he who keeps all these requirements will live, not he who keeps only one of them" (b. Sanh. 81a). See the similar story in b. Makk. 24a regarding the 613 laws.

Chapter 5

Romans 2.17-3.8: The Self-Righteous Jew

1. Introduction

Many commentators take Rom. 2.17-29 with Rom. 2.1-16.[1] However, although there may be certain common elements in 2.1-16 and 2.17-29, I believe it makes more sense to take Rom. 2.17-29 with 3.1-8.[2] There are two main considerations here. First, I have already argued that Rom. 1.18-2.16 forms a unit.[3] Secondly, Rom. 2.17-3.8 concerns Jews whereas the vast majority of the text in Rom. 1.18-2.16 concerns both Jew and Gentile (1.18-2.11) or concerns Gentiles (2.14-16). In fact it may be that 2.12a (ὅσοι γὰρ ἀνόμως ἥμαρτον, ἀνόμως καὶ ἀπολοῦνται) acts as a heading for 2.14-16 (Gentiles) and 2.12b (καὶ ὅσοι ἐν νόμῳ ἥμαρτον, διὰ νόμου κριθήσονται) as a heading for 2.17-3.8 (Jews).[4] After this section on the Jews, Paul then returns to speak of Jews and Gentiles in 3.9-20.

2. Romans 2.17-24: The Jew is just as guilty as the Gentile

Rom. 2.17-24 is related to 2.1-5. This can be seen both in the content of these passages[5] and in the fact that they both occur in the second person singular.[6] But whereas 2.1-5 concerns any self-righteous person, 2.17-24 concerns the self-righteous Jew.[7] But why the *self-righteous* Jew? Is not

---

[1] E.g. Godet, *Romans*, p. 113; C. Hodge, *A Commentary on the Epistle to the Romans*, Grand Rapids ²1950, (¹1864), p. 46.

[2] Cf. *GNT*⁴ and Stott, *Romans*, p. 90.

[3] See chapter 1 above.

[4] Cf. Berger, *Exegese*, p. 24.

[5] Cf. Ziesler, *Romans*, p. 89, who sees Rom. 2.17-24 as a repetition and expansion of 2.1-3.

[6] Berger, *Exegese*, p. 23.

such language a step backwards in the light of the "progress" made in Pauline studies? I think not, for there are indications in the Pauline writings that Paul can write about the self-righteous Jew. First, if Rom. 2.1-5 refers to the self-righteous person generally, why cannot 2.17-24 refer to the self-righteous Jew? Not only are both passages in the second person singular, but also the content is similar. Both passages deal with people who think they are righteous and judge others, but in fact are really no better than those they judge. So the whole point of 2.17-24 is that the Jew addressed believes himself to be in a superior position. He believes himself to be a guide to the blind, a light to those in darkness (v. 19), a corrector of the foolish and teacher of children (v. 20).[8] Further he "boasts in God" (v. 17) and "boasts in the law" (v. 23). Does this not show that Paul is concerned with the self-righteous Jew? And just as Jesus is portrayed as attacking the self-righteous Pharisees in Mt. 23.1-36, so Paul here attacks the self-righteous Jew.

The passage has a striking rhetorical structure, consisting of two sections, vv. 17-20 and vv. 21-24[9]. Whether one can speak of a diatribe,[10] I am not so sure. As noted in chapter 4, the second person singular is characteristic of, but not peculiar to, the Hellenistic diatribe[11] and, as in 2.1-5, may be used for the sake of vividness. On a more general level I agree with Norden that Paul's letters do have a certain rhetorical elegance (2 Cor. 10.10) which is lacking in the Gospels but not such as he obtained by reading Greek authors.[12] On the particular issue of the diatribe I tend towards the more sceptical positions of Judge[13] and Schmeller.[14]

---

[7] Lightfoot, *Notes*, p. 258, compares Rom. 2.17-19 with the opening of the parable of the Pharisee and Publican (Lk. 18.9).

[8] See below, where I argue that Paul is not being entirely ironical is describing the Jew's privileged position.

[9] See Wilckens, *Römer*, 1:146-47.

[10] See S.K. Stowers, *The Diatribe and Paul's Letter to the Romans*, Chico, California 1981, and more recently S. K. Stowers, *A Rereading of Romans*, New Haven/London 1994, p. 150.

[11] Cranfield, *Romans*, 1:142.

[12] E. Norden, *Die antike Kunstprosa vom VI. Jahrhundert v. Chr. bis in die Zeit der Renaissance, II*, Leipzig/Berlin 1909, pp. 506-7.

[13] E.A. Judge, "St Paul and Classical Society", JAC 15 (1972) 33 (19-36). See also Bell, *Provoked to Jealousy*, p. 75 n. 180.

Nevertheless, an interesting parallel to 2.17-24 can be found in Epictetus, *Discourses* 2.19.19-20 and 3.7.17, where he taunts his contemporary Stoics for not being true Stoics.[15] Epictetus, though, is obviously too late to influence Paul.[16]

In v. 17 Paul refers to the Jew explicitly for the first time in chapter 2. The person who calls himself a Jew relies on the law and boasts in God (2.17). The use of the verb καυχᾶσθαι here and in 2.23 raises the issue of the nature of this boasting. Is it a boasting in God (v. 17) and in the law (v. 23) in the sense that the Jew believes he has a special status?[17] Or is the Jew boasting in his performance of the law which involves an element of self-reliance?[18] Bultmann's general point about Paul's use of καυχᾶσθαι is that it "discloses the basic attitude of the Jew to be one of self-confidence which seeks glory before God and which relies upon

---

[14] T. Schmeller, *Paulus und die 'Diatribe'*, Münster 1987. He argues that the "diatribe" is no actual Gattung, "sondern ein in jeder Hinsicht ausgesprochen vielgestaltiges und schwer bestimmbares Phänomen mündlicher, dann auch literarischer Rede" (p. 428). Any influence from the so-called "Diatribe" is weak (p. 431) and there are significant differences in both content and style. For example, as far as content is concerned, he writes: "Während die 'Diatribe' konkrete, existentiell betreffende und verbreitete Lebensprobleme behandelt, geht es Paul um Probleme, die aus dem christlichen Glaubensvollzug und/oder seiner Reflexion resultieren, die demnach ausschließlich Glaubende betreffen" (p. 432).

[15] See Fridrichsen, "Jude", 45; Fitzmyer, *Romans*, p. 315. See, for example, *Discourses* 2.19.19, where Epictetus criticises the so called Stoics for their baseness, cowardice and bragging. "Why did you pride yourself upon things that were not your own? Why did you call yourself a Stoic?" (Epictetus (LCL), 1:365).

[16] Dodd, *Romans*, pp. 148-49, considers Rom. 9-11 to be highly reminiscent of Epictetus, who, he believes, is the best familiar example of the diatribe. Stowers, *Diatribe*, pp. 112-13 (p. 223 nn. 139-142) points to a number of parallels between Rom. 2.17-24 and Epictetus. For example, he points to the ὁδηγός of Epictetus, *Discourses* 2.12.3, who leads the person who goes astray to the right path. This may be compared to Rom. 2.19a: πέποιθάς τε σεαυτὸν ὁδηγὸν εἶναι τυφλῶν. But the biblical text he also mentions form a much more appropriate background (i.e. Is. 42.6; 49.6; Mt. 15.14; 23.16, 24). Likewise he compares the Jew being a παιδευτής to *Discourses* 3.22.77 and 1.9.18-20. However, a more appropriate parallel can be discovered simply by consulting Hatch and Redpath, *Concordance* (see Sir. 37.19: ἔστιν ἀνὴρ πανοῦργος πολλῶν παιδευτής, καὶ τῇ ἰδίᾳ ψυχῇ ἐστιν ἄχρηστος).

[17] Sanders, *Paul, the Law, and the Jewish People*, pp. 32-33.

[18] R. Bultmann, καυχάομαι κτλ, *TDNT* 3:648-52 (643-54).

itself".[19] On 2.17, 23 he writes that "boasting in God and the Law which Judaism requires has been perverted into an ἐπαναπαύεσθαι νόμῳ" and that "this καυχᾶσθαι is in truth a πεποιθέναι ἐν σαρκί (Phil. 3:3f)".[20] I believe it is difficult to fault Bultmann's analysis. In fact his analysis is more subtle than many commentators have allowed, for implicit in his remarks is the idea that the Jew boasts in his possession of the law. There is both the element of performance and the element of relying on the law, giving rise to a complacent attitude. So the alternatives *either* boasting in possession of the law *or* boasting in performance of the law are false alternatives in Rom. 2.17-24. I suggest that *both* ideas are to be found in 2.17 and 2.23. It is instructive to compare 2 Bar. 48.22: "In you we have put our *trust*, because, behold, *your Law is with us*, and we know that *we do not fall as long as we keep your statutes*".[21] However, in Rom. 3.27-4.2, where cognates of καυχᾶσθαι occur (καύχησις in 3.27 and καύχημα in 4.2), boasting seems to be in the doing of the law, not in the possession of the law. For a discussion of Rom. 3.27 see the concluding discussion in chapter 7 below.

Paul goes on to criticise this boasting. On what basis? Thompson believes that boasting in itself is not wrong; Paul criticises boasting because the Jew has failed to keep the law.[22] There is certainly support in the text that Paul criticises the boasting of the Jew because he fails to keep the law, but I wonder whether this is the whole story. Although it is the case that the Old Testament can speak positively of boasting[23], wherever boasting involves self-confidence, it is condemned.[24] I suggest that Rom. 2.17-24 concerns not only transgressing the law but also an attitude of

---

[19] Bultmann, καυχάομαι, 648-49.

[20] Bultmann, καυχάομαι, 649.

[21] Translation of Klijn, in Charlesworth, *Pseudepigrapha*, 1:636.

[22] R.W. Thompson, "Paul's Double Critique of Jewish Boasting: A Study of Rom 3,27 in Its Context", *Bib* 67 (1986) 523 (520-31): "God is not dishonored by boasting but by transgressions. The boasting, in and of itself, receives no criticism".

[23] See Jer. 9.24, taken up by Paul in 1 Cor. 1.31.

[24] See S. Travis, "Paul's Boasting in 2 Corinthians 10-12", in E.A. Livingstone (ed.), *Studia Evangelica Vol VI*, Berlin 1973, 527 (527-32), who points to 1 Kgs 20.11; Prov. 25.14; 27.1. For the specific idea of boasting before God see Judg. 7.2; 1 Sam. 2.2-3.

self-confidence. It is significant that although the pre-Christian Paul considered himself blameless under the law (Phil. 3.6), he nevertheless as a Christian considered this boasting to be wrong.[25]

Paul then continues in vv. 18-20 to put forward the Jew's self-understanding. So in v. 18 the Jew is said to know God's will (γινώσκεις τὸ θέλημα) and to distinguish the things that matter (δοκιμάζεις τὰ διαφέροντα)[26] being taught by the law (κατηχούμενος ἐκ τοῦ νόμου). Barth rightly comments: "Though there may be some irony in these words, they are not merely ironical, but also a sincere acknowledgement of the position and the mission which the Jews have in fact been given in the Gentile metropolis and in the whole Gentile world".[27] He goes on to make the valid point that in the Old Testament Israel was regarded as "a guide to the blind, a light to those who are in darkness, a corrector of the foolish" (vv.19b-20a).[28] Paul therefore is by no means relativising the elec-

---

[25] In Phil. 3.4b he says he had every reason for confidence in the flesh. He then lists four items related to his birth and upbringing (περιτομῇ ὀκταήμερος, ἐκ γένους Ἰσραήλ, φυλῆς Βενιαμίν, Ἑβραῖος ἐξ Ἑβραίων). These are followed by three items over which he had a choice: he was a Pharisee (κατὰ νόμον Φαρισαῖος), he was a persecutor of the Church (κατὰ ζῆλος διώκων τὴν ἐκκλησίαν) and was blameless under the law (κατὰ δικαιοσύνην τὴν ἐν νόμῳ γενόμενος ἄμεμπτος). As R.H. Gundry, "Grace, Works and Staying Saved in Paul", *Bib* 66 (1985) 13 (1-38), points out, Paul begins with boasting in his Jewish status "but climaxes with confidence in personal accomplishments". Further, in opposition to Sanders, *Law*, p. 44, he rightly argues that in Phil. 2.3-11 "we are dealing with an autobiographical as well as a dispensational shift" (13).

[26] So Cranfield, *Romans*, 1:166.

[27] Barth, *Shorter Commentary*, p. 37. Cf. Schlatter, *Gottes Gerechtigkeit*, p. 105, who writes: "von Ironie ist hier gar nichts vorhanden". Contrast J.-M. Cambier, "Le jugement de tous les hommes par Dieu seul, selon la vérité, dans Rom 2₁-3₂₀", *ZNW* 67 (1976) 205 (187-213).

[28] See, for example, Is. 42.6b-7a (εἰς φῶς ἐθνῶν 7 ἀνοῖξαι ὀφθαλμοὺς τυφλῶν) and 49.6b (ἰδοὺ τέθεικά σε εἰς διαθήκην γένους εἰς φῶς ἐθνῶν τοῦ εἶναί σε εἰς σωτηρίαν ἕως ἐσχάτου τῆς γῆς). See also Wis. 18.4 (through Israel "the imperishable light of the law was to be given to the world"); Sib. 3.194-95 ("And then the people of the great God will again be strong who will be guides in life for all mortals" (translation of J.J. Collins, in Charlesworth, *Pseudepigrapha*, 1:366)); 1 En. 105.1b ("Reveal it to them your wisdom, for you are their guides; and (you are) a reward upon the whole earth" (translation of E. Isaac, in Charlesworth, *Pseudepigrapha*, 1:86)).

tion of Israel. This becomes absolutely clear in Rom. 3.1-8 (and, of course, in Rom. 9-11).

Then in v. 20 are the striking words: ἔχοντα τὴν μόρφωσιν τῆς γνώσεως καὶ τῆς ἀληθείας ἐν τῷ νόμῳ.[29] Barth comments: "In its Law it really does possess 'the embodiment (the form) of knowledge and truth'".[30] Barth continues: "But only their form, and, in spite of all endeavours to live according to that form, not knowledge and truth themselves. For Jesus Christ is knowledge and truth, the essence and the sum total of the Law (10.4)".[31] I largely agree with Barth. The word μόρφωσις can mean the act of forming or the result of such activity (i.e. a form, meaning roughly the same as μορφή).[32] Here the word is to be taken is this second sense. But then a further distinction can be made. μόρφωσις could then either mean "form" in the sense of "embodiment" or it could mean "external form" or "appearance". Paul in Rom. 2.20 probably means the former (the latter meaning being found in 2 Tim. 3.5).[33] The law then does contain the embodiment of knowledge and of truth.

Although the Jew knows the will of God, is instructed from the law (v. 18), and considers himself a teacher of others (19-20), he does not teach himself (v. 21a).[34] In 2.21b-22 Paul makes specific accusations against the self-righteous (but hypocritical) Jew: ὁ κηρύσσων μὴ κλέπτειν κλέπτεις; 22 ὁ λέγων μὴ μοιχεύειν μοιχεύεις; ὁ βδελυσσόμενος τὰ εἴδωλα ἱεροσυλεῖς; So the Jew condemns theft, adultery and he abhors idols. But the Jew himself is guilty of theft and adultery itself, and is guilty of

---

[29] The word νόμος here may mean "book of the law" as in Josephus, *Antiquitates* 12.256.

[30] Barth, *Shorter Commentary*, p. 37. Contrast J. Behm, μορφή κτλ, *TDNT* 4:754 (742-59), who writes that the judgement "which is stated with obvious irony by Paul, is not the same as his own estimate of the significance of the Law, in spite of R. 7:7ff.; 2:13ff.; 3:31; 9:4; 13:8".

[31] Barth, *Shorter Commentary*, p. 37.

[32] Behm, μορφή κτλ, *TDNT* 4:754.

[33] See *BA* p. 530.

[34] Cf. Mt. 23.3. See also Aboth R. Nathan 29: "'A man who taught others but did not teach himself' — how is this? A man learnt an Order or two or three [of the Mishnah] several times and taught them to others, but he did not occupy himself with them so that he forgot them — he is one who taught others but did not teach himself".

temple robbery[35]. The first two sins refer to commands in the decalogue[36] and the third to Dt. 7.25-26.[37] Taken at face value the sins in 2.21b-22 (theft, adultery and temple robbing) would only be committed by a small minority of Jews (the questions are clearly rhetorical). In view of this, some believe that Paul is referring to every Jew and has radicalised the law here as Jesus does in Mt. 5.21-48. On this basis theft may involve

---

[35] The verb ἱεροσυλέω can mean "rob a temple" or "commit sacrilege". I believe Paul has in mind the idea of Jews profiting from selling idols to Gentiles. According to Josephus, *Antiquitates* 4.207, Moses commanded Israel: "Let none blaspheme the gods which other cities revere, nor rob foreign temples (μηδὲ συλᾶν ἱερὰ ξενικά), nor take treasure that has been dedicated in the name of any god" (Josephus (LCL), 4:575). Although Josephus does not use ἱεροσυλέω, the text may provide a clue to Paul's meaning. Josephus may be referring to a contemporary practice (Morris, *Romans*, p. 137 n. 136) and Paul may have precisely this practice in mind. Also Morris, *Romans*, p. 137 n. 136, points to the slander of Lysimachus, that Jerusalem was originally called Ἱερόσυλα because the inhabitants engaged in temple robbery and the name of the city was subsequently changed to Ἱεροσόλυμα (*Contra Apionem* 1.311). So although the Jew does not worship idols, he profits from them. I therefore translate ὁ βδελυσσόμενος τὰ εἴδωλα ἱεροσυλεῖς as "You abominate idols, but do you rob temples?" Cf. J.D. Derrett, "'You abominate False Gods; But do you rob Shrines?' (Rom 2.22b)", *NTS* 40 (1994) 570 (558-71), who paraphrases v. 22b as: "You abominate idols (as the written law requires); but do you never profit illegitimately at the expense of an idol's wealth (which the law of conscience forbids)". Another possible clue to Paul's question "do you rob temples" (and "do you steal") is the incident related by Josephus, *Antiquitates* 18.81-84 (cf. Watson, *Paul*, p. 114). A high ranking Jewish proselyte in Rome, Fulvia, was encouraged by four Jews to give "purple and gold" for the Jerusalem temple. But these Jews, one of whom had fled Palestine with a criminal record and in Rome played the part of an "interpreter of the Mosaic law and its wisdom", appropriated her gifts for themselves. Fulvia's husband, the senator Saturninus, reported this to Tiberius, who then ordered the expulsion of Jews from Rome. H.J. Leon, *The Jews of Ancient Rome*, Peabody ²1995, (¹1960), p. 17-18, relates this incident to the expulsion in AD 19 mentioned by Tacitus (*Annals* 2.85) and Suetonius (*Tiberius* 36). This incident must have been acutely embarrassing for Roman Jews even as late as the time of receiving Paul's letter.

[36] This may explain why Paul uses κηρύσσειν and λέγειν respectively for theft and adultery, but not for temple robbery (H. Gese, "Psalm 50 und das alttestamentliche Gesetzesverständnis", in *Alttestamentliche Studien*, Tübingen, 1991, 167 n. 47 (149-69)).

[37] Barrett, *Romans*, p. 54, points to Philo, *De confusione linguarum* 163, where theft (κλέπτειν), adultery (μοιχεύειν), murder (ἀνδροφονεῖν) and sacrilege/temple robbery (ἱεροσυλεῖν) stand together. Paul uses all these words (except ἀνδροφονεῖν).

robbing God (cf. Mal. 3.8-9); adultery may involve being unfaithful to God (Hos. 1-3); robbing temples may involve profaning God's temple (Jer. 7.1-15). However, I wonder whether this captures the sense of the text. Also unlikely, I believe, is the view that Paul is concerned with the Jews' rejection of Jesus.[38] The best solution, I believe, is that Paul is referring precisely to theft, adultery and temple robbery. Although Paul may be exaggerating, it is instructive to compare inner Jewish judgement texts such as Ps. Sol. 8.7-13; Test. Naph. 4.1; 8.6; 4 Ezr. 8.20-36[39] as well as the words attributed to R. Johanan ben Zakkai in t. Sot. 14.1ff.[40]

In v. 23 Paul argues that although the Jew boasts in the law he dishonours God by transgressing the law. Rom 2.21-23 may allude to Ps. 50.16-21.[41] Although Haldane may be going too far in claiming that Ps. 50 "predicts the change which God was to make in His covenant at the coming of the Messiah, and likewise His rejection of His ancient people", he may be right in pointing to the fact that the Psalm "reproaches them (i.e. his people) with their crimes, and more especially with hypocrisy, which are precisely the charges made against them in this place by the Apostle".[42] Note also that as in Ps. 50, theft and adultery are placed side by side in Rom. 2.21b-22a.[43] Ps. 50 may possibly have formed one of

---

[38] Barth, *Shorter Commentary*. pp. 37-38: "The Jews are thieves, adulterers, desecrators by what they did to Jesus Christ on the day of Golgotha and which, in spite of his resurrection(,) they continue to do by declining to accept the glad message of the grace which has appeared in him, and by persecuting the Church which praises that grace".

[39] Referred to by Stuhlmacher, *Römer*, p. 47.

[40] Billerbeck writes concerning Rom. 2.21-23: "Eine Bestätigung u. Ergänzung finden diese Worte des Apostels durch das Sittenbild, das R. Jochanan b. Zakkai († um 80) von den inneren Zuständen des jüdischen Volkes aus den letzten Dezennien vor der Tempelzerstörung entworfen hat" (*Kommentar*, 3:105-6). In t. Sot. 14.1ff R. Johanan b. Zakkai speaks of the. increase in murder, adultery, sexual immorality, judicial corruption (giving rise to the distancing of God's Shekinah), commercial injustice, envy, pride and so on (Billerbeck, *Kommentar*, 3:106-7). See also b. Sot. 47b. Although these words attributed to R. Johanan may not reflect the historical truth, they do nevertheless illustrate what Paul is saying in Rom. 2.21b-22.

[41] See R. Haldane, *An Exposition of the Epistle to the Romans*, London 1958 (repr.), p. 98. Cf. Fitzmyer, *Romans*, p. 317.

[42] Haldane, *Romans*, p. 98.

[43] Gese, "Psalm 50", 167 n. 47.

Paul's "text-plots"[44] although there is no other quotation and probably no other allusion to the Psalm in the writings of Paul.[45]

Paul's accusation against the Jew comes to a climax in vv. 23-24. In v. 23b he makes the striking point: διὰ τῆς παραβάσις τοῦ νόμου τὸν θεὸν ἀτιμάζεις and then he links directly his modified quotation from Is. 52.5 LXX.[46]

Is. 52.5c: δι' ἡμᾶς διὰ παντὸς τὸ ὄνομά μου βλασφημεῖται ἐν τοῖς ἔθνεσιν.

Rom. 2.24: τὸ γὰρ ὄνομα τοῦ θεοῦ δι' ὑμᾶς βλασφηεῖται ἐν τοῖς ἔθνεσιν.

Paul has brought forward τὸ ὄνομα and explicitly added τοῦ θεοῦ, so giving this quotation special emphasis.[47] Further the direct link between v. 23 and v. 24 is particularly striking in view of the fact that this is the only case where Paul has καθὼς γέγραπται at the *end* of a quotation.[48] But striking though the quotation may be, it is quoted somewhat out of context. In Isaiah God's name is blasphemed because of the helpless situation of the Jews in exile;[49] for Paul, God's name is being blasphemed because of the hypocrisy of the Jews.[50]

---

[44] Cf. C.H. Dodd, *According to the Scriptures*, London 1952.

[45] It is unlikely that 1 Cor. 10.26 alludes to Ps. 50.12 (49.12) for Paul here quotes exactly from Ps. 24.1 (23.1).

[46] Is. 52.5 may be compared to Ezek. 36.20.

[47] See D.-A. Koch, *Die Schrift als Zeuge des Evangeliums*, Tübingen 1986, p. 105.

[48] See Koch, *Schrift*, p. 105.

[49] Although the MT and LXX differ, they both agree on this point.

[50] S.L. Edgar, "Respect for Context in Quotations from the Old Testament", *NTS* 9 (1962) 56 (55-62), writes: "It is true that God's name was being brought into reproach because the Jews of Paul's time did not practice what they preach; but Isaiah's passage does not support this at all, for it states that God's name was blasphemed because of the helplessness of the Jews, who had been slaves in Egypt and in Babylon; God was said to be powerless to save them". On the anti-Jewish use of Is. 52.5 in the apostolic Fathers and Patristic period, see B. Lindars, *New Testament Apologetic*, London 1961, pp. 22-24. I should also add that it is unlikely that Paul is considering ideas of Israel *now* being in exile in this passage, even though Is. 52.5 is quoted. Contrast R.B. Hays, *Echoes of Scripture in the Letters of Paul*, New Haven/London 1989, pp. 44-46; N.T. Wright, "The Law in Romans 2", in J.D.G. Dunn (ed.), *Paul and the Mosaic Law*, Tübingen 1996, 139 (131-50). If the continued

Before moving on to the next section it must be stressed that Paul is by no means relativising the election of Israel. He really does believe that Israel is to be a guide to the blind. Yahweh has chosen Israel to be a light to the nations and this mission still stands, even though Israel has failed in her mission. To say that Paul is "undermining ethnocentric covenantalism by disqualifying the ethical claim of 'the Jew'"[51] misses the point of the passage.[52] Paul is not concerned with ethnic pride "but with the assumption that the knowledge of God's will mediated by the Law brings moral superiority".[53] The issue whether Paul relativises Israel's election has been important for the exegesis of Rom. 2.25-29 and it is to these verses that I now turn.

3. Romans 2.25-29: Circumcision by itself will not save

Paul now turns to the issue of circumcision. He argues in Rom. 2.25 that circumcision is only of value if the Jew obeys the law. He makes the radical point that if the Jew breaks the law his circumcision is not only worthless, but it is as if he were uncircumcised.[54] His circumcision becomes uncircumcision: Περιτομὴ μὲν γὰρ ὠφελεῖ ἐὰν νόμον πράσσῃς· ἐὰν δὲ παραβάτης νόμου ᾖς, ἡ περιτομή σου ἀκροβυστία γέγονεν. Paul, again, probably has perfect obedience of the law in mind. Paul's view is that circumcision means you have to obey the whole law, as Gal. 5.3 demonstrates.[55]

Paul in 2.26 then takes the argument a stage further and says that if the uncircumcised keeps the requirements of the law, will not his uncircumcision be regarded as circumcision? (ἐὰν οὖν ἡ ἀκροβυστία τὰ δικαιώματα

---

exile were a theme in Paul, one would expect more *explicit* mention of it (e.g. references to Israel returning from exile).

[51] B.W. Longenecker, *Eschatology and the Covenant*, Sheffield 1991, p. 91.

[52] I am also unconvinced by Wright, "The Law in Romans 2", 139, that Paul is attacking "National Righteousness".

[53] M.A. Seifrid, *Justification by Faith*, Leiden 1992, p. 65.

[54] Althaus, *Römer*, p. 27.

[55] Gal. 5.3: μαρτύρομαι δὲ πάλιν παντὶ ἀνθρώπῳ περιτεμνομένῳ ὅτι ὀφειλέτης ἐστὶν ὅλον τὸν νόμον ποιῆσαι.

τοῦ νόμου φυλάσσῃ, οὐχ ἡ ἀκροβυστία αὐτοῦ εἰς περιτομὴν
λογισθήσεται;) The future λογισθήσεται could be just a logical future,
but it is more likely that there is a reference to the future judgement
here.[56] Many commentators believe that the Gentile who keeps the
precepts of the law (τὰ δικαιώματα τοῦ νόμου) is the Gentile Christian.[57]
It is, however, extremely unlikely that Paul is referring to the Gentile
Christian in v. 26 (or in vv. 27-29 for that matter).[58] There are no clear
indications here that Paul is speaking of Gentile Christians and there is a
much simpler explanation: Paul speaks of the pious Gentile who keeps the
law.[59] And in v. 27 Paul says that this pious Gentile who keeps the law (ἡ
ἐκ φύσεως ἀκροβυστία τὸν νόμον τελοῦσα) will judge the Jew who,
although having the written code (γράμμα, i.e. the law)[60] and circumcision, is a transgressor of the law.[61] The Gentile will not take on the role
of a judge (as in 1 Cor. 6.2)[62]; rather the Gentile by his deeds will expose
the deeds of the Jew.[63] It becomes clear in 3.9-20 that the person
described here simply does not exist.[64] As Fridrichsen writes: ". . . das

---

[56] See J. Denny, "St. Paul's Epistle to the Romans", in W. Robertson Nicoll, *The
Expositor's Greek Testament*, Grand Rapids 1976 (repr), 601 (555-725), who points
to the use of the futures in 2.12-16 which refer to the final judgement.

[57] Barrett, *Romans*, p. 58; Cranfield, *Romans*, 1:173.

[58] Although Paul speaks in Rom. 8.4 of the Christian in whom τὸ δικαίωμα τοῦ
νόμου is fulfilled, Paul in Rom. 2.26-27 is making a quite different point.

[59] The expression τὰ δικαιώματα τοῦ νόμου refers to the whole law (Käsemann,
Römer, p. 68). The objection may be raised that circumcision itself was a commandment of the law. How then can Gentiles keep the whole law if they are not circumcised? However, as I argued in chapter 4 above, the law of God has been manifest in
different ways to Jews and Gentiles.

[60] On the meaning of γράμμα, see the discussion below on Rom. 2.29.

[61] Note that with Käsemann I take διά in the expression διὰ γράμματος καὶ
περιτομῆς not to be instrumental but to describe the "accompanying circumstances"
(*Romans*, p. 74; "Geist und Buchstabe", in *Paulinische Perspektiven*, ²1972, (¹1969),
246 (237-85)). Contrast Schlatter, *Gottes Gerechtigkeit*, p. 110.

[62] Such an interpretation could be plausible if Paul were speaking of Gentile
Christians.

[63] G.P. Carras, "Romans 2,1-29: A Dialogue on Jewish Ideals", *Bib* 73 (1992)
205 (183-207). On Gentiles exposing the sins of Jews see Mt. 12.41 and Lk. 11.31.

[64] One of the main points in Rom. 1.18-3.20 is that no one will be justified by
works of the law. In Rom. 5.12ff it is made especially clear that the pious person cannot exist for all are in Adam.

Bild des gesetzerfüllenden Heiden ist ein nur gedachtes, ist ein dialektisches Moment in der Auseinandersetzung mit dem stolzen, selbstgerechten Juden".[65]

The section 2.25-29 comes to a climax in 2.28-29 which I set out with supplements.[66]

οὐ γὰρ ὁ ἐν φανερῷ ('Ιουδαῖος) 'Ιουδαῖός ἐστιν, οὐδὲ ἡ ἐν τῷ φανερῷ ἐν σαρκὶ (περιτομὴ) περιτομή (ἐστιν)· (29) ἀλλ' ὁ ἐν τῷ κρυπτῷ 'Ιουδαῖος ('Ιουδαῖός ἐστιν), καὶ περιτομὴ καρδίας ἐν πνεύματι οὐ γράμματι (περιτομή ἐστιν), οὗ ὁ ἔπαινος οὐχ ἐξ ἀνθρώπων (ἐστὶν) ἀλλ' ἐκ τοῦ θεοῦ.

The distinction is made between the person who appears a Jew (ὁ ἐν φανερῷ 'Ιουδαῖος) and the one who is inwardly a Jew (ὁ ἐν τῷ κρυπτῷ 'Ιουδαῖος). Not all outward Jews are Jews in the special sense and not all Jews in the special sense are outward Jews. The Jew ἐν τῷ κρυπτῷ has circumcision of heart (περιτομὴ καρδίας)[67] but the Jew ἐν τῷ φανερῷ has circumcision in flesh (ἐν σαρκί). It is widely assumed that Paul also speaks of Gentile Christians is vv. 28-29.[68] In fact Schreiner, who takes 2.26-29 to refer to Gentile Christians, writes that "the 'for' (γάρ) introducing verses 28-29 is decisive for the Gentile Christian interpretation", and the expression ἐν πνεύματι οὐ γράμματι of v. 29 is "the primary reason we know that verses 26-27 speaks of Gentile Christians".[69] The view that Paul refers to Christians in Rom. 2.29 has a long and distin-

---

[65] Fridrichsen, "Jude", 43.

[66] See Cranfield, *Romans*, 1:175.

[67] See Dt. 10.16; 30.6.

[68] This is seen as early as Justin Martyr. See the probable allusion to Rom. 2.29 in his discussion of Gentile Christians in *Dialogue* 92.4: Καὶ ἡμεῖς οὖν, ἐν ἀκροβυστίᾳ τῆς σαρκὸς ἡμῶν πιστεύοντες τῷ θεῷ διὰ τοῦ Χριστοῦ καὶ περιτομὴν ἔχοντες τὴν ὠφελοῦσαν ἡμᾶς τοὺς κεκτημένους, τοῦτ' ἔστι τῆς καρδίας, δίκαιοι καὶ εὐάρεστοι τῷ θεῷ ἐλπίζομεν φανῆναι . . .). Justin's exegesis of Paul can be accounted for by the fact that he wished to disinherit Israel.

[69] T.R. Schreiner, *The Law and its Fulfillment: A Pauline Theology of Law*, Grand Rapids 1993, p. 198.

guished history. I give three examples.[70] First, Chrysostom, *Commentarius in epistulam ad Romanos* homilia 6.4:

Εἰπὼν δὲ, Ἐν πνεύματι, προοδοποιεῖ λοιπὸν τῇ τῆς Ἐκκλησίας πολιτείᾳ, καὶ τὴν πίστιν εἰσάγει· καὶ γὰρ αὕτη ἐν καρδίᾳ καὶ πνεύματι τὸν ἔπαινον ἀπὸ τοῦ Θεοῦ ἔχει.[71]

Second, Pseudo-Oecumenius, *Commentarius in epistulam ad Romanos* on 2.29

Εἰπὼν δὲ Ἐν πνεύματι, προοδοποιεῖ τῇ πίστει. Οἱ γὰρ πιστοὶ διὰ Πνεύματος ἁγίου τὴν περιτομὴν ἔχουσι τῶν ἁμαρτιῶν.[72]

Third, Augustine, *De spiritu et littera* 8 (13)

circumcisionem autem cordis dicit, puram scilicet ab omni inlicita concupiscentia uoluntatem; quod non fit littera docente et minante, sed spiritu adiuuante atque sanante. ideo laus talium non ex hominibus, sed ex deo est, qui per suam gratiam praestat unde laudentur . . .[73]

However, I question the tradition that Paul refers to Christians in Rom. 2.29. First, I consider the antithesis γράμμα/πνεῦμα, which occurs in the New Testament only in Rom. 2.29; 7.6 and 2 Cor. 3.6, and is completely lacking in the Old Testament. There are two basic interpretations of the terms.[74] In the "formalistic" interpretation, γράμμα is the literal sense and πνεῦμα the spiritual sense of any document. The originator of this was Origen[75] and was characteristic of the Alexandrian school.[76] In the

---

[70] There are taken from B. Schneider, "The Meaning of St. Paul's Antithesis: 'The Letter and the Spirit'", *CBQ* 15 (1953) 174-75, 177 (163-207), where English translations are given.

[71] *MPG* 60:436. English translations of this text (and of the following texts) are given by Schneider, "The Letter and the Spirit", 174-75, 177.

[72] *MPG* 118:368 (307-638).

[73] *CSEL* 60:165-66 (*MPL* 44:208).

[74] See Schneider, "The Letter and the Spirit", 164.

[75] See Schneider, "The Letter and the Spirit", 166. See, for example, *Contra Celsum* 6.70 (E. Klostermann (ed.), *Origenes Werke: Dritter Band* (GCS), Leipzig 1961, p. 140; *MPG* 11:1404), where 2 Cor. 3.5-6 is discussed.

[76] See Athanasius (*Epistula I ad Serapionem* 8 (*MPG* 26:549 (529-608)) and Cyril of Alexandria (*In epistulam II ad Corinthios* on 3.6, *MPG* 74:929 (915-52)). This formalistic interpretation is also found in Gregory of Nyssa (e.g. *Commentarius in Canticum Canticorum*, prooemium, *MPG* 44:757-60). Didymus of Alexandria gives a formalistic interpretation of 2 Cor. 3.6 and Rom. 2.29 in *Liber de Spiritu Sancto* 57 (*MPG* 39:1081 (1033-86)) but gives both realistic and formalistic interpretations of 2

"realistic" interpretation, γράμμα refers to the Mosaic law itself and πνεῦμα refers to the Holy Spirit. This view is found in Marcion⁷⁷ and became characteristic of the Antiochene school.⁷⁸ Many who argue for the realistic interpretation of Rom. 2.29 do so because of a realistic interpretation of Rom. 7.6 and 2 Cor. 3.6. But it is instructive to note that among commentators who have realistic and formalistic interpretations of the γράμμα/πνεῦμα texts, the texts can be arranged in the spectrum 2 Cor. 3.6 (generally taken as realistic), Rom. 7.6 (often taken as realistic) and Rom. 2.29 (usually taken as formalistic).⁷⁹ Further, even if some sort of realistic interpretation in Rom. 2.29 if adopted, which may well be correct in that γράμμα refers to the Mosaic law,⁸⁰ and πνεῦμα *may possibly* refer to the Holy Spirit, the reference does not have to be to

---

Cor. 3.6 in *Commentarius in epistolam secundam Pauli Apostoli ad Corinthios* (*MPG* 39:1693-96 (1679-1732)).

⁷⁷ See the discussion of Rom. 2.29 in Tertullian, *Adversus Marcionem* 5.13 (*CSEL* 47:620). As Schneider points out, Tertullian does not object to Marcion's realistic interpretation ("The Letter and the Spirit", 166).

⁷⁸ See Chrysostom (e.g. *Commentarius in epistulam ad Romanos* homilia 12.3 (*MPG* 60:498-99)) and his followers (John of Damascus, Ps.-Oecumenius, Theophylactus and Euthymius Zigabenus) and Theodoret (see e.g. *Interpretatio epistulae II ad Corinthios* on 3.6 (*MPG* 82:393). See also Ephraem, Augustine (e.g. *De Spiritu et littera* 5 (7-8) (*CSEL* 60:159-60; *MPL* 44:204-5)), Pelagius (e.g. see his comments on Rom. 2.27, 29, A. Souter, *Pelagius's Exposition of Thirteen Epistles of St. Paul: II. Text*, Cambridge 1926, p. 27), Apollinaris of Laodicea (Staab, *Pauluskommentare*, pp. 63-65) and Ambrosiaster (see his comments on 2 Cor. 3.6; Rom. 2.29; 7.6 (for Rom. 2.29, for example, see *CSEL* 81.1:90-93)).

⁷⁹ See Schneider, "The Letter and the Spirit", 184-85, who points out that among early medieval authors who present both formalistic and realistic interpretation, there is a preponderance for the realistic interpretation of 2 Cor. 3.6. Thomas Aquinas has a realistic interpretation of 2 Cor. 3.6 and Rom. 7.6 but on Rom. 2.29 gives both views without any preference (*In omnes d. Pauli apostoli epistolas commentaria*, 3 vols, Liège 1857-58, 2:20-30; 1:60, 126, referred to by Schneider, "The Letter and the Spirit", 185).

⁸⁰ See especially G. Schrenk, γράφω κτλ, *TDNT* 1:765-68 (742-73), and O. Hofius, "Gesetz und Evangelium nach 2. Korinther 3", in *Paulusstudien*, 82 (75-120). Note expressions such as ποιεῖν πάντα τὰ ῥήματα τοῦ νόμου τούτου τὰ γεγραμμένα ἐν τῷ βιβλίῳ τούτῳ (Dt. 28.58, used in Gal. 3.10) and ποιεῖν πάντα τὰ γεγραμμένα ἐν τῷ βιβλίῳ τοῦ νόμου Μωυσῆ (Jos. 23.6).

Christians. In fact this is rather unlikely; for Paul and his hearers it was obvious that the Christian does the good. See in particular the comment of Theodore of Mopsuestia:

Τῷ πνεύματι, οὐ τῷ ἁγίῳ· οὐ γὰρ περὶ τῶν ἐν τῇ χάριτι κατορθούντων διαλέγεται, ἀλλ᾽ ὑποτίθεται δι᾽ ὅλου τοὺς ἔξω τὰ τοῦ νόμου ποιοῦντας, καὶ δείκνυσι κρείττονας τῶν ἐν τῷ νόμῳ παραβαινόντων.[81]

Further, the whole context goes against a reference to Christians.[82] The expression ἐν πνεύματι has the general sense "in a spiritual way"[83] although I would not necessarily want to rule out completely the idea of the Holy Spirit.[84] According to Rom. 2.29 the circumcision that counts is that of the heart (Dt. 10.16; 30.6; Jer. 4.4; 9.25); such circumcision is not from the written law, but exists is in a spiritual sense.[85] Therefore the passage makes perfect sense without any reference to Christians and it is interesting to note that Jub. 1.16, 20-21 and 23 form a useful background to aspects of Rom. 2.25-29. In Jub. 1.20-21 Moses says:

O Lord, let your mercy be lifted up upon your people, and create for them an *upright spirit*. And do not let the spirit of Beliar rule over them to accuse them before you and ensnare them from every path of righteousness so that they might be destroyed from before your face. 21 But they are your people and your inheritance, whom you saved by your great might from the hand of the Egyptians. Create a *pure heart* and a *holy spirit* for them. And do not let them be ensnared by their sin henceforth and forever.[86]

---

[81] Theodore of Mopsuestia, *In epistulam ad Romanos commentarii fragmenta* (Staab, *Pauluskommentare*, p. 116).

[82] Schreiner, *Law*, p. 199, points to the "remarkable similarity" between Phil. 3.3 (ἡμεῖς γὰρ ἐσμεν ἡ περιτομή, οἱ πνεύματι θεοῦ λατρεύοντες καὶ καυχώμενοι ἐν Χριστῷ Ἰησοῦ καὶ οὐκ ἐν σαρκὶ πεποιθότες) and Rom. 2.29. I take the point that Paul refers to the Holy Spirit in Phil. 3.3 (there is a text critical problem but θεοῦ rather than θεῷ is the most likely reading), but in Phil. 3.3 the context makes it absolutely clear that Paul is talking of Christians. I see no evidence from the context that Paul is speaking of Christians in Rom. 2.29.

[83] See Barrett, *Romans*, p. 58.

[84] The possible allusions to Jer. 31.31-34; Ezek. 11.19; 36.25-29 and Jub. 1.20-21, 23, may point to the Holy Spirit.

[85] Cf. Althaus, *Römer*, p. 28, who speaks of an obedience "der nicht durch das geschriebene Gesetz von außen her erzwungen, sondern vom 'Geiste' als die innerliche Bewegung freudiger Hingabe geschaffen wird".

[86] O.S. Wintermute's translation in Charlesworth, *Pseudepigrapha*, 2:53-54 (my emphasis).

God then replies to Moses in vv. 22-26 and in v. 23 we read:

But after this they will return to me in all uprighteousness and with all (their) *heart* and soul. And I shall *cut off the foreskin of their heart* and the *foreskin of the heart* of their descendants. And I shall create for them a *holy spirit*, and I shall purify them so that they will not turn away from following me from that day and forever.[87]

It is therefore unnecessary to bring in Gentile Christians (or Jewish Christians) at this point. In fact to do so would go against the context Rom. 1.18-3.20, where Paul is arguing that no one, Jew nor Gentile, will be justified by works of law. There may possibly be allusions to Jer. 31.31-34; Ezek. 11.19; 36.25-29. However, that does not necessarily mean Paul is referring to Gentile Christians.

There are in fact a number of other factors which support the idea that Paul is referring simply to pious Jews or Gentiles and not to Christians in vv. 28-29. First, there are a number of expressions here which are unusual for Paul.[88] This is the only text in Paul where there is the positive use of κρυπτόν, where Paul speaks of the circumcision of the heart, and where the heart is placed in opposition to the flesh.[89] This unusual use of these words suggests that Paul here is referring to pious Jews and Gentiles, for nowhere else does he refer to such hypothetical figures, although in many other passages he speaks about Christian existence. Secondly, it makes perfect sense to use language such as "hidden" and "heart" to refer to a pious person.[90] Thirdly, there are a number of parallels between Rom. 2.28-29 and Rom. 2.12-16. In 2.16 Jesus Christ will judge τὰ κρυπτὰ τῶν ἀνθρώπων (note also the reference in v. 14 to

---

[87] Wintermute, in Charlesworth, *Pseudepigrapha*, 2:54 (my emphasis). Wintermute dates Jubilees in the period 161-140 BC. Käsemann, "Geist und Buchstabe", 249-50, also appeals to Jub. 1.23.

[88] See E. Schweizer, "'Der Jude im Verborgenen . . ., dessen Lob nicht von Menschen, sondern von Gott kommt'. Zu Röm 2,28f und Mt 6,1-18", in J. Gnilka (ed.), *Neues Testament und Kirche: Für Rudolf Schnackenburg*, Freiburg/Basel/Wien 1974, 115-16 (115-24).

[89] Schweizer, "Jude", 116 n. 4, highlights the unusual nature of the opposition of heart and flesh by pointing to 2 Cor. 3.3, where heart and flesh are placed *together* in opposition to the tablets of stone.

[90] See 1 Sam. 16.7b: "man looks on the outward appearance, but the LORD looks on the heart".

Gentiles, and to their *hearts* in v. 15 (τὸ ἔργον τοῦ νόμου γραπτὸν ἐν ταῖς καρδίαις αὐτῶν)). If Rom. 2.12-16 concerns the judgement according to works whereby pious persons will be acquitted (cf. Rom. 2.13), it would seem that Rom. 2.28-29 concerns such pious persons also and not Christians. Fourthly, Rom. 2.28-29 has a number of parallels with Mt. 6.1-6, 16-18.[91] Although the teaching in Matthew is clearly directed at the Christian Church, this teaching and that found in Rom. 2.28-29 can be traced back simply to the Old Testament and Judaism[92] and there is nothing to suggest that the teaching im Mt. 6.1-6, 16-18 is distinctively Christian.[93] So such a text could just as well apply to pious Jews and pious Gentiles as well as Christians. To return to Rom. 2.28-29, I therefore conclude that this is not concerned with Christians but with pious Jews and Gentiles.[94]

To sum up on Rom. 2.25-29, I believe that Paul argues that circumcision by itself will not save. What matters is keeping the law. I stress again that Paul does not relativise the election of Israel. This has been argued by Dunn who writes that in Romans 2 "it becomes progressively clearer that Paul is seeking to undermine a Jewish assumption of national distinctiveness and privilege . . .".[95] The issue is not about groups, but about salvation, and the point of Rom. 2.25-29 is that circumcision by itself will not save. In fact the focus throughout Romans 2 has not been on issues of the relationship between Jews and Gentiles, but about questions of the final judgement.[96]

---

[91] See Fridrichsen, "Jude", 46; Schweizer, "Jude"; W.D. Davies and D.C. Allison, *A Critical and Exegetical Commentary on the Epistle to the Gospel According to Saint Matthew*, vol. 1, Edinburgh 1988, pp. 576-77.

[92] See Schweizer, "Jude".

[93] See Davies and Allison, *Matthew*, pp. 576-77.

[94] Note that although I have drawn from the work of Schweizer in this paragraph, Schweizer himself does not make it clear whether Paul refers to Christians in Rom. 2.28-29.

[95] J.D.G. Dunn, "What was the Issue between Paul and 'Those of the Circumcision'?", in M. Hengel and U. Heckel (ed.), *Paulus und das antike Judentum: Tübingen-Durham-Symposium im Gedenken an der 50. Todestag Adolf Schlatter*, Tübingen 1991, 311 (295-313). See also Longenecker, *Covenant*, p. 194, who argues that Paul wished "to discredit an ethnocentric understanding of God's ways".

[96] See the comment of P. Stuhlmacher following the discussion of J.D.G. Dunn's paper, in Hengel and Heckel (ed.), *Paulus*, 315: "Es gehe nicht nur um das

4. Romans 3.1-8: Objections

I disagree with Dodd when he writes that "the whole argument of 3.1-8 is obscure and feeble. . . . The argument of the epistle would go much better if this whole section were omitted".[97] I believe these verses make perfect sense in their position in Paul's argument. However, it does need to be stressed that to some extent these verses form a digression[98] for in his argument Paul does seem to move away from the central concern of Rom. 1.18-32, 2.1-16 and 2.17-29.[99] The issues raised are more fully addressed in Rom. 9-11. However, although there may be some points of contact between 3.1-8 and Rom. 9-11 (mentioned in the exegesis below), the arguments are in many ways quite different. The main reason for this is that Rom. 3.1-8 is written from a perspective before the revelation of the righteousness of God. Although he has briefly spoken of the revelation of the δικαιοσύνη θεοῦ in 1.16-17, he does not develop it until 3.21ff (and in fact 3.21 forms the major turning point in the argument).[100] I therefore take a quite different line to that of Cosgrove who, in addition to stressing a number of parallels between Rom. 3.1-8 and Rom. 9-11, believes that Paul is indicting torah-faithful Jews.[101] So, according to Cosgrove's inter-

---

Verhältnis zwischen Juden und Heiden, nicht nur um die abgrenzende Funktion, die das Gesetz im Blick auf die Heiden erfüllt, also nicht um ein letztlich soziales Problem, sondern um die theologische Frage: Was brauchen der Jude wie auch der Heide angesichts des letzten Gerichts?"

[97] Dodd, *Romans*, p. 46.

[98] S.K. Stowers, "Paul's Dialogue with a Fellow Jew in Romans 3:1-9", *CBQ* 46 (1984) 708 (707-22), points out that the view that Paul digresses here goes back at least to Calvin, Melanchthon, Bucer and Bullinger. Stowers himself believes 3.1-9 (note he takes vv. 1-9 as a unit and not v. 1-8) does not form a digression ("Romans 3:1-9", 721). See also C.H. Cosgrove, who, for different reasons, argues that 3.1-8 is not to be taken as a digression ("What if Some Have Not Believed? The Occasion and Thrust of Romans 3₁₋₈", *ZNW* 78 (1987) 92 (90-105)).

[99] See Schlier, *Römerbrief*, p. 97, who after his comment on Rom. 3.8, writes: "Paulus ist weit von seinem Ausgangsthema, Kap. 2, abgekommen. In den VV 9ff holt er sich wieder zum Thema zurück, erst zu 3,1 und dann zu 2,1ff bzw. auch 1,18ff". See also Käsemann, *Römer*, p. 73; M. Black, *Romans*, London 1973, pp. 61-63.

[100] See chapter 1 above.

[101] Cosgrove, "Romans 3₁₋₈".

pretation, even if they were to keep the torah, they have not believed in Jesus the Messiah and so show themselves to be sinners. Thereby Rom. 3.1-8 acts as a preparation for 3.9. Interesting though Cosgrove's exegesis is, my main problem with it is that Paul writes in 3.1-8 from the perspective of justification by works. Christ is important in Rom. 1.18-3.20 but his role is that of judge (Rom. 2.16) and one whose "pre-existent" nature is revealed through the created order (1.19-21a). In 1.18-3.20 Christ is not the one upon whom one believes in order to be acquitted at the final judgement. Paul here is concerned with the justification of the godly.

As far as the structure of 3.1-8 is concerned, I put forward the following analysis (based on that of Hall).[102]

3.1-2: The Jew has the advantages of the covenant and promises.
3.3-8: God's judgement on Jews does not contradict the covenant for:

    3.3-4: the Old Testament recognizes that judgement is consistent with righteousness

    3.5-8: if God were not free to exercise wrath, there would be intolerable moral consequences.

One of the issues involved in the exegesis is whether Paul is using some sort of diatribe (putting in questions of some imaginary objector) or possibly putting in real questions which his opponents had, or whether some of the questions (or all of them) are Paul's own.

4.1 Romans 3.1-2

In view of what Paul has said in 2.25-29 the question is raised in 3.1 whether there is any advantage in being a Jew and in circumcision. Τί οὖν τὸ περισσὸν τοῦ Ἰουδαίου ἢ τίς ἡ ὠφέλεια τῆς περιτομῆς; According to Dodd, the answer to this question based on Paul's argument is: "None whatever!"[103] Paul's answer, however, is πολὺ κατὰ πάντα τρόπον, "much in every way". Paul's reply is not as illogical as Dodd would sug-

---

[102] D.R. Hall, "Romans 3.1-8 Reconsidered", *NTS* 29 (1983) 185 (183-97).

[103] Dodd, *Romans*, p. 68.

gest. There is, according to Paul, a clear advantage in being a Jew. Jews are entrusted with the oracles of God (τὰ λόγια τοῦ θεοῦ, 3.2). There are various ways of understanding τὰ λόγια τοῦ θεοῦ: as τὰ δικαιώματα τοῦ νόμου;[104] as the law as given on Sinai together with the promises relating to the Messiah;[105] as the Law and the Prophets;[106] as the whole Heilsgeschichte of the Old Testament and the New Testament[107]. I think it unlikely that Paul would include the New Testament promises in τὰ λόγια τοῦ θεοῦ.[108] The most likely meaning is the Law and the Prophets. As Wilckens, writes: "τὰ λόγια (τοῦ θεοῦ) ist in LXX, bei Philon und Apg 7,38 eine pauschale Bezeichnung der Offenbarungsworte in der Schrift und dürfte hier entsprechend gebraucht sein".[109] Paul therefore firmly asserts the special position of the Jew. One reason for doing this is that he most likely had Jewish Christian opponents in Rome who claimed that Paul smoothed over the distinction between Jew and Gentiles in salvation history. Therefore behind the question in 3.1 may well lie a real concern of these Jewish Christian opponents.[110]

4.2 Romans 3.3-4

Paul then continues in 3.3: τί γάρ; εἰ ἠπίστησάν τινες, μὴ ἡ ἀπιστία αὐτῶν τὴν πίστιν τοῦ θεοῦ καταργήσει; This question I suggest is Paul's, not that of an opponent (real or imaginary).[111] What does Paul mean by

---

[104] P. Stuhlmacher, *Gerechtigkeit Gottes bei Paulus*, Göttingen ²1966, (¹1965), p. 85.

[105] Sanday and Headlam, *Romans*, p. 70.

[106] Hall, "Romans 3", 185; J.W. Doeve, "Some note with reference to τὰ λόγια τοῦ Θεοῦ", in J.N. Sevenster and W.C. van Unnik (ed.), *Studia Paulina in honorem J. de Zwaan*, Haarlem 1953, 111-23. Doeve relates v. 2 to v. 21.

[107] G. Kittel, λέγω κτλ, *TDNT* 4:138 (77-143).

[108] See Doeve, "ΤΑ ΛΟΓΙΑ ΤΟΥ ΘΕΟΥ". Doeve criticises G. Kittel for deriving the meaning of τὰ λόγια τοῦ θεοῦ from etymology. Kittel writes: "Literally (wortmäßig), τὰ λόγια τοῦ θεοῦ is simply a reference to God's speaking, which for Paul takes place just as much in OT as NT salvation history" (λέγω κτλ *TDNT* 4:138 (77-143)). Doeve comments that it is necessary to inquire how a word is used (113).

[109] Wilckens, *Römer*, 1:164.

[110] See Bell, *Provoked to Jealousy*, pp. 74-75.

[111] Cf. H. Räisänen, "Zum Verständnis von Röm 3,1-8", *SNTU* 10 (1985) 98 (93-108): "Der 'Einwand' ist in V.3 völlig vom Standpunkt des Paulus aus formuliert".

the words ἀπιστεῖν and ἀπιστία in v. 3? The use of ἐπιστεύθησαν in 3.2 suggests that ἀπιστεῖν and ἀπιστία mean "be unfaithful" and "unfaithfulness" respectively. This is certainly an important component. But in addition to this, Paul probably also wishes to include the idea of unbelief and not just unfaithfulness and this unbelief includes not believing in Christ.[112] After all, do not the Law and the Prophets witness to Christ (cf. Rom. 3.21)? However, what sort of unbelief is this? There are two possibilities. First, there is not believing the *gospel* of Jesus Christ. Compare Rom. 11.23 where Paul says Jews will be grafted in again if they do not continue in their unbelief (ἀπιστία), i.e. unbelief in Christ and the gospel of Christ. If Rom. 3.1-8 anticipates Rom. 9-11, it may be that Paul is thinking of Jews not believing the gospel of Christ.[113] But, as noted above, 3.1-8 seems to be written from a pre-gospel perspective. The second and more likely possibility is therefore that Paul refers to not believing God and because his view of God included Christ, this involves not believing Christ. Such a view could be supported in view of the fact that Rom. 1.18-3.20 (apart from 2.16) does not consider the gospel but speaks from the perspective of justification by works (Rom. 2.1-16) and knowing God (including Christ) through creation (Rom. 1.19-21a). Note also the interesting use of ἀπιστία in Rom. 4.20 (εἰς δὲ τὴν ἐπαγγελίαν τοῦ θεοῦ οὐ διεκρίθη τῇ ἀπιστίᾳ). Could this be a reference to Abraham's belief in the pre-existent Christ?

The use of the word τινες (in the phrase εἰ ἠπίστησάν τινες) at first seems strange. Surely all Israel has not believed. Does not Rom. 3.9-20 make that clear? But the use of τινες is simply part of Paul's rhetoric, for in 3.4 he asserts πᾶς δὲ ἄνθρωπος ψεύστης.[114] These words of 3.4 also make it clear that Paul cannot be talking in v. 3 from a post-gospel per-

---

[112] Sanday and Headlam, *Romans*, p. 71.

[113] The use of the aorist ἠπίστησαν may well suggest not believing the gospel (Räisänen, "Röm 3,1-8", 97). See also Cosgrove, "Romans 3₁₋₈", 92.

[114] Cf. A.T. Lincoln, "From Wrath to Justification: Tradition, Gospel and Audience in the Theology of Romans 1:18-4:25", in E.H. Lovering Jr (ed.), *SBL Seminar Papers*, Atlanta 1993, 201 (194-226). I argue below that ψεύστης includes the idea of being faithless.

spective, that is asking "What if some Jews have not believed the gospel". If Paul were asking that he would have to acknowledge that some Jews have in fact believed the gospel and could not write πᾶς δὲ ἄνθρωπος ψεύστης.

So Paul's question of v. 3 is whether the unfaithfulness and unbelief of Israel nullifies[115] the faithfulness (πίστις) of God? Paul answers with μὴ γένοιτο. This again puts in question the view that Paul wishes to relativise the election of Israel. Paul argues in the strongest way for the opposite point. As Hofius argues: "Mit diesen Worten stellt der Apostel betont heraus, daß die den Israeliten gegebenen Verheißungen Gottes unwiderruflich sind und auch durch Israels Bundesbrüche nicht hinfällig werden".[116] After denying that Israel's unfaithfulness nullifies God's faithfulness, Paul continues in 3.4: γινέσθω δὲ ὁ θεὸς ἀληθής, πᾶς δὲ ἄνθρωπος ψεύστης, καθὼς γέγραπται· ὅπως ἄν δικαιωθῇς ἐν τοῖς λόγοις σου καὶ νικήσεις ἐν τῷ κρίνεσθαί σε (quotation from Ps. 50.6b). The idea of God being true includes the idea that God is faithful and likewise the idea of every person being a liar includes the idea of every person being faithless.[117] As Cranfield points out, Paul's words πᾶς δὲ ἄνθρωπος ψεύστης are reminiscent of Ps. 115.2: ἐγὼ εἶπα ἐν τῇ ἐκστάσει μου Πᾶς ἄνθρωπος ψεύστης. Paul's words, although focused on the Jews, refer in a wider sense to all people. Every man is a liar, and if every man is a liar, only God is true.[118] This and the quotation from Ps. 51 point to the fallen nature of every human being.[119]

---

[115] On the meaning of καταργεῖν see G. Delling, ἀργός, ἀργέω, καταργέω, *TDNT* 1:452-54, and H. Hübner, καταργέω, *EDNT* 2:267-68.

[116] O. Hofius, "Die Unabänderlichkeit des göttlichen Heilsratschlusses", *ZNW* 64 (1973) 145 (135-45).

[117] Cf. the discussion below on ἀλήθεια in Rom. 3.7.

[118] O. Hofius, Lectures on Romans, Tübingen, Winter Semester 1986-87. The other way to argue this is that all men are seen as sinners when set alongside God. See 1QH 9.26-27 (= 1QH 1.26-27): "To you, God of knowledge, belong all the works of justice 27 and the foundation of truth; to the sons of man the service of sin and the deeds of deception" (F.G. Martínez, *The Dead Sea Scrolls Translated*, Leiden 1994, p. 327).

[119] Note also Ps. 50.7 LXX: ἰδοὺ γὰρ ἐν ἀνομίαις συνελήμφθην, καὶ ἐν ἁμαρτίαις ἐκίσσησέν με ἡ μήτηρ μου. This follows directly from the words quoted by Paul in 3.4. Note also Ps. 50.8a LXX: ἰδοὺ γὰρ ἀλήθειαν ἠγάπησας and compare Rom. 3.4a: γινέσθω δὲ ὁ θεὸς ἀληθής.

Paul's point in quoting the Psalm is that when God makes a judgement he is justified (i.e. in the right).[120] He is not saying with the use of Ps. 50.6 LXX "daß die Weltgeschichte mit dem Siege Gottes über seine Feinde und mit der Manifestation seines Rechtes über den Geschöpfen endet".[121]

The train of thought in Rom. 3.3-4 is therefore that God has remained faithful even though Israel herself has been unfaithful and not believed. This again confirms that God's covenant relationship to Israel has not been destroyed, despite Israel's unbelief. Therefore to some extent vv. 3-4 anticipate what Paul writes in Rom. 9-11.

4.3 Romans 3.5-8

In vv. 5-8 Paul digresses somewhat from his main argument. So in v. 5 he puts the question εἰ δὲ ἡ ἀδικία ἡμῶν θεοῦ δικαιοσύνην συνίστησιν, τί ἐροῦμεν; μὴ ἄδικος ὁ θεὸς ὁ ἐπιφέρων τὴν ὀργήν; A number of commentators believe that Paul has in mind Ps. 50.6b LXX (just quoted) and Ps. 50.6a LXX (σοὶ μόνῳ ἥμαρτον καὶ τὸ πονηρὸν ἐνώπιόν σου ἐποίησα). This verse then could possibly be taken to mean that the Psalmist sinned in order to demonstrate God is just.[122] Note that whereas Paul usually understands δικαιοσύνη θεοῦ as "salvation of God",[123] here it is used in the sense of a *iustitia distributiva*. This point gives confirmation to my view that Rom. 1.18-3.20 is to some extent written as though there were no revelation of the righteousness of God as we find in Rom. 3.21.[124] Many have taken the verb συνίστησιν to mean "show up"[125]; others take the meaning "prove".[126] But both ideas are probably present.[127]

---

[120] Hall, "Romans 3.1-8", 187, points to Lam. 1.18 and Neh. 9.33.

[121] Käsemann, *Römer*, p. 76.

[122] Barrett, *Romans*, p. 61.

[123] See the discussion of δικαιοσύνη θεοῦ in chapter 1 above.

[124] I write "to some extent" because in Rom. 1.18-3.20 humankind is seen in the light of the cross of Christ.

[125] Cranfield, *Romans*, 1:184.

[126] Käsemann, *Römer*, p. 78.

[127] Schlier, *Römerbrief*, p. 94, writes that συνιστάναι in Rom. 3.5 means

At the end of v. 5a Paul asks τί ἐροῦμεν. The question τί (οὖν) ἐροῦμεν can be used by Paul in two ways: first to introduce a false conclusion from the preceding argument, which he then rejects (Rom. 6.1; 7.7); secondly, to introduce a true conclusion from the preceding argument which he accepts (Rom. 8.31; 9.30). Many commentators take the first alternative and believe that v. 5b is the objection of an imaginary objector. However, if that is the case, why is the question introduced by μή which anticipates the answer "no". Barrett sees the problem in this, writing, unconvincingly I believe, that Paul alters the expression "out of reverence".[128] Therefore I believe it is much better with Godet and Hall to say Paul is speaking here.[129] So the sense of v. 5b is that in the light of Ps. 50.6 LXX "we clearly cannot accept the suggestion that God's wrath is unjust, can we? Of course not!"[130] By way of confirmation of this understanding, the only other case in Romans where τί ἐροῦμεν is followed by a question introduced by μή is Rom. 9.14: μὴ ἀδικία παρὰ τῷ θεῷ; Here also it is more convincing to say this is part of Paul's reasoning rather than being a question put in the mouth of an opponent.[131]

In v. 6 Paul argues that it is unthinkable that God is unjust to exercise his wrath for how could God otherwise judge the world (ἐπεὶ πῶς κρινεῖ ὁ θεὸς τὸν κόσμον;). Jews accepted that God was judge and Paul reminds Jews that they too will be subject to God's judgement.

Many see in v. 7 the objection of v. 5 is brought forward again. εἰ δὲ ἡ ἀλήθεια τοῦ θεοῦ ἐν τῷ ἐμῷ ψεύσματι ἐπερίσσευσεν εἰς τὴν δόξαν αὐτοῦ, τί ἔτι κἀγὼ ὡς ἁμαρτωλὸς κρίνομαι; However, Hall gives good reasons for the reading εἰ γάρ instead of the commonly accepted εἰ δέ.[132] The reading εἰ γάρ is well attested (B D G W) and could be considered the harder reading.[133] Further, if this is seen as an objection, Paul dis-

---

"herausstellen", "erwirken", "erweisen" as in Rom. 5.8. So he writes: "Unsere Ungerechtigkeit bringt seine Gerechtigkeit an den Tag".

[128] Barrett, *Romans*, p. 61.
[129] Godet, *Romans*, p. 136; Hall, "Romans 3.1-8", 190.
[130] Hall's paraphrase, "Romans 3.1-8", 190.
[131] Hall, "Romans 3.1-8", 190-91.
[132] Hall, "Romans 3.1-8", 192.
[133] Cranfield, *Romans*, 1:185 n. 3.

misses it by just five words: ὧν τὸ κρίμα ἔνδικόν ἐστιν. As Hall writes: "If Paul is not willing to answer the question, why does he raise it in such detail?"[134] Hall rightly suggests taking the reading εἰ γάρ and sees v. 7 not as an objection but as Paul clarifying v. 6.[135] As regards the question τί ἔτι κἀγὼ ὡς ἁμαρτωλὸς κρίνομαι; Hall argues that κἀγώ refers to Paul himself[136] and argues for a parallel with Gal. 2.17.[137] Cosgrove objects to this, pointing out that "Paul the 'Christian' does not understand himself as a sinner".[138] However, could it not be that Paul is even presenting himself in 3.1-8 from a pre-gospel perspective?[139]

Hübner believes that ἀλήθεια in 3.7 (and in 15.8) signifies the covenant faithfulness of God in the sense of the word אֱמֶת.[140] Faithfulness may well be an important component (cf. v. 4b: γινέσθω δὲ ὁ θεὸς ἀληθής). In this case the ψεῦσμα of v. 7 refers not only to the human "lie" but also to human "unfaithfulness" (cf. v. 4c: πᾶς δὲ ἄνθρωπος ψεύστης).

Cranfield writes that v. 8 "is unusually clumsy and tangled".[141] Added to this is the uncertainty in punctuation. Both GNT[4] and NA[26] place a question mark after τὰ ἀγαθά and a full stop at the end of the verse: καὶ μὴ καθὼς βλασφημούμεθα καὶ καθώς φασίν τινες ἡμᾶς λέγειν ὅτι ποιήσωμεν τὰ κακά, ἵνα ἔλθῃ τὰ ἀγαθά; ὧν τὸ κρίμα ἔνδικον ἐστιν.

---

[134] Hall, "Romans 3.1-8", 192.

[135] Note the parallel between Rom. 3.7 and 9.20: τί με ἐποίησας οὕτως;

[136] Hall, "Romans 3.1-8", 194 and 197 n. 28. So καί is taken with ἐγώ meaning "I, Paul" and not taken with κρίνομαι (as in Käsemann, *Römer*, p. 73, and Lietzmann, *Römer*, p. 46).

[137] Hall, "Romans 3.1-8", writes: "Paul had often pondered on God's purpose in the history of salvation, and been tempted to accuse God of unfaithfulness to the covenant in making Jew and Gentile equally liable to this eschatological wrath. But to suggest this would be to deny a basic truth of the gospel, and of his own religious experience, — that he, Paul, as Jew and a Pharisee, was a sinner under judgement just as much as a Gentile. There is thus a close parallel between εὑρέθημεν καὶ αὐτοὶ ἁμαρτωλοί in Gal. 2.17 and the words κἀγὼ ὡς ἁμαρτωλὸς κρίνομαι in Rom. 3.7".

[138] Cosgrove, "Romans 3₁₋₈", 94 n. 14. Among the texts he mentions are Rom. 5.19; 6.1-11; 8.1-4.

[139] Cf. Rom. 7.14-25, which can be viewed as Paul looking at his pre-Christian life (though through Christian spectacles).

[140] H. Hübner, ἀλήθεια κτλ, *EDNT* 1:59 (57-60).

[141] Cranfield, *Romans*, 1:186.

However, many translate v. 8a as though it were not a question.[142] Cranfield, however, does translate it as a question, and I find his translation the most satisfactory: "And do we then say (as certain people slanderously allege that we say), 'Let us do evil, that good may come of it'"?[143] So in v. 8 Paul makes the point that if the idea of v. 5 is accepted (that God is unjust to inflict wrath on Jews) then there is a further problematic consequence: if Jews are not to be judged, they can do whatever they wish. Such people, not Paul, are the antinomians.[144]

So Paul in vv. 6-8 has disproved the idea in v. 5 (that it would be unjust for God to be wrathful) by showing what the logical consequences would be. He has during 3.1-8 moved away from his main theme (hence my argument that the verses form a digression). But he returns to it in the next section, Rom. 3.9-20, to which I now turn.

---

[142] See Wilckens, *Römer*, 1:161; Michel, *Römer*, p. 136.

[143] Cranfield, *Romans*, 1:137. He therefore takes μή as introducing a question which expects a negative answer, assumes an ellipsis of λέγομεν and takes ὅτι outside the parenthesis (Cranfield, *Romans*, 1:187). Cf. *BDF* 427.4 which takes μή with the subjunctive.

[144] The issue of Paul's alleged antinomianism is raised again in Rom. 6. It was clearly an accusation which grieved Paul.

Chapter 6

Romans 3.9-20: Jew and Gentile
under the Power of Sin

1. Introduction

In this chapter I examine Rom. 3.9-20 and I hope to show that in these verses Paul not only summarises much of his earlier argument, but also takes his argument a crucial stage further.

2. Romans 3.9-20

2.1 Romans 3.9

Rom. 3.9 belongs to 3.10-20 (rather than to 3.1-8 as Stowers suggests[1]) and with the verb προῃτιασάμεθα looks back to 1.18-2.29 (giving some confirmation to the view that 3.1-8 is a digression). However, as I will presently show, there is also a link in 3.9 back to 3.1-8 seen in the use of the verb προεχόμεθα.

Rom. 3.9 is by no means straightforward and I begin by considering the text-critical problems of 3.9a. The various texts are helpfully presented by Dahl[2]. The text as found in *NA*26 and *GNT*4 is Τί οὖν; προεχόμεθα; οὐ πάντως. προῃτιασάμεθα γὰρ . . . which is based on the Egyptian-Byzantine texts (ℵ B K 33 1739). Dahl in a fascinating and ingenious argument says that the reading as found in P (025, ninth century) is most likely the original. Here we have the single question Τί

---

[1] Stowers, "Romans 3:1-9".

[2] N.A. Dahl, "Romans 3:9: Text and Meaning", in M.D. Hooker and S.G. Wilson (ed.), *Paul and Paulinism: Essays in honour of C.K. Barrett*, London 1982, 186-87 (184-204).

οὖν προεχόμεθα; and the negation οὐ πάντως is missing. Such a reading is found only in P. The other important text form is the so-called "Antiochene" text Τί οὖν κατέχομεν περισσόν. Dahl admits that the arguments given for the change from the Egyptian-Byzantine text to the Antiochene text do work well up to a point. So the form προεχόμεθα probably caused difficulties and one can readily understand why it was changed to κατέχομεν περισσόν. He suggests that the change from προῃτιασάμεθα to ἠτιασάμεθα may have occurred at the same time.[3] But he believes the arguments for the omission of οὐ πάντως are "much less convincing".[4]

The text I favour is in fact the Egyptian-Byzantine text (Τί οὖν; προεχόμεθα; οὐ πάντως) and I will shortly give justification for accepting this. But first, I need to examine the verb προεχόμεθα. There are three possibilities. First, it could be taken as middle with an active force. The verse would then be asking if Jews have an advantage (over Gentiles). This is found in the Vulgate *Quid igitur praecellimus eos*. The answer οὐ πάντως could then be taken to mean either "certainly not"[5] or "not altogether".[6] If the answer is taken as "certainly not", there would be a stark contradiction with 3.1-2a (Τί οὖν τὸ περισσὸν τοῦ Ἰουδαίου ἢ τίς ἡ ὠφέλεια τῆς περιτομῆς; 2 πολὺ κατὰ πάντα τρόπον). Secondly, the verb could be understood as a passive: "Are we (Jews) excelled by them". This is adopted by a number of commentators.[7] But does this make sense of the context? Stowers believes it does. But he wrongly takes 3.9 with 3.1-8 and even then it makes little sense. Why, after 3.1-8, would Paul want to ask whether Jews are at a disadvantage? He says in 3.1-2 that they are at an advantage in that they are entrusted with τὰ λόγια τοῦ θεοῦ and has made it absolutely clear already in 2.1-29 that Jews and Gentiles are treated the same when it comes to the final judgement. The third possibility and the one which makes the most sense is to take προεχόμεθα as a middle with a middle force: "Are we making excuses?"[8] The logic then

---

[3] Dahl, "Romans 3.9", 188.

[4] Dahl, "Romans 3.9", 188. See my comments in n. 11 below.

[5] Murray, *Romans*, 1:102. Compare again the Vulgate *nequaquam*.

[6] Cranfield, *Romans*, 1:190.

[7] E.g. Sanday and Headlam, *Romans*, p. 77; Lightfoot, *Notes*, p. 267.

[8] See Stuhlmacher, *Römer*, pp. 51-52 (cf. RV margin and J.A. Beet, *A Com-*

is that Paul asks in view of the slanderous charge made in 3.8 whether he (and his fellow Christians) are making excuses for themselves (as though they were claiming to be blameless).[9] His answer is οὐ πάντως, "not at all". The reason for this denial is given in v. 9b: προῃτιασάμεθα γὰρ Ἰουδαίους τε καὶ Ἕλληνας πάντας ὑφ᾽ ἁμαρτίαν εἶναι ("for we have already charged that Jews and Gentiles are all under the power of sin").[10] So the argument of 3.9 is that Paul asks whether he is making excuses for himself. Is he pretending that he himself is without sin? He has, after all, insisted in 3.8 that the charge brought against him that he is an antinomian is a slanderous charge. Paul replies by saying that he is not making excuses (and implying that he is not without excuse). For he has already charged that all, Jews and Greeks, are under the power of sin. So Paul himself cannot pretend he is without sin.

Many copyists probably found this reasoning not the most obvious and it is clear why it was changed to the various texts we now have.[11] In par-

---

mentary on St. Paul's Epistle to the Romans, London [10]1902, p. 100). The basis for this translation is Sophocles, *Antigone* 80: σὺ μὲν τάδ᾽ ἂν προὔχοι·· ἐγὼ δὲ δὴ τάφον χώσουσ᾽ ἀδελφῷ φιλτάτῳ πορεύσομαι (You may offer that excuse; but I shall go to heap up a tomb for my dearest brother!) (*Sophocles* (LCL), 2:11). I take Dahl's point that Thucydides, *History of the Peloponnesian War* 1.140.4 (he mistakenly gives 1.40.4), which is frequently cited, does not support this translation. Concerning 1 En. 99.3, we have here a transitive use of the verb: προέχεσθε τὰς ἐντεύξεις ὑμῶν εἰς μνημόσυνον. Dahl, "Romans 3.9", 194, translates this as "hold your supplications before you, that they may be remembered" (cf. E. Isaac (in Charlesworth, *Pseudepigrapha*, 1:80) who translates the Ethiopic as "raise up your prayers as a memorial"). The translation I adopt "Are we making excuses?" is made more plausible when one considers the first person plural of Rom. 3.9a and 3.9b. See *BA* and *BAG*: ". . . if the 'we' in 9a must of necessity be the same as in 9b, i.e. Paul himself, he is still dealing w. the opponents whom he has in mind in vss. 7,8, and asks ironically: *am I protecting myself?, am I making excuses?*"

[9] See Morris, *Romans*, p. 165.

[10] The AV has "we have before proved", which is rightly rejected by Lightfoot, *Notes*, p. 267. Likewise, Morris, *Romans*, p. 166, points out that "it is the laying of a charge (αἰτία) beforehand that προαιτιάομαι signifies. Although Morris' argument is based on etymological grounds, the verb προαιτιάομαι is nowhere else attested and may well be Paul's own invention. In this case determining the meaning on etymological grounds is not unreasonable.

[11] Dahl argues that it is easier to see how things were changed from the reading in P. For example it is easier, he claims, to account for how οὐ πάντως was inserted than omitted. On my understanding, the οὐ πάντως had to be omitted, for a reading

ticular the change to P may have occurred because in the form Τί οὖν; προεχόμεθα; οὐ πάντως the verb is intransitive. Would it not make more sense to have a transitive middle in which case τί could act as the object? In which case there has to be just one question and not two: Τί οὖν προεχόμεθα; The reading I favour is then the harder reading. Added to this is the fact that the Egyptian-Byzantine reading is so well attested.

I turn now to the interpretation of 3.9. This is in fact a key verse for in it Paul takes his argument forward in two crucial respects. First, he asserts that all are under the *power* of sin. This is the first occurrence of ἁμαρτία in Romans.[12] As Cranfield points out Paul rarely uses the plural to denote actual sins committed.[13] Paul prefers the singular and uses it to show the power of sin. Sin for Paul is primarily an ontological problem, not simply a functional problem.[14] This has central implications for Paul's view of the atonement.[15] The second way in which the argument is carried forward is the idea that *all without exception* are under the power of sin. προῃτιασάμεθα γὰρ Ἰουδαίους τε καὶ Ἕλληνας πάντας ὑφ' ἁμαρτίαν εἶναι. Note particularly the wording: for the first time Paul uses Jews and Greeks (i.e. Gentiles) in the plural.[16] This suggests, with

---

such as that in P (Τί οὖν προεχόμεθα;) requires an οὐδέν. As regards the "Antiochene" texts (Τι ουν (προ)κατεχομεν περισσον), Dahl writes: "It is unlikely that any corrector or scribe would substitute (προ-)κατεχομεν περισσον for προεχομεθα ου παντως" ("Romans 3.9", 188). This point, however, is by no means clear. As Cranfield, *Romans*, 1:189, points out, the question in the Antiochene texts τί οὖν προκατέχομεν περισσόν is much easier.

[12] Note, however, that in 2.12 Paul uses the verb ἁμαρτάνω and in 3.7 the noun ἁμαρτωλός.

[13] Cranfield, *Romans*, 1:191. In fact among the cases where the plural occurs, there may well be a pre-Pauline formulae (1 Cor. 15.3; Rom. 3.25).

[14] H. Hübner, *Das Gesetz bei Paulus: Ein Beitrag zum Werden der paulinischen Theologie*, Göttingen 1978, p. 94 comments on Rom. 3.9: "Es fällt auf, daß in dieser zusammenfassenden Anklage die Rede ist vom Sein unter der Sündenmacht, nicht aber von den eigenen zu verantwortenden Sündentaten". See also G. Klein, "Gesetz III", *TRE* 13:71 (58-75): "Niemals sind es die Taten, die über das Sein entscheiden, vielmehr bringt des Menschen Sein allemal seine Taten hervor".

[15] See Bell, "Sin Offerings", 25-28. I hope to develop this in a future study on Paul's view of the atonement.

[16] Previously in Rom. 1.16; 2.9, 10 he has used the singular for the Jew and Greek (see also 10.12). (He does however refer to Greeks and barbarians in 1.14.) In addi-

the use of πάντας, that Paul refers to every single Jew and Gentile without exception. Up until now Paul has made the charge that generally people fail to keep the law. But there appear to be exceptions (Rom. 2.7, 10, 12-16). So he has not in fact "already charged" that every single person is under the power of sin. There appears, then, to be some discrepancy between what he *thinks* he has charged and what he *has actually* charged. I suggest that Paul was aware of this discrepancy and for this reason made it absolutely clear in 3.10-20 that everyone without exception is under the power of sin.

But there is another possibility which needs exploring. Perhaps Paul is not in fact arguing that everyone without exception is a sinner. He could be simply using a rhetorical hyperbole.[17] Or he could mean Jews and Gentiles as a whole.[18] So Stowers points to cases where although the Jewish nation may have turned away, there were nevertheless faithful Jews, sometimes a great number.[19] Stowers argues that it was commonplace in Jewish, Greek and Roman culture to speak of the sinfulness of human beings. It is true that pagan authors did not speak of universal sinfulness, but neither did Paul, according to Stowers.[20] And so Stowers claims that ancient readers would more likely greet Rom. 3.9 "with a yawn, than a gasp".[21] Nothing could be further from the truth. Paul's anthropology stands out against the Jewish and Graeco-Roman background. Although there are elements in the Hebrew bible which point to the sinfulness of humankind, even the sinfulness of some of the spiritual

---

tion he refers to the Jew in the singular in 2.17, 28, 29; 3.1. Note also the plural Jews and Gentiles in 3.29; 9.24.

[17] See Paul's use of "all" in positive senses in Rom. 10.18; Acts 19.10; Col. 1.23 (see *Provoked to Jealousy*, pp. 93-94) and Acts 17.21 (given by Stowers, *Rereading*, p. 181).

[18] Stowers, *Rereading*, p. 181, compares Rom. 11.26 which he takes to mean Israel as a whole being saved.

[19] Stowers gives the example of 4 Mac. 4.15-20, where Jason "changed the nation's way of life and altered its form of government in complete violation of the law" (4.19). But many of the Jews resisted and remained faithful (4.24-27).

[20] He points to Rom. 2.14-15 (which assumes some pious Gentiles) and Rom. 3.3 (which says *some* Jews have been disobedient).

[21] Stowers, *Rereading*, p. 181.

giants (e.g. David, Ps. 51), Paul's view of human nature is much more extreme. Paul would no doubt see that some were worse sinners than others. But the fundamental point is that all are under the power of sin. So Stowers' judgement that vv. 9-18 "do not mean that all humans, including Enoch, Moses, and Elijah, have been horrible sinners, no better than the worst gentiles"[22] really misses the point. It may be that some great figures in the Old Testament were not sexual perverts or idolaters or murderers. But Paul still considers even Abraham as "godless" (Rom. 4.5) and any positive things which can be said about them are in the light of their being *justified* sinners.[23]

So I do not believe Paul is simply referring to groups in using πάντας and neither is he saying that sinners are to be found among both Jews and Gentiles.[24] This last view could possibly be supported by pointing to texts like Rom. 2.7-10; 14-16; 25-29 and Rom. 3.3. But I believe it becomes clear in 3.9 and 3.10-18 (and of course in 3.19-20) that any righteous Jews and Gentiles which may have been hinted at do not in fact exist.[25] I will argue presently that Paul uses the scripture quotations to show that *all without exception* are under the power of sin. Rom. 3.10-18 is therefore far from being a rather superfluous addition to the argument. It is not just giving scriptural support for his argument so far (important though this is); it carries the argument a crucial step further.

2.2 Romans 3.10-18

I turn now to the catena itself, vv. 10-18. This has a clear structure. There is an inclusio (3.10/3.18)[26] and speech organs play a prominent

---

[22] Stowers, *Rereading*, p. 184.

[23] See the argument in Romans 4 concerning Abraham and David.

[24] Contrast G.N. Davies, *Faith and Obedience in Romans: A Study in Romans 1-4*, Sheffield 1990, p. 96, who believes Paul simply wishes to "establish the distributive presence of sinfulness . . . across the covenantal boundaries of Jew and Gentile".

[25] In chapter 5 I also noted that τινες of Rom. 3.3 (εἰ ἠπίστησάν τινες) is relativised by πᾶς ἄνθρωπος ψεύστης of 3.4.

[26] L.E. Keck, "The Function of Rom 3:10-18: Observations and Suggestions", in J. Jervell and W.A. Meeks (ed.), *God's Christ and His People: Studies in Honour of Nils Alstrup Dahl*, Oslo/Bergen/Tromsö 1977, 143 (141-57). See the use of οὐκ ἔστιν and the similar content of v. 10 and v. 18.

role in vv. 13-14 (throat; tongue; lips; mouth).[27] The reference to speech may have influenced Paul's wording in 3.19b: ἵνα πᾶν στόμα φραγῇ. But perhaps the most important structural element is the six times repeated οὐκ ἔστιν (five times in vv. 10-12, once more than in the original Psalm passage, and once in v. 18). This repeated use of οὐκ ἔστιν and the πάντες in v. 12 leaves the reader in no doubt whatsoever that sin has a hold on everyone. Further it become clear at this point in the argument that the pious Jews and Gentiles of Rom. 2.7, 10, 14-16, 26-29 do not exist. Further the catena shows not only that there are no pious Jews or Gentiles. It suggests also that *no one does any good*. It puts over the most serious view of human kind under the power of sin. Sin affects all human life[28] and it seems that no part of the human person is exempt from the effects of the fall.

The text of the catena (with Old Testament references) is as follows:

10b οὐκ ἔστιν δίκαιος οὐδὲ εἷς

11 οὐκ ἔστιν ὁ συνίων,
οὐκ ἔστιν ὁ ἐκζητῶν τὸν θεόν.
12 πάντες ἐξέκλιναν, ἅμα ἠχρεώθησαν·
οὐκ ἔστιν ὁ ποιῶν χρηστότητα,
[οὐκ ἔστιν] ἕως ἑνός. (Ps. 13.1-3)

13 τάφος ἀνεῳγμένος ὁ λάρυγξ αὐτῶν,
ταῖς γλώσσαις αὐτῶν ἐδολιοῦσαν, (Ps. 5.10b)
ἰὸς ἀσπίδων ὑπὸ τὰ χείλη αὐτῶν, (Ps. 139.4b)
14 ὧν τὸ στόμα ἀρᾶς καὶ πικρίας γέμει· (Ps. 9.28a)
15 ὀξεῖς οἱ πόδες αὐτῶν ἐκχέαι αἷμα,
16 σύντριμμα καὶ ταλαιπωρία ἐν ταῖς ὁδοῖς αὐτῶν,
17 καὶ ὁδὸν εἰρήνης οὐκ ἔγνωσαν. (Is. 59.7-8)

---

[27] Keck, "Rom 3:10-18", 143. Keck also points to the balance of singular and plural nouns: λάρυγξ (singular); γλώσσαις (plural); χείλη (plural); στόμα (singular). Perhaps he is reading too much into the text when he points also to the fact that λάρυγξ and στόμα are "openings for sound" and γλώσσαις and χείλη are "moveable organs for forming words".

[28] Lincoln, "Wrath to Justification", 211, points out that the catena refers to the throat, tongue, lips, mouth, feet and eyes.

18 οὐκ ἔστιν φόβος θεοῦ ἀπέναντι τῶν ὀφθαλμῶν αὐτῶν. (Ps. 35.2).

Some have claimed that 3.10 is actually a quotation from Eccl. 7.20a (ὅτι ἄνθρωπος οὐκ ἔστιν δίκαιος ἐν τῇ γῇ). It is more likely that Paul has worked on Ps. 13.1-3 LXX missing out certain sections which did not suit his theological purpose. The text of Ps. 13.1-3 LXX is:

1 Εἶπεν ἄφρων ἐν καρδίᾳ αὐτοῦ Οὐκ ἔστιν θεός· διέφθειραν καὶ ἐβδελύχθησαν ἐν ἐπιτηδεύμασιν, οὐκ ἔστιν ποιῶν χρηστότητα, οὐκ ἔστιν ἕως ἑνός.
2 κύριος ἐκ τοῦ οὐρανοῦ διέκυψεν ἐπὶ τοὺς υἱοὺς τῶν ἀνθρώπων τοῦ ἰδεῖν εἰ ἔστιν συνίων ἢ ἐκζητῶν τὸν θεόν.
3 πάντες ἐξέκλιναν, ἅμα ἠχρεώθησαν, οὐκ ἔστιν ποιῶν χρηστότητα, οὐκ ἔστιν ἕως ἑνός.

So taking 13.1 it is clear that the idea of the fool needs to be removed, for the Psalm implies that only the fool does not do the right. The Psalm says such fools have no knowledge and all are evildoers (13.4: οὐχὶ γνώσονται πάντες οἱ ἐργαζόμενοι τὴν ἀνομίαν; οἱ κατεσθίοντες τὸν λαόν μου βρώσει ἄρτου τὸν κύριον οὐκ ἐπεκαλέσαντο). But the case of the righteous is quite different (13.5b: ὅτι ὁ θεὸς ἐν γενεᾷ δικαίᾳ). Therefore Paul leaves out the first section of 13.1. He can, however, adopt the last two clauses: οὐκ ἔστιν ποιῶν χρηστότητα, οὐκ ἔστιν ἕως ἑνός. If Paul then omits the section on the fool, it makes sense for Paul also to omit Ps. 13.2a (κύριος ἐκ τοῦ οὐρανοῦ διέκυψεν ἐπὶ τοὺς υἱοὺς τῶν ἀνθρώπων τοῦ ἰδεῖν), "denn hier wird genau das dargestellt, womit der 'Tor' nicht rechnet: Daß Gott sein Handeln keineswegs übersieht".[29] Paul, however, can adopt 13.2b (εἰ ἔστιν συνίων ἢ ἐκζητῶν τὸν θεόν) in Rom. 3.11. Rom. 3.12 is virtually identical to Ps. 13.3.

Rom. 3.13ab is an exact quotation from Ps. 5.10b and Rom. 3.13c is an exact quotation from Ps. 139.4b. Rom. 3.14 is a free quotation from Ps. 9.28a.[30]

---

[29] Koch, *Schrift*, p. 119.
[30] Note that Ps. 139.4a and Ps. 9.28b both contain the word γλῶσσα (cf. Ps. 5.10b).

In Rom. 3.15-17, Is. 59.7-8 is quoted but a large part of Is. 59.7 has been omitted. Again the theme of foolishness has been omitted (καὶ οἱ διαλογισμοὶ αὐτῶν διαλογισμοὶ ἀφρόνων).

Finally in Rom. 3.18 there is an almost exact quotation from Ps. 35.2b (with αὐτῶν instead of αὐτοῦ). By omitting the reference to ὁ παράνομος in 35.2a Paul is able to apply 35.2b to the whole of humanity (and therefore needs to change αὐτοῦ of the Ps. 35.2b to αὐτῶν).[31]

Note that all the Psalms quoted (Psalms 5, 9, 13; 35 and 139) begin with the superscript Εἰς τὸ τέλος.[32] This may possibly point to these Psalms having an eschatological use already in the LXX.[33]

There has been some debate whether Paul has taken over an already existing florilegium. There is a parallel in Justin, *Dialogue* 27.3, which I set out as follows to highlight the structure[34]:

καὶ
πάντες γὰρ ἐξέκλιναν,
βοᾷ,
πάντες ἄρα ἠχρειώθησαν

---

[31] See Koch, *Schrift*, p. 112; C.D. Stanley, *Paul and the Language of Scripture*, Cambridge 1992, p. 99.

[32] Εἰς τὸ τέλος translates למנצח, which is a pi'el participle of נצח meaning "to be pre-eminent", the pi'el having the sense "act as overseer". This title is often translated as "to the choirmaster" in the RSV and occurs in 55 Psalms and in Hab. 3.19. The septuagintal Εἰς τὸ τέλος is understood by Eusebius and Theodoret in an eschatological sense (see C.A. Briggs and E.G. Briggs, *The Book of Psalms*, 2 vols, Edinburgh 1906-7, 1:lxxiii). See Eusebius' comment on Εἰς τὸ τέλος in his commentary on Psalm 4 (*Commentaria in Psalmos*, in *MPG* 23:101). Aquila has νικοποιοῦ and Symmachus ἐπινικίους for למנצח.

[33] On the general issue of the eschatological use of the septuagintal Psalter, see J. Schaper, "Der Septuaginta-Psalter als Dokument jüdischer Eschatologie", in M. Hengel and A.M. Schwemer (ed.), *Die Septuaginta zwischen Judentum und Christentum*, Tübingen 1994, 38-61, and J. Schaper, *Eschatology in the Greek Psalter*, Tübingen 1995.

[34] The text may be found in E.J. Goodspeed (ed.), *Die ältesten Apologeten: Texte mit kurzen Einleitungen*, Göttingen 1914, p. 121.

οὐκ ἔστιν ὁ συνίων,
οὐκ ἔστιν ἕως ἑνός.

ταῖς γλώσσαις αὐτῶν ἐδολιοῦσαν,
   τάφος ἀνεῳγμένος ὁ λάρυγξ αὐτῶν,
   ἰὸς ἀσπίδων ὑπὸ τὰ χείλη αὐτῶν,
   σύντριμμα καὶ ταλαιπωρία ἐν ταῖς ὁδοῖς αὐτῶν,
καὶ ὁδὸν εἰρήνης οὐκ ἔγνωσαν.

Keck concludes that this text "provides evidence that Rom 3:10-18 once existed independently".[35] He puts forward three arguments. First, Justin, begins with the texts Ps. 105.37 LXX; Is. 1.23, 15; 3.16 and then he gives a number of texts also occurring in Rom. 3.10-18 which are introduced by βοᾷ. Keck argues: "This βοᾷ is the same sort of clue to an originally independent tradition as καὶ ἔλεγεν αὐτοῖς is in the synoptics (e.g., Mark 7:9)". However, Justin could just as well be pointing back to Rom. 3.10-18 by using βοᾷ. Keck's second argument is that it is not clear why Justin would shorten Rom. 3.10-18 and he suggests Justin relies on a shorter and possibly earlier version of the same catena. But Koch has put forward a perfectly plausible reason for Justin's abbreviated form: "Justin konzentriert sich auf möglichst konkrete Anklagen, um τὸ σκληροκάρδιον der Juden (27,2) zu erweisen".[36] Keck's third argument is that Justin's catena "has a clear internal structure and cannot be regarded as a mutilated form of Rom. 3".[37] However, Justin could simply have carefully rearranged Paul's catena so giving it this new structure.

In the discussion as to whether there was an independent catena, the burden of proof must be on those who posit such a catena. I do not believe that Keck has put forward strong enough arguments for an independent catena. The most economical hypothesis to account for the texts we have is that Paul himself brought these texts together and Justin

---

[35] Keck, "Rom 3:10-18", 150.

[36] Koch, *Schrift*, p. 182. See also below on Justin and Paul's quotations of the Old Testament in Romans 2-4.

[37] Keck, "Rom 3:10-18", 150.

adopted his catena from Paul.[38] In fact one may go further and say there
is an indication that Justin did in fact use Romans. When Romans is compared with Justin, it becomes apparent that Justin has taken over Paul's
quotations in blocks. So of the eight Old Testament texts quoted in
Romans 2-4, Justin uses five of them.[39] Also the quotations in common
with Romans are concentrated in two blocks in the *Dialogue*.[40] Further, it
is striking that in Romans 2-4 Justin has omitted texts which Paul has
quoted to prove that every man is a sinner, i.e. Ps. 51.4; Ps. 143.2[41] and,
as already mentioned, the catena of Rom. 3.10-18 is turned into an anti-
Jewish text.

I return now to the theological point Paul wishes to make in this catena.
One of the striking things about the Psalms quoted is that they do *not*
point to the universality of sin.[42] Rather they point to a group within
humanity, the "wicked". We have seen this is the case of Ps. 13.1-3
LXX. There the "fool" is criticised. In Ps. 5, the Psalmist is clearly dif-
ferentiating himself from the "trangressors" ($\pi\alpha\rho\acute{\alpha}\nu o\mu o\iota$) (5.6) and those
of v. 10 of whom the Psalmist says "their throat is an open sepulchre".[43]
Again in Ps. 139 LXX there are those who have venom of asps under
their lips (Ps. 139.4 LXX), but the Psalmist asks to be delivered from
such people. Likewise in Ps. 9 God is a refuge for the poor (9.10), even
though the Psalmist's enemies have a mouth filled with cursing, bitterness
and deceit (9.28). In Ps. 35 LXX we find that although the Psalmist can
say "there is no fear of God before his eyes" (35.2), there are those, the
Psalmist included, who "trust in the shelter of thy wings" (35.8) and who
are "upright in heart" (35.11). As far as these Psalms are concerned, I

---

[38] The appearance of this catena in some of the texts of the LXX text of Ps. 13
provides no evidence for an independently existing catena. This text of Ps. 13
obviously came into being in view of the Christian use of this Psalm.

[39] See O. Skarsaune, *The Proof from Prophecy: A Study of Justin Martyr's Proof-
Text Tradition*, Leiden 1987, pp. 93-95. In this reckoning, Rom. 3.10-18 counts as
one quotation.

[40] See Skarsaune, *Proof from Prophecy*, pp. 95-96.

[41] Skarsaune, *Proof from Prophecy*, p. 97.

[42] See Edgar, "Respect for Context", 56.

[43] Cf. S. Moyise, "The Catena of Romans 3:10-18", *ExpT* 106 (1995) 368 (367-
70).

suggest that Paul has gone largely against the context.[44] But is there some hermeneutical principle at work? Dunn believes that "it can hardly be accidental that in this case all the Psalm quotations work with an antithesis between those self-consciously favoured by God and the rest variously described as the fool, the unrighteous, the lawless, the wicked, the sinner. Whether his first readers would have recognised the allusions or not, it is hard to doubt that Paul intended the Psalm citations as a turning of the tables on Jewish overconfidence in their nations favoured status before God".[45] This is one possible explanation, although I feel there is a danger in Dunn's approach in that he perhaps reads in too often the idea that Paul is wishing to deny Jewish people their privileges.[46] Another possible explanation is that for Paul there was only one righteous person, Jesus Christ. Paul, I believe, had the view that only Jesus Christ is righteous and it is interesting that he, like other New Testament writers, saw Jesus as the righteous sufferer of Ps. 69 (68 LXX).[47]

So in the Psalms quoted in Rom. 3.10-18, Paul has radically altered the original meaning. The case of Is. 59.7-8, however, is somewhat different. Although there are references not far away in Is. 57.1 to the "righteous man" (ὁ δίκαιος) and "righteous men" (ἄνδρες δίκαιοι), such people are clearly in a small minority and it is striking that in Is. 59 itself the impression is given that everyone in Judah is a sinner. So the chapter begins by referring to the iniquities of the people which separate them from God (59.2). Their hands are defiled with blood and their lips have spoken iniquity (59.3). Their works are works of iniquity (τὰ γὰρ ἔργα αὐτῶν, ἔργα ἀνομίας, 59.6). After the verses from which Paul quotes (59.7-8) the chapter continues to stress the hopeless situation of the people. Then God saw that there was no one to intervene and so God himself will intervene to save his people (59.16-19). So in the case of Is. 59.7-8, Paul did, it appears, pay some attention to the context. The major change is, of

---

[44] Note Edgar's conclusion ("Respect for Context", 62) that "Old Testament passages quoted by Jesus were used with a respect for the original context that is unmatched by other New Testament writers".

[45] J.D.G. Dunn, *Romans*, 2 vols, Dallas, Texas 1988, p. 151.

[46] See the discussion of ἔργα νόμου below.

[47] So Paul quotes from Ps. 68.10 in Rom. 15.3. He uses verses from the same Psalm to point to the unbelief of Israel (Ps. 68.23-24 quoted in Rom. 11.9-10).

course, that he applied the text not only to Judah but to everyone. This is significant, for Is. 59.20-21 is quoted in Rom. 11.26-27.[48] But the other texts quoted are not elsewhere quoted or alluded to.[49]

Rom. 3.9 has summed up the accusation against humankind. Rom. 3.10-18, I believe, acts as a further accusation, stressing that no one is exempt from God's condemnation.[50] To a certain extent I therefore agree with Keck that the catena has a semi-legal status. However, I believe he is going too far in arguing that Rom. 1.18-3.9, 19 "is a sustained theological exposition of the catena, an exposition developed neither as pesher nor midrash, but as a forensic indictment, a statement of God's 'case' against the world".[51] Rather the catena functions to take Paul's argument a step further: no one does the good. Such a view is reinforced in the conclusion of Paul's argument, Rom. 3.19-20.

2.3 Romans 3.19

Having put forward his catena, Paul summarises his argument in Rom. 3.19-20. Rom. 3.19: Οἴδαμεν δὲ ὅτι ὅσα ὁ νόμος λέγει τοῖς ἐν τῷ νόμῳ

---

[48] An issue which is here raised is the way Paul understood the extent of the "text-block". C. Westermann, *Isaiah 40-66*, London 1969, p. 344, believes Is. 59.1-21 is "plainly a unity". However, he believes that v. 21 is misplaced, a view Paul would not seem to share in view of his quotation of vv. 20-21a. A. Motyer, *The Prophecy of Isaiah*, Leicester 1993, has a different analysis, taking 59.1-13 as one unit and 59.14-63.6 (concerning the anointed conqueror) as the next (see his analysis of Is. 56-66, p. 461). However Paul understood the text, 59.7-8 and Is. 59.20-21 certainly have a proximity.

[49] A possible exception is Ps. 13.7 LXX. This may have influenced Paul's citation of Is. 59.20 in Rom. 11.26. Is. 59.20 has ἥξει ἕνεκεν Σιων ὁ ῥυόμενος whereas Paul has ἥξει ἐκ Σιων ὁ ῥυόμενος. Paul may have changed ἕνεκεν to ἐκ in view of Ps. 13.7 (Τίς δώσει ἐκ Σιὼν τὸ σωτήριον τοῦ Ἰσραήλ; ἐν τῷ ἐπιστρέψαι Κύριον τὴν αἰχμαλωσίαν τοῦ λαοῦ αὐτοῦ, ἀγαλλιάσθω Ἰακὼβ, καὶ εὐφρανθήτω Ἰσραήλ) or Ps. 49.2 LXX (ἐκ Σιων ἡ εὐπρέπεια τῆς ὡραιότητος αὐτοῦ, ὁ θεὸς ἐμφανῶς ἥξει).

[50] Again contrast Davies, *Faith*, p. 96, who claims: "The effect of the catena as a whole enables Paul to demonstrate that God's condemnation of unrighteousness is cross-cultural, including Jew and Gentile alike. That there are those who are righteous and who do fear God, is no more excluded by Paul than it was by the psalmist and the prophet when their words were first recorded".

[51] Keck, "Rom 3:10-18", 152.

λαλεῖ, ἵνα πᾶν στόμα φραγῇ καὶ ὑπόδικος γένηται πᾶς ὁ κόσμος τῷ θεῷ. The phrase ὅσα ὁ νόμος λέγει points back to the catena of 3.10-18. This is a case where νόμος clearly means the Old Testament for Paul has quoted from the Writings and Prophets (cf. 1 Cor. 14.21). To whom does Paul refer in τοῖς ἐν τῷ νόμῳ? Comparing the phrase οἱ ἐν τῷ νόμῳ of Rom. 2.12, Cranfield believes τοῖς ἐν τῷ νόμῳ refers to those who possess the law, i.e., the Jews. The logic of therefore Rom. 3.19 is that if Jews are guilty, the whole world is guilty.[52] Another possible interpretation is that Jews would assume Gentiles do the sins of 3.10-18 and Paul surprises them by saying that these are sins are committed by the Jews also.[53] Murray, however, believes that the πᾶν and πᾶς of 19b suggests Paul is referring to Jews and Gentiles in 19a as well as 19b. As far as the Gentiles are concerned, he writes: "The Gentiles are therefore regarded as 'in the law', that is to say, in the sphere within which the law of which Paul had quoted samples had relevance".[54] Note also that for Paul the Mosaic law condemns both Jews and Gentiles and so the Gentiles also can be said to be in the sphere of the law.[55] Therefore I believe Murray is probably correct.

It was noted that Paul employs forensic language in 3.9. The same is true in 3.19 (and in 3.20). Cranfield points out that the words στόμα φραγῇ evoke the picture of the defendant in court, who, given the

---

[52] Cranfield, *Romans*, 1:196, writes: "If the Jews are shown by Scripture to be ὑφ᾽ ἁμαρτίαν, there is no question of any Gentile's not being ὑφ᾽ ἁμαρτίαν". See also the similar argument of J.C. Beker, *Paul the Apostle*, Edinburgh 1980, p. 80.

[53] Schlier, *Römerbrief*, p. 99. Cf. Wilckens, *Römer*, 1:173: "Was die Tora hier sagt, zielt darauf, daß den Juden, die wie die Heiden zu Frevlern geworden sind, ihr καυχᾶσθαι (2,17ff vgl. 3,27) vergeht und so die gesamte Welt, Juden wie Heiden (V 9), dem göttlichen Recht des Zorngerichts verfallen".

[54] Murray, *Romans*, 1:106.

[55] See especially Rom. 2.14-15. Note also F. Hahn's comments on Rom. 3.19-20: "Im 'Bereich des Gesetzes' stehen zunächst einmal unbestritten die Juden, jedoch nach den Ausführungen von 2₁₄ff. gilt dies eben grundsätzlich auch für die Heiden" ("Das Gesetzesverständnis im Römer- und Galaterbrief", *ZNW* 67 (1976) 34 (29-63)). He also writes: "Wo immer der Mensch der Rechtsforderung Gottes begegnet, hat er es direkt oder indirekt mit dem in der Tora dokumentierten Willen Gottes zu tun" ("Gesetzesverständnis", 57).

opportunity to speak in his own defence, is speechless because of the weight of evidence brought against him.[56]

2.4 Romans 3.20

Rom. 3.20 is a crucial verse and I will spend some time discussing it. Rom. 3.20: διότι ἐξ ἔργων νόμου οὐ δικαιωθήσεται πᾶσα σὰρξ ἐνώπιον αὐτοῦ, διὰ γὰρ νόμου ἐπίγνωσις ἁμαρτίας. The first half of this verse sums up the main argument of the whole section 1.18-3.20. No one will be justified through works of law.[57] There is an allusion to Ps. 142.2 LXX: καὶ μὴ εἰσέλθῃς εἰς κρίσιν μετὰ τοῦ δούλου σου, ὅτι οὐ δικαιωθήσεται ἐνώπιόν σου πᾶς ζῶν.[58] Paul in fact had alluded to this same verse earlier in Gal. 2.16b: ὅτι ἐξ ἔργων νόμου οὐ δικαιωθήσεται πᾶσα σάρξ. In both cases he has changed Ps. 142.2 LXX in two respects. First, he has replaced πᾶς ζῶν with πᾶσα σάρξ. Secondly, he has added the words ἐξ ἔργων νόμου. While the former does not change the sense of the Psalm,[59] the latter does,[60] for it adds the specific idea that through works of law no one will be justified.

One of the major questions here is the meaning of ἔργα νόμου, which has been the subject of much recent debate.[61] I begin by considering Billerbeck's discussion.[62] He points to 2 Bar. 57.2,[63] arguing that "Werke

---

[56] Cranfield, *Romans*, 1:196-97.

[57] The future may well be gnomic (cf. Bultmann, *Theologie*, p. 274; Käsemann, *Römer*, p. 84).

[58] Ps. 143.2 MT is וְאַל־תָּבוֹא בְמִשְׁפָּט אֶת־עַבְדֶּךָ כִּי לֹא־יִצְדַּק לְפָנֶיךָ כָל־חָי:

[59] The term πᾶσα σάρξ simply refers to human beings and does not carry the negative connotation. This is seen clearly in Gal. 2.16 (see F. Mußner, *Der Galaterbrief*, Freiburg/Basel/Wien 1974, p. 172).

[60] P. Vielhauer, "Paulus und das Alte Testament", in *Oikodome: Aufsätze zum Neuen Testament*, München 1979, 214 (196-228).

[61] A discussion on the precise significance of the preposition ἐκ will be reserved for chapter 7.

[62] See Billerbeck, *Kommentar* 3:160-62. Billerbeck's work is referred to in the recent discussion on "works of law" but few consider his actual argument in much detail. Billerbeck's great commentary has been greatly maligned by certain scholars over the last 15 or 20 years. Although one may not always agree with his methodology, his achievement was colossal. Hengel and Deines believe that Billerbeck "did more to spread the knowledge of rabbinic texts in academic theology than any

der Gebote" are "genau dasselbe, was der Apostel ἔργα νόμου nennt, nur
daß das singularische νόμος durch die Vielheit der einzelnen Gebote
ersetzt ist".[64] I will later question this. He also points to 2 Bar. 48.38:
"And it will happen in that time that a change of times will reveal itself
openly for the eyes of everyone because they polluted themselves in all
those times and caused oppression, and each one walked in his own
works and did not remember the Law of the Mighty One".[65] Billerbeck
comments that if the wicked were guided instead by the torah, their "own
works" would become *opera praeceptorum*, "d.h. Werke, zu denen die
Tora Anleitung gibt, die auf Grund der Tora vollbracht werden, die aus
der Beobachtung der Tora hervorgehen".[66] He argues that Paul's ἔργα
νόμου have just the same meaning: "es sind Werke, die das Ergebnis der
Gesetzesbeobachtung oder der Gebotserfüllung sind".[67] Billerbeck writes
that although the Rabbis do not use the Hebrew equivalent to ἔργα νόμου,
מַעֲשֵׂי תּוֹרָה, they do use מעשים (e.g. Aboth 3.17), sometimes adding
טובים.[68] However, he goes on to argue that the expressions מעשים and
מעשים טובים are not generally used to refer to works of law; rather the
terminus technicus is מִצְוָה/ מִצְוֹת which can either mean commandment
(ἐντολή) or "das aus der Gebotserfüllung resultierende Werk" (ἔργον
νόμου).[69] Billerbeck's view has influenced many. So he is supported by

---

other Christian theologian" (M. Hengel and R. Deines, "E.P. Sanders' 'Common
Judaism', Jesus, and the Pharisees", *JTS* 46 (1995) 69 (1-70)).

[63] "For at that time *the unwritten law* (l' ktb' nmws') was in force among them
(i.e. Abraham, Isaac, Jacob), and *the works of the commandments* ('bd' dpwqdn')
were accomplished at that time, and the belief in *the coming judgement* (dyn' d'tyd)
was brought about . . ." (translation of Klijn, in Charlesworth, *Pseudepigrapha*,
1:641). This passage was discussed in chapter 4 above.

[64] Billerbeck, *Kommentar*, 3:160.

[65] Translation of Klijn, in Charlesworth, *Pseudepigrapha*, 1:637.

[66] Billerbeck, *Kommentar*, 3:160.

[67] Billerbeck, *Kommentar*, 3:161.

[68] Billerbeck, *Kommentar*, 3:161, points to Aboth 3.11 (Danby, 3.12).

[69] See, for example, the use of מִצְוֹת in Sifre Num. 15.31 (112): "R. Eleazar the
Modite said, 'He who desecrates the Holy Things, despises the holy seasons, or nullifies the covenant of Abraham, our Father, even though he has to his credit many
religious duties (מִצְוֹת), is worthy of being driven out of the world" (J. Neusner, *Sifré
to Numbers*, 2 vols, Atlanta 1986, 2:170). What Neusner has translated as "religious
duties", Billerbeck has translated more precisely as "Gebotserfüllungen". I have dis-

Bertram[70] and by commentators like Käsemann[71] and Schlier.[72] Billerbeck did not have the advantage of having the Qumran texts to illumine the meaning of ἔργα νόμου. Nevertheless, I believe he has made many valuable points.

Although indebted to Billerbeck's insights, Lohmeyer had a somewhat different approach. He argues that the expression "works of law" does not primarily refer to the performance of specific acts demanded by the law. Rather the reference is to the "Dienst des Gesetzes".[73] I believe Käsemann correctly describes Lohmeyer's work as an "ebenso anregenden wie kritisch zu lesenden Artikel".[74] There are interesting insights, but at the same time there are, I believe, a number of problems in his approach. He reaches his conclusion by among other things considering the septuagintal use of ἔργα with a genitive. So he considers expression like ἔργα τῆς σκηνῆς (e.g. Ex. 35.21), ἔργα τῆς λειτουργίας (e.g. 1 Chr. 9.19) and ἔργα τῆς θυσίας (e.g. 1 Chr. 9.31), such expressions applying to the Priests and Levites. "Auch hier gibt der Genitiv einen bestimmten Tätigkeitskreis an, in dem die Handelnden ihr 'Werk' vollbringen".[75] Focusing on ἔργα τῆς σκηνῆς Lohmeyer argues that such work is "service" as is suggested by the usual Hebrew equivalent of עֲבֹדָה rather than מַעֲשֶׂה.[76] But there are two problems with such an argument. First, an expression like ἔργα τῆς σκηνῆς is an objective genitive: they are works performed for the tabernacle. But ἔργα νόμου can hardly be taken in this way (and Lohmeyer himself rejects the objective genitive for

---

cussed Sifre Num. to Num. 15.30-31 in my article "Sin Offerings and Sinning with a High Hand", *JPJ* 4 (1995) 46-48 (25-59).

[70] G. Bertram, ἔργον κτλ, *TDNT* 2:646 (635-55).

[71] Käsemann, *Römer*, p. 83.

[72] See H. Schlier, *Der Brief an die Galater*, Göttingen [14]1971, ([10]1949), pp. 91-92; Schlier, *Römerbrief*, pp. 100-101.

[73] E. Lohmeyer, "Probleme paulinischer Theologie. II. 'Gesetzeswerke'", *ZNW* 28 (1929) 202 (177-207) (= *Probleme paulinischer Theologie*, Stuttgart (no date), 67 (33-74)).

[74] Käsemann, *Römer*, p. 83.

[75] Lohmeyer, *Probleme*, p. 38.

[76] See Num. 3.7, 8; 4.30, 43.

ἔργα νόμου). Such works are not works which serve the law.[77] They are rather "konkrete Werke . . . die die Tora fordert und die als getane Werke die Tora erfüllen".[78] Secondly, an expression like ἔργα τῆς σκηνῆς (Num. 3.7, 8), while suggesting general service, does have the emphasis "on a series of concrete acts which make up that service".[79] It may be that this was not the emphasis in the Hebrew (which often uses עֲבֹדָה); but in the LXX the emphasis is on the individual acts (as suggested by the use of the plural ἔργα).[80] Lohmeyer also points to texts where "Werk" essentially means "Gesetz", "so daß 'Werk' nicht von der Tatsache der Erfüllung, sondern von der Forderung einer solchen Erfüllung spricht".[81] He points to texts like Test. Lev. 19.1 and 2 Bar. 57.2. I take the point that in 2 Bar. 57.2, "ist der Ausdruck 'Werk' nur eine Variante des Begriffes Gebot, die auf die Forderung des 'Vollbringens', nicht auf die Tatsache des 'Vollbrachtseins' tendiert".[82] But I maintain that the expression "works of the commandments" parallels the expression τὸ ἔργον τοῦ νόμου (Rom. 2.15) and not so much the expression ἔργα νόμου.[83] Many other things could be said of Loh-

---

[77] As J. Tyson points out, Lohmeyer himself did not classify the genitive ἔργα νόμου. But Tyson claims Lohmeyer's interpretation assumes a "qualitative genitive" (Tyson, "'Works of Law' in Galatians", *JBL* 92 (1973) 425 n. 13 (423-31). points to A.W. Slaten, "The Qualitative Use of νόμος in the Pauline Epistles", *AJT* 23 (1919) 213-19). Note, however, that Lohmeyer himself denies that ἔργα νόμου is to be understood as a qualitative genitive. He writes that law is not a quality "sondern eine Norm, um Qualitäten, sittliche oder unsittliche, fromme oder unfromme zu bestimmen" (*Probleme*, p. 35) and his conclusion is this: "So bleibt die Art dieses Genetives grammatisch unklar" (*Probleme*, p. 73). Note also that although Lohmeyer claims the expression "Dienst des Gesetzes" is in one sense a genitivus qualitatis (*Probleme*, p. 73) it is also in a certain sense a *genitivus auctoris* and a *genitivus objectivus* (*Probleme*, p. 73).

[78] Schlier, *Galater*, p. 91.

[79] D. Moo, "'Law,' 'Works of the Law,' and Legalism in Paul", *WTJ* 45 (1983) 94 (73-100).

[80] If the emphasis were not on the individual acts, expressions such as λειτουργία τῆς σκηνῆς or perhaps διακονία τῆς σκηνῆς could have been used.

[81] Lohmeyer, *Probleme*, p. 40.

[82] Lohmeyer, *Probleme*, p. 40.

[83] Therefore I disagree with Billerbeck's point that "works of the commandments" parallels Paul's ἔργα νόμου.

meyer's thought-provoking study, but I turn to the more recent discussion.

Related to Lohmeyer's view is that of Tyson.[84] Although he was discussing works of law in Galatians, some of his conclusions need mentioning. He writes that the expression "works of law" "refers specifically to a life dedicated to nomistic service", such service being "primarily associated with circumcision and food laws". Paul's point in Galatians is that "God's people are marked by faith and the spirit rather than by circumcision and food laws".[85] However, "works of law" cannot be limited to circumcision and food laws as I hope to show below.

Dunn's views on "works of law" bear a resemblance to Tyson's.[86] Dunn, although indebted to Sanders, expresses dissatisfaction with his view (and Räisänen's view) that Paul's view on the law is self-contradictory, and believes that they have "failed to grasp the full significance of *the social function of the law*".[87] For Dunn, Paul is negative about "works of law" because it is "the law as identity and boundary marker which is in view".[88] He concludes: "The recognition that what Paul is attacking is a particular and restrictive understanding of the law provides the key to many of the tensions perceived in Paul's writing on the law. Freed from that too narrow understanding of the law, the Jewish Christian (and Gentile) is able to recognize that the law has a continuing positive role, to be fulfilled in love of neighbour".[89] So for Dunn "works of the law" are "badges" and "are simply what membership of the covenant people involves"[90] and take on a sociological dimension. The stress is then on laws like circumcision and food laws which mark out the

---

[84] J. Tyson, "'Works of Law' in Galatians", *JBL* 92 (1973) 423-31.

[85] Tyson, "Works of Law", 431.

[86] See J.D.G. Dunn, "The New Perspective on Paul", *BJRL* 65 (1983) 95-122; "The Works of the Law and the Curse of the Law (Galatians 3:10-14)", *NTS* (1985) 523-42. He has been criticised, for example, by C.E.B. Cranfield, "'The Works of the Law' in the Epistle to the Romans", *JSNT* 43 (1991) 89-101. See Dunn's reply "Yet Once More—'The Works of the Law'", *JSNT* 46 (1992) 99-117.

[87] Dunn, "The Works of the Law and the Curse of the Law", 524.

[88] Dunn, "The Works of the Law and the Curse of the Law", 531.

[89] Dunn, "The Works of the Law and the Curse of the Law", 538.

[90] J.D.G. Dunn, "The New Perspective on Paul", *BJRL* 65 (1983) 110 (95-122).

Jew from other people. As regards Rom. 3.20, which especially interests me here, Dunn writes:

. . . 'works of the law' are *not* the same as *doing* the law (2:13-14), or *fulfilling* the law (2:27). . . . 'Works of the law' are rather something more superficial, at the level of 'the letter' (2:27, 29), an outward mark indicative of ethnic solidarity (2:28).[91]

Although Dunn appeals to Jewish texts from Qumran and 2 Bar. 57.2 I do not think they actually support his view and I believe his view of "identity markers" makes little sense of the Pauline texts. In fact Rom. 3.20 makes it clear that his position is wrong. Schreiner points out that 3.20 cannot be separated from what Paul says in Rom. 2.[92] As I argued in chapter 5 above, "works of law" is related to practising the law (νόμου πράσσῃς, 2.25) observing the ordinances of the law (τὰ δικαιώματα τοῦ νόμου φυλάσσῃ, 2.26) and keeping the law (τὸν νόμον τελοῦσα, 2.27). Paul also speaks of doers of the law (ποιηταὶ νόμου, 2.13). It is striking to see what Paul actually has in mind when he criticises the Jews for not keeping the law. In 2.21-22 he refers to sins of theft, adultery and temple robbery. On the other hand Paul by no means has a negative view of circumcision per se. This is clear from the discussion in Rom. 2.25-29. Jews are not criticised for circumcision. He makes the point, rather, that circumcision does not profit if one does not keep the law.

There are two further problems with Dunn's approach. First, Rom. 3.20b says that through the law comes knowledge of sin. But there is no hint here that the problem is an exclusive spirit. Secondly, going further to Rom. 4.2, Paul refers to "works" which can be regarded as a shorthand for "works of law".[93] But Romans 4 refers to works in the broadest sense. Also the example of David makes it clear that Paul is thinking not of "boundary markers" but failure to obey the law. Paul refers to David's ἀνομίαι and ἁμαρτίαι (4.7). As Schreiner writes: "Paul is not implying that David's sins consisted in an overemphasis on circumcision and other 'boundary markers' so that Gentiles were excluded from the people of God. His 'lawless acts' and 'sins' described here are general

---

[91] Dunn, *Romans*, pp. 158-59.

[92] T.R. Schreiner, "'Works of Law' in Paul", *NovT* 33 (1991) 226 (217-44).

[93] See Hofius, "Rechtfertigung des Gottlosen", 127 n. 35. He points to the use of ἔργα in Rom. 4.2, 6; 9.12, 32; 11.6).

terms for one who sins by disobeying the law".[94] In fact the sins for which David is remembered are murder and adultery.

Another view to be rejected is that of Gaston who understands ἔργα νόμου as a subjective genitive. According to Gaston Paul refers to works which are produced by the law and these can only be evil.[95] Gaston points to the genitives τὰ ἔργα τῆς σαρκός (Gal. 5.19) and ὁ καρπὸς τοῦ πνεύματος which refer to works done by the flesh and fruit produced by the spirit[96] and places special emphasis on Rom. 4.15, where Paul writes "for the law works wrath" (ὁ γὰρ νόμος ὀργὴν κατεργάζεται).[97] There are two problems with this approach. First, the Jewish texts which most clearly parallel Paul's ἔργα νόμου refer to the works demanded by the law or the works as actually done. In both cases such works are not evil. Secondly, I do not think Gaston's interpretation makes sense of the Pauline texts. For example, it makes little sense of Rom. 3.20: why would Paul wish to make the point that no one is justified by evil works? No one is going to disagree with such an idea.[98]

Having examined and criticised a number of views, I put forward my own. I believe the phrase ἔργα νόμου means "observance of the Torah", such observance being of the *whole Torah*. So observance of the law would involve keeping the ten commandments and various other moral laws contained in the Old Testament (for example the laws concerning sexual behaviour in Lev. 20). Observing the law also involves the various ceremonial laws such as the food laws and circumcision. Such a view can be supported by the texts from Qumran where the equivalent expression (מַעֲשֵׂי תוֹרָה) occurs. First I consider 4QFlor 1.6-7 (4Q174 3.6-7). The text as commonly given is[99]:

---

[94] Schreiner, "Works of Law", 229.

[95] L. Gaston, "Works of Law as a Subjective Genitive", in *Paul and the Torah*, Vancouver 1987, 100-6 (= *SR* 13 (1984) 39-46).

[96] Gaston, "Works of Law", 104.

[97] Gaston, "Works of Law", 105.

[98] Cf. Schreiner, "Works of Law", 231.

[99] See, for example, J.M. Allegro (A.A. Anderson), *Discoveries in the Judaean Desert of Jordan V: Qumrân Cave 4, I (4Q158-4Q186)*, Oxford 1968, p. 53; E. Lohse, *Die Texte aus Qumran, Hebräisch und Deutsch mit Masoretischer Punktation, Übersetzung, Einführung und Anmerkungen*, Darmstadt ⁴1986, (¹1964), p. 256.

ויומר לבנות לוא מקדש אדם להיות מקטירים בוא לוא לפניו מעשי תורה

I give my own fairly literal translation:

And he (God) said that he would build for himself a sanctuary among men (lit. sanctuary of man),[100] for there to be smoking sacrifices in it for him[101] in his presence, that is works of law.

However, some Qumran scholars have questioned the reading מעשי תורה. So Brooke,[102] following a suggestion of Strugnell,[103] reads מעשי תודה, i.e. "works of thanksgiving", as does Steudel in a recent book.[104] However, I wonder whether one can be as confident as Steudel when she writes: "Die ansonsten in der Literatur vertretene Lesung מעשי תורה ist paläographisch nicht möglich".[105] Further, the reading מעשי תורה would make excellent sense in view of the stress in Qumran on keeping the law[106] although the reading מעשי תודה would also make sense, relating "smoking sacrifice" to thanksgiving. I will work with the assumption that מעשי תורה could be read. If it is read, it is significant that there is no hint in the text that "works of the law" are to be restricted to ceremonial law

---

[100] There is some disagreement whether מקדש אדם should be rendered "sanctuary among men" (Lohse, *Texte*, p. 257; Vermes, *Dead Sea Scrolls*, p. 293), or "sanctuary of men" (G.J. Brooke, *Exegesis at Qumran: 4QFlorilegium in its Jewish Context*, Sheffield 1985, p. 92; cf. J.P.M. Sweet, "A House Not Made with Hands", in W. Horbury (ed.), *Templum Amicitiae: Essays on the Second Temple presented to Ernst Bammel*, Sheffield 1991, 369 (368-90)).

[101] As Brooke, *Exegesis at Qumran*, p. 107, points out, the appearance of לו and בו with א is frequent at Qumran.

[102] Brooke, *Exegesis at Qumran*, p. 108.

[103] J. Strugnell, "Notes en Marge du Volume V des 'Discoveries in the Judaean Desert of Jordan", *RQ* 7 (1970) 221 (163-276).

[104] A. Steudel, *Der Midrasch zur Eschatologie aus der Qumrangemeinde (4QMidrEschat^{a.b})*, Leiden/New York/Köln 1994, pp. 25, 44. Her translation is: "Und er sagte, daß man ihm ein Heiligtum von Menschen bauen solle, damit darin seien für ihn Rauchopfer (?) vor ihm, Taten/Werke des Dankes" (p. 31). The reading "works of thanksgiving" is also accepted by Gaston, "Works of Law", 220 n. 8.

[105] Steudel, *Midrasch*, p. 44. Steudel points out that the surface of the leather has peeled off at the top of what she believes is a ד. But she adds: "doch ist ד noch zu erkennen".

[106] This is a point which Brooke, *Exegesis*, p. 108, concedes.

or even that there is an emphasis on such law. The whole law is clearly meant.[107]

Second there is the text 4QMMT מִקְצָת מַעֲשֵׂי הַתּוֹרָה "Some of the precepts of the law". In this fragment the teacher of righteousness writes to his opponent in Jerusalem: he says that he has

. . . written a part of the commandments of the law (מקצת מעשי התורה), which we believe to be especially important, for your good (salvation?) and the good (salvation?) of your people (i.e. Israel) (לטוב לך ולעמך).

The teacher of righteousness then wishes that the wicked priest

. . . finds joy at the end of time in that you find our words correct and that this may be reckoned to you as righteousness (ונהשבה לך לצדקה) when you do the right and the good before God (בעשותך הישר והטוב) for your good (salvation?) (טוב) and the good (salvation?) of your people (טוב).

Parts of this translation, which is based on that of H. Stegemann, may be disputed. Compare the translation given by Qimron and Strugnell:

26 We have (indeed) sent you 27 some of the precepts of the Torah according to our decision, for your welfare and the welfare of your people. For we have seen (that) 28 you have wisdom and knowledge of the Torah. Consider all these things and ask Him that He strengthen 29 your will and remove from you the plans of evil and the device of Belial 30 so that you may rejoice at the end of time, finding that some of our practices are correct. 31 And this will be counted as a virtuous deed of yours, since you will be doing what is righteous and good in His eyes, for you own welfare and 32 for the welfare of Israel.[108]

The key difference in the translations is whether טוב is to be understood as "salvation" or as "welfare". In favour of "salvation" is the fact that the text is clearly concerned with the last things, i.e. finding "joy at the end of time". Also this טוב is related to צדקה, which, as I have argued in chapter 1, can mean very much the same as salvation in various texts in the Psalms and Deutero-Isaiah.[109] But in favour of Qimron and Strugnell

---

[107] See especially 4Q174 4.2 (4QFlor 2.2): ועשו את כול התורה, also mentioned in chapter 4 above in the exegesis of Rom. 2.12-13.

[108] E. Qimron and J. Strugnell, *Discoveries in the Judaean Desert X: Qumran Cave 4, V: Miqṣat Ma'aśe Ha-Torah*, Oxford 1994, p. 63.

[109] Note also how I translated the final part of 4QMMT above: "reckoned to you as righteousness". Cf. Rom. 4.3: τί γὰρ ἡ γραφὴ λέγει; Ἐπίστευσεν δὲ Ἀβραὰμ τῷ θεῷ καὶ ἐλογίσθη αὐτῷ εἰς δικαιοσύνην. Paul quotes Gen. 15.6. The Hebrew is וְהֶאֱמִן בַּיהוָה וַיַּחְשְׁבֶהָ לּוֹ צְדָקָה. Cf. לצדקה ונהשבה לך of 4QMMT.

is that the noun טוב can mean "welfare" in the Hebrew Bible and I have found no other texts where טוב means salvation. Perhaps the wisest translation for טוב is simply "good", but in view of the eschatological emphasis in the passage, I would favour the interpretation "salvation" rather than "welfare". If I am right in interpreting טוב in this way there is a strong parallel to what I believe is the emphasis in Paul's use of ἔργα νόμου: the relation of such works to salvation at the final judgement. But whether the idea is "salvation" or "welfare", it seems clear that the "precepts of the law" here involve the whole torah. Note, however, that here the idea is not so much the works as actually done, but the demands of the law.[110]

In addition to these two texts where מעשי התורה/מעשי תורה occur, there is in the Community rule the related term "his works in the law" (מַעֲשָׂיו בַּתּוֹרָה, 1QS 5.21; 6.18)[111] and the context makes it clear that the complete obedience of the law is in view again.[112]

Then there is a text from Syriac Baruch which has been discussed above and in the exegesis of Rom. 2.14-15. 2 Bar. 57.2: "For at that time the unwritten law was in force among them, and the works of the commandments were accomplished at that time, . . ."[113] Although "works of the commandments" corresponds more to τὸ ἔργον τοῦ νόμου of Rom. 2.15 rather than ἔργα νόμου, again it is significant that reference is to the whole law (although this law was an unwritten law, not the Mosaic law).

On the basis of these Jewish texts, it seems that "works of law" means observance of the whole law. But what about Paul's own use of ἔργα νόμου? In what way does it correspond to these Jewish usages? First, for Paul, as for the Qumran texts and 2 Baruch, ἔργα νόμου refers to the

---

[110] Qimron and Strugnell, *Miqsat Maʿaśe Ha-Torah*, p. 139, note that in MMT laws are not referred to as מצוות but rather מעשים (B2) and מעשי התורה (C27). In Ex. 18.20 מעשה refers to law and it is only in the second temple period that the plural מעשים is commonly used for commands of the bible.

[111] The expression מַעֲשָׂיו בַּתּוֹרָה refers to the law as done, not the demand of the law. Qimron and Strugnell, *Miqsat Maʿaśe Ha-Torah*, p. 139 n. 43, seem to make the mistake of taking מעשים in 1 QS to have the same meaning as in 4QMMT.

[112] Schreiner, *Law*, p. 53, points to 1QS 5.8: "to return to the law of Moses according to *all* that he commanded".

[113] Translation of Klijn, in Charlesworth, *Pseudepigrapha*, 1:641.

whole law.[114] Paul's usage is also closer to that in 4QFlor. 1.7 (4Q174 3.7) in that he speaks of the works as actually performed (whereas in 4QMMT and in 2 Bar. 57.2, the reference is to the demand of the law). Further, if Stegemann's translation of 4QMMT is correct, there is a striking parallel in that works of law are linked to the final judgement.[115] In Paul this is seen very clearly in Rom. 3.20. If works of law have this fundamental significance for the final judgement, focusing on "boundary markers" misses the point.

Some confirmation of the above view is that Paul often simply writes of ἔργα. This is a shortened form of ἔργα νόμου[116] as can be seen by comparing their uses. So both ἔργα νόμου and ἔργα can be used with the prepositions ἐκ and χωρίς to put forward the idea that salvation is not by works/works of law.[117] If these terms are equivalent, one is justified in then looking back into the Old Testament and Jewish literature to see how the word "work(s)" was employed. Moo points to a number of texts where "work(s)" are used "to refer to actions with moral significance and which constitute a basis for judgment".[118] So a text like Is. 66.18 in both the LXX and MT points to the eschatological significance of works as does Ps. 61.13 LXX, quoted in Rom. 2.6.

---

[114] See Theodoret, *Interpretatio epistolae ad Romanos*, on 3.20 (*MPG* 82:82). This point was also made clear by J. Calvin, *The Epistles of Paul The Apostle to the Romans and to the Thessalonians*, translated by R. Mackenzie, Grand Rapids 1976 (repr.) (Edinburgh ¹1960), pp. 70-71, in his comment on Rom. 3.20.

[115] I am assuming that there was some idea in Qumran of a final judgement according to works. The idea is not only suggested by 4QMMT but also by the fact that fragments have been found corresponding to 1 Enoch including substantial fragments from book 5, i.e. 4Q204, fragment 5 (= 1 En. 104.13-106.2 + 106.13-107.2, Martinez, *Dead Sea Scrolls*, pp. 253-54) and 4Q212 (= 1 En. 91.18-92.2 + 92.5-93.4 + 93.9-10 + 91.11-17 + 93.11-94.2, Martínez, *Dead Sea Scrolls*, pp. 258-59).

[116] See Hofius, "Rechtfertigung des Gottlosen", 127 n. 35, referred to in n. 93 above.

[117] Cf. Moo, "Legalism", 94, and his table (93) showing the uses of ἔργον in Paul. Moo, however, makes the consistent mistake of writing τὰ ἔργα τοῦ νόμου. The expression is in fact anarthrous (except for the expression τὸ ἔργον τοῦ νόμου in Rom. 2.15).

[118] Moo, "Legalism", 92.

So works of law are the works done to fulfil the law. But is there an emphasis on the individual works (as in Billerbeck)? Or is Hofius correct when he writes that ἔργα νόμου does not mean "die einzelnen 'Gebotserfüllungen' (מצות)" but rather "der ganzheitliche Toragehorsam, die Tora-Observanz im ganz umfassenden Sinn"?[119] In view of the plural ἔργα I think Billerbeck's view must be given some weight.

Paul's point then in Rom. 3.20a is that no one is justified by torah observance, by doing the works demanded of the law. Paul was attacking the Jewish view that justification, i.e., salvation, can be achieved through observing the torah. Although there were many different Jewish groups in Paul's time, it is striking that they essentially agreed that salvation was achieved through keeping the law, i.e., they had a view of salvation by works. Such a view is seen in 4QMMT and in 2 Bar. 51.7: "Miracles, however, will appear at their own time to those who are saved because of their works and for whom the Law is now a hope . . ."[120]

Such then is my interpretation of Rom. 3.20a. One issue, however, has not been answered. Did Paul believe that if a Jew were to fulfil the law, then he would be righteous? Related to this is the question whether Paul uses the expression ἔργα νόμου in a negative sense such as "works done in the flesh".[121] There is no suggestion in the Jewish background that "works of law" should be considered in this sense. Whether Paul himself so understood ἔργα νόμου is, however, slightly more difficult to determine. This issue will be addressed in the final chapter when I discuss in more general terms Paul's view of the Mosaic law.

I turn now to the second half of the 3.20: "For through the law comes knowledge of sin". This could be taken in a number of different ways. "Knowledge of sin" (ἐπίγνωσις ἁμαρτίας) may refer to a subjective

---

[119] Hofius, "Rechtfertigung des Gottlosen", 127 n. 35.

[120] Klijn, in Charlesworth, *Pseudepigrapha*, 1:638.

[121] This is the view of Snodgrass, "Romans 2", 84, who writes: "Other than the quotation in 2.6 where ἔργα appears, Paul used the singular and qualifications so that it is clear that he is referring to godly obedience of Romans 2 (2.7 καθ᾽ ὑπομονὴν ἔργου ἀγαθοῦ; 2.10 τῷ ἐργαζομένῳ τὸ ἀγαθόν; and 2.15 τὸ ἔργον τοῦ νόμου). I would suggest that for Paul ἔργα νόμου, γράμμα, σάρξ and ἁμαρτία belong together on one side and that ἔργον, πνεῦμα and such phrases as δικαιώματα τοῦ νόμου φυλάσσειν belong together on the other side." Cf. Hübner's view of ἔργα νόμου.

knowledge (the usual interpretation)[122] or it may refer to objective knowledge in the sense that the law shows sin to be sin.[123] But there may be an additional point being made by Paul: not only does the law show sin to be sin, but it is through the law that one experiences sin. The logic of v. 20 is then that far from bringing justification, the law brings sin.[124] In this case Rom. 3.20 is seen in the light of Rom. 7.7ff. Conzelmann makes these significant comments which support my approach: "The law does not lead to subjective despair about one's own wickedness, but into an objectively desperate situation, which one understands on hearing the gospel".[125] He later adds: "At the moment that my situation is disclosed through the gospel, I know that I am — and always have been — dominated by the law, and recognize that this is not the position that God intends".[126]

So in Rom. 3.9-20 Paul argues that all are under the power of sin. Paul is only able to say this in the light of the cross of Christ and through faith. As Luther wrote:

---

[122] See, for example, K. Sullivan, "Epignosis in the Epistles of St. Paul", in *Studiorum Paulinorum Congressus Internationalis Catholicus 1961*, 2 vols, Rome 1963, 2:407 (405-16), who translates 3.20b as "All that the Law can do is to make man conscious of sin".

[123] Hofius, "Das Gesetz des Mose und das Gesetz Christi", *Paulusstudien*, 57: "Unter der ἐπίγνωσις ἁμαρτίας versteht Paulus ausschließlich die *reale Erfahrung* der Sündenmacht. Das Gesetz bringt objektiv an den Tag, daß der Mensch rettungslos jener Krankheit zum Tode verfallen ist, die Sünde heißt".

[124] Schlier, *Römerbrief*, p. 101: "Niemand wird durch Gesetzesleistungen gerechtfertigt. Das hat seinen Grund darin, daß das Gesetz das Gegenteil bewirkt. Es läßt die Sünde zur Erfahrung werden, es ruft die Sünde hervor". So Schlier writes concerning ἐπίγνωσις ἁμαρτίας: "Es meint also nicht, daß wir durch das Gesetz über das Bescheid bekommen können, was Sünde ist, sondern daß wir durch das Gesetz die Sünde erfahren". Schlier compares Rom. 4.15; 5.20; 7.8; 2 Cor. 5.21. A similar view is put forward by Klein, "Gesetz III", 71, who, commenting on ἐπίγνωσις ἁμαρτίας, writes: "Das ist keine kognitive, sondern eine zutiefst praxisbezogene Aussage. . . . In der Einlassung auf das Gesetz wird der Mensch von der Sünde übermächtigt und zeitigt sich das 'ursprünglich' lebensfreundliche Gesetz als sein eigenes Gegenteil (Röm 7,10)".

[125] H. Conzelmann, *An Outline of the Theology of the New Testament* ET, London 1969, p. 227.

[126] Conzelmann, *Outline*, p. 228.

Etsi nos nullum peccatum in nobis agnoscamus, Credere tamen oportet, quod sumus peccatores. Vnde Apostolus: 'Nihil mihi conscius sum, Sed non in hoc Iustificatus sum.' Quia sicut per fidem Iustitia Dei viuit in nobis, Ita per eandem et peccatum viuit in nobis, i.e. sola fide credendum est nos esse peccatores, Quia non est nobis manifestum, immo sepius non videmur nobis conscii.[127]

But what about Rom. 3.20 (διὰ γὰρ νόμου ἐπίγνωσις ἁμαρτίας)? Is it not through the law that one can say what Paul has said in Rom. 3.9-20? No. As I have already argued, subjective knowledge of sin comes only through the gospel. Rom. 3.20 refers to an objective knowledge of sin through the law and to the fact that it is through the law that one experiences sin. And one can only make the statement "through the law comes knowledge of sin" from the perspective of faith in Christ.[128]

Having completed the exegesis of Rom. 1.18-3.20 I turn in the final chapter to draw some of the threads together and discuss a number of key issues which have been raised.

---

[127] *WA* 56:231 (Scholion to Rom. 3.5).

[128] Cf. H-J. Eckstein, *Verheißung und Gesetz: Eine exegetische Untersuchung zu Galater 2,15-4,7*, Tübingen 1996, p. 133. He writes that it is clear from Gal. 3.10, 13-14, "daß Paulus *von der Christologie und der Soteriologie her* die Aussagen über die Bedeutung der Tora und die Situation des Menschen vor Gott enfaltet . . . ".

Chapter 7

Concluding Discussion

1. Introduction

In this final chapter I will draw the threads together, looking at a number of key themes which have arisen in the above discussion. Note, however, that a number of themes have already been addressed in chapter 3 (e.g. natural theology) and in the excursuses in chapter 4.

2. Coherence of Romans 1.18-3.20

Although some contradictions can be found across the letters of Paul[1], I believe that at the time of writing of Romans, probably his last letter,[2]

---

[1] I take the genuine letters to be Romans, 1 and 2 Corinthians, Galatians, 1 Thessalonians, Philippians and Philemon.

[2] I believe that it is likely that both Philippians and Philemon were written from Ephesus. Concerning Philippians, scholars such as W. Michaelis (e.g. *Die Datierung des Philipperbriefs*, Gütersloh 1933) and G.S. Duncan (e.g. *St. Paul's Ephesian Ministry*, London/New York 1929) have argued for Philippians being written during an Ephesian imprisonment. See also G. Friedrich, "Der Brief an die Philipper", in H.W. Beyer, P. Althaus, H. Conzelmann, G. Friedrich and A. Oepke, *Die kleineren Briefe des Apostels Paulus*, Göttingen [13]1972, 93-95 (92-130); R. Jewett, "Conflicting Movements in the Early Church as reflected in Philippians", *NovT* 12 (1970) 362-90; J. Gnilka, *Der Philipperbrief*, Freiburg/Basel/Wien [4]1987, ([1]1968), pp. 19-25 (see also J. Gnilka's recent study *Paulus von Tarsus: Apostel und Zeuge*, Freiburg/Basel/Wien 1996, pp. 119-21). However, two recent commentators on Philippians, P.T. O'Brien, *Commentary on Philippians*, Grand Rapids 1991, pp. 21-23 and G.F. Hawthorne, *Philippians*, Waco 1983, pp. xxxviii-xl, are both sceptical about the Ephesian origin of Philippians. R.P. Martin, *Philippians*, London 1976, pp. 48-56, offers a more positive assessment of the Ephesian hypothesis. As regards Philemon, Lohse, *Colossians and Philemon*, p. 188, points out that there are problems with the view that Paul wrote from Caesarea or Rome. Both are so far from Colossae that it is difficult to see how Onesimus could have travelled so far without

Paul had worked out a fairly coherent theological system. But Paul does not conform to medieval, reformed or modern systematic theologies. Whereas these present their theological ideas in a somewhat static system, Paul often expresses his ideas in a dynamic form. There is often a movement in his argument and often he employs some sort of story. One example of this is Rom. 1.18-3.20, where Paul argues that no one will be justified by works of law (3.20). Whereas some of Paul's stories are often described as a *Heilsgeschichte* ("History of Salvation", e.g. Rom. 9-11), Rom. 1.18-3.20 may be termed a *Verdammnisgeschichte* ("History of Damnation"). I believe serious mistakes are made in the theological interpretation of 1.18-3.20 by those who have not recognised the dynamic of the argument. One issue which is of special importance is judgement according to works and it is to this that I now turn.

3. Judgement according to Works

In the exegesis of Rom. 2.1-16 it was seen that judgement according to works is an Old Testament idea which continued into later Judaism. So in the Old Testament there is the general idea of divine retribution[3] and the particular view that God recompenses human beings according to their works.[4] This view is continued in the Apocrypha and Pseudepigrapha, Qumran, Hellenistic Judaism and Rabbinic Judaism. There has, however, been some controversy as to the nature of this judgement. Was a perfect obedience necessary? Was it necessary to have a preponderance of good works over evil works? And has Judaism not been grossly misrepresented by ignoring God's grace in judgement and the role of sacrifice and repentance as a means of atonement?

In the Apocrypha and Pseudepigrapha there is the idea that God recompenses human beings in this life but in the apocalyptic works it

---

detection and how Paul could hope to visit to Colossae in the near future. Gnilka, *Paulus*, pp. 119-21, again supports an Ephesian imprisonment.

[3] See the discussion of Rom. 1.22-31 in chapter 2 above. See also Travis, *Judgment*, pp. 9-10.

[4] See Jer. 25.14; Lam. 3.64; Ps. 62.12 (61.12); Prov. 24.12; Is. 3.10-11. See Bertram, ἔργον κτλ, 647.

becomes especially clear that people will be judged according to their works at the final judgement.[5] In this connection it is necessary to stress that the claim that the righteous are judged by mercy whereas the sinners are punished according to strict rules of justice is misleading in the extreme. So Sanders has claimed to find the idea of judgement according to grace in 2 Bar. 84.11[6]: "For if he judges us not according to the multitude of his grace, woe to all us who are born".[7] However, it is crucial to consider the context which is concerned with keeping the law.[8] It is also necessary to understand what such Jewish writers mean by "mercy" and "grace". Carson writes: "God may be 'gracious' to his people, but it is no longer grace in defiance of demerit and rooted in the sovereign goodness of God. Rather, it is a kind response to merit".[9] God does then appear to be gracious to the "righteous" and disciplines them. But the righteous are elected precisely because of their "works". So in 2 Baruch, election is based on human worth. 2 Bar. 48.20: "For these are the people whom you have elected, and this is the nation of which you found no equal." So the "elect" now means the "righteous".[10] A roughly similar idea is found in the Psalms of Solomon. In these Psalms there are some texts which speak of God being merciful to the righteous, although it is

---

[5] See the discussion in chapter 4 above.

[6] See E.P. Sanders, "The Covenant as a Soteriological Category and the Nature of Salvation in Palestinian and Hellenistic Judaism", in R. Hamerton-Kelly and R. Scroggs (ed.), *Jews, Greeks and Christians: Religious Cultures in Late Antiquity*, Leiden 1976, 17-20 (11-44).

[7] Translation of Klijn, in Charlesworth, *Pseudepigrapha*, 1:651.

[8] See, for example, 2 Bar. 84.6b-8: "if you obey the things which I have said to you, you shall receive from the Mighty One everything which has been prepared and has been preserved for you. 7 Therefore let this letter be a witness between me and you that you may remember the commandments of the Mighty One, and that it also may serve as my defense in the presence of him who has sent me. 8 And remember Zion and the Law . . . and do not forget the festivals and the sabbaths".

[9] Carson, *Divine Sovereignty*, p. 69. Note also that although in 2 Bar. 84.10 the readers are encouraged to pray that the Mighty One may accept them in mercy, he is also asked to remember the integrity of the fathers.

[10] Note also that in a range of apocalyptic literature, the "righteous" are those who keep the law. See J. Stock-Hesketh, "Law in Jewish Intertestamental Apocalyptic", Nottingham Ph.D. Thesis 1993. See, for example, pp. 103-7 (on 1 En. 72-82) and pp. 317-21 (on 2 Baruch).

not entirely clear whether the idea is that God is merciful in judgement itself or whether he is merciful in that he delivers the righteous from the oppression of the unrighteous.[11] But whatever the case, the author of the Psalms of Solomon clearly believed that the "righteous" had merited this position.

The same idea is found in Qumran. Those who wish to join the community may do so by a free decision: "This is the rule for the men of the Community who freely volunteer to convert from all evil and to keep themselves steadfast in all he prescribes in compliance with his will".[12] Then if they do the right they will be saved at the final judgement.[13]

I turn now to Rabbinic Judaism. The general Rabbinic view does seem to be that one is judged according to the majority of works. This is clearly pointed to in R. Akiba's saying in Aboth 3.15 (3.16). The text as translated by Danby is: "All is foreseen, but freedom of choice is given; and the world is judged by grace, yet all is according to the excess of works".[14] הַכֹּל צָפוּי וְהָרְשׁוּת נְתוּנָה: וּבְטוֹב הָעוֹלָם נִדּוֹן: וְהַכֹּל לְפִי רֹב הַמַּעֲשֶׂה. I suggest that a better translation is: "All is known, and freedom of choice is given; the world is judged by good nature (fairness), and all is according to excess of works". Urbach argues that the verb צפה as used by the tannaim "does not signify knowledge of the future, but seeing that which exists and is present . . ."[15] Therefore "R. Akiba's intention was not to

---

[11] Ps. Sol. 2.33-35: "Praise God, you who fear the Lord with understanding, for the Lord's mercy is upon those who fear him with judgment. 34 To separate between the righteous and the sinner to repay sinners forever according to their actions 35 And to have mercy on the righteous (keeping him) from the humiliation of the sinner, and to repay the sinner for what he has done to the righteous" (translation of Wright, in Charlesworth, *Pseudepigrapha*, 2:654). See also 13.9-12, where "the Lord's mercy is upon the devout" (v. 12) but this mercy involves discipline.

[12] 1QS 5.1 (Martínez, *Dead Sea Scrolls*, p. 8).

[13] On the issue of the final judgement in Qumran, see 4QMMT (discussed in chapter 6 above).

[14] Danby, *Mishnah*, p. 452.

[15] Urbach, *Sages*, p. 257. Urbach points to the use of the verb in Prov. 15.3 and Suk. 3.9. Prov. 15.3: "The eyes of the LORD are in every place, keeping watch (צֹפוֹת) on the evil and the good"; Suk. 3.9, which quotes R. Akiba: "I once watched (צוֹפֶה) Rabban Gamaliel and R. Joshua, and while all the people were shaking their Lulabs, they shook them only at 'Save now, we beseech thee, O Lord'" (Danby, *Mishnah*, p. 177). See also Aboth 2.1: "Consider three things and thou wilt not fall into the hands of transgression: know what is above thee — a seeing eye and a hearing

resolve the contradiction between [God's] foreknowledge and [man's] freewill, but to make man realize his responsibility for his actions".[16] So the text is not saying that God foresees but rather watches, examines, to see what men do. Further, I believe one can say that according to this text judgement by grace actually means that God is forebearing and not too severe in his judgement.[17] The world is judged by fairness. Carson points to the later view of R. ḤHanina (b. Ḥama) as found in b. Ber. 33b: "Everything is in the hand of heaven except fear of God". Ḥanina b. Hama's view is confirmed by R. Ḥanina b. Papa who said (b. Nid. 16b):

The name of the angel in charge of conception is 'Night' and he takes up a drop and places it in the presence of the Holy One, blessed be He, saying, 'Sovereign of the universe, What shall be the fate of this drop? Shall it produce a strong man or a weak man, a wise man or a fool, a rich man or a poor man?' Whereas 'wicked man' or 'righteous man' he does not mention, in agreement with the view of R. Ḥanina.

The result of this is that although God can determine many things, he does not determine whether one is wicked or good. This is left to human free choice.

The text Aboth 3.15 (3.16) therefore points clearly to the principle of judgement according to the majority of works,[18] and perhaps a similar idea is being put forward by R. Eleazar ha-Kappar in Aboth 4.22: "And know that everything is according to the reckoning"[19]. Note also the idea

---

ear and all thy deeds written in a book" (Danby, *Mishnah*, p. 447). Urbach also points out that he has only found the verb used in the sense of "to know beforehand" or "to see beforehand" in the Amoraic sayings. C. Taylor, *Sayings of the Jewish Fathers*, New York [2]1969, ([1]1897), p. 59 n. 38, defends the idea of foreknowing in Aboth 3.15 (3.16), in view of Ps. 139.1-2. However, the verb צפה does not occur there.

[16] Urbach, *Sages*, p. 257.

[17] Cf. Carson, *Divine Sovereignty*, p. 102.

[18] See Avemarie, *Tora und Leben*, p. 39, for a critique of Sanders' treatment of this passage (see E.P. Sanders, *Paul and Palestinian Judaism*, London 1977, p. 139, who can only conclude that "Aboth 3.15 remains enigmatic"). Avemarie suggests that Sanders' problem here is trying to harmonise Aboth 3.15 with y. Kid. 61d and b. Sanh. 81a. He points to S. Safrai, "And All is According to the Majority of Deeds" (Hebrew), *Tarbiz* 53 (1983-84) 33-40.

[19] Danby, *Mishnah*, p. 455.

of book-keeping as found in Aboth 2.1.[20] It may be, however, that Kid. 1.10a is saying something slightly different.

> If a man performs but a single commandment it shall be well with him and he shall have length of day and shall inherit the Land; but if he neglects a single commandment it shall be ill with him and he shall not have length of days and shall not inherit the Land.[21]

This is rather concerned with encouraging good works, not giving some systematic view about being judged according to the majority of works.[22]

There is the idea therefore that judgement is according to the majority of works. Such a view is found in only a few texts though. But although this view is not that common, it was clearly essential to accumulate as many good works as possible. See also Gen. R. 9.9 (on 1.31) which speaks of heaping up fulfilments of the law: "Thus for him who heaps up fulfilments of the law and good works (מסגל במצות ומעשים טובים), Gan Eden is there; but for him who does not heap up fulfilments of the law and good works (מסגל במצות ומעשים טובים) Gehinnom is there".[23]

So it appears that in Rabbinic Judaism, perfect obedience was not generally required. But there was obviously a spectrum of opinion. There may well have been a few Rabbis/Pharisees[24] who regarded virtually perfect obedience as necessary for salvation and one such person was Paul of

---

[20] Quoted above.

[21] Danby, *Mishnah*, p. 323.

[22] On this point I agree with Sanders, *Palestinian Judaism*, p. 129. Cf. t. Kid. 1.13-16; b. Kid. 39b.

[23] Translation of Bertram, ἔργον, 648. Cf. Gen. R. 9.10. See also Billerbeck, *Kommentar*, 4:11.

[24] I assume some degree of continuity between the Pharisees before 70AD and the "Rabbis". S.J.D. Cohen, "The Significance of Yavneh: Pharisees, Rabbis, and the End of Jewish Sectarianism", *HUCA* 54 (1984) 27-53, argues for discontinuity. P. Schäfer, "Der vorrabbinische Pharisäismus", in M. Hengel - U. Heckel (ed.), *Paulus und das antike Judentum: Tübingen-Durham-Symposium im Gedenken an der 50. Todestag Adolf Schlatter*, Tübingen 1991, 125-72, has some sympathy with the views of Cohen, especially his criticism of Neusner. However, in the debate, 172-75, M. Hengel argues for continuity. For example he makes the point that according to Josephus, the New Testament and Essene sources the Pharisees were highly influential; in fact their movement was the most influential between the Maccabean revolt and the destruction of Jerusalem. "Where should the Sages of Jabneh find the point of contact to unite the people, if not here?" (173).

Tarsus who belonged to the "right wing" of the Rabbinic spectrum. Compare Gamaliel II who wept when he came to the end of the 13 requirements of Ezek. 18.5-9. He said: "Only he who does all these things shall live, but not merely one of them" (b. Sanh. 81a).[25]

But the idea of perfect obedience is found elsewhere. I noted in chapter 4 above the view in the Isaiah Targum.[26] Philo believes that repentance involves a turning "to a blameless life" ($\pi\rho\dot{o}\varsigma$ $\dot{\alpha}\nu\nu\pi\alpha\dot{\iota}\tau\iota\nu$ $\zeta\omega\dot{\eta}\nu$)[27] and he considers sinning after repentance to be impossible.[28] Like Philo, Josephus assumes that repentance will lead to a sinless life. Repentance for Josephus involves a turning away from law breaking and a turning to the law and he assumes that it is possible to keep the law perfectly.[29] Dietrich suggests that Josephus was the sort of Pharisee who considered he did not require repentance. He kept the commandments and for this reason repentance plays no major role in his writings.[30] There was also

---

[25] See the similar story in b. Mak. 24a regarding Ps. 15.5b: "he that doeth these things shall never be moved". "Whenever R. Gamaliel came to this passage he used to weep, saying: [Only] one who practised all these shall not be moved; but anyone falling short in any of these [virtues] would be moved!" b. Mak. 24a says that David reduced the 613 commandments to eleven in Ps. 15. Galamiel's words do not exclude occasional disobedience followed by repentance. Rather, they point to the expectation that the main principles of the Torah (as given by Ezekiel and David) would be kept. Note that in both b. Sanh. 81a and b. Mak. 24a the words of Gamaliel are reported in Aramaic whereas the context is Hebrew. Also whereas in b. Sanh. 81a the text commented upon is Ezek. 18.5-9 and Gamaliel's words are followed by a quotation from R. Akiba, in b. Mak. 24a the text is Ps. 15.5b and the response to Gamaliel comes from "his colleagues".

[26] The Isaiah Targum speaks of "righteous people which have kept the law with a perfect heart" (26.2). The view of perfect obedience does, however, include an element of repentance (cf. Rom. 2.4). So 7.3 and 10.21, 22, speaks of "the remnant that have not sinned, and they that have turned from sin".

[27] *De virtutibus* 177. Cf. *De Abrahamo* 19.

[28] *De fuga et inventione* 160; *Quod Deus immutabilis sit* 8-9.

[29] See *Antiquitates* 7.153, where we read that David was "a god-fearing man and never sinned in his life except in the matter of Uriah's wife" (cf. 1 Kgs 15.5) and *Antiquitates* 19.315, where Jonathan, referring to his brother Matthias, says: "I have a brother, pure of all sin against God and against you, O king". Both texts are mentioned in Schlatter, *Die Theologie des Judentums nach dem Bericht des Josephus*, p. 157.

[30] E.K. Dietrich, *Die Umkehr (Bekehrung und Buße) im Alten Testament und im Judentum*, Stuttgart, p. 313.

the tradition in Judaism of certain people being sinless. The Testament of Abraham (A) says Abraham was sinless (cf. Jub. 17.15, 17). Other texts speak of figures being virtually sinless.[31] So sinlessness, although not being literally demanded, is clearly seen as a possibility in a variety of Jewish texts.

I now turn to Paul's view. First of all I believe that in Galatians, perfect obedience of the law is required if salvation is by works of law (Gal. 3.10; 5.3). This view has not been universally held[32] but I think it is the most convincing explanation of the texts.[33] But for Romans there has been some understandable disagreement among scholars as to whether perfect obedience was required. Snodgrass argues that perfect obedience is not required in Romans and nor was it required in Judaism.[34] He argues that perfect obedience was an issue in Galatians for the issue was works-righteousness and Paul had to answer the Judaisers. That, however, is not the issue in Romans 2. Further: "There is nothing in Romans 2 to suggest that perfection is required for salvation. 2.7 refers only to seeking glory, honour, and immortality according to a good work".[35] One could add that according to Rom. 2.4 there is the possibility of repentance, repentance implying that perfect obedience is not required.

However, I believe that in Romans perfect obedience was in fact required. This was argued in the exegesis of Rom. 2.12-16. One of the reasons why Paul believed perfect obedience of the law was required was

---

[31] Test. Zeb. 1.5: "Nor do I recall having committed a transgression, except what I did to Joseph in ignorance (τὴν ἄγνοιαν ἣν ἐποίησα ἐπὶ τοῦ Ἰωσήφ) because in a compact with my brothers I kept from telling my father what had been done, although I wept much in secret".

[32] See, for example, G. Howard, *Paul: Crisis in Galatia. A Study in Early Christian Theology*, Cambridge 1979, p. 53.

[33] See T.R. Schreiner, "Is Perfect Obedience to the Law Possible? A Re-examination of Galatians 3:10", *JETS* 27 (1984) 151-160.

[34] See 1QH 4.30-31; 9.14-15; 12.19-20; Wis. 15.2; 2 Bar. 84.11; 4 Ezr. 4.38; 7.46, 68. However, Snodgrass also points out that in Jub. 23.10 Abraham is considered perfect and Issachar and Zebulun are presented as not being conscious of having committed sin (Test. Is. 7.1; Test. Zeb. 1.4). Also b. Hag. 4b views Samuel as perfect.

[35] Snodgrass, "Romans 2", 83.

because of Dt. 27.26 LXX, the first part of which is quoted in Gal. 3.10 (with some changes in the light of Dt. 28.58 and 30.10).

Dt. 27.26 LXX: Ἐπικατάρατος πᾶς ἄνθρωπος, ὃς οὐκ ἐμμενεῖ ἐν πᾶσιν τοῖς λόγοις τοῦ νόμου τούτου τοῦ ποιῆσαι αὐτούς· καὶ ἐροῦσιν πᾶς ὁ λαός Γένοιτο.

Gal. 3.10: ὅσοι γὰρ ἐξ ἔργων νόμου εἰσίν, ὑπὸ κατάραν εἰσίν· γέγραπται γὰρ ὅτι ἐπικατάρατος πᾶς ὃς οὐκ ἐμμενεῖ πᾶσιν τοῖς γεγραμμένοις ἐν τῷ βιβλίῳ τοῦ νόμου τοῦ ποιῆσαι αὐτά.

Compare Dt. 27.26 MT:

אָרוּר אֲשֶׁר לֹא־יָקִים אֶת־דִּבְרֵי הַתּוֹרָה־הַזֹּאת לַעֲשׂוֹת אוֹתָם וְאָמַר כָּל־הָעָם אָמֵן:

So Dt. 27.26 LXX has the inserted ἐν πᾶσιν.[36] So this is one reason why Paul believed that perfect obedience was necessary.[37] Because perfect obedience is not possible, the law acts as a curse.[38]

One of the interesting things about Rom. 2.1-16 is that Paul seems to assume that repentance is possible and therefore Paul's view of "perfect obedience" in Romans has to take this into account. However, it needs stressing that Paul considered such repentance to play a minor part in consideration of the final judgement, one reason being his pessimistic view of human nature.[39] Paul therefore shared the view of the apocalypses, where "Die Umkehr nimmt . . . einen sehr begrenzten Raum ein".[40] In Rabbinic literature there is more room for repentance. But even here there are cases where repentance is impossible or almost impossible: if someone misuses repentance[41]; if someone does not or can-

---

[36] Note also that in Gal. 3.10 Paul has inserted πᾶς in his quotation from Dt. 27.26 LXX.

[37] Note also the language of the Isaiah Targum mentioned above and in chapter 4.

[38] For a helpful summary of the various interpretations of the use of Dt. 27.26 in Gal. 3.10, see J.M. Scott, "'For as Many as are of Works of the Law are under a Curse' (Galatians 3.10)", in C.A. Evans and J.A. Sanders (ed.), *Paul and the Scriptures of Israel*, Sheffield 1993, 188-94 (187-221). However, I find myself unconvinced by Scott's own theory that Paul is referring to the curse upon Israel in her "exile".

[39] See Bell, "Teshubah", 47-48.

[40] Sjöberg, 250. On apocalyptic views of repentance see Bell, "Teshubah", 30-31.

[41] Yoma 8.9: "If a man said, 'I will sin and repent, and sin again and repent', he will be given no chance to repent".

not make a complete restitution;[42] if someone sins persistently;[43] if someone leads people astray;[44] if someone desecrates God's name[45]. Also

---

[42] For sins between men repentance must involve reconciliation and restitution (cf.
Yoma 8.9: "For transgressions that are between man and God the Day of Atonement
effects atonement, but for transgressions that are between a man and his fellow the
Day of Atonement effects atonement only if he has appeased his fellow").

[43] See the legend of Elisha b. Abuja, who was excluded from repentance. One day
he heard a bath kol crying out "Return, ye backsliding children (Jer. 3.22), Return
unto Me, and I will return unto you (Mal. 3.7), with the exception of Elisha b.
Abuyah who knew My might and yet rebelled against Me!" (Eccl. R. 7.8.1, Soncino,
p. 185); cf. Ruth R. 6.4; b. Hag. 15a; y. Hag. 77b (2.1). However, the story does go
on to speak of Elisha's eventual salvation. First R. Meir rejoices because his teacher,
Elisha, appears to have died in a mood of repentance. However, Elisha's grave is
consumed with fire (indicating he was not forgiven). R. Meir, however, spread his
cloak over his grave, and prayed (including the words of Ruth 3.13: "But if He [God]
will not redeem thee, then I [Meir] redeem thee, as the Lord liveth" (y. Hag. 77c
(2.1); Eccl. R. 7.8.1; Ruth R. 6.4; cf. b. Hag. 15b). The fire is then extinguished,
indicating forgiveness.

[44] See Aboth 5.18 (quoted in b. Sot. 47a and b. Sanh. 107b in reference to
Gehazi): "But he that leads the many to sin, to him shall be given no means for
repentance" (Danby, *Mishnah*, p. 458; cf. Taylor, *Sayings of the Jewish Fathers*, p.
94, has "they grant him not the faculty to repent"). However, according to M.
Jastrow, *A Dictionary of the Targumim, the Talmud Babli and Yerushalmi, and the
Midrashic Literature*, New York 1982 (repr.), (¹1950), p. 1016, this text is saying
that no *opportunity* will be given to him to repent (אֵין מַסְפִּיקִין בְּיָדוֹ לַעֲשׂוֹת תְּשׁוּבָה).
There are two possible reasons for this. The ostensible one in b. Yoma 87a is that it is
unjust that the one who leads people astray is in Gan Eden whilst those he has
deceived are in Gehinnom (cf. Aboth R. Nathan 40). Another reason is that restitution
is essential to repentance and if one has led many astray it is impossible to make a
complete restitution. There are, however, one or two possible exceptions to the view
that those who lead people astray cannot repent. One is Manasseh (see the view of R.
Judah b. Ilai, Sanh. 10.2) and another is Ahab (Pirke de Rabbi Eliezer, 43 (G. Friedlander, *Pirke de Rabbi Eliezer*, New York ⁴1981 (¹1916), pp. 337-38)). Note,
however, that according to the anonymous tradition in Sanh. 10.2, neither Manasseh
nor Ahab have a share in the world to come.

[45] Sifre Dt. 328: "The Holy One, blessed be He, will forgive anything, but
desecration of His name He will requite immediately" (Hammer, *Sifre*, p. 339). See,
however, t. Yoma 4.8 C-D: "But he through whom the Name of Heaven is profaned
deliberately but who repented - repentance does not have the power to suspend [the
punishment], nor the Day of Atonement to atone, D but repentance and the Day of
Atonement atone for a third, suffering atones for a third, and death wipes away the
sin, with suffering" (J. Neusner, *The Tosefta: Moed*, New York 1981, p. 208).

sometimes it is said that those who desecrate the sabbath will not be for-given.[46] And as we have seen above, there may well have been a few Rabbis/Pharisees who regarded virtually perfect obedience as necessary for salvation. It also needs stressing that repentance belonged to "works" in that there was the tendency to see it as a meritorious work.[47]

If Paul allowed a limited role for repentance, what about the other major means of atonement, sacrifice? Does not the very existence of the cult already imply that perfect obedience to the law was not required?[48] Surprisingly, perhaps, Paul simply does not take the cult into account. He uses sacrificial imagery for the death of Christ[49] and for the life of the Christian,[50] but does not reckon with sacrifice as a means of atonement in Rom. 1.18-3.20.[51] Why should this be? The reason is that with the sacrifice of Christ, all cultic atoning sacrifice was rendered invalid. This makes sense, for Rom. 1.18-3.20 is viewing men and women in the light of the cross. An alternative explanation is that cultic atoning sacrifice was not important anyway for Paul the Pharisee. But this explanation is unlikely to be true. Although there was a close link between the Sad-ducees and the priesthood,[52] and the Pharisees were opposed to the Sad-

---

[46] Midr. Tann. Dt. 5.15 (Hoffmann 23).

[47] See Bell, "Teshubah", 28-30, 42-45.

[48] See Howard, *Crisis*, p. 53, who, commenting on Gal. 3.10, writes: "To keep the law then was, among other things, to find cultic forgiveness for breaking the law. For Paul to have argued that the law demanded absolute obedience and that one legal infraction brought with it unpardonable doom would have been for him to deny what all the world knew, namely, that the Jerusalem temple stood as a monument to the belief that Yahweh was a forgiving God who pardoned his people when they sinned".

[49] See Rom. 8.3, which says God "sent his own Son in the likeness of sinful flesh and as a sin offering (περὶ ἁμαρτίας)". Note also the use of ἱλαστήριον (כַּפֹּרֶת) in Rom. 3.25: Paul writes here that God publicly set forth Christ Jesus as a mercy seat (ἱλαστήριον). Even if 2 Cor. 5.21 does not refer to Christ being made a "sin offering" (ἁμαρτία), the whole argument in 2 Cor. 5.14-21 is rooted in Paul's understanding of Christ's death as a sin offering (see Hofius, "Sühne und Versöhnung", 38-42). In a future study I wish to look in more detail at Christ's sacrificial death.

[50] See Rom. 12.1.

[51] This is true also for Galatians and all other letters of Paul.

[52] J. Jeremias, *Jerusalem in the Time of Jesus* ET, Philadelphia 1969, p. 230; A.C. Sundberg, "Sadducees", *IDB* 4:160 (160-63).

ducees, issues of temple sacrifice were nevertheless of great interest to the Pharisees. After all, the origins of the movement go back to the temple[53] and the Pharisees taught on matters of cultic atonement.[54] In fact Hengel and Deines suggest that in view of the Pharisees' minute knowledge of commandments relating to the cult, there may have been a Pharisaic "faction" among the temple personnel.[55] It is well known that the Pharisees wished to apply to the people as a whole in their everyday lives the ritual purity of the priests.[56] But this does not mean that the cult was in any way relativised, for there was an ascending scale of holiness. Kel. 1.6-9 speaks of ten degrees of holiness: the land of Israel — the walled cities — Jerusalem — temple mount — the rampart — court of women — court of Israelites — court of priests — area between the porch and the altar — sanctuary — holy of holies.[57] In view of this interest in the cult, it is doubtful whether Saldarini is correct in saying that Pharisees

---

[53] See Jeremias, *Jerusalem*, p. 257; Hengel and Deines, "E.P. Sanders' 'Common Judaism', Jesus, and the Pharisees", 48-49.

[54] See, for example, J. Neusner, *From Politics to Piety*, Englewood Cliffs, N.J. 1973, pp. 23-29, 119-20; Hengel, *Pre-Christian Paul*, pp. 52-53. In fact Hengel and Deines, "E.P. Sanders' 'Common Judaism', Jesus, and the Pharisees", 47-48, argue that a large proportion of Rabbinic regulations regarding the temple go back to before AD 70.

[55] Hengel and Deines, "E.P. Sanders' 'Common Judaism', Jesus, and the Pharisees", 50,

[56] See Hengel, *Pre-Christian Paul*, pp. 30-31. So the whole people are to be holy (Lev. 19.2) and a nation of priests (Ex. 19.6). O. Betz, "Pharisäer, Pharisäismus II: Antikes Judentum und Neues Testament", *HWP* 7:537 (536-39), writes; "Das eigene Haus sollte einem Heiligtum, der Tisch einem Altar ähnlich sein".

[57] In fact according to this list there appear to be eleven degrees of holiness. Commentators of this passage are understandably puzzled especially since Kel. 1.1-4 give eleven degrees of uncleanness. See J. Neusner, *A History of the Mishnaic Law of Purities, Part One: Kelim 1-11*, Leiden 1974, p. 39; W. Bunte, *Die Mischna: Text, Übersetzung und ausführliche Erklärung: Kelim*, Berlin/New York 1972, p. 76; D. Hoffmann in D. Hoffmann, J. Cohn and M. Auerbach, *Mischnajot: Die sechs Ordnungen der Mischna. Hebräischer Text mit Punktation, deutscher Übersetzung und Erklärung, Teil VI: Ordnung Toharot*, Basel ³1968, p. 13. Bunte, *Kelim*, p. 76, suggests the possible bracketing of the "land of Israel" or the equating of the "area between the porch and altar" and the "sanctuary". Another possibility is to consider not the levels of holiness themselves but the gaps between them of which there are ten.

were more concerned with issues like tithing, ritual purity and sabbath observance than temple sacrifices.[58] I therefore conclude that the reason Paul ignored sacrifice as a means of atonement in Rom. 1.18-3.20 is not because of any disinterest in sacrificial cult as a former Pharisee, but rather because Christ's sacrificial death had rendered all cultic sacrifice void.

In view of the what has been said about judgement according to works, I now ask what Paul's logic was in Romans 1.18-3.20? He certainly rejected the view of normative Judaism which can be expressed as follows:

(1) one is saved by works in the sense that one must have the basic intention of keeping the law to be saved (any sins being atoned for by repentance and cult);
(2) those who either sin seriously or abuse the means of atonement are therefore lost.

But Paul's logic is not precisely the same as in Galatians either,[59] where he argues:

(1) One must obey the law perfectly to be saved;
(2) No one obeys the law perfectly;
(3) Therefore, no one can be saved by works of law.[60]

Rather, I believe the logic is slightly more complex in that he did allow a limited role for repentance. I therefore put forward two possible solutions. First, is a solution which is closer to the Jewish model which would be something like this:

(1) One must have a basic intention to do the law to be saved (any sins being atoned for by repentance);

---

[58] See A.J. Saldarini, "Pharisees", *ABD* 5:302 (289-303).

[59] Note that in a number of respects Paul's view on the law is somewhat different in Galatians and Romans. This is to some extent explained by the fact that Paul is not facing the Judaising controversy in Romans. See Hahn "Gesetzesverständnis", and Hübner, *Gesetz*, passim.

[60] T.R. Schreiner, "Paul and Perfect Obedience of the Law: An Evaluation of the View of E.P. Sanders", *WTJ* 47 (1985) 278 (245-78), believes this is Paul's logic in Galatians but not in Rom. 1.18-3.20.

(2) No one has this basic intention (in fact no one does any good (3.10-11) and all are unrepentant (2.5));

(3) Therefore no one can be saved by works of law.

Or one could adopt a view closer to the Galatian model:

(1) One must keep the law perfectly to be saved (repentance taking on a strictly limited role);

(2) No one keeps the law perfectly (Rom. 3.9-20) and all are unrepentant (2.5);

(3) Therefore no one can be saved by works of law.

In view of what I have said earlier about Rom. 2.12-13 I believe that in Romans, Paul has a scheme nearer to the last one.

I now want to examine the precise nature of judgement according to works in Romans 2 and compare this with the view found elsewhere in Paul. The teaching of judgement according to works in Romans 2 is I believe unique in the seven letters of Paul in two respects. First, all other texts refer only or primarily to the judgement of *Christians*.[61] But in Romans 2 Paul seems to be speaking of non-Christians. Second, Romans 2 is the only text in Paul which clearly states that judgement according to works determines whether one is saved or damned. I now develop this second point in more details.

Outside of Rom. 1.18-3.20, judgement texts in Paul's letters can be divided into two categories: first, texts which speak of the reward Christians will receive; secondly, texts which are warnings to Christians. The idea of the reward for Christians is seen at its clearest in 1 Cor. 3.13-15. But this is also the case, I believe, in a text such as 2 Cor. 5.10.[62]

---

[61] Rom. 14.10-12; 1 Cor. 3.13-15; 2 Cor. 5.10; 9.6; 11.15; Gal. 6.7. See also Eph. 6.8; 1 Tim. 5.24-25; 2 Tim. 4.14. A possible exception is 1 Thes. 2.16 (God's judgement upon Jews) but there is no explicit reference to judgement according to works. A number of texts are of course relevant to both Christians and non-Christians but Paul seems more concerned with their relevance to Christians (e.g. 1 Cor. 6.1-11; 10.1-12).

[62] See P.E. Hughes, *The Second Epistle to the Corinthians*, Grand Rapids 1962, p. 182, and J. Héring, *The Second Epistle of Saint Paul to the Corinthians*, London 1967, pp. 39-40, who relate 2 Cor. 5.10 to 1 Cor. 3.10-15. See also the comments on 2 Cor. 5.9-10 by H. Lietzmann, *An die Korinther I/II*, Tübingen ⁵1969 (supplemented by W.G. Kümmel), pp. 122-23.

There are in fact a number of judgement texts which are concerned with the reward Christians receive. As Kühl writes:

Das Endgericht wird für den Christen nur noch die Bedeutung haben, daß es den relativ höheren oder geringen Wert seiner sittlichen Lebensarbeit zum Ausdruck bringt, und danach wird sich Lohn und Lob aus Gottes Munde bestimmen.[63]

But there are other texts which do appear to put in question whether a believer will attain final salvation. This second category of texts, though, are to be seen as warnings for those who are presuming on God's grace.[64] Such threats of exclusion from salvation are not the final word. Rather they are meant to alert the complacent Christian to the possible consequences of his actions and lead him to cast himself upon the grace of God again.[65] The *final word* in Paul's letters for Christians is salvation.[66] Therefore I totally reject the view of K.P. Donfried who writes:

---

[63] Kühl, *Römer*, p. 78.

[64] It is significant that such warnings are especially prominent in 1 Corinthians, where there was much licentious behaviour. See, for example, 1 Cor. 5.1-13; 6.9-11; 10.1-12.

[65] See N.M. Watson, "Justified by Faith; Judged by Works - An Antinomy?", *NTS* 29 (1983) 220 (209-21): "The message of judgment is the valid word of God, not for those whose sins have found them out but for those who are presuming on God's grace, those who are 'at ease in Zion', and its aim is always to make possible a renewed encounter with the gospel". Watson builds upon the work of W. Joest, *Gesetz und Freiheit: Das Problem des Tertius Usus Legis bei Luther und die neutestamentliche Parainese*, Göttingen ³1968, who uses the Lutheran law/gospel dialectic. See, for example, p. 185: "Denn nach dem Gerichtswort kommt noch einmal, und zwar oft in unmittelbarer Folge, das ganze Evangelium, die volle Gewißheit zu Wort: Gott ist treu, er wird es tun. Das kann und muß dem Erschrockenen gesagt werden, nachdem dem Sicheren gesagt war: Alles kannst du verlieren. So wird die Parainese zuletzt wieder Ruf zum Glauben, nachdem sie zuvor noch einmal in vollem Ernste Ruf zum Wirken wurde. Oder anders und genauer gesagt: sie ruft zum Glauben an das mit dem Heile geschenkte Wirken, nachdem sie zuvor noch einmal zu dem um des Heiles willen geforderten Wirken gerufen hat. Nach dem Evangelium spricht noch einmal das Gesetz. Aber nach dem Gesetze spricht wiederum neu das Evangelium". Although such an analysis is fitting for a number of judgement texts, it is not appropriate for Romans 2 (Joest does apply the idea to Romans 2 in *Gesetz und Freiheit*, pp. 177-78).

[66] See again Lietzmann, *An die Korinther I/II*, p. 122: "Daß ein Mitglied der Gemeinde Christi, auch wenn es die schlimmste Todsünde begangen hätte, der ἀπώλεια anheimfallen könne, erscheint dem Apostel zwar durchaus möglich, wie die pädagogischen Drohungen I Th 4₆ I Cor 8₁₁ 10₁₁. ₁₂ II Cor 5₁₀ beweisen, aber

Paul expects a last judgment for Christians which can have different results: salvation for the Christian who has been obedient in faith and wrath for the the one who has been disobedient to his calling in Christ.[67]

If this analysis is correct, it seems that outside of Romans 2, Paul speaks of judgement in terms *either* of the reward Christians are to receive *or* speaks in terms of warnings of possible exclusion from salvation. Rom. 2.1-16 therefore stands out because it is the only text which unambiguously says that judgement according to works determines whether one is saved or not.[68]

Can this view of justification by works in Romans 2 be reconciled to Paul's theology of justification *sola fide, sola gratia*? Lietzmann tried to reconcile Romans 2 with justification by faith alone by arguing that Paul's argument in Romans 2 was hypothetical.[69] I believe that the argument in Romans 2 is not *entirely hypothetical* for there *will be* a judgement according to works through Jesus Christ according to the gospel (2.16). But there are two hypothetical elements in Paul's argument. First, in 3.9-20 it becomes clear that no one will be acquitted through works of law: both Jew and Gentile are under the power of sin (3.9) as scripture makes clear (3.10-18). On reading 3.9-20 one must conclude that the pious Jews and pious Gentiles of Romans 2 (6-11; 14-15; 27-29) *do not exist*.[70] The

---

tatsächlich doch unwahrscheinlich, weil der Sünder das $\pi\nu\varepsilon\hat{\upsilon}\mu\alpha$ einmal erhalten hat I Cor 3_{15} 5_5 vgl. 11_{32} . . . ".

[67] K.P. Donfried, "Justification and Last Judgment in Paul", *ZNW* 67 (1976) 103-4 (90-110). For criticism of Donfried see, for example, Travis, *Christ and the Judgment of God*, pp. 62-63. Travis criticises Donfried for trying to make Paul tidier than he actually is in claiming Paul has the view that justification is a past event, sanctification is a present event and salvation is a future event. See also C.H. Cosgrove, "Justification in Paul: A Linguistic and Theological Reflection", *JBL* 106 (1987) 654 (653-70), who criticises Donfried for not taking seriously Paul's future statements about justification. However, I am unhappy about Cosgrove's own understanding. See my criticisms below.

[68] One of the problems with the approach of the work of Joest, *Gesetz und Freiheit*, is that he does not distinguish between Rom. 2.1-16 and other texts in Paul which speak of a judgement according to works.

[69] See Lietzmann, *Römer*, pp. 39-40, quoted in chapter 4 above.

[70] It is interesting to compare the theme of seeking in Rom. 2.7 ($\tau o\hat{\imath}\varsigma$ $\mu\grave{\varepsilon}\nu$ $\kappa\alpha\theta$' $\dot{\upsilon}\pi o\mu o\nu\grave{\eta}\nu$ $\check{\varepsilon}\rho\gamma o\upsilon$ $\dot{\alpha}\gamma\alpha\theta o\hat{\upsilon}$ $\delta\acute{o}\xi\alpha\nu$ $\kappa\alpha\grave{\imath}$ $\tau\iota\mu\grave{\eta}\nu$ $\kappa\alpha\grave{\imath}$ $\dot{\alpha}\phi\theta\alpha\rho\sigma\acute{\imath}\alpha\nu$ $\zeta\eta\tauο\hat{\upsilon}\sigma\iota\nu$ $\zeta\omega\grave{\eta}\nu$ $\alpha\dot{\imath}\acute{\omega}\nu\iota o\nu$) with 3.11b ($o\dot{\upsilon}\kappa$ $\check{\varepsilon}\sigma\tau\iota\nu$ $\dot{o}$ $\dot{\varepsilon}\kappa\zeta\eta\tau\hat{\omega}\nu$ $\tau\grave{o}\nu$ $\theta\varepsilon\acute{o}\nu$). This was first brought to my attention by my student Esther Elliott.

second hypothetical element in Romans 2 is that Paul says nothing about believers being justified by faith. Later it becomes clear that those who believe in Christ will be saved from the future wrath: δικαιωθέντες νῦν ἐν τῷ αἵματι αὐτοῦ σωθησόμεθα δι᾽ αὐτοῦ ἀπὸ τῆς ὀργῆς (Rom. 5.9, cf. 1 Thes. 1.9-10) and so the judgement of Romans 2 does not apply to Christians. Interestingly, Paul never relates the judgement of unbelievers (as found in Rom. 2.1-16) to the judgement of believers (Rom. 14.10-12; 1 Cor. 3.13-15; 2 Cor. 5.10; 9.6; 11.15; Gal. 6.7[71]). Also Brandenburger[72] is absolutely correct to question what Conzelmann writes on "Gericht": "Rechtfertigung allein (!) aus Glauben und Gericht allein (!) nach Werken bilden einen in sich einheitlichen Gedanken".[73] Judgement is definitely not according to works alone, for believers and unbelievers are treated on quite different terms.

I maintain that in Rom. 1.16-3.31 judgement according to works and justification by faith stand in a dialectical relationship. In fact I believe this is the general pattern in Paul.[74] Such a view, however, has been challenged by Roetzel.[75] So he believes "it is a distortion of Paul's thought to view justification by faith and judgment in a dialectical relationship".[76] He points out that Paul can speak of judgement without mentioning justification by faith.[77] But some of the passages he mentions have nothing to

---

[71] Note Paul is not saying here that one can lose salvation. Gundry Volf, *Paul and Perseverance*, pp. 141-154, makes the important point that Paul is not attacking a Galatian libertarianism; rather he is showing that his gospel does not give rise to libertarianism (see 5.13ff; 6.6-10). So in 6.6-10 Paul "is continuing his defense of the ethical integrity of Spirit-led Christian behaviour" (p. 154).

[72] E. Brandenburger, "Gericht Gottes III", *TRE* 12:478 (469-83).

[73] H. Conzelmann, "Gericht Gottes III", *RGG*[3] 2:1421 (1419-21) (Conzelmann's exclamation marks).

[74] It needs stressing that I am not making the point *here* that there is a *constant* dialectic between judgement and gospel for the Christian, although this idea may be found in some Pauline texts concerning judgement. See my discussion above of the work of W. Joest and N.M. Watson.

[75] See C.J. Roetzel, *Judgement in the Community: A Study of the Relationship between Eschatology and Ecclesiology in Paul*, Leiden 1972, pp. 9-10, 177-78.

[76] Roetzel, *Judgement*, p. 78.

[77] Roetzel, *Judgement*, p. 10, mentions 1 Cor. 3.10-16; 4.1-5; 5.1-8; 6.1-11; 10.1-12; 11.27-32; 2 Cor. 5.10; 2 Thes. 2.1-12.

do with judgement in the sense of salvation versus damnation, but rather concern the reward the Christian will receive.[78] Further, as Travis has argued, although Paul may not always explicitly mention both judgement and justification by faith together, it is clear that judgement comes upon all and those who are justified by faith are delivered from this judgement. Also Paul contrasts condemnation with salvation through faith in Jesus.[79]

To return to Rom. 1.18-3.20, judgement according to works shows the necessity of the revelation of the δικαιοσύνη θεοῦ. And so I believe Rom. 2.1-16 only makes sense if it is seen as part of the argument of Rom. 1.18-3.20 where, according to my understanding, Paul is establishing that Jews and Gentiles are heading for condemnation on the day of judgement. The argument comes to a climax in 3.20 when Paul concludes that there will be no acquittal at the final judgement on the basis of observing the law — in fact the law reveals sin to be sin (διότι ἐξ ἔργων νόμου οὐ δικαιωθήσεται πᾶσα σὰρξ ἐνώπιον αὐτοῦ, διὰ γὰρ νόμου ἐπίγνωσις ἁμαρτίας). In 1.18-3.20 Paul has thereby demonstrated the necessity of the revelation of the righteousness of God from faith to faith. If 1.18-3.20 is understood in this way one can make perfect sense of the γάρ in 1.18 ('Αποκαλύπτεται γὰρ ὀργὴ θεοῦ ἀπ' οὐρανοῦ . . .). In Rom. 1.16-17 Paul has spoken of the revelation of the righteousness of God in the gospel. The γάρ of 1.18 can then be understood as introducing the argument which establishes the necessity of this revelation.[80] Once he has established this in 1.18-3.20 he returns to the revelation of the righteousness of God in 3.21-26.

---

[78] See 1 Cor. 3.10-16; 2 Cor. 5.10. 1 Cor. 4.1-5 may concern the reward but there are arguments for taking ἔπαινος in 4.5 to refer to salvation. See Mattern, *Verständnis*, pp. 183-84, although she equates ἔπαινος with μισθός, *despite* these arguments (p. 184). Note the use of ἔπαινος in Rom. 2.29, the only other text which speaks of praise from God. As far as the other Pauline texts mentioned by Roetzel are concerned, they are concerned with warnings for Christians: 1 Cor. 5.1-8; 6.1-11; 10.1-12; 11.27-32.

[79] Among the texts Travis mentions (*Judgment*, p. 62) are 1 Thes. 1.8-10 and 1 Cor. 15.2.

[80] See Sanday and Headlam, *Romans*, p. 40; Käsemann, *Römer*, p. 31.

If salvation were to be dependent on works as well as faith, the theological implications would be astounding. For if works are required for justification, faith is insufficient, and by implication God's grace is also insufficient.[81] In view of this it is lamentable that a number of scholars in the protestant tradition have put forward a view which one could legitimately call double justification. See, for example, the comment of Godet on Rom. 2.6:

> . . . justification by faith alone applies to the time of *entrance* into salvation through the free pardon of sin, but not to the time of judgment. When God of free grace receives the sinner at the time of his conversion, He asks nothing of him except faith; but from that moment the believer enters a wholly new responsibility; God demands from him, as the recipient of grace, the fruits of grace.[82]

Such a view is unfaithful to Paul (and also deviates from what I consider to be orthodox protestant theology).[83] Apart from the different terminology, it is difficult to distinguish Godet's view from that of Contarini's *duplex iustitia*.[84] Godet's view is more directly linked to a view of sanctification (*sanctificatio*) and regeneration (*renovatio*) which emerged in the second half of the seventeenth century[85] and which later found widespread expression in Pietism.[86]

---

[81] Cf. Gundry Volf, *Paul and Perseverance*, p. 205.

[82] Godet, *Romans*, p. 118.

[83] Note also the criticisms made of Godet by T.W. Chambers in the Appendix to the American edition of Godet's commentary (pp. 517-31, especially pp. 524-26).

[84] At Regensburg Contarini tried to reach agreement with protestants on justification. On Ratisbon/Regensburg, see Th. Kolde, "Regensburger Religionsgespäch und Regensburger Buch 1541", *RE*³ 16:545-52, and D. Fenlon, *Heresy and Obedience in Tridentine Italy*, Cambridge 1972, pp. 53-61. Calvin, on the other hand, was more careful to avoid the idea that works complete justification (see J.T. McNeill (ed.), *Calvin: Institutes of the Christian Religion*, 2 vols, Philadelphia 1960, 1:811 n. 9). Contrast canon 24 of the Council of Trent: *Si quis dixerit, justitiam acceptam non conservari, atque etiam non augeri coram Deo per bona opera; sed opera ipsa fructus solummodo et signa esse justificationis adeptae, non autem ipsius augendae causam: anathema sit* (P. Schaff, *The Creeds of Christendom*, 3 vols, Grand Rapids 1993 (repr.), (⁶1931), 2:115).

[85] See Elert, *Glaube*, pp. 486-87. He points for example to the problems in Quenstedt's view of justification and regeneration. He writes that Quenstedt "den Unterschied zwischen Rechtfertigung und Erneuerung darin erblickt, daß jene ausschließlich Handeln Gottes sei, bei dieser aber der wiedergeborene Mensch mit Gott zusammenwirkte" (p. 486). On Quenstedt, see J.K. Tholuck, "Quenstedt", *RE*³

This brings me to the specific issue of Romans 2 and the question of the obedience of the Christian.

4. Romans 2 and the Question of Christian Obedience

In the exegesis of Romans 2 I have been critical of those who argue that the passages about justification by works apply to Christians. Luther believed that the "doers of the law" of Rom. 2.13 are believers.[87] In a similar way Calvin thought Rom. 2.7 referred to Christian believers.[88] Such views have been fairly widespread down to the present day. I give four examples.

First, I take the example of Adolf Schlatter. I find many of his arguments that Romans 2 refers to Christians unsatisfactory. For example, he writes that Romans 2 is "sicher mit Kenntnis der parallelen Worte Jesu geschrieben, da Paulus die Erklärung Jesu über die Ehescheidung kennt, 1 Kor. 7,10".[89] It may be that some of Jesus words have influenced Paul in Romans 2.[90] But that does not necessarily mean that Romans 2 is then concerned with the obedience of the "Christian". Schlatter also writes:

16:380-83. On the dangers of making too radical a separation between justification and sanctification, see W. Joest, "Heiligung III: Dogmatisch", *RGG*[3] 3:180 (180-81): "Eine strenge Unterscheidung von Rechtfertigung und Heiligung als zweier getrennter Gottesakte ist indessen den biblischen Texten gegenüber nicht möglich". Later he writes: "Nicht von der Rechtfertigung selbst also, wohl aber von der Frage nach der *Begründung* oder *Bedingung* der Rechtfertigung muß die Heiligung sorgfältig getrennt werden. Beides gehört zusammen; aber nicht so, daß Gott rechtfertigt, *weil* er geheiligt hat (geschweige denn: weil wir selbst uns geheiligt hätten), sondern so, daß Gott heiligt, weil und indem er aus freier Gnade, vom Menschen her ohne positive Voraussetzung, gerechtspricht" (181).

[86] See H. Brandenburg, "Heiligungsbewegung", *RGG*[3] 3:182.

[87] See *WA* 56:248.

[88] Calvin, *Romans*, p. 44.

[89] A. Schlatter, *Der Glaube im Neuen Testament*, Stuttgart [6]1982 (mit einer Einführung von P. Stuhlmacher), ([4]1927), p. 325 n.1.

[90] See, for example, my analysis of Rom. 2.17-24 in chapter 5 above.

"Wie soll Paulus irgendeine Kenntnis Jesu haben, ohne zu wissen, daß Jesu Verheißung und Lob galt, 'der das Gute wirkt'".[91] But did Paul necessarily agree with Jesus on the issue of obedience and promise?[92] Or, putting it more precisely, did Paul believe that Jesus' teaching on judgement is directly applicable to Christians? I suggest that Paul was perhaps influenced by Jesus' teaching on judgement, but he applied it in such a way that everyone was a "goat" and no one was a "sheep".[93] Paul has therefore put in a dialectical dimension to Jesus' teaching. And even if Paul did apply Jesus' teaching directly to Christians in the sense that doing good means salvation and doing evil means damnation, it does not necessarily mean Paul is speaking of the Christian in Romans 2. A roughly similar exegetical mistake is made by scholars who argue that Rom. 7.14-25 refers to Christian experience, for the Christian experiences precisely the tension of knowing what is the right and not being able to do it (e.g. Rom. 7.15).

Ridderbos also believes Romans 2 is applicable to Christians and stresses that "the whole idea that Paul's concept of faith is in fundamental conflict with such a retribution according to works must be rejected".[94] He writes that "justification and sanctification . . . are inseparable in Paul's preaching, not merely as indicative and imperative, but in the first place as two redemptive realities coinciding in Christ's death and resurrection".[95] Commenting on Romans 4, he argues that "faith cannot remain empty and work-less, but becomes known as faith precisely in works".[96] Further, "works are indispensible as the demonstration of the true nature of faith and as the evidence of having died and been raised together with Christ".[97] Thus Ridderbos puts forward a position often

---

[91] Schlatter, *Glaube*, p. 326.

[92] This is a enormous question. Although it is not straightforward to determine the teaching of Jesus, it seems likely that he did teach some sort of judgement according to works, such judgement not only being relevant for the "reward" (Mt. 6.1-4) but also for the issue of salvation and damnation.

[93] I am not suggesting that Mt. 25.31-46 necessarily goes back to Jesus; but it does seem highly likely that Jesus taught some sort of eschatological separation of the righteous from the wicked on the basis of works.

[94] Ridderbos, *Paul*, p. 179.

[95] Ridderbos, *Paul*, p. 179.

[96] Ridderbos, *Paul*, p. 180.

found in reformed theology that sanctification is a significant sign of election.[98] I wonder, though, whether this is faithful to Paul's theology. Paul certainly believed that faith should result in works (Gal. 5.6). But the fundamental sign of election for Paul is confession of faith (Rom. 10.9).[99] This, not sanctification, is the ultimate criterion that one is chosen by God.[100]

This brings me to the work of Cosgrove. He believes that although one is not made right by means of works, one can still have a justification by works as in Rom. 2.13. The phrase ἐξ ἔργων νόμου in Rom. 3.20 simply refers to the instrumentality of works. So Paul is saying that *by means of* works of law no flesh will be justified. But it does not mean *on the basis of* works of law no flesh will be justified. Cosgrove points to the fact that if Paul were wishing to point to the reason in the widest sense for the judgement expressed by δικαιοῦν, he could use διά with accusative, ἕνεκα/ἕνεκεν or χάριν; and if he wanted to express the evidential basis he could use ἐπί with the dative or κατά with the accusative. In fact κατά with the accusative is so widely used in the LXX that it seems strange, he argues, that Paul does not use this if he wished to point to the evidential basis rather than simply to the instrument.[101] He finds confirmation for his view in that Chrysostom, when formulating Paul's statements, uses ἀπό but never κατά with the accusative or ἐπί with the dative.[102] Therefore he believes it unlikely that ἐξ ἔργων νόμου points to the forensic grounds of justification.[103] Justification can therefore be on the basis of

---

[97] Ridderbos, *Paul*, p. 180.

[98] There is some disagreement as to whether Calvin himself saw works as a sign of election. W. Niesel, *The Theology of Calvin* ET, London 1956, pp. 169-81, denies Calvin's use of the so-called *syllogismus practicus*. For an alternative view see G.C. Berkouwer, *Divine Election* ET, Grand Rapids 1960, pp. 279-306.

[99] This may raise the question of false confession. However, Paul does not seem to reckon with this possibility. See 1 Cor. 12.3b: καὶ οὐδεὶς δύναται εἰπεῖν· Κύριος Ἰησοῦς, εἰ μὴ ἐν πνεύματι ἁγίῳ.

[100] See the discussion below, and especially the discussion of 1 Thes. 5.9-10.

[101] See Ps. 61.13 LXX and other texts given by Heiligenthal, *Werke*, pp. 172-75.

[102] Cosgrove, "Justification", 659-60. See, for example, Chrysostom, *Commentarius in epistulam ad Romanos* homilia 8 on Rom. 4.2: Δύο γάρ ἐστι καυχήματα, τὸ μὲν ἀπὸ τῶν ἔργων, τὸ δὲ ἀπὸ τῆς πίστεως (*MPG* 60:455).

[103] Cosgrove, "Justification", 659.

works, works taking on an evidential function. This is precisely what is going on in Rom. 2.1-16 according to Cosgrove. So he can write: "The expectation of the believer is that judgment according to works will mean *justification*".[104]

Cosgrove has produced an extremely interesting and thoughtful argument. But it does not hold for a number of reasons. First, I again stress that there is nothing in the context of Rom. 2.10, 13 to suggest that Paul is referring to the judgement of Christians. The other texts he mentions refer either to the reward Christians are to receive, or simply do not concern justification by works.[105] Second, I believe there are serious problems with his view that ἐξ ἔργων νόμου of Rom. 3.20 refers simply to the instrumental use and not the evidential use. The verse I believe refers to the last judgement; even if the future δικαιωθήσεται is gnomic as I have earlier suggested, there is still some reference to the eschatological judgement. And if there is a reference to the final judgement, Paul must have in mind the basis of justification, i.e. that there is no justification *on the basis of* works of law.[106] My third point regards the unusual nature of the preposition ἐκ with δικαιοῦν. Cosgrove points out that outside of Paul and authors dependent on his phraseology (James and Greek Fathers quoting or alluding to Paul), he has found only two instances of δικαιοῦν with ἐκ. First, there is Athanasius, *Expositiones in Psalmos* 100 (MPG 27:424). Commenting on v. 1 Athanasius writes: Ἐδικαίωσε γὰρ ἐκ τῶν ἐχθρῶν ἡμῶν τὴν δίκην ἡμῶν (for he vindicates our cause from our enemies). Second there is Mt. 12.37: ἐκ γὰρ τῶν λόγων σου δικαιωθήσῃ, καὶ ἐκ τῶν

---

[104] Cosgrove, "Justification", 661.

[105] In addition to Rom. 2.10, 13, Cosgrove mentions 1 Cor. 4.3-5; 2 Cor. 5.10 and Rom. 8.33. But 1 Cor. 4.3-5 does not concern "justification" as such. As Eckstein points out (*Syneidesis*, p. 205), Paul argues that his position in the last judgement does not depend on any "good conscience" he may have. 2 Cor. 5.10 concerns the reward, not the issue whether one is going to be saved or not and Rom. 8.33 has nothing to do with justification by works. I find Cosgrove's treatment of Rom. 8 ("Justification", 667-69) rather unsatisfactory. I have no space to pursue this here.

[106] The same can be said of the parallel in Gal. 2.16b: ὅτι ἐξ ἔργων νόμου οὐ δικαιωθήσεται πᾶσα σάρξ. H.D. Betz, *Galatians*, Philadelphia 1979, p. 118, is therefore not incorrect to translate: "For all flesh will not be justified on the basis of works of [the] law".

λόγων σου καταδικασθήσῃ. This text could present problems for Cosgrove's thesis for any distinction between justification by and justification on the basis of seems artificial here. Cosgrove admits a possible problem, but believes that ἐκ could be used here on stylistic grounds.[107] But one thing is clear: Paul is using an unusual expression in ἐξ ἔργων νόμου. In the LXX ἐκ is only used with ἔργων in Judg. 19.16 (ἐκ being used in the sense of ἀπό).[108] How then did Paul come to use the expression ἐξ ἔργων νόμου? Although Cosgrove denies the use of a semitism (he considers only עַל, בְּ, כְּ), perhaps behind Paul's use of ἐκ is מִן. According to *BDB* this in the Hebrew bible can, among other things, be used for an "immediate, or efficient, cause" and also for a "remoter cause", the latter including "on account of", "by reason of". There is also another line of argument. Paul believes faith is the mode of salvation and therefore he avoids the term διὰ πίστιν, using instead ἐκ πίστεως or διὰ πίστεως.[109] So justification is ἐκ πίστεως; it cannot be ἐξ ἔργων νόμου. Cosgrove is perhaps guilty of reading Paul too woodenly. I suggest that the idea put forward by article 11 of the 39 articles of the Church of England is thoroughly Pauline: *per fidem, non propter opera et merita nostra, justi coram Deo reputamur*.[110] So Paul would obviously be unhappy to use διὰ πίστιν or κατὰ πίστιν. If one is to use κατά with anything, it is with χάρις. So in Rom. 4.16 Paul can write Διὰ τοῦτο ἐκ πίστεως, ἵνα κατὰ χάριν and in Rom. 4.4 τῷ δὲ ἐργαζομένῳ ὁ μισθὸς οὐ λογίζεται κατὰ χάριν ἀλλὰ κατὰ ὀφείλημα. I suspect then that Cosgrove has misread

---

[107] Cosgrove, "Justification", 658 n. 16. He notes that Mt. 12.33-35 "abounds with ἐκ-formulations".

[108] Compare Judg. 19.16 A with 19.16 B.

[109] See J.B. Lightfoot, *St. Paul's Epistle to the Galatians*, Peabody 1993 (repr.), (¹1865), p. 115.

[110] For the text see E.C.S. Gibson, *The Thirty-Nine Articles of the Church of England*, London ³1902, (¹1896), p. 388. Gibson (p. 401) rightly stresses that justification is *per fidem*, not *propter fidem*. See also W.H. Griffith Thomas, *The Principles of Theology: An Introduction to the Thirty-Nine Articles*, London 1963, p. 191, who, commenting on article 11, writes: "Faith is never associated with the ground of Justification, but only as its means or channel". Article 11 is indebted for some of its phrases to the confessions of Augsburg and Würtemberg (see Schaff, *The Creeds of Christendom*, 1:626, for a comparison of article 11 with Augsburg confession article 4, and 1:629 for a comparison with Würtemberg confession article 5).

Paul's intentions. I suggest then that Cosgrove has been too restrictive in interpreting Rom. 3.20. My fourth problem with Cosgrove's approach is his more general interpretation of Paul's view of justification. I believe faith is more than simply the means to producing good works. And if judgement is according to works, what happens to the assurance of salvation for the believer which is so central to Paul's theology?[111]

Finally, in a recent monograph Schreiner argues that Rom. 2.7, 10, 26-29 refer to Gentile Christians. In the exegesis in chapters 4 and 5 above I was critical of the view where Romans 2 is applied to Christians. But the problems in Schreiner's exegesis are compounded by two further factors. First, he insists that Rom. 2.14-15 refers to unbelievers, which gives rise to a strange inconsistency. Secondly, Schreiner argues that the law cannot be the basis of salvation for perfect obedience is necessary. But he does not require perfect obedience of Christians but rather "obedience that is significant, substantial, and observable".[112] Is this not inconsistent?

5. Paul and the Law

Paul and the law is a vast theme and in this section I am only able to point to some key issues relevant to Rom. 1.18-3.20.

Paul asserts in Rom. 3.20 that no one will be justified by works of law. I now ask why Paul believes this to be the case. Often the distinction is made between the quantitative critique of the law and the qualitative critique.[113] In the quantitative critique Paul says that the Jews tried to fulfil the law but in fact they were unable to do so. In the qualitative critique, it is said that human being are not even intended to fulfil the law.

The quantitative critique actually needs to be subdivided,[114] for there are some who simply argue that Paul's point is that human beings are unable to fulfil the law and that is why there is no justification by works of law.[115] There are then those who make the additional point that not

---

[111] On this, see Gundry Volf, *Paul and Perseverance*.

[112] Schreiner, *Law*, p. 204.

[113] Cf. D. Moo, "Paul and the Law in the Last Ten Years", *SJT* 40 (1987) 297-98 (287-307).

[114] Cf. Schreiner, "Works of Law", 218-220.

only are human beings unable to fulfil the law but they try to fulfil it in a legalistic manner.[116] Both these points carry roughly equal weight. This, of course, was an approach adopted by the reformers and has a long history down to the present day.[117]

I believe there can be little doubt that Paul believes human beings are unable to fulfil the law. The whole section Rom. 3.9-20 makes that clear. So there is no justification by works of law because all men and women are in Adam and they have all fallen short of the glory of God. It is simply impossible to fulfil the law. But what about the supplementary idea

---

[115] See U. Wilckens, "Was heißt bei Paulus: 'Aus Werken des Gesetzes wird kein Mensch gerecht'?", in *Rechtfertigung als Freiheit: Paulusstudien*, Neukirchen-Vluyn 1974, 77-109; *Römer*, pp. 173-78, 244-50; S. Westerholm *Israel's Law and the Church's Faith: Paul and His Recent Interpreters*, Grand Rapids 1988, pp. 120-21.

[116] I use the term "legalism" to refer not only to keeping the law (or trying to keep it) but also to a constellation of negative aspects: externalism, casuistry, and, above all, the attitude that one is earning salvation and thus giving rise to an attitude of boasting and self-righteousness. This, I believe, is how the word is usually used by theologians. So my term "legalism" corresponds to what Räisänen calls "hard" or "anthropocentric" legalism, as opposed to "soft" or "torah-centric" legalism (H. Räisänen, "Legalism and Salvation by the Law", in S. Pederson (ed.), *Die paulinische Literatur und Theologie*, Aarhus 1980 (63-83), referred to in Westerholm, *Israel's Law*, pp. 132-33). Cf. R. Longenecker, *Paul, Apostle of Liberty*, Grand Rapids 1980 (repr.), (¹1964), pp. 78-84, who makes a distinction between "acting legalism" and "reacting nomism". My experience is that very few theologians use the word as defined in the Shorter Oxford English Dictionary: "Adherence to the Law as opposed to the Gospel; the doctrine of justification by works, or teaching which savours of it".

[117] Luther can be placed in this category, although there are instances where he seems to be saying that even the one who obeys the whole law will not be justified. See his Commentary on Galatians (*WA* 40.1:218): *Quidquid non est gratia, Lex est, sive sit Iudicialis, Ceremonialis, sive Decalogus; Idea si etiam feceris opus legis secundum hoc praeceptum: 'Diliges Dominum Deum tuum ex toto corde tuo' etc., tamen non iustificaberis coram Deo, Quia ex operibus legis non iustificatur homo.* That Luther's view was not simply that "Judaism was not Christianity" is clear from his comments on Rom. 3.20 in his lectures on Romans (*WA* 56:248): *Apostolus distinguit inter legem et fidem, siue inter literam et gratiam, ita et inter opera earum. Opera legis dicit, quę fiunt extra fidem et gratiam et ex lege per timorem cogente Vel promissionem temporalium alliciente facta. Opera autem fidei dicit, quę ex spiritu libertatis amore solo Dei fiunt. Et hęc fieri non pussunt nisi a Iustificatis per fidem, ad quam Iustificationem opera legis nihil cooperantur, immo vehementer impediunt, dum non sinunt hominem sibi iniustum videri et Iustificatione indigentem.*

that it is legalistic to try to fulfil the law? This, I believe, has some basis
in Paul. But I need to spend a little time defending this.

I take the point that in Rom. 3.20 there is no explicit reference to
legalism. But Rom. 3.27-4.5 makes it clear that Paul does have legalism
in mind,[118] not to mention other Pauline texts.[119] I focus now on Rom.
3.27-4.5. One of the mistakes in the exegesis of Romans is to sever Rom.
3.27-31 from Rom. 4. This cannot be done. Much better sense is made if
Rom. 3.27-31 is seen to run into chapter 4.[120] Schreiner rightly stresses
the connection between Rom. 3.27-28 and Rom. 4.2. In 3.27-28 boasting
is excluded for a man is justified by faith apart from works of law. In
Rom. 4.2 it is said that if Abraham was justified by works he has a reason
for boasting. As Schreiner points out, Rom. 3.27-28 and Rom. 4.2 have
the three key words in common: "works", "justify", boasting".[121] It is
true that whereas Rom. 3.28 has ἔργα νόμου, Rom. 4.2 simply has ἔργα.
But the latter is simply a shortened form of the former.[122] Also whereas
3.27 has καύχησις, 4.2 has καύχημα. But these are clearly related, the
former expressing the act of boasting and the latter the claim upon
God.[123] Such boasting is wrong.[124] In addition, it can be said that there
are elements in Rom. 1.18-3.20 which point to legalism. First, Rom. 2.1-

---

[118] Note that Calvin does not discuss legalism in his commentary on 3.20 but does
bring it in in his comment on 3.27 (Calvin, *Romans*, pp. 78-79).

[119] I think especially of Rom. 9.30-10.4 (discussed in my *Provoked to Jealousy*,
pp. 186-91).

[120] If Rom. 3.27-31 is taken with Rom. 4, the otherwise puzzling statement in
Rom. 3.31b (ἀλλὰ νόμον ἱστάνομεν) makes perfect sense if νόμος is taken to mean
"pentateuch". Paul then establishes the pentateuch in Rom. 4 by showing that the
stories about Abraham (Gen. 15, 17, 18) support justification by faith.

[121] Schreiner, "Works of Law", 232.

[122] See the discussion of ἔργα νόμου in chapter 6 above (see the exegesis of Rom.
3.20). See also Käsemann, *Römer*, p. 83.

[123] See Bultmann, καυχάομαι, 649 n. 35; Cranfield, *Romans*, 1:165. Cf. Hübner,
Gesetz, p. 100, who understands καύχησις as "Sich-Rühmen" and καύχημα as
"Ruhm . . . worauf sich ein Sich-Rühmen stützen könnte".

[124] Contrast the view of J. Lambrecht, "Why is Boasting Excluded? A Note on
Rom 3,27 and 4,2", *ETL* 61 (1985) 366 (365-69): "it would seem that the boasting
terminology in 2,17; 2,23; 3,27 and 4,2 is rather neutral; by itself it does not point to
a morally perverse 'Selbstruhm'". See also Thompson, "Paul's Double Critique of
Jewish Boasting".

4 refers to the self-righteous judge.[125] Secondly, Rom. 2.17-24 refers specifically to the self-righteous Jew.[126]

So much for the quantitative critique of the law. But what about the qualitative view? This view is typified by Bultmann. He believed that according to Paul men and women are incapable of fulfilling the law but he makes this crucial addition: "But Paul goes much further still; he says not only that man *can* not achieve salvation by works of the Law, but also that he is not even *intended* to do so".[127] Bultmann continues, appealing to both Rom. 3.20 and Gal. 2.16:

Paul thinks in this manner in consequence of his concept of God, according to which whatever factually is or happens, is or happens according to divine plan. In its context, Rom. 3:20—'no human being will be justified . . . by works of the law' — means, 'no one can be justified on the basis of works of the Law,' but that this impossibility was also *intended* is indicated by Gal. 2:16, where the same sentence means in this context: 'no one *is to be* justified on the basis of works of the Law'.[128]

In fact, he argues, "the way of works of the Law and the way of grace and faith are mutually exclusive opposites". Why? "Because *man's effort to achieve his salvation by keeping the Law* only leads him into sin, indeed this effort itself in the end *is already sin*".[129] So according to this position the view that man is not even intended to fulfil the law is the predominant point. The fact that one cannot fulfil the law *is a subsidiary point*. So even complete obedience, if that were possible, would be sin. "*Selbst der vollkommene Mensch* — nochmals: gäbe es ihn! doch es gibt ihn ja nicht! — *ist Sünder!*"[130] The pious Jew then boasts in his performance. He feels he has a claim upon God. This idea of the self-righteous Jew is found not only in Bultmann but also in Käsemann,[131] Bornkamm[132] and Conzelmann[133] and in the work of Klein.[134]

---

[125] See the discussion in chapter 4.

[126] I therefore question Westerholm's point (*Israel's Law*, p. 120) that "one searches the argument (i.e. Rom. 1.18-3.20) in vain for the notion that Jewish obedience to the law's statutes is marked by a 'legalistic spirit'".

[127] Bultmann, *Theology*, 1:263.

[128] Bultmann, *Theology*, 1:263.

[129] Bultmann, *Theology*, 1:264 (Bultmann's emphasis).

[130] Hübner, *Gesetz*, p. 99 (Hübner's emphasis).

[131] Käsemann, *Romans*, p. 89.

[132] See G. Bornkamm, "The Letter to the Romans as Paul's Last Will and

Although Bultmann's view has received considerable criticism, I believe there is something in his view that God does not intend people to be justified by works. First, Bultmann, as we have seen, makes this point: "Paul thinks in this matter in consequence of his concept of God, according to which whatever factually is or happens, is or happens according to divine plan".[135] Also one could say that God intended that human beings would be unable to fulfil the law in view of the fact that human beings find themselves in Adam. Second there are a number of passages in Paul which seem to make it clear that God does not intend human beings to be justified by works. I give three such passages.

First, Rom. 9.30-10.4 suggests that God does not wish human beings to pursue the law ἐξ ἔργων.[136] Secondly, according to Rom. 9.11-12, salvation does not depend on whether one does good or evil but depends on God's call.[137] Third, and this is of especial importance, is the whole argument in Rom. 3.27-4.8. Paul says in Rom. 3.27 that boasting is excluded through the "law of faith" and not through the "law of works". Hübner, rightly I believe, takes this a step further by saying that the law seen as a "law of works" is a perverted way of understanding the law.[138] Such a

---

Testament", in K.P. Donfried (ed.), *The Romans Debate*, Peabody [2]1991 ([1]1977), 26 (16-28), where the Jew represents the pious man in general.

[133] Conzelmann, *Outline*, p. 226: "If I try to bring about my salvation by fulfilling the law, my wish is not for what befits God and his law; what I seek is my own righteousness".

[134] See Klein, "Gesetz III". See also G. Klein, "Individualgeschichte und Weltgeschichte bei Paulus", in *Rekonstruktion und Interpretation: Gesammelte Aufsätze zum Neuen Testament*, München 1969, 180-224; "Sündenverständnis und theologia crucis bei Paulus", in C. Anderson and G. Klein (ed.), *Theologia crucis - signum crucis: Festschrift für Erich Dinkler zum 70. Geburtstag*, Tübingen 1979, 249-82.

[135] Bultmann, *Theology of the New Testament*, 1:263.

[136] See Bell, *Provoked to Jealousy*, pp. 186-91.

[137] Rom. 9.11-12: μήπω γὰρ γεννηθέντων μηδὲ πραξάντων τι ἀγαθὸν ἢ φαῦλον, ἵνα ἡ κατ' ἐκλογὴν πρόθεσις τοῦ θεοῦ μένῃ, 12 οὐκ ἐξ ἔργων ἀλλ' ἐκ τοῦ καλοῦντος, ἐρρέθη αὐτῇ ὅτι Ὁ μείζων δουλεύσει τῷ ἐλάσσονι.

[138] Hübner, *Gesetz*, pp. 100-101, writes: "Wer Gottes Gesetz und somit Gottes heiligen Willen von den Werken her angeht, hat das *Gesetz Gottes zum 'Gesetz der Werke'* pervertiert . . ." (Hübner's emphasis). See also Michel, *Römer*, p. 155: "Paulus meint mit dem Begriff νόμος τῶν ἔργων ein Verständnis des Gesetzes, das den Gehorsam in Einzelakte zerlegt und den Willen Gottes mißversteht. Dem νόμος τῶν ἔργων entsprechen auf Seiten des Menschen die ἔργα νόμου (Röm 3,20). Das

view finds boasting a necessity.[139] "Siehe, o Gott, hier sind meine gerechten Werke! Siehe, hier bin ich in meinen gerechten Werken, wie du sie vor dich zu stellen befohlen hast!"[140] Now the issue of boasting in this sense does not come to the fore in Rom. 1.18-3.20 although I believe it is implied.[141] Also one could perhaps gain the impression that there is nothing wrong in being justified by works and by fulfilling the law (see Rom. 2.6, 7, 10, 13). In fact Wilckens writes that Bultmann's view of God not intending men to be righteous through the law finds no basis in Rom. 1-3.[142] Perhaps if 1.18-3.20 is taken alone, one could gain this impression. But these verses cannot be considered in isolation; Rom. 3.21-31 and Rom. 4ff must also be taken into account. After all, Paul could only write Rom. 1.18-3.20 on the basis of Rom. 3.21-31 and Rom. 4ff. For I concluded my exegesis of 3.9-20 by saying that Paul could only write what he writes in the light of the cross of Christ. Returning to Rom. 3.27-4.8, I believe Paul makes it quite clear that God does not intend human beings to be made righteous on the basis of works. I do not have time to engage in detailed exegesis, but Rom. 4.2 I believe makes the point. εἰ γὰρ Ἀβραὰμ ἐξ ἔργων ἐδικαιώθη, ἔχει καύχημα, ἀλλ᾽ οὐ πρὸς θεόν. In view of 3.9-20 it is clear that Abraham cannot have been justified by works. But if he had, he could have a reason for boasting (and in this sense the verse is *realis*) but not before God.[143] So any boasting would

---

jüdische Verständnis des Gesetzes ruft notwendig den Selbstruhm des Menschen hervor".

[139] Hübner, *Gesetz*, p. 96 (*Law*, p. 116).

[140] Hübner, *Gesetz*, p. 96.

[141] See the references to the self-righteous person in Rom. 2.1-4 and the self-righteous Jew in 2.17-24. Note also the reference to boasting in 2.17 and 2.23 (which, as I have argued, refers to both boasting in possessing the law and boasting in doing the law).

[142] Wilckens, "Was heißt bei Paulus: 'Aus Werken des Gesetzes wird kein Mensch gerecht'?", 82-83.

[143] G. Klein, "Römer 4 und die Idee der Heilsgeschichte, in *Rekonstruktion und Interpretation*, München 1969, 151-52 (145-69), supported by Hahn, "Gesetzesverständnis", 39, argues for an *irrealis*, by which he means a hypothetical statement. Arguing against Lipsius, "Der Brief an die Römer", 115, Klein, "Römer 4", 151 n. 25, makes the point that Rom. 4.2 can be understood as *irrealis* although ἄν is missing (see *BDF* 360.1) even though a present is used in the apodosis (see *BDF* 360.4). An alternative view is that of Lambrecht ("Why is Boasting Excluded?"; "Unreal

not count at all before God. As Hübner writes: "Selbst vollkommene Werkgerechtigkeit im Rahmen der Torah bedeutet nicht Gerechtigkeit vor Gott!"[144] In addition to 4.2 one should also consider Rom. 4.4: τῷ δὲ ἐργαζομένῳ ὁ μισθὸς οὐ λογίζεται κατὰ χάριν ἀλλὰ κατὰ ὀφείλημα. So as far as salvation is concerned, "working" is totally opposed to "grace". God has chosen to justify people on the basis of faith and grace, and not through working and reward.[145]

What about Rom. 3.20 itself? Is there anything here to suggest that God does not intend human beings to be justified by works? I have already mentioned Bultmann's treatment. Perhaps a more penetrating analysis is put forward by Klein. Criticising Wilckens' treatment of 3.20,[146] Klein argues that had Paul wished to say that no one is justified by works of law because no one has produced them, then Paul would have put it differently such as: "Keiner wird gerechtfertigt, der die vom Gesetz geforderten Werke *nicht* vorzuweisen hat".[147] Klein adds:

Conditions in the Letters of Paul: A Clarification", *ETL* 63 (1987) 153-56). He argues that there is a "mixed" construction in 4.2a,b, the protasis standing in the *irrealis*, the apodosis standing in the *realis*. So in the protasis "Paul implies that Abraham's justification through works as a matter of fact did not take place" ("Boasting", 367). In the apodosis however, Paul, by using the *realis*, focuses on the works-boasting connection. The apodosis then has the form of a simple condition, a condition of fact (*realis*). But this construction "points only to the logical connection between the two clauses. . . In a 'realis' the form itself does not contain a reference to whether the condition is in fact fulfilled or not" ("Boasting", 366; cf. D. Zeller, "Zur neueren Diskussion über das Gesetz bei Paulus", *ThPh* 62 (1987) 491 (481-99)). So far I would accept Lambrecht's analysis. However, I part company with him on the final section of Rom. 4.2: αλλ' οὐ πρὸς θεόν. I maintain that Paul is conceding a possible boasting before men (contrast the views of Klein, "Römer 4", 152 n. 26, and Michel, *Römer*, p. 162 n. 3). I therefore agree with Kuss, *Der Römerbrief*, 1:181, when he writes: "es gibt überhaupt keinen menschlichen Selbstruhm vor Gott" (quoted by Lambrecht, "Why is Boasting Excluded?", 367 n. 14).

[144] Hübner, *Gesetz*, p. 99 (Hübner's emphasis).

[145] Note, however, that Paul can speak of a reward when it comes to discussing one's state in the world to come. See the discussion above.

[146] Wilckens, "Aus Werken des Gesetzes wird niemand gerecht", 81-82.

[147] Klein, "Sündenverständnis", 260.

Aber die in das Zitat eingesprengte und seinen Sinn umstürzende Wendung ἐξ ἔργων νόμου hebt ja nicht auf faktische Gesetzesverletzung, sondern darauf ab, das Gesetzeswerke *überhaupt*, unabhängig von der Frage nach ihrer Verwirklichung, keinen möglichen Rechtfertigungsgrund hergeben.[148]

Klein is also rightly critical of Wilckens' idea that Paul is opposing an idea that through good works one can compensate for evil works.[149] Such an idea cannot be found in the text.

So already in 3.20 there is a hint that human beings are not intended to be justified by works of law.[150] Further, the thoughts that are implicit in Rom. 1.18-3.20 are made explicit in Rom. 3.21-4.25. In this respect I differ slightly from Hübner's view. He argues that in 1.18-3.20 "war nicht die Rede davon, daß durch die Befolgung des vom Gesetz Gebotenen rechtfertigende Werke eben um der Rechtfertigung willen intendiert werden sollten".[151] So according to Hübner, the argument in Rom. 1.18-3.20 is consecutive, not final. There was no question of doing works *in order to gain salvation*: "Aus dem Nichttun des Gebotenen ergibt sich als Konsequenz die Ungerechtigkeit".[152] However, I am not sure this is a convincing way to understand the text. Likewise, Hübner argues that 1.18-3.20 says little about works, the law being much more important. So he makes the distinction between works-righteousness (that found in 3.27-4.8) and law-righteousness (that found in Romans 2). So he argues that in 2.17-29 "works" does not occur, and in Rom. 2 it is only in the quotation from Ps. 62 that the terms appears. I find this unconvincing. Note, for example, Rom. 2.10 and the use there of ἐργάζομαι: δόξα δὲ καὶ τιμὴ καὶ εἰρήνη παντὶ τῷ ἐργαζομένῳ τὸ ἀγαθόν, Ἰουδαίῳ τε πρῶτον καὶ

---

[148] Klein, "Sündenverständnis", 260.

[149] Wilckens, *Römer*, 1:175, writes: "Ungerechte aber, deren Ungerechtigkeit in ihren Taten manifest und wirksam ist, können nicht dadurch gerecht werden, daß sie Geboterfüllungen als Ersatzleistung erbringen, durch die die Sünde etwa aufgehoben würde". Compare Schlatter's view on boasting (*Die Theologie der Apostel*, Stuttgart ⁴1984, (¹1910), p. 282), discussed below.

[150] See also the discussion of Rom 3.20 by H. Weder, "Einsicht in Gesetzlichkeit: Paulus als verständnisvoller Ausleger des menschlichen Lebens", *Judaica* 43 (1987) 22-24 (21-29).

[151] Hübner, *Gesetz*, p. 103.

[152] Hübner, *Gesetz*, p. 103.

Ἕλληνι· Interestingly, such an approach is simliar to that of Snodgrass, although in other respects his approach is quite different.[153]

So I would give qualified support to Hübner. However, a possible objection could be raised to this approach. Schlatter, writing earlier this century, criticised a standard protestant view (although such a view was perhaps not so extreme as Bultmann's). He wrote:

> Das Urteil, daß die Werke des Gesetzes verwerflich seien, ist nicht paulinisch. Sein Satz, daß sich aus den Werken des Gesetzes die Rechtfertigung des Menschen nicht ergebe, darf nicht in den anderen Gedanken umgebogen werden, die Werke des Gesetzes seien sündlich. Dieser Satz trüge den Antinomismus in sich, während sich Paulus das Gesetz immer als Gottes Gesetz denkt und deshalb als die Macht beschreibt, die über das Geschick des Menschen entscheidet und Gottes Verhalten gegen ihn bestimmt.[154]

In certain respects Schlatter anticipated Wilckens' article on works of law. Such a view, however, has its problems. Käsemann says that "the distinction between works of the law as the good and Christ's works as the best . . . is thoroughly non-Pauline".[155] Also the words of Hahn are especially helpful in pointing to the fallacy of Schlatter's position.

> Die Dialektik des paulinischen Gesetzesverständnis ist zerstört, wenn man meint, die Aussagen des Römer- und Galaterbriefes so verstehen zu können, daß es dabei zwar wegen der Macht der Sünde um die faktische Unmöglichkeit des Menschen, gute Werke aufgrund des Gesetzes zu vollbringen, gehe, daß aber sehr wohl dem Menschen durch die im Glauben angenommene Gnadentat Gottes das Tun der ἔργα νόμου ermöglicht worden sei.[156]

He adds the significant point: "Es ist kaum zufällig, daß Paulus den Begriff ἔργα für das Handeln der Glaubenden weitgehend vermeidet".[157] Hahn points out that Paul prefers the ideas καρπός (Rom. 6.22; Gal. 5.22; Phil. 1.11; 4.17), καρποφορεῖν (Rom. 7.4) and if he uses ἔργον he employs the singular.[158]

---

[153] See Snodgrass, "Romans 2", 84, quoted in chapter 6.

[154] Schlatter, *Theologie der Apostel*, p. 281.

[155] Käsemann, *Romans*, p. 89.

[156] Hahn, "Gesetzesverständnis", 61. Perhaps "die faktische Unmöglichkeit" should be replaced by "prinzipielle Unmöglichkeit"? Cf. Hofius, "Rechtfertigung des Gottlosen", 127.

[157] Hahn, "Gesetzesverständnis", 61.

[158] 1 Cor. 15.58 (ἔργον τοῦ κυρίου); 16.10 (ἔργον κυρίου); 2 Cor. 9.8 (ἔργον ἀγαθόν); Gal. 6.4; see also καρπὸς ἔργου Phil. 1.22.

These reservations concerning Schlatter are confirmed by his continuing argument:

Er hat darum nie bestritten, daß der Jude fromm sei und für Gott eifere, und im Rückblick auf seine eigene jüdische Zeit seinen Pharisäismus nicht als seine Versündigung, sondern als das für die vorchristliche Zeit richtige Verhalten beschrieben.[159]

Perhaps this describes the sort of picture one gains from Luke 1[160] but it seems a far cry from Paul's own theological position. Schlatter does see the negative aspect of boasting but he puts forward the somewhat unconvincing view that in Rom. 3.27 Paul attacked the Rabbinic view that good works can compensate for evil works.[161] His view of boasting is: "Wer die Sünde durch die neben ihr stehenden frommen Leistungen decken will, benützt die guten Werke zum eigenen Ruhm".[162] I wonder whether this is really what Paul had in mind. I suggest that Lk. 18.9-14 forms the best commentary. The Pharisee boasts yet there is nothing about covering evil deeds with good deeds.

I therefore conclude that Paul's critique of works of law in Rom. 1.18-3.20 is the human inability to keep the law. But in these verses it is hinted that the problem with justification by works is that human beings feel they have a claim on God and 3.20 does also suggest that Paul felt that human beings are not even intended to be justified by works of law. This view, however, is developed and made more explicit in Rom. 3.27ff. Further, human beings are *in principle* unable to keep the law, for they are all in Adam. I therefore question Wilckens' view:

---

[159] Schlatter, *Theologie der Apostel*, pp. 281-82.

[160] See the description given of Zacharias and Elizabeth in Lk. 1.6: ἦσαν δὲ δίκαιοι ἀμφότεροι ἐναντίον τοῦ θεοῦ, πορευόμενοι ἐν πάσαις ταῖς ἐντολαῖς καὶ δικαιώμασιν τοῦ κυρίου ἄμεμπτοι.

[161] Schlatter, *Theologie der Apostel*, p. 282: "Die Theorie des Rabbinats, wonach böses Handeln durch gutes Handeln aufgewogen werden kann und Gott schließlich berechnet, auf welcher Seite sich der Überschuß befinde, hat Paulus deshalb verworfen, weil sie gleichzeitig das Gesetz als Gottes heiligen Willen anruft, wenn das Werk des Gesetzes als Gerechtigkeit gelten soll, und es als nebensächlich entwertet, wenn seine Übertretung die Rechtfertigung nicht verhindern soll".

[162] Schlatter, *Theologie der Apostel*, p. 283.

Daß alle Menschen Sünder und der Sünde als dem Herrn der Welt unterworfen sind, ist nicht ein Urteil, das von jenseits irdischer Wirklichkeit her an diese herangetragen wäre, sondern das Ergebnis eines radikalen Ernstnehmens faktischen menschlichen Tuns, . . . [163]

Paul writes what he writes in Rom. 1.18-3.20 in the light of the cross, and this implies in the light of his theology that all are in Adam. Paul is not making an empirical statement.

Paul's view that no one can be justified by works has a certain parallel with the view that no one can know God through the created order. So in Rom. 1.19-21a Paul puts forward the view of people knowing God through creation; then in 1.21b-32 he says this is an impossible way, for any such knowledge has been lost, for "they became futile in their thinking and their senseless minds were darkened" (1.21b). Likewise, in Rom. 2.1-29 he puts forward the view that one can be justified by works; then in 3.9-20 he makes it clear that this way is impossible because all are under the power of sin. So we have this situation:

	Natural knowledge of God	Justification by works
Plan A:	Rom. 1.19-21a	Rom. 2.1-29
Plan B:	Rom. 1.21b-32	Rom. 3.9-20

But Paul, I have argued, also believed that human beings were not *intended* to be justified by works. The situation therefore of Rom. 2.1-29 (Plan A) whereby people can be justified on the basis of their works is therefore not an ideal plan. Perhaps Paul also saw the dangers in a natural theology and likewise questioned this "Plan A" as well. Such natural theology would be a *theologia gloriae*, for the cross of Christ is not considered. One is reminded of Luther's nineteenth and twentieth theses from the Heidelberg disputation, interestingly related to Rom. 1.20, 22 and 1 Cor. 1.21, 24 respectively.

Non ille digne Theologus dicitur, qui inuisibilia Dei, per ea, quae facta sunt, intellecta conspicit. Patet per eos, qui tales fuerunt, Et tamen ab Apostolo Roma. I.

---

[163] Wilckens, *Römer*, 1:178-79.

stulti uocantur. . . 20 Sed qui uisibilia (et) posteriora Dei, per passiones (et) crucem conspecta intelligit. Posteriora (et) uisibilia Dei sunt opposita inuisibilium, id est, humanitas, infirmitas, stulticia. Sicut I. Corinth. I. uocat infirmum (et) stultum Dei, Quia enim homines cognitione Dei ex operibus abusi sunt, uoluit rursus Deus ex passionibus cognosci (et) reprobare illam sapientiam inuisibilium, per sapientiam uisibilium, ut sic, qui Deum non coluerunt manifestum ex operibus, colerent absconditum in passionibus. Sicut ait I. Corinth. I. Quia in Dei sapientia non cognouit mundus Deum per sapientiam, placuit Deo per stulticiam praedicationis saluos facere credentes. Ita, ut nulli iam satis sit ac prosit, qui cognoscit Deum in gloria (et) maiestate, nisi cognoscat eundem in humilitate (et) ignominia crucis. . . .[164]

So building upon Luther, I believe that provided someone has faith in the crucified Christ, a natural theology (knowing Christ in his glory and majesty) does not have to be excluded.[165]

6. Justification sola fide, sola gratia

In the above discussion the question whether Romans 2 puts in question justification sola fide, sola gratia has been raised. As long as Romans 2 is seen in its proper place in Rom. 1.18-3.20, I do not believe one can question Paul's central idea of justification by faith and by grace alone. Justification is forensic language used to express the acquittal at the day of judgement. The verdict the Christian now receives (acquittal) *must* correspond to the verdict he receives at the last judgement. For someone such as myself who believes Paul had a basically coherent theology, if salvation is sola gratia, sola fide, then this salvation must be independent of works. As I argued above, if works are required for justification, faith is insufficient, and by implication God's grace is also insufficient. I therefore find the following idea of Schlier unacceptable for an understanding of Romans 2:

Mit dem von Christus gebrachten Glauben ist vielmehr das Mittel gegeben, vor dem Gericht in Werken des Glaubens oder im wirksamen Glauben zu bestehen.[166]

---

[164] H.-U. Delius (ed.), *Martin Luther: Studienausgabe Band 1*, Berlin 1979, pp. 207-8.

[165] See the discussion in chapter 3 above.

[166] H. Schlier, "Von den Juden: Römerbrief 2,1-29", in *Die Zeit der Kirche: Exegetische Aufsätze und Vorträge*, Freiburg: Herder 1956, 41 (38-47).

Such may be the view of Matthew's gospel[167] or the Epistle of James. It is, however, a far cry from Paul.

The Uppsala theologian Gillis P:son Wetter wrote this:

Es gibt also in der Welt zweierlei Arten von Menschen, und beide gehen mit unerbittlicher Konsequenz dem ihnen von Gott gestellten Ziele entgegen; und das Ziel heißt für die Christen περιποίησις σωτηρίας, für die anderen Menschen ὀργή.[168]

I believe these comments on 1 Thes. 5.9 sum up the essence of Paul's theology of judgement. For Christians there is περιποίησις σωτηρίας; for others there is wrath. Further, 1 Thes. 5.9-10 is saying that salvation is not dependent on sanctification.[169] Of course, good works are important, and Paul writes of "faith working through love" (Gal. 5.6). And in the dogmatic discussion it has been rightly emphasised that a sharp distinction between "justification" and "santification" is unhelpful.[170] But ultimately, salvation is not dependent on good works.[171] Many have believed that

---

[167] Schlier refers to Mt. 25.14-30 immediately before the above quotation.

[168] Wetter, *Vergeltungsgedanke*, pp. 42-43.

[169] See Lautenschlager, "Εἴτε γρηγορῶμεν εἴτε καθεύδωμεν". The text of 1 Thes. 5.9-10 is: ὅτι οὐκ ἔθετο ἡμᾶς ὁ θεὸς εἰς ὀργὴν ἀλλὰ εἰς περιποίησιν σωτηρίας διὰ τοῦ κυρίου ἡμῶν Ἰησοῦ Χριστοῦ 10 τοῦ ἀποθανόντος ὑπὲρ ἡμῶν, ἵνα εἴτε γρηγορῶμεν εἴτε καθεύδωμεν ἅμα σὺν αὐτῷ ζήσωμεν. The translation of the RSV is: "For God has not destined us for wrath, but to obtain salvation through our Lord Jesus Christ, 10 who died for us so that whether we wake or sleep we might live with him". Such a translation suggests that εἴτε γρηγορῶμεν εἴτε καθεύδωμεν simply means whether we are alive or dead (cf. 1 Thes. 4.13). But Lautenschlager makes the following crucial observations: 1. γρηγορεῖν means "to be awake" or "be alert". Never does it mean "be alive". 2. καθεύδειν and κοιμᾶσθαι can be used for natural sleeping. 3. Only κοιμᾶσθαι can be used in the metaphorical sense of "to be dead". There is no reference in the whole Greek literature to καθεύδειν meaning "to be dead". 4. καθεύδειν can mean "to be sleepy" in the sense of morally asleep.

[170] See the discussion above.

[171] Note that in the Konkordienformal 4 "Von guten Werken", 4.6 affirms: "Daß gute Werk dem wahrhaftigen Glauben, wann derselbige nicht ein toter, sondern ein lebendiger Glaub ist, gewißlich und ungezweifelt folgen als Früchte eines guten Baumes". But it does go on to say this (4.7): "Wir glauben, lehren und bekennen auch, daß die gute Werke gleich, sowohl wann von der Seligkeit gefragt wird, als im Artikel der Rechtfertigung vor Gott, *gänzlichen ausgeschlossen werden sollen*, wie der Apostel mit klaren Worten bezeugnet" (my emphasis). Then Rom. 4.6-8 and Eph. 2.8 are quoted (*BSELK* 787.19-39). Further, we read in 4.16: "Demnach verwerfen und verdammen wir diese Weise zu reden, wann gelehret und geschrieben wird, daß gute Werk nötig sein zur Seligkeit. Item, daß niemand jemals ohne gute Werk sei

Romans 2 creates problems for a view that stresses that salvation is independent of works.[172] But Romans 2, correctly understood in the context 1.18-3.20, does not contradict this sentiment. Justification is *sola gratia, sola fide, propter Christum.*

---

selig worden. Item, daß es unmuglich sei, ohne gute Werk selig werden" (*BSELK* 789.15-21).

[172] It is worth adding that Romans 2 was not just a problem for reformation theologians, but also for the Church Fathers (see K.H. Schelkle, *Paulus Lehrer der Väter*, Düsseldorf ²1959, (¹1956), p. 80). A number saw problems in reconciling Rom. 2.13 with Rom. 3.20. See, for example, Origen's treatment of this in his discussion of Rom. 2.11 (See Hammond Bammel, *Der Römerbriefkommentar des Origenes*, pp. 129-30). See also Apollinarius (in Staab, *Pauluskommentare*, p. 60).

Bibliography

1. Primary sources

1.1. *Bible*

Aland, Kurt, et al., (ed.), *The Greek New Testament*, Stuttgart: Deutsche Bibelgesellschaft [4]1993.

Aland, Kurt, et al., (ed.), *Novum Testamentum Graece*, Stuttgart: Deutsche Bibelstiftung [26]1979.

Aland, Kurt, (ed.), *Synopsis quattuor evangeliorum*, Stuttgart: Deutsche Bibelgesellschaft [13]1985, ([1]1963).

The Aramaic New Testament, Estrangelo Script, New Knoxville, Ohio: American Christian Press 1983.

Die Bibel nach der Übersetzung Martin Luthers mit Apokryphen, Stuttgart: Deutsche Bibelgesellschaft 1984.

Biblia sacra iuxta vulgatam versionem, 2 vols, Stuttgart: Deutsche Bibelgesellschaft 1983.

Elliger, K. - Rudolph, W., et al., (ed.), *Biblia Hebraica Stuttgartensia*, Stuttgart: Deutsche Bibelstiftung 1967/77.

Field, F., (ed.), *Origenis Hexaplorum quae supersunt*, Oxford: Clarendon Press 1875.

Frede, Hermann Josef, (ed.), *Ein neuer Paulustext und Kommentar, Bd II: Die Texte* (Vetus Latina 8), Freiburg: Herder 1974.

Die heilige Schrift des Alten und des Neuen Testaments, Zürich: Verlag der Zürcher Bibel 1987.

The Holy Bible: Revised Standard Version with Apocrypha, New York/Glasgow/London/Toronto/ Sydney/Auckland: Collins 1973.

The Holy Bible: New Revised Standard Version with Apocrypha, Nashville: Thomas Nelson Publishers 1989.

Luther, Martin, *Die gantze Heilige Schrift Deudsch (Wittenberg 1945)*, edited by Heinz Blanke and Hans Volz, 3 vols, München: Rogner & Bernhard 1972.

Menge, Hermann, (ed.), *Die heilige Schrift*, Stuttgart: Württembergische Bibelanstalt 1926.

Moffatt, James, (ed.), *The New Testament: A New Translation*, London: Hodder & Stoughton 1913.

The New Covenant Commonly Called the New Testament: Peshitta Aramaic Text With a Hebrew Translation, Jerusalem: The Bible Society 1986.

The New English Bible with Apocrypha, Oxford: OUP/Cambridge: CUP 1970.

Rahlfs, Alfred, (ed.), *Septuaginta: Id est Vetus Testamentum graece iuxta LXX interpretes*, 2 vols, Stuttgart: Württembergische Bibelanstalt 1935.

The Septuagint Version of the Old Testament with an English Translation, London: S. Bagster (n.d.).

Swete, Henry Barclay, (ed.), *The Old Testament in Greek According to the Septuagint*, 3 vols, Cambridge: CUP 1 1925 (repr.), ([1]1887); 2 1922 ([1]1891); 3 1912 ([1]1894).

Syriac Bible, United Bible Societies 1979.

Syriac NT and Psalms, Stuttgart: United Bible Societies 1993.

Tischendorf, Constantinus, (ed.), *Novum Testamentum Graece*, 4 vols, Leipzig 1884-94.

Westcott, Brooke Foss — Hort, Fenton John Anthony, (ed.), *The New Testament in the Original Greek*, London: Macmillan 1956 (repr.), ([1]1881).

1.2. *Apocrypha, Pseudepigrapha and Hellenistic Jewish literature*

Box, G.H., (ed.), *The Apocalypse of Ezra (II Esdras II-XIV)* (Translations of Early Documents, Series I: Palestinian Jewish Texts), London: SPCK 1917.

Charles, R.H., (ed.), *The Apocrypha and Pseudepigrapha of the Old Testament in English*, Oxford: OUP 1977 (repr.), ([1]1913).

Charles, R.H., (ed.), *The Greek Version of the Testaments of the Twelve Patriarchs*, Oxford: OUP/Darmstadt: Wissenschaftliche Buchgesellschaft [2]1960 ([1]1908).

Charlesworth, James H., (ed.), *The Old Testament Pseudepigrapha*, 2 vols, London: Darton, Longman & Todd 1 1983; 2 1985

Colson, F.H. — Whitaker, G.H. — Marcus, R. — Earp, J.W., (ed.), *Philo* (LCL), 10 vols with 2 supplements, London: William Heinemann/Cambridge, Mass.: Harvard University Press 1929-62.

Dedering, S, (ed.), *Apocalypse of Baruch* (VTS 4.3), Leiden: E.J. Brill 1973.

de Jonge, Marinus, (ed.), *The Testaments of the Twelve Patriarchs: A Critical Edition of the Greek Text* (PVTG 1.2), Leiden: E.J. Brill 1978.

Kmosko, Michael, (ed.), *Liber apocalypseos Baruch filii Neriae*, PS 1.2:1058-1306, Paris 1907.

Lévi, Israel, (ed.), *The Hebrew Text of the Book of Ecclesiasticus* (SSS 3), Leiden: E.J. Brill 1951 (repr.), ([1]1904).

Picard, J.-C., (ed.), *Apocalypsis Baruchi Graece* (PVTG 2), Leiden: E.J. Brill 1967.

Thackeray, H. St. John — Marcus, Ralph — Wikgren, Allen — Feldman, Louis H., (ed.), *Josephus* (LCL), 9 vols, London: William Heinemann/Cambridge, Mass.: Harvard University Press 1926-65.

1.3. *Qumran literature*

Allegro, John M. (with Arnold A. Anderson) (ed.), *Discoveries in the Judaean Desert of Jordan V: Qumrân Cave 4, I (4Q158-4Q186)*, Oxford: Clarendon Press 1968.

Baillet, Maurice, (ed.), *Discoveries in the Judaean Desert VII: Qumrân Grotte 4, III (4Q482-4Q520)*, Oxford: Clarendon Press 1982.

Barthélemy, D. — Milik, J.T., (ed.), *Discoveries in the Judaean Desert I: Qumran Cave I*, Oxford: Clarendon Press 1956 (repr.), (¹1955).

Lohse, Eduard, (ed.), *Die Texte aus Qumran, Hebräisch und Deutsch mit Masoretischer Punktation, Übersetzung, Einführung und Anmerkungen*, Darmstadt: Wissenschaftliche Buchgesellschaft ⁴1986, (¹1964).

Maier, Johann, (ed.), *Die Tempelrolle vom Toten Meer* (UTB 829), München/Basel: Ernst Reinhardt Verlag 1978.

Martínez, F.G., (ed.), *The Dead Sea Scrolls Translated* ET, Leiden: E.J. Brill 1994.

Qimron, Elisha — Strugnell, John, (ed.), *Discoveries in the Judaean Desert X: Qumran Cave 4, V: Miqṣat Ma'aśe Ha-Torah* (DJD 10), Oxford: OUP 1994.

Vermes, Geza, (ed.), *The Dead Sea Scrolls in English*, Sheffield: JSOT Press ³1987, (¹1962).

1.4. *Rabbinic literature*

Braude, William G., (ed.), *The Midrash on the Psalms* (YJS 13), 2 vols, New Haven: Yale University Press 1959.

Braude, William G., (ed.), *Pesikta Rabbati* (YJS 18), 2 vols, New Haven/London: Yale University Press 1968.

Buber, S., (ed.), *Midrash Tehillim*, Jerusalem 1966 (repr.), (¹1891, Wilna).

Clarke, E.G., et al., (ed.), *Targum Pseudo-Jonathan of the Pentateuch: Text and Concordance*, Hoboken, N.J.: Ktav 1984.

Cohen, A., (ed.), *Midrash Rabbah: Ecclesiastes*, London/New York: Soncino ³1983.

Cohen, A., (ed.), *Midrash Rabbah: Lamentations*, London/New York: Soncino ³1983.

Cohen, A., (ed.), *The Minor Tractates of the Talmud (Massekoth Ketannoth)*, London: Soncino 1 ²1971, (¹1965); 2 ²1971, (¹1965).

Danby, Herbert, (ed.), *The Mishnah*, Oxford: OUP 1985 (repr.), (¹1933).

le Déaut, Roger, (ed.), *Targum du pentateuque, tome I: Genèse* (SC 245), Paris: Les éditions du Cerf 1978.

le Déaut, Roger, (ed.), *Targum du pentateuque, tome II: Exode et lévitique* (SC 256), Paris: Les éditions du Cerf 1979.

Díez Macho, Alejandro, (ed.), *Ms. Neophyti 1 Tomo I: Génesis* (Texts y etudios 7), Madrid: Consejo superior de investigaciones científicas 1968.

Díez Macho, Alejandro, (ed.), *Ms. Neophyti 1 Tomo II: Éxodo* (Texts y etudios 8), Madrid: Consejo superior de investigaciones científicas 1970.

Drazin, Israel, (ed.), *Targum Onkelos to Deuteronomy: An English Translation of the Text With Analysis and Commentary (Based on A. Sperber's Edition)*, New York: Ktav 1982.

Epstein, I., (ed.), *The Babylonian Talmud*, 35 vols, London: Soncino 1938-52.

Epstein, I., (ed.), *The Hebrew-English Edition of the Babylonian Talmud*, 30 vols, London: Soncino 1994 (repr.).

Etheridge, J.W., (ed.), *The Targums of Onkelos and Jonathan Ben Uzziel on the Pentateuch with the Fragments of the Jerusalem Targum (from the Chaldee)*, New York: Ktav 1968.

Freedman, H. — Simon, Maurice, (ed.), *Midrash Rabbah*, 10 vols, London/New York: Soncino [3]1983.

Freedman, H., (ed.), *Midrash Rabbah: Genesis*, 2 vols, London/New York: Soncino [3]1983.

Friedlander, G., (ed.), *Pirke de Rabbi Eliezer*, New York: Sepher Hermon Press [4]1981 ([1]1916).

Ginsburger, M., (ed.), *Pseudo-Jonathan (Thargum Jonathan ben Usiël zum Pentateuch)*, Berlin: S. Calvary & Co. 1903.

Hammer, Reuven, (ed.), *Sifre: A Tannaitic Commentary on the Book of Deuteronomy* (YJS 24), New Haven/London: Yale University Press 1986.

Hoffmann, D., (ed.), *Midrasch Tannaim zum Deuteronomium*, Berlin 1908-9.

Hoffmann, David — Cohn, John — Auerbach, Moses, (ed.), *Mischnajot: Die sechs Ordnungen der Mischna. Hebräischer Text mit Punktation, deutscher Übersetzung und Erklärung, Teil VI: Ordnung Toharot*, Basel: Victor Goldschmidt Verlag [3]1968.

Horovitz, H.S., (ed.), *Siphre d'be Rab* (Corpus Tannaiticum, sectio tertia, pars tertia), Leipzig: Gustav Fock 1917.

Horowitz, Charles, (ed.), *Der Jerusalemer Talmud in deutscher Übersetzung. Band I: Berakhoth*, Tübingen: J.C.B. Mohr (Paul Siebeck) 1975.

Hyman, A. — Shiloni, J, (ed.), *Yalqut Shim'oni: Bemidbar*, Jerusalem: Mossad Harav Kook 1986.

Klein, Michael L., (ed.), *The Fragment Targums of the Pentateuch According to their Extant Sources* (AnBib 76), 2 vols, Rome: Biblical Institute Press 1980.

Lauterbach, Jacob Z., (ed.), *Mekilta de-Rabbi Ishmael* (SLJC), 3 vols, Philadelphia: The Jewish Publication Society of America 1 [2]1949, ([1]1933); 2 [2]1949, ([1]1933); 3 [2]1949, ([1]1935).

Lehrman, S.M., (ed.), *Midrash Rabbah: Exodus*, London/New York: Soncino [3]1983.

Lieberman, Saul, (ed.), *The Tosephta According to Codex Vienna with Variants from Codices Erfurt, Genizah Mss. and Editio Princeps (Venice 1521)*, 5 vols, New York: Louis Rabinowitz Institute in Rabbinics/Jewish Theological Seminary of America 1955-88.

Midrash Rabbah, 3 vols, Jerusalem 1923 (repr.), (Wilna [1]1887).

Neusner, Jacob, (ed.), *Sifre to Deuteronomy: An Analytical Translation* (BJS 98 and 101), 2 vols, Atlanta: Scholars Press 1987.

Neusner, Jacob, (ed.), *Sifré to Numbers: An American Translation and Explanation* (BJS 118-19), 2 vols, Atlanta: Scholars Press 1986.

Neusner, Jacob, (ed.), *The Tosefta. Translated from the Hebrew*, 6 vols, New York: Ktav 1977-86.

Rabinowitz, L., (ed.), *Midrash Rabbah: Ruth*, London/New York: Soncino [3]1983.

Rabbinovicz, R.N.N., *Sefer dikdukei sofrim. Variae Lectiones in Mischnam et in Talmud Babylonicum*, 16 vols, Munich/Mainz/Przemysl 1866-97.

Rabbinowitz, J., (ed.), *Midrash Rabbah: Deuteronomy*, London/New York: Soncino [3]1983.

Simon, Maurice, (ed.), *Midrash Rabbah: Song of Songs*, London/New York: Soncino [3]1983.

Slotki, Judah J., (ed.), *Midrash Rabbah: Numbers*, 2 vols, London/New York: Soncino [3]1983.

Salomonsen, Børge, (ed.), *Die Tosephta. Seder IV: Nezikin 3: Sanhedrin - Makkot* (RT IV.3), Stuttgart/Berlin/Köln/Mainz: Verlag W. Kohlhammer 1976.

Sperber, Alexander, (ed.), *The Bible in Aramaic*, 5 vols, Leiden: E.J. Brill 1959-73.

Stenning, J.F., (ed.), *The Targum of Isaiah*, Oxford: OUP 1949.

Taylor, Charles, *Sayings of the Jewish Fathers* (LJC), New York: Ktav [2]1969, ([1]1897).

1.5. *Early Christian literature*

Bernardi, Jean, (ed.), *Grégoire de Nazianze, Discours 4-5: Contre Julien* (SC 309), Paris: Les éditions du Cerf 1983.

Borret, Marcel, (ed.), *Origène: Contre Celse* (SC 132, 136, 147, 150), Paris: Les éditions du Cerf 1:1967; 2:1968; 3-4:1969.

Chadwick, Henry, (ed.), *Origen: Contra Celsum*, Cambridge: CUP 1965 (repr.), ([1]1953).

Evans, Ernst, (ed.), *Adversus Marcionem, Books 4 and 5*, Oxford: Clarendon Press 1972.

Falls, Thomas B., (ed.), *Saint Justin Martyr* (The Fathers of the Church 6), Washington, D.C.: The Catholic University of America Press 1965 (repr.), ([1]1948).

Ferrar, W.J., (ed.), *Eusebius of Caesarea: The Proof of the Gospel being the Demonstratio Evangelica* (Translation of Christian Literature, Series I: Greek Texts), 2 vols, London: SPCK/New York: Macmillan 1920.

Goldbacher, A., (ed.), *S. Aureli Augustini Hipponiensis Episcopi Epistulae* (CSEL 34), Prague/Vienna: F. Tempsky/Leipzig: G. Freytag 1895.

Goodspeed, Edgar J., (ed.), *Die ältesten Apologeten: Texte mit kurzen Einleitungen*, Göttingen: Vandenhoeck & Ruprecht 1914.

Hall, Stuart George, (ed.), *Melito of Sardis: On Pascha and fragments* (OECT), Oxford: OUP 1979.

Hammond Bammel, Caroline P., (ed.), *Der Römerbriefkommentar des Origenes: Kritische Ausgabe der Übersetzung Rufins, Buch 1-3* (Vetus Latina 16), Freiburg: Herder 1990.

Hartel, Guilelmus, (ed.), *S. Thascii Caecilii Cypriani, Opera Omnia* (CSEL 3.1), Prague/Vienna: F. Tempsky/Leipzig: G. Freytag 1868.

Heikel, I.A., (ed.), *Eusebius Werke, Band. 6: Die Demonstratio evangelica* (GCS), Leipzig: J.C. Hinrichs'sche Buchhandlung 1913.

Hennecke, E. - Schneemelcher, W., (ed.), *New Testament Apocrypha* ET, 2 vols, London: SCM 1973-74, ([1]1963-65).

Klostermann, Erich, (ed.), *Origenes Werke: Dritter Band* (GCS), Leipzig: J.C. Hinrichs'sche Buchhandlung 1961.

Koetschau, Paul, (ed.), *Origenes Werke: Erster Band* (GCS), Leipzig: J.C. Hinrichs'sche Buchhandlung 1899.

Koetschau, Paul, (ed.), *Origenes Werke: Zweiter Band* (GCS), Leipzig: J.C. Hinrichs'sche Buchhandlung 1899.

Lake, Kirsopp, (ed.), *Apostolic Fathers* (LCL), 2 vols, London: William Heinemann/Cambridge, Mass.: Harvard University Press 1985 (repr.), ([1]1912).

Lake, Kirsopp, (ed.), *Eusebius: The Ecclesiastical History* (LCL), 2 vols, London: William Heinemann/Cambridge, Mass.: Harvard University Press 1 1965; 2 1964.

Migne, Jacques-Paul, (ed.), *Patrologiae cursus completus*, Paris 1845ff.

Mras, Karl, *Eusebius Werke, Bd. 8: Die Praeparatio Evangelica* (GCS), 2 vols, Berlin: Akademie-Verlag 1954-56.

Pusey, P.E., (ed.), *Sancti patris nostri Cyrilli Archiepischopi Alexanrini in D. Joannis Evangelium Vol. III*, Bruxelles: Culture et civilisation 1965 (repr.), ([1]1872).

Roberts, Alexander — Donaldson, James — Coxe, A. Cleveland, (ed.). *Ante-Nicene Fathers*, 10 vols, Peabody: Hendrickson 1994 (repr.), ([1]1885-1896) (repr. of vol. 10 contains a newly prepared *Annotated Index of Authors and Works of the Ante-Nicene, Nicene and Post-Nicene Fathers, First and Second Series*).

Rousseau, Adelin, (ed.), *Irénée de Lyon: Contre les hérésies IV* (SC 100.1-2), Paris: Les éditions du Cerf 1965.

Schaff, Philip, (ed.), *Nicene and Post-Nicene Fathers: First Series*, 14 vols, Peabody: Hendrickson 1994 (repr.), ([1]1886-1889).

Schaff, Philip, — Wace, Henry, (ed.), *Nicene and Post-Nicene Fathers: Second Series*, 14 vols, Peabody: Hendrickson 1994 (repr.), ([1]1890-1900).

Souter, Alexander, (ed.), *Pelagius's Exposition of Thirteen Epistles of St Paul: II. Text* (TaS 9.2), Cambridge: CUP 1926.

Stählin, Otto, (ed.), *Clemens Alexandrinus, Bd 2* (GCS), Leipzig: J.C. Hinrichs'sche Buchhandlung 1906.

Stählin, Otto, (ed.), *Clemens Alexandrinus, Bd 3* (GCS), Leipzig: J.C. Hinrichs'sche Buchhandlung 1909.

Urba, C.F. — Zycha, I., (ed.), *Sancti Aureli Augustini opera (Sect. VIII pars I)* (CSEL 60), Vienna: F. Tempsky/Leipzig: G. Freytag 1913.

Vogels, H.I., (ed.), *Ambrosiastri qui dicitur commentarius in epistulas Paulinas, pars 1: In epistulam ad Romanos* (CSEL 81.1), Vienna: Hoelder/Pichler/Tempsky 1961.

1.6. *Greek and Roman literature*

Arnim, Ioannes ab (ed.), *Stoicorum veterum fragmenta*, 4 vols, Stuttgart: In aedibus B.G. Teubner [2]1964 ([1]1903-24).

Basore, John W., (ed.), *Seneca, Moral Essays III, De Beneficiis* (LCL), London: William Heinemann/Cambridge, Mass.: Harvard University Press 1958 (repr.), ([1]1935).

Bury, R.G., (ed.), *Plato VII: Timaeus, Critias, Cleitophon, Menexenus, Epistles* (LCL), Cambridge, Mass./London: Harvard University Press 1989, ([1]1929).

Bury, R.G., (ed.), *Plato X: Laws Books I-VI* (LCL), Cambridge, Mass./London: Harvard University Press 1994, ([1]1926).

Bury, R.G., (ed.), *Plato XI: Laws Books VII-XII* (LCL), Bury, R.G., (ed.), *Plato X: Laws Books I-VI* (LCL), London: William Heinemann/Cambridge, Mass.: Harvard University Press 1984, ([1]1926).

Corcoran, Thomas H., (ed.), *Seneca X: Naturales quaestiones II* (LCL), London: William Heinemann/Cambridge, Mass.: Harvard University Press 1972.

Diels, Hermann — Kranz, Walther, (ed.), *Die Fragmente der Vorsokratiker Band 1*, Berlin: Weidmannsche Verlagsbuchhandlung [6]1951, ([1]1903).

Diels, Hermann — Kranz, Walther, (ed.), *Die Fragmente der Vorsokratiker: Band 2*, Dublin/Zürich: Weidmann [12]1966, ([1]1903).

Falconer, William Armistead, (ed.), *Cicero XX: De senectute, De amicitia, De divinatione* (LCL), Cambridge, Mass./London: Harvard University Press 1992, ([1]1923).

Fowler, Harold North, (ed.), *Plato I: Euthyphro, Apology, Crito, Phaedo, Phaedrus* (LCL), Cambridge, Mass./London: Harvard University Press 1995, ([1]1914).

Fowler, Harold North — Lamb, W.R.M., (ed.), *Plato VIII: Statesman, Philebus, Ion* (LCL), Cambridge, Mass./London: Harvard University Press 1990, ([1]1925).

Forster, E.S. — Furley, D.J., (ed.), *Aristotle: On Sophistical Refutations; On Coming-to-be and Passing-away; On the Cosmos*, London: William Heinemann/Cambridge, Mass.: Harvard University Press 1955.

Freese, John Henry, (ed.), *Aristotle: The "Art" of Rhetoric* (LCL), London: William Heinemann/Cambridge, Mass.: Harvard University Press 1959.

Haines, C.R., (ed.), *Marcus Aurelius* (LCL), Cambridge, Mass./London: Harvard University Press 1994 (repr.), ([1]1916).

Hicks, R.D., (ed.), *Diogenes Laertius: Lives of Eminent Philosophers* (LCL), 2 vols, London: William Heinemann/Cambridge, Mass.: Harvard University Press 1 1950 (repr.), ([1]1925); 2 1995 (repr.), ([1]1925).

Jackson, John, (ed.), *Tacitus: The Histories, the Annals* (LCL), 4 vols, London: William Heinemann/Cambridge, Mass.: Harvard University Press 1962-63.

Jones, W.H.S., (ed.), *Pausanias: Description of Greece I: Books I and II* (LCL), London: William Heinemann/Cambridge, Mass.: Harvard University Press 1954 (repr.), ([1]1918).

Keyes, C.W., (ed.), *Cicero: De re publica, De legibus* (LCL), Cambridge, Mass./London: Harvard University Press 1994, ([1]1928).

Lacy, Phillip H. de - Einarson, Benedict, (ed.), *Plutarch's Moralia vol. VII*, London: William Heinemann/Cambridge, Mass.: Harvard University Press 1959.

Lloyd-Jones, Hugh, (ed.), *Sophocles* (LCL), 2 vols, Cambridge, Mass./London: Harvard University Press 1994.

Marchant, E.C. — Todd, O.J., (ed.), *Xenophon: Memorabilia, Oeconomicus, Symposium, Apology* (LCL), Cambridge, Mass./London: Harvard University Press 1992 (repr.), ([1]1923).

Nock, A.D. — Festugière, A.-J., (ed.), *Corpus hermeticum*, 4 vols, Paris: Société de'édition 'les belles lettres' 1945-54.

Oldfather, W.A., (ed.), *Epictetus* (LCL), 2 vols, London: William Heinemann/Cambridge, Mass.: Harvard University Press 1 1925; 2 1928.

Pease, Arthur Stanley, (ed.), "M. Tullii Ciceronis: De divinatione liber primus", *University of Illinois Studies in Languages and Literature* 6 (1920) 3-338.

Rackham, H., (ed.), *Cicero: De natura deorum, Academica*, London: William Heinemann/Cambridge, Mass.: Harvard University Press [2]1951, ([1]1933).

Rolfe, J.C., (ed.), *Suetonius* (LCL), 2 vols, London: William Heinemann/Cambridge, Mass.: Harvard University Press 1964-79.

Rouse, W.H.D. — Smith, Martin F., (ed.), *Lucretius: On the Nature of Things* (LCL), Cambridge, Mass./London: Harvard University Press 1992 (repr.), ([1]1975).

Schlesinger, Alfred C., (ed.), *Livy XIII: From the Founding of the City, Books 43-45* (LCL), London: William Heinemann/Cambridge, Mass.: Harvard University Press 1951.

Shorey, Paul, (ed.), *Plato: The Republic vol. 2: Books VI-X* (LCL), London: William Heinemann/Cambridge, Mass.: Harvard University Press 1946 (repr), (¹1935).

Smith, Charles Forster, (ed.), *Thucydides: History of the Peloponnesian War* (LCL), 4 vols, London: William Heinemann/Cambridge, Mass.: Harvard University Press 1962-66.

Tredennick, Hugh, (ed.), *Aristotle: Metaphysics Books I-IX* (LCL), Cambridge, Mass./London: Harvard University Press 1996 (repr.), (¹1933).

Tredennick, Hugh — Armstrong, G. Cyril, (ed.), *Aristotle: Metaphysics Books X-XIV, Oeconomica, Magna Moralia* (LCL), Cambridge, Mass./London: Harvard University Press 1990 (repr.), (¹1935).

Way, A.S., (ed.), *Euripides I: Iphigeneia at Aulis, Rhesus, Hecuba, Daughters of Troy, Helen* (LCL), London: William Heinemann/Cambridge, Mass.: Harvard University Press 1988 (repr.), (¹1912).

2. Reference works and exegetical aids

Allenbach, J., et al., *Biblia Patristica: Index des citations et allusions bibliques dans la littérature patristique*, 4 vols with Supplement (Philon d'Alexandrie), Paris: Éditions du centre national de la recherche scientifique 1975-87.

Altaner, Berthold - Stuiber, Alfred, *Patrologie: Leben, Schriften und Lehre der Kirchenväter*, Freiburg/Basel/Wien: Herder ⁸1978.

Bachmann, H. — Slaby, W.A., *Concordance to the Novum Testamentum Graece*, Berlin/New York: Walter de Gruyter ³1987.

Balz, Horst — Schneider, Gerhard, (ed), *Exegetical Dictionary of the New Testament* ET, 3 vols, Grand Rapids: Wm. B. Eerdmans 1990-93.

Bauer, Walter, *Griechisch-deutsches Wörterbuch zu den Schriften des Neuen Testaments und der frühchristlichen Literatur*, Berlin: Walter de Gruyter ⁶1988 (völlig neu bearbeitet von Kurt und Barbara Aland).

Bauer, W. — Arndt, W.F. — Gingrich, F.W., *Greek-English Lexicon of the New Testament and Other Early Christian Literature*, Chicago and London: University of Chicago Press 1961.

Blass, F. — Debrunner, A., *A Greek Grammar of the New Testament*, translated and revised by R.W. Funk, Chicago/London: University of Chicago Press 1961.

Botterweck, G. Johannes — Ringgren, Helmer, (ed.), *Theological Dictionary of the Old Testament* ET, Grand Rapids: Wm B. Eerdmans ²1974ff.

Bromiley, Geoffrey W., (ed.), *The International Standard Bible Encyclopedia*, 4 vols, Grand Rapids: Wm. B. Eermanns 1979-88.

Brown, Colin, (ed.), *The New International Dictionary of New Testament Theology*, 3 vols, Exeter: Paternoster 1975-78.

Brown, F. — Driver, S.R. — Briggs, C.A., *A Hebrew and English Lexicon of the Old Testament based on the Lexicon of W. Gesenius*, Oxford: Clarendon Press 1978 (repr.).

Buchberger. Michael, (ed.), *Lexikon für Theologie und Kirche*, 10 vols, Freiburg: Herder 1930-38.

Buttrick, George A., (ed.), *The Interpreter's Bible*, 12 vols, New York/Nashville: Abingdon-Cokesbury Press 1952-57.

Buttrick, George A., (ed.), *The Interpreter's Dictionary of the Bible*, 4 vols, New York/Nashville: Abingdon-Cokesbury Press 1962 (supplement 1976).

Cremer, Hermann, *Biblico-Theological Lexicon of New Testament Greek* ET, Edinburgh: T. & T. Clark ⁴1895.

Cremer, Hermann, *Biblisch-Theologisches Wörterbuch des neutestamentlichen Griechisch* (bearb. von J. Kögel), Gotha ¹¹1923.

Cross, F.L. — Livingstone, E.A., (ed.), *The Oxford Dictionary of the Christian Church*, Oxford: OUP ²1978, (¹1957).

Dalman, Gustaf H., *Grammatik des jüdisch-palästinischen Aramäisch und aramäische Dialektproben*, Darmstadt: Wissenschaftliche Buchgesellschaft 1981 (repr.), (²1905).

Davies, W.D. — Finkelstein, Louis, (ed.), *The Cambridge History of Judaism*, 2 vols, Cambridge: CUP 1984-89.

Denis, Albert-Marie, (ed.), *Concordance grecque des Pseudépigraphes d'Ancien Testament*, Louvain-la-Neuve: Université catholique de Louvain 1987.

Encyclopaedia Judaica, 16 vols, Jerusalem: Keter Publishing House 1978 (repr.), (¹1971-72).

Fitzmyer, Joseph A., *An Introductory Bibliography for the Study of Scripture* (Subsidia Biblica 3), Rome: Biblical Institute Press 1981.

France, R.T., (ed.), *A Bibliographical Guide to New Testament Research*, Sheffield: JSOT Press 1979.

Frede, Hermann Josef, (ed.), *Ein neuer Paulustext und Kommentar, Bd I: Untersuchungen* (Vetus Latina 7), Freiburg: Herder 1973.

Freedman, David Noel, (ed.), *The Anchor Bible Dictionary*, 6 vols, New York: Doubleday 1992.

Galling, Kurt, (ed.), *Die Religion in Geschichte und Gegenwart: Handwörterbuch für Theologie und Religionswissenschaft*, 7 vols, Tübingen: J.C.B. Mohr (Paul Siebeck) ³1957-65.

Gunkel, Hermann — Zscharnack, Leopold, (ed.), *Die Religion in Geschichte und Gegenwart: Handwörterbuch für Theologie und Religionswissenschaft*, 7 vols, Tübingen: J.C.B. Mohr (Paul Siebeck) ²1927-32.

Hatch, Edwin — Redpath, Henry A., *A Concordance to the Septuagint*, 2 vols, Grand Rapids: Baker Book House 1983 (repr.), (¹1897).

Hauck, Albert, (ed.), *Realencyklopädie für protestantische Theologie und Kirche*, 22 vols, Leipzig: J.C. Hinrichs'sche Buchhandlung ³1896-1909.

Hawthorne, Gerald F. — Martin, Ralph P., (ed.), *Dictionary of Paul and his Letters*, Leicester: IVP 1993.

Höfer, J. — Rahner, K., (ed.), *Lexikon für Theologie und Kirche*, 11 vols, Freiburg: Herder 1957-67.

Hornblower, Simon — Spawforth, Antony, (ed.), *The Oxford Classical Dictionary*, Oxford: OUP ³1996.

Jastrow, Marcus, *A Dictionary of the Targumim, the Talmud Babli and Yerushalmi, and the Midrashic Literature*, New York: Judaica Press 1982 (repr.), ¹1950.

Jenni, Ernst — Westermann, Claus, (ed.), *Theologisches Handwörterbuch zum Alten Testament*, 2 vols, München: Chr. Kaiser Verlag/Zürich: Theologischer Verlag 1 1971; 2 1976.

Kautzsch, E., (ed.), *Gesenius' Hebrew Grammar* ET, Oxford: Clarendon Press ²1910 (revised by A.E. Cowley).

Kittel, G. — Friedrich, G., (ed.), *Theological Dictionary of the New Testament* ET, 10 vols, Grand Rapids: Wm B. Eerdmans 1964-76.

Kittel, G. — Friedrich, G., (ed.), *Theologisches Wörterbuch zum Neuen Testament*, 10 vols, Stuttgart: W. Kohlhammer Verlag 1933-78.

Kluge, Friedrich, *Etymologisches Wörterbuch der deutschen Sprache* (neu bearbeitet von Elmar Seebold), Berlin/New York: Walter de Gruyter ²²1989.

Koehler, L. — Baumgartner, W., *Lexicon in Veteris Testamenti libros*, Leiden: E.J. Brill 1953.

Koehler, L. — Baumgartner, W. - Stamm, J.J., *Hebräisches und Aramäisches Lexikon zum Alten Testament*, 3 vols, Leiden: E.J. Brill 1967-83.

Krause, G. — Müller, G., (ed.), *Theologische Realenzyklopädie*, 17 vols, Berlin/New York: Walter de Gruyter 1977-88.

Krauß, Samuel, *Griechische und lateinische Lehnwörter im Talmud, Midrasch und Targum*, 2 vols, Berlin: S. Calvary & Co. 1898-99.

Kuhn, Karl Georg, *Konkordanz zu den Qumrantexten*, Göttingen: Vandenhoeck & Ruprecht 1960.

Kuhn, Karl Georg, "Nachträge zur 'Konkordanz zu den Qumrantexten'", *RQ* 4 (1963-64) 163-234.

Lampe, G.W.H., (ed.), *Patristic Greek Lexicon*, Oxford: Clarendon Press 1961-68.

Leisegang, Joannes, *Indices ad Philonis Alexandrini opera* (Philonis Alexandrini: Opera quae supersunt 7), Berlin: Walter de Gruyter 1926.

Levy, Jacob, *Wörterbuch über die Talmudim und Midraschim*, 4 vols, Darmstadt: Wissenschaftliche Buchgesellschaft 1963.

Lewis, Charlton T. — Short, Charles, *A Latin Dictionary*, Oxford: Clarendon Press ²1962 (¹1879).

Liddell, H.G. — Scott, R., *Greek-English Lexicon*, Oxford: Clarendon Press 1985 ([1]1843) (revised by H.S. Jones and R. McKenzie with a Supplement 1968).

Lisowsky, Gerhard, *Kondordanz zum Hebräischen Alten Testament*, Stuttgart: Deutsche Bibelgesellschaft [2]1966, ([1]1958).

Lust, J. — Eynikel, E. — Hauspie, K. — Chamberlain, G., *A Greek-English Lexicon of the Septuagint: Part I, A-I*, Stuttgart: Deutsche Bibelgesellschaft 1992.

Mayer, Günter, *Index Philoneus*, Berlin/New York: Walter de Gruyter 1974.

Metzger, Bruce M., *A Textual Commentary on the Greek New Testament*, London/New York: United Bible Societies 1971.

Morgenthaler, Robert, *Statistik des neutestamentlichen Wortschatzes*, Zürich/ Frankfurt am M.: Gotthelf-Verlag 1958.

Moule, C.F.D., *An Idiom Book of New Testament Greek*, Cambridge: CUP [2]1977, ([1]1953).

Moulton, James Hope — Turner, Nigel, — Howard, Wilbert Francis, *A Grammar of New Testament Greek*, 4 vols, Edinburgh: T. & T. Clark 1978-80 (repr.), ([1]1908-76).

Nöldeke, Theodor, *Kurzgefasste syrische Grammatik*, Darmstadt: Wissenschaftliche Buchgesellschaft 1966 (repr.), ([1]1880).

Parker, T.H.L., *Commentaries on the Epistle to the Romans 1532-1542*, Edinburgh: T. & T. Clark 1986.

Paulys Realencyclopädie der classischen Altertumswissenschaft, Neue Bearbeitung von Georg Wissowa, Wilhelm Kroll, Karl Mittelhaus et al., Stuttgart: Alfred Druckenmüller Verlag 1894ff., 2. Reihe 1914ff.

Pfeifer, Wolfgang, (ed.), *Etymologisches Wörterbuch des Deutschen*, 3 vols, Berlin: Akademie-Verlag 1989.

Pritchard, James B., (ed.), *The Ancient Near East in Pictures*, Princeton: Princeton University Press [2]1969, ([1]1954).

Rehkopf, Friedrich, *Septuaginta-Vokabular*, Göttingen: Vandenhoeck & Ruprecht 1989.

Rengstorf, Karl Heinrich, *A Complete Concordance to Flavius Josephus*, 4 vols, Leiden: E.J. Brill 1973-83.

Radermacher, Ludwig, *Neutestamentliche Grammatik: Das Griechisch des Neuen Testaments im Zusammenhang mit der Volkssprache* (HzNT 1), Tübingen: J.C.B. Mohr (Paul Siebeck) [2]1925.

Robinson, Theodore H., *Syriac Grammar*, Oxford: Clarendon Press [4]1962 (ed. by L.H. Brockington), ([1]1915).

Rosenthal, Franz, *A Grammar of Biblical Aramaic* (PLO 5), Wiesbaden: Otto Harrassowitz 1983 (repr.), ([1]1961).

Safrai, Shmuel, (ed.), *The Literature of the Sages. First Part: Oral Tora, Halakha, Mishna, Tosefta, Talmud, External Tractates* (CRINT 2.3.1), Assen: Van Gorcum/Philadelphia: Fortress Press 1987.

Schiele, Friedrich Michael — Zscharnack, Leopold, (ed.), *Die Religion in Geschichte und Gegenwart: Handwörterbuch in gemeinverständlicher Darstellung*, 5 vols, Tübingen: J.C.B. Mohr (Paul Siebeck) [1]1909-13.

Schwyzer, Eduard — Debrunner, Albert, *Griechische Grammatik* (Handbuch der Altertumswissenschaft, 2. Abteilung, 1. Teil), 4 vols, München: C.H. Beck'sche Verlagsbuchhandlung 1 1939; 2 1950; 3 1953; 4 1971.

Segal, M.H., *A Grammar of Mishnaic Hebrew*, Oxford: Clarendon Press 1958 (repr.), ([1]1927).

Smith, Jessie Payne, (ed.), *A Compendious Syriac Dictionary Founded upon the Thesaurus Syriacus of Robert Payne Smith*, Oxford: Clarendon Press 1985 (repr.).

Souter, Alexander, *A Glossary of Later Latin to 600 A.D.*, Oxford: Clarendon Press 1949.

Spicq, Ceslas, *Theological Lexicon of the New Testament* ET, 3 vols, Peabody: Hendrickson 1994.

Stern, Menahem, *Greek and Latin Authors on Jews and Judaism*, 3 vols, Jerusalem: Israel Academy of Sciences 1974-84.

Stone, Michael E., (ed.), *Jewish Writings of the the Second Temple Period* (CRINT 2.2), Assen: Van Gorcum/Philadelphia: Fortress Press 1984.

Strack, Hermann L. — Stemberger, Günter, *Einleitung in Talmud und Midrasch*, München: Verlag C.H. Beck [7]1982.

Temporini, H. — Haase, W., (ed.), *Aufstieg und Niedergang der römischen Welt*, Berlin/New York: Walter de Gruyter 1972ff.

Thesaurus Linguae Graecae (Data Bank); Theodore F. Brunner (Director), University of California, Irvine, CA 92717, USA.

Weber, Otto, *Karl Barths Kirchliche Dogmatik: Ein einführender Bericht*, Neukirchen-Vluyn: Neukirchener Verlag [11]1989, ([1]1950).

Weingreen, J., *A Practical Grammar for Classical Hebrew*, Oxford: Clarendon Press 1978 (repr.), ([1]1939).

Würthwein, Ernst, *Der Text des Alten Testaments: Eine Einführung in die Biblia Hebraica*, Stuttgart: Deutsche Bibelgesellschaft [3]1988, ([1]1952).

Zerwick, M., *Graecitas Biblica* (SPIB 92), Rome: E Pontificio Instituto Biblico [3]1955, ([1]1944).

van Zijl, J.B., *A Concordance to the Targum of Isaiah* (SBL Aramaic Studies 3), Missoula: Scholars Press 1979.

3. Secondary literature

Alexander, Philip S., "Jewish Aramaic Translations of Hebrew Scriptures", in Martin Jan Mulder (ed.), *Mikra: Text, Translation, Reading and Interpretation of the Hebrew Bible in Ancient Judaism and Early Christianity* (CRINT 2.1), Assen: Van Gorcum/Philadelphia: Fortress Press 1987, 217-253.

Althaus, Paul, *Der Brief an die Römer* (NTD 6), Göttingen: Vandenhoeck & Ruprecht [10]1966.

Althaus, Paul, *Die christliche Wahrheit*, Gütersloh: C. Bertelsmann [3]1952, ([1]1947).

Althaus, Paul, *Die Theologie Martin Luthers*, Gütersloh: Güterloher Verlagshaus Gerd Mohn [6]1983 ([1]1962).

Althaus, Paul, "Ur-Offenbarung", *Luthertum* 46 (1935) 4-24.

Amir, Yehoshua, "Measure for Measure in Talmudic Literature and in the Wisdom of Solomon", in Henning Graf Reventlow and Yair Hoffman (ed.), *Justice and Righteousness: Biblical Themes and their Influence* (JSOTSup 137), Sheffield: JSOT Press 1992, 29-46.

Anderson, A.A., *The Book of Psalms* (NCB), 2 vols, London: Oliphants 1972.

Anderson, B.W., "Creation", *IDB* 1:725-32.

Avemarie, Friedrich, *Tora und Leben: Untersuchungen zur Heilsbedeutung der Tora in der frühen rabbinischen Literatur* (TSAJ 35), Tübingen: J.C.B. Mohr (Paul Siebeck) 1996.

Baillie, John, *The Idea of Revelation in Recent Thought*, New York: Columbia University Press 1956.

Barr, James, *Biblical Faith and Natural Theology* (The Gifford Lectures for 1991 Delivered in the University of Edinburgh), Oxford: OUP 1993.

Barrett, C.K., *The Gospel according to John: An Introduction with Commentary and Notes on the Greek Text*, London: SPCK [2]1978, ([1]1955).

Barrett, C.K., *A Commentary on the Epistle to the Romans* (BNTC), London: A. & C. Black [2]1991, ([1]1957).

Barrett, C.K., (ed.), *The New Testament Background: Selected Documents*, London: SPCK 1957.

Barrow, John D. — Tipler, Frank J., *The Anthropic Cosmological Principle*, Oxford/New York: OUP 1986.

Barth, Karl, *Church Dogmatics* ET, 4 vols, Edinburgh: T. & T. Clark 1936-60.

Barth, Karl, *Church Dogmatics: Index Volume with Aids for the Preacher* ET, Edinburgh: T. & T. Clark 1977.

Barth, Karl, *The Epistle to the Romans* ET (translated from the sixth edition by E.C. Hoskyns), London/Oxford/New York: OUP 1968 (repr.), ([1]1933).

Barth, Karl, *Die Kirchliche Dogmatik*, 4 vols, Zürich: Evangelischer Verlag A.G. Zollikon 1932-1967.

Barth, Karl, *Der Römerbrief*, München: Chr. Kaiser Verlag [6]1929.

Barth, Karl, *A Shorter Commentary on Romans* ET, London: SCM 1959.

Barth, Markus, *Ephesians* (AB 34), 2 vols, Garden City, New York: Doubleday & Co. 1974.

Barth, Markus, "Speaking of Sin", *SJT* 8 (1955) 288-96.

Barth, Markus — Blanke, Helmut, *Colossians* (AB 34B), New York: Doubleday 1994.

Bassler, Jouette M., *Divine Impartiality: Paul and a Theological Axiom* (SBLDS 59), Chico: Scholars Press 1982.

Bassler, Jouette M., "Divine Impartiality in Paul's Letter to the Romans", *NovT* 26 (1984) 43-58.

Bavinck, J.H., "Human Religion in God's Eyes: A Study of Romans 1:18-32", *SBET* 12.1 (1994) 45-46.

Becker, Jürgen, *Untersuchungen zur Entstehungsgeschichte der Testamente der Zwölf Patriarchen* (AGAJU 8), Leiden: E.J. Brill 1970.

Beet, Joseph Agar, *A Commentary on St. Paul's Epistle to the Romans*, London: Hodder and Stoughton [10]1902.

Behm, Johannes, μορφή κτλ, *TDNT* 4:742-59.

Behm, Johannes, - Würthwein, Ernst, νοέω κτλ, *TNDT* 4:948-1022.

Beker, J. Christiaan, *Paul the Apostle: The Triumph of God in Life and Thought*, Edinburgh: T. & T. Clark 1980.

Bell, Richard H., *Provoked to Jealousy: The Origin and Purpose of the Jealousy Motif in Romans 9-11* (WUNT 2.63), Tübingen: J.C.B. Mohr (Paul Siebeck) 1994.

Bell, Richard H., "Sin Offerings and Sinning with a High Hand", *JPJ* 4 (1995) 25-59.

Bell, Richard H., "Teshubah: The Idea of Repentance in Ancient Judaism", *JPJ* 5 (1995) 22-52.

Bell, Richard H., Review of A.J. Guerra, *Romans and the Apologetic Tradition*, *JTS* 47 (1996) 226-30.

Bell, Richard H., Review of M. Meiser, *Paul Althaus als Neutestamentler: Eine Untersuchung der Werke, Briefe, unveröffentlichten Manuskripte und Randbemerkungen*, *SEÅ* 61 (1996) 53-55.

Bengel, Johann Albrecht, *Gnomon Novi Testamenti*, Berlin: Gust. Schlawitz 1855 ([3]1773).

Berger, Klaus, *Exegese des Neuen Testaments: Neue Wege vom Text zur Auslegung* (UTB 658), Heidelberg: Quelle & Meyer [2]1984, ([1]1977).

Berkouwer, G.C., *Divine Election* ET (Studies in Dogmatics), Grand Rapids: Wm B. Eerdmans 1960.

Berkouwer, G.C., *General Revelation* ET (Studies in Dogmatics), Grand Rapids: Wm B. Eerdmans 1955.

Bertram, Georg, ἔργον κτλ, *TDNT* 2:635-55.

Betz, Hans Dieter, *Galatians* (Hermeneia), Philadelphia: Fortress Press 1979.

Betz, Otto, "Pharisäer, Pharisäismus II: Antikes Judentum und Neues Testament", *HWP* 7:536-39.

Beyschlag, Karlmann, *Die Erlanger Theologie* (EKGB 67), Erlangen: Martin-Luther-Verlag 1993.

Bietenhard, Hans, "Natürliche Gotteserkenntnis der Heiden", *ThZ* 12 (1956) 275-88.

Billerbeck, Paul, (Strack, Hermann L.), *Kommentar zum Neuen Testament aus Talmud und Midrasch*, 4 vols, München: C.H. Beck'sche Verlagsbuchhandlung 1-3 ³1961; 4 ²1956.

Black, Matthew, *Romans* (NCB), London: Oliphants 1973.

Bockmuehl, Markus N.A., "Das Verb φανερόω im Neuen Testament", *BZ* 32 (1988) 87-99.

Bockmuehl, Markus N.A., *Revelation and Mystery in Ancient Judaism and Pauline Christianity* (WUNT 2.36), Tübingen: J.C.B. Mohr (Paul Siebeck) 1990.

Bonhöffer, Adolf, *Epiktet und das Neue Testament* (RVV 10), Gießen: Alfred Töpelmann 1911.

Bornkamm, Günther, "Gesetz und Natur: Röm 2₁₄₋₁₆", in *Studien zu Antike und Urchristentum*, München: Chr. Kaiser Verlag 1970, 93-118.

Bornkamm, Günther, "Glaube und Vernunft bei Paulus", in *Studien zu Antike und Urchristentum: Gesammelte Aufsätze Band II*, München: Chr. Kaiser Verlag 1970, 119-37.

Bornkamm, Günther, "Paulus", *RGG³* 5:166-90.

Bornkamm, Günther, *Paulus* (Urban-Taschenbücher 119), Stuttgart: Verlag W. Kohlhammer ⁶1987, (¹1969).

Bornkamm, Günther, "The Letter to the Romans as Paul's Last Will and Testament", in Karl P. Donfried (ed.), *The Romans Debate*, Peabody: Hendrickson ²1991 (¹1977), 16-28.

Bornkamm, Günther, "The Revelation of God's Wrath: Romans 1-3", in *Early Christian Experience* ET, New York: Harper & Row 1969, 47-70.

Bousset, Wilhelm, *Die Religion des Judentums in neutestamentlichen Zeitalter*, Berlin: Reuther & Reichard 1903.

Bousset, Wilhelm - Greßmann, Hugo, *Die Religion des Judentums im späthellenistischen Zeitalter* (HzNT 21), Tübingen: J.C.B. Mohr (Paul Siebeck) ³1926.

Boylan, Patrick, *St. Paul's Epistle to the Romans*, Dublin: M.H. Gill 1934.

Brandenburg, H. "Heiligungsbewegung", *RGG³* 3:182.

Brandenburger, Egon, "Gericht Gottes III", *TRE* 12:469-83.

Braun, Herbert, *Gerichtsgedanke und Rechtfertigungslehre bei Paulus* (UNT 19), Leipzig: J.C. Hinrichs'sche Buchhandlung 1930.

Briggs, Charles Augustus - Briggs, Emile Grace *The Book of Psalms*, 2 vols, Edinburgh: T. & T. Clark 1906-7.

Brooke, George J., *Exegesis at Qumran: 4QFlorilegium in its Jewish Context* (JSNTSup 29), Sheffield: JSOT Press 1985.

Brown, Colin, *Karl Barth and the Christian Message*, London: Tyndale Press 1967.

Bruce, F.F., *The Epistle of Paul to the Romans: An Introduction and Commentary* (TNTC), London: Tyndale 1963.

Bruce, F.F., "Is the Paul of Acts the Real Paul", *BJRL* 58 (1975-76) 282-305.

de Bruyne, D., "Étude sur le texte latin de la Sagesse", *RBén* 41 (1929) 101-33.

Büschel, Friedrich, θυμός κτλ, *TDNT* 3:167-72.

Bultmann, Rudolf, ἀλήθεια κτλ, *TDNT* 1:238-251.

Bultmann, Rudolf, γινώσκω κτλ., *TDNT* 1:689-719 (= *ThWNT* 1:688-719).

Bultmann, Rudolf, καυχάομαι κτλ, *TDNT* 3:645-54.

Bultmann, Rudolf, "Die Bedeutung des geschichtlichen Jesus für die Theologie des Paulus", in *Glauben und Verstehen: Gesammelte Aufsätze, Bd 1* (UTB 1760), Tübingen: J.C.B. Mohr (Paul Siebeck) [9]1993, ([1]1933), 1:188-213.

Bultmann, Rudolf, "Glossen im Römerbrief", in *Exegetica: Aufsätze zur Erforschung des Neuen Testaments*, Tübingen: J.C.B. Mohr (Paul Siebeck) 1967, 278-84.

Bultmann, Rudolf, *Theologie des Neuen Testaments* (UTB 630), Tübingen: J.C.B. Mohr (Paul Siebeck) [9]1984 (durchgesehen und ergänzt von Otto Merk), ([1]1948).

Bultmann, Rudolf, *Theology of the New Testament* ET, 2 vols, London: SCM 1 1952; 2 1955.

Bultmann, Rudolf, "Untersuchungen zum Johannesevangelium", *ZNW* 29 (1930) 169-92.

Bultmann, Rudolf — Lührmann, Dieter, φαίνω κτλ, *ThWNT* 9:1-11.

Bunte, Wolfgang, *Die Mischna: Text, Übersetzung und ausführliche Erklärung: Kelim*, Berlin/New York: Walter de Gruyter 1972.

Byrne, Brendan J., *Romans* (SPS 6), Collegeville, Minnesota: Liturgical Press 1996.

Byrne, Brendan J., Review of R.H. Bell, *Provoked to Jealousy: The Origin and Purpose of the Jealousy Motif in Romans 9-11* (WUNT 2.63), Tübingen: J.C.B. Mohr (Paul Siebeck) 1994, in *JTS* 46 (1995) 277-79.

Caird, G.B., *The Language and Imagery of the Bible*, London: Duckworth 1980.

Calvin, John, *The Epistles of Paul The Apostle to the Romans and to the Thessalonians*, translated by Ross Mackenzie (Calvin's Commentaries 8), Grand Rapids: Wm B. Eerdmans 1976 (repr.) (Edinburgh: Oliver and Boyd [1]1960).

Cambier, J.-M., "Le jugement de tous les hommes par Dieu seul, selon la vérité, dans Rom 2_1-3_{20}", *ZNW* 67 (1976) 187-213.

Carras, George P., "Romans 2,1-29: A Dialogue on Jewish Ideals", *Bib* 73 (1992) 183-207.

Carson, D.A., *Divine Sovereignty and Human Responsibility: Biblical Perspectives in Tension* (MTL), London: Marshall, Morgan & Scott 1981.

Carson, D.A., *The Gospel according to John*, Leicester: IVP 1991.

Clarke, Ernest G., "The Bible and Translation: The Targums", in Bradley H. McLean (ed.), *Origins and Method: Towards a New Understanding of Judaism and Christianity. Esssays in Honour of John C. Hurd* (JSNTSup 86), Sheffield: JSOT Press 1993, 380-93.

Cohen, S.J.D., "The Significance of Yavneh: Pharisees, Rabbis, and the End of Jewish Sectarianism", *HUCA* 54 (1984) 27-53.

Collins, John J., *Apocalypticism in the Dead Sea Scrolls* (LDSS), London/New York: Routledge 1997.

Collins, John J., "Early Jewish Apocalypticism", *ABD* 1:282-88.

Collins, John J., "Genre, Ideology and Social Movements in Jewish Apocalypticism", in John J. Collins and James H. Charlesworth (ed.), *Mysteries and Revelations: Apocalyptic Studies since the Uppsala Colloquium* (JSPSup 9), Sheffield: JSOT Press 1991, 11-32.

Conzelmann, Hans, *Der erste Brief an die Korinther* (KEK 5), Göttingen: Vandenhoeck & Ruprecht ²1981, (¹1969).

Conzelmann, Hans, "Gericht Gottes III", *RGG*³ 2:1419-21.

Conzelmann, Hans, *Grundriß der Theologie des Neuen Testaments* (UTB 1446), Tübingen: J.C.B. Mohr (Paul Siebeck) ⁴1987 (revised by Andreas Lindemann), (¹1967).

Conzelmann, Hans, *An Outline of the Theology of the New Testament* (NTL) ET, London: SCM 1969 (translation of the second edition of *Grundriß der Theologie des Neuen Testaments*).

Conzelmann, Hans, "Paulus und die Weisheit", in *Theologie als Schriftauslegung: Aufsätze zum Neuen Testament* (BEvTh 65), München: Chr. Kaiser Verlag 1974 (= *NTS* 12 (1965) 231-44).

Cosgrove, Charles H., "What if Some Have Not Believed? The Occasion and Thrust of Romans 3_{1-8}", *ZNW* 78 (1987) 90-105.

Cosgrove, Charles H., "Justification in Paul: A Linguistic and Theological Reflection", *JBL* 106 (1987) 653-70.

Cranfield, C.E.B., *A Critical and Exegetical Commentary on the Epistle to the Romans* (ICC), 2 vols, Edinburgh: T. & T. Clark 1 ²1977, (¹1975); 2 1979.

Cranfield, C.E.B., "'The Works of the Law' in the Epistle to the Romans", *JSNT* 43 (1991) 89-101.

Dahl, Nils Alstrup, "Romans 3.9: Text and Meaning", in M.D. Hooker and S.G. Wilson (ed.), *Paul and Paulinism: Essays in honour of C.K. Barrett*, London: SPCK 1982, 184-204.

Davies, Glenn N., *Faith and Obedience in Romans: A Study in Romans 1-4* (JSNTSup 39), Sheffield: JSOT Press 1990.

Davies, W.D. — Allison, Dale C., *A Critical and Exegetical Commentary on the Epistle to the Gospel According to Saint Matthew* (ICC), vol. 1, Edinburgh: T. & T. Clark 1988.

Davies, W.D., *Paul and Rabbinic Judaism: Some Rabbinic Elements in Pauline Theology*, London: SPCK ²1955, (¹1948).

Deißmann, Adolf, *Licht vom Osten: Das Neue Testament und die neuentdeckten Texte der hellenistisch-römischen Welt*, Tübingen: J.C.B. Mohr (Paul Siebeck) ⁴1923 (¹1908).

Delius, Hans-Ulrich, (ed.), *Martin Luther: Studienausgabe Band 1*, Berlin: Evangelische Verlagsanstalt 1979.

Delling, Gerhard, ἀργός, ἀργέω, καταργέω, *TDNT* 1:452-54.

Dembowski, Hermann, "Natürliche Theologie - Theologie der Natur", *EvTh* 45 (1985) 224-48.

Denny, James, "St. Paul's Epistle to the Romans", in W. Robertson Nicoll, *The Expositor's Greek Testament*, Grand Rapids: Wm B. Eerdmanns 1976 (repr), 555-725.

Denzinger, Heinrich, *Enchiridion symbolorum definitionum et declarationum de rebus fidei et morum* (ed. P. Hünermann), Freiburg: Herder 1991.

Derrett, J.D., "'You abominate False Gods; But do you rob Shrines?' (Rom 2.22b)", *NTS* 40 (1994) 558-71.

Dietrich, E.K., *Die Umkehr (Bekehrung und Buße) im Alten Testament und im Judentum*, Stuttgart: W. Kohlhammer Verlag 1936.

Dietzfelbinger, Christian, *Die Berufung des Paulus als Ursprung seiner Theologie* (WMANT 58), Neukirchen-Vluyn: Neukirchener Verlag 1985.

von Dobschütz, E., "Zum Wortschatz und Stil des Römerbriefs", *ZNW* 33 (1934) 51-66.

Dodd, C.H., *According to the Scriptures: The Sub-structure of New Testament Theology* (Stone Lectures 1950), London: Nisbet & Co. 1952.

Dodd, C.H., *The Epistle of Paul to the Romans* (MNTC), London: Hodder and Stoughton ¹²1949, (¹1932).

Doeve, J.W., "Some Notes with Reference to ΤΑ ΛΟΓΙΑ ΤΟΥ ΘΕΟΥ in Romans III 2", in J.N. Sevenster and W.C. van Unnik (ed.), *Studia Paulina in Honorem Johannis de Zwaan*, Haarlem: De Erven F. Bohn N.V. 1953, 111-23.

Donfried, Karl Paul, "Justification and Last Judgment in Paul", *ZNW* 67 (1976) 90-110.

Duncan, G.S., *St. Paul's Ephesian Ministry*, London: Hodder and Stoughton 1929.

Dunn, J.D.G., "'A Light to the Gentiles': the Significance of the Damascus Road Christophany for Paul", in L.D. Hurst and N.T. Wright (ed.), *The Glory of Christ in the New Testament: Studies in Christology*, Oxford: Clarendon Press 1987, 251-66.

Dunn, J.D.G., "The New Perspective on Paul", *BJRL* 65 (1983) 95-122.

Dunn, J.D.G., *Romans* (WBC 38), 2 vols, Dallas, Texas: Word Books 1988.

Dunn, J.D.G., "The Works of the Law and the Curse of the Law (Galatians 3:10-14)", *NTS* 31 (1985) 523-42.

Dunn, J.D.G., "What was the Issue between Paul and 'Those of the Circumcision'?", in Martin Hengel and Ulrich Heckel (ed.), *Paulus und das antike Judentum: Tübingen-Durham-Symposium im Gedenken an der 50. Todestag Adolf Schlatter*, Tübingen: J.C.B. Mohr (Paul Siebeck) 1991, 295-313.

Dunn, J.D.G., "Yet Once More—'The Works of the Law'", *JSNT* 46 (1992) 99-117.

Dupont, Jaques, "The Conversion of Paul, and its Influence on his Understanding of Salvation by Faith", in W. Ward Gasque and Ralph P. Martin (ed.), *Apostolic History and the Gospel: Biblical and Historical Essays presented to F.F. Bruce on his 60th Birthday*, Exeter: Paternoster 1970, 176-94.

Eberle, Adolf, "Naturgesetz", *LThK*[1] 7:451-53.

Eckstein, Hans-Joachim, *Der Begriff Syneidesis bei Paulus* (WUNT 2.10), Tübingen: J.C.B. Mohr (Paul Siebeck) 1983.

Eckstein, Hans-Joachim, "'Denn Gottes Zorn wird vom Himmel her offenbar werden'. Exegetische Erwägungen zu Röm 1$_{18}$", *ZNW* 78 (1987) 74-89.

Eckstein, Hans-Joachim, *Verheißung und Gesetz: Eine exegetische Untersuchung zu Galater 2,15-4,7* (WUNT 86), Tübingen: J.C.B. Mohr (Paul Siebeck) 1996.

Edgar, S.L., "Respect for Context in Quotations from the Old Testament", *NTS* 9 (1962) 55-62.

Ego, Beate, *Im Himmel wie auf Erden: Studien zum Verhältnis von himmlischer und irdischer Welt im rabbinischen Judentum* (WUNT 2.34), Tübingen: J.C.B. Mohr (Paul Siebeck) 1989.

Eichholz, Georg, *Die Theologie des Paulus in Umriß*, Neukirchen-Vluyn: Neukirchener Verlag [5]1985, ([1]1972).

Elert, Werner, *Der christliche Glaube: Grundlinien der lutherischen Dogmatik*, Erlangen: Martin-Luther-Verlag [6]1988, ([1]1940).

Eltester, W., "Schöpfungsoffenbarung und natürliche Theologie im frühen Christentum", *NTS* 3 (1956-57) 93-114.

Fascher, Erich, "Deus invisibilis: Eine Studie zur biblischen Gottesvorstellung", *MThS* (1931) 41-77.

Fee, Gordon, *The First Epistle to the Corinthians* (NICNT), Grand Rapids: Wm. B. Eerdmans 1987.

Feine, Paul, *Das gesetzesfreie Evangelium des Paulus*, Leipzig: Hinrichs' 1899.

Feine, Paul, *Theologie des Neuen Testaments*, Berlin: Evangelische Verlagsanstalt 81953.

Fenlon, D., *Heresy and Obedience in Tridentine Italy: Cardinal Pole and the Counter Reformation*, Cambridge: CUP 1972.

Fichtner, J., *Die altorientalische Weisheit in ihrer israelitisch-jüdischen Ausprägung: Eine Studie zur Nationalisierung der Weisheit in Israel* (BZAW 62), Gießen: Verlag von Alfred Töpelmann 1933.

Fitzmyer, Joseph A., *Romans* (AB 33), New York: Doubleday 1993.

Flückiger, F., "Die Werke des Gesetzes bei den Heiden", *ThZ* 8 (1952) 17-42.

Fox, Michael V., "'Amon Again", *JBL* 115 (1996) 699-702.

Fridrichsen, Anton, "Zur Auslegung von Röm 1,19f.", *ZNW* 17 (1916) 159-68.

Fridrichsen, Anton, "Der wahre Jude und sein Lob", *Symbolae Arctoae* 1 (1927) 39-49.

Friedrich, Gerhard, "Der Brief an die Philipper", in Hermann W. Beyer, Paul Althaus, Hans Conzelmann, Gerhard Friedrich and Albrecht Oepke, *Die kleineren Briefe des Apostels Paulus* (NTD 8), Göttingen: Vandenhoeck & Ruprecht 131972, 92-130.

Gärtner, Bertil, *The Areopagus Speech and Natural Revelation* (ASNU 21), Uppsala: Almquist & Wiksell 1955.

Garland, David, "The Composition and Unity of Philippians: Some Neglected Literary Factors", *NovT* 27 (1985) 141-73.

Gaston, Lloyd, "Works of Law as a Subjective Genitive", in *Paul and the Torah*, Vancouver: University of British Columbia Press 1987, 100-106 (= *SR* 13 (1984) 39-46).

Gemser, Berend, *Sprüche Salomos* (HzAT 1.16), Tübingen: J.C.B. Mohr (Paul Siebeck) 11937.

Gerleman, G., "The Septuagint Proverbs as a Hellenistic Document", *OTS* 8 (1950) 15-27.

Gerson, L.P., *God and Greek Philosophy: Studies in the Early History of Natural Theology*, London: Routledge 1990.

Gese, Hartmut, "Die Einheit von Psalm 19", in *Alttestamentliche Studien*, Tübingen: J.C.B. Mohr (Paul Siebeck) 1991, 139-48.

Gese, Hartmut, *Lehre und Wirklichkeit in der alten Weisheit: Studien zu den Sprüchen Salomos und zu dem Buche Hiob*, Tübingen: J.C.B. Mohr (Paul Siebeck) 1958.

Gese, Hartmut, "Psalm 50 und das alttestamentliche Gesetzesverständnis", in *Alttestamentliche Studien*, Tübingen: J.C.B. Mohr (Paul Siebeck) 1991, 149-69 (= Johannes Friedrich, Wolfgang Pöhlmann and Peter Stuhlmacher (ed.), *Rechtfertigung: Festschrift für Ernst Käsemann zum 70. Geburtstag*, Tübingen:

J.C.B. Mohr (Paul Siebeck)/Göttingen: Vandenhoeck & Ruprecht 1976, 57-77).

Gese, Hartmut, "Die Sühne", in *Zur biblischen Theologie: Alttestamentliche Vorträge*, Tübingen: J.C.B. Mohr (Paul Siebeck) [3]1989, ([1]1977), 85-106.

Gese, Hartmut, Die Weisheit, der Menschensohn und die Ursprünge der Christologie als konsequente Entfaltung der biblischen Theologie", in *Alttestamentliche Studien*, Tübingen: J.C.B. Mohr (Paul Siebeck) 1991, 218-48.

Gibson, Edgar C.S., *The Thirty-Nine Articles of the Church of England*, London: Methuen & Co. [3]1902, ([1]1896).

Gilbert, M., "Wisdom Literature", in Michael E. Stone (ed.), *Jewish Writings of the the Second Temple Period*, Assen: Van Gorcum/Philadelphia: Fortress Press 1984, 283-324.

Ginzberg, Louis, *The Legends of the Jews* ET, 7 vols, Philadelphia; Jewish Publication Society of America 1909-38.

Gleßmer, Uwe, *Einleitung in die Targume zum Pentateuch* (TSAJ 48), Tübingen: J.C.B. Mohr (Paul Siebeck) 1995.

Gnilka, Joachim, *Der Epheserbrief* (HThKNT 10.2), Freiburg/Basel/Wien: Herder [4]1990, ([1]1971).

Gnilka, Joachim, *Der Kolosserbrief* (HThKNT 10.1), Freiburg/Basel/Wien: Herder [2]1991, ([1]1980).

Gnilka, Joachim, *Paulus von Tarsus: Apostel und Zeuge* (HThKNTSup 6), Freiburg/Basel/Wien: Herder 1996.

Gnilka, Joachim, *Der Philipperbrief* (HThKNT 10.3), Freiburg/Basel/Wien: Herder [4]1987, ([1]1968).

Godet, Frederic L., *Commentary on Romans* ET, Grand Rapids: Kregel Publications 1977 (repr.), ([1]1883).

Godet, Frederic L., *Commentaire sur l'épitre aux Romains*, 2 vols, Paris: Librarie Sandoz & Fischbacher 1 1879; 2 1880.

Grafe, Eduard, "Das Verhältniss der paulinischen Schriften zur Sapientia Salomonis", in *Theologische Abhandlungen: Carl von Weizsäcker zu seinem siebzigsten Geburtstage 11. December 1892 gewidmet*, Freiburg: J.C.B. Mohr (Paul Siebeck) 1892, 253-86.

Gray, John, "Idol", *IDB* 2:673-75.

Gray, John, "Idolatry", *IDB* 2:675-78.

Griffith Thomas, W.H., *The Principles of Theology: An Introduction to the Thirty-Nine Articles*, London: Church Book Room Press 1963.

Guerra, A.J., *Romans and the Apologetic Tradition: The Purpose, Genre and Audience of Paul's Letter* (SNTSMS 81), Cambridge: CUP 1995.

Gundry, Robert H., "Grace, Works and Staying Saved in Paul", *Bib* 66 (1985) 1-38.

Gundry Volf, Judith, *Paul and Perseverance: Staying in and Falling Away* (WUNT 2.37), Tübingen: J.C.B. Mohr (Paul Siebeck) 1989.

Gutbrod, W. — Kleinknecht, H., νόμος κτλ, *TDNT* 4:1022-91.

Habel, Norman C., *The Book of Job* (OTL), London: SCM Press 1985.

Hackenberg, Wolfgang, ἐπιγινώσκω, *EDNT* 2:24-25.

Hackenberg, Wolfgang, ἐπίγνωσις, *EDNT* 2:25.

Hadas, Moses, *The Third and Fourth Books of Maccabees*, New York: Ktav 1953.

Hahn, Ferdinand, "Das Gesetzesverständnis im Römer- und Galaterbrief", *ZNW* 67 (1976) 29-63.

Haldane, Robert, *Exposition of the Epistle to the Romans*, London: The Banner of Truth Trust 1958 (repr.).

Hall, David R., "Romans 3.1-8 Reconsidered", *NTS* 29 (1983) 183-97.

Hanson, Anthony Tyrrell, *The Wrath of the Lamb*, London: SPCK 1957.

Hanson, Paul D., "Apocalypticism", *IDBSup* 28-34.

Hawthorne, Gerald F., *Philippians* (WBC 43), Waco: Word Books 1983.

Hays, Richard B., *Echoes of Scripture in the Letters of Paul*, New Haven/London: Yale University Press 1989.

Hays, Richard B., "Psalm 143 and the Logic of Romans 3", *JBL* 99 (1980) 107-15.

Hays, Richard B., "Relations Natural and Unnatural: A Response to John Boswell's Exegesis of Romans 1", *JRE* (1986) 184-215.

Hayward, Robert, "The Date of Targum Pseudo-Jonathan: Some Comments", *JJS* 60 (1989) 7-30.

Heiligenthal, Roman, *Werke als Zeichen: Untersuchungen zur Bedeutung der menschlichen Taten im Frühjudentum, Neuen Testament und Frühchristentum* (WUNT 2.9), Tübingen: J.C.B. Mohr (Paul Siebeck) 1983.

Heinemann, I., "Die Lehre vom ungeschriebenen Gesetz im jüdischen Schrifttum", *HUCA* 4 (1927) 149-71.

Hendry, George S., *Theology of Nature*, Philadelphia: Westminster Press 1980.

Hengel, Martin, *The 'Hellenization' of Judaea in the First Century after Christ* (in collaboration with Christoph Markschies) ET, London: SCM 1989.

Hengel, Martin, *Judaism and Hellenism: Studies in their Encounter in Palestine during the Early Hellenistic Period* ET, 2 vols, London: SCM 1974.

Hengel, Martin, "The Origins of the Christian Mission", in *Between Jesus and Paul: Studies in the Earliest History of Christianity*, London: SCM 1983, 48-64 (= "Die Ursprünge des christlichen Mission", *NTS* 18 (1971) 15-38).

Hengel, Martin, *The Pre-Christian Paul*, London: SCM 1991.

Hengel, Martin - Deines, Roland, "E.P. Sanders' 'Common Judaism', Jesus, and the Pharisees", *JTS* 46 (1995) 1-70.

Hengel, Martin - Schwemer, Anna Maria, *Paul between Damascus and Antioch: The Unknown Years*, London: SCM 1997.

Héring, Jean, *The First Epistle of Saint Paul to the Corinthians* ET, London: Epworth 1962.

Héring, Jean, *The Second Epistle of Saint Paul to the Corinthians* ET, London: Epworth 1967.

Hermisson, Hans-Jürgen, "Observations on the Creation Theology in Wisdom", in John G. Gammie et al. (ed.), *Israelite Wisdom: Theological and Literary Essays in Honor of Samuel Terrien*, Missoula: Scholars Press 1978, 43-57.

Hodge, Charles, *A Commentary on the Epistle to the Romans*, Grand Rapids: Wm B. Eerdmans ²1950, (¹1864).

Hofius, Otfried, "Erwägungen zur Gestalt und Herkunft des paulinischen Versöhnungsgedankens", *ZThK* 77 (1980) 186-99 (= *Paulusstudien*, 1-14).

Hofius, Otfried, "Das Gesetz des Mose und das Gesetz Christi", *ZThK* 80 (1983) 262-86 (= *Paulusstudien*, 50-74).

Hofius, Otfried, "Gesetz und Evangelium nach 2. Korinther 3", in *Jahrbuch für Biblische Theologie Band 4: "Gesetz" als Thema Biblischer Theologie*, Neukirchen-Vluyn: Neukirchener Verlag 1989, 105-50 (= *Paulusstudien*, 75-120).

Hofius, Otfried, *Paulusstudien* (WUNT 51), Tübingen: J.C.B. Mohr (Paul Siebeck) 1989.

Hofius, Otfried, "'Rechtfertigung des Gottlosen' als Thema biblischer Theologie", in *Paulusstudien*, 121-47.

Hofius, Otfried, "Sühne und Versöhnung: Zum paulinischen Verständnis des Kreuzestodes Jesu", in W. Maas (ed.), *Versuche, das Leiden und Sterben Jesu zu verstehen* (Schriftenreihe der Katholischen Akademie der Erzdiözese Freiburg), München/Zürich: Verlag Schnell & Steiner 1983, 25-46 (= *Paulusstudien*, 33-49).

Hofius, Otfried, "Wort Gottes und Glaube bei Paulus", in *Paulusstudien*, 148-74.

Hofius, Otfried, "Die Unabänderlichkeit des göttlichen Heilsratschlusses", *ZNW* 64 (1973) 135-45.

Hoheisel, Karl, "Homosexualität", *RAC* 16:289-364.

Hollander, Harm W., θυμός, *EDNT*, 2:159-60.

Hollander, Harm W. - de Jonge, Marinus, *The Testaments of the Twelve Patriarchs: A Commentary* (SVTP 8), Leiden: E.J. Brill 1985.

Holtzmann, Heinrich J., *Lehrbuch der Neutestamentlichen Theologie*, 2 vols, Tübingen: J.C.B. Mohr (Paul Siebeck) ²1911 (ed. by A. Jülicher and W. Bauer).

Hooker, Morna D., "Adam in Romans I", *NTS* 6 (1959-60) 297-306.

Hooker, Morna D., "A Further Note on Romans I", *NTS* 13 (1966-67) 181-83.

Horbury, William, "The Christian use and the Jewish origins of the Wisdom of Solomon", in John Day, Robert P. Gordon and H.G.M. Williamson (ed.), *Wisdom in ancient Israel: Essays in honour of J.A. Emerton*, Cambridge: CUP 1995, 182-96.

Howard, George, *Paul: Crisis in Galatia. A Study in Early Christian Theology* (SNTSMS 35), Cambridge: CUP 1979.

Howey, Matthew, "A Study in the Theological Exegesis of Karl Barth", Nottingham M.Th. Thesis 1996.

Hübner, Hans, ἀλήθεια κτλ, *EDNT* 1:57-60.

Hübner, Hans, καταργέω, *EDNT* 2:267-68.

Hübner, Hans, *Das Gesetz bei Paulus: Ein Beitrag zum Werden der paulinischen Theologie*, Göttingen: Vandenhoeck & Ruprecht 1978.

Hughes, Philip Edgcumbe, *The Second Epistle to the Corinthians* (NICNT), Grand Rapids: Wm B. Eerdmans 1962.

Hunsinger, George, *How to Read Karl Barth: The Shape of his Theology*, Oxford: OUP 1991.

Hyldahl, N., "A Reminiscence of the Old Testament at Romans i.23", *NTS* 2 (1955-56) 285-88.

Janowski, Bernd, *Sühne als Heilsgeschehen: Studien zur Sühnetheologie der Priesterschrift und zur Wurzel KPR im Alten Orient und im Alten Testament* (WMANT 55), Neukirchen-Vluyn: Neukirchener Verlag 1982.

Janowski, Bernd, "Tempel und Schöpfung: Schöpfungstheologische Aspekte der priesterschriftlichen Heiligtumskonzeption", *Jahrbuch für Biblische Theologie Band 5: Schöpfung und Neuschöpfung*, Neukirchen-Vluyn: Neukirchener Verlag 1990, 37-69.

Jensen, Philip Peter, *Graded Holiness: A Key to the Priestly Conception of the World* (JSOTSup 106), Sheffield: JSOT Press 1992.

Jeremias, Joachim, "Chiasmus in den Paulusbriefen", *ZNW* 49 (1958) 145-56 (= *Abba: Studien zur neutestamentlichen Theologie und Zeitgeschichte*, Göttingen: Vandenhoeck & Ruprecht 1966, 276-90).

Jeremias, Joachim, "Die Gedankenführung in Röm 4: Zum paulinischen Glaubensverständnis", in Markus Barth and C.K. Barrett (ed.), *Foi et Salut selon S. Paul (Épitre aux Romains 1,16)* (AnBib 42), Rome: Biblical Institute Press 1970, 51-58.

Jeremias, Joachim, *Die Gleichnisse Jesu*, Göttingen: Vandenhoeck & Ruprecht ⁹1977, (¹1947).

Jeremias, Joachim, *Jerusalem in the Time of Jesus* ET, Philadelphia; Fortress Press 1969.

Jeremias, Joachim, "Zu Rm 1 22-32", *ZNW* 45 (1954) 119-21 (= *Abba: Studien zur neutestamentlichen Theologie und Zeitgeschichte*, Göttingen: Vandenhoeck & Ruprecht 1966, 290-92).

Jeremias, Joachim, "Zur Gedankenführung in den paulinischen Briefen", in *Abba: Studien zur neutestamentlichen Theologie und Zeitgeschichte*, Göttingen: Vandenhoeck & Ruprecht 1966, 269-76 (= J.N. Sevenster and W.C. van Unnik (ed.), *Studia Paulina in Honorem Johannis de Zwaan*, Haarlem: De Erven F. Bohn N.V. 1953, 146-54).

Jervell, Jacob, "Bild Gottes I", *TRE* 6:491-98.

Jervell, Jacob, *Imago Dei: Gen 1,26f. im Spätjudentum, in der Gnosis und in den paulinischen Briefen*, Göttingen: Vandenhoeck & Ruprecht 1960.

Jewett, Robert, "Conflicting Movements in the Early Church as reflected in Philippians", *NovT* 12 (1970) 362-90.

Joest, W., *Gesetz und Freiheit: Das Problem des Tertius Usus Legis bei Luther und die neutestamentliche Parainese*, Göttingen: Vandenhoeck & Ruprecht ⁴1968.

Joest, W., "Heiligung III: Dogmatisch", *RGG³* 3:180-81.

de Jonge, Marinus, *The Testaments of the Twelve Patriarchs: A Study of their Text, Composition, and Origin*, Leiden: E.J. Brill 1953.

Judge, Edwin A., "St Paul and Classical Society", JAC 15 (1972) 19-36.

Jülicher, Adolf, "Der Brief an die Römer", in Wilhelm Bousset and Wilhelm Heitmüller (ed.), *Die Schriften des Neuen Testaments*, 4 vols, Göttingen: Vandenhoeck & Ruprecht ³1917, 3:223-335.

Jüngel, Eberhard, "Das Gesetz zwischen Adam und Christus", in *Unterwegs zur Sache: Theologische Bemerkungen* (BEvTh 61), München: Chr. Kaiser Verlag ²1988, (¹1972), 145-72 (= *ZThK* 60 (1963) 42-69).

Jüngel, Eberhard, "Ein paulinischer Chiasmus; Zum Verständnis der Vorstellung vom Gericht nach den Werken in Röm 2,2-11", *Unterwegs zur Sache: Theologische Bemerkungen* (BEvTh 61), München: Chr. Kaiser Verlag ²1988, (¹1972), 173-78 (= *ZThK* 60 (1963) 70-74).

Jüngel, Eberhard, *Paulus und Jesus: Eine Untersuchung zur Präzisierung der Frage nach dem Ursprung der Christologie* (HUTh 2), Tübingen: J.C.B Mohr (Paul Siebeck) ⁶1986, (¹1962).

Kamlah, Ehrhard, *Die Form der katalogischen Paränese im Neuen Testament* (WUNT 7), Tübingen: J.C.B. Mohr (Paul Siebeck) 1964.

Kamm, Anthony, *The Romans*, London: Routledge 1995.

Käsemann, Ernst, *An die Römer* (HzNT 8a), Tübingen: J.C.B. Mohr (Paul Siebeck) ⁴1980, (¹1973).

Käsemann, Ernst, *Exegetische Versuche und Besinnungen, Bd 2*, Göttingen: Vandenhoeck & Ruprecht ³1970, (¹1964).

Käsemann, Ernst, "Geist und Buchstabe", in *Paulinische Perspektiven*, Tübingen: J.C.B. Mohr (Paul Siebeck) ²1972, (¹1969), 237-85.

Käsemann, Ernst, "Rechtfertigung und Heilsgeschichte im Römerbrief", in *Paulinische Perspektiven*, Tübingen: J.C.B. Mohr (Paul Siebeck) ²1972, (¹1969), 108-139.

Kaufman, Stephen A., "On Methodology in the Study of the Targums and their Chronology", *JSNT* 23 (1985) 117-24.

Kaufman, Stephen A., "Dating the Language of the Palestinian Targums and their Use in the Study of First Century CE Texts", in D.R.G. Beattie and M.J. McNamara (ed.), *The Aramaic Bible: Targums in their Historical Context* (JSOTSup 166), Sheffield: JSOT Press 1994, 118-141.

Kaylor, R. David, *Paul's Covenant Community: Jew and Gentile in Romans*, Atlanta: John Knox Press 1988.

Keck, Leander E., "The Function of Rom 3:10-18: Observations and Suggestions", in Jacob Jervell and Wayne A. Meeks (ed.), *God's Christ and His People: Studies in Honour of Nils Alstrup Dahl*, Oslo/Bergen/Tromsö: Universitetsforlaget 1977, 141-57.

Kim, Seyoon, *The Origin of Paul's Gospel* (WUNT 2.4), Tübingen: J.C.B. Mohr (Paul Siebeck) 1981.

Kittel, Gerhard, λέγω κτλ, *TDNT* 4:77-143.

Kittel, Gerhard — von Rad, Gerhard — Kleinknecht, Hermann, εἰκών, *TDNT* 2:381-97.

Klein, G., *Der älteste christliche Katechismus und die jüdische Propaganda-literatur*, Berlin: Georg Reimer 1909.

Klein, Günter, "Individualgeschichte und Weltgeschichte bei Paulus", in *Rekonstruktion und Interpretation: Gesammelte Aufsätze zum Neuen Testament* (BEvTh 50), München: Chr. Kaiser Verlag 1969, 180-224.

Klein, Günter, "Gesetz III", *TRE* 13:58-75.

Klein, Günter, "Römer 4 und die Idee der Heilsgeschichte", in *Rekonstruktion und Interpretation: Gesammelte Aufsätze zum Neuen Testament* (BEvTh 50), München: Chr. Kaiser Verlag 1969, 145-169 (= *EvTh* 24 (1963) 424-47).

Klein, Günter, "Sündenverständnis und theologia crucis bei Paulus", in Carl Anderson and Günther Klein (ed.), *Theologia crucis - signum crucis: Festschrift für Erich Dinkler zum 70. Geburtstag*, Tübingen: J.C.B. Mohr (Paul Siebeck) 1979, 249-82.

Kleinknecht, Hermann — Gutbrod, Walter, νόμος κτλ *TDNT* 4:1022-91.

Kleinknecht, Hermann — Grether, Oscar — Procksch, Otto — Fichtner, Johannes — Sjöberg, Erik — Stählin, Gustav, ὀργή κτλ, *TDNT* 5:382-447.

Klöpper, A., "Die durch natürliche Offenbarung vermittelte Gotteserkenntnis der Heiden bei Paulus. Röm. 1,18ff.", *ZWTh* 47 (1904) 169-80.

Klostermann, E, "Die adäquate Vergeltung in Rm 1₂₂₋₃₁", *ZNW* 32 (1933) 1-6.

Knox, Wilfred L., *St Paul and the Church of the Gentiles*, Cambridge: CUP 1939.

Koch, Dietrich-Alex, *Die Schrift als Zeuge des Evangeliums* (BHTh 69), Tübingen: J.C.B. Mohr (Paul Siebeck) 1986.

Koch, Klaus, "Einleitung", in Klaus Koch und Johann Michael Schmidt (ed.), *Apokalyptik* (WdF 365), Darmstadt: Wissenschaftliche Buchgesellschaft 1982, 1-29.

Kolde, Theodor, "Regensburger Religionsgespäch und Regensburger Buch 1541", ³*RE* 16:545-52.

Kühl, Ernst, *Der Brief des Paulus an die Römer*, Leipzig: Quelle & Meyer 1913.

Kuhlmann, Gerhardt, *Theologia naturalis bei Philon und bei Paulus: Eine Studie zur Grundlegung der paulinischen Anthropologie* (NTF 1.7), Gütersloh: C. Bertelsmann 1930.

Küng, Hans (with Josef van Ess, Heinrich von Stietencron and Heinz Bechert), *Christianity and the World Religions: Paths of Dialogue with Islam, Hinduism, and Buddhism* ET, London 1987.

Kuss, Otto, *Der Römerbrief*, 3 vols, Regensburg: Verlag Friedrich Pustet 1:1957; 2:1959; 3:1978.

Lackmann, Max, *Vom Geheimnis der Schöpfung: Die Geschichte der Exegese von Römer I, 18-23, II, 14-16 und Acta XIV, 15-17, XVII, 22-29 vom 2. Jahrhundert bis zum Beginn der Orthodoxie*, Stuttgart: Evangelisches Verlagswerk 1952.

Lagrange, M.-J., *Saint Paul: Épitre aux Romains* (Étbib 13), Paris: J. Gabalda ²1922, (¹1915).

Lambrecht, Jan, "Unreal Conditions in the Letters of Paul: A Clarification", *ETL* 63 (1987) 153-56.

Lambrecht, Jan, "Why is Boasting Excluded? A Note on Rom 3,27 and 4,2", *ETL* 61 (1985) 365-69.

Lane, William L., *The Gospel according to Mark* (NICNT), Grand Rapids: Wm B. Eerdmans 1974.

Lang, Friedrich, *Die Briefe an die Korinther* (NTD 7), Göttingen: Vandenhoeck & Ruprecht 1986.

Laporte, Jean, "Philo in the Tradition of Wisdom", in R.L. Wilken (ed.), *Aspects of Wisdom in Judaism and Early Christianity* (University of Notre Dame Center for the Study of Judaims and Christianity in Antiquity 1), Notre Dame/London: University of Notre Dame Press 1975, 103-41.

Larsson, Edvin, *Christus als Vorbild: Eine Untersuchung zu den paulinischen Tauf- und Eikontexten* (ASNU 23), Uppsala: Almquist & Wiksell 1962.

Larsson, Edvin — Schiffman, L.H. — Strugnell, John, "4Q470, Preliminary Publication of a Fragment Mentioning Zedekiah", *RevQ* 63.16 (1994) 335-49.

Lautenschlager, Markus, "Εἴτε γρηγορῶμεν εἴτε καθεύδωμεν: Zum Verhältnis von Heiligung und Heil in 1 Thess 5,10", *ZNW* 81 (1990) 39-59.

Leenhardt, Franz J., *The Epistle to the Romans: A Commentary* ET, London: Lutterworth 1961.

Leon, Harry J., *The Jews of Ancient Rome* (The Morris Loeb Series), Peabody: Hendrickson ²1996 (Philadelphia: The Jewish Publication Society of America ¹1960).

Levenson, Jon D., *Sinai and Zion: An Entry into the Jewish Bible*, Minneapolis/Chicago/New York: Winston Press 1985.

Levenson, Jon D., "The Sources of the Torah: Psalm 119 and the Modes of Revelation in Second Temple Judaism", in Patrick D. Miller Jr., Paul D. Hanson and S. Dean McBride (ed.), *Ancient Israelite Religion: Essays in Honor of Frank Moore Cross*, Philadelphia: Fortress 1987, 559-74

Levison, John R., *Portraits of Adam in Early Judaism: From Sirach to 2 Baruch* (JSPSup 1), Sheffield: JSOT Press 1988.

Lietzmann, Hans, *An die Korinther I/II* (HzNT 9), Tübingen: J.C.B. Mohr (Paul Siebeck) ⁵1969 (supplemented by Werner Georg Kümmel).

Lietzmann, Hans, *An die Römer* (HzNT 8), Tübingen: J.C.B. Mohr (Paul Siebeck) ⁵1971.

Lightfoot, J.B., *The Apostolic Fathers: Clement, Ignatius, Polycarp*, 5 vols, Peabody: Hendrickson 1989 (¹1889-90).

Lightfoot, J.B., *Notes on the Epistles of St. Paul*, Peabody: Hendrickson 1993 (repr.), (¹1895).

Lightfoot, J.B., *St. Paul's Epistle to the Galatians*, Peabody: Hendrickson 1993 (repr.), (¹1865).

Lincoln, Andrew T., *Ephesians* (WBC 42), Dallas, Texas: Word Books 1990.

Lincoln, Andrew T., "From Wrath to Justification: Tradition, Gospel and Audience in the Theology of Romans 1:18-4:25", in E.H. Lovering Jr (ed.), *SBL Seminar Papers*, Atlanta, Georgia: Scholars Press 1993, 194-226.

Lindars, Barnabas, *New Testament Apologetic*, London: SCM 1961.

Lindeskog, Gösta, *Studien zum neutestamentlichen Schöpfungsgedanken* (AUU 11), Uppsala: Almquist & Wiksell 1952.

Link, Christian, *Die Welt als Gleichnis: Studien zum Problem der natürlichen Theologie* (BEvTh 73), München: Chr. Kaiser Verlag 1976.

Lipsius, R.A., "Der Brief an die Römer", in H.J. Holtzmann (ed.), *Handkommentar zum Neuen Testament*, 3 vols, Freiburg/Leipzig: J.C.B. Mohr (Paul Siebeck) ²1892-93, 2.2:70-206.

Locke, John, *An Essay Concerning Human Understanding*, ed. by Peter H. Nidditch (The Clarendon Edition of the Works of John Locke), Oxford: Clarendon Press 1975.

Locke, John, *A Paraphrase and Notes on the Epistles of St Paul*, ed. by Arthur W. Wainwright (The Clarendon Edition of the Works of John Locke), 2 vols, Oxford: Clarendon Press 1987.

Lohmeyer, Ernst, "Probleme paulinischer Theologie. II. 'Gesetzeswerke'", *ZNW* 28 (1929) 177-207 (= *Probleme paulinischer Theologie*, Stuttgart: W. Kohlhammer Verlag (no date), 33-74).

Lohse, Eduard, *Colossians and Philemon* ET (Hermeneia), Philadelphia: Fortress Press 1971.

Longenecker, Bruce W., *Eschatology and the Covenant: A Comparison of 4 Ezra and Romans 1-11* (JSNTSup 57), Sheffield: JSOT Press 1991.

Longenecker, Richard N., *Paul, Apostle of Liberty*, Grand Rapids: Baker Book House 1980 (repr.), (¹1964).

Lüdemann, Hermann, *Die Anthropologie des Apostels Paulus und ihre Stellung innerhalb seiner Heilslehre*, Kiel: Universitäts-Buchhandlung 1872.

Lührmann, Dieter, *Das Offenbarungsverständnis bei Paulus und in paulinischen Gemeinden* (WMANT 16), Neukirchen-Vluyn: Neukirchener Verlag 1965.

Lyonnet, Stanislaus, "Lex naturalis et iustificatio Gentilium", *Verbum Dei* 41 (1963) 238-42.

Lyonnet, Stanislaus, *Études sur l'épître aux Romains* (AnBib 129), Rome: Pontificio Istituto Biblico 1990.

Martens, J.W., "Romans 2.14-16: A Stoic Reading", *NTS* 40 (1994) 55-67.

Martin, Ralph P., *Philippians* (NCB), London: Oliphants 1976.

Mattern, Lieselotte, *Das Verständnis des Gerichtes bei Paulus* (AThANT 47), Zürich/Stuttgart: Zwingli Verlag 1966.

Maurer, C., σύνοιδα κτλ, *ThWNT* 7:897-918.

McCurdy, J. Frederic, "Animal Worship", *JE* 1:604-6.

McCurdy, J. Frederic, "Brazen Serpent", *JE* 3:358-59.

McKane, William, *Proverbs* (OTL), London: SCM 1970.

McNeill, John T., (ed.), *Calvin: Institutes of the Christian Religion* (LCC 20-21), 2 vols, Philadelphia: Westminster Press 1960.

Meiser, Martin, *Paul Althaus als Neutestamentler: Eine Untersuchung der Werke, Briefe, unveröffentlichten Manuskripte und Randbemerkungen* (CThM A15), Stuttgart: Calwer Verlag 1993.

Meyer, Gottlob, *Der Römerbrief*, Gütersloh: C. Bertelsmann 1913.

Meyer, H.A.W., *Critical and Exegetical Handbook to the Epistle to the Ephesians and the Epistle to Philemon* ET, Edinburgh: T. & T. Clark 1880.

Meyer, Rudolf, *Hellenistisches in der rabbinischen Anthropologie: Rabbinische Vorstellungen vom Werden des Menschen* Stuttgart: W. Kohlhammer Verlag 1937.

Michaelis, Wilhelm, *Die Datierung des Philipperbriefes*, Gütersloh: C. Bertelsmann 1933.

Michel, Otto, *Der Brief an die Römer* (KEK 4), Göttingen: Vandenhoeck & Ruprecht ¹⁴1978, (¹⁰1955).

Miller, James E., "The Practices of Romans 1:26: Homosexual or Heterosexual", *NovT* 37 (1995) 1-11.

Moo, Douglas J., *The Epistle to the Romans* (NICNT), Grand Rapids: Wm B. Eerdmans 1996.

Moo, Douglas J., "'Law,' 'Works of the Law,' and Legalism in Paul", *WTJ* 45 (1983) 73-100.

Moo, Douglas J., "Paul and the Law in the Last Ten Years", *SJT* 40 (1987) 287-307.

Moore, George Foot, *Judaism in the First Centuries of the Christian Era: The Age of the Tannaim*, 3 vols, Cambridge, Mass.: Harvard University Press 1 1962 (repr.), (¹1927); 2 1962 (repr.), (¹1927); 3 1962 (repr.), (¹1930).

Morris, Leon, *The Apostolic Preaching of the Cross*, Leicester: IVP ³1965, (¹1955).

Morris, Leon, *The Epistle to the Romans*, Leicester: IVP/Grand Rapids: Wm B. Eerdmanns 1988.

Motyer, Alec, *The Prophecy of Isaiah*, Leicester: IVP 1993.

Moyise, Steve, "The Catena of Romans 3:10-18", *ExpT* 106 (1995) 367-70.

Mueller, John Theodore, *Christian Dogmatics: A Handbook of Doctrinal Theology*, St. Louis: Concordia Publishing House 1934.

Müller, Paul-Gerd, φανερόω, *EDNT* 3:413-14.

Mundle, W., "Zur Auslegung von Röm 2,13ff.", *ThBl* 13 (1934) 249-56.

Murphy, Roland E., "The personification of Wisdom", in John Day, Robert P. Gordon and H.G.M. Williamson (ed.), *Wisdom in ancient Israel: Essays in honour of J.A. Emerton*, Cambridge: CUP 1995, 222-33.

Murphy, Roland E., "Wisdom in the OT", *ABD* 920-31.

Murphy, Roland E., "Wisdom — Theses and Hypotheses", in John G. Gammie et al. (ed.), *Israelite Wisdom: Theological and Literary Essays in Honor of Samuel Terrien*, Missoula: Scholars Press 1978, 35-42.

Murray, John, *The Epistle to the Romans: The English Text with Introduction, Exposition and Notes* (NICNT), 2 vols, Grand Rapids: Wm B. Eerdmans 1982 (repr.), (1 ¹¹959; 2 ¹¹965).

Mußner, Franz, *Der Galaterbrief* (HThKNT 9), Freiburg/Basel/Wien: Herder 1974.

Neusner, Jacob, *A History of the Mishnaic Law of Purities, Part One: Kelim 1-11* (SJLA 6), Leiden: E.J. Brill 1974.

Neusner, Jacob, *Jews and Christians: The Myth of a Common Tradition*, London: SCM 1991.

Neusner, Jacob, *From Politics to Piety: The Emergence of Pharisaic Judaism*, Englewood Cliffs, N.J.: Prentice-Hall 1973.

Nickelsburg, George W.E., *Jewish Literature between the Bible and the Mishnah: A Historical and Literary Introduction*, Philadelphia: Fortress Press 1981.

Niesel, Wilhelm, *The Theology of Calvin* ET (LL 48), London: Lutterworth Press 1956.

Nilsson, Martin P., "The High God and the Mediator", *HTR* 56 (1963) 101-20.

Norden, Eduard, *Agnostos Theos: Untersuchungen zur Formengeschichte religiöser Rede*, Stuttgart: B.G. Teubner ⁴1956, (¹1912).

Norden, Eduard, *Die antike Kunstprosa vom VI. Jahrhundert v. Chr. bis in die Zeit der Renaissance, II*, Leipzig/Berlin: B.G. Teubner 1909.

Norden, Eduard, "Beiträge zur Geschichte der griechischen Philosophie", in Alfred Fleckeisen (ed.), *Jahrbücher für classische Philologie: Neunzehnter Supplementband*, Leipzig: B.G. Teubner 1893, 365-462.

Nygren, Anders, *Commentary on Romans* ET, Philadelphia: Fortress Press ⁶1983, (¹1949).

O'Brien, Peter T., *Commentary on Philippians* (NIGTC), Grand Rapids: Wm B. Eerdmans 1991.

Oepke, Albrecht, καλύπτω κτλ, *ThWNT* 3:558-97.

Ollenburger, Ben C., *Zion the City of the Great King: A Theological Symbol of the Jerusalem Cult* (JSOTSup 41), Sheffield: JSOT Press 1987.

Oltmanns, Käte, "Das Verhältnis von Röm 1,18-3,20 zu Röm 3,21ff.", *ThBl* 8 (1929) 110-116.

O'Neill, John Cochrane, *The Epistle to the Romans*, Harmondsworth: Penguin 1975.

Ott, Heinrich, "Röm 1,19ff als dogmatisches Problem", *TZ* 15 (1959) 40-50.

Owen, H.P., "The Scope of Natural Revelation in Rom. I and Acts XVII", *NTS* 5 (1958-59) 133-43.

Pauck, Wilhelm, (ed.), *Martin Luther: Lectures on Romans* (LCC 15), Philadelphia: Westminster Press 1961.

Pease, Arthur Stanley, "Caeli Enarrant", *HTR* 34.4 (1941) 163-200.

Pesch, Rudolf, *Das Markusevangelium* (HThKNT 2), 2 vols, Freiburg/Basel/Wien: Herder 1 ⁵1989, (¹1976); 2 ⁴1991, (¹1977).

Pesch, Rudolf, *Die Apostelgeschichte* (EKK 5), 2 vols, Zürich/Einsiedeln/Köln: Benziger Verlag/Neukirchen-Vluyn: Neukirchener Verlag 1986.

Peterson, Erik, *Eis theos: Epigraphische, formgeschichtliche und religionsgeschichtliche Untersuchungen*, Göttingen: Vandenhoeck & Ruprecht 1926.

Pfleiderer, Otto, *Der Paulinismus: Ein Beitrag zur Geschichte der urchristlichen Theologie*, Leipzig: Reisland ²1890.

Pfleiderer, Otto, *Das Urchristentum: seine Schriften und Lehren*, 2 vols, Berlin: Georg Reimer ²1902, (¹1887).

Philippi, Friedrich Adolph, *Commentar über den Brief Pauli an die Römer*, Frankfurt am M./Erlangen: Verlag von Heyder & Zimmer ²1856.

Pierce, C.A., *Conscience in the New Testament* (SBT), London: SCM Press 1955.

Piper, John, "The Righteousness of God in Romans 3,1-8", *ThZ* 36 (1980) 3-16.

Plöger, Otto, *Sprüche Salomos* (BKAT 17), Neukirchen-Vluyn: Neukirchener Verlag 1984.

Pohlenz, Max, "Paulus und die Stoa", in Karl Heinrich Rengstorf (ed.), *Das Paulus-bild in der neueren deutschen Forschung*, Darmstadt: Wissenschaftliche Buch-gesellschaft 1982, 522-64.

Pohlenz, Max, *Vom Zorne Gottes. Eine Studie über den Einfluß der griechischen Philosophie auf das alte Christentum* (FRLANT 12), Göttingen: Vandenhoeck & Ruprecht 1909.

Popkes, Wiard, "Zum Aufbau und Charakter von Römer 1.18-32", *NTS* 28 (1982) 490-501.

Porter, Stanley E., *Idioms of the Greek New Testament* (BLG 2), Sheffield: JSOT Press ²1994, (¹1992).

Rabbinowitz, A.H., "The 613 Commandments", in *EJud* 5:760-83.

von Rad, Gerhard, *Wisdom in Israel* ET, London: SCM 1972.

Räisänen, Heikki, "Legalism and Salvation by the Law", in S. Pederson (ed.), *Die paulinische Literatur und Theologie*, Aarhus: Aros 1980, 63-83.

Räisänen, Heikki, *Paul and the Law* (WUNT 29), Tübingen: J.C.B. Mohr (Paul Siebeck) 1983.

Räisänen, Heikki, "Zum Verständnis von Röm 3,1-8", *SNTU* 10 (1985) 93-108.

Reese, James M., *Hellenistic Influence on the Book of Wisdom and its Consequences* (AnBib 41), Rome: Biblical Institute Press 1970.

Reicke, Bo, "Natürliche Theologie nach Paulus", *SEÅ* 22/23 (1957/58) 154-67.

Reicke, Bo, "Syneidesis in Röm. 2,15", *ThZ* 12 (1956) 157-61.

Richmond, James, *Ritschl: A Reappraisal*, London: Collins 1978.

Ridderbos, Herman, *Paul: An Outline of His Theology* ET, London: SPCK 1977.

Riesner, Rainer, *Die Frühzeit des Apostels Paulus: Studien zur Chronologie, Mis-sionsstrategie und Theologie* (WUNT 71), Tübingen: J.C.B. Mohr (Paul Siebeck) 1994.

Ringgren, Helmer — Zimmerli, Walter — Kaiser, Otto, *Sprüche/Prediger/Das Hohe Lied/Klagelieder/ Das Buch Esther* (ATD 16), Göttingen: Vandenhoeck & Ruprecht 1962.

Ritschl, Albrecht, *Die christliche Lehre von der Rechtfertigung und Versöhnung Bd II: Der biblische Stoff der Lehre*, Bonn: Adolph Marcus 1874.

Robinson, James M., (ed.), *The Nag Hammadi Library in English*, Leiden/New York/ Kφbenhavn/Köln: E.J. Brill ³1988, (¹1977).

Roetzel, Calvin J., *Judgement in the Community: A Study of the Relationship between Eschatology and Ecclesiology in Paul*, Leiden: E.J. Brill 1972.

Rosin, Hellmut, "To gnoston tou Theou", *ThZ* 17 (1961) 161-65.

Rüger, Hans-Peter, "'Amôn — Pflegekind. Zur Auslegungsgeschichte von Prv 8:30a", in *Übersetzung und Deutung: Festschrift A.R. Hulst*, Nijkerk: Callenbach 1977, 154-63.

Safrai, Shmuel, "And All is According to the Majority of Deeds" (Hebrew), *Tarbiz* 53 (1983-84) 33-40.

Saldarini, Anthony J., "Pharisees", *ABD* 5:289-303.

Sand, Alexander, νοῦς, *EDNT* 2:478-79.

Sanday, W. - Headlam, A.C., *A Critical and Exegetical Commentary on the Epistle to the Romans* (ICC), Edinburgh: T. & T. Clark, [2]1896.

Sanders, E.P. "The Covenant as a Soteriological Category and the Nature of Salvation in Palestinian and Hellenistic Judaism", in R. Hamerton-Kelly and R. Scroggs (ed.), *Jews, Greeks and Christians: Religious Cultures in Late Antiquity*, Leiden: E.J. Brill 1976, 11-44.

Sanders, E.P., *Paul and Palestinian Judaism: A Comparison of Patterns of Religion*, London: SCM 1977.

Sanders, E.P., *Paul, the Law, and the Jewish People*, London: SCM 1985 (Philadelphia: Fortress Press 1983).

Sandmel, Samuel, "Parallelomania", *JBL* 81 (1962) 1-13.

Sasse, Hermann, αἰών, αἰώνιος, *TDNT* 1:197-209.

Schäfer, Peter, "Der vorrabbinische Pharisäismus", in Martin Hengel - Ulrich Heckel (ed.), *Paulus und das antike Judentum: Tübingen-Durham-Symposium im Gedenken an der 50. Todestag Adolf Schlatter*, Tübingen: J.C.B. Mohr (Paul Siebeck) 1991, 125-72.

Schaff, Philip, *The Creeds of Christendom: With a History and Critical Notes*, 3 vols, Grand Rapids: Baker 1993 (repr.), ([6]1931).

Schaper, Joachim, *Eschatology in the Greek Psalter* (WUNT 2.76), Tübingen: J.C.B. Mohr (Paul Siebeck) 1995.

Schaper, Joachim, "Der Septuaginta-Psalter als Dokument jüdischer Eschatologie", in Martin Hengel and Anna Maria Schwemer (ed.), *Die Septuaginta zwischen Judentum und Christentum* (WUNT 72), Tübingen: J.C.B. Mohr (Paul Siebeck) 1994, 38-61.

Scharnagl, Anton, "Naturrecht", *LThK*[1] 7:453-55.

Schechter, Solomon, *Aspects of Rabbinic Theology*, New York: Schocken Books [2]1961, ([1]1909).

Schelkle, Karl Hermann, *Paulus Lehrer der Väter: Die altkirchliche Auslegung von Römer 1-11*, Düsseldorf: Patmos Verlag 1956.

Schenke, Hans-Martin, "Aporien im Römerbrief", *TLZ* 92 (1967) 881-888.

Schjött, P.O. "Eine religionsphilosophische Stelle bei Paulus. Röm. 1,18-20", *ZNW* 4 (1903) 75-78.

Schlatter, Adolf, *Der Glaube im Neuen Testament*, Stuttgart: Calwer Verlag [6]1982 (mit einer Einführung von Peter Stuhlmacher), ([4]1927).

Schlatter, Adolf, *Gottes Gerechtigkeit: Ein Kommentar zum Römerbrief*, Stuttgart: Calwer Verlag [5]1975, ([1]1935).

Schlatter, Adolf, *Die Theologie der Apostel*, Stuttgart: Calwer Verlag [4]1984 (mit einem Vorwort von Hans Stroh und Peter Stuhlmacher), ([1]1910).

Schlatter, Adolf, *Die Theologie des Judentums nach dem Bericht des Josephus*, Gütersloh: C. Bertelsmann 1932.

Schlier, Heinrich, *Der Brief an die Galater* (KEK 7), Göttingen: Vandenhoeck & Ruprecht [14]1971, ([10]1949).

Schlier, Heinrich, "Die Erkenntnis Gottes nach den Briefen des Apostels Paulus", in *Besinnung auf das Neue Testament: Exegetische Aufsätze und Vorträge II*, Freiburg/Basel/Wien: Herder [2]1967 ([1]1964), 319-339.

Schlier, Heinrich, "Über die Erkenntnis Gottes bei den Heiden (Nach dem Neuen Testament)", *EvTh* 2 (1935) 9-26.

Schlier, Heinrich, "Kerygma und Sophia - Zur neutestamentlichen Grundlegung des Dogmas", *Die Zeit der Kirche*, Freiburg: Herder 1955, 206-232.

Schlier, Heinrich, *Der Römerbrief* (HThKNT 6), Freiburg/Basel/Wien: Herder 1977.

Schlier, Heinrich, "Von den Heiden: Römerbrief 1,18-32", in *Die Zeit der Kirche: Exegetische Aufsätze und Vorträge*, Freiburg: Herder 1956, 29-37.

Schlier, Heinrich, "Von den Juden: Römerbrief 2,1-29", in *Die Zeit der Kirche: Exegetische Aufsätze und Vorträge*, Freiburg: Herder 1956, 38-47.

Schlink, Edmund, "Die Offenbarung Gottes in seinen Werken und die Ablehnung der natürlichen Theologie", *ThBl* 20 (1941) 1-14.

Schmeller, Thomas, *Paulus und die 'Diatribe': Eine vergleichende Stilinterpretation* (NTA NF 19), Münster: Aschendorff 1987.

Schmeller, Thomas, "Stoics, Stoicism", *ABD* 6:210-14.

Schmitz, E.D., "Knowledge", *NIDNTT* 2:390-406.

Schnabel, Eckhard J., *Law and Wisdom from Ben Sira to Paul: A Tradition Historical Enquiry into the Relation of Law, Wisdom, and Ethics* (WUNT 2.16), Tübingen: J.C.B. Mohr (Paul Siebeck) 1985.

Schnabel, Eckhard J., "Wisdom", in G.F. Hawthorne - R.P. Martin - D.G. Reid (ed.), *Dictionary of Paul and his Letters*, Leicester: IVP 1993, 967-73.

Schneider, Bernardin, "The Meaning of St. Paul's Antithesis: 'The Letter and the Spirit'", *CBQ* 15 (1953) 163-207.

Scholder, Klaus, *The Churches and the Third Reich, Vol 2* ET, London: SCM 1988.

Schrage, Wolfgang, *Der erste Brief an die Korinther: 2. Teilband 1Kor 6,12-11,16* (EKK 7.2), Solothurn/Düsseldorf: Benziger Verlag/Neukirchen-Vluyn: Neukirchener Verlag 1995.

Schreiner, Thomas R., "Is Perfect Obedience to the Law Possible? A Re-examination of Galatians 3:10", *JETS* 27 (1984) 151-160.

Schreiner, Thomas R., *The Law and its Fulfillment: A Pauline Theology of Law*, Grand Rapids: Baker 1993.

Schreiner, Thomas R., "Paul and Perfect Obedience of the Law: An Evaluation of the View of E.P. Sanders", *WTJ* 47 (1985) 245-78.

Schreiner, Thomas R., "'Works of Law' in Paul", *NovT* 33 (1991) 217-44.

Schrenk, Gottlob, γράφω κτλ, *TDNT* 1:742-73.

Schulte, Hannelis, *Der Begriff der Offenbarung im Neuen Testament*, München: Chr. Kaiser Verlag 1949.

Schulz, Siegfried, "Die Anklage in Röm. 1,18-32", *ThZ* 14 (1958) 161-73.

Schürer, Emil, *Geschichte des jüdischen Volkes im Zeitalter Jesu Christi*, 4 vols, Leipzig: J.C. Hinrichs'sche Buchhandlung ⁴1901-11, (¹1886-90).

Schürer, Emil, *The History of the Jewish People in the Age of Jesus Christ* (revised and edited by Geza and Pamela Vermes, Fergus Millar, Martin Goodman and Matthew Black), 3 vols, Edinburgh: T. & T. Clark 1973-86.

Schürer, Emil, *A History of the Jewish People in the Time of Jesus Christ*, 3 vols, Peabody: Hendrickson 1994 (repr.), (Edinburgh: T. & T. Clark ¹1890).

Schweizer, Eduard, "'Der Jude im Verborgenen . . ., dessen Lob nicht von Menschen, sondern von Gott kommt'. Zu Röm 2,28f und Mt 6,1-18", in Joachim Gnilka (ed.), *Neues Testament und Kirche: Für Rudolf Schnackenburg*, Freiburg/Basel/Wien: Herder 1974.

Scott, James M., "'For as Many as are of Works of the Law are under a Curse' (Galatians 3.10)", in Craig A. Evans and James A. Sanders (ed.), *Paul and the Scriptures of Israel* (JSNTSup 83/SSEJC 1)), Sheffield: JSOT Press 1993, 187-221.

Scott, R.B.Y., "Wisdom in Creation: The 'Āmôn of Proverbs VIII 30", *VT* 10 (1960) 213-23.

Scroggs, Robin, *The New Testament and Homosexuality: Contextual Background for Contemporary Debate*, Philadephia: Fortress Press 1983.

Seifrid, Mark A., *Justification by Faith: The Origin and Development of a Central Pauline Theme* (NovTSup 68), Leiden: E.J. Brill 1992.

Shinan, Avigdor, "Dating Targum Pseudo-Jonathan: Some More Comments", *JJS* 61 (1990) 57-61.

Sider, R.D., (ed.), *Annotations on Romans* (Collected Works of Erasmus 56), Toronto: University of Toronto Press 1994.

Siegert, Folker, *Argumentation bei Paulus gezeigt an Röm 9-11* (WUNT 34), Tübingen: J.C.B. Mohr (Paul Siebeck) 1985.

Siegfried, G., "Wisdom, Book of", *HDB* 4:928-31.

Sjöberg, Erik, *Gott und die Sünder im palästinischen Judentum*, Stuttgart/Berlin: W. Kohlhammer Verlag 1938.

Skarsaune, Oskar, *The Proof from Prophecy: A Study of Justin Martyr's Proof-Text Tradition: Text-Type, Provenance, Theological Profile* (NovTSup 56), Leiden: E.J. Brill 1987.

Skehan, Patrick W. - Di Lella, Alexander A., *The Wisdom of Ben Sira* (AB 39), New York: Doubleday 1986.

Slaten, A. Wakefield, "The Qualitative Use of νόμος in the Pauline Epistles", *AJT* 23 (1919) 213-19.

Smith, J., "De Interpretatione Sap. 13.9", *Verbum Dei* 27 (1949) 287-290.

Smith, Mark D., "Ancient Bisexuality and the Interpretation of Romans 1:26-27", *JAAR* 64 (1996) 223-56.

Snodgrass, K.R., "Justification by Grace — to the Doers: The Place of Romans 2 in the Theology of Paul", *NTS* 32 (1986) 72-93.

Spencer, Stephen R., "Is Natural Theology Biblical", *GTJ* 9 (1988) 59-72.

Staab, Karl, *Pauluskommentare aus der griechischen Kirche* (NTA 15), Münster: Aschendorff 1933.

Stanley, Christopher D., *Paul and the Language of Scripture: Citation Techniques in the Pauline Epistles and Contemporary Literature* (SNTSMS 74), Cambridge: CUP 1992.

Steinmetz, R., *Das Gewissen bei Paulus*, Berlin 1911.

Stelzenberger, Johannes, *Syneidesis im Neuen Testament* (AMT 1), Paderborn: Ferdinand Schöningh 1961.

Stendahl, Krister, *Paul among Jews and Gentiles and Other Essays*, London: SCM 1976.

Steudel, Annette, *Der Midrasch zur Eschatologie aus der Qumrangemeinde (4QMidrEschat[a.b])* (STDJ 13), Leiden/New York/Köln: E.J. Brill 1994.

Stock-Hesketh, Jonathan, "Law in Jewish Intertestamental Apocalyptic", Nottingham Ph.D. Thesis 1993.

Stoevesandt, Hinrich, "Meditation zu Joh 1,35-42", *GPM* 35 (1981) 336-45.

Stott, J.R.W., *Romans*, Leicester: IVP 1994.

Stowasser, Martin, "Homosexualität und Bibel: Exegetische und hermeneutische Überlegungen zu einem schwierigen Thema", *NTS* 43 (1997) 503-26.

Stowers, Stanley Kent, *The Diatribe and Paul's Letter to the Romans* (SBLDS 57), Chico, California: Scholars Press 1981.

Stowers, Stanley Kent, "Paul's Dialogue with a Fellow Jew in Romans 3:1-9", *CBQ* 46 (1984) 707-22.

Stowers, Stanley Kent, *A Rereading of Romans: Justice, Jews, and Gentiles*, New Haven/London: Yale University Press 1994.

Strathmann, Hermann, μάρτυς κτλ, *ThWNT* 4:477-520.

Strecker, Georg, "Befreiung und Rechtfertigung: Zur Stellung der Rechtfertigungslehre in der Theologie des Paulus", in Johannes Friedrich, Wolfgang Pöhlmann, and Peter Stuhlmacher (ed.), *Rechtfertigung: Festschrift für Ernst Käsemann zum 70. Geburtstag*, Tübingen: J.C.B. Mohr (Paul Siebeck)/Göttingen: Vandenhoeck & Ruprecht 1976, 479-508.

Strugnell, John, "Notes en Marge du Volume V des 'Discoveries in the Judaean Desert of Jordan", *RQ* 7 (1970) 163-276.

Stuhlmacher, Peter, *Biblische Theologie des Neuen Testaments, Band 1: Grundlegung: Von Jesus zu Paulus*, Göttingen: Vandenhoeck & Ruprecht 1992.

Stuhlmacher, Peter, *Der Brief an die Römer* (NTD 6), Göttingen: Vandenhoeck & Ruprecht 1989.

Stuhlmacher, Peter, "'Das Ende des Gesetzes': Über Ursprung und Ansatz der paulinischen Theologie", in *Versöhnung, Gesetz und Gerechtigkeit*, Göttingen: Vandenhoeck & Ruprecht 1981, 166-91.

Stuhlmacher, Peter, *Gerechtigkeit Gottes bei Paulus* (FRLANT 87), Göttingen: Vandenhoeck & Ruprecht ²1966, (¹1965).

Stuhlmacher, Peter, "Das paulinische Evangelium", in *Das Evangelium und die Evangelien: Vorträge vom Tübingen Symposium 1982* (WUNT 28), Tübingen: J.C.B. Mohr (Paul Siebeck) 1983, 157-82.

Stuhlmacher, Peter, "Sühne oder Versöhnung?", in U. Luz und H. Weder (ed.), *Die Mitte des Neuen Testaments. E. Schweizer FS*, Göttingen: Vandenhoeck & Ruprecht 1983, 291-316.

Stuhlmacher, Peter, "Zur neueren Exegese von Röm 3,24-26", in *Versöhnung, Gesetz und Gerechtigkeit*, Göttingen: Vandenhoeck & Ruprecht 1981, 117-35.

Sullivan, Kathryn, "Epignosis in the Epistles of St. Paul", in *Studiorum Paulinorum Congressus Internationalis Catholicus 1961* (AnBib 17-18), 2 vols, Rome: E Pontificio Instituto Biblico 1963, 2:405-16.

Sundberg, A.C., "Sadducees", *IDB* 4:160-63.

Sweet, J.P.M., "A House Not Made with Hands", in W. Horbury (ed.), *Templum Amicitiae: Essays on the Second Temple presented to Ernst Bammel* (JSNTSup 48), Sheffield: JSOT Press 1991 368-90.

Synofzik, Ernst, *Die Gerichts- und Vergeltungsassagen bei Paulus: Eine traditionsgeschichtliche Untersuchung* (GThA 8), Göttingen: Vandenhoeck & Ruprecht 1977.

Szekeres, Attila, "Karl Barth und die natürliche Theologie", *EvTh* 24 (1964) 229-42.

Tasker, R.V.G., *The Biblical Doctrine of the Wrath of God*, London: Tyndale Press 1951.

Temple, William, *Nature, Man and God* (The Gifford Lectures Delivered in the University of Glasgow in the Academical Years 1932-1933 and 1933-1934), London: Macmillan 1964.

Tennant, F.R., *The Sources of the Doctrines of the Fall and Original Sin*, Cambridge: CUP 1903.

Thackeray, H. St. John, *The Relation of St Paul to Contemporary Jewish Thought*, London: Macmillan 1900.

Theißen, Gerd, "Theologie und Exegese in den neutestamentlichen Arbeiten von Günther Bornkamm", *EvTh* 51 (1991) 308-22.

Thiselton, Anthony C., "Barr on Barth and Natural Theology: A Plea for Hermeneutics in Historical Theology", *SJT* 47 (1994) 519-28.

Tholuck, Johannes Kunze, "Quenstedt", *RE*³ 16:380-83.

Thomas Aquinas, St., *In omnes d. Pauli apostoli epistolas commentaria*, 3 vols, Liège: Dessain 1857-58.

Thomas Aquinas, St., *Summa Theologiae: Latin Text and English Translation, Introductions, Notes, Appendices and Glossaries*, 61 vols, London: Eyre & Spottiswoode/New York: McGraw-Hill 1964-81.

Thompson, Richard W., "Paul's Double Critique of Jewish Boasting: A Study of Rom 3,27 in Its Context", *Bib* 67 (1986) 520-31.

Thrall, Margaret, "The Pauline Use of ΣΥΝΕΙΔΗΣΙΣ", *NTS* 14 (1967-68) 118-25.

Tiedtke, E., μάταιος, *NIDNTT*, 1:549-53.

Torrance, Thomas F., *The Ground and Grammar of Theology*, Charlottesville: University of Virginia Press 1980.

Toy, Crawford H., *A Critical and Exegetical Commentary on the Book of Proverbs* (ICC), Edinburgh: T. & T. Clark 1899.

Travis, Stephen H., "Paul's Boasting in 2 Corinthians 10-12", in E.A. Livingstone (ed.), *Studia Evangelica Vol VI* (TU 112), Berlin: Akademie-Verlag 1973, 527-32.

Travis, Stephen H., *Christ and the Judgment of God: Divine Retribution in the New Testament*, Basingstoke: Marshall, Morgan & Scott 1986.

Travis, Stephen H., "Wrath of God (NT)", *ABD* 6:996-98.

Tyson, Joseph, "'Works of Law' in Galatians", *JBL* 92 (1973) 423-31.

Ulrichsen, Jan Henning, *Die Grundschrift der Testamente der Zwölf Patriarchen: Eine Untersuchung zu Umfang, Inhalt und Eigenart der ursprünglichen Schrift* (AUU.HR 10), Uppsala: Almquist & Wiksell 1991.

Urbach, E.E., *The Sages - Their Concepts and Beliefs* ET, Cambridge/London: Harvard University Press ²1979, (¹1975).

Vielhauer, Philipp, "On the 'Paulinism' of Acts", in Leander E. Keck and J. Louis Martyn (ed.), *Studies in Luke-Acts: Essays presented in honor of Paul Schubert*, London: SPCK 1968, 33-50.

Vielhauer, Philipp, "Paulus und das Alte Testament", in *Oikodome: Aufsätze zum Neuen Testament* (ThBü 65), München: Chr. Kaiser Verlag 1979, 196-228.

Vögtle, Anton, *Die Tugend- und Lasterkataloge im Neuen Testament exegetisch, religions- und formgeschichtlich untersucht* (NTA 16), Münster i.W: Verlag der Aschendorfschen Verlagsbuchhandlung 1936.

Walker, R., "Die Heiden und das Gericht: Zur Auslegung von Römer 2,12-16", *EvTh* 20 (1960) 302-14.

Wanamaker, Charles A., *The Epistles to the Thessalonians: A Commentary on the Greek Text* (NIGTC), Grand Rapids: Wm B. Eerdmans/Exeter: Paternoster 1990.

Watson, Francis, *Paul, Judaism and the Gentiles: A Sociological Approach* (SNTSMS 56), Cambridge: CUP 1986.

Watson, Nigel M., "Justified by Faith; Judged by Works - An Antinomy?", *NTS* 29 (1983) 209-21.

Watson, Philip S. *Let God be God: An Interpretation of the Theology of Martin Luther*, London: Epworth Press 1947.

Weber, Emil, *Die Beziehung von Röm. 1-3 zur Missionspraxis des Paulus* (BFCTh), Gütersloh: C. Bertelsmann 1905.

Wedderburn, A.J.M., "ἐν τῇ σοφίᾳ τοῦ θεοῦ — 1 Kor 1 $_{21}$", *ZNW* 64 (1973) 132-34.

Wedderburn, A.J.M., "Adam in Paul's Letter to the Romans", in E.A. Livingstone (ed.), *Studia Biblica 1978 III. Papers on Paul and Other New Testament Authors, Sixth International Congress on Biblical Studies, Oxford 3-7 April 1978* (JSNTSup 3), Sheffield: JSOT Press 1980, 413-30.

Weder, Hans, "Einsicht in Gesetzlichkeit: Paulus als verständnisvoller Ausleger des menschlichen Lebens", *Judaica* 43 (1987) 21-29.

Weinel, H., *Biblische Theologie des Neuen Testaments* (GThW 1.19), 2 vols, Tübingen: J.C.B. Mohr (Paul Siebeck) [3]1920-21.

Weisengoff, J.P., "The Impious of Wisdom 2", *CBQ* 11 (1949) 40-65.

Weiß, Bernhard, *Der Brief an die Römer* (KEK 4), Göttingen: Vandenhoeck & Ruprecht [9]1899, ([6]1881).

Weiß, Johannes, *Das Urchristentum*, Göttingen: Vandenhoeck & Ruprecht 1917.

Wendland, Paul, *Die hellenistisch-römische Kultur in ihren Beziehungen zu Judentum und Christentum: Die urchristlichen Literaturformen*, Tübingen: J.C.B. Mohr (Paul Siebeck) [2]1912.

Wenham, David, "The Paulinism of Acts again: two historical clues in 1 Thessalonians", *Themelios* 13 (1988) 53-55.

Wenham, Gordon, *Genesis 1-15* (WBC 1), Waco: Word Books 1987.

Wernle, Paul, *Der Christ und die Sünde bei Paulus*, Freiburg/Leipzig: J.C.B. Mohr (Paul Siebeck) 1897.

Wesley, John, *The New Testament with Explanatory Notes*, London: Epworth Press 1954 (repr.), ([1]1754).

Westerholm, Stephen, *Israel's Law and the Church's Faith: Paul and His Recent Interpreters*, Grand Rapids: Wm B. Eerdmans 1988.

Westermann, Claus, *Genesis, I. Teilband: Genesis 1-11* (BKAT I/1), Neukirchen-Vluyn: Neukirchener Verlag 1974.

Westermann, Claus, *Isaiah 40-66* ET (OTL), London: SCM 1969.

Wetter, Gillis P:son, *Der Vergeltungsgedanke bei Paulus: Eine Studie zur Religion des Apostels*, Göttingen: Vandenhoeck & Ruprecht 1912.

Whybray, R.N. *Proverbs* (NCB), Grand Rapids: Wm B. Eerdmanns 1994.

Wibbing, E., "Die Tugend- und Lasterkatalog im Neuen Testament", Heidelberg Dissertation 1955.

Wilckens, Ulrich, *Der Brief an die Römer* (EKK 6), 3 vols, Zürich/Einsiedeln/Köln: Benziger Verlag/Neukirchen-Vluyn: Neukirchener Verlag 1 1978; 2 1980; 3 1982.

Wilckens, Ulrich, "Was heißt bei Paulus: 'Aus Werken des Gesetzes wird kein Mensch gerecht'?", in *Rechtfertigung als Freiheit: Paulusstudien*, Neukirchen-Vluyn: Neukirchener Verlag 1974, 77-109.

Wilckens, Ulrich, *Weisheit und Torheit: Eine exegetisch-religionsgeschichtliche Untersuchung zu 1. Kor. 1 und 2* (BHTh 26), Tübingen: J.C.B. Mohr (Paul Siebeck) 1959.

Winston, David, "Solomon, Wisdom of", *ABD* 6:120-27.

Winston, David, *Wisdom of Solomon* (AB 43), New York: Doubleday 1979.

Wrede, William, *Paulus*, Halle 1904 (= Karl Heinrich Rengstorf (ed.), *Das Paulusbild in der neueren deutschen Forschung* (WdF 24), Darmstadt: Wissenschaftliche Buchgesellschaft 1982, 1-97).

Wright, David, "The Watershed of Vatican II: Catholic Attitudes Towards Other Religions", in Andrew D. Clarke and Bruce W. Winter (ed.), *One God, One Lord in a World of Religious Pluralism*, Cambridge: Tyndale House 1991, 153-71

Wright, N.T., *The Climax of the Covenant: Christ and the Law in Pauline Theology*, Edinburgh: T. & T. Clark 1991.

Wright, N.T., "The Law in Romans 2", in J.D.G. Dunn (ed.), *Paul and the Mosaic Law: The Third Durham-Tübingen Research Symposium on Earliest Christianity and Judaism* (WUNT 89), Tübingen: J.C.B. Mohr (Paul Siebeck) 1996 131-50.

Wright, N.T., *The New Testament and the People of God*, London: SPCK 1992.

York, Anthony D. "The Dating of the Targumic Literature", *JSJ* 5 (1971) 49-62.

Zahn, Theodor, *Der Brief des Paulus an die Römer* (KzNT 6), Leipzig: A. Deichertsche Verlags-buchhandlung [3]1925.

Zeller, Dieter, "Zur neueren Diskussion über das Gesetz bei Paulus", *ThPh* 62 (1987) 481-99.

Ziesler, John, *Paul's Letter to the Romans* (TPINTC), London: SCM/Philadelphia: Trinity Press International 1989.

Zimmerli, Walter, "The Place and Limit of the Wisdom in the Framework of Old Testament Theology", *SJT* 17 (1964) 146-58 (= "Ort und Grenze der Weisheit im Rahmen der alttestamentlichen Theologie", in *Gottes Offenbarung: Gesammelte Aufsätze zum Alten Testament* (ThBü 19), München: Chr. Kaiser 1963, 300-315).

Index of Authors

Index of References

14. Other Rabbinic Works

15. Early Christian Writings and Patristic Literature

Index of Subjects and Names

Wissenschaftliche Untersuchungen zum Neuen Testament

Alphabetical Index of the First and Second Series

Feldmeier, Reinhard and *Ulrich Heckel*
(Ed.): Die Heiden. 1994 *(70)*.

Fletcher-Louis, Crispin H.T.: Luke-Acts:
Angels, Christology and Soteriology.
1997 *(II/94)*.

Forbes, Christopher Brian: Prophecy and
Inspired Speech in Early Christianity and
its Hellenistic Environment. 1995 *(II/75)*.

Fornberg, Tord: see *Fridrichsen, Anton.*

Fossum, Jarl E.: The Name of God
and the Angel of the Lord. 1985 *(36)*.

Frenschkowski, Marco: Offenbarung und
Epiphanie Volume 1 1995 *(II/79)* –
Volume 2 1997

Eugen Drewermann und die biblische
Exegese. 1995 *(II/71)*.

– Die johanneische Eschatologie Volume I.
1997 *(96)*.

Fridrichsen, Anton: Exegetical Writings.
Ed. by C.C. Caragounis and T. Fornberg.
1994 *(76)*.

Garlington, Don B.: ›The Obedience
of Faith‹. 1991 *(II/38)*.

– Faith, Obedience, and Perseverance.
1994 *(79)*.

Garnet, Paul: Salvation and Atonement
in the Qumran Scrolls. 1977 *(II/3)*.

Gese, Michael: Das Vermächtnis
des Apostels. 1997 *(II/99)*.

Gräßer, Erich: Der Alte Bund im Neuen.
1985 *(35)*.

Green, Joel B.: The Death of Jesus.
1988 *(II/33)*.

Gundry Volf, Judith M.: Paul and
Perseverance. 1990 (II/37).

Hafemann, Scott J.: Suffering and the Spirit.
1986 *(II/19)*.

– Paul, Moses, and the History of Israel.
1995 *(81)*.

Hartman, Lars: Text-Centered New
Testament Studies. Ed. by D. Hellholm.
1997 *(102)*.

Heckel, Theo K.: Der Innere Mensch.
1993 *(II/53)*.

Heckel, Ulrich: Kraft in Schwachheit.
1993 *(II/56)*.

– see *Feldmeier, Reinhard.*

– see *Hengel, Martin.*

Heiligenthal, Roman: Werke als Zeichen.
1983 *(II/9)*.

Hellholm, D.: see *Hartman, Lars.*

Hemer, Colin J.: The Book of Acts in the
Setting of Hellenistic History. 1989 *(49)*.

Hengel, Martin: Judentum und Hellenismus.
1969, [3]1988 (10).

– Die johanneische Frage. 1993 *(67)*.

– Judaica et Hellenistica Volume 1.
1996 *(90)*.

Hengel, Martin and *Ulrich Heckel* (Ed.):
Paulus und das antike Judentum.
1991 *(58)*.

Hengel, Martin and *Hermut Löhr* (Ed.):
Schriftauslegung im antiken Judentum
und im Urchristentum. 1994 *(73)*.

Hengel, Martin and *Anna Maria Schwemer*
(Ed.): Königsherrschaft Gottes
aund himmlischer Kult. 1991 *(55)*.

– Die Septuaginta. 1994 *(72)*.

Herrenbrück, Fritz: Jesus und die Zöllner.
1990 *(II/41)*.

Herzer, Jens: Paulus oder Petrus?
1998 *(103)*.

Hoegen-Rohls, Christina: Der nachösterliche
Johannes. 1996 (II/84).

Hofius, Otfried: Katapausis. 1970 *(11)*.

– Der Vorhang vor dem Thron Gottes.
1972 *(14)*.

– Der Christushymnus Philipper 2,6–11.
1976, [2]1991 *(17)*.

– Paulusstudien. 1989, [2]1994 *(51)*.

Hofius, Otfried and *Hans-Christian
Kammler:* Johannesstudien. 1996 *(88)*.

Holtz, Traugott: Geschichte und Theologie
des Urchristentums. 1991 *(57)*.

Hommel, Hildebrecht: Sebasmata. Volume 1
1983 *(31)* – Volume 2 1984 *(32)*.

Hvalvik, Reidar: The Struggle for Scripture
and Covenant. 1996 *(II/82)*.

Kähler, Christoph: Jesu Gleichnisse
als Poesie und Therapie. 1995 *(78)*.

Kammler, Hans-Christian: see *Hofius,
Otfried.*

Kamlah, Ehrhard: Die Form der katalogischen Paränese im Neuen Testament.
1964 *(7)*.

Kieffer, René and *Jan Bergman* (Ed.):
La Main de Dieu / Die Hand Gottes.
1997 *(94)*.

Kim, Seyoon: The Origin of Paul's Gospel.
1981, [2]1984 *(II/4)*.

– »The ›Son of Man‹« as the Son of God.
1983 *(30)*.

Kleinknecht, Karl Th.: Der leidende
Gerechtfertigte. 1984, [2]1988 *(II/13)*.

Klinghardt, Matthias: Gesetz und Volk
Gottes. 1988 *(II/32)*.

Köhler, Wolf-Dietrich: Rezeption des Matthäusevangeliums in der Zeit vor Irenäus. 1987 *(II/24).*

Korn, Manfred: Die Geschichte Jesu in veränderter Zeit. 1993 *(II/51).*

Koskenniemi, Erkki: Apollonios von Tyana in der neutestamentlichen Exegese. 1994 *(II/61).*

Kraus, Wolfgang: Das Volk Gottes. 1996 (85).
– see *Walter, Nikolaus.*

Kuhn, Karl G.: Achtzehngebet und Vaterunser und der Reim. 1950 *(1).*

Laansma, Jon: I Will Give You Rest. 1997 *(II/98).*

Lampe, Peter: Die stadtrömischen Christen in den ersten beiden Jahrhunderten. 1987, ²1989 *(II/18).*

Lau, Andrew: Manifest in Flesh. 1996 (II/86).

Lichtenberger, Hermann: see *Avemarie, Friedrich.*

Lieu, Samuel N.C.: Manichaeism in the Later Roman Empire and Medieval China. ²1992 *(63).*

Loader, William R.G.: Jesus' Attitude Towards the Law. 1997 *(II/97).*

Löhr, Gebhard: Verherrlichung Gottes durch Philosophie. 1997 *(97).*

Löhr, Hermut: see *Hengel, Martin.*

Löhr, Winrich Alfried: Basilides und seine Schule. 1995 *(83).*

Maier, Gerhard: Mensch und freier Wille. 1971 *(12).*
– Die Johannesoffenbarung und die Kirche. 1981 *(25).*

Markschies, Christoph: Valentinus Gnosticus? 1992 *(65).*

Marshall, Peter: Enmity in Corinth: Social Conventions in Paul's Relations with the Corinthians. 1987 *(II/23).*

Meade, David G.: Pseudonymity and Canon. 1986 *(39).*

Meadors, Edward P.: Jesus the Messianic Herald of Salvation. 1995 *(II/72).*

Meißner, Stefan: Die Heimholung des Ketzers. 1996 *(II/87).*

Mell, Ulrich: Die »anderen« Winzer. 1994 *(77).*

Mengel, Berthold: Studien zum Philipperbrief. 1982 *(II/8).*

Merkel, Helmut: Die Widersprüche zwischen den Evangelien. 1971 *(13).*

Merklein, Helmut: Studien zu Jesus und Paulus. Volume 1 1987 *(43).* – Volume 2 1998 *(105).*

Metzler, Karin: Der griechische Begriff des Verzeihens. 1991 *(II/44).*

Metzner, Rainer: Die Rezeption des Matthäusevangeliums im 1. Petrusbrief. 1995 *(II/74).*

Mittmann-Richert, Ulrike: Magnifikat und Benediktus. 1996 *(II/90).*

Niebuhr, Karl-Wilhelm: Gesetz und Paränese. 1987 *(II/28).*
– Heidenapostel aus Israel. 1992 *(62).*

Nissen, Andreas: Gott und der Nächste im antiken Judentum. 1974 *(15).*

Noormann, Rolf: Irenäus als Paulusinterpret. 1994 *(II/66).*

Obermann, Andreas: Die christologische Erfüllung der Schrift im Johannesevangelium. 1996 *(II/83).*

Okure, Teresa: The Johannine Approach to Mission. 1988 *(II/31).*

Paulsen, Henning: Studien zur Literatur und Geschichte des frühen Christentums. Ed. by Ute E. Eisen. 1997 *(99).*

Park, Eung Chun: The Mission Discourse in Matthew's Interpretation. 1995 *(II/81).*

Philonenko, Marc (Ed.): Le Trône de Dieu. 1993 *(69).*

Pilhofer, Peter: Presbyteron Kreitton. 1990 *(II/39).*
– Philippi Volume 1 1995 *(87).*

Pöhlmann, Wolfgang: Der Verlorene Sohn und das Haus. 1993 *(68).*

Pokorný, Petr and *Josef B. Souček:* Bibelauslegung als Theologie. 1997 *(100).*

Prieur, Alexander: Die Verkündigung der Gottesherrschaft. 1996 *(II/89).*

Probst, Hermann: Paulus und der Brief. 1991 *(II/45).*

Räisänen, Heikki: Paul and the Law. 1983, ²1987 *(29).*

Rehkopf, Friedrich: Die lukanische Sonderquelle. 1959 *(5).*

Rein, Matthias: Die Heilung des Blindgeborenen (Joh 9). 1995 *(II/73).*

Reinmuth, Eckart: Pseudo-Philo und Lukas. 1994 *(74).*

Reiser, Marius: Syntax und Stil des Markusevangeliums. 1984 *(II/11).*

Richards, E. Randolph: The Secretary in the Letters of Paul. 1991 *(II/42).*

Riesner, Rainer: Jesus als Lehrer. 1981, ³1988 (II/7).
– Die Frühzeit des Apostels Paulus. 1994 *(71).*

Rissi, Mathias: Die Theologie des Hebräerbriefs. 1987 *(41).*

Röhser, Günter: Metaphorik und Personifikation der Sünde. 1987 *(II/25)*.

Rose, Christian: Die Wolke der Zeugen. 1994 *(II/60)*.

Rüger, Hans Peter: Die Weisheitsschrift aus der Kairoer Geniza. 1991 *(53)*.

Sänger, Dieter: Antikes Judentum und die Mysterien. 1980 *(II/5)*.

– Die Verkündigung des Gekreuzigten und Israel. 1994 *(75)*.

Salzmann, Jorg Christian: Lehren und Ermahnen. 1994 *(II/59)*.

Sandnes, Karl Olav: Paul – One of the Prophets? 1991 *(II/43)*.

Sato, Migaku: Q und Prophetie. 1988 *(II/29)*.

Schaper, Joachim: Eschatology in the Greek Psalter. 1995 (II/76).

Schimanowski, Gottfried: Weisheit und Messias. 1985 *(II/17)*.

Schlichting, Günter: Ein jüdisches Leben Jesu. 1982 *(24)*.

Schnabel, Eckhard J.: Law and Wisdom from Ben Sira to Paul. 1985 *(II/16)*.

Schutter, William L.: Hermeneutic and Composition in I Peter. 1989 *(II/30)*.

Schwartz, Daniel R.: Studies in the Jewish Background of Christianity. 1992 *(60)*.

Schwemer, Anna Maria: see *Hengel, Martin.*

Scott, James M.: Adoption as Sons of God. 1992 *(II/48)*.

– Paul and the Nations. 1995 *(84)*.

Siegert, Folker: Drei hellenistisch-jüdische Predigten. Part I 1980 (20) – Part II 1992 *(61)*.

– Nag-Hammadi-Register. 1982 *(26)*.

– Argumentation bei Paulus. 1985 *(34)*.

– Philon von Alexandrien. 1988 *(46)*.

Simon, Marcel: Le christianisme antique et son contexte religieux I/II. 1981 *(23)*.

Snodgrass, Klyne: The Parable of the Wicked Tenants. 1983 *(27)*.

Söding, Thomas: Das Wort vom Kreuz. 1997 *(93)*.

– see *Thüsing, Wilhelm.*

Sommer, Urs: Die Passionsgeschichte des Markusevangeliums. 1993 *(II/58)*.

Souček, Josef B.: see *Pokorný, Petr.*

Spangenberg, Volker: Herrlichkeit des Neuen Bundes. 1993 *(II/55)*.

Speyer, Wolfgang: Frühes Christentum im antiken Strahlungsfeld. 1989 *(50)*.

Stadelmann, Helge: Ben Sira als Schrift-gelehrter. 1980 *(II/6)*.

Strobel, August: Die Stunde der Wahrheit. 1980 *(21)*.

Stuckenbruck, Loren T.: Angel Veneration and Christology. 1995 *(II/70)*.

Stuhlmacher, Peter (Ed.): Das Evangelium und die Evangelien. 1983 *(28)*.

Sung, Chong-Hyon: Vergebung der Sünden. 1993 *(II/57)*.

Tajra, Harry W.: The Trial of St. Paul. 1989 *(II/35)*.

– The Martyrdom of St.Paul. 1994 *(II/67)*.

Theißen, Gerd: Studien zur Soziologie des Urchristentums. 1979, [3]1989 *(19)*.

Thornton, Claus-Jürgen: Der Zeuge des Zeugen. 1991 *(56)*.

Thüsing, Wilhelm: Studien zur neutesta-mentlichen Theologie. Ed. by Thomas Söding. 1995 *(82)*.

Tsuji, Manabu: Glaube zwischen Vollkommenheit und Verweltlichung. 1997 *(II/93)*.

Twelftree, Graham H.: Jesus the Exorcist. 1993 *(II/54)*.

Visotzky, Burton L.: Fathers of the World. 1995 *(80)*.

Wagener, Ulrike: Die Ordnung des »Hauses Gottes«. 1994 *(II/65)*.

Walter, Nikolaus: Praeparatio Evangelica. Ed. by Wolfgang Kraus and Florian Wilk. 1997 *(98)*.

Wander, Bernd: Gottesfürchtige und Sympathisanten. 1998 *(104)*.

Watts, Rikki: Isaiah's New Exodus and Mark. 1997 *(II/88)*.

Wedderburn, A.J.M.: Baptism and Resurrection. 1987 *(44)*.

Wegner, Uwe: Der Hauptmann von Kafarnaum. 1985 *(II/14)*.

Welck, Christian: Erzählte ›Zeichen‹. 1994 *(II/69)*.

Wilk, Florian: see *Walter, Nikolaus.*

Wilson, Walter T.: Love without Pretense. 1991 *(II/46)*.

Zimmermann, Alfred E.: Die urchristlichen Lehrer. 1984,[2]1988 *(II/12)*.

For a complete catalogue please write to the publisher
Mohr Siebeck, P.O. Box 2040, D–72010 Tübingen, Germany.

DATE DUE

MAY 0 8 2000			

HIGHSMITH #45230

Printed
in USA